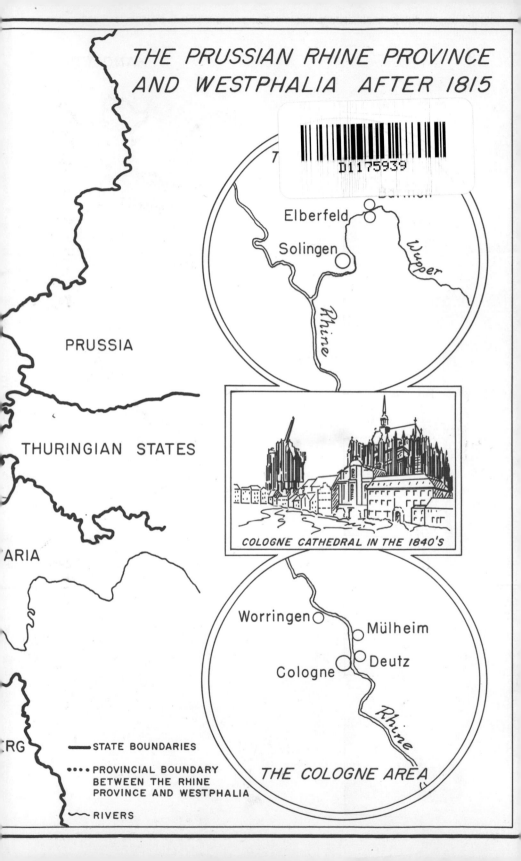

THE PRUSSIAN RHINE PROVINCE AND WESTPHALIA AFTER 1815

PRUSSIA

THURINGIAN STATES

ARIA

RG

Elberfeld

Solingen

Wupper

Rhine

COLOGNE CATHEDRAL IN THE 1840'S

Worringen

Mülheim

Cologne

Deutz

Rhine

THE COLOGNE AREA

STATE BOUNDARIES

PROVINCIAL BOUNDARY
BETWEEN THE RHINE
PROVINCE AND WESTPHALIA

RIVERS

The Red '48ers

KARL MARX AND FRIEDRICH ENGELS

The Red '48ers

KARL MARX AND FRIEDRICH ENGELS

by

OSCAR J. HAMMEN

CHARLES SCRIBNER'S SONS · NEW YORK

Endpaper maps drawn under the author's supervision
BY ARTHUR J. JETTE

All illustrations were provided through
the courtesy of the *Internationaal Instituut
voor Sociale Geschiedenis*, Amsterdam

To Philip, Richard, *and* John
and their generation

ACKNOWLEDGMENTS

THE author accepts full responsibility for the contents of this book. He wishes in particular to note that all translations are his own. Frequently he has paraphrased sentences and phrases of Marx, Engels and others, with the aim of retaining some of the color, humor, romanticism and occasionally flamboyant phraseology of the age. Everything appearing in quotation marks has been taken from Marx, Engels or some other contemporary source. All italicized words are as they appear in the original source. (The author has not used italics of his own for emphasis, excepting several obvious occasions.) The title of the book may appear sensational, but the author believes it is historically most descriptive and appropriate, one that Marx and Engels themselves might have adopted.

In the preparation of the manuscript the author has received assistance over the years from a number of people and sources, which he now acknowledges with gratitude. He wishes to pay special tribute to the late Chester Penn Higby of the University of Wisconsin in whose Modern European Seminar he developed an appreciation for the value of critical analysis, perspective and balance in history. A similar debt of gratitude goes to Chester V. Easum, Emeritus Professor of History of the University of Wisconsin, under whom the author was first exposed to the study of German history, and to whom he is indebted for help over many years.

The author wishes to acknowledge with deep gratitude the courtesy and special aid provided by Dr. Werner Blumenberg, the noted Marxist scholar and Director of the *Internationaal Instituut voor Sociale Geschiedenis* in Amsterdam. He likewise is most deeply grateful for the courtesies extended by Dr. Theodor Scheider, Rector of the University of Cologne, during his research in Cologne. The staffs of various libraries and depositories were uniformly gracious and helpful, notably at the universities in Cologne and Bonn, the Bonn City Archives, the Bremen State Library (catalog of German newspaper holdings), the Internationaal Instituut in Amsterdam, and the New York City Public Library.

vii

Acknowledgments

Thanks are also extended to Professor William O. Shanahan of Hunter College, Professor John L. Snell of the University of Pennsylvania and to Professor Robert T. Turner of the University of Montana for their encouragement in this project. The author gratefully acknowledges financial assistance from the Social Science Research Council and the American Philosophical Society in helping to cover the cost of travel and research in Europe, as well as in the microfilming of sources. He likewise acknowledges financial aid from the University of Montana for the typing of the manuscript and for some microfilming.

A large part of the manuscript was read by an old friend, Dr. Ellis Waldron, Professor of Political Science at the University of Montana, who offered valuable suggestions and comments. Thanks also go to a family friend, Dr. Peter Lapiken, Professor of Russian, for assistance of a special character. The constant help of the author's wife, Barbara, in the preparation of the manuscript requires no formal expression of gratitude.

OSCAR J. HAMMEN

MISSOULA, MONTANA
October, 1967

FOREWORD

"Encore la Russie" was the apology of the French writer Marc Fournier in 1844 for offering to the world, already saturated with works concerning the proportions and nature of the Russian menace, still another study on the subject. Likewise, in the 1960's a work on Karl Marx must also be prefaced with the comment, "Once again Marx," and Friedrich Engels also.

Marx and Engels, who in their own times complained about a "conspiracy of silence," no longer suffer from neglect. New articles, special studies and books on this subject appear without end. But the real Marx and Engels as individuals living in and reacting to the age that saw them in the flesh are often lost. The distillation of Marx has reached a point where many who hover over the Marxian brandy are ignorant of the original savor and color of the grape, as also of the soil, rain and sunshine that account for the unique quality of the fruit. It is necessary to return to the native landscape.

The scholars often referred to as "Intellectual Marxists" have done much to create a lopsided picture of Marx and Engels. Inspired perhaps with the desire to save the name of Marx from association with Stalinist Russia, they placed their Marx in an ivory tower by removing him from the world in which he lived. Yet the integrity and stature of many Intellectual Marxists was such that even a distinguished historian like H. R. Trevor-Roper (see *The New York Times Magazine,* January 30, 1949) accepted their conclusions. Trevor-Roper accordingly depicted Marx as lacking any competence in revolutionary tactics, as indeed challenging the 19th century but not with the "threat of force," and as having dismissed the peasants as being incurably conservative. The exact opposite of the above and similar assertions comes closer to the historically real Marx.

A more recent school of Marxian enthusiasts has turned to the writings of a "Young Marx" as revealing the essential Marx. The Marx whom they present is first of all a philosopher who wrote of "alienation" and envisioned a future society resembling a colony of artists working har-

ix

moniously together. They have taken a part of Marx and magnified it to the point where it overshadows the rest of the man.

Such an idealized Marx, introduced as the complete flesh-and-blood Marx, has attracted some followers among the idealistic youth of college age. In becoming a Marxist of a sort, often in the most unsystematic way, that youth escapes the isolation that accompanies a protest without a name. He gains a certain identity and status through a self-identification with a great name, a recognized philosophy and the company of nameless others with the same idealistic urge. If Marx had not existed, perhaps he would have had to be invented to satisfy such a demand.

The prime need in the study of Marx is a return to the original Marx, the complete Marx, as well as to the times in which he acted and to which he reacted. This calls for more than a survey of the *Communist Manifesto*, key parts of *Das Kapital* and other partly theoretical works, for Marx was more than a mere theorist, historical analyst and humanist philosopher. Friedrich Engels, his collaborator in the making of Marxism and the man who knew him best, pointed to the complete Marx.

In a brief graveside talk at Marx's burial on March 17, 1883, Engels sketched the dominant characteristics and achievements of the deceased Marx. Emphasizing the primacy of the revolutionist in Marx, after having paid due tribute to the theorist and thinker, Engels stated the following:

> The scientist and theorist in Marx represented only half of the man. Science for Marx was a great historical lever, a revolutionary power in the strongest and true sense of the word. No matter how purely elated he was over a new discovery in any theoretical field . . . he felt an entirely different joy when a discovery involved an immediate revolutionary application to industry, to historical developments in general. . . . *For Marx was above all a revolutionist.* [Italics by this writer.] To participate in one way or another in the destruction of capitalist society and the state institutions which it established, to take part in the liberation of the modern proletariat . . . that was his real calling. Combat was his element. And he fought with a passion, a tenacity and success as few others did.

Marx's uninhibited correspondence with Engels alone is sufficient to verify the above.

The purpose of the present work is to concentrate on Marx and Engels as men, actively engaged in their "real calling." The author hopes to give due emphasis to the historical framework in which they played their roles. The stress will be on their evolution along revolutionary lines—both in a theoretical and in a practical sense—culminating in their direct participation in the Revolutions of 1848/49. The work will attempt to show their early and persistent interest in what it takes to engineer a successful revolution.

A study of Marx and Engels as revolutionists, finally, may also suggest that a portion of that which passes for Marxian theory and scientific findings was partly a revolutionary expedient. Early in his career Marx declared in a didactic manner that, in order to bring about a successful revolution, it was necessary to make one class appear as the champion of humanity as against another class that was charged with the responsibility for all evil, misery and tyranny. Was the dark picture that Marx painted of the bourgeoisie and the capitalist class the product of pure and objective research? Or was it partly a concession to this revolutionary demand? These are questions that will challenge a generation greatly interested in the Young Marx.

CONTENTS

Contents

LIST OF ILLUSTRATIONS

PART ONE

The Evolution

= I =

The Setting

By one of the strange quirks of history, Karl Marx and Friedrich Engels were native sons of Prussia. Yet, for all the scorn and anger both of them reserved for that state, neither one regretted being Prussian citizens from the Rhineland, a province that Prussia had acquired only a few years before they were born. The transfer of territory containing their birthplaces had been made in 1814/15 at the Congress of Vienna. The fate of Germany at large, of individual German states, and of specific Germans more often was decided by the wider collective interests of the big powers—or the whim of a prince—than by any decisions of the Germans as to what was best for the German world. Early 19th century German liberals compared the process to a deal in cattle. Prussia's acquisition of the Rhine Province occurred in connection with a deal involving the Polish nation so fiercely championed by Marx and Engels in later years. Tsar Alexander I of Russia wanted to resurrect a small Polish kingdom, with himself as its king. The new Poland would be formed solely from territories which Prussia and Austria had annexed during the earlier partitionings by the three powers of the once large and independent Poland. As compensation for her loss of Polish soil, Prussia received scattered German territories, including land on both sides of the Rhine River. The latter regions, separated from the main body of the Prussian state, were there for the taking, once the big powers agreed on a taker. Prussia accepted this western area very reluctantly. These annexations, later organized into the Prussian Rhine Province and Westphalia, represented such a challenge that a leading Prussian statesman protested that the big powers were forcing Prussia into greatness by allowing her no other choice.

The Rhine Province included an area that once had been divided into dozens of petty states ruled by archbishops, bishops, abbots or imperial knights. But the French Revolution and Napoleon swept aside this diver-

3

sity in favor of French uniformity and advanced institutions. Certainly the Rhine Province, separated from the main body of the old Prussian state lying several hundred miles to the east, was more western and advanced. The modernity of institutions in countries east of the Rhine was generally in an inverse ratio to the distance from Paris.

Besides a geographic separation from Prussia proper, there was also a religious division. Most of the Rhineland was Catholic while Prussia since 1648 was the leading Protestant state in the German world. The Rhineland Catholics, touched by the revival and militancy of the early 19th century church, developed a minority complex, acutely sensitive to every trace of discrimination.

An awakening national and cultural consciousness and pride in all things purportedly German also operated against old Prussia. The Rhineland regarded itself as the true heart of the original Germany. It was the age when romanticists glorified the *German* Rhine in verse and song. Prussia, in contrast, included territories whose German character was not above reproach. The Prussians were twitted for being half Slavic or Lithuanian in racial makeup. The similar ring of the two names also made it possible to suggest that the *Prussians* were the westerly *Russians.*

The Rhineland, though backward in an economic sense when compared with England or even neighboring Belgium, was entering the industrial age. An industrial revolution had brought the steam engine, factories and growing cities. Commerce and communications received an energizing boost from the advent of the steamboat and the tugboat. The peacemakers at the Congress of Vienna had freed traffic on the Rhine from a return of the dozen toll stations, shipping monopolies, and other impedimenta that had once added to the cost and slowness of river traffic. The steam locomotive and the railway came after 1830, opening up vistas of limitless speed. Man broke through the barrier that in all past times had restricted the speed of travel and transportation to that of his own legs, or those of animals, or to the propulsion of wind. It was an exhilarating experience comparable to the contemporary excursions into outer space, but with greater immediate benefits. All this bred a spirit of optimism and enterprise in the Rhineland. In a political sense, this helped to nurture that liberal temper which characterized the middle classes in the early 19th century. Here also, the old Prussia lagged behind.

Prussia, nevertheless, introduced economic policies which were considered progressive. Partly in response to her need for making the Rhineland area prosperous and contented, Prussia launched a program designed to remove the barriers to the free movement of commerce between most of the thirty-nine sovereign German states. The breakthrough came in 1834 when most German states joined Prussia in a German Tariff Union (*Zollverein*).

4

For Karl Marx and Friedrich Engels, the growing cities and industry made the Rhineland a place fit to live in. They had no romantic, Rousseau-like adulation for the plowman who plods homeward and finds his reward in a good night of sleep. They always considered agricultural localities "barbarian." Cities, commerce and industry, on the other hand, represented progress and a civilization which gave birth to the two classes which were to be the main forces behind revolutions. The middle class, or *bourgeoisie,* came first in historic order. With a political outlook that called for change in the direction of constitutions, representative government, and a bill of individual rights, this class was the backbone of 19th century liberalism. Industrial progress also produced a second class—the factory workers, or the *proletariat*—that would furnish the shocktroops of the ultimate communist revolution, as Marx and Engels saw it.

The Rhineland with its advancing bourgeoisie and proletariat was the ideal setting for later Marxian operations. It is not surprising, in the light of the above, that Marx and Engels should return to their homeland when revolution broke out in 1848. There all the actors existed, or were being rapidly bred, who were to revolutionize and shape history to the end of all time. In their own way, Marx and Engels might have paraphrased the chamber-of-commerce-like boast of the liberal businessmen of Cologne who backed the *Rheinische Zeitung*—a newspaper ultimately edited by Marx in 1842/43—which spoke of Cologne, the chief city of the Prussian Rhineland, as the gateway through which the progressive ideas of the modern world poured into the rest of Germany. Marx and Engels shared in this Rhenish confidence, and were ready to use it for their own ends. It was undoubtedly presumptuous to believe that the Rhenish tail could wag the larger and more conservative Prussian head. But so it was.

The Rhineland had another special advantage, as a privileged sanctuary in the Prussian state. Prussia wanted to win the loyalty of her new, avowedly reluctant Rhineland subjects. Hence, in her dealings with the Rhenish populace, Prussia was less strictly Prussian. Thus, Prussia allowed the French code of laws, the *Code Napoléon,* to remain in force in the Rhineland. This meant that a trial by jury operated in most cases when an individual became the object of an unfriendly interest on the part of the authorities. A Rhineland jury was apt to be cool towards charges by a government which it distrusted, or which it wanted to obstruct. Engels, in retrospect, affirmed that the existence of the trial by jury was a factor in causing him and Marx to take up headquarters in Cologne during the Revolution of 1848/49. The advantages were clearly demonstrated in 1849 when a jury acquitted Marx from a charge of inciting the people to insurrection and armed resistance to the government. Several months later, when the last curtain fell on the revolution, the Prussian authorities merely ordered Marx to leave the country within twenty-four

5

hours or be bodily deposited across the frontier. Prussia evidently did not want to offend Rhenish sensibilities by more arbitrary procedures. Thus Marx was saved from a martyrdom that other revolutionists earned by years behind bars. Neither Marx nor Engels had any taste for that form of fame. Martyrdom, as Marx once wrote to Engels in another connection, should be reserved for a Christian with the proper capacity for renunciation and suffering. For a revolutionary, it was better to be free to act.

In contrast to most Rhinelanders who were generally cool towards Prussia, the families of both Marx and Engels belonged to a minority which, by virtue of religion, occupation and inclination, favored the new Fatherland. The Engelses were residents of Barmen, a distinctly Protestant city. The Marxes, however, had their home in Trier, close to the French frontier. Trier, the oldest of German towns dating back to Roman times, was better known as the former residential city of the archbishops of Trier, who for centuries as electoral princes had governed wide territories on the left bank of the Rhine, until they were swept out of power by the French Revolution. Trier remained a stronghold of Catholicism.

Marx's father, who changed his name from Hirschel to Heinrich upon being baptized as a Christian in 1817, was of Jewish origin. The conversion, however, was not to the typically Rhenish Catholicism, but to the official Prussian Evangelical Church, the product of a recent fusion of Lutheranism and Calvinism officially promulgated in 1817. The change also may have been professionally advantageous to the elder Marx; as a successful lawyer, he had numerous contacts with Prussian officialdom. It was apparent that he was not repelled by what he met.

Heinrich Marx's veneration of Prussia rested on foundations which were typical among some of the admirers of the Hohenzollern state. Reared during the age of enlightenment, he developed a humanist, rationalist and tolerant spirit, quite apart from the orthodox, exclusive and seclusive outlook not yet overcome by many Jews in Germany. The elder Marx saw Prussia as the land that carried on the heritage of Frederick the Great, the enlightened despot who had corresponded with the philosophers and had invited Voltaire to reside in Berlin. The great reform era in Prussia after 1807 later had seemed to reaffirm that view. Against the petulant and occasionally sincere Rhineland complaint that things had been better under French rule, Heinrich Marx would argue that a larger measure of freedom and human dignity existed in Prussia than in Napoleonic France. Thus a reasoned respect and perhaps devotion to Prussia existed in the Marx household, as was true for similar reasons with the Engelses.

=II=

Young Marx

1. THE GLÜCKSKIND

KARL HEINRICH MARX was born on May 5, 1818, the second child in a family of eight children. The other seven find their names in history only because Karl was their brother. Aside from an early attachment to his oldest sister, Sophie, Marx showed little interest in any of them.

The life of Karl Marx belies any belief that poverty, family conflicts and youthful frustrations are a necessary part of an environment that breeds revolutionary leaders. Marx had the benefits of a sheltered childhood in a prosperous bourgeois home. Heinrich Marx's success as a legal counsellor assured his son a respected position in society. The cultured and intellectual interests of the father stimulated the mind of one who would receive the best educational opportunities which the German world could provide.

At the age of six, Karl with the rest of the Marx children was baptized and registered as a Christian. Unlike the German poet Heinrich Heine, Marx suffered no shock from the change. He was too young when it happened. Although his ancestors, on both the paternal and maternal side, had over the centuries furnished rabbis for Jewish communities, the roots of a Hebrew faith had dried up in the home of Heinrich Marx. The adoption of a new religion also represented little more than the formal entry into the Evangelical Church. Neither the parents nor the children experienced the spiritual travail that goes with the loss or the gain of a deep faith. Heinrich Marx believed in God and warned his children against any atheistic outlook. But his was a God with rationalistic and pantheistic features, and with few of the attributes of the Biblical figure.

Marx's Jewish origins in other ways had no visible effect in shaping his outlook on life. His father had been assimilated to the point where he showed no signs of a Jewish consciousness, setting him apart from other

7

people who spoke German. A Marx was the same as any other German. This lack of all racial consciousness was transmitted to the son and nothing in the youthful experience of Karl Marx caused him to think or feel otherwise.

Karl was the favored child in the family. His mother spoke of him as a *"Glückskind,"* a child of Fortune whom providence had endowed with exceptional natural gifts. His enlightened and cultured father placed all hopes in this only gifted child out of a family otherwise made up of girls and less promising boys. It was he who gave to Karl the nickname of "the Moor." Taken from Shakespeare, the name seemed appropriate for a person with a dark complexion, a rather broad nose, and lively black eyes. Marx's own children and Engels still used it when a grey beard and hair in later years made the name less fitting.

Heinrich Marx always treated his son as an equal and enjoyed the process of being "pumped dry" by the latter's enquiring mind. The precocious child noted that his precocity was recognized and encouraged. Karl Marx retained a reverent respect for and attachment to his father to the very end, although this did not prevent him from practicing some deceit towards a parent who certainly was indulgent (though not blind) to certain character defects that appeared in his gifted offspring.

Through his father's contacts with Prussian officialdom, Karl also was introduced to a family which exercised a considerable influence on him, beginning during his formative years. This was the family of Ludwig von Westphalen, Prussian official and aristocrat, the father of Marx's future wife, Jenny von Westphalen.

Ludwig von Westphalen was one of the not entirely rare members of the aristocracy who, because of a liberal and cultured outlook, demonstrated that not all Prussians were unredeemedly militaristic, autocratic, bureaucratic and narrow. He contributed to the favorable image of Prussia that Marx assimilated in his early years.

Von Westphalen's father had earned the ennobling *von* because of a distinguished career in the Seven Years War. His mother was from one of the most venerable families of Scotland, the Campbells. As Earls and then Dukes of Argyle, the Campbells played a prominent role in Scottish and also British history. Glamor and romance invested the family name and Marx who came to enjoy the novels of Sir Walter Scott was bound to be impressed.

But there was more in the Westphalen family than historic greatness and a glamorous ancestry. Ludwig von Westphalen was an enlightened man with wide cultural interests. He knew much of Homer from memory and could quote whole passages from Shakespeare. It was the time when Shakespeare was probably more read, admired and staged among the Germans than in England. Marx himself became a lifelong reader of Shakespeare.

The association with the Prussian aristocrat was stimulating and produced a lasting influence on young Marx. It increased his self-confidence, for here was another cultivated adult who obviously was struck by his talent and probing mind. Ludwig von Westphalen even paid Karl the compliment of showing more interest in him than in his own son. It may be also that these contacts with Von Westphalen left Marx—later the self-appointed champion of the common man—with a trace of a hushed admiration for aristocracy and even noble titles. Many years later he occasionally had his wife register her name in a manner that called attention to her aristocratic origins; or he instructed her to enclose in her letters a card which carried the legend: *Mme. Jenny Marx, née Baronesse de Westphalen.*

Henriette Marx, Karl's mother, was not a cultured person nor an intellectual in any sense of the word, though she came from a family in Holland that was not devoid of intellectual interests. Many of her ancestors had been rabbis and her brother, a wealthy merchant in Zalt-Bommel, became most appreciative of his nephew's unorthodox genius. Henriette Marx, on the other hand, had the virtue of being without pretense. She possessed a motherly pride in her gifted son—her *Glückskind* —but lacked a comprehension of his intellectual aspirations. Her lack was epitomized in later years when she made the practical, homespun comment that all would have been better if her "Karell," as she pronounced his name, had made some capital instead of merely writing about it.

The mother's horizon did not extend beyond an elemental love for her family, best expressed by a constant solicitude for their physical well-being. Her letters to Karl, while he was away at the university in Berlin, plyed him with questions as to his mode of living. Health and contentment, she advised, depended on cleanliness and order; a proper "economy" played a major role in all households. Almost apologetically, she expressed the whimsical hope that her son's "beloved muse" would not be offended by the "prose" of his mother. She exhorted him to keep God and his parents constantly in mind. Her German was pathetically, almost charmingly, faulty and burdened with Dutch peculiarities. But this did not trouble her. Like the emperor of an earlier century, she was above grammar. Her sentences flow on endlessly, past misspelled words, neglected capital letters and omitted commas or periods. Her indifference to correct German undoubtedly annoyed Marx. He always took pride in the correctness of his own language and singled out the linguistic lapses of his opponents as proof of illogical and undisciplined thought.

Although Marx seems to have been fond enough of his mother in his youth, in later years a strain developed in their relations because of money questions. It is hard to avoid the impression that Marx turned to her only when he needed money. On the other hand, there is the myth of a hard-hearted mother who refused to help her talented son. That son, however, felt sufficiently sure of his mother's sentiments to resort to pressure tactics on one desperate occasion. In the 1850's, while an exile in London, he once threatened to return to Prussia to allow the police to arrest him, unless she advanced the desired sum. The mother balked, and her son evidently concluded that there was nothing to be gained in a Prussian prison. Actually, Marx received various advances from an inheritance that was supposed to be withheld until after the death of his mother. On her death, furthermore, Marx and his three surviving sisters inherited equal sums.

While Heinrich Marx appreciated his son's latent talents, he discovered that Karl's personality was deficient in sentiment and feeling. When Karl was studying at the universities in Bonn and Berlin, his father repeatedly wrote to him, expressing concern that egotism was his ruling passion, more than was needed in a competitive world. The father pointed out that this was a defect in his otherwise noble character and emphasized the need of a human heart and finer feelings. But parental or any other preachings seldom produce a cure and egotism was to remain in the core of Marx's personality.

Marx's youth in some ways failed to foreshadow the intellectual interest of his later years, though his first preferences were along speculative and literary lines. The practical and scientific side of life produced no response in him. He had no interest in politics. Nor did the scientific, technological and industrial gains of the time succeed in moving him. If he was aware of the existence of a working class and rumblings of future social conflict (signs of which had appeared in the Rhineland), he did not go beyond a mere mental cataloging of a fact which otherwise was of no concern to him.

Early proof of Marx's intellectual powers occurred largely in private. In school his record was far from meteoric or even consistently outstanding. Upon completing his work in the *Gymnasium,* he took the usual exams in the traditional subjects, including Latin, Greek, religion, history, French, mathematics and natural sciences. The examinations together with the teachers' comments have been preserved.

The German essay on the topic, "The thoughts of a youth on the choice of a profession," was the high point of the examination for Marx who already had literary ambitions. After commenting in red ink that Marx's reflections were "interesting" and buttressed by a wealth of thought, the professor then criticized Marx for falling into his usual error, an exaggerated search after unusual and picturesque modes of expression which beclouded the subject. This lack of clarity was a shortcoming that Marx never overcame. In later life, when dealing with items where conviction was strong but clarity of thought and logical proof were weak, Marx customarily masked the weakness in a cloud of "Nordic" verbiage, as one writer put it.

One sentence of the essay disclosed the conflict which Marx already faced: "We cannot always follow the calling for which we feel ourselves predestined; our position in society to a certain extent already has been established before we are in a position to determine it." Family background and preference pointed to a career in law, with a judgeship or something higher to crown his career. But Marx wanted fame in other fields. The conflict marked the university years that followed.

2. BONN AND BERLIN

MARX began his university study in the field of law at the nearby university in Bonn, newly-founded by the Prussian state. At the age of seventeen and away from home for the first time, Marx went the way of those German students who regarded the university as a proper place for a life unspoiled by things strictly academic; study seems not to have been a major part of Marx's routine at Bonn. Perhaps this resulted from an inner repugnance towards the subject of law. In any event, the reports that his father received from Bonn were in violent contrast to the hopes he had nourished. His son was arrested by the police for drunkenness and brawling during hours when settled citizens wanted sleep. He spent much time in nearby Cologne; a larger city has greater diversions. He fought a duel with pistols, although the sabre was more in accord with German academic tradition. At one point the police considered him worthy of investigation. Forbidden weapons were found in his possession, but the matter was dropped. There was no evidence connecting him with politically-suspect groups or individuals.

All the while Marx spent more money than his liberal father had allowed for. Marx, quite understandably, never made clear to his father, and perhaps was not clear in his own mind, as to where all the money had gone. Heinrich Marx was ready to forget and to spare his son the necessity of answering too many questions. But it was obvious that the gateway to an expected brilliant career was not through Bonn. Another way had to be tried. In the meantime Karl returned to Trier.

The temporary homecoming was decisive for Marx in that he fell in love with Jenny von Westphalen. Always a welcomed guest in the Prussian official's home, Marx now saw much of Jenny. This was possible mainly because of the good offices of his oldest sister, Sophie, who was Jenny's schoolmate and inseparable friend.

Marx's success in winning Jenny's love was a remarkable achievement. She was four years older than he and her position in society assured a good match. She was also a recognized beauty, long-remembered as the "prettiest girl in Trier," and as "the queen of the ballroom." She, however, was fascinated by Marx's sparkling conversation and certain facets of his personality. He could be extremely eloquent, gallant and romantic in addressing an attractive woman. And there was no doubt regarding his devotion to Jenny. It was a case of mutual attraction. But marriage was possible only after Karl had completed his education and established himself. Jenny was prepared to wait.

The news of the informal engagement was withheld from the Von Westphalen family. Heinrich Marx was both pleased and frightened when Karl and Jenny privately told him their plans. His promising son and the beautiful daughter of a Prussian nobleman! No better match could be found. But he also thought too highly of the Von Westphalen family and of Jenny in particular to expose her to what must be a "dangerous and uncertain future." Although it cost Heinrich Marx some qualms, he agreed to keep the news from the Von Westphalen family. The strength of the attachment first had to be tested by a long period of separation.

The trial by separation lasted for seven years, most of which Marx spent in Berlin.

After the disappointments of the year at Bonn University, Marx resumed his studies at the university in Berlin. His father probably chose the Prussian capital; Berlin was hundreds of miles from Trier, and far enough to make effective the separation from Jenny. Possibly there was an even more important consideration. Berlin had a world-wide fame as a veritable workshop of learning and scholarship. In such an atmosphere his son might develop a sounder appreciation for the purposes for which a university existed. But Karl, neither then nor later, showed any liking for the Prussian capital. Nevertheless he spent the next five years there, presumably as a full-time student.

Marx's life in Berlin was as undisciplined as it had been in Bonn, only in a different sense. He registered for various courses, but attended relatively few lectures. For lack of anything better he continued the study of law, although his father had suggested a change in fields, perhaps to a science such as chemistry. Before the first year was over, however, his letters began to speak of jurisprudence as a subordinate subject—perhaps a mere bread-and-butter consideration. He preferred history and philosophy.

Actually, the first year in Berlin saw Marx frantically trying to find himself. In an early letter to his father he reported that he had ties with no one and saw people only rarely and with reluctance. He spent most of his time in writing, independent study and self-directed reading. Formal study seemed almost irrelevant, and too slow for an impatient youth. In what field was he to find fame, success, or immortality? Law and jurisprudence, crowned by a judgeship or high administrative post? Marx never felt the proper enthusiasm for a future so prosaic, so circumscribed.

Not without cause did Heinrich Marx write of the "demon" in his son. In that romantic age the demon (*Dämon*) represented that rare genial or creative force which spelled out greatness, or the makings of greatness. On the other hand, the same demon could work in a destructive manner, if it were not properly controlled. Marx's father was beset with worry that the latter might happen. But he hoped for the best, and granted his son the opportunity to find himself.

The younger Marx first turned to poetry. Here he was a child of the age, dazzled by the lustre surrounding the names of Schiller, Goethe, Heine, Lord Byron, Shelley, Lamartine, and other poets, living or recently deceased. All Germans tried their hand at poetry, as a medium for any subject, emotion and experience. A whole series of Greek and Polish lyrics had expressed the German sympathy with the cause of Greek and Polish independence. Then, in the 1830's, a bevy of young poets won acclaim overnight by publishing a poetry of political and radical protest. Later, when the French talked of marching to the Rhine in 1840, the German response found its most typical form in the writing and singing of a host of Rhine songs—attesting to the German character of the Rhine, a love for the Rhine, and a will to defend it against the French. Bismarck, the realist in politics, asserted that the first of the Rhine lyrics, sung in over a hundred melodic variations, had the force equivalent to the presence on the Rhine of several additional army corps. If the force of a lyric could be measured in terms of a small army, the career of a poet was not to be despised by even the most ambitious person.

Marx, having an enduring interest in literature anyway, had to turn loose his demon in the field of poetry. Poetry, in any event, was a proper chariot for love. Love lyrics had a high rank among the immortal works of a Goethe or Dante.

Unfortunately, Marx's demon brought him no literary fame. Jenny von Westphalen, the "eternally beloved" to whom Marx dedicated and sent two "Books of Love," followed by a "Book of Songs," alone appreciated the effort. She received the poems with "tears of joy and pain" and kept the copies over the years, but ultimately they were lost. So we do not know whether love made a poet out of Marx or whether the "Books" were dear to Jenny merely as proof of a monumental devotion and emotional exertion.

Marx's literary hopes ranged beyond the lyric of love. He wrote a twenty-four page dialogue, poetic in form and philosophic in content, named "Cleantes." Satire then entered the field in the "strained humor" (as Marx later described it) of a novel, "Scorpion and Felix." He also tried his hand at tragedy in the classical style, a play, "Oulanem," probably inspired by Goethe's *Faust*. His father even encouraged these literary strivings, as a fast way to gain recognition, and helpfully suggested a long poem of a patriotic character, perhaps an ode glorifying Prussia and the role of her kings—the Battle of Waterloo might serve as the central theme.

Except for the private appreciation of Jenny von Westphalen, Marx's literary flights went unnoticed. The fact that others were unimpressed helped Marx to practice some of that self-criticism which his admirers attribute to him in such large measure. When he awoke to the fact that his scribblings were largely forced, artificial and full of rhetorical outbursts, it was a "devastating blow." There was nothing left for him, except to become a critic. He briefly thought of founding a critical review, confident that the leading critics of the age would collaborate. But nothing came of it.

Marx next turned to philosophy, another specialty in which the Germans had gained world fame. A joke of the age had the French as masters of the land, the British dominant on the seas, with the Germans reigning in the skies (the zone of the intellect). The figures of Kant, Fichte and the colossal Hegel stood in the near past. Berlin and Prussia had housed all of them, adding to the stature of Prussia as the home of the intellect.

As an offshoot to his study of jurisprudence, Marx turned out a manuscript on the philosophy of law. This was followed by a "new system of metaphysics" designed to supplant the reign of Hegel and all past philosophers.

But again Marx had overreached himself. He was like a healthy but slow runner, running by himself. Impressed by his own efforts, such a runner feels that he is breaking all records, until a check with the timeclock brings to light the true measure of things. These philosophical excursions, as Marx wrote in one of the few surviving letters to his father, were tiresomely prolix and merely demonstrated that an unwarranted force had been used to make the ideas fit into his system. Marx also was feverishly occupied with endless reading, the translation of a number of classical Greek and Latin works, and an abortive study of English and Italian grammar.

The failures of this first year left Marx with "fantastically gloomy thoughts." His father detected a tendency to go to pieces over every failure. Such a *Weltschmerz* was disgusting—a sign of conceit, self-dramatization and weakness. Heinrich Marx was worried, all the more so because he felt that Karl was sufficiently indifferent to all advice to use his letters as matches (*Fidibus*) for lighting a pipe.

Marx's restless striving, irregular habits and repeated disappointments produced a physical breakdown during the first year in Berlin. His doctor prescribed the proper cure: fresh country air and exercise. Although Marx's health had improved by the following year when he volunteered for service in the Prussian army, the medical examiner found him unfit because of a weakness of the lungs and periodic expectoration of blood. In 1841 Marx was finally freed of all military obligation as a "complete invalid" because of sensitive lungs. Marx, however, developed into a person who took pride in the depth of his chest, and in a capacity to endure long and vigorous walks.

At the time of his illness, Marx burned all his poems, outlines of intended novels, and other materials. During the rest of his years in Berlin, he tried almost no writing. But he read all the more.

In a letter to his father at the end of the first year, he listed a number of works on law and jurisprudence which he had read. He still spoke of an "official career" in law, pointing out that in certain provincial regions of Prussia, it was possible to advance to the post of an assistant judge in three years. If then one became a doctor of law, a professorship in law might be just around a nearby corner. It is evident that Marx wrote of the above prospects largely to reassure a troubled father, because he already had admitted a superior interest in history and philosophy. The field of law was more and more neglected.

As for history, Marx's study and grasp of the subject was superficial during the Berlin years. He professed a striving for "modernity" yet he seemed unaware of, or untouched by, the revolution that was going on in Berlin University in the field of historical study and criticism where Leopold von Ranke had introduced the seminar method. It is not surprising that Ranke's aim to picture the past as it was, with no attempt to distil guidance and inspiration for the future, did not appeal to a Marx who was falling under the influence of Hegelian philosophy. Ranke's method ran counter to the Hegelian dialectic which looked for law, order and a purpose in history. Moreover, Ranke was a moderate conservative, and Marx was uninspired by conservative lines of thought, professorial or otherwise.

Philosophy monopolized most of Marx's attention during his last four years in Berlin. Hegel and Hegelian dialectics and philosophy of history became his first true intellectual love. Yet on first sight, Hegel's "grotesque rock-melody" had repelled Marx. The system was too overwhelming and definitive; it left no room for a youth who wanted to devise a metaphysics of his own. Then during his illness he again looked at Hegel and saw its dynamic possibilities. Marx became wedded to Hegel, or rather, to a radical offshoot of Hegelianism.

3. HEGEL AND THE
YOUNG HEGELIANS

WHEN Marx first turned to Hegel he seemed unaware of the conflict that was smoldering in the German world between the philosophers and the political realities of the day. Germany then was a patchwork of thirty-nine separate and sovereign states leagued together in the German Confederation (*Bund*). Austria and her chief statesman, Prince Metternich, exercised a preponderant influence within the Confederation—an influence that was mainly conservative or reactionary. According to the Carlsbad Decrees of 1819 (not uniformly executed in every German state), all printed materials under twenty *Bogen* (320 pages) were subject to censorship. This measure was aimed at newspapers and pamphlets. Writers occasionally stretched their work or used large print to enjoy the safety which lay in numbers. But the authors of longer books were not free from harassments either, while universities, professors and student organizations were kept under close scrutiny. Earlier, an investigating committee had operated with results that brought an aura of martyrdom to its victims.

Yet in tribute to the German veneration for learning, governments showed an uncertain respect for "academic freedom." He who studies the age is always surprised at what was thought and taught in the universities and the intellectual world. Intelligent observers sensed what was happening. As Heinrich Heine predicted from a safe domicile in Paris, if the Germans ever "struck out," their revolution would put all past revolutions to shame. Several years later Marx confidently asserted that the Germans *thought* the revolutions that other nations had carried out; ultimately the German intellect would carry through the complete revolution, a revolution to end all revolutions.

French observers were struck by the gap between German revolutionary thought and concrete action. A conservative clerical writer was appalled at the "fury of destruction" that he found in Heidelberg University. Others asserted that France had nothing to compare with it; if ideas moved men, then the Germans ought to have a revolution every few years. Yet they did not.

The explanation lay partly in the fact that most of this ferment was confined to academic and narrow intellectual circles. The expounders of philosophies were locked in a combat whose battle cries were incomprehensible to most other Germans.

The philosophy which Georg Wilhelm Friedrich Hegel (1770–1831) himself had devised was essentially conservative. Called to occupy a professorial chair in Berlin University, Hegel propounded views that became almost the official doctrine of the Prussian state—a bastion of the prevailing order and an awesome obstacle to forceful innovation. So great was Hegel's prestige that many spoke of him as the philosopher of the century. Then the Asiatic cholera swept him away with countless others in 1831. Still, the Hegelian tradition and influence lived on in Berlin.

It was Hegel's dialectics and philosophy of history that gave Marx the framework for a philosophical system invested with hope, faith and an intellectual assurance of a final triumph. Hegel's system was a factor in producing that sense of infallibility which Marx later ascribed to Communists in general. The dialectics, or logic, of Hegel was a device for discovering the truth and the advancement of understanding. Structurally it was made up of a thesis (affirmation), and antithesis (negation) and a synthesis (negation of the negation). The thesis in this logical procedure could be a simple affirmation or an observed fact. In a historic and more complex sense, the thesis could stand for a set of values, a particular ideology, and even the total culture of a given period. The thesis, as an accepted fact, belief or status then meets with opposition, an inner contradiction (antithesis or negation) that must be resolved. (This aspect had a special appeal in a romantic age that revelled in an awareness of conflict, of polarity—as of two souls in one body.) If the dialectic then proceeds along classical lines, a synthesis will emerge reconciling the contradictions in the form of a more advanced truth. Knowledge grows through struggle; so does progress.

The dialectical process became a vital element in Marxian thinking. For a time it even influenced his style of writing, with catchy sentences, epigrams and clever inversions, sometimes at the cost of clarity. This appears in the titles of works, as also in the texts themselves. *The Poverty of Philosophy* was Marx's devastating answer to Proudhon's *Philosophy of Poverty*. An early article was entitled, "Moralizing Criticism and Critical Morality." He used such phrases and sentences as : "If the censor doesn't censor my censure . . ."; "[Luther] destroyed faith in authority by bringing back the authority of faith." Each sentence appears like a self-contained Hegelian world, with more than a whisper of a negation.

Hegel's application of the dialectical process to history was to have a special importance in shaping Marx's concept of it. Hegel believed that humanity was on an uneven course, ever moving upward. This concept of history as progress naturally had an affinity to the optimism of the period. Man was harnessing the limitless power of steam, constantly increasing production, and eliminating distance behind the sooty puffing of the locomotive; it was easy to believe that he was moving ahead with his own hand on the throttle.

For Hegel, the dominant force behind observed history was God, rational and powerful. History was the march of God through time. Hegel, however, seemed to imply at times that the higher intelligence, which gave direction to history, lay in the mind of man himself, or operated through that mind. So he refers to it as the "Absolute Idea," the "World Spirit" and similar all-encompassing terms. Reason seemed to be the guiding force, with action being an expression or manifestation of the *Idea*. Whatever the driving force may have been, Hegel's theory of history saw it as operating along dialectic lines in the direction of progress.

The appeal of Hegel lay in the fact that he gave meaning to history.

17

Man, if he read the signs correctly, could explain the past, interpret the present rationally, and predict the future shape of things. Marx was to appropriate the method of Hegel, also the conviction that he had the key to an understanding of human development. But instead of God or the *Idea* of Hegel, he placed man, as influenced by material circumstances, economic forces and earthly considerations, in control of his own destiny.

At the time when Marx first turned to Hegel, Hegelianism was afflicted with the same stress and strain, inner contradictions and negations that the master had accepted as operating everywhere else. A younger generation of philosophers questioned some of the assumptions that they had inherited. Here was a proper proof that the dialectical process allowed for no exceptions.

First of all, Hegel had used many words and concepts without a clear definition, thus opening the way for conflicting interpretations. Second, Hegel seemed to give to God or the *Idea* a too-decisive role in history, change and progress. In time of stress, impatient men were unwilling to wait for the *Idea* to move in its own calculated manner.

The Old Hegelians, probably reflecting the cautious spirit of the mature Hegel, were essentially conservative in outlook. Hegel certainly had enjoyed the favor of the Prussian state. Many of his ideas could be used to prove the folly of protest and rebellion. All that existed was rational—and therefore right for any rationally-minded person. Existing institutions, as the product of the dialectical process, were the ripest fruits of an evolutionary process. If certain evils existed, they were merely a small part of an overall situation which was just. Change and improvement would come when the time was right. Acceptance, a product of a higher understanding of history, was a virtue and a mark of intelligence.

The Young Hegelians were impatient—they found a call to action in Hegel. Hegel had asserted that what was real was rational. But this line of argument could be reversed to prove that everything which was irrational was unreal, and did not exist, or ought not to be allowed to delay the progress of history. Through a chorus of criticism, negation, and ridicule of institutions and modes of thought that they considered irrational, the Young Hegelians could sharpen the conflict and speed up the dialectical process, thereby provoking change. The Young Hegelians were out to help history move along. They would unseat the gods who only remained enthroned because no one had dared to shake their accustomed chairs.

Marx identified himself with the Young Hegelian rebels when he turned to Hegel. He abandoned his solitary ways and found a new center of existence in the Doctors' Club (*Doktorklub*), an informal group of Young Hegelian intellectuals who met regularly at 2 P.M. at Stehelys, a well-known confectionary and coffee shop in Berlin. There, the members "talked wisely" (*klugscheissen*) while looking through the newspaper, to cite Engels' scornful description of the Club in 1845 when he and Marx had become disillusioned with their former associates. At that time, however, Marx found the atmosphere congenial and stimulating, in harmony with his own mood and latest intellectual inclinations. The discussions seemed to be of world-shaking importance.

Most of the members of the Doctors' Club were ten years older than Marx, had their Ph.D.'s, and were active professionally as teachers, professors, writers and editors. Marx's youth proved to be no barrier to his belonging. As always he was able to command admiration because of his sharp mind and challenging questions. In the Club he could compare notes with the others, test his own ideas, and discover the measure of his own capacity. He soon shone even in this august company.

One reason for Marx's prominence among the Doctors may have been that he was quite free in spending money incidental to Club sessions or otherwise. Perhaps he was helpful to an associate in need. In any event, Heinrich Marx's letters complained of excessive expenditures. Karl again had spent nearly 700 *Taler* in a year, contrary to an agreement and all usage. Even the richest persons consumed less than 500. The father recognized that his son was not a wastrel; but how could a person who invented a new system every two weeks bother about petty pecuniary details? Everybody had their hands in his pockets and made a fool of him, his father complained. But perhaps the son was a willing fool! None could ever accuse Marx of pinching a coin, if he had one.

Heinrich Marx at the time was deeply concerned over the future. His own health was failing. Medical expenses increased while income declined. A younger son contacted tuberculosis and died of it. The father denied himself a trip to Berlin to visit Karl. There was also the matter of providing for the future of six other children, most of them girls and younger than Karl. None had any special capacity or natural gifts guaranteeing an assured future.

In a last letter, Heinrich Marx, already fatally ill, again complained despairingly that Karl had spent over 280 *Taler* in three months. The son seemed unimpressed and lived on the illusion that the family fountain would never run dry. Heinrich Marx died in March, 1838. Karl continued to receive remittances from Trier during the remainder of the Berlin years, even though the Doctors' Club had replaced the classroom and formal instruction.

Among the members of the Club, Marx at first referred to Adolf Rutenberg as his most intimate friend. Rutenberg, like Marx, was not tied to the rigors of a time schedule. He had lost his position as a geography teacher in the Berlin school for cadets. He had been cashiered, ostensibly, for having been found drunk in the gutters of Berlin at an unhallowed hour of the early morning. As often occurs in such cases, it was rumored that the *real* cause of the dismissal was different. Rutenberg was suspected of writing hostile articles for several newspapers.

Karl Friedrich Köppen was another member of the Club, in better standing with the authorities. He taught history in a technical school and published a treatise on Frederick the Great in 1840. The manuscript, which held up that enlightened despot as a model for contemporary Prussia, had been submitted to Marx for criticism. Marx's name appeared in print for the first time when Köppen dedicated the work to "Karl Marx from Trier," as his "dear friend." We can assume that Köppen's admiration for Frederick the Great was shared by Marx. For the Young Hegelians, Prussia was still regarded as the state of the intellect, as a country with a mission. But it was an idealized Prussia, following the rationalist and enlightened precepts ascribed to Frederick II.

Arnold Ruge offered the Young Hegelians a literary outlet for their works, even if he was not specifically connected with the Doctors' Club. Ruge had begun his adult career by spending six years in prison. Such was the penalty for unusual zeal shown in the service of outlawed student organizations. Then, after marrying a wealthy woman, Ruge had the leisure and means to practice his calling as an editor and writer. He became the directing force on the editorial staff of the *Hallische Jahrbücher* (*Halle Yearbooks*), which were founded in a Young Hegelian spirit and with a pro-Prussian bias. Ruge solicited contributions from Young Hegelians in Berlin. He also recognized the potential that lay in Marx, even if Marx very belatedly got around to writing the anticipated articles for the *Jahrbücher*. But the friendship and mutual admiration bore fruit several years later when Marx and Ruge collaborated briefly in Paris.

In this Young Hegelian atmosphere Marx ripened in a philosophical sense. He became a conscious rebel, and directed his first charges against religion under the banner of a militant atheism. Politics, economic questions, industry, labor problems and the crying issue of poverty were ignored or remained unnoticed by the "eagle eye" of the Young Hegelians who were shaping the world anew.

In politics, the Young Hegelians at first simply accepted Prussia as the promised land, or as the state with the greatest promise. The 20th century which considered Prussia as an unfortunate blot on the map of Europe finds it difficult to grasp this fact. In the early 19th century, however, the Hegelians found it easy to be prejudiced in Prussia's favor. Hegel himself, in glorifying the state as the highest expression of the Absolute *Idea,* had regarded Prussia as the best example of such a state. Again, although Prussia was despotically governed, various Germans in the 1830's as well as some French and English writers felt that this despotism was tempered by a rational spirit, benevolent and just laws, and a model bureaucracy.

No miraculous measure of faith was required among those who looked to Prussia as the state destined to have a special role in history. The Young Hegelians felt that they could play a part in making that state conscious of its true mission.

The Young Hegelians saw themselves in the role of liberators and champions of humanity. Rationalism was to be the guide and governor. Their task was that of freeing Prussian policy via the spirit that informs from current pietistic and religious influences that operated in a reactionary way. With the confidence peculiar to intellectuals, and especially philosophers, the Young Hegelians were convinced that the destiny of man was being decided by what they thought, and by the death of opposing systems which they killed in the process. Marx later, after he had turned to other means of producing revolutions, ridiculed his former friends for this conviction that he also shared at the time.

The Young Hegelian crusade against Christianity, God and ultimately anything religious appeared in a sense like a resumption of the rationalist outlook of the 18th century. More immediately it represented a reaction against the religious revival in the early 19th century, as manifested in the reappearance of the Jesuit Society, the creation of Bible Societies, and the formation of missionary societies by the dozens. Romanticism, with a stress on emotion, instinct and the stirrings of the heart—with a veneration for past history, ways and institutions—again made it intellectually respectable to go to church. Many disillusioned elders returned to the church, and the young found it fashionable to flock to religious services. The reinvigorated churches showed a distinctly conservative bias, partly as a reaction to the French Revolution which had plundered, demoted and degraded the church. As a repository of eternal and lasting values, the church was also bound to be essentially conservative.

New theories of state and government, conservative and often authoritarian in character, were stressing the virtue of an alliance between princes and religions. Altar and throne mutually buttressed each other. Germany, where the conservative theories of Edmund Burke already had a wider following than in the British Isles, was blessed with a whole school of political theories that announced the virtues of the "Christian State." Karl Ludwig Haller and others were out to destroy the "hydra of revolution" and the "serpent of Jacobinism" with the motto of "One God, one King and father." The ruler was described as the father of his people, paternal indeed but also the master of the household.

Under the circumstances it was easy enough for the Young Hegelians to assume that an attack on religion represented a direct assault on authority. For them, the rights of man called for the destruction of the power of God. They would enthrone humanity, as the measure of all things. Through historical criticism they first cast doubt upon the validity of the

Bible and then proceeded to the denial of all religion and God. This was negation operating at full speed.

The opening battles already had been fought before Marx was exposed to Hegel. In 1835 David Friedrich Strauss had caused a sensation with his *Life of Jesus* in which he applied the Hegelian method and modern historical criticism to a study of the *New Testament*. Strauss denied that the Gospels could be accepted as historical; they were mere "myths" and a product of the myth-making consciousness. Strauss' work inaugurated the role of higher criticism as applied to the Bible.

At the very time when Marx was beginning his association with the Doctors' Club, Catholic militancy thrust the church question into the foreground by asserting itself in defiance of the Prussian state. What began as a local Rhineland question in 1837—the so-called Cologne disturbances (*Wirnisse*)—soon had repercussions throughout Europe.

Prussia had a reputation for tolerance and equity in the handling of her Catholic minority. But the Catholics showed the sensitivity which often characterizes a minority whose status and self-confidence are rising. In the Prussian Rhineland and Westphalia, moreover, any conflict with the church was easily magnified by the fact that the populace was already critical of Prussia. Smoldering grievances found a safe outlet in a religious protest.

A revolution in neighboring Belgium, where a Catholic opposition had played a leading role in overthrowing an unpopular Dutch, Protestant rule, had emboldened the Catholics. Belgium in the process had acquired her independence in 1830, with a most liberal constitution and a favored status for the Catholic Church. Some Rhineland Catholics felt that the Belgian example was relevant to the special conditions that prevailed in Prussia.

But the actual explosion in 1837 resulted directly from a series of inexplicable Prussian blunders. Most important, Prussia made the mistake of approving the selection of Klemens von Droste-Vischering as the next Archbishop of Cologne. The new Archbishop possessed a religious zeal and courage which made him insensitive to the views and needs of the Prussian state. When he began to disregard past agreements and established compromises, the Prussian authorities suspected treason and rebellion. They ignored the usual legal procedures, arrested the Archbishop, and confined him to a distant military fortress. The storm broke when Prussia failed to find any real evidence to justify her arbitrary action. Rhenish opposition and distrust of the state rallied around the Church—a safe platform. Catholics in Germany and abroad—and in fact everyone who opposed the growing prestige of the Hohenzollern state—drew hope from Prussia's embarrassment. Even Protestants and many liberals who normally looked to Prussia for leadership were abashed.

The Cologne controversy inspired bitter polemics for several years.

Steadfast Prussians, including the Young Hegelians, attempted to exonerate the state. Marx himself offered some helpful suggestions to his father who, during the last year of his life, worked at a pamphlet defending Prussia. But the Young Hegelians were inspired more by a strong animus against the church than by any admiration for the way Prussia had handled the problem; they believed that the secular state had to keep the church in its place.

Most Germans became weary of the whole affair by 1840 although fanatics on both sides would not contemplate any settlement short of a complete victory. Two events then helped to push religious differences into the background. When France, perhaps encouraged by divisions within Germany, threatened to march to the Rhine, most Germans forgot their domestic quarrels and joined together in a fiery display of national feeling against the western neighbor. Also in 1840, Frederick William IV succeeded to the Prussian throne. As a deeply religious and romantic person, the King actually favored a broader role for religion in all spheres of life. (Some suspected him of having a romantic predilection for Catholic tradition.) Therefore, aside from a few face-saving stipulations, he was ready to make extensive concessions to the Catholic position. The negotiations with Rome, extending into 1842, ended in a substantial triumph for the Catholic Church.

The Young Hegelians were appalled by Prussia's retreat. They had hoped for the triumph of the Prussian state. In 1839 Bruno Bauer, a close associate of Marx, had announced that science and knowledge would not cease to defend the *Idea* of the state against the encroachments of the church. But when the views of the Young Hegelians were ignored in the councils of the Prussian state, Frederick William IV then was denounced and derided for having "bowed down to kiss the sandal of the pope" (as expressed by Marx in 1842).

From the Young Hegelian point of view, the evil was compounded in Prussia when Protestant pietism of a narrow orthodox variety simultaneously gained strength in the councils of the Prussian state. Berlin University was affected by the change when even the basic rationalism of a conservatively-interpreted Hegel became suspect. In 1842 the philosopher Friedrich von Schelling was called to Berlin to counteract the "pernicious" influence of the once officially honored Hegel. Although this event occurred after Marx had left Berlin, Friedrich Engels was on the scene then, taking part in the defense of Hegel, an issue of world-shaking importance for the Young Hegelians. For them, the destiny of Prussia and the future of humanity and progress were being decided in the lecture halls of the university. Most literate Germans, let alone the rest of Europe, took little note of the event. Or if they did, they dismissed it as a 19th century equivalent of a medieval squabble among monks.

The events in Prussia between 1840 and 1842 caused the Young Hegelians to intensify their attacks on the church, religion and God. Bruno Bauer published a work in 1841 which went beyond Strauss in a critical debunking of Christ and the Bible. Bauer, however, already regarded Marx as his ablest ally in all future assaults aimed at dethroning God and eliminating religion from the life of man. In fact all the Young Hegelians expected great things from Marx, awed as they were by his critical powers. For them, criticism was comparable to the force which kept the stars and planets from going astray.

A Young Hegelian in South Germany, Ludwig Feuerbach, described religion as nothing but an invention of man, with God as the central figure. In his *Essence of Christianity*, Feuerbach asserted that man took what was noblest and best in himself and transferred it to an imaginary being whom he then worshipped. By doing this, man alienated his own best qualities and failed to recognize the high potentialities that lay in humanity. To be really human, to regain his own self, man had to replace God with humanity. There was nothing in man's existence other than man, this life and nature, the physical setting in which humanity moved. Man's business was to make the most of this and of the humanity of which he was a part. Although some rationalists already had rejected religion and God, it took Feuerbach's philosophical demonstration to make the matter conclusive for most Young Hegelians. Engels in later years recalled the "liberating" effect of the book.

Having accepted Feuerbach and atheism, the Young Hegelians faced the necessity of making an atheist of Hegel. The Hegel who had emphasized God, *Idea*, or World Spirit as the driving force in human progress and history was out of date. In 1841 Bruno Bauer and Marx made the necessary correction by explaining away Hegel's references to God and the *spirit* as camouflage which hid his real atheism. There remained the practical labor of liberating the state, notably Prussia, from the bondage of religion. Prussia must cease to be a "Christian state" so as to pursue her true destiny as the state of intelligence and rationalist outlook.

Besides the burning issues of the day, Marx also had to deal with the distracting question of a career. A professorship at some university seemed the most practical solution for the time being. But to obtain such a position, Marx needed a Ph.D. degree. Though never one to take the high degree lightly, he was almost embarrassingly slow in obtaining it.

The members of the Doctors' Club almost lost patience with Marx; a man of his intellectual brilliance should have acquired the Ph.D. in quick order. In 1839 Bruno Bauer had urged him to finally have done with the "lousy exams" which any fool could pass. To hurry matters along, Bauer made enquiries and then informed him that the Berlin University exams invariably dealt with the philosophies of Aristotle, Spinoza and Leibnitz. Marx prepared himself accordingly. Still he hesitated to face the scrutiny of the Berlin professors whose lectures he had not attended. Bruno Bauer also had suggested that he might take the exams in Bonn University where it would be easy to "bowl over" the professors. But Marx finally found a way with even fewer hazards.

In Saxe-Weimar, the most liberal of small German states, the whole matter could be settled by mail. All that was necessary were letters of application for the doctoral degree, certain testimonials from Bonn and Berlin regarding courses for which Marx had registered, and the enclosure of an acceptable doctoral dissertation. Marx had a dissertation ready for the purpose. The subject, a comparison of the materialistic philosophies of Democritus and Epicurus, was orthodox enough, and also safe. The work had no special merits; it was never published.

The dissertation, together with the rest of the required package, was sent away on April 6, 1841. Marx asked the Jena University to act with all possible speed since he was at the point of leaving Berlin. One wonders whether Jena went beyond a perfunctory check to see that everything needed had been sent. The diploma conferring the doctoral title on *Carolo Henrico Marx, Trevierensi,* bore the date of April 15, 1841. The Dean promised to send Marx the change for the twelve *Friedrich d'or* which Marx had sent to pay for the operation. The circumstances lacked academic regularity, but there is no doubt that Marx possessed the knowledge and critical ability to wear the doctoral title without blushing.

Marx was in a hurry in the spring of 1841. For more than a year Bruno Bauer had been urging Marx to join him in Bonn where he had been lecturing at the university since late in 1839. Bauer was confident his recommendation would assure Marx of a position in philosophy, once he had the Ph.D. and a published book to demonstrate his scholarship. With this in mind, and even before Jena found the dissertation worthy, Marx had written a special introduction for the otherwise undistinguished study. He dedicated the work to Jenny's father, Ludwig von Westphalen, in words rhetorically romantic in their praise of the "still youthfully strong old man."

The introduction otherwise revealed Marx's mood. He saw himself as another Prometheus who stole fire from the heavens for the benefit of man, but in direct defiance of the command of the gods. Prometheus had had to endure an endless routine of torture for having opposed divine authority. Marx now assigned to Prometheus a place in the calendar of the philosophers, as a martyr and saint. Even the Young Hegelians needed heroes and holy ones to fill the gap left by the evicted Christian saints.

Several generations of romantic rebels already had exalted Prometheus as a champion of humanity against a presumably despotic and irrational tyranny, whether exercised by God, religion, or man. Marx's own personal manifesto now stated that philosophy identified itself with the Promethean declaration, "In plain words, I harbor a hate of all gods."

Marx must have felt that the faculty at Bonn would be impressed by this Promethean manifesto which advertised his membership in the avant-garde. But Bruno Bauer warned him that he was waving the flag too furiously—he should stick to philosophy until he had the job. In any event Marx's prospects for a professorship were not strong.

Marx hoped to teach philosophy, yet, aside from logic, he had not even registered for any courses in the subject. Under such circumstances he scarcely could expect glowing recommendations from Berlin's professors. Turning to Jena for the Ph.D. had not helped the matter either. Nor had he published anything to prove his scholarship and mental calibre. His sole chance rested on Bruno Bauer's ability to convince the faculty and the authorities that Bonn needed another transfusion of Young Hegelian blood and that Marx's brilliant endowments made him the man to supply the need. But Bauer's own status at the university was very uncertain.

Bauer had acknowledged earlier in letters to Marx that he owed his initial appointment as a Professor of Theology at Bonn University to the Prussian Ministry of Culture which earlier had preferred the Young Hegelians. Bauer recognized that he would obtain tenure more easily if he won the approval of the faculty. (The state did the hiring and firing, but usually it did not disregard the views of an almost unanimous faculty.)

Bauer, however, never gained the confidence of the Bonn professors who were suspicious of the Young Hegelians. Bauer tried to be diplomatic and to reassure his colleagues, but that was difficult for a person who was convinced of the intellectual superiority of his views; his attempts at diplomacy appeared like condescension. He spoke of a "stifling atmosphere."

Already in 1839 some students preparing for the Protestant ministry openly declared that they would avoid Bauer's classes. Bauer told of a "holy panic" which affected the professors when he announced that he would lecture on "The Life of Christ" and a "Critique of the Fourth Gospel." He then altered the latter title because it was regarded as "too philosophical and frivolous." Stormy scenes occurred between Bauer and some of the professors of theology. At the end of 1841 he mockingly wrote to Arnold Ruge that an "evil demon" possessed him when he lectured, and his "blasphemies" were so terrible that "the hair of innocent students stood on end."

Bauer's "evil demon" followed him outside the lecture hall. In collaboration with Marx he then published an anonymous work, *The Trump of the Last Judgment on Hegel*, in which the authors posed as pious and indignant Christians who damned Hegel as a disguised atheist and cited passages to prove their point. It was a device to demonstrate that the Young Hegelians, as atheists, were the true disciples of the master and heirs to the grand realm of Hegelian thought. After the work had produced the desired sensation, other Young Hegelians revealed the identity of the real authors. Marx and Bauer thereafter prepared to write a sequel to *The Trump*.

Marx and Bauer also made plans to publish a new journal, the "Archive of Atheism," once they were together in Bonn. The mere thought of the new journal caused a fellow Young Hegelian to write: "It was time for all angels to hover about the Lord God because Marx, Bauer and Feuerbach [whom they hoped to enlist] would surely throw Him out of His heaven and hang a summons on His neck to boot."

In view of such sensational prospects, the repugnance felt by the Bonn professors, especially the theologians, towards Bruno Bauer and anyone he might recommend is not too difficult to grasp. Yet Marx optimistically joined Bauer in Bonn during July, 1841. The reception Marx received was so chilly that his usual capacity to impress everyone with his mental sharpness was of no aid. According to Bauer, the Bonn professors regarded Marx with the trepidation reserved for an "emissary appearing to preside over the Last Judgment."

Yet, Marx was not discouraged. As late as September he still gave friends the impression that he would teach at Bonn. The call never came. Bauer, however, continued to lecture through the winter semester. Then he was dismissed. His departure met with the heartfelt approval of the Bonn faculty.

Marx's dim prospects for a professorship had completely vanished. He expressed no regrets; he never felt attracted to an academic career. But the problem of money was more important than ever. Jenny von Westphalen was still waiting and he could no longer depend on remittances from home. His family was beginning to insist that he accept financial responsibility.

Although no immediate prospects for earning a livelihood were in sight, Marx was supremely self-confident, certain that his intellectual prowess and critical talents guaranteed recognition. The Young Hegelians were unanimous in expecting great things from him. A typical example of the impression he made on others was recorded by Moses Hess in September, 1841.

Moses Hess was a radical Jewish writer from the Rhineland, who enjoyed the patronage of a wealthy father. Hess was to anticipate Marx and Engels in concluding that the Hegelian dialectic ineluctably pointed towards a triumph of communism. It took only one meeting to convince him that Marx was the greatest, perhaps the only *real* philosopher then living, upon whom all German eyes would turn when he appeared as a professor and a writer. Marx was his "idol," a man who combined the deepest philosophical earnestness with the most biting wit—Rousseau, Voltaire, Holbach, Lessing, Heine and Hegel, all in one.

As Marx approached his twenty-fourth birthday, he was clearly in a revolutionary mood, impatient to strike out and to leave his mark. A series of personal frustrations may have helped to persuade him that a world which did not automatically take care of a genius needed a radical reorganization. Bruno Bauer spoke of a "beserk fury" which possessed Marx when he was crossed. Other friendly witnesses used the word "desperate or frenzied" (*verzweifelt*) in describing his revolutionary disposition. Members of the former Doctors' Club must have given Friedrich Engels a similar impression of his future collaborator. Engels, who was then in Berlin, had not yet met Marx when he wrote a satirical poem on the subject of Bruno Bauer's dismissal from Bonn University. In it he twice used the word tempestuous or violent (*ungestüm*) in characterizing Marx. Engels' sympathies were clearly with the "black fellow from Trier" as, in poetic fantasy, he had Marx leaping up from his heels with a fierce intensity, trying to drag the heavens down to earth, moving about with clenched fists held high, and raging on without rest, as if ten thousand devils were trying to drag him down by the hair. With some allowance for poetic exaggeration, Engels' description had the same common denominator as appears in other accounts. No witness noted anything like intellectual serenity and an academic calm in Marx.

By early 1842 it was clear that Marx would no longer restrict his attacks to religious authority. The sword of negation would strike out more widely. Moses Hess saw Marx as the man who would give the death blow to medieval religion and *politics*. Marx's writings indicate the trend. In the first month of 1842 he wrote an essay on Prussia's new censorship rules. In a letter to Ruge, he spoke of undertaking a critique of Hegel in which constitutional monarchy would be attacked as a thoroughly self-contradictory and self-liquidating bastard (*Zwitterding*). The dialectical process was at work. Constitutional monarchy was a mongrel that, because of its own inner contradictions, would help to bring about its own destruction.

But a constitutional monarchy, with representative parliamentary government and safeguards for individual freedom, was the ideal for which most liberals were then striving. It was the political credo of the middle classes, the *bourgeoisie*. In Marx's mind, however, the political forms and the ideals of the bourgeoisie already faced demolition. About two years later he discovered the proletariat, or working class, as the agents to carry through the destruction via the means of class conflict.

= III =

Young Engels

1. THE BUSINESS APPRENTICE

BARMEN, the birthplace of Friedrich Engels, and its twin industrial city Elberfeld lie in the Wuppertal, the narrow valley of a tributary of the Rhine. Already in the early 19th century the Wupper River was polluted and discolored by industrial wastes, mainly in the form of textile dyes. Friedrich Engels had an early view of the two faces of the rising manufacturing town—optimism and well-being on the one hand; misery, grime and disease on the other. Today in Barmen a wide, handsome street named *Friedrich Engels Strasse* passes a small park. In this park is a stone slab marking the site of the home of Barmen's "great citizen," the "co-founder of scientific socialism."

Friedrich Engels, the oldest child in a family of eight children, was born November 28, 1820. His father, also named Friedrich, possessed enough of the spirit of the entrepreneur to keep abreast of the times. Besides owning a cotton manufacturing plant in Barmen, the "Manchester of Germany," the elder Engels was a partner in the firm of Ermen and Engels in England's own Manchester. The immediate environment in which young Friedrich spent the first eighteen years of his life, therefore, normally would have produced a moderately liberal businessman, a conscientious Protestant church-goer and a loyal Prussian.

Friedrich's childhood was sheltered and happy, though interspersed with stormy moments. The father reared the children in a respect for God, the various Commandments, and the existing state and society. Nevertheless, he possessed a penchant for life and action which kept him from being an unbending pietist. But the young Friedrich early showed a zest for living, a nonconformity and even rebellion which a father who believed in strict discipline and responsibility could not ignore. It is told that on one occasion the youth, Diogenes-like, searched

29

the paternal home from room to room, using a lantern in broad daylight, avowedly looking for a human being. That was hardly the gesture of a completely submerged child.

Engels later described life in the parental home as intolerable. But by then the family knew that their eldest son was a rebel against the religion of the household, as well as its political and economic beliefs. Often enough there were tears, lamentations and reproaches, spoken or left unsaid, over the error of the son's views and ways. The father, nonetheless, possessed a bourgeois liberalism and paternal sentiments which made vast allowances for an erring son. Friedrich Engels was never confronted with the irrevocable alternative of renouncing a philosophy aimed at the destruction of private business or of doing without the income derived from said business. Without that income, Marx and Engels might have been denied much of the opportunity to promote and sell Marxism. Ultimately, Marxists are bound to observe a moment of silence in honor of the elder Engels.

Engels retained a close attachment to his mother, a person with a strong zest for life and fun, easily carried away by laughter to the point of tears. She had a tolerance based on a great love that could not admit the evidence of mortal sin, though she might grieve silently over the indications that pointed in that direction. Engels often regretted the sorrow he brought his mother.

Engels' parents regarded their oldest child with great hopes mixed with some doubts. In spite of strict disciplining during childhood, Friedrich continued to display a self-assertiveness and non-conformist behavior that marred the otherwise good qualities they recognized in him. Once, while he was away from home attending the *Gymnasium* in Elberfeld, his father was dismayed to find a "dirty" (*schmieriges*) book—a 13th century romance drawn from a local loan library—left openly on his son's desk. What was most upsetting was the brashness his son had displayed by leaving the book in a place where anyone might notice it.

Engels' record at Elberfeld's *Gymnasium* was far from spectacular, but he certainly profited from the liberal arts curriculum of a school he later described as one of the best in Prussia. His formal academic study, however, ended in 1837 (when he was seventeen), a year short of graduation from the *Gymnasium*. The reason for this is not clear, but it appears that he no longer wanted to prepare for the legal profession and his father opposed further study in the absence of a practical goal. In any event, it was agreed that Engels would follow a business career, though there are indications he would have preferred going on to a university. With a business career in mind, the first step was an apprenticeship involving office work and practical experience in commercial procedures.

Engels may have become reconciled to a business apprenticeship because he saw that it would not seriously interfere with his real, inner interest, the writing of poetry. In Barmen itself, Ferdinand Freiligrath was working in an office, yet was able to turn out inspiring poetry. Engels must have confided his ambitions to the Director of the *Gymnasium*, for the latter noted on Engels' withdrawal report that the youth had selected a business career as his "external profession."

Engels possessed the gift of versification, the ability to express himself in meter and rhyme. True to the age, his poetry was of an extravagant, romantic sort, about Moors, Negroes and Indians (the noble savages), tumbling, torrential mountain streams, and mythology of the heroic sort, especially from the German *Nibelungenlied*. In keeping with his mood, Engels depicted Siegfried as one who was impatient with conventions and parental admonitions, ready to roam in the woods testing his strength with bears.

Like Marx and countless other young Germans, Engels soon recognized that he lacked a sustained poetic talent. Like Marx also, he then turned to prose, journalism, criticism. Engels, however, never completely disavowed the rhymed verse, when used for satire and mimicry. The results could be decidedly clever, though marred by some footweary lapses.

In July, 1838, Engels left the Wuppertal for the free, republican and sovereign city-state of Bremen. But he did not go as a naive youth, later to succumb to the allurements of a strange and broader world. His rebellious spirit made him receptive to everything liberal and iconoclastic that Germany had to offer. And there was enough of that in a reactionary, censorship-ridden land. A rebel in search of ideas could find anything to fit his tastes, even if not on display on the open counters of the market place.

Engels went to Bremen as an apprentice to learn commercial procedures in a business office. His father probably picked the place of the business, the export firm of Heinrich Leupold who was as conservative in politics as in commercial practices. Engels lived in the home of a Protestant pastor, G. G. Treviranus, where he was treated as a member of the family. Bremen, if we accept Engels' description of the old Hanseatic city, matched the philistinism and Calvinism of Barmen.

The routine of office work was easy for Engels to master, so he had ample time for outside pursuits. He made one attempt to stir up dormant waters by persuading other young apprentices in various business houses to wear moustaches in defiance of local custom, and to organize in defense of the right to do so. Engels' revolutionary instincts were becoming restive. But this was only a minor effusion—otherwise, as in later life, he preserved an external appearance of urbanity, cultivated agreeable manners, and ably performed his duties during scheduled business hours.

Bremen appeared dull to Engels. He sang in a choral society and occasionally joined friends for an evening in the celebrated *Ratskeller*. As a devotee of physical vigor and the strenuous life, the youth improved his skill as a swordsman and horseman; in later years he prided himself on being able to outride most Englishmen in a fox hunt. As a swimmer who could cross the Weser River several times in succession, he expressed contempt for people who were afraid of cold water, "like dogs with hydrophobia." He soon showed a similar scorn for persons who made it a point of honor to evade military service.

It was in Bremen that Engels discovered he had a special aptitude for languages. He was able to obtain English, French and Scandinavian newspapers and he met many people who spoke in foreign tongues. Soon he was writing to his sister (in that big-brother, fanfaronade style which he used when addressing a beloved but naive inferior) that he could speak in twenty-four languages. He might have become a distinguished linguist. As it was, he cultivated this natural gift which later helped qualify him as the expert in foreign affairs, nationality questions and anything involving languages in the Marx-Engels "company business," as Marx later termed it.

The Bremen period, above all, give Engels the opportunity to educate himself and to develop a philosophy of life. In his search for a satisfactory amalgam, he plunged headlong into the "sheer ideas of the century." His rebellious dispositions and thirst for action, coupled with a confidence that he had a call to help shape the future, led him to the revolutionary and iconoclastic ideals of the Young Germans.

The Young German school of writers found much in a reactionary and seemingly stagnant Germany to be angry about. They called for liberty, equality and a free play of the senses. They denounced princes, aristocrats and often the clergy as faithless and tyrannical—costly and shopworn to say the least. A strong note of social protest appeared in Georg Büchner's call for "peace to the cottages, war against palaces." The age was able to indulge in the romantic fantasies of free love in the writings of Theodor Mundt. Many Young Germans were fervent nationalists, waving the forbidden black-red-gold colors of an envisioned strong, united, free and respected Germany. There was also a strong vein of cosmopolitanism among them, founded on the romantic belief that free nations would respect the rights of other free people, thus allowing each to develop its peculiar genius to the greater enrichment of humanity.

The Young German writers had gained a special recognition in 1835 when the Diet of the German Confederation, representing the thirty-nine German states, condemned their works as subversive. The edict produced mixed results. It brought tragedy and martyrdom to some. On the other hand, young poets soon found that the publication of something sufficiently revolutionary to merit official condemnation guaranteed immediate fame. Much artistic talent probably was wasted in the process, but it could no longer be said that German writers were indifferent to politics and social issues.

Engels devoured the radical literature of the Young German writers. He found modernity and fulfillment by identifying himself with the hopes and hatreds of the movement. He used the word *wurzelhaft* (radical) most frequently to describe his own inclinations, as well as those of the writers whom he favored (especially Ludwig Börne, the "John the Baptist of the new times," a German Jew who had written from exile in Paris). Börne's uncomplicated republicanism, expressed as a hatred of all tyranny, servility, aristocratic privileges and power, suited Engels' mood. Engels exulted in the privilege of sitting on a branch of the "oak tree of Börne."

Soon, however, Engels recognized that even the most inspiring poem and revolutionary prose were not enough. The sword was also necessary. In ecstatic visions Engels then saw himself as a dedicated hunter and horseman, sounding the horn to open the hunt against the tyrant, while the glow of burning castles lighted the way from the hilltops, and thrones and altars trembled on all sides. He expressed a newly-found hatred for the Prussian King; in fantasy he heard the shrill clatter of palace windows shattered by stones. In all his fury, however, Engels did not lose a characteristic sense of humor. Replying to his sister who had described the thrilling experience of being presented to the Grand Duchess of Baden, Engels stated that in the future he was only interested in the question of whether the woman was good looking. A year later in Berlin, Engels trained his dog to howl when told that an aristocrat was in sight. All jesting aside, Engels had reached the point where he was in rebellion against most of the existing authorities and institutions. He was in search of a new revolutionary theory and force, as a lever to move the universe. The Young German radicals no longer suited him; they were too unsystematic, undisciplined, incoherent and inconclusive.

During this time in Bremen, Engels turned to journalism and pamphleteering. He had a clarity of style and pungency of wit that the more pedestrian Marx occasionally envied and often used in later years. Engels' first journalistic articles, "Letters out of the Wuppertal," were published in the Hamburg *Telegraph für Deutschland* edited by Karl Gutzkow, the "arch heretic" who accepted contributions from Young German writers. Engels' articles, describing life in the Wuppertal, appeared under the pseudonym of Friedrich Oswald. Though in later years Engels used the device of anonymity for various reasons, he probably chose a pen name at this time to spare his parents the pain of knowing that their son was the author of radical works, highly critical of religion, pietism and nearly everything else in the "blessed valley."

When Engels wrote his scathing description of the Wuppertal, he had already rejected Christianity. As a child he had accepted the Protestant faith of the household as a matter of course. During the period of religious instruction before Confirmation, he even seems to have been deeply moved. In a poem written in 1837, he entreated Christ to save him, as he swore off his sinful ways and promised to avoid worldly distractions. But the spell did not last long.

In letters to a friend who was studying theology, Engels indicated that the question of Christianity stirred him to the bottom of his soul. He had "asked for bread and was given stones." The Calvinist belief in predestination which damned or saved separate souls in accordance with the will and foreknowledge of an omnipotent God appeared appalling. In view of Engels' other interests and activities, it seems unlikely, however, that the question of God and of individual salvation became an all-absorbing obsession. Perhaps the young man was indulging in self-dramatization. It made his final apostasy seem almost natural, logical and inevitable. Engels, moreover, always had a talent for parody, as when he posed as a pious Christian for the purpose of making religion ridiculous.

Yet we may assume that Engels' break with the church was not an easy step. It flew in the face of the beliefs of his family. When he spoke of the "thousand hooks" with which Christianity kept a person captive, he probably recognized that family ties would be strained or ruptured if he renounced religion. Christianity, moreover, had been one of the foundations of Western culture for fifteen hundred years. Its contemporary relevance seemed to be reaffirmed by the 19th century revival of the church. Furthermore, in Bremen Engels had had the chance to witness a practical expression of the resurgent Christianity; Pastor Treviranus, in whose home he lived, taught and helped the poor and brought comfort to such unfortunates as released prisoners and penniless emigrants awaiting passage to America. But that kind of direct action in support of an immediate need was not the "bread" for Engels.

Judging from his letters, Engels finally paused at a point where he was ready to preserve a formal recognition of God, shared by an inner repudiation of much of the framework of Christianity as he understood it. He was not the rugged individualist or crank who could take a stand, usually ineffective, on the basis of his private inclinations alone. He needed a replacement onto which he could hitch himself with the "thousand hooks," with the assurance that his rebellion was a part of a wide cosmic movement. Then he could move with the consciousness that the current seconded his motions and carried others along behind him.

Early in 1839 Engels discovered Strauss's *Life of Jesus*. Here was proof, in the best dialectical form, that the Bible was merely another historical document. By October, 1839, Engels could write to Wilhelm Graeber, his theological friend, "If you can disprove Strauss, very well, then I'll be-

'come a pietist again." The tone of the letter suggests that Engels had viewed the final inspiration, or latest product of the critical mind.

Through a study of Strauss, Engels soon came to Hegel and the Young Hegelians. The majestic scope of Hegel's philosophy of history and concept of God left him exhilarated and breathless. Finally, via the road of Young Hegelianism, Engels came to atheism.

Engels returned to Barmen after the end of his apprenticeship in March, 1841. As a young man slightly past twenty, he was glad to leave the "boresome nest where one could do nothing but fence, drink, sleep and be a drudge." He had done justice in each field. Friedrich Engels, the outward man, had met all the tests for a career in business. All the while, the real Engels, known to the outside world as Friedrich Oswald, had remained concealed from his associates in Bremen.

Engels' mind now turned to Berlin, the Mecca for the followers of Hegel. But to go there he needed the financial help of an approving parent. His father, however, was still averse to university study without a definite goal in mind; he urged his son to continue business training by accepting a position in Milan, Italy. There undoubtedly were heated discussions regarding the matter. Ultimately Engels did go to Italy, but only as a tourist, probably to escape the entanglements of a love affair.

The trip to Italy during the summer of 1841 gave Engels the opportunity to spread the fame of his literary alter ego, Friedrich Oswald. He wrote articles wherein scenes of Alpine grandeur and the irresistible force of cascading waters alternated with reflections on revolutionary persons and the burial place of Ulrich von Hutten, Germany's 16th century rebel and man of action. Published in a Young Hegelian weekly in the Prussian capital, the articles later enabled Engels to make his bow before the Young Hegelians, once he revealed the identity of Friedrich Oswald.

2. ARTILLERY AND HEGEL

THE requirements of Prussia's system of universal military service made it possible to postpone a decision regarding Engels' future career after his return from Italy. The conscript in Prussia normally served for two years, but the state also paid homage to the value of learning; young men with an education on par with that of Engels could fulfill their military obligations by enlisting as volunteers for one year. Such volunteers could pick the place where they would receive training, as well as the branch of service they preferred. Engels' father probably felt that military discipline would have a stabilizing effect on his son. As for Engels himself, it gave him the chance to go to Berlin. He selected the artillery, perhaps because it had the smallest percentage of officers of aristocratic origin.

Military service extended from September, 1841, into August, 1842. The company commander certified that Engels' conduct was very good, both in performance of his military duties and in his personal behavior. Engels seems to have enjoyed wearing the uniform. In a letter to his sister, he showed a very human zest for colorful incidentals. No anti-militarist compunctions interfered with the pleasure of it all. Military science and the assessment of the war potential later became one of his minor specialities, much treasured by Marx. Engels' close friends ultimately honored him with the nickname, "The General."

Engels' duties as a military conscript did not interfere with his major purpose in Berlin—going to the university (which lay close to his quarters) and exploring all the roots and ramifications of Hegelian thought or anything else the great world had to offer. He was like the bold youth whom he described in an article published in a South German journal, a youth who was unafraid of the deep, dark forest and chopped his way through the dense woods wherein the "Palace of Ideas" was hidden to "kiss the sleeping princess" there.

Engels experienced an intellectual development during the year he was in Berlin that illustrates Marx's later statement that Engels had the quicker gift of comprehension. It was an exciting time. A confrontation was at hand between the Young Hegelians and the Prussian state. Many of the Young Hegelians believed that history was being decided by the philosophical battles in the Prussian capital. Responding to the Christian, feudal romantic concepts of Frederick William IV, the government was preparing to dislodge Hegelianism from the theological chairs and all citadels of learning. Almost immediately Engels identified himself with the Young Hegelian crowd and worked his way to the front. Having experienced the "liberating effect" of Ludwig Feuerbach's *Essence of Christianity,* he became an embattled atheist.

Not surprisingly, Engels took his place in the same circle that Marx had frequented—the Doctors' Club. His welcome into the Club was assured when he identified himself as the author of the Friedrich Oswald articles. In 1842, the Club adopted a new name, "The Free" (*Freien*), and, according to one witness, pursued the particular goal of overthrowing "any dependence upon an outside God in all thinking, and of getting the human mind recognized as the God of this world." The change in name also led to an abandonment of an external sedateness suggested by the earlier designation. The group became more bohemian, pursued the sensational in its mockery of bourgeois morals and ideals.

Engels was never a mere joiner or follower. He believed in an active strategy aimed at confounding and disorganizing the opposition. He was a leader among men, with a zest for action and a genius for witty speech and ridicule. If the "sleeping princess" was to be kissed, he was going to be in on the act, even if behind the mask of Friedrich Oswald. The initiated would know the secret.

When the philosopher Friedrich Wilhelm Joseph von Schelling was called to Berlin University in 1842, Engels was among the listeners in Auditorium No. 6, as the professor attempted to oust the Hegelians from the philosophy chairs. It seemed to Engels that the destiny of Germany was being decided and he leaped into the melee, though he had no certified training in philosophy.

In one of several anonymous articles against Schelling and the cause which he represented, Engels parodied the indignation of a pious Christian at the blasphemies of the Young Hegelians. But the anonymity was preserved only as long as it served a purpose. Engels' friends then revealed that "Friedrich Oswald" was behind the scenes, manipulating the strings which produced the grimaces of the pious puppet. Later, in 1843, Engels pointed with pride to this article as the first open admission that the Young Hegelians were indeed atheists.

Engels jumped to the rescue of Bruno Bauer when the latter was refused the anticipated theological chair at Bonn University. This time he used his poetic talent in imitation of Goethe's *Faust*, with God and the Devil contending over Bruno Bauer's destiny. It was a mixture of satire and burlesque under the misleading title, "The Brazenly Threatened, Yet Nonetheless Miraculously Rescued Bible, or Triumph of Faith."

The work has a special interest for the biographer because it contains character sketches of many of the Young Hegelians. Although Engels recognized Bruno Bauer's leadership, his dramatic sympathies clearly leaned towards the two angriest characters—Karl Marx and "Friedrich Oswald." The picture of the rampant Marx has been noted earlier. No assumed modesty kept Engels from describing "Oswald" as the most radical of all, with "hide and hair." Oswald is dressed in a grey coat with pepper-colored trousers, and also "peppery within," as he tears across the stage on his long legs to the far left where he plays a musical instrument—the guillotine. To the tune of a "Song of Hell" Oswald bellows out a refrain, "Form your battalions! To arms, citizens!"

Engels also wrote for the *Rheinische Zeitung* in Cologne, edited by and for Young Hegelians. He established himself as a literary critic with an article, published in a Berlin periodical, in which he attacked writers and critics who tried to reconcile political and social conflicts. The Young German writers were now passé. Even Gutzkow, who had given "Friedrich Oswald" his literary debut, could not survive unless his *Telegraph* fell in line. Only the deceased Ludwig Börne remained on a pedestal.

37

The Young Hegelians—with Strauss, Feuerbach and Bauer contending over the life and death of Christianity—alone were in step with the "movement of the time."

Engels' last article under the "Friedrich Oswald" pseudonym was a direct attack on Frederick William IV and his Prussian policies. Probably written after Engels had returned to Barmen in October, it appeared belatedly in 1843 in a collective volume published in Switzerland in order to evade German censorship. "Oswald" there compared the position of Prussia with that of "France before——." The missing date could have been either 1789 or 1830. The odds favor 1789, after which the "good king" lost his French throne and head, with Oswald's "musical instrument" taking care of the latter.

The *Freien,* meanwhile, were verging towards communism. Several members of the Berlin group declared that political change no longer sufficed; a social revolution founded on communal ownership of property alone could satisfy their abstract principles. A year later when Engels described the above events in the *New Moral World,* the journal founded by Robert Owen, he referred to the Young Hegelians' clique as "the Party." Marx, who was then editor of the *Rheinische Zeitung* in distant Cologne, failed to grasp the new trend and was protesting sourly that some of the Berlin contributors to his paper, by smuggling an entirely new world outlook (*Weltanschauung*) into theatrical criticism, etc., were guilty of an inappropriate, yes, even unmoral conduct!

Engels himself, although more advanced than Marx, did not become an immediate convert to communism. Sentiment was not enough. He had previously noted the misery of the masses in Barmen and Bremen, yet such observations were merely a minor item in a wider indictment of a society already condemned. But now a host of serious scholars, sentimental writers as well as a governmental investigation were advertising the revolutionary potential of the proletariat and even the inevitability of socialism and communism. Here was a negation in the existing order that might command millions of followers egged on by despair and the vision of a better future.

As one who swore by the Hegelian philosophy of history that saw progress as the offspring of conflict between the old and the new, Engels could not ignore the possibilities. But a time for adjustment was needed. Up to this point, he had inveighed mostly against castles, thrones and altars. It was also a little difficult for a person accustomed to fighting with philosophical and critical weapons to envision the unschooled and hungry masses as a reliable force with which to revolutionize the world in the right direction. It took several months for him to be persuaded that communism was the "necessary consequence" of the Young Hegelian philosophy.

Engels' final conversion to communism occurred after he had returned to Barmen in the fall. It was Moses Hess who then persuaded him during a meeting in Cologne that Young Hegelian thought, if logically pursued, pointed infallibly to communism. Hess, describing the occasion the following summer (June 19, 1843), gloated that he had "spread devastation" —Engels left as a most enthusiastic Communist, a revolutionist of the "Year I." Engels himself subsequently named Moses Hess as the "first communist in the party," though he and Marx later ridiculed Hess as a man of unsystematic thinking, patronizingly calling him the "Communist Rabbi." But it was this son of a Rhenish merchant who raised some of the signposts that Marx and Engels followed in the next years. Hess was first among the Young Hegelians to recognize the force latent in the problem of poverty and social conflict. He also was the first to elaborate on the converging roles of England (the most advanced economically), France (the classical land of political revolutions), and Germany (the mother of philosophical revolution) in the coming upheavals. This triple combination, or "triarchy," was bound to shove the world out of its old orbit. It was a prospect which made Engels eager to go to England.

3. ENGELS IN ENGLAND

THERE was no disagreement between father and son regarding the next step in Engels' career; he would go to Manchester, England, to serve in the cotton-spinning firm of Ermen and Engels, as another move towards the completion of a thorough apprenticeship in business. The father may have felt that a change in climate, away from the philosophical radicalism in Germany, would be healthful. Engels himself was enthusiastic over the prospects since Moses Hess had opened his eyes to England's importance in a coming social revolution. Now he would have the opportunity to examine directly the status of English society, proletarian unrest and the impact of the industrial revolution, as well as to study political economy.

Engels left Barmen for Manchester in November, 1842, stopping in Cologne for a brief visit with Karl Marx at the office of the *Rheinische Zeitung*. It was their first meeting, an uneventful affair, one that was marked by an atmosphere of restraint and formal courtesy, as when two people recognize each other's potentialities, but have reservations regarding their respective aims and associations. Marx at that time, though a revolutionist, was unimpressed by such subjects as socialism, communism, social unrest and economic theory. He was not yet ripe for Engels. But in the coming months the *Rheinische Zeitung* printed several articles by Engels, merely reports of conditions in England, though selective as to subject matter and conclusions.

Though the *Rheinische Zeitung* carried no further writings by Engels after 1842 (the reasons are unclear), Engels became a medium through which the continent heard of the social crises in England. His four "Letters out of London" were published in 1843 in a Swiss republican newspaper, soon suppressed for being communistic. Simultaneously, in the Owenite *New Moral World* Engels advised the English of a gathering avalanche of socialism and communism in Germany, France and Switzerland. By 1844 he again established contacts with Marx who was then co-editor of a publication in Paris. Engels had become the expert on England, as also the best-read Young Hegelian on the subject of political economy.

Engels also had broader plans—a big book or two—and gathered materials for one of them, a comprehensive social history of England. Since the English had been examining themselves and reporting on their findings for several generations, he was able to consult a wide variety of "authentic sources," such as governmental reports and published works. In addition, he went out into the byways, to the factories and slums, to see for himself. "I forsook the company and the dinner-parties, the port-wine and champagne of the middle classes, and devoted my leisure-hours almost exclusively to the intercourse with plain Working Men," Engels stated in English in the preface of his book on the condition of the working class in England.

Engels' activities outside business hours were not limited to study, research and writing. He neglected no opportunity to establish contact with any movement or group which had the proper revolutionary potential. This included the formidable Chartist movement, which demanded universal manhood suffrage and a role for the English worker in politics. The Chartists, however, were too purely political in their outlook to satisfy Engels; they lacked a real proletarian instinct. With an eye for the essentials, he did establish a friendship with George Julian Harney, the editor of the Chartist paper, *Northern Star*, thus opening up another channel for future articles.

More significant for the future, during a stay in London, Engels became acquainted with Karl Schapper, Joseph Moll and Heinrich Bauer, three stalwarts in the League of the Just, a German communist group in that city. They were the first "revolutionary proletarians" Engels had met— "real men," resolute in action and not hindered by reservations, especially mental. Though they lacked a proper grasp of theory, they showed the needed spirit and physical strength. Many years later Engels again expressed admiration for Joseph Moll, a "medium-sized Hercules," who together with the giant Schapper had so often successfully fought off the invasion of hundreds of hostile intruders at the door of a meeting hall. Such talent can be useful.

Engels also developed a unique interest in the Irish. Thousands were leaving impoverished Ireland to become the lowest rank in England's labor hierarchy. He saw them as "carefree, gay, potato-eating children of nature" who had become genuine proletarians in England, wild untrammelled fanatic Gaels, consumed by an inner rage and capable of anything. With 200,000 Irish at his command, Engels felt that he could overthrow the whole British monarchy. Though he and Marx later were to label the lowest fringe of the working populations as a "ragged proletariat" (*Lumpenproletariat*), useless and perhaps even embarrassing for communist purposes, they never lost a certain interest in the Irish whose liberation seemed a necessary prologue to an English revolution. Yet it is possible that even then in England, Engels sensed that the Irish would never follow his banner.

The Irish entered the private life of Engels in the person of Mary Burns, a working woman and an uneducated child of nature. She filled Engels' needs perfectly. Educated women never had the same appeal to him. His tie with Mary Burns lacked legal formality and some critics have called her his mistress. But it is more appropriate to classify her as his common-law wife. The union lasted many years until Mary's death. Engels thereafter took up a similar life with her sister Lizzie. Engels ultimately married Lizzie, as a death-bed concession when Lizzie wished to die as an honest woman.

Engels spent nearly two years in England, mostly in Manchester. He left with a far greater knowledge of political economy, backed by a first-hand acquaintance with an advanced industrial society, than Marx possessed when the two again met, in Paris late in August, 1844. Marx, with a stronger grounding in philosophy and pure intellectualism, had found it more difficult to accept the economic factor, class conflict and the proletariat as alone capable of crashing through the barriers that stood in the way of a revolutionary dream. But by then he also had arrived, after trying and eliminating other possibilities.

=IV=

The Rheinische Zeitung

1. INTERIM

DURING the time that Engels was serving in the artillery and absorbing Hegel in Berlin, Marx was at loose ends. He stayed on in Bonn, though all hope for a professorship at the university had vanished. There at least he enjoyed a certain freedom from the pressures he would encounter if he returned to Trier. His family felt that he should become self-supporting and, most painful of all, Jenny von Westphalen was still waiting. After a six-year engagement he was not yet in a position to marry her. Moreover, in Trier he would feel "completely excluded" from the literary world where he hoped to win recognition. He would be in a better position to establish himself from Bonn and nearby Cologne where he was immersed in the movements of the time.

Just then the Young Hegelian philosophers were beginning to make a full-fledged debut into journalism and politics—the "movement of 1842/43," as it was later called. Convinced that their philosophy represented the highest revelation of human wisdom, they were out to change the course of Prussian and perhaps world history. Under the circumstances, Marx had cause for optimism, for he possessed the most incisive philosophic mind of all. His Young Hegelian admirers were waiting for him to show "what he really was."

After the New Year, 1842, Marx busied himself with all sorts of writings, but he failed to complete the promised articles. For a time he was sick. Then his future father-in-law and friend, Ludwig von Westphalen, was mortally ill for three months before his death on March 2, 1842. During this time Marx could do little.

Later in March, Marx went to Cologne to set up a "new domicile." Life with the Bonn professors was becoming unbearable—no one liked to talk constantly with "intellectual skunks." But life in Cologne proved to be

42

too stirring—he had too many friends there. He returned to Bonn early in April, with the comforting thought that it would be too bad if no one remained there to offend the pious.

During this period Marx was never out of contact with the publishing world. He constantly corresponded with Arnold Ruge, editor of the former *Hallische Jahrbücher,* which since July 1, 1841, had been appearing under a new name, *Deutsche Jahrbücher.* The change occurred when the Prussian government ordered Ruge to submit to censorship, if he wished to distribute his *Jahrbücher* in the big Prussian market. Ruge, however, knew the tricks of the trade; he simply moved across the frontier to Dresden in the Kingdom of Saxony where a lighter censorship prevailed. Disillusioned in Prussia, Ruge adopted a more radical and critical policy in the new *Jahrbücher.* Under the circumstances, contributions from Marx were especially welcomed.

Marx sent his first article to Ruge in February, 1842, a criticism of the liberalized Prussian censorship rules issued late in 1841. Ruge, however, found the article too strong for the *Jahrbücher,* even under the milder censorship in Saxony. But he did suggest that it might be published in a collective volume (of "cute and piquant things" rejected by the censor) that he planned to have printed in Switzerland. In April, Marx mentioned the titles of four additional articles that might be included—he needed just a few more days to complete the stuff. But the promised articles (on Religious Art, The Romanticists, The Philosophical Manifesto of the Historical School of Law, and The Hegelian Natural Law) were never completed. When Ruge's collective volume, *Anecdotes on the Latest in German Philosophy and Publicity,* appeared in Switzerland in 1843, only Marx's censorship article and a two-page piece on "Luther as Umpire between Strauss and Feuerbach" were included. The censorship article appeared under the anonymous by-line of "A Rhinelander," the latter piece, "No Berliner."

The question of proclaiming authorship had kept Marx on tethers. On February 10, 1842, he had asked Ruge not to print his name under the article on censorship. By March he decided that a "demonstration" like the *Anecdotes* forbade anonymity; Ruge could use his name. People were to see that one had a "good conscience." But then Marx changed his mind again and decided that it was best to maintain anonymity. By that time he had become editor of a Cologne newspaper and he may have felt that his position would be endangered. Tactical considerations, in all good conscience, could not be ignored.

The four articles which Marx promised Ruge never got beyond the manuscript state, except for a few parts published later. On July 9, he complained to Ruge that at best he had had only four weeks free for work since April. A family death had taken him back to Trier; six weeks in all had been spoiled by the most "repulsive family controversies." His family was no longer willing to give him the accustomed allowance in spite of the "wealth" which he accused them of having.

Unquestionably, outside distractions and interests kept Marx from concentrating on unfinished articles. But he was beset already with a weakness that plagued him to the end. Ideas and theories that stood out in frigid clarity in Marx's own mind looked less logical when spelled out in ink. Hence, there was the need for added research. Then critiques were stacked against critiques; evidence was amassed on evidence; mountains were pulled down around other mountains to smother a molehill. The result was impressive by its massiveness, and the shimmering passages here and there suggested buried treasure. In later times Engels and others who knew Marx best usually suffered a letdown whenever Marx came out with a "learned volume." The print never looked as convincing as Marx's oral exposition, accompanied by the appropriate emotional tone and eloquent gestures. Marx could and did write superb prose, but only when deeply aroused in response to a current situation or when expounding a concept of history or theories accepted as articles of faith.

2. COLOGNE'S NEW PAPER

By summer, 1842, Marx was no longer greatly interested in Ruge's publication in Switzerland. He had become increasingly involved in the affairs of a new newspaper in Cologne, which held considerable promise for the future. The paper, the *Rheinische Zeitung für Politik, Handel und Gewerbe* (*Rhenish Newspaper for Politics, Trade and Industry*) is a classical example of a newspaper that went astray from its original purpose.

Financed by members of the banking, industrial and business elite of Cologne, the founders of the new paper hoped to create a moderately liberal, pro-Prussian organ. They wanted to break the monopoly which the *Kölnische Zeitung*, with its eight thousand subscribers, had successfully maintained in the Rhineland metropolis—an appalling situation because that paper had favored the anti-Prussian stand of the Catholic opposition during the recent Cologne church struggle. Since the founders of the *Rheinische Zeitung* were generally loyal to Prussia, Prussia favored their undertaking and gladly granted the company a concession to publish. The chief Prussian administrator was even listed among the early stockholders.

Ludolf Camphausen (banker, railroad promoter and liberal Catholic) stood out prominently as a stockholder in the company. Thoroughly loyal to Prussia, he advocated a moderately liberal, constitutional monarchy. The climax of his public career came during the Revolution of 1848 when for three months he headed the first liberal government in Prussia. Gustav Mevissen, the son of a manufacturer, was another prominent stockholder. He distinguished himself as a liberal and humanist of the highest order. On visiting England, Mevissen noted with genuine sympathy the debased lot of the working man, but unlike Engels, he was convinced that human society would correct the situation without revolution.

Since most of the stockholders were practical men of business and finance, they allowed their sons, the self-confident younger generation, to publish the paper. Georg Jung and Dagobert Oppenheim, university-trained lawyers and the sons of wealthy parents, were charged with the management of the *Rheinische Zeitung*. Both were Young Hegelians and admirers of Marx. Georg Jung, already well enough known to have been included in that galaxy which Engels celebrated in verse, was mainly responsible for the acquisition of an editorial staff and correspondents. Dagobert Oppenheim was in charge of business affairs. Moses Hess all the while displayed his usual promotional zeal and enlisted the services of his friends as correspondents and editors.

From the first the new paper was expected to match the established *Kölnische Zeitung* (*Cologne Newspaper*) in both size and format. It was to be second to none, even contesting the field with the *Augsburger Allgemeine Zeitung* (*Augsburg General Newspaper*) and the *Leipziger Allgemeine Zeitung* (*Leipzig General Newspaper*), the two leading German newspapers. Georg Jung emphasized that money was no consideration in acquiring the best correspondents and editors; he felt free to lose 20,000 *Taler* the first year.

As managing editor (*Gerant*), Georg Jung attempted to give the paper a Young Hegelian stamp. He informed Arnold Ruge that he was making certain that all correspondents were of their "view" (*Richtung*). Such Young Hegelians would know what to say and how to say it, except that they had to observe two conditions: they must show the "greatest indulgence" towards Catholicism and their writings must be in a "popular manner," using only veiled expressions when discussing politics. They must not alienate the Catholic stockholders and potential subscribers. And censorship still existed, even under the somewhat liberalized rules issued by the Prussian state in 1841.

Moses Hess, in contrast to Jung, was not discriminating enough. He did not comprehend that a proper philosophical outlook was the soul of the true liberal and he, therefore, was unable to winnow out the Young Hegelians from the general liberal chaff. Some of those whom he selected for the staff, consequently, were rejected or told to adapt themselves to the editorial slant of the paper.

Almost from the beginning Marx had had a hand in shaping the affairs of the *Rheinische Zeitung* through his influence on Georg Jung. Jung rejected a capable liberal who had offered his services as editor-in-chief because Marx blackballed him. Ludwig Braunfels, to whom Hess had promised the post of co-editor, experienced a similar rebuff. Braunfels later blamed the "Hegelei" of the managing editor for his "enforced withdrawal; Bruno Bauer and Marx despised him as a non-Hegelian, and they controlled Georg Jung like a puppet."

When the *Rheinische Zeitung* first appeared on January 1, 1842, however, the post of editor-in-chief was filled by a non-Hegelian—Gustav Höfken, a liberal writer with a major interest in economic questions. This represented a temporary concession to the liberal bourgeois stockholders. Höfken's career was brief; he suffocated the philosophical views of the Young Hegelians in too much "cotton and twist," according to Jung. Höfken, by his own account, soon saw that a struggle for control of the paper was developing between a "clique of Catholic liberals and the Young Hegelian communists" (some were already attracted to communism), with the latter group, "as the more intellectual, though not the most sensible," emerging on top. Höfken left before the end of the month, when he saw that he could not check that trend. The Young Hegelians were in control. Moses Hess was asked to step into the vacancy.

Hess "danced for joy," but his joy did not survive the month. The Young Hegelians could use him to fill a gap, but not to hold a position. In the early days of February, 1842, Adolf Rutenberg arrived from Berlin to replace Hess. Rutenberg's appointment as editor resulted from Marx's recommendation.

This was the same Adolf Rutenberg whom Marx had admired and called his closest friend during the early university years in the Prussian capital, a fact which seems to have been Rutenberg's major qualification for the chief editorial post. Marx always accepted responsibility for bringing Rutenberg into the *Rheinische Zeitung* even after he had proven to be entirely unsuitable for the position.

The newspaper was a sensation of a sort from the first, an *enfant terrible*, more talked about than read. A year later Friedrich Engels, blandly referring to the *Rheinische Zeitung* as a "political organ of the Party," attributed the momentary success of the Young Hegelians' journalism to the suddenness and energy of their assault. He boasted that German papers, although published under the eyes of a censor, carried materials that in France would have been condemned as treasonous, while other items, if printed in Britain, would have been considered blasphemous.

The *Rheinische Zeitung*, nevertheless, lacked popular appeal; people were more angered than impressed by it. The critical and irreverent tone offended religious and other sensibilities. Various newspapers accused the newcomer of brash immaturity, paired with a philosophically superior know-it-all tone. They even rebuked the Prussian censor for being lax and indulgent towards the paper. The Young Hegelians, however, were confident that Germany was ready to buy their philosophical prescriptions as a "bitter medicine" that cured all ills. They were certain that the paper would be financially successful. But in spite of extensive promotional activities, there were only eight hundred subscribers by July, 1842. According to Ludolf Camphausen, five hundred more were added by August, but even so, he reported on August 12, the *Rheinische Zeitung* faced a grave financial crisis; three-fourths of the original capital had been eaten up.

The greatest immediate threat to the survival of the paper came from the Prussian government, which was appalled by the monster it had sponsored. The *Rheinische Zeitung* actually negated the very principles upon which the government of Frederick William IV rested, though it occasionally praised a few Prussian policies. Hess boasted that the editorial staff paid no attention to the censors. But the censors were spending much time on the *Rheinische Zeitung*. Even so, the Prussian government found that the printed pages were provocative, odious and subversive. The situation was absurd. Having passed through the hands of the censor, the paper carried the official stamp of Prussian approval. Yet the published copy met a general condemnation in governmental quarters. Here were enough contradictions to delight any Young Hegelian. An end to censorship seemed the logical answer; in the Prussia of the 1840's, suppression was the more likely result.

The Prussian state always took the position that the license to publish the *Rheinische Zeitung* was temporary and provisional, thus allowing a review of the question at the end of every quarter. At the end of the first quarter in March, 1842, and again in May, the Ministry of Interior was ready to suppress the paper by refusing to renew the concession. The official report classified the paper as "partisan and oppositionist"; in order to win a popular following, it used the "despicable method of distorting facts, as well as attacking the government and casting doubts on official measures. The paper attacked Christianity while professing Protestantism, but it was a type of Protestantism which no Evangelical Christian could accept." Furthermore, the report continued, as an organ of Young Hegelian propaganda the paper tried to prove that the changes it recommended for society were a necessary consequence of German philosophy. The *Rheinische Zeitung*, however, was saved on both occasions because it was a Rhineland product, financed by families whose loyalties to Prussia were above reproach. The same tolerance would not have prevailed in the older, eastern provinces. Meanwhile, with so few readers, notably in the Rhineland, the paper represented no great danger.

Marx himself did not write anything for the *Rheinische Zeitung* until May, 1842, but he maintained a deep interest in its affairs. In a letter of

July 9, he sounded as if the whole weight and woe of an editorship rested on him. Rutenberg was "completely impotent"; sooner or later he would have to be dismissed. On August 25, Marx wrote a long letter to Dagobert Oppenheim, outlining his views on how to edit a paper in a world cluttered with censorship. Marx pointed out that the main object was to avoid any general discussion of constitutional theory lest it provoke more stringent censorship or even suppression. Also, openly hostile attacks of that sort would offend the liberal, practical men who were fighting for freedom within the existing constitutional framework. The Young Hegelians could hardly expect financial support from the liberals if they, "from the comfortable chair of abstraction," set out to prove that the ideal of a liberal constitutional monarchy (favored by most of the stockholders) was a contradictory and therefore futile dream. There was no need to thrust "true theory under peoples' noses for all to smell." It could be brought out by indirection, within the framework of a criticism of concrete conditions, Marx advised.

There is a myth about Marx as the fearless man, who was above concealment of his own objectives. He did have courage, the courage of a person with the superior mind who has the conviction that history marches with him, and he marches with history, at double time. But Marx already recognized that the tactics of a frontal assault with flying banners did not always guarantee an otherwise certain victory.

Marx's first contribution to the *Rheinische Zeitung* appeared on May 5, when, under the by-line of "A Rhinelander," he began a series of six articles on the Proceedings of the Sixth Rhenish Diet of 1841. He selected the debate on freedom of the press as a backdrop for his own observations on the subject. Marx here defended the customary right of journalists to remain anonymous with the flippant remark: "Indeed, Adam, when he gave names to all the animals in Paradise, forgot to do the same for German newspaper correspondents; and nameless they would remain throughout eternity." Anonymity, however, meant that the general reader had no occasion to applaud, ignore, condemn or to be aware of the existence of a Karl Marx in connection with the *Rheinische Zeitung*. Only a select few knew the identity of the author of a specific article.

In these censorship articles Marx avoided any direct reference to Prussian policies. But in citing the views of members of the Diet, he took the opportunity to expound his own views, in the way of a rebuttal, amplification or clarification of the debate. Here was the technique he had suggested to Oppenheim, of bringing out the "true theory" while reporting on concrete events. Simultaneously, Marx could paint the "desolate and disagreeable impression" which the artificially-reconstituted feudal character of the Prussian provincial diets (with representation along class lines and the nobility being favored) made on him. The members of the Diet,

Marx asserted, did not express their personal views, but merely reflected those of a specific class.

Marx next used the debates of the Diet of 1841 on the Cologne Church controversy, together with Prussia's concessions to the Catholics, for an attack on the "Ultramontane Party," the "most dangerous in the Rhineland." Employing a clever line of argument, Marx hoped to fool the "stupid Cologne Catholics" and win subscriptions from them for the *Rheinische Zeitung* by an apparent defense of the deposed Archbishop. But the intelligence of the Catholics was never put to the test because the Prussian censor forbade publication. After this rebuff, Marx left the Proceedings of the Rhenish Diet of 1841 alone for several months.

Beginning on July 10, Marx wrote a series of articles attacking the *Kölnische Zeitung* which had accused the upstart *Rheinische Zeitung* of assault on Christianity and religion, and questioned the propriety of bringing philosophy into the daily newspaper. The *Kölnische Zeitung* had even suggested that the Prussian censor needed to be more vigilant in guarding the world against such "repulsive outpourings of youthful arrogance."

Marx always felt like a cow in fresh clover when he set out to answer such attacks. He excelled in a form of criticism designed to pick apart the arguments of others, making them appear contradictory, ridiculous and even stupid, prompted moreover by motives which were less than noble.

The articles reached an apex in an almost rhapsodic defense of philosophy, "the intellectual quintessence" of the age. The philosophers had left the academic halls behind to become newspaper correspondents, thereby mingling and interacting with the real world—and "philosophy becomes worldly and the world becomes philosophical." When that happens, Marx asserted, philosophy "ceases to be a question of one specific system competing with other specific systems; it becomes the philosophy as such against the world; it becomes the philosophy of the contemporary world"—the "true philosophy of the present."

Marx apparently felt that competing views and systems were possible only as long as it was a mere academic matter. But when philosophy entered the arena of reality, all argument ceased; there could be only one true philosophy of and for that real world. Marx obviously believed that the Young Hegelians had that true philosophy. Later, after Marx opted for communism, he similarly defined communism as not just another system competing with various systems, but as the actual reflection of reality, of what was happening and destined to happen. The strength of Marx rested on such a faith and certitude.

Aside from a journalistic misfit, "The Philosophical Manifesto of the Historical School of Law," published on August 9, Marx wrote nothing for the *Rheinische Zeitung* for several months. By October, 1842, the af-

49

fairs of the paper reached a crisis. Adolf Rutenberg had proven to be weak and completely incompetent as editor and had to be pushed aside. An iron hand was needed to discipline the Berlin correspondents from the ranks of "The Free"; they were becoming too reckless and outspoken in their communist views. The situation was compounded by a financial crisis. Regardless of increasing subscriptions, the stockholders had to be approached for additional money. It was under such circumstances that Marx moved from Bonn to Cologne to become the chief editor of the *Rheinische Zeitung* on October 15. His appointment assured the stockholders of the presence of an unusually intelligent person and an energetic and even ruthless hand in dealing with the overall situation.

The selection of Marx as editor-in-chief was the logical outcome of the influence which he exerted over the Young Hegelians who managed the paper and a tribute to the awesome respect he commanded from them. Moreover, the common sense views he had expressed to Oppenheim in August, concerning the editing of a paper with radical aims, certainly played a role. Under Marx there would be no bold, forthright declaration of the actual aims of the Young Hegelians which would offend the stockholders and the Prussian authorities to the point where it would be fatal for the *Rheinische Zeitung*. This observation contradicts the common view that Marx at once gave to the *Rheinische Zeitung* a special democratic, radical and outspoken twist.

The change in editors produced no immediate miracle, although Franz Mehring, usually regarded as the best biographer of Marx, asserts that it brought an increase of subscriptions, from 885 to 1820 between October 15 and November 10. This is contradicted by Camphausen's letter which indicates that about 1300 were in hand by the preceding mid-August. Actually, Marx's rise to the chief editorial post was unheralded and unannounced. Most readers were unaware of a change in editors. Even the Prussian authorities assumed that Rutenberg was still at the helm.

Marx's first article as editor appeared on October 16, unsigned as usual.* It was a reply to the South German *Augsburger Allgemeine Zeitung* that had accused the *Rheinische Zeitung* of being a "Prussian communist" paper, or of at least flirting with communism. The Augsburg paper also had taken some gentle jabs at the rich sons of Cologne merchants who innocently played with socialist ideas without any intentions of sharing their wealth with the stonemasons working on the Cathedral or the dock laborers in the harbor. Actually, the *Augsburger's* charge rested on flimsy foundations. But the accusation had been made by one of the foremost German papers; an answer was in order.

* Most of Marx's unsigned articles have been identified through references to such articles in the Marx-Engels correspondence, in other writings, or in their correspondence with others. The subject and style offer additional clues.

Marx twisted the dagger around and accused the Augsburg paper of having its own dalliance with communism. Beyond that he flatly refused to discuss the theory of communism and the chances of its practical realization. Such matters required profound study and could not be disposed of through a few superficial remarks on the level of the "frothy phraseology" of the *Augsburger*. Marx then expressed a "firm conviction" that the real danger of communism came from the theoretical development of communist ideas, not from any attempt to introduce it in practice. Practical attempts, even if backed by the masses, could be answered with cannon. But *Ideas* which conquer our minds, they are the real "demons which man can overcome only by subjecting himself to them."

In later years Marx once stated that this controversy with the Augsburg paper soured his interest in the *Rheinische Zeitung* and hastened the decision to get back to his studies, presumably to catch up on the neglected subjects of communism, socialism, economics and poverty. Even Franz Mehring does not place much faith in this bit of Marxian retrospection. Other biographers have concluded that the incident embarrassed Marx since he was unprepared to say anything profound on the subject of communism. That is unlikely also. Why should Marx be discommoded here when, as a matter of editorial policy he avoided discussions of principle and theory even in subjects where he was best informed? The whole tone of Marx's reply indicates that he welcomed the attack as an opportunity to demonstrate the superiority of the *Rheinische Zeitung*. It also gave him a chance to repeat that his paper believed that such problems could be solved in a "peaceful manner." Such affirmations were not amiss in October, 1842, and could be made without a chapter of profound commentary.

The paper faced another of the almost chronic quarterly threats of suppression by the Prussian government. The matter was doubly serious this time because mounting subscriptions erased the government's hope that the *Rheinische Zeitung* would die of its own accord. It was Marx's own pronounced urge to be the first to print the news that precipitated the crisis on October 20 when he published the text of a new divorce law then being considered in the Prussian Council of State. A copy of the law had come to him from some unauthorized source before the government was ready to release the text. Marx simply printed it without any editorial comment. Other newspapers, however, immediately attacked the draft law which was designed to make divorce more difficult, in line with religious considerations. These attacks offended the King who had taken a very personal interest in the measure. The government's anger, however, was directed solely at the *Rheinische Zeitung* for having printed the text prematurely. Official wrath increased when the paper refused to reveal how or through whom the text had found its way to Cologne.

The Prussian government confronted the *Rheinische Zeitung* with an ultimatum. Unless the paper changed its hostile tendency, the concession to publish would not be renewed at the end of the year. A bill of particulars, mainly a recapitulation of already chronic complaints, was sent to the paper. But the Prussian authorities revealed their ignorance regarding the inner workings of the *Rheinische Zeitung* by calling for the dismissal of Adolf Rutenberg as chief editor.

Rutenberg had become merely a tolerated nullity whose sole responsibility, according to Marx, was the harmless task of checking the punctuation of the essays. Judging from letters of Hess and Marx, the Prussian demand merely relieved the *Rheinische Zeitung* of the "embarrassing step" of firing Rutenberg. Now it could be made to appear that the management was bowing to a higher authority when it dismissed him, after registering a feeble protest.

Marx's reply to the Prussian government's charges was a masterpiece of diplomatic finesse, respectful in tone yet without surrendering much in substance. Writing under the name of the responsible publisher, J. E. Renard, Marx stressed some of the positive features of the *Rheinische Zeitung*. He maintained that it aimed at turning the German gaze away from France by cultivating a truly German liberalism. The paper always mirrored Prussian North German ideas, in contrast to the South German papers that looked to France. As for religious and church questions, the *Rheinische Zeitung* would show its good will by avoiding the subject, unless other newspapers and political developments made it necessary to break the silence. Marx was not giving away much in the latter promise; hardly a day would pass when the exception could not be invoked. But the general tone of Marx's statement was satisfactory. The *Rheinische Zeitung* was assured of its existence into a second year.

Prussia, however, took the precaution of replacing the old censor with another, presumably more intelligent and therefore more vigilant person. Moses Hess soon concluded that the change helped more than it hurt. Marx himself later called the new censor an "honorable fellow." This may have been fatal since the paper was judged by what appeared in print; it could not therefore afford a censor who was too lenient.

Ludolf Camphausen at this time also reported an illusion which existed in the inner circles of the *Rheinische Zeitung*—the belief that Berlin would not dare to suppress the newspaper since too many respected and loyal Rhinelanders had invested money in the company. But there was always the question of how far the paper could go before other considerations would prevail. Marx appears to have been confident that he could walk the tightwire, but in the end he overestimated his own cleverness, or underestimated the intelligence of the Prussian authorities in recognizing the disguised but persistently hostile tendency of the *Rheinische Zeitung*.

Marx initially acted with energy to bring some discipline into the affairs of the paper. More and more he depended on the able journalistic talents of Konrad Heinzen, an arch-republican and anti-Prussian writer, unspoiled by socialistic predilections. The unpredictable Moses Hess was expedited to Paris with increased pay, to edit the French articles from that point. But it was more difficult to bridle his former friends, "The Free," in Berlin. Marx had been worried over the doings and writings of these Berlin correspondents as early as the previous July. He persisted in the belief that a paper could accomplish more by not flaunting its theoretical views in a provocative manner. Therefore, when the censor was not strict enough, Marx himself suppressed some of the items. To the Berlin *Free*, this appeared like a compromise; they demanded a bold affirmation of their position. Marx, in turn, demanded less talk of atheism, less preaching, fewer ringing phrases, more exactitude, a greater stress on concrete circumstances, a better knowledge of practical facts. An irreparable break occurred in November.

One of the Berlin *Free*, Eduard Meyen, called Marx a conservative (in an "insolent letter," as Marx termed it) and demanded that the *Rheinische Zeitung* not compromise. Marx declared that the Young Hegelian demands would entail a foolhardy sacrifice of the paper to the police and censorship authorities. To save a "political organ" like the *Rheinische Zeitung*, he was ready to sacrifice a "few Berlin windbags." It is not surprising that Marx was incapable of giving Friedrich Engels, who had just come from Berlin, a sympathetic reception when the latter passed through Cologne in November, right in the middle of the showdown with the Berlin *Free*. Engels was suspect for having associated with them.

Writing for the *Rheinische Zeitung* on October 24, Marx returned to the unexciting Proceedings of the Sixth Rhenish Diet of 1841. This time he analyzed the debates on a law designed to stiffen the penalties for the "theft" of wood (dead wood, fallen branches, and live berries in the forest, customarily gleaned by the rural population in former ages). He commented later that here, for the first time, he had to write about material interests for which there was no guide in Hegel. But it was a matter of choice and not necessity, because at one point he stated succinctly that he used that example to show what might be expected from a diet based on separate classes, if such a body ever gained real legislative power.

This attack on the nobility for their indifference to the lot of the rural poor shows Marx for the first time painting a stirring and sympathetic picture of the common man. At the same time he extolled the state as the great equalizer and protector of the helpless. "The state also sees in the wood criminal a human being, a living limb in which its own heart blood flows, a soldier who defends the Fatherland, a witness whose testimony is valid before a court, a family father whose being is sacred, above all things a citizen of the state . . . The state amputates itself whenever it makes a criminal out of a citizen."

On December 19, Marx took up the subject of the divorce law which had raised such a storm in October. The *Rheinische Zeitung,* Marx stated later, stood in an "isolated position" among other papers when it insisted that the new law contained improvements over the "previously numerous and frivolous grounds for divorce." Although Marx listed a number of objections to the law where it was based too broadly on religious considerations, his criticism was respectful. Furthermore, he condemned the "eudaemonistic" view, favored by many writers in that romantic age, which made the happiness of two wedded people the crucial consideration; they ignored the family and placed the rights of the children at the mercy of the arbitrary whims and desires of the parents. Marx insisted upon the essentials. It is obvious that he wanted to rule out the church and religious considerations, but he did not say so. He maintained that a divorce was only a declaration that a marriage no longer existed in fact. It was the state that should determine when a marriage, by its "essential nature" had ceased to exist.

Towards the end of 1842, journalism in Prussia (and in some other German states) faced new troubles. Frederick William IV was offended and appalled by the audacity with which everything he valued was being attacked. A Berlin observer spoke of endless governmental consultations that tried to solve the riddle of how to allow newspapers a certain freedom without having them use this freedom to print something exasperating. The censors seemed ineffectual where a given paper had a chronically hostile tendency. Repression was the only certain answer.

On December 28, 1842, the Prussian government took the first step by prohibiting the distribution in Prussia of an outside paper, the *Leipziger Allgemeine Zeitung,* a liberal and somewhat Young Hegelian paper from the neighboring Kingdom of Saxony. The Saxon authorities, responding to the Prussian example, then suppressed it. Young Hegelian and liberal journalism seemed threatened everywhere when Arnold Ruge's *Deutsche Jahrbücher* was likewise suppressed after coming out with a bold pronouncement in favor of democracy.

Marx recognized the "gloomy auspices," but he appeared unabashed, perhaps because he still counted on the immunity of the Rhineland. He at once took up the cause of the banished Leipzig paper and the question of a free press, but he was cautious enough not to condemn Prussia directly. He had plenty of opportunities, however, to lash out in all directions at other newspapers who applauded or condoned the actions of the Prussian state in this matter. In a series of articles running from January 1 to 13, Marx deplored the outlawing of the Leipzig newspaper, derided the *Kölnische Zeitung* for thinking differently, drafted a brief comparison of the "good and bad press," replied to the attack of a "moderate newspaper," did the same against the denunciations of a "neighboring paper," followed this with a rebuttal of another denunciation from the Cologne competitor as also the "polemic" of the Catholic *Rhein-und-Mosel Zeitung,* and ended with a second assault on the last-named paper. In these articles Marx was typically *Marxian,* using either the stiletto or blunderbuss as seemed most fitting in each case, innuendo here and a barrage of facts there.

Marx admitted that the so-called *Young Press* in Germany (the *Volks-presse,* as he also called it now) was inferior to French and English standards. It was unstable, indiscreet, raw, filled with a "pathos of infallibility" and redolent with odious passions. It was "awkward and fairytale-like" even in reporting the facts. But a *Young Press* was bound to be "unripe and raw." It stirred up discontent and anger, "but that anger turned peoples' minds toward the state, created a real interest in the state, thereby making the state a matter of the heart and home." Moreover, Marx argued, the anger that it aroused was a *German* discontent. Berlin, Dresden and Hanover thereby replaced St. Petersburg, Paris and London as the intellectual capital cities of the Germans. Marx, with some justice, could claim that the *Rheinische Zeitung* was German, and more specifically, Prussian. Even Heinrich von Treitschke, the Prussian national historian, rated the paper favorably, later stating that it promoted a vigorous Prussian pride, then still rare in the Rhineland.

Marx dropped the fight with other newspapers after a final fling against the Catholic press on January 13. The Board of Directors of the *Rheinische Zeitung,* noting the rash of suppressive measures against publications with a "malevolent tendency," concluded that a critical moment was at hand in the attitude of the Prussian government. The government indeed hardly need fear even a "quiet reproach" if it suppressed the *Rheinische Zeitung,* in view of the many attacks on it by other papers. Under the circumstances, the Board believed it "very advisable" to avoid offending the government, insofar as this was possible without jettisoning the *tendency* of the paper. Marx ended his attacks on other papers, but he took up a sensitive Rhineland issue he had laid aside for nearly a month.

Several articles by the *Rheinische Zeitung's* Moselle correspondent had been published during November and December, describing the chronic depression and misery that the grape growers of the Moselle Valley had experienced for years. The Moselle, with vineyards on rolling, mountainous hills, was Marx's own homeland, though previously he had seemed unaware of its problems. But here was an opportunity to use a local, down-to-earth example to demonstrate that even the material well-being of the people benefited from a freer press.

In publishing the correspondent's reports from the Moselle, Marx almost certainly gave a special editorial twist to the contents. After describing the depressed conditions, the articles stated that Prussian officials formerly had shown a callous indifference to suffering and had squelched complaints coming from the Moselle. Hence, the winegrowers had welcomed Prussia's liberalization of the censorship laws in 1841. This suggested that a free press, by exposing bureaucratic omissions and derelictions, might have spared the people a generation of unbroken misery. Naturally the Prussian authorities resented the implications in the article; Prussia prided herself and was often credited with being especially benevolent and paternal. An official protest followed, challenging the soundness and veracity of the articles, and accusing the *Rheinische Zeitung* of distorting the facts and slandering the officials.

Marx ignored the government's protest for several weeks in order to gather enough facts so he could reply with a cannonade. Then between January 15 and 20 the "Vindication of the Moselle Reports" appeared in five issues of the *Rheinische Zeitung,* all written by Marx, though unsigned. In this answer to the official protest, Marx presented an especially strong case against Prussia's bureaucracy. He elaborated on his earlier charge that a free press could have spared the winegrowers much misery, would have helped to clarify official thinking, and might have prevented certain callous and arbitrary decisions of the officials.

At first glance Marx here appears most courageous, even reckless, in giving such a black-on-white demonstration of bureaucratic derelictions after the Board of Directors of the *Rheinische Zeitung* had called for caution and restraint. But the baiting of bureaucrats was not necessarily dangerous; some blatant examples were found in the most conservative journals. Of greater significance, however, was the fact that the romantic King of Prussia himself disliked the bureaucracy, regarding it as a soulless machine operating along rationalist lines and reflecting an accursed enlightenment that had its roots in the 18th century. During a recent tour of the Rhine Province, Frederick William IV had even given public proof that he could side with the people against his own bureaucracy. A criticism of the bureaucrats by itself was not needlessly provocative, although it would hardly sweeten the disposition of those officials with whom the *Rheinische Zeitung* had to deal.

Marxian scholars are usually aghast or somewhat amused by the naive and cavalier manner in which Marx brushed aside economic considerations in the Moselle articles. To overcome the chronic depression, Prussia had suggested a more diversified farming to reduce a grape acreage that otherwise produced its annual surplus of Moselle wines. Prussia also had advised a halt to the endless parcelling and subdivision of farms into units too small to keep a family above poverty.

There is evidence that Marx was not uninformed and unresponsive to basic economic considerations. Nor did he question the soundness of Prussia's recommendations in the matter. He simply dismissed such recommendations with the statement, "The people had asked for help and not for advice." He thereafter injected an appeal to Rhineland sensibilities and suspicions by suggesting that Prussia's advice against the unlimited subdivision of farms was another covert attack on the French code of laws that included clauses on equal inheritance for all the children of a family. (Rhinelanders were usually ready to defend their Napoleonic Code of Laws even against beneficial changes.) The people would not surrender a right in order to get relief, Marx asserted.

There is a tradition, faithfully repeated by scholar after scholar, that the *Rheinische Zeitung* under Marx's editorship took a more provocative, radical and democratic turn. The conclusion seems to rest largely on the assumption that it must have been so under a man like Marx. This ignores the fact that Marx deliberately bridled himself and others, with a fairly accurate sense as to what was practical and tactically safe, even if it is possible to detect a democratic trend in certain articles. When he writes on the poverty along the Moselle and the "theft" of wood, he does get down to some of the problems of the common man, paints a sympathetic picture of the rural poor, condemns the selfish interests of privileged (especially noble) classes and makes an unusually effective declaration of the equality and value of each person in the eyes of the state. But if this had the effect of making him into a political democrat, it never appears in the newspaper. Marx to the end adhered to the policy of making no positive and recognizable declarations as to the real political aims of the paper.

Marx, however, did use occasional editorial footnotes to endorse a specific policy. Thus he identified himself with what is usually called Pan-Germanism. He backed the aspirations of a "German Party" in Belgium (the Flemish movement, which cultivated the use of Flemish, a Low German dialect native to half of the Belgians, in opposition to the culturally-dominant French). Every effort to bring recognition to the German nationality in foreign lands, Marx declared, was welcome as a significant anticipation of a better future.

In another editorial footnote on December 16, 1842, Marx stated that it was the duty of all German papers to support their German compatriots in Schleswig-Holstein against Denmark. Asserting that it was a "great, honorable and unheard-of event" for Germany that its separated members yearned to return, Marx ascribed the change to a growth of freedom in Germany. "Only a land of freedom could be the Fatherland of *men*." The "internal revival" of Germany would lead to the return of all lost German lands—Holland, half of Belgium, most of Switzerland, Alsace-Lorraine and Schleswig-Holstein. This was a grandiose vision for an awakening German nation.

To conclude from the preceding and similar declarations in later times that Marx was a rampant German nationalist, and a Pan-German at that, would be sheer folly. All the sounder evidence shows that Marx lacked any pronounced German national sentiments. At this time, however, it was just good politics, and even business, to identify the *Rheinische Zeitung* with German national pains and aspirations. Ever since 1840, when France threatened to march to the Rhine, German national feeling had become a militant force that no journalist and revolutionist could ignore. An advocate of reform or revolution could argue that internal change in Germany was the prerequisite for the fulfillment of the broadest national hopes. Freedom, Marx declared, would make Germany a land of *"men"* that all outside Germans would want to join.

3. SUPPRESSION BRINGS SUCCESS

THE decision to suppress the *Rheinische Zeitung* was formulated in Berlin on January 21, 1843. Notice of the step, together with a bill of particulars explaining the reason, reached the Board of Directors on the 25th. The suppression was not immediate. Out of consideration for the stockholders, the government allowed the paper to appear until April 1, the end of the quarter. During the interim, however, the paper was to be subjected to a double consorship and other restrictions.

Several hours before learning the news of the suppression, Ludolf Camphausen had written that the *Rheinische Zeitung* was doing well materially; subscriptions had risen to thirty-three hundred. But, he added wryly, its "inner value" had not grown in the same measure. He regretted the lack of clear and definitive principles in regard to the questions of the day and suggested that the editorship had failed to define its political beliefs in a positive sense.

The main charges raised by the Prussian authorities justifying the suppression actually differed little from the complaints registered in March, May and October, 1842, except that now they were spelled out in greater detail. One new item stands out—the paper was accused of printing materials inciting hostility to friendly foreign countries. Several articles critical of foreign governments, notably Russia, had indeed been published in the *Rheinische Zeitung* early in January. But such attacks were not uncommon in other papers, since many liberals and radicals sensed that Nicholas I of Russia influenced Prussian policy in a reactionary sense. Nicholas I, however, could hold the Prussian government responsible whenever the official censorship failed to suppress anything that was offensive to Russia.

Frederick William IV, related to the Tsar through marriage, wanted friendly ties with St. Petersburg. Prussia, moreover, regarded Russian friendship as vital for her survival. She needed the insurance that a friendly eastern neighbor could provide, faced as she was with a chronic French desire, demonstrated anew in 1840, to seize the Rhineland. At a time when various French writers also pointed to the mutual advantages of a Franco-Russian alliance at the expense of the German world in between, Prussia could recognize the wisdom of not offending Nicholas I.

The Russians had stumbled across the offending articles in the *Rheinische Zeitung*. A Russian protest followed. A few biographers of Marx feel that this was the decisive factor leading to the suppression of the paper. If so, it was just the proverbial last straw. Frederick William IV was becoming increasingly incensed by the irreverent, critical and negative tone of the newspaper, which in his colorful prose he now called the "harlot-sister on the Rhine." When some of the major Rhenish papers simultaneously attacked the *Rheinische Zeitung*, Berlin could well hope that its suppression might even be applauded by the Catholic populace.

Essentially, the *Rheinische Zeitung* was suppressed because Prussia was not ready to tolerate the type of journalism that it represented. The liberalized censorship instructions of 1841 had granted a freedom to criticize and a right to discuss public affairs, provided that such criticism was constructive, discreet and well-intentioned. The stress was always on the proper attitude or tendency (*Gesinnung*).

There was slight doubt concerning the essentially hostile *tendency* of the *Rheinische Zeitung* in regard to the status quo, and especially the religious and political principles of the Prussian King. This was true even though Marx had avoided open attacks, direct declarations of principles and discussions of theoretical issues. In reply to the Prussian charges, Marx could even argue that it was an exaggeration to say that the tendency of the paper was completely hostile, for it had fought for the "tariff union and for Prussian hegemony"; it had hailed Prussia as the "state of progress," with ample praise for such Prussian "democratic institutions as the army, administrations, etc." Such affirmations, however, seemed to have a hollow ring when they were contradicted by the negative tone of the whole.

From the Prussian point of view, suppression seemed the only solution. A change of editors would be futile, in view of the makeup of the Board of Directors. The only other "remedy," that of an "unusually strict censorship," was rejected. The censors were there merely to catch occasional aberrations and indiscretions in papers that generally remained "within the framework of the law and morality, where no hostile intentions were evident." The prestige of the government was also at stake. "It was a question of showing that the Prussian Government possessed the power to suppress such monstrosities, completely and instantaneously," the Interior Minister stated.

Marx's immediate, angry reaction (recorded in a letter to Arnold Ruge on January 25) was to resign, to get out then and there. It was a number of articles and actions for which he personally was responsible that had led to the suppression of the paper, he asserted. He mentioned especially the Moselle articles in which the "highest officials were strongly blamed." (It is unlikely, however, that the Moselle articles, published between January 15 and 20, could have contributed much to a decision that was formally drawn up in Berlin on the 21st, although it may have appeared advantageous to Marx to convey that idea.) He was tired of "doing menial services even in the name of freedom, fighting with needles instead of clubs." To make matters worse, there now would be a double censorship. The Administrative President in Cologne, "a passive, submissive blockhead," was to play the role of a second censor. Even after the double scrutiny, the printed issue was to be submitted again to the noses of the police. If they smelled anything "un-Christian or un-Prussian," the paper could not appear at all. Marx planned to leave Germany where a "man had to falsify himself." He was tired of disguising the *real* Marx as he had done while editing the *Rheinische Zeitung*.

Marx, however, had some second thoughts and decided to remain at his editorial post, regardless of double censorship and all. It soon became evident that the *Rheinische Zeitung* was to gain its chief fame and popularity by virtue of the fact that it was suppressed. Association with such a paper in its last months of martyrdom was a distinct asset. In the popular mind, the *Rheinische Zeitung* became a symbol of resistance against a government veering towards repression. Men began to ascribe to the paper a greater daring in expounding radical and democratic views than had occurred in any positive sense under Marx's adept hand. It became almost popular in the Rhineland. Franz Mehring, however, probably erred in speaking of a jump in subscriptions up to 3200 following the notice of suppression. Camphausen, after all, had reported a similar figure before the news reached Cologne on the 25th. But a legend was born and persisted. Thus, years later Heinrich von Treitschke (in his monumental history of Germany in the 19th century) even has the *Rheinische Zeitung* pushing the rival *Kölnische Zeitung* into the background.

Camphausen thought that the belated interest in the paper resulted from the fact that any unprejudiced person would believe that the Prussian government had acted unjustly. A paper that could print nothing except material approved beforehand by an official censor ought not be condemned after it appeared in print. "Censorship and yet forbidden; I can't get that through my head," was the oft-cited remark of one peasant subscriber.

The editor of the hostile *Kölnische Zeitung*, C. H. Hermes, described the situation as follows: Before its suppression, the *Rheinische Zeitung* had no influence in most of the Rhineland where a strong Catholic feeling prevailed. The contempt shown for all positive religion had stirred up an intense bitterness among citizens. Suppression changed all that. The past sins of the hated paper were at once forgotten, when people felt that an injustice had been done. Of the hundreds to whom he had spoken, Hermes stated, not one justified the suppression.

A movement to petition Berlin to save the *Rheinische Zeitung* was started immediately in Cologne. It was drafted in a manner that made it possible for many to sign who otherwise disapproved of the contents of the *Rheinische Zeitung*. In Cologne, where the paper had less than 300 subscribers, 911 persons signed the petition. Some other Rhineland cities, including several towns in the Moselle Valley, followed Cologne's example. But the Prussian government remained unresponsive to the above petitions as well as to the efforts of the stockholders.

Marx himself abandoned some of his earlier caution. After deciding on January 25 that he definitely would leave Germany, he now neglected no opportunity to stir up popular discontent. He urged the stockholders to take a firm stand against the suppression of the paper. This same mood is illustrated most clearly in a letter of March 13, 1843, to Arnold Ruge wherein he states that the leader of the Cologne "Israelites" had called on him to get his support for a petition to the Rhenish Diet in favor of the Jews. He had decided to go along with it, no matter how repulsive the "Israelite faith" was to him, for it was a question of poking as many holes as was possible in the "Christian state" and smuggling in the rational things, as far as was possible. That was the least one could do, Marx went on; bitterness would grow with every petition that was rejected by the authorities.

Prussia paid the *Rheinische Zeitung* the compliment of sending an unusually intelligent censor to Cologne in the person of Wilhelm Saint-Paul, to see that no slip occurred after January 25. Here was a censor with diversified talents. From the memoirs of a Prussian general we know that Saint-Paul earlier had spoken in favor of a freer press. Other contemporaries refer to him as a "Don Juan." Marxian scholars are apt to point to his excursions away from traditional morality. Franz Mehring calls him a "young Bohemian" who had caroused with "The Free" in Berlin. In Cologne he also had brawls with policemen in the precincts of a house of prostitution. Perhaps a censor needed a few distractions after office hours.

It was a difficult matter to censor a paper such as the *Rheinische Zeitung*. A contemporary Prussian liberal stated that Marx daily attacked the government but in such a flowery disguise that the censors failed to see what was going on. But the matter was less simple, and Marx was seldom flowery. Again, while the censors usually were taken from the ranks of the less able bureaucrats, they were not entirely blind.

The new censor, Saint-Paul, almost at once saw through the screen of anonymity and obfuscation that surrounded the inner workings of the *Rheinische Zeitung*, perhaps because Marx was now less interested in hiding his role. Saint-Paul reported to Berlin that Dr. Marx was the "doctrinaire nexus, the living source of the theories of the paper." The tone of the despatches indicates that Saint-Paul was impressed by Marx's intelligence. He made a point of becoming acquainted with Marx, thus gaining an "insight into the intellectual movement of the present." Nowhere in these reports to Berlin, however, did Saint-Paul spell out what Marx's real views were—information that he had acquired only through private conversations.

Saint-Paul, without any obvious anger or irritations, pointed out various tactics that were used to get around the censor or to put pressure on him. When an article was deleted seriously, the paper would appear with wider spaces and larger print to indicate where the cuts had been made—as a "silent accusation." Saint-Paul mentioned a number of other ruses. On February 9, he admitted that he should have censored a certain article more severely. But the original copy had come to him in very rough shape, with an enormous number of mechanical errors. The printed copy later had an entirely different meaning, once the misspelled words and other errors had been corrected by the editor.

Due to Saint-Paul's suggestion, the double censorship was dropped almost immediately. Early in February Saint-Paul argued that a very liberal censorship during the remaining weeks of the *Rheinische Zeitung* would have tactical advantages. That would reveal the tendency of the paper in a naked manner; nothing would be more likely to turn the majority of the people against the paper again. In line with this procedure, Saint-Paul reported that he had allowed an article on divorce, with strong polemics against the Church, to be printed.

Marx was faced with a perplexing problem after January 25. Now that the *Rheinische Zeitung* was popular, he wanted to capitalize on the fact that he was the editor. But the situation was a little awkward since he had repeatedly insisted on the virtues of anonymity. The wider public that now sympathized with, and even lionized, the martyred newspaper knew nothing of Marx. He could not break out suddenly with naming of names, with himself most directly involved. It might also appear a little boastful to announce that he was the real mind and force in the *Rheinische Zeitung*. But Marx was entitled to this recognition, and he was not the man to avoid publicity when it was helpful. As a person interested in revolutionizing the world in accordance with his own superior philosophical findings, he recognized the importance of promoting his name. The capacity to establish a certain image of himself in the public mind certainly contributed to Marx's ultimate success. Whenever it was possible, however, he allowed others to do the advertising.

At this time an anonymous friend acted as a medium in giving out the inside story of the *Rheinische Zeitung*. Marx probably wrote the story himself, to spare the friend the effort as well as to make certain that it was done right. In any event, the account is reprinted in the complete works of Marx and Engels, as something that was either written by Marx, or inspired by him, or drafted by someone very close to him.

The story appeared in the *Mannheimer Abendzeitung* (published in the South German state of Baden) on February 28, 1843, ostensibly to enlighten the public as to who was who and what in the operations of the *Rheinische Zeitung*. The article names the responsible publisher, the managing editors, the Board of Directors, and the editorial staff. But everything leads up to the "real editor," to "Dr. Marx," who gave the paper its "decisive color." There is a brief sketch of Marx's background together with a list of the articles that he wrote for the *Rheinische Zeitung*. Most of the polemics appearing in the paper were written by Marx, as the "polemicist par excellence." The article then describes the sharp incisive intellect, the admirable dialectic, the marvelous gifts and the rare diversity of talents that were all combined in the said Dr. Marx.

The *Mannheimer* story closes with the "rumor" that Dr. Marx, in association with Dr. Ruge, planned to resume publication of the *Deutsche Jahrbücher* under a "foreign title." In Dr. Marx, "to say the least, [Ruge] would have an associate who would help with all his soul to carry the flag which he had raised in recent times."

In this way the name of Dr. Marx was introduced to a wider public. A contemporary allegorical sketch thereafter depicted the suppression of the *Rheinische Zeitung* with Marx towering above everything, as an athletic, chained Prometheus, chained to an equally chained printing press, while the Prussian eagle pecks away at his liver, all on the banks of the Rhine with Cologne Cathedral silhouetted across the stream.

On March 18, 1843, the following declaration was published in the *Rheinische Zeitung*:

> The undersigned declares that he, because of the present status of censorship, on this day has stepped out of the editorship of the *Rheinische Zeitung*
> Cologne, March 17, 1843
>
> Dr. Marx.

Had Marx remained two weeks longer until the end of publication, there would have been no occasion for such a declaration. As it was, the censor graciously permitted Marx to bow out with flying flags, not anonymously, but with a formal, signed statement. Perhaps Wilhelm Saint-Paul felt that he could do no less for a worthy foe.

=V=

Kreuznach and Paris
1843–1845

1. PHILOSOPHY DISCOVERS
THE PROLETARIAT

WHEN Marx resigned as editor of the *Rheinische Zeitung* on March 17, 1843, his immediate future appeared secure since he had the promise of a position as co-editor of a periodical, with a definite and satisfactory salary. Once out of Germany he could give full rein to his talents, uninhibited by the self-imposed restrictions under which he had operated in Cologne. The new position grew out of his decision on that fateful January 25 when he had turned to Arnold Ruge for help and advice, stating that he was determined to leave Germany with Jenny beside him. At the same time he had also written to Georg Herwegh, offering his services as co-editor of a journal that the latter expected to publish in Zurich.

Herwegh, a radical republican poet, had risen to fame recently, with the usual meteoric speed reserved for those who provoked the authorities. Aside from revolutionary verses, he was the author of an insulting and much-publicized letter to the Prussian King. Its publication in the *Leipziger Allgemeine Zeitung* had been mainly responsible for the exclusion of that paper from Prussian soil. Marx's own defense of the *Leipziger* had placed him in rapport with Herwegh who thereafter had contributed to the *Rheinische Zeitung*. Herwegh was delighted with Marx's proposal and suggested that Marx write "some ruthless, censorship-worthy observations" on the suppression of the *Rheinische Zeitung* and Ruge's *Deutsche Jahrbücher*. But nothing came of it because Herwegh was soon ordered out of Zurich. Marx, meanwhile, had become interested in the more promising prospect that Arnold Ruge offered.

64

Ruge planned to revive his *Deutsche Jahrbücher,* probably on Swiss soil. He envisioned the new yearbooks as appearing in a dramatic manner, edited with a great deal of esprit, like the French *Revue Indépendente.* Considering Marx to be a "most extraordinary brain," better suited to edit a periodical than a daily newspaper, he offered Marx the position of co-editor with an annual salary of 550 or 600 *Taler,* plus additional fees of 250–300 *Taler* for the articles Marx himself wrote. But it would require several months of preparation so that the new publication would be "in full armor when it sprang out among the philistines."

On February 18 Ruge informed Marx that he had released the news that they would jointly publish the revived *Jahrbücher* in some foreign land. Everything else was of a "protean nature," with the time and place of publication remaining uncertain. Switzerland, Belgium and France (Paris or Strasbourg) were considered. On March 13 Marx suggested that they publish a German-French yearbook, as a "principle and event" that really made him enthusiastic. It would unite the Gallic heart with the German head. French revolutionary esprit and an instinct for politics would follow the lead of German superiority in philosophy, naturally in its latest Hegelian form. Ruge immediately approved this Gallo-Germanic principle, which would enlist the aid of French as well as German radical writers.

It is often asserted that Feuerbach's writings inspired Marx to think of an alliance of the French revolutionary heart with the German philosophical head. Nevertheless, it was merely a new version of an old scheme to promote Gallo-Germanic cooperation, proposed by various French and German writers—Moses Hess, Heinrich Heine, Edgar Quinet, Saint-Marc Girardin and others. The thought was in the air, even if it had lost support among the Germans after the most recent threat from the French.

In the same letter in which Marx suggested the German-French yearbook idea, he confided to Ruge that he was going to marry Jenny, for "without any romanticizing [he] was in love from head to foot and in all seriousness." During an engagement of more than seven years, his "bride" had fought the hardest battles in his defense, to the point of undermining her health. It had been a war on two fronts, partly against her own "pietistic aristocratic relatives to whom the Lord in Heaven and the Lord in Berlin were equal objects of worship"; partly with his own family where "several priests [*Pfaffen*]" and other enemies had entrenched themselves. Whatever the opposition may have been, Marx seemed to have had no doubts that he would be free to claim his bride. Moreover, he and Jenny planned to stay with her mother after the marriage until the new publication was launched.

Towards the end of March, Marx went to Holland to visit a wealthy uncle, Lion Philips, the husband of his mother's sister. Philips, a merchant and banker, handled the financial affairs of the Marx family. Cultivation of closer ties with this uncle might be advantageous. The prospect was all the more alluring because Philips was known to be a person who flirted with unorthodox views. Marx and his uncle were mutually impressed; Marx established a contact that was profitable at a later date.

Marx left Cologne late in May for Kreuznach where the Westphalen family had been living since the death of the father. On June 12, 1843, a civil marriage contract was officially registered, witnessed and notarized between "Mr. Carl Marx, Doctor of Philosophy, resident in Cologne" and "Miss Johanna Berta Julia Jenny von Westphalen, without a profession, resident in Kreuznach." The formal wedding was on June 19. The bride and groom then remained in the Westphalen home for four months, until late in October, 1843.

All the evidence indicates that Marx's conversion to communism occurred before and during the honeymoon in Kreuznach. Since Marx left no account, we do not know whether the transition from mere radicalism and atheism to communism resulted from a sudden philosophical insight or from slower reflection. During this time, however, he did study history intensively, with an emphasis on the French Revolution. He also wrote a "Critique on the Hegelian Constitutional Law" that was never published. Some scholars assume that this critical dissection of Hegel brought Marx to the conclusion that the dialectic pointed towards a communist finale.

Engels had two explanations, spaced fifty-one years apart, as to the manner in which Marx came to communism. In the *New Moral World* of February 3, 1844, Engels stated that Marx belonged to the "learned communists" of Germany who had arrived at communism as the inevitable consequence and logical result of philosophic conclusions along Young Hegelian lines. In 1895, in response to an enquiry, Engels wrote that Marx had always told him that it was preoccupation with the debates on the theft of wood and with the depressed conditions of the Moselle winegrowers that had carried him from ordinary politics to economic questions, thence to socialism. The first explanation has a suspicious similarity to what Engels himself apparently experienced. The second leaves one with the impression that that is the sort of answer one would like posterity to believe.

But there is a third element, or combination of elements, in the picture. Marx was a revolutionary philosopher; he was also a realist. As a realist he recognized that the philosopher must take into account the world of 1842/43 that he hoped to shape for the future. What he experienced was bound to affect his judgment.

Philosophy in 1842/43 had turned to journalism for the purpose of subverting an outmoded order through criticizing and debunking the old. Marx and the Young Hegelians then had hoped to enlist the aid of the liberal world, the middle classes and educated people at large. The effort failed in the face of repressive measures when the bourgeoisie lacked the strength and courage—or inclination—to hurry history along. Marx himself was directly affected by the failure. It was evident that philosophy had to marshall new forces if it were to fulfill its mission. Not surprisingly, Marx then concluded that an alliance of philosophy and the proletariat, leading to communism, alone promised revolutionary results. The climate of the age suggested such a conclusion.

The danger of so-called communism, the threat posed by the impoverished workers, the likelihood of bloody conflict between classes and the stress on the importance of economic factors were commonplace items of conversation in Germany in 1843, as elsewhere in Western Europe. The German scholar E. G. Adler actually traced the start of socialistic propaganda in Germany back to 1818—to Ludwig Gall, right in Trier where Marx was born. It is even possible that Marx's father and Ludwig von Westphalen were sympathetic to the ideas of the French socialist, Saint-Simon, which Gall expounded. Gall used the phraseology that became so familiar in the decades to come. He presented the worker as the source of all national wealth, yet that same worker lived in abject poverty. Class conflict entered the picture with the growing misery of the working population. Gall declared that society owed everyone a real *human* existence.

The well-informed German, if he were interested in the matter, thereafter had a large literature that he could consult. The apocalyptic prognostications of the French "communist" Abbé Lamennais regarding world revolutions were known to various Germans in the 1830's. After a tour of Britain in the early 1830's, the German liberal historian Friedrich von Raumer published an account of conditions and institutions there, which contained much information on economic problems. The book became a best seller in Germany. The academic world likewise demonstrated an interest in this mundane subject. Eduard Gans, Marx's own favorite professor in Berlin (in a semi-autobiographical work appearing in 1836), had turned to poverty and class conflict in past history with pronouncements that read very much like portions of the *Communist Manifesto* of 1848. The writings of the noted Westphalian industrialist, Friedrich Harkort, often were filled with sympathetic consideration for the problem of poverty and the industrial worker. The desperate revolt of the workers in Lyons in 1831 was widely noted in Germany. When the French journalist Saint-Marc Girardin referred to the uprising as a new "invasion of barbarians," coming not from the outside but from within the ranks of society, the expression found its way to Germany also.

Governments took action to meet some of the problems. In 1839 Prussia had her first child labor law, drafted with a knowledge of England's experience in the same field. Impressed by the arguments of Malthus, various smaller German states drafted laws to make marriage impossible for those unable to support a family.

For those interested in the study of political or national economy, as it was usually called, most of the best works of the English and French political economists were available in translation. Germany also had her own economists. Professor K. H. Rau's classical text appeared in successive editions in the 1830's and 1840's. J. H. von Thünen published a work in 1842 that tied up class conflict with the Hegelian dialectics; but he believed a peaceful solution to be the more humane.

The importance of the study of political economy for governments and individuals was strongly stressed by 1840. Some were calling it the most important branch of knowledge. When the developments in the sciences and technology held out the prospect of an unlimited increase in goods, the science of the "wealth of nations" was bound to command attention. The economists had even reached the point where they were writing histories of the science of political economy.

Marx and Engels later tended to deprecate the amount of information available in Germany before the 1840's on the problems of poverty, economic questions, class conflict and socialism. It was easier for them to explain their own omissions by making it appear as a general German failing. The Germans have a saying that "that which fills the heart flows from the mouth." In Marx's case we see little coming from the heart, or head, until after he was able to fit the revolutionary potentialities of the proletariat into the Hegelian concept of history, as he saw it. If Marx had had any specific interest in the status of the worker, accompanied by a humanistic indignation over the lot of the rising proletariat, he would have found plenty of material about which to write.

Indeed, it can be said that virtually every economic principle initially adopted by Marx merely could be plucked from the tree or picked up from the ground like an over-ripe apple. This extended to the idea of class conflict. In France since 1830 the government of Louis Philippe was daily praised, denounced or ridiculed as a *bourgeois* regime. Histories of specific classes existed in England. The French writer, Robert du Var, was gathering materials for a monumental four-volume history of the working class. Marx himself later stated quite honestly, and in self-defense, that he did not invent class conflict; he picked up the idea from French *bourgeois* historians like Guizot and Thierry.

Another cornerstone upon which Marx built his theory of an inevitable proletarian revolution was the current belief that the industrial revolution produced an increasing concentration of wealth. The rich became richer, while the poor became poorer in everything but numbers. This contradiction baffled the political economists and troubled most informed observers. Something was wrong with the capitalist system when the capacity for increasing wealth and goods merely brought a greater poverty to the worker whose labor produced this wealth. Reflections of this nature made many people receptive to socialist ideas in the 1840's. The sentiment of humanity, to which all paid tribute, demanded a solution.

A few keen observers, like the French economist, B. C. P. Dunoyer, already noted that labor in England, the most industrialized country, enjoyed a better standard of living than the worker in less advanced states. But such observations were isolated and were smothered by the contrary and prevailing impression that persisted for another generation, and even longer. Marx and Engels adopted the commonplace assumption and clung to it to the end.

Romanticism, the cultural trend of the period, ultimately placed a halo on the unkempt head of the worker and even gave to his suffering, degradation, hopelessness and grime a romantic glamor. In literature, the novelists who had first looked to the medieval age, as in the case of Sir Walter Scott, now turned to the slums and alleys and workshops for materials. The writings of Charles Dickens, Victor Hugo and Eugène Sue come to mind. The famous caricaturist, Honoré Daumier, denied the right to indulge in political caricatures, turned to the streets and sketched the poor and deformed. The dignity of man and his humanity shone through the grime and suffering in heroic proportions. Contrastingly, Daumier sketched the bourgeoisie with characteristics so repulsive they seemed sub-human.

A contempt and even hatred for the bourgeoisie, as the class that dedicated its life to the prosaic matter of business, became a phenomenon of the romantic movement. Romanticism preferred extremes and colorful contrasts, whereas the bourgeoisie was inclined to see virtue in a golden mean, the *juste milieu*. The word *philistine*, dear to the romantic, became a favorite expression of Marx and Engels, as applied to the middle classes. There was an element of intellectual snob-appeal in it all.

Thus, when Marx turned to communism, it seemed that he was almost moving with a tide, except that he struck out along a revolutionary side-current of his own. Almost every informed person in Germany seemed to become social-minded between 1842 and 1844. Alarmed over the prospect of class conflict, they were open to the arguments of socialism. Lorenz von Stein's book, *Socialism and Communism in Contemporary France,* published in 1842, therefore attracted wide attention. Four editions appeared in the next few years. The book was largely concerned with an account of the various schools of socialist and communist thought in France. The big impact lay in Stein's conclusions that the proletariat represented the chief revolutionary danger. The machine, the growth of industry, was producing a class that could not rise. The proletariat, therefore, would look to revolution to improve its position.

Stein linked the above observations with the assertion that people were becoming conscious of a conflict in society along class lines. Every revolution brought power to a new social class, so that it was hard to distinguish between the interests of that class and the policy pursued by the state. Since power fell into the hands of one class, new conflict would follow. The proletariat would try to oust the bourgeoisie, who in France at least seemed very much in the saddle. The concept that the state ruled society was gradually being twisted around, with society dominating the state and determining its form. Stein, of course, proposed that timely remedies and reforms be administered so as to correct the situation.

It is evident that Stein, a moderate Young Hegelian himself, expressed many lines of thought similar to those that went into the Marxian complex, although most Marxian scholars deny that Marx was influenced by Stein's book. Engels, however, paid tribute to its importance by calling it a "miserable" work. In any event, it is another demonstration of the fact that many of the ideas that went into the Marxian explanation of history and society were already fluttering around, ready to be fixed into a pattern by a man with a genius for systematizing things, and the will to do so along the most revolutionary lines.

2. DEUTSCH-FRANZÖSISCHE JAHRBÜCHER

PREPARATION for the publication of the German-French yearbooks (*Deutsch-Französische Jahrbücher*) required considerably more time than Ruge originally anticipated. He had no difficulty finding a publisher —Julius Fröbel, who was trying to make a business out of printing radical and liberal works. But then Fröbel insisted that more capital was needed. Ruge tried to sell stocks in Cologne, but abandoned further attempts when it became evident that people were wary of investing money in anything slightly suspicious. As a last resort, Ruge took 6000 *Taler* from the fortune of his wealthy wife to finance the venture. The question of a place of publication involved a survey of the best possibilities—Brussels and Paris. Paris, having a large German population (from 85,000 to 100,000), was chosen since it was recognized that most of the subscribers initially would be German.

The task of recruiting German and French writers largely fell on Ruge. There was no lack of German radicals to give the paper a respectable debut. The *Mannheimer Zeitung* reported on August 9 that Moses Hess had accompanied Arnold Ruge to Paris to create a revolutionary alliance between France and Germany, after which they would cross the channel to bring the English into the "Triarchy." Johann Jacoby, the forthright radical democrat in East Prussia agreed to contribute. Georg Herwegh had moved to Paris. Michael Bakunin, Russia's 19th century anarchist and prodigy, had moved there from Saxony. Marx, for his part, tried to get Ludwig Feuerbach to make a "glorious debut" in the *Jahrbücher* by writing something devastating against the philosophic "windbag" Schelling. But Feuerbach refused to waste his time on a straw man. He did, however, agree to write a letter for publication in the first issue. All in all a very commendable group was assembled to represent the German end of the *Jahrbücher*. The French end fell flat.

Ruge hopefully contacted a variety of French scholars—liberals, radicals, anarchists, socialists, communists and finally just plain feminine feminists. The names of Victor Cousin, Pierre Leroux, Alphonse de Lamartine, Abbé Lamennais, Louis Blanc, Étienne Cabet, Victor Considérant, Pierre-Joseph Proudhon appear on the list. But the French were wary of the philosophic abandon of these German radicals. When it began to appear that none of the better known French writers was ready to collaborate, Ruge asked Marx if they should "serenade" the ladies— George Sand and Flora Tristan; they at least had the virtue of being more radical than Louis Blanc and Lamartine. But the French were not to be had for this type of rapprochement and their part of the *Jahrbücher* remained an aspiration in the title.

The first issue of the *Jahrbücher* was scheduled to appear in November, 1843. The Marxes moved to Paris late in October. To save expenses for everyone, Ruge found a house that could be occupied by three or four parties. The Marxes, the Herweghs, the Ruges, and another German couple then set up a single ménage, with one cook, one kitchen, a single dining room and common shopping and cleaning services. This "piece of communism" was designed to offset the high cost of living in Paris.

Publication of the *Jahrbücher*, however, was again delayed when Ruge became ill. Marx willingly assumed responsibility as editor, but he could not get the copy ready for the press on schedule. Finally, towards the end of February, 1844, the *Jahrbücher* made its debut, as a double issue. The name of Arnold Ruge was listed first on the title page, much to Marx's annoyance. But the contents and tone carried the special imprint of Marx. Ruge was not at all pleased with the results.

The *Jahrbücher* opened with an exchange of letters between Marx, Ruge, Feuerbach and Bakunin, which bemoan, satirize and denounce the horrible state of affairs in the German world. This was followed by an exposition of the future role of the philosophers and enlightened gentry. It was an artificial contrivance designed to set the tone and to state the purpose of the periodical. Marx was now openly contemptuous and hostile to Prussia, as a land of naked and repulsive despotism when stripped of its Sunday-clothes liberalism. He depicted Germany as a whole as being plagued with philistinism and philistines. Indeed, a pilloried *philistine* stares at the reader from virtually every paragraph. Nonetheless, Marx professed to be full of good hope. The philosopher now had a new ally in the system of production and trade that was rapidly producing a split in the existing society. The presence of a "suffering humanity which thinks and of a thinking humanity which is oppressed would become indigestible for the animal world of philistinism."

Marx's final letter, defining the program of the "real thinking heads," stressed the tactics and strategy of attack. As a matter of broad strategy, Marx opposed raising a "dogmatic banner" that announced the design of the world-to-be. The prime task, rather, was the *"ruthless criticism of all that exists,* ruthless in the sense that criticism does not become frightened by its own conclusions nor by a conflict with the existing powers." Negation, the repudiation and annihilation of the old, came first.

Criticism, Marx then indicated, would also extend to the many existing schools of socialist and communist thought, as being too dogmatic in anticipating the future shape of society. The numerous current communist systems were merely diverse and one-sided expressions of the humanistic principle, reacting against the system of private property. Each satisfied only a part of the "reality of the true human essence." Marx demanded more than this; criticism also had to take note of the "theoretical existence of man, as religion, science etc." (Marx used the "etc." more often and perhaps more deliberately than is usual among scientific thinkers. Evidently, he did not want to say everything and yet wished to suggest endless unsaid things. As he once stated, "for the initiated, enough has been said.")

Marx, likewise, took issue with the "crass socialism" that operated on the lofty assumption that mixing in politics was beneath its principles and that any mere change in political systems was irrelevant, offering no solution to the problems of poverty and social change. Marx insisted that nothing stand in the way of active participation in politics, thus creating a link with "real conflicts and identifying oneself with them." To gain the support of a "large party," he advocated supporting the liberals in their demands for true representative systems. Nothing would be lost in the mix-up; the victory of the liberals simultaneously would be their defeat, as the tide of revolution that briefly brought them to the top swept over and beyond them. Tactical elasticity became a matter of principle with Marx; certainly he always advocated and practiced it.

Marx, as always, sketched the future in general philosophical formulas. The shape of the coming world would emerge from a criticism of the old, through negation. A recognized evil would be replaced by its opposite, as when private property was supplanted by communism, competition yielded to cooperation or association, government gave way to no government.

Yet there was also a positive, formative force at work. Mankind, Marx asserted, long had cherished a dream; man merely had to become fully conscious of it in order to realize his true human essence. There was no question of gap between the past and the future, but the fulfillment of the thoughts of the past. "Reason always existed, but not always in a reasonable form," Marx declared. Philosophy in the 1840's presumably had discovered the "reasonable form." Still, when humanity, reason and fulfillment are added to the required negations, the picture we see is an abstraction. It always remained thus. Marx never made clear whether there was any place for those who arrived at conclusions that were contrary to the "reasonable form."

Aside from the three opening letters, Marx contributed two full-length articles to the *Jahrbücher*. The first one, "Zur Judenfrage," takes up the Jewish question, a very lively topic among the Germans just then. The Young Hegelians had turned to the subject, while numerous liberals petitioned their governments in favor of an equal status for the Jews. Marx himself, on somewhat special grounds, had signed a similar petition before leaving Cologne. In the *Jahrbücher*, however, he used the Jewish question as a vehicle for an attack or critique of Bruno Bauer, simply because the latter had just published two works on the subject. Marx was out to demonstrate the more advanced character of his own latest views through an expose of the faulty opinions of Bauer. Marxian scholars and Marx himself described the process as one of "self-clarification" in which he disposed of certain modes of thought that he had shared with Bauer in the recent past. When Marx indulged in such self-clarification, however, he was often guilty of striving for strained effects to illustrate the novelty, bold originality and superiority of his own latest line of thought. This may explain some of the curious features in the article on the Jewish question.

It is possible to charge Marx with anti-Semitism on the basis of this article and certain private letters in which he applied offensive and derogatory names to specific Jews. If name-calling alone is enough, the proof is there. But Marx used equally colored and offensive designations for particular Germans, Russians, Frenchmen and Englishmen who offended him. That was Marx. He was not above an appeal to prejudice, but there was nothing exclusively anti-Semitic about it. If Marx stated that the Jewish religion was repulsive to him, he said the same thing a thousandfold more often in regard to the Christian faith.

Marx's article does show what strange results the dialectic can produce in the absence of much knowledge of the history, mode of life, and business practices of the Jews. When Marx proclaimed first principles under such circumstances, the world always received something that could be gripped by the hair—occasionally a monstrosity. In this case he set out to look for the "mystery of the Jews not in their religion, but to find the mystery of their religion in the real Jews." When the dialectic revealed itself through such epigrammatic inversions, it flashed brightly but produced an uncertain light.

Analyzing the Jewish people in a catechistic manner, Marx made them appear synonymous with the bourgeois, capitalist class. "What is the real foundation of Judaism? Practical necessity and self-interest. . . . What is the worldly cult of the Jews? Petty huckstering [*Schacher*]. . . . What is his worldly God? Money. . . . Money is the jealous God of Israel beside whom no other God is permitted."

In the light of the above, Marx as a Communist saw no problem in connection with the emancipation of the Jews. Once the power of money, usury and capitalism (which Marx identified with Judaism) were ended, Judaism would end of itself. The Jews then would be emancipated by ceasing to be Jews. Thus, "the emancipation of the Jews is the emancipation of society from Judaism." With an almost equal insouciance Marx later brushed aside the significance of all other national differences. They also would cease to exist for all practical purposes once communism triumphed and the proletariat recognized that a common interest united the workers of all lands.

Marx's second article in the *Jahrbücher*, a "Critique of the Hegelian Philosophy of Law, An Introduction," has a special significance because it illustrates the revolutionary temperament of Marx as an avowed Communist. It not only presents the revolutionary dialectics that promised the triumph of communism, but also the particular strategy and tactics that would expedite the destruction of the old order.

Beginning with the assertion that nothing new could be said on the subject of religion, Marx then threw in his classical definition of religion as the "groan of the oppressed creature . . . the opiate of the people." Having settled with religion, he asserted that criticism was ready to turn to earth, to law and to politics, with Germany as the first target. He declared war on that Germany which he thereupon denounced as hopeless, backward and inhuman.

Criticism for Marx, however, was not of the calm and analytical variety groping its way towards the light. As he stated, criticism "is no passion of the mind; it is the mind of passion. It is not an anatomical knife; it is a weapon. Its target is the enemy, whom it does not want to disprove but to destroy." Criticism is a "means; its essential pathos is *indignation;* its

74

essential task is *denunciation.*" Marx's writings show no lack of the necessary *indignation,* and *denunciation* was never far away. Finally, in such
a hand-to-hand fight it was immaterial "whether the enemy is a noble,
equal or interesting individual; the purpose is to hit him."

Marx was certain that the struggle would not be restricted to a futile
war of words. While the Germans were backward in most ways, they
were the leaders in thought and philosophy. The Germans, he maintained, had "thought" the politics that other nations had acted out on
the world stage. The Germans had a surplus of theory, and theory became a material force as soon as it took hold of the masses. Theory,
therefore, would conquer the masses as soon as it appealed to man—to
human needs and instincts.

A mass following, however, alone did not guarantee victory. The
strategic requirements of revolution demanded what has been called a
"revolutionary class." A particular class, Marx asserted, could carry
through a successful bid for power only if it acted (for the time being)
as if it were the spokesmen for all humanity, representing the claims and
rights of everyone. Only in the name of the general rights of society could
a specific class justify its demand for general domination.

But, continued Marx, revolutionary theory and energy, mated with a
specific class posing as the representative of all humanity, needed yet
another stock character in the drama of revolution. "If one class is to
appear as the liberating class *par excellence,* it is necessary to have, in
reverse, another class which blatantly stands for subjection." So the
revolutionary class has to set up a contrasting class as the scapegoat,
made up as the universal villain in whom all evil in society originated
and was concentrated. It was to be labelled as guilty of a "universal
offense"; its position in society was to be stigmatized as the "notorious
crime against all human society." The dialectic undoubtedly operated
best in such a conflict of marked opposites. A study of history also
showed Marx that a black-on-white situation was a blessing in revolution
and war. He made a passing reference to the French Revolution in the
above context.

In view of the preceding, the scholar is uncertain as to what extent
the demands of the dialectic and of effective revolutionary strategy
colored the contents of that which passes for Marxian theory, as well as
the direction and results of Marx's economic and historical research.
When Marx denounced the bourgeoisie and capitalism so indiscriminately and praised the proletariat so unreservedly, to what degree was he
prompted by that *revolutionary imperative* which demanded that one
class be made to appear most odious and another as the universal
liberator of humanity? Certainly that imperative was a factor in
Marxism.

Turning to the revolutionary prospects in Germany, Marx declared that no class had the "broadness of soul" to play the revolutionary role. A step-by-step liberation thus was not practical; only a complete and universal revolution was possible. How the second conclusion flows out of the first is not fully clear, except as a dialectical opposite. Marx then announced that the German proletariat alone had the makings of a revolutionary class, with philosophy added to provide the required "broadness of soul." This conclusion was justified in the following series of dialectical contrasts, negations and inversions:

The proletariat is

> a class in civil society without being a class in civil society, an estate which is the dissolution of all estates, a sphere which has a universal character because of its universal suffering, which claims no *particular right* because it is oppressed with no *particular wrong* but *wrong in general,* which no longer can raise a *historical* claim but only a *human* one . . . a class, finally, which cannot emancipate itself without liberating itself from all other classes of society and thereby freeing all other classes of society; a class which in one word represents the *total loss* of humanity, and thus can gain control over its own destiny only through the *total reconquest of humanity.* . . . If the proletariat proclaims the *dissolution of the past world order,* it merely expresses the *mystery of its own existence.* . . . If the proletariat is the *negation of private property* it merely exalts as a *principle of society* that which society exalted as *its* principle.

In the following catchy sentences, Marx established the connection between philosophy and the proletariat:

> As philosophy finds in the proletariat its *material* weapons, so the proletariat sees in philosophy its *intellectual* weapons, and as soon as the lightning of ideas has struck thoroughly into this naive popular soil, the emancipation of the Germans into *human beings* will be fulfilled. . . . In Germany *no* type of slavery can be ended without the elimination of *every* variety of subjugation. . . . The *emancipation of the German* is the *emancipation of man.* The *head* of this emancipation is the *philosophy,* its *heart* the *proletariat.* The philosophy cannot become reality without the dissolution of the proletariat, the proletariat cannot dissolve itself without realizing the philosophy.

In the fullness of time the *"German day of resurrection"* would be announced by the *"crowing of the Gallic cock."* In borrowing the last phrase from Heinrich Heine, Marx reserved at least a small role for France in a future shaped by a union of philosophy and the proletariat—unto communism.

Friedrich Engels, writing from Manchester, contributed an article to the *Deutsch-Französische Jahrbücher* that set the tone for a subject that soon became Marx's speciality. Engels' "Outlines of a Critique of National Economy" was an analysis of political economy, the status of the proletariat, and the consequences of the "industrial revolution," an expression that he frequently used at this early date. Engels also displayed the proper dialectical perspective in calling the liberal economic theories of Adam Smith—the "economic Luther"—a necessary stage in historical evolution, which replaced the "barbarism" of peasant life with the industry of the cities.

Engels accepted the prevalent view that industrial progress was accompanied by a growing poverty among the masses. The national wealth of England was very large, but the English were the "poorest people under the sun." The "centralization," or concentration, of wealth was an "imminent law," with the strong worker displacing the weak, the big capitalist swallowing the small, and the large landowner absorbing the acres of the little farmer. In the end, the world would be divided into "millionaires and paupers, large landowners and poor daily laborers." Nothing could stop this trend except a social revolution, Engels asserted; this trend, in fact, made such a revolution inevitable.

Engels stressed the role of economic crises or depressions, as the best illustration of the contradictions in a capitalist society—suffering in the midst of surplus goods, or because of such abundance. As one who looks for the rules governing historical events, Engels discovered that depressions reappeared with the regularity of a comet, in cycles averaging from five to seven years. Predictability was important because economic crises hastened the impoverishment of workers and increased their numbers through the bankruptcy of many capitalists. The later correspondence of Marx and Engels shows how they kept a weather eye open for signs of a coming depression, as harbingers of revolution. They greeted such signs like the first flowers of spring.

As a replacement for the capitalist free enterprise system, Engels adopted the two fundamental ideas advocated by most early 19th century socialists, whether of the Utopian brand or otherwise, that were summed up in the expressions *Organization of Labor* and *Association*. To the 19th century the *Organization of Labor* meant a planned economy, the conscious planning and organization of all human labor or effort, while *Association* generally meant social, group or state control and ownership in contrast to private ownership and competition.

Engels' articles ended on a confident note. However strongly he denounced the "horrible immorality" of the free enterprise system and the "hypocrisy of the economists," yet even they had their place in a world governed by a dialectical providence. As for the poor economist, Engels stated, "He knows not that he, with all of his egoistic line of arguments, is just a link in a chain of universal human progress. He knows not that he, with his dissolution of all special interests, merely paves the way for the great transformation which the century was approaching, the reconciliation of humanity with nature and with himself." Only the philosopher could know that. The minds of Engels and Marx were ready to meet.

Engels' second article in the *Jahrbücher*, "The Condition of England," hinged on a review of Thomas Carlyle's *Past and Present* (1843). This book, Engels stated, was the only recent English work worth reading because it struck a human note, described human conditions, and had a trace of human outlook. He translated sections of Carlyle's coruscating prose, as a native's description of the condition of England. But for all of Carlyle's good sentiments, Engels insisted that Carlyle did not go far enough. Instead of demanding the abolition of private property, Carlyle placed his faith in heroes and the emergence of a true aristocracy. Carlyle lacked a thorough grounding in German philosophy and, as a pantheist, was still too religious.

Engels attempted to correct the views of many Germans who looked to England for political inspiration on the false assumption (according to Engels) that the English were independent men. On the contrary, the educated Briton was the "most contemptible slave under the sun." Engels could not forgive the English because no "respectable" person among them was ready to translate Strauss' *Life of Jesus,* and no printer would publish it, except ultimately a socialist. Popular prejudice was stronger in Britain than anywhere, except in the United States where "such prejudice is given legal recognition in lynch law." Even the English socialists, who knew nothing of German philosophy, were still too English when they ought to be human beings. Marx and Engels, in all the years to come, were to deplore the imperviousness of the English to the dialectic, or their inability to grasp it.

The first number of the *Deutsch-Französische Jahrbücher* also proved to be the last one. The grand conception of a union of the Gallic revolutionary heart and the Germanic philosophic head had failed to materialize. The French ignored it, and of the more than eighty thousand Germans in Paris, there were few who were willing to buy a copy. Arnold Ruge, with years of success as an editor behind him, ascribed its failure to a wrong style. Part of it was too crude; the rest, because of Marx's exaggerated style (*Ueberform*), was too ingenious (*künstlich*).

Originally it had been anticipated that a large number of copies would be sold in Germany. But in the 1840's the auspices were not good for a periodical that suggested Franco-German collaboration. Also, the Prussian market was closed, mainly because of Marx's insulting comments about the Prussian King. Marx was, in fact, so disrespectful and provocative that the government charged him with treason and lese majesty. On April 18, 1844, an order from Berlin called for his arrest, in case he set foot on Prussian soil. Marx was safe enough in Paris, but the Prussian officials were unusually vigilant in intercepting shipments of the *Jahrbücher;* nearly all of the three hundred copies sent to Prussia were confiscated.

After publication of the first issue, Julius Fröbel needed more capital to continue. But Arnold Ruge, having already lost 6000 *Taler,* was unwilling to risk more of his wife's fortune. In any event, he had lost his original enthusiasm because of the tone and contents of the first number, more specifically, of Marx's new communist views. Marx, for his part, was exasperated when he found that a portion of his salary as editor even had to be paid in goods, some of the unsold copies. He apparently felt that Ruge should furnish the additional capital.

An open clash between Marx and Ruge followed in March, 1844, ostensibly over an argument involving the irregular habits of Georg Herwegh, the "iron lark" of democracy. When Ruge called Herwegh a bum (*Lump*) for succumbing to the temptations of Paris, Marx answered with a long letter, defending the poet as a genius and denouncing Ruge's "inhuman and philistine" views on marriage.

Ruge frequently referred to the quarrel in private letters. He spoke of it as a senseless wrangle and apparently tried to persuade Marx that the whole thing was unnecessary. But that only made matters worse. Marx was irritated because his name did not appear first on the title page of the *Jahrbücher.* Marx even resented the fact that his name had been associated with him (Ruge) in any way. Worst of all, Ruge wrote, Marx expected him to use his private fortune to finance future publication of the *Jahrbücher.*

The Marx-Ruge feud went on into the summer with Ruge continuing to deplore Marx's "tasteless hate" and "madness." Ruge, however, retained a respect for Marx's capacity, expecting much from him "unless Marx worked himself to death and failed to make his work fruitful and published."

Arnold Ruge's letters are the source of most of the meagre details available about Marx during the spring and summer of 1844. Ruge wrote of Marx's irritation and vehemence, especially after having made himself sick by not getting to bed for two or three nights in succession, reading and working with an unusual intensity, but finishing nothing. Marx would break off with everything he started to plunge anew into an "endless sea of books." He was, Ruge stated, a born scholar and writer, but spoiled completely as a journalist.

The sustained break with Ruge (as also with Bruno Bauer) illustrates a certain characteristic of Marx—the compulsion to destroy those whom he had once admired, with whom he had worked and shared many enthusiasms, when such a person failed to move forward along the same ideological lines. It may also have reflected the inner rage of a man who, conscious of his own intellectual superiority, strikes out at a world that failed to reward him with that which he considered his deserts. Family considerations and financial uncertainties probably acted as another irritant.

Marx's salary as co-editor of the *Jahrbücher* had come to an end after February. Likewise, the "bit of communism" practiced by the Marxes, Ruges and Herweghs ceased with the quarrel. Furthermore, Jenny was pregnant and her health was not good.

It was at this time that Jenny's mother sent a peasant girl—Lenchen Demuth—to her daughter, as "the best thing [she] could send." Lenchen was to remain with the Marxes as their loyal servant, literally as part of the household, during the rest of their lives. Marx's first child, named after her mother, was born in May, 1844. Shortly thereafter, Jenny returned to Trier temporarily, ostensibly to let the grandmother see her new granddaughter.

In spite of financial uncertainties, Marx managed to dispose of considerable sums. The Westphalens apparently sent some money. In March, Marx received 1000 *Taler* collected by Georg Jung from friends and former stockholders of the *Rheinische Zeitung*. At the end of July, he obtained an additional sum from the same Jung—800 *francs* as compensation for one hundred copies of the *Jahrbücher* that the Prussian authorities had seized, copies that Marx had received in place of salary. In addition, Lion Philips, the wealthy uncle and a truly capital fellow whom Marx had visited in Holland, apparently sent some aid. The accumulative sums Marx thus acquired during the spring and summer of 1844 certainly were adequate. At this time, a worker-family in Paris with an annual income of 1000 *francs* was very fortunate indeed. In Cologne a person with an annual income of 500 *Taler* (nearly 2000 *francs*)—the minimum qualification as a voter in the elections for the upper house of Prussia's new parliament in January, 1849—enjoyed a middle class existence above the petty bourgeoisie.

3. FORWARD WITH *VORWÄRTS*

THE Marx-Ruge feud entered a new phase on August 7 and 10, 1844, when Marx attacked Ruge in a two-part article in *Vorwärts*, a bi-weekly German radical paper edited by Heinrich Börnstein and published in Paris. Previously, with signed articles in that same paper, Ruge had defended Marx's writings in the defunct *Deutsch-Französische Jahr-*

bücher against Börnstein's criticism. In Ruge's case this probably represented a gesture of appeasement. Marx, however, seems to have regarded it as an insult. The climax came when Ruge, signing himself as "A Prussian," published another article in *Vorwärts* highly critical of Prussia's policy and King. Technically, Ruge was a citizen of the Kingdom of Saxony, and not of Prussia. In this case, Ruge probably called himself a Prussian so as to give more force to the damnatory impact of the article. One expected a Saxon—and Arnold Ruge—to be uncomplimentary to Prussia; when "A Prussian" said the same thing, it carried more weight and heightened the impression that there were inner tensions in the Hohenzollern realm.

At that time, however, Marx's state of mind was such that he apparently suspected that Ruge was plotting some skullduggery when he signed himself as "A Prussian." Except for Marx, there were few Prussians in Paris then who were capable of writing the article on Prussia. In any event, Ruge's article revolved about a subject that offered Marx the opportunity to advance his own interpretation of events, while deriding and denouncing Ruge.

In this *Vorwärts* article, Marx pushed his dexterity as a polemist to the limit. It was entitled, "Critical Marginal Comments to the Article, 'The King of Prussia and Social Reform by a Prussian.'" An accompanying footnote stated, "Special circumstances compel me to declare that the present article is the first which I have submitted to *Vorwärts*." Marx wanted to make doubly sure that no one would mistake him for the "Prussian" whose article he was attacking. Employing a favorite technique whereby the stylistic and grammatical lapses of a foe were used to suggest mental fuzziness and confusion, if not outright stupidity, Marx immediately picked out one of Ruge's sentences to belittle him. Thereafter, in an unceasing barrage of unflattering and ironical adjectives and nouns, Marx, without directly mentioning Ruge's name, called him the "pretended Prussian," a "wise Prussian," a "too clever Prussian" who showed the "stamp of mediocrity," a "rare naivete" and much more of the same. Accusing Ruge of "literary charlatanry," Marx ended his attack by asking the reader to decide whether the anonymous "Prussian" did not owe it to the public to stop writing about political and social questions while he undertook a serious self-examination of his own private condition.

The subject of Ruge's Prussian-signed article was the revolt of the impoverished Silesian weavers, which had occurred on June 4–6. Soldiers were required to restore order. Although Ruge had condemned Prussia for this act, he otherwise had dismissed the event as of no significance in an unpolitical land like Germany. Marx could not permit this view to go unchallenged.

In contrast to Ruge, Marx hailed the Silesian revolt as a portent of the coming proletarian revolution. He helped to persuade Heinrich Heine to write a poem on the subject—gruesome and unsentimental in tone—describing the weavers as weaving, weaving without cease, the funeral pall of the old Germany. With the aid of such a famous introduction, the Silesian revolt later inspired social dramas and other literary works.

In the *Vorwärts* article, Marx himself sought to prove that the revolt was an "event," and a "frightening event." When not a single soldier had been required to subdue the liberal bourgeoisie who wanted freedom of press and a constitution (Marx was referring to the events of 1842/43), it was an *event* when soldiers were needed to suppress the workers, when the workers even had been victorious in the first encounter.

Marx constantly stressed the special aptitude of the Germans for social revolution and communism, because of their grasp of the proper philosophy and the dialectic. No single French or English worker revolt, Marx declared, showed the same advanced "theoretical and conscious character" as the Silesian uprising, nor a like bravery, tenacity and deliberation. Germany possessed a "classical" calling for social revolution, proportionate to her incapacity for political revolution. Marx even saw a virtue in the political innocence of the Germans. The more universal and mature the political understanding of a people, the more the proletariat would waste its strength in senseless riots choked in blood, at least at the start of the movement. A proletariat with a grounding in politics would see the root of all evil in specific political forms, thus creating confusion and sending the proletariat off on a false trail.

Marx also cited the "weak reaction of the German bourgeoisie against socialism" as added proof that a philosophical people could find salvation only in socialism. All liberal German papers, which were the "organ of the liberal bourgeoisie," were full of materials on "organization of labor, reform of society, attacks on monopoly and competition, etc." Marx interpreted the widespread, open-minded and human preoccupation of the Germans with the question of poverty, reforms and even socialism as proof that a philosophical people recognized that socialism was inevitable and were ready to join forces with it.

Marx also turned briefly to England, the land "which invented the word *poverty*." In condemning the "cynicism" of English economists, especially John Ramsey MacCulloch, Marx applied that "pathos of indignation" he had recommended in the *Jahrbücher*. Thus he wrote of the "good clear air of English cellar dwellings . . . pale wrinkled flesh of women, consumed by work and misery; children who lie on manure piles; the cripples produced by excessive work at the monotonous machines in a factory. The most beloved of final details of the practice:

prostitution, murder and the gallows." Marx, like Engels, already had adopted the view that crime had an economic basis. As for prostitution, which involved a sale of services, probably including competition and the law of supply and demand, Marx occasionally threw it in as the ultimate thrust against the capitalist system.

Marx expressed a contrasting, romantically exaggerated confidence in the potentialities of the worker. He cited the example of Christian Wilhelm Weitling, a tailor by profession, often called the first German Communist, as proof of the capacity of the German worker to think along theoretical lines. "Where," Marx asked, "could the bourgeoisie with their philosophers and writers produce a writing on the political emancipation of the bourgeoisie which could be compared to what Weitling had done for the worker?" * This was a "measureless and brilliant literary debut" of the German worker. If one compared the "gigantic *infant shoes* of the proletariat with the dwarflike size of the down-at-the-heel political shoes of the German bourgeoisie, one had to admit that the *German Cinderella* would grow into a strong, athletic figure." One had to concede, Marx reiterated, that the German proletariat was the "theorist" of the European proletariat—as the English worker had a penchant for economics and the French for politics.

Marx thereafter defined the lot of the proletariat in generalized philosophical terms, followed by the envisioned solution. The worker by virtue of his position "is isolated from life itself, the physical and intellectual life, human morality, human activity, human gratification, *human essence*. The *human essence* is the *true universal essence of the human.*" With such universal grievances, Marx stated, a proletarian revolt to end this human isolation would have a more universal character than a mere political revolt designed to gain mere political power, just as the "*man is more infinite than the state citizen, and human life than political life.*" After clarifying the distinction between "social and political" revolutions, Marx continued: "Without *revolution*, however, *socialism* cannot be carried into effect. It needs this *political* act insofar as it requires the acts of *destruction* and *liquidation.* But when its *organizing activity* starts, its real *end*, its *soul* emerges, then socialism flings away the *political husk.*" Such was Marx's version of the future, directly translated from the long article in *Vorwärts.* On this occasion (in contrast to his writings in the *Jahrbücher*) Marx used the word socialism in preference to communism.

Some biographers consider the year in Paris as the most fruitful of Marx's life. According to his own account, this was the time when he turned to the study of economics. After adopting the proletariat as the

* Weitling had published *Guarantees of Harmony and Freedom* in 1841; his *Gospel of the Poor Sinner* was about to appear. Less than two years later Marx mercilessly cut down the same Weitling as incompetent, inconsequent and soft.

champion of humanity, the thoroughgoing Marx wanted to be solidly informed on the nature and practical workings of a capitalist system he was out to destroy. Notebooks from the period show that he perused the English and French classics of Adam Smith, David Ricardo, and Jean Baptiste Say. Marx's article in *Vorwärts*, as well as unpublished manuscripts, indicates that he read additional works on the condition of England. In 1844 he was ready to write a book on the subject—a two-volume "Critique of Politics and National Economy."

Arnold Ruge reported in May, 1844, that Marx also had plunged into a study of the French Revolution, expecting to write a history of the Convention. Again the work was never completed. But the French Revolution left its mark on Marx's own revolutionary analyses, tactics, strategy and politics.

During this time also, Ruge reported that Marx associated with the German workers in Paris in order, "to have a party and people under his command." Actually, most of the German workers in Paris were craftsmen and not the more proletarian factory worker. Yet some of them had fought beside the French behind the celebrated barricades of 1830, and were going to do the same in 1848. Marx also associated with remnants of the *League of the Just,* a small secret German revolutionary group with communist inclinations. It was the London branch of this *League* that was to form the nucleus for Marx and Engels' Communist League.

Marx likewise attended some meetings of French workers, which he described in a manner reminiscent of the romantic literature of the period:

> When communist craftsmen meet, their first purpose is doctrine and propaganda etc. But immediately the workers acquire a new need, the need for union [*Gemeinschaft*]. . . . Smoking, drinking, eating etc. are no longer there as a medium for union or a uniting medium . . . the brotherhood of man is no mere phrase, but a reality with them, and the nobility of man shines forth on us from their work-hardened features.

One thinks of the sketches of Daumier.

Marx, however, spent more time with people of recognized abilities and rank, ranging from socialists, Communists and literary figures to Russian noblemen. He was especially impressed with the anarchist Pierre-Joseph Proudhon, author of the oft-cited sentence, "Property is theft." During long discussions, often late into the night, Marx tried to implant some needed Hegelianism into Proudhon. But the Frenchman never became a convert.

Marx also saw Bakunin quite frequently. The Russian admired Marx's mental power and devotion to the cause of the worker, except for an ingredient of personal vanity in it. Bakunin enjoyed Marx's conversation as being witty, when it was not colored by spitefulness, as happened often enough. But there was a clash of temperaments even if both were interested in subverting the existing world. Bakunin declared that Marx considered him to be too much of a man of sentiment, while he in turn called Marx "gloomy, egoistic and deceitful."

Heinrich Heine was one of Marx's most frequent associates. Although some scholars maintain that it was a special predilection for poets that drew Marx to Heine, Marx mainly appreciated him as a writer of satiric works in the war against the old Germany. Heine showed the true tact of a revolutionist—the capacity to disregard questions of principle in a common assault on a mutual foe. Thus, in 1830 he had concentrated his attacks on nobility and church, even though he admitted privately that he hated the bourgeois aristocracy far more. Then in the 1840's Heine reached a point where he could "almost love the communists," as destined to destroy the German nationalists whom he hated. So it was not out of character for him to "board a new ship" and to sail along with Marx in 1844. Actually, Heine lacked the philosophic commitment to the dialectic that was necessary for a Communist in the Marxian sense—and he never was one.

Marx's meeting with Engels in August was the biggest event in 1844. At that time, a "company business" (as Marx once called it) was to be initiated, dealing with revolution and the propagation of a philosophy of history that was unique. The way had been prepared by Engels' contributions to the *Jahrbücher*.

PART TWO

The Revolutionary Partnership

=I=
Historical Backdrop

WHEN Marx and Engels formed their revolutionary partnership in 1844, Europe was in the midst of the Hungry Forties with the three hungriest years just ahead. Europe was also in an intellectual and emotional turmoil. Contrasting and conflicting ideals and ideas jostled each other in a hothouse atmosphere that was exciting to those who embraced the Hegelian dialectic and to the Romanticists who also exalted extremes and polar opposites. On the one side there flourished a revivified church, a new respect for tradition and the force of continuity in history. On the other extreme there was a flight into revolution, even towards complete anarchy with its rejection of all inhibitions, customs, institutions, perhaps even of man's limited and sinful nature as pictured in the annals of the past. Europe dreamed of revolution, held up the threat of revolution, even while dreading any repetition of the spectacle of terror that the French upheaval of 1789/99 had offered to the world.

The masses as always faced the immediate problems of making ends meet so they could bridge their way safely into the next day, month and year. Yet even the common man, impressed by the new wonders of the industrial revolution and pricked by some poorly-comprehended information that seeped down from the learned world, began to suspect that a change in governments, the social order and the way in which goods were produced might be of some help. Not without cause did De Tocqueville assert that "false ideas on political economy" produced the Revolutions of 1848. Utter despair and destitution may turn men to violence and revolution; but more often men are moved to revolt when they are persuaded that only false institutions, systems and rulers stand between them and an improved existence.

The "Silent Revolution," as a contemporary English writer called the Industrial Revolution (a term already used by Engels), was speeding along. On the one side lay the prospect of endless wealth, as devised by the advance of science and technology. The other side of the picture offered a ghastly contrast—increased poverty, or at least an increased awareness of it. The large industrial town had appeared, built by men who were ignorant of the elemental rules of sanitation and good health. The small independent craftsman was being crushed by the competition of the machine. The lot of the factory worker was appalling. The belief then grew that a diabolic contradiction existed in the 19th century society. Even as the rich became wealthier and the total sum of goods multiplied, so the lot of the worker and his share in the goods seemed to diminish. This conclusion was accepted all the more readily because the age respected the sanctity of simple opposites and contrasts. Many observers concluded that the system of private ownership, competition and the laws of supply and demand were at fault. The word *capitalism*, of course, was new in the 1840's, though much was said about capitalistic ways, investment and exploitation, as well as capital itself. The concept of capitalism, however, had been pretty well established and elaborated by earlier socialists such as Saint-Simon, Fourier and Proudhon in their analyses and criticism of the political economists. Credit for the neologism goes to Proudhon.* Karl Grün, who helped to popularize Proudhon in Germany, used the word in the socialist *Trier'sche Zeitung* of February 11, 1848, in speaking of a "conflict of capitalism and the proletariat." Marx himself does not use the term "capitalism" in the *Communist Manifesto*.

National feeling, or nationalism, represented another revolutionary force in the 1840's. Fertilized by the romantic movement, nationalism flourished in Central and Eastern Europe. The nations were demanding self-realization and emancipation. Invariably, the memory of past grievances (real or imaginary), and the identification of a neighboring nation as the eternal enemy, oppressor and despoiler, served to fire the desired emotional ecstasy of the aspiring nation.

Among the Germans and Italians national feeling called for the unification (or closer union) of existing states. The movements were revolutionary since they could only be realized against the will and at the cost of existing governments. National movements also had a revolutionary impact on international relations—a unified Germany or Italy would stand forth as a great power that the established states would have to recognize as an equal. An infuriating sense of weakness, of being flouted and ignored by the great powers, stimulated national feeling among the Germans and Italians. They also wanted a place in the sun. Elsewhere in Europe such submerged peoples as the Czechs, Croats, Rumanians and

* *Le Grand Dictionnaire Universel Du XIXe Siècle* (Larousse) cites the following example from Proudhon: "La terre est encore la fortresse du *capitalisme*."

Hungarians were busy forging a uniform literary language and a new culture out of a diversity of peasant dialects. Romanticism in general blessed the cultivation of native languages and traditions as a contribution to civilization. Once the submerged nations advanced to the point where they demanded political autonomy and even complete independence, national movements served as a disruptive force in a conservative and multi-national empire such as Austria.

The Polish national cause commanded the widest sympathy. The thousands of Polish refugees living in exile reminded Europeans of the destruction and partitioning of the once territorially great Polish state. The Poles were glorified in romantic verse and prose. Many Europeans also regarded a free Poland as a necessity, since the power of Russia, grown to dread proportions under Nicholas I, seemed like a threat to Western and Central European freedom and security. The revival of a large and independent Poland would serve as a bulwark against Russia.

Parallel with the growth of nationalism, liberalism was developing rapidly as a challenge to the traditional authority of kings and aristocracies. Often regarded as the ideology of the rising bourgeoisie, its impact was primarily domestic, although the victory of liberalism in one country usually excited the hopes of liberals in other lands, leading to new demands and the possibility of revolution.

Democracy was also on the march. Democratic sentiment was ill-defined, often not extending beyond a vague conviction that the popular will, however discovered and implemented, was the arbiter of a nation's destiny. The idea of democracy, moreover, was associated frequently with a program of social reform. In Britain, the Chartist movement demanded universal manhood suffrage, which would give labor a voice in Parliament, perhaps even a decisive control. In France, there was a social democratic movement that joined in the rising cry for "reform," a demand that was indefinite enough so all who were dissatisfied could rally around it. To many, reform meant primarily an extension of the right to vote. The Germans regarded the latest developments in the advanced western states with hope, mixed feelings, or horror. In any event, change seemed imminent.

The mood of these years was still one of fading romanticism. But already it was giving way here and there to a new realism that revealed itself to the world like the metallic clacking of the newly-introduced telegraph. Romanticism, which once had gilded the past until it appeared golden, now looked to the future—the best was yet to be, at the end of the distant rainbow that arched over the throes of the present.

Wide-scale food shortages after 1844, aggravated later by a business depression in 1847, transformed the economic distress of millions into an outright disaster in some regions of Europe. Millions lived on a margin so small that unexpected shortages and high prices could be fatal. Europe was shocked to learn of actual famine in some localities. Governments were blamed for not responding to the danger in time, and then only with insufficient means. The period had heard so much about poverty that it responded almost with disbelief when reports of a real calamity came.

The basic disaster resulted from a potato blight that caused that "prolific but uncertain root," as an English historian called the potato, to rot in the ground or soon after it was harvested. The result was stark tragedy for the potato-eating Irish. Its effects were also serious in France, Belgium and Germany. Late in September, 1845, a Royal Prussian Cabinet Order, taking note of reports that most fields were affected with the blight, and expressing a special concern for the "highly populated factory regions," prohibited the export of potatoes. In Belgium, the "suffering of Flanders" was compared to famines in the Middle Ages.

The virtually complete destruction of the potato crop persisted until 1848. In 1846 and 1847 there was also a partial failure of the two main bread crops, wheat and rye, resulting in a catastrophic rise in the cost of food. Simultaneously, wages dropped and unemployment increased, as Europe experienced a commercial crisis or depression that became acute in 1847. In the Rhineland as early as December, 1846, the chief Prussian official reported that the business depression and the continuing high food prices were causing hardship among the working classes. As a relief measure, he suggested public works—railroads, highway and canal construction. A liberal Rhineland merchant noted in 1847 that the poor were becoming "bloody-poor" and that craftsmen and members of the petty bourgeoisie were sinking to the ranks of the poor, never to rise again. These were but typical observations taken from many. It was a misery so appalling that no informed person could ignore it.

It is always difficult to assess the role of actual physical suffering in producing or helping to bring on revolutions. But there is no question that many believed (governments included) that desperation increased popular unrest. Food riots and demonstrations occurred. The fear of mass uprisings was added to the almost chronic preoccupation with the "spectre of communism." Contemporaries gave the potato blight credit for dramatic and lasting changes. The calamities of the Hungry Forties helped to create the fear that revolution was certain to come. Many governments resigned themselves to the inevitable and, in doing so, reduced their capacity and will to survive. Those who welcomed revolution had cause to be confident.

= II =

From Each According
to His Abilities

1. THE TEN DAYS IN PARIS

AFTER nearly two years in England, Friedrich Engels left Manchester during the latter part of August, 1844, to return to his home in Barmen. He chose the longer route via Paris because he wanted to see Karl Marx again. The time was ripe for a second and decisive meeting. Marx's articles in the *Deutsch-Französische Jahrbücher*, where he had boldly announced his conversion to communism, had spoken a language that Engels could applaud. While German philosophy and French revolutionary examples still dominated Marx's thinking, economics was coming into the picture as the clinching, down-to-earth materialist argument. Engels was beating the bushes in a somewhat different manner, but it was evident that both were chasing the same game.

Engels was in Paris for ten days. Forty years later he stated briefly: "When I visited Marx in Paris in the summer of 1844, it was clear that we were in complete agreement on all theoretical questions; our joint work dated from that time." The partnership that was to last a lifetime was launched during those epochal days.

The discussion of theory and revolutionary strategy did not occupy the entire time. Both Marx and Engels had a zest for living and enjoyed convivial evenings in the company of congenial associates. Marx introduced Engels to Bakunin, to August Hermann Ewerbeck, a physician from East Prussia and the radical leader of the German Communist League of the Just in Paris, and to F. C. Bernays, a German journalist and editor of the Paris *Vorwärts*, as well as to others who frequented the *Quai* Voltaire each evening. Such contacts produced one immediate re-

93

sult. On August 31 *Vorwärts* published the first in a series of articles by Engels on the "Condition of England," a continuation of the critical survey inaugurated by his article on Carlyle in the *Jahrbücher*.

Marx and Engels both had a thirst for action and they lost no time in planning their course. As a first move, they surveyed each philosophy and system that might contest their supremacy. The next step was to remove the contestants. Since both Marx and Engels had come to communism via Hegelian philosophy, it was quite natural that they should first attack those who had started from the same philosophical basis but had strayed into the wrong conclusions. This applied to the Young Hegelians, especially Bruno Bauer and "consorts."

The attack on the Bauers is cited as another case of Marxian "self-clarification." Franz Mehring calls it a "settling of accounts with their philosophical consciences." The Marx of today fought against no one more vehemently than the Marx of yesterday, and those associated with his earlier illusions. In the process Marx undoubtedly experienced a clarification of his own position; but it was also an application of the criticism that aimed to destroy. The latter unquestionably was its major purpose.

Bruno Bauer and his Young Hegelian followers in Germany certainly helped to provoke this conflict. Since December, 1843, they had been publishing a monthly *Allgemeine Literatur-Zeitung* (*General Literary Gazette*) that contained veiled attacks on Marx. Georg Jung in Cologne had sent copies of the *Literatur Zeitung* to Marx and had urged him to answer Bruno Bauer. Now Marx and Engels worked themselves into a rage as they surveyed the eight copies that lay before them. There in black and white were indirect attacks on Marx and the direction he had taken since 1842. There were references to the "wise men of *Anno* 1843," and to the *Rheinische Zeitung* of "blessed memory," together with the threat to expose the "liberalism and radicalism of 1842 in its full superficiality and empty phraseology." The conversion to communism was called a proof of philosophical desperation; nothing great could ever come from an appeal to the masses. This, of course, was in direct contradiction to Marx and Engels' new faith in the proletariat as the vehicle of human progress and emancipation.

It is easy to understand the fury of Marx and Engels. Both had proclaimed that philosophy ineluctably pointed to communism and the certainty of social revolution, especially among the Germans. The effect was spoiled when "Bruno Bauer and Consorts" from the same Berlin Hegelian stables demonstrated that philosophy could produce horses of an entirely different color. Marx was not the person to allow such an affront to pass unanswered. Anyway, he and Engels had once been admirers of Bruno Bauer; it was easy enough for them to fear that others might stop to pray where they themselves had worshipped. Bruno Bauer had to be refuted, briefly, decisively and without an appeal. This would be accomplished by publishing a short but shattering polemic.

Work on the polemic was begun at once. A title—*Kritik der kritischen Kritik. Gegen Bruno Bauer & Consorten* (*Critique of Critical Criticism. Against Bruno Bauer & Consorts*)—was chosen. Engels jotted down his contribution, about twenty-five pages in all. As a specialist on England he exposed and then corrected the ignorance displayed by Bauer's "consorts" whenever they wrote on English affairs. Deriding their philosophical pretensions, he now denied that Hegelianism any longer represented a vital force. He ridiculed the "withered and widowed Hegelian philosophy" as an old woman who painted and primped her body, already dried up into a "repulsive abstraction," in order to attract a suitor somewhere in Germany. Marx, for his part, was to cover any other questions that he decided to take up in this, their first joint work.

In the *Foreword*, dated "Paris in September, 1844," the co-authors stated that this *"Polemik"* would be followed by independent works in which each would portray his "own positive views and thereby [his] positive reactions to the more recent philosophical and social doctrines." Engels, for his part, had already completed most of the research for a social history of England with the major aim of painting a darkly vivid picture of the condition of the working class in the most advanced industrial country. Marx also was ready to furnish a few "learned volumes"; he spoke of being far along on a two-volume critique of politics and national economy. The "company business" was well under way.

Engels was in an exalted and optimistic mood when he left Paris. He was under the impression that Marx would complete and publish the *Kritische Kritik* with no delay and follow it with the two clinching volumes on politics and economics. Writing from Barmen about a month later, he spoke of the "gay and human mood" that he had experienced during the ten days with Marx in Paris.

2. MARX: "POSITIVE VIEWS" FROM PARIS

ALONE in Paris Marx set about the task of completing the *Kritische Kritik*. But he just could not pile enough into the polemic. The tie-up with Engels had effected no change in his writing habits and mental processes. By the end of November the projected pamphlet had grown into a volume of over three hundred pages. Before the manuscript was published, he could add a "Historical Epilogue" that stated: "As we have heard subsequently, not the world but the critical *Literatur-Zeitung* has perished." This made Marx's efforts of nearly three months appear slightly redundant.

Meanwhile in Barmen, Engels was waiting impatiently for the appearance of the *Kritische Kritik* as well as the two learned volumes. He wanted to utilize them for propaganda purposes in the Rhineland. Writing to Marx on October 8–10, he asked how the "pamphlet" was coming along; it surely had to be finished by then. On November 19 he hopefully requested Marx to send him a few copies of the *Kritische Kritik*, if it were finished. By January 20, 1845, he was writing that he had given up waiting for it. He was quite astonished that Marx had broadened the work into more than three hundred pages (*zwanzig Bogen*); but that was all to the good; it meant that a lot of material would come out that otherwise would have stayed in Marx's desk for "who knows how long." But he thought that it would give a most "curious" impression if his name remained on the title page, since he had written only about twenty-four pages. Dismayed by the delays, he commented that it was ridiculous that they, the "theoretical Germans," just did not get around to an exposition of their theories; they had not even been able to publish their "Critique of Nonsense."

Apparently late in November Marx had sent the *Kritische Kritik* to a publisher in Frankfurt, who paid an honorarium of 1000 *francs* for it. The book was published around the end of February, 1845, under a new title, *The Holy Family*. The complete title was *Die heilige Familie, oder Kritik der kritischen Kritik. Gegen Bruno Bauer & Consorten. Von Friedrich Engels und Karl Marx.* The new title, picked by the publisher with Marx's approval (somewhere in the text he had rather casually referred to the Bauer family as "the holy family"), was more sensational than the chillingly compounded *Critique of Critical Criticism* which remained as the alternate title. Likewise the publisher in placing Engels' name first, apparently felt that as an author his name carried more sales appeal. (Engels himself had commented on the "enormous repute" that his article on Carlyle had earned for him among the "mass.")

The change in title had occurred without Engels' knowledge. He was quite naturally surprised and somewhat taken aback. Writing to Marx on February 22 he stated that the title (with its blasphemous connotation) would lead to a family quarrel with his "pious, already highly exasperated old man." He charitably assumed that Marx could not have been aware of the circumstances. But he also asked why his name was placed first on the title page, when he had done little and everyone would recognize Marx's style anyway.

In a long letter to Marx on March 17, Engels included a short critique of *The Holy Family*. It evidently struck the right note, down to the use of specific words and phrases, because it was the pattern that Engels followed in future evaluations of Marx's works. Referring to the book as the *Kritische Kritik* (*The Holy Family* title still appeared a little strange), he praised it as *"ganz famos,"* (entirely splendid—his standard phrase for such occasions). Then he singled out certain parts on the Jewish question, the history of materialism and Eugène Sue's *Mysteries of Paris* as being "splendid," as destined to have "extraordinary effects." But for all of that, the work was too long. The pose of "sovereign contempt" that they adopted towards the *Literatur-Zeitung* was in startling contrast to the 350 pages that they dedicated to it. Moreover, the public would neither understand nor be interested in most of the materials involving the "critique of speculation and of the abstract essence." Otherwise, Engels continued, the whole book was "splendidly written" and fit to make a person "laugh himself sick." The Bauers would find it impossible to say a word. (Marx apparently appreciated the laughing-oneself-sick [*kranklachen*] compliment because Engels frequently used it later when praising Marx's works.)

The Holy Family is very little more and certainly no less than a polemic and a critique, as announced in the foreword and title. Marx had thumbed through the various articles in the *Literatur-Zeitung*, copying sentences or paragraphs that displeased him or that he could use as proof that Bruno Bauer and "Consorts" were ridiculous. The isolated fragments were then subjected to an attack from all sides. Sometimes there is the boom of a big gun, but much of it is more like the rattle of small arms and a guerrilla ambush. Scattered here and there like oases are some of Marx's own ideas, illustrating the latest phase of Marxian evolution. Marxian scholars read *The Holy Family* in search of such isolated pearls. As Engels himself recognized, most of the work is largely a meaningless chaos to anyone not acquainted with the full contents or lines of thought of the *Literatur-Zeitung*. Today, even the most ardent admirers of the "Young Marx" indulge in what Marx called a "conspiracy of silence" when confronted with some of the subject matter in his early writings. No coherent account of the contents of *The Holy Family* is possible. The book was a catch-all; every offense that Marx saw in the *Literatur-Zeitung* was immortalized by being included in *The Holy Family*. The range was indiscriminate—all the way from the Jewish question to the French Revolution, prostitution, punishment of criminals, Flora Tristan, the masses, Eugène Sue, emancipation of women, Pierre-Joseph Proudhon and finally love.

In his critique of others, Marx occasionally fell into a trap of his own devising, as when he praised with much zeal and little foresight those whom his enemies condemned. In *The Holy Family* he overreached himself in an extensive defense of Proudhon. Praising Proudhon's work on property as the "Scientific Manifesto" of the French proletariat that first exposed private property to a ruthless, critical and scientific investigation, he credited it with revolutionizing the subject of political economy. Within two years he was writing a book that condemned Proudhon as vigorously as this work praised him.

Marx devoted a few pages to his new speciality, the study of economics. But he treated the subject like the pelt of a skinned animal by stretching it to conform to the shape of the Hegelian dialectic. Contradictions and negations make up the framework upon which his political economy is racked. Somewhat abbreviated quotations from several successive paragraphs illustrate his use of the dialectic:

> Proletariat and wealth are opposites. As such, they make up a whole. . . . Private property as private property, as wealth, is forced to preserve its *own* existence and therewith its own opposite, the proletariat. . . . The proletariat, in contrast, as a proletariat is forced to destroy itself and thereby its opposite, private property, which is responsible for its existence.

The proletariat is

> to use an expression of Hegel, the *rebellion* against degradation in the midst of degradation, a rebellion to which it is driven because of the conflict between its human *nature* and its situation in life, which is the avowed, decisive and comprehensive negation of this nature. . . . The proletariat executes the sentence which private property brings upon itself through its creation of the proletarian. . . . It cannot free itself without destroying its condition of life. . . . It cannot end its own condition of life without destroying *all* inhuman living conditions of contemporary society which are summarized in its own situation.

In later years, when the quality and sophistication of Marx's economic coat improved, the dialectical elbows did not stick out quite so far.

Preoccupation with *The Holy Family* kept Marx from speeding along with the writing of his great and learned two-volume *Kritik der Politik und Nationalökonomie* (*Critique of Politics and National Economy*) which both he and Engels believed would be revolutionary, definitive and intellectually persuasive. Engels constantly stressed the importance and need of such a guide line. "As long as it was not demonstrated through a couple of volumes that the principles were the products of past viewpoints of history and a continuation of them, everything added up to mere half doses and a blind groping in most cases," Engels complained from the Rhineland. He urged Marx to take the materials that he had gathered and "hurl them out into the world. It was damnable high time!" Engels' call for such a set of learned volumes from Marx runs like a refrain through their lives until Marx came out with the first volume of *Das Kapital* in the late 1860's.

On January 20, 1845, Engels returned to the same theme. The all-important need was a "pair of bigger works to serve as a foothold for the many half-informed persons who were very willing but unable to make their own way." He urged Marx to finish his books on "national economics" even if he was not fully satisfied with the results. It did not matter; the minds of the people were receptive; one must hammer the iron while it was hot. The work should be finished by April. Marx should follow his example by setting a deadline when he "positively wanted to finish it." But Marx, like Engels, shared a fault that Marx once ascribed to Germans in general; they judged a book by its "cubic contents." The work became bigger and bigger and never reached a satisfying conclusion.

Since Marx's letters during this period have been lost, there is little information as to his progress. He certainly had given Engels the impression in Paris that he was far along with the work. On February 1, 1845, Marx signed a contract with C. W. Leske, a German publisher from Darmstadt who made a business of printing socialist and radical works, to publish the two volumes. It is probable that Marx set an April deadline for himself and informed Engels of the fact. In any event, Engels' article in the Owenite *New Moral World* of May 10, 1845 (apparently written during the first week of April), stated specifically that Dr. Marx's *Kritik der Politik und Nationalökonomie* was in press. The notice was premature. Only a few fragments of the original manuscript have survived. In the 1930's they were finally published under the novel title of *Economic and Philosophic Manuscripts of 1844*.

In the *Manuscripts of 1844*, Marx established his own theoretical position partly through ridicule and damnation of certain persons and partly through a nearly indiscriminate praise of others. After a brief, contemptuous curtsey to some unnamed "critical theologians" (unmistakably Bruno Bauer and followers), he placed Ludwig Feuerbach on a pedestal. Feuerbach was the man in whom "positive, humanistic and naturalistic criticism" had its beginnings. Many years later while re-reading a similar line of praise in *The Holy Family*, Marx indulgently referred to this "Feuerbach cult" as something that affected him "very humoristically."

When Marx wrote the *Manuscripts of 1844*, he already had read his way into the literature of the political economists. In the preface he carefully noted that the informed reader would see that his conclusions rested on a "conscientious critical study of political economy." By accepting the premises of political economy, with its languages and laws, Marx's accusations had the virtues of a case that rested on the phrases and professed principles of the accused. His notebooks dating back to the Paris period suggest the thought that he turned to economics and descriptions of economic conditions to support conclusions that had their origins elsewhere—in philosophy and in his own revolutionary humanistic temperament. His notes are accompanied by passionate, impulsive and angry comments, as of one whose mind is already made up before research is completed.

As a scholar Marx knew what was expected of him. He paid due tribute to the classics of political economy. But among the writers whom he cited extensively, his sympathies obviously lay with the critics of the classical economists and of the current industrial society. Marx's bibliography already included the works of Sismondi, Charles Loudon, Michel Chevalier, Antoine-Eugène Buret (the author of a two-volume study of the poverty of the working classes in England and France), and others.

In his discussions of wages, capital, profit, rent and similar items, Marx expressed many of the views that stayed with him thereafter. Much of it was commonplace, widely accepted or at least currently known. Many of Marx's observations were little more than accepted clichés of the age. Wages were the product of a hostile struggle between capitalist and worker. The worker was subject to the law of supply and demand like any other commodity, with wages tending to fall to a level just adequate to keep a necessary labor force alive. Even in the best times, the worker earned so little that "of four children, two must starve and die." Other statements were somewhat more unique with Marx. Private property was the "material expression of estranged human life." The more the worker produced, the less he received; the more value he created, the more worthless he became; and the worst was yet to come.

The *Manuscripts of 1844* are unique among Marxian writing only where they dwell on the subject of man's "alienation" or "estrangement," and the overcoming of the same. Here Marx was sufficiently idealistic and humanistic, as also complex, esoteric, abstract, unresolved and unclear to meet anybody's requirements. In later decades, when Marx showed similar lapses into the abstract and the obscure, Engels tolerantly placed the blame on the physical distractions of boils and carbuncles that plagued his partner often enough to account for a lot of things.

The concept of human *alienation* and *estrangement,* with all its involvements, represented a segment of the vast system of Hegel. The Young Hegelians met the challenge by searching for the philosopher's stone that would transmute the riddle into a golden realization of the full human essence. Feuerbach had helped when he presumably recovered for man that part of his human essence that had been alienated when man transferred a part of himself to an outside God. Other

Young Hegelians also speculated as to the path that led to full human realization. So Lorenz von Stein, who had written a widely-influential work on French socialism two years earlier, wrote in 1844 that the goal of man was his own completion or the realization of every capacity that lay in him.

Marx, however, having announced an alliance between philosophy and proletariat, applied the concept of alienation directly to the peculiar status of labor and the role of work. Hegel, to cite Marx's own words, regarded labor "as man's act of self-genesis" in an abstract way. Marx himself conceived of labor as satisfying a human need for self-expression and action, rather than in the light of a job that was required to take care of the individual's needs. Under the existing system, Marx declared, the worker was estranged from the goods that he produced, from his fellow men, from nature and from his own human essence. Since the worker did not affirm himself or express his human essence through his labor, work failed to stimulate him physically and mentally. Such labor was not voluntary, it was bondage and dehumanization.

Private property came out of it all as the highest expression of human estrangement. Man could not overcome this alienation except through the abolition of private property and capital. Here communism entered the picture as a system that transcended private property as the embodiment of human self-estrangement; communism therefore represented the real acquisition of the human essence, by and for man. Communism was the same as humanity, the solution of the mystery of history. In speaking thus, Marx was using language that a Hegelian-trained German world might comprehend and follow. But it was otherwise with the rest of mankind, as Marx later deplored—non-Germans seemed incapable of distinguishing the heads from the tails of Hegelian terms. The *Manuscripts of 1844*, if they had been published, would have baffled, and rebuffed, many readers—except for the fact that they were larded with such familiar concepts as alienation and human realization.

The Marx family had been living in Paris for fifteen months when an order of expulsion came from the French government. The order was not the result of anything Marx had done or written against the July Monarchy. Like Heinrich Heine, Marx respected the sensibilities of the state that happened to be his current host. On the whole he had lived quietly. Personal contacts had not been successful. Except for Proudhon, he had failed to establish friendly ties with French radicals. He had recently met Étienne Cabet, communist writer and promoter, but that meeting was fruitless. The pretext for Marx's expulsion from Paris ostensibly resulted from his almost casual ties with the German-language *Vorwärts*. He had not published anything in that bi-weekly since his attack on Arnold Ruge, though both he and Engels seem to have regarded the paper as an instrument that might be useful and therefore worthy of support. But the Prussian government had been taking a special interest in *Vorwärts*.

Under Bernays' editorship the paper sought popularity by baiting Prussia and especially her King. Prussia had been attempting to kill the newspaper through diplomatic channels by urging the French government to expel everybody associated with it. Paris was reluctant at first. There was no point in pursuing repressive measures when no French interests were affected. Any action against *Vorwärts* would also touch Heine who was the recipient of an annual income from the secret funds of the French Foreign Office. Again, the government of Louis Philippe, which tolerated no attacks against itself, was inclined to be liberal in allowing the publication on French soil of critical attacks on other governments. But when *Vorwärts* published an unbalanced article that praised a would-be assassin of the Prussian King, Paris was more responsive. The French King, himself the intended victim of several assassination plots, could appreciate the evil of regicide under any flag. On January 11, 1845, the French government then issued an expulsion order against Marx, Ruge, Heine, Bakunin, Börnstein and Bernays. But in Paris such difficulties could often be settled out of court. The order was generally evaded in one way or another. Marx made no such attempt.

It is commonly assumed that Marx was above any back-door dealings with reactionary governments, as contrary to his principles and revolutionary integrity. Marx, however, was also a person who recognized the value of the martyrdom associated with such an expulsion—several inches would be added to his stature as a foe of existing governments. Little was to be gained by staying in Paris anyway. He had failed to establish himself as a force and had gained no noteworthy following among the French. On the other hand, there were practical advantages in a move to Brussels, which lay closer to the Rhineland and Germany. And living was cheaper there than in Paris. On February 3, 1845, Marx therefore moved to Brussels. His family arrived a few days later. On May 1 they moved into a permanent home at 5–7 Rue d'Alliance in a suburb of Brussels, Saint Josse-ten-noode.

The extraordinary costs involved in the move to Brussels were taken care of "in a communist manner" by Engels, Georg Jung and socialist friends who collected funds from sympathizers in Cologne, Elberfeld and other towns in the Rhineland and Westphalia. The "dogs," Engels wrote, "were not to have the pleasure of seeing Marx exposed to pecuniary embarrassment as a result of their infamy." Over the next months Marx received several recorded shipments of money from such sources

—50 *Taler,* 122 *francs,* and finally 750 *francs.* Engels also promised to contribute the 100 *Taler* that he expected soon from the publisher of his recently completed manuscript on the condition of the working class in England.

Heinrich Bürgers, a radical writer from Cologne, had accompanied Marx to Brussels. They were welcomed by Ferdinand Freiligrath, the revolutionary poet whom Marx had not met previously. Karl Heinzen soon arrived. The Marxes therefore were among friends. Externally Marx's life in Brussels was very quiet at first. Soon after his arrival, the Administration of Public Security demanded and received a written promise from Marx that he would write nothing on contemporary politics in Belgium.

3. ENGELS: ACTION FROM BARMEN

ENGELS left Paris for Barmen in September, 1844, expecting to rejoin Marx within a few weeks. His main purpose in going home was to arrange a gracious and satisfactory understanding with his family. That was not a simple matter in view of the fact that he wanted the assurance of a monthly allowance to enable him to continue a literary and revolutionary career that flew in the face of all principles and traditions that were sacred to them. Such an arrangement took longer than he had anticipated and the weeks grew into months. Meanwhile he had the leisure to write and to cultivate revolutionary connections in the Rhineland and Westphalia.

During the first half-year of the revolutionary partnership Engels certainly was the more productive. His articles on "The Condition of England" (*Die Lage Englands*) continued to appear in Paris through September and into October as front-page features of the German-language *Vorwärts.* Since the articles were written before he met Marx in Paris, they are important because they reveal the stock of ideas that Engels brought into the revolutionary partnership.

In sentences that reveal the humanist and the philosopher, Engels condemned the English industrial society. "Cash payment" had become the only tie between men. To complete the "alienation," property and money had become the lords of the universe. Yet it was all a part of a necessary process that would make humanity conscious of itself again, leading to an escape from its existence as a "mass of isolated, mutually-repelling atoms."

Originally written for publication in two installments under the respective titles, "The 18th Century" and "The English Constitution," the articles appeared instead in eleven editions of the paper. In the first series, dealing with the 18th century, Engels declared that England since 1750 had been going through the greatest revolution. Scientific advances expedited this "industrial revolution." Such words as spinning-jenny, Wedgwood, Watt, Macadam and railroads marked some of the milestones of its progress. But its most significant product was the proletariat, the class that would destroy the economic and political structure of old England. A social revolution would follow in the wake of the industrial transformation.

Engels maintained that nationality differences accounted for variations in philosophic reflections, which in turn helped to shape the destiny of peoples, as did economic and material considerations. Applying the dialectic to certain national traits, Engels concluded that the English nationality rested on an unresolved conflict, the union of the sharpest contrasts. The English were the most religious people in the world and at the same time the most irreligious; they tortured themselves more over the question of the hereafter than any other nation but at the same time they lived as if the present were their one and all. Unable to solve their inner conflict, they were driven towards action that led to colonization, conflict, industry and an enormous practical activity.

The series of articles dealing with the English Constitution were very timely. Most German liberals praised the English model above anything that France could offer. Engels, however, set out in a debunking manner to prove that behind the well-known English facade lay a fundamental fraud, institutionalized hypocrisy and incarnate deception.

Defining the "essence of the state" (as also of religion) as representing "mankind's fear of itself," Engels maintained that this fear found its loftiest expression in England's constitutional monarchy. People feared a government based on pure democracy, or absolute monarchy, or undiluted aristocracy (the three classical forms of government). But instead of drawing the conclusion that all forms of government were inhuman and a negation of humanity, the English decided that several negatives when joined together resulted in something positive. They believed that the union of the three "immoral" forms of government formed a "moral" product, in the shape of a constitutional monarchy. "Property ruled. . . . England, of course, is a democracy, but in the same sense as Russia is a democracy, insofar as the people everywhere unconsciously rule and in all states the government is merely another expression of the cultural level of the people." Under such a definition, anything could be called democratic. If the despotism and autocracy of Nicholas I merited a democratic badge, Engels (and Marx also) was not stretching the concept too far when he elsewhere spoke of the communist movement as being democratic.

Engels scoffed at the traditional English freedoms and safeguards, so much admired in a Europe where arbitrary force was not uncommon. Under his coating of tar and feathers, freedom of press, assembly and association, trial by jury, and *habeas corpus* are scarcely recognizable as they march through the last three articles in *Vorwärts*. Oddly enough, what disturbed Engels most was the respect and protection granted to the accused person. "English law declares that the accused is sacred and turns itself against the society for whose protection it really exists."

As for the fate of England, "democracy" lay in the immediate future —a "*social* democracy." But such a democracy was incapable of curing any social evil and could be only a transitional state, the "last purely political means" before a new principle entered the picture, a principle that transcended all politics, the principle of "socialism." Such was England's destiny.

Between November, 1844, and mid-March, 1845, in Barmen, Engels wrote his best-known book, *Die Lage der arbeitenden Klasse in England. Nach eigner Anschauung und authentischen Quellen* (*The Condition of the Working Class in England. Based on Personal Observations and Authentic Sources*). Although he wrote Marx on November 19, 1844, that he was buried up to his ears in English newspapers and books, the research had been virtually completed while he was in Manchester. Most of his information came from published books, articles, governmental reports (Bluebooks), and newspapers. He was not the first to use these sources. Furthermore, he seems to have been unaware of the excellent study by Eugène Buret, *De la misère des classes laborieuse en Angleterre et en France* (Paris, 1840), to which Marx does refer in the so-called *Manuscripts of 1844.*

Engels did not present the objective, purely descriptive study that he promised his readers. Instead, he wrote with that "pathos of indignation" and "denunciation" that matched the Marxian recipe for revolutionary propaganda. Bruno Hildebrand, an informed contemporary critic and an economist, rated the work as "accurate in its details but misleading as a whole." Engels himself wrote to Marx on November 19 that the book would charge the English bourgeoisie with "murder, robbery and all other crimes"—a "beautiful registry of sins committed." He confessed that he was "beating the pack when the blows were intended for the donkey," namely, he was really berating the German bourgeoisie who were just as bad as the English, only "less bold, consequent and skilled in extortion."

The *Condition of the Working Class* described the lot of all segments of the laboring population, including the lowly Irish and the neglected farm worker. The picture was rounded out with descriptions of the big city, housing, mortality statistics, the increase of crime (Engels always called this the first symptom of proletarian protest), strikes, poorhouses, poverty and prostitution. Engels made the position of the workers appear worse than that of the traditional slave, while painting their character and potentialities in radiant colors. The curse of national prejudice and arrogance was not in them. They admired all that was "noble and good," whether of native or foreign origin. The worker was not just an Englishman, a citizen of a single isolated nation. Instead, he was a human being, "the citizen of a great and international family of mankind . . . a human being in the most weighty sense of the word."

Engels, however, observed that wages did not necessarily sink to a level just sufficient to keep the worker alive and able to breed enough children to stock the labor market. The "degree of civilization" of the worker played a role. If he were accustomed to eating meat several times a week, the capitalist had to pay enough to allow for this. But Engels ruled out the possibility that future advances in the "civilization" of the workers might be accompanied by continuing improvements in wages. Economic depressions, chronically recurring every five years, made this impossible under the capitalist system. Such crises, as the "mightiest levers for all independent growth of the proletariat," guaranteed the ultimate triumph of revolution. The war of the poor against the rich would be the bloodiest ever experienced, he prophesied.

Engels denounced the bourgeoisie as a class that profited from the existing system and had an interest in its defense. Therefore their "pretense" of humanity, even the genuine human feelings that some possessed, did not alter the picture. When the roll call was taken, the forces that make history and revolutions would divide along class lines. The French revolutionary "Terror" of 1794 would appear mild in comparison to the events that lay ahead.

Having held up a spectre of inevitable bloody terror and class warfare, Engels added that the worst might still be avoided. At that time he very optimistically believed that he was gaining converts to communism from the middle classes and that they might even aid in its propagation. With their conversion in mind, Engels held out the hope that the inescapable revolution might take a milder course, if enough "socialist and communist elements" (recruited from the bourgeoisie) joined the ranks of the proletariat. The "spilling of blood, revenge and fury" would diminish proportionally. Communism recognized that the proletarian hatred for the bourgeoisie was necessary as the most important "lever for the beginning labor movement." Since communism, however, was "concerned with humanity and not just the workers," the Communists had no thought of taking revenge on individuals or of believing that the bourgeois person could act differently under prevailing circumstances. If the proletariat gained the same "clarity in social questions," the Communist Party might be able to "overcome the brutal element of the revolution in the long run." The book ended on this optimistic note.

The manuscript was completed by the middle of March, 1845, and published in Leipzig towards the end of May. It was the most successful work of the revolutionary partners during the "youthful" period before 1848.

Engels realized, however, that writing alone was not enough; theory must be implemented through the mobilization of human beings marching in step with the proper ideas and resentments. He found that he even preferred standing before "real, corporeal men and speaking to them directly, sentiently and openly," instead of the "damned abstract scribbling directed at an abstract public."

Much of the information of Engels' political and promotional work in Germany during this period comes from the famous Marx-Engels correspondence that started with Engels' arrival in Barmen. Though all but one of Marx's letters to Engels between 1844 and 1848 were lost, it is possible to guess at much that Marx wrote from Engels' replies. This correspondence remains as a valuable source of information on their actions and thoughts throughout their lives. The letters are unusually frank and unreserved, as between persons who understand each other fully and are in complete agreement. An almost chronic suspicion that the postal or police authorities were opening or intercepting their letters alone caused them to be somewhat cautious. To mislead the officials and to detect any missing letters, Engels recommended a number of ruses such as a "feminine appearing letter," a "businessman-like handwriting" and the tactic of numbering their letters consecutively so they would immediately discover any gap. In turn, their rivals and enemies later accused them of opening and intercepting letters. The "Party Archive" undoubtedly contained copies of various such letters. In a letter to Engels on September 28, 1852, Marx described how *Lupus* (Wilhelm Wolff, one of their most trusted followers) had opened a letter "in a masterly fashion," while Ernst Dronke, another Communist, copied the most important things.

During these months in the Rhineland, Engels began his lifetime career as the chief promoter and salesman of Marx and Marxism. At this time the English readers of the *New Moral World* saw the name of "Dr. Karl Marx" at the head of a list of the chief German Communists; the same Marx was praised as the author of a forthcoming monumental definitive critique of politics and economics. The aforesaid Marx was also Engels' ally in a declared war on those German philosophers who failed to draw practical conclusions from their pure theories. As for the new union of philosophy and proletariat, it was the same ubiquitous Marx who had first announced this alliance a year earlier. The English also read that the conservative French government had forced Marx to leave Paris; he might even be forced to find refuge in England, if he were not allowed to live in peace in Brussels. When Engels, a man of impressive credentials in his own right, continued to point to Marx as the man to be noted, it was bound to rouse curiosity and to suggest the idea that here was a rare bird indeed.

Engels lost no time in starting an energetic campaign to promote and sell communism in the Prussian Rhineland and Westphalia. Every letter to Marx spoke of new prospects, contacts and converts. Karl Lessing, the historical painter, had announced his conversion. Karl Hübner was exhibiting an eloquent painting of the cruel lot of the Silesian weavers—the face of the industrialist, red and feelingless as brass, contrasted sharply with the agony of the working mother, child and aging father. This generated more agitative power than a hundred pamphlets, Engels asserted. In Elberfeld he discovered an artist who would be "very useful as a caricaturist." Everywhere on steamboats, railroad coaches and just ordinary mail coaches, he was bumping into Communists and persons interested in social problems. He was astounded by the "enormous propaganda" they had achieved in Cologne during a stay of three days. For once he was also proud of his native Wuppertal; there he found that the humanistic principles had become flesh and blood. The young generation lectured the fathers when they handled their servants or workers in an "aristocratic" manner. In Barmen the police commissioner was a Communist. Engels even discovered six or more socialists in his own "very pious and loyal family."

Engels' optimism in regard to their cause rested on an illusion that both he and Marx still shared. As they saw it, philosophical Germany was destined to become communist. Humanism was almost a religion in the ranks of the bourgeoisie and among educated people in general. Consequently Marx and Engels regarded the widespread interest in socialism and social questions as being synonymous with communism, or as needing only a little clarification before maturing into communism.*

* The term communism was used as a label for all types of mass unrest. The word socialism occurred with equal frequency. There was no clear distinction between the two. In general usage the word communism was employed when speaking of the danger and threat of mass uprising; socialism was more frequently applied to the various systems proposed as the cure for social evils. Both obviously opposed private property, competition and capitalism in general. Both generally stood for a planned economy and social control of property, as illustrated in the favored catchwords "organization of labor," and "association." So it was easy to use the word interchangeably. Theodor Oelchers, the respected German writer on socialism, stated in 1844 that there was no good definition of communism yet. He himself then defined communism as the "idea of absolute freedom driven to extremes." But this use of an abstraction as a definition for the undefined was of little help.

The distinction between socialism and communism ultimately narrowed down to a question of ways and means in which the desired change would be realized. So-

Germany seemed like a promised land to anyone operating on the above assumptions. Alerted to the problem of poverty by the revolt of the Silesian weavers and a flood of socialist literature, the creation of "Societies for the Improvement of the Lot of the Workers" became almost a fad, initially with the encouragement of the Prussian authorities. The Communists helped to give such societies a proper orientation. This caused a "colossal stir," Engels wrote to Marx, as the social question was brought to the attention of the "philistine world." After such a promising start, the Prussian government intervened when it became clear that the societies were being "infected" with communism. But even this short-lived movement had benefited the Communists, according to Engels; it had shown that the bourgeoisie was trying to hoodwink the workers through hypocrisy and a false philanthropy.

Engels acknowledged that the bourgeoisie made up the bulk of the socialist movement that was spreading like an epidemic. As for the workers, he could merely hope that this class would soon support them. The time was ripe. The Wuppertal workers were beginning to protest against the old social order—the streets were unsafe at night; bourgeois citizens were assaulted, stabbed and robbed. The proletarians would soon discover, Engels continued, that such isolated protests were useless; then they would resort to force as "human beings," in a conscious, disciplined communist manner. Apparently Engels never risked making contacts with the workers. "If we could work directly on the people, we would soon be on top," he explained to Marx. "But that is virtually impossible, because we writers have to be quiet in order to avoid arrest."

Before long a shadow of doubt darkened Engels' first optimistic expectations. People had the right will, but there was much confusion and a lack of clarity as to the proper goals. What was needed was a suitable work by Marx, a "few bigger books," to serve as a compass. Engels himself, aided by the ubiquitous and enterprising Moses Hess, promoted a new monthly *Gesellschaftsspiegel* (*Mirror of Society*) that would describe the "social misery and the bourgeois regime." He and Marx then thought of publishing a veritable "library" that would include translations of the leading foreign socialist writers. Marx would edit the French works while Engels took care of the English. As Engels en-

cialism was usually regarded as favoring a peaceful, humane, intelligently guided and gradual change. Thus the French economist Vidal asserted in 1843 that the socialists did not want social war; on the contrary, they wished to prevent it through reforms. Far from provoking hatred between different classes, they preached concord and cooperation. The socialist appealed to the intelligence and humanity of all classes.

Communism, in contrast, was regarded as a more distinctly proletarian movement. The emphasis was on the hostile interests and clash of classes. The forceful annihilation of the old society was necessary in order to establish the rule of the working class. Even so, the respective communist and socialist trademarks continued to be used somewhat indiscriminately. Certainly Étienne Cabet, a self-styled French Communist, was anything but an advocate of class warfare and wholesale revolution.

visioned the undertaking, it was best to jettison anything of a mere "theoretic" interest in favor of subjects that were closest to their own principles and had a practical, direct and telling impact on the Germans. The lack of funds and a publisher ultimately deprived the German world of such a selectively edited library.

Engels' direct promotion of communism reached its climax in Elberfeld, the center of the industrial area of the Prussian Rhineland, where "wonderful things" occurred when three "regular communist meetings" were held on the 8th, 15th and 22nd of February, 1845. Forty persons attended the first meeting, one hundred and thirty were at the second, while the third drew at least two hundred. "All of Elberfeld and Barmen were represented, from the moneyed aristocracy to the corner groceryman. Only the proletariat was excluded," Engels reported.

The meetings were rather typical of such gatherings in an age when full freedom of assembly was lacking. A dose of culture and other entertainment came first, partly to camouflage the true purpose of the meeting and perhaps also to serve as an added attraction. Music and declamation—several female harpists were followed by the reading of German socialist poems and selections from Shelley—set the tone and established a sympathetic mood for that which followed. Since the Communists had a majority at the first meeting, they controlled the organization and procedure. Moses Hess, who worked closely with Engels at this time, proposed that Gustav Köttgen, a communist painter, be elected as the presiding officer. The motion was carried. Hess then gave the first speech. Engels was next in order, as the main speaker.

Engels was never successful as a popular speaker; his printed speeches seem tedious and prolix. He read excerpts from romantically enthusiastic reports of such utopian settlements in America as Pleasant Hill, New Lebanon, Zoar (Ohio), Equality (Wisconsin) and New Harmony. On the basis of such examples, Engels insisted that in a communist society people lived better with less effort, had more leisure for the edification of their minds, and were better and more moral persons than their neighbors who owned property. Communism was "neither contrary to human nature, intelligence and the heart, nor was it a theory rooted in sheer fantasy which ignored reality."

Engels tried to persuade his bourgeois listeners that they should join with the inevitable instead of waiting until they were crushed by it. Once the workers united in favor of communism, they would be "endlessly stronger than the rich." Moreover, the better and more sensible members of the wealthy class would side with the workers, as some were already. A revolution, more terrible than the upheavals of the past, was bound to come unless the bourgeoisie themselves took the first step in the direction of communism. Engels assured his listeners that there was no thought of introducing "communist ownership overnight and against the will of the nation."

All of the oratory for the three meetings was furnished by the Communists, but the opposition had its opportunity during the discussion period that lasted until after midnight. According to one report, many factory owners attended the second and third meetings to get a kick out of the affair, thus accounting for the greatly increased attendance. Roderick Benedix, a writer of comedies and the director of the city theatre, was their spokesman. But Engels seems not to have been disturbed by such interruptions. "People speak of nothing but communism and we are gaining new followers each day," he wrote to Marx. ". . . Wuppertal communism is a verity, yes, almost a power. The most stupid, indolent philistine people" were becoming almost fanatical over communism.

Up to this point Engels and his followers had avoided any references to the state, politics and religion. The omissions were deliberate. Engels did not want to alienate the audience by appearing too revolutionary in too many ways. Perhaps also he wanted to spare the feelings of his own family. And the Prussian state could not be ignored. Engels assured Marx that they had been "clever enough" not to give the authorities any cause for interference. But evidently the Communists were not clever enough.

After the third meeting Engels, Hess and Köttgen received an official notice that such meetings were illegal and that, if need be, force would be used to prevent them. When a fourth meeting was held anyway, the mayor and public prosecutor, with an escort of armed policemen, were present. Under the circumstances there were no speeches and the assembly was restricted to the secondary attraction—"beefsteak and wine." Engels was not entirely depressed, however; the meetings had attracted attention, and people were impressed by the way the Communists had handled themselves. Even persons who had come to ridicule left with a greater respect for the Communists.

Six months had passed since Engels met Marx in Paris. The original purpose of his return to Barmen was not accomplished; he had not been able to persuade his family to finance a career as a writer and communist agitator. Writing to Marx in November, he had stated that he could not yet come to Paris "without falling out with the whole family." All sorts of "petty considerations and superstitious fears" stood in the way. The situation called for a strategy of attrition and not of assault, for he was too attached to his family, especially his mother, to break with them. The time had flown rapidly enough. In addition to writing and propagating his communist views, there had been a number of digressions.

The engagement of a favorite sister, Marie, to Emil Blank, a "Communist from London," was the occasion for a number of festivities and diversions. Then in January, 1845, Engels himself was involved in a love affair that had to be settled. He asked Marx to excuse him from spelling out the "boring" details, since an entire evening would be wasted if he explained the "whole paltry show." And so posterity can only guess how near Engels was to marriage.

At this time Engels agreed to try his hand at the family business again, as a concession to the "sad faces of his two parents," the pleas of Emil Blank, and the exigencies of the love affair. For two weeks he worked behind a desk. But "business was too abominable," he informed Marx. So was Barmen and the waste of time. It was especially outrageous to pose as a bourgeois, even worse, as a manufacturer. One could not write communist propaganda in a grand style and be active at the same time in trade and industry. Moreover, the "debilitating life in a completely radical-Christian Prussian home" would make a *philistine* out of him and bring philistinism into communism. He then assured Marx that he would only stay in business as long as it suited him. After that, he would write something that the police would find objectionable, thus giving him the pretext for a graceful flight across the frontiers. Easter would be the deadline for his exit from Barmen.

The series of communist meetings in Elberfeld during February then produced a crisis in the Engels family. The "old man" was determined to support his son only in connection with his "*Studia*" (study at the university in Bonn), and not for "communist purposes of any sort." In view of Engels' dislike for a business career, his father evidently was now ready to finance any university study in preparation for another calling. But Engels had already picked his profession, and only the "money question" remained uncertain.

From this point forward, Engels lived a "veritable dog's life," as he wrote Marx on March 17. Because of the communist meetings and the "slovenliness" of some of the Communists with whom he associated, the "whole religious fanaticism" of his father had been awakened again. Parallel with it, a "sterling bourgeois fanaticism" had been aroused by his renunciation of a business career and aggravated by his public appearance as a Communist. Wherever he turned, he saw the "godly-woeful countenance" of the family; the same "damned child-of-God look" followed his every move. It was impossible to describe the "malignity of this Christian chase after his soul." Since he expected to leave Barmen in fourteen days or so, he bore everything in silence. He did regret the pain that he caused his mother—there was a "beautiful human stock" in her. Whenever she became especially exasperated with him, she endured a headache for eight days. Except for her, Engels declared, he would not make even the most miserly concession to his "despotic and fanatic old man." And, as he had written earlier, there was still the question of money.

In the end the Prussian state came to Engels' aid. The police began to show an interest of a sort that made it possible to envision an arrest. This would have been a hard blow for the loyal and law-abiding Engels family. A fast move across the frontier seemed advisable. In view of the special circumstances, he probably did not even have to press his excellent bargaining position. He left home with the assurance that a monthly allowance would ease his exile.

= III =

Union in Brussels:
The New Tone

1. THE MATERIALISTIC CONCEPTION
OF HISTORY

THE ten days in Paris had been too brief for Marx and Engels to establish a complete coordination of views. It was in Brussels that they really became acquainted. Engels found lodging in the house right next to Marx's residence, so they were together almost constantly, comparing notes, experiences, impressions and ideas. A new note, emphasis, orientation, singlemindedness or just toughness of mind became evident in their actions and pronouncements. The impact of the study of economics had broadened Marx's perspective. The famed Marxian process of self-clarification had been at work during the preceding months. As a maker of systems in which all pieces had their proper place, Marx had progressed towards a theory that would explain all human history. Engels apparently had sensed the same need of a coherent, all-inclusive explanation as early as October, 1844, when he wrote Marx that "so long as the principles were not logically explained on the basis of previous concepts and earlier history, and as a necessary continuation of the same," everything would remain as "half doses and a groping in the dark for most people."

The answer came now in Brussels. It was the materialistic conception of history, historical materialism, economic determinism, or the economic interpretation of history, as it has been variously named. This explanation of history (the materialistic conception, as it is perhaps most commonly named) starts with the assertion that man's first need is to feed himself and to provide for his offspring. "Production and reproduction [as Engels put it late in his life] is the determining force in history." As man rose above the primitive level, a division of labor developed when each produced different wares, leading to an exchange of goods and commerce. In the course of time, this process brought about the division of society into classes, in conformity with the way the individuals work and what they own. Class conflict entered the picture. Those who were economically strong became dominant—the exploiters and rulers. It was they who established governments, religions, moral codes and a culture—the ideological superstructure—that merely reflected the interests of the economically favored class.

But history does not stand still; societies change when a shift occurs in the methods of production and the exchange of goods. When the productive forces (soil, natural power, machines, new techniques, etc.) are altered, a new class comes to the fore, challenging the previously dominant class. Revolution occurs when an existing society and order acts like a straitjacket that keeps in check the new economic forces and the class that benefits from them. The new class favored by the latest economic forces then seizes power and establishes a new government. Marx and Engels illustrated class conflict through the ages with such examples as slave versus freeman; serf versus nobleman; bourgeois versus nobility. In the most advanced countries, the final clash was approaching—that of the proletariat versus the bourgeoisie (capitalism and private property). (Germany, of course, lagged one step behind; there the bourgeoisie was destined to seize power in the next revolutionary round.) Each change represented progress in history; revolution ushered in a higher development of humanity—this was its justification. Revolution was a necessary and inevitable process.

It is necessary to note that the dialectic remained the director of the whole process, however economically determined it might be. Change and progress resulted from conflict, negation, negation of negation, and so on. Conflicts and contradiction developed as a given order clashed with the changing economic basis. This conflict expressed itself in class competition and warfare. The issues were simplified as the final round approached when the proletariat and bourgeoisie would square off against each other. The proletariat would crush the adversary and establish its own dictatorial power, accompanied by a socialist order. After that, with the consolidation of a classless society, the state and political power would gradually vanish as the final communist society emerged. Then the real *human* history would start, or in another sense, all history would end for lack of anything exciting to report.

The dialectic was basic in the thinking of Marx and Engels. They approached history with the assumption that it had to keep in step with the dialectical progression. There was just enough in history and in the contemporary economic developments to give this view a superficial plausibility. Everything seemed to hang together; out of the past and the present the future could be projected. It provided a certain answer for those who needed certainty above all and for those who liked a simple scientific explanation for the phenomena that have always puzzled man.

The credit for formulating the materialist conception of history is usually assigned to Marx. Engels always insisted that Marx had shown him the blueprint when he arrived in Brussels in April. On the other hand, Marx later indicated that Engels too had been coming towards the same conclusions. As for the emphasis on sheer economic factors and the role of class conflicts, Engels had plowed the first ground in his studies on English conditions. To Marx probably belongs the credit for creating an artistic whole that hung together in a pattern or system.

But there is a puzzling hiatus at this point in the primary records of Marx's development. Nothing of his new discovery found its way into print, or even into his unpublished papers. The first fairly extensive account of the new theory appeared in scattered places in *The German Ideology*, a work that both Marx and Engels started in the fall and that they were unable to publish. In 1888 Engels discovered the so-called "Theses on Feuerbach" in Marx's notebooks. Since Marx apparently had jotted them down in the spring of 1845, they appeared like a missing link. In the absence of anything else, Engels had them published and attributed an exaggerated importance to them. The "Theses" were eleven in number, about two printed pages in length. Engels described them as having been "rapidly scribbled off, absolutely not intended for publication, but priceless as the first document wherein the genial bud of the new interpretation of the world was implanted." With this introduction by Engels, the "Theses," brief like so many commandments and orphic in their incompleteness, have attracted an unwarranted degree of attention. Where a mere "bud" or "embryo" (*Keim*) shows, speculation is encouraged.

Thesis No. 11 (which reads, "The philosophers have only interpreted the world in various ways; it is necessary to *change* it") is often cited to illustrate the new trend. But this stress on practice, action and reality was not a revelation of something new in Marx. The structural design of the new theory of history does not appear here. The "Theses" do make clear, however, that the "Feuerbach cult" of *The Holy Family* was a thing of the past, to be replaced by a war on Feuerbachian humanism and those concepts of humanity that were not rooted in the earth and expressed in action.

A new tone accompanied the adoption of the new theory of history. There is a change in tactics and alignments, a greater stress on history and concrete developments, coupled with a rejection of philosophy as an unreliable vehicle. Most of the documentation of the new outlook first appeared in the writings of Engels. The change in attitude towards Ludwig Feuerbach is very noticeable. A month before joining Marx in Brussels, Engels had written in the *New Moral World* that Feuerbach's conversion to communism was the most important item that he could report. The same jubilant note was evident in his letter of March 7 to Marx. After April, however, Engels denounced Feuerbach for his humanism, as being too abstract—it did not point to action and revolution. Actually Marx and Engels turned against Feuerbach because too many German reformers and socialists who wanted a peacefully humane transformation of society took their stand on his humanism. As advocates of revolution and class conflict, Marx and Engels had to deprecate the philosopher who once had commanded their unlimited praise.

The adoption of the new theory of history produced a second change, a reversal of their attitude towards most other socialists and Communists. Before the Brussels reunion, Engels had referred to Hermann Püttmann, Otto Lüning, Karl Grün and Wilhelm Weitling as being in their camp. After joining Marx in April, the same socialists and Communists became the target of ridicule and denunciation, though Weitling enjoyed a temporary reprieve. Simultaneously, there was a change in Engels' vocabulary—and also Marx's. Words and expressions such as "humanity," "humanism," "alienation" and the "realization of humanity" were largely discontinued, even ridiculed, since those noble words were widely employed by socialists who wished to avoid class conflict, hatred and violent revolution.

The above changes stand out starkly in Engels' "A Fragment from Fourier on Trade." In the introduction, written between April and July, 1845, Engels openly derided the Germans for being at the point of "spoiling the communist movement." This was the first skirmish in a virulent campaign against "True Socialism." Engels mocked the "comical arrogance of German theory" that was at work when a "whole army of speculative heads" took over the newly-imported communist principle and supposedly "elevated it to the level of German theory." They thought they had done miracles when they translated and "Hegeled" the French and English ideas into the fundamentals of a "true, pure, German theoretical communism and socialism." Engels frankly stated that he did not exempt some of his own previous works from this criticism.

Engels also accused the Germans of noting only the visions of utopian societies while they ignored the actual, existing conditions that Fourier and others criticized. In doing so, the Germans brought out only the "worst and the most theoretical parts, the schematization of future societies, the *social systems*"; they calmly ignored the other side, "the *critique of existing society*, the real foundation, the chief purpose of any preoccupation with social questions." Again comparing Fourier with the Germans, Engels showed how Fourier's method was superior. Fourier constructed his future, after he had correctly grasped the past and the present; German theory, in contrast, "first remade past history in line with their wishes and then similarly told the future what directions it should take." Engels knew his Germans well, especially those who had graduated from Hegel.

The Germans, Engels continued, relied too much on "impure sources" of information. That was why their "absolute socialism" was so "terrifyingly poor."

> A little "humanity," as the thing is entitled of late, a little "realization" of this humanity (or, better yet, monster), a little bit about property taken from Proudhon—via third or fourth hand, a little proletarian compassion, organization of labor . . . side-by-side with a boundless ignorance of political economy and the real society—that is the whole story, which, moreover, because of a theoretical objectivity, a "complete serenity of thought," loses its last drop of blood, the last trace of energy and elasticity. And with this boring stuff they want to revolutionize Germany, set the proletariat in motion, make the masses think and act?

In the light of the above, it is not surprising that Marx himself never completed the celebrated *Economic and Philosophic Manuscripts of 1844.* It contained too much talk of "humanity," "realization" of humanity and similar things now regarded as synonymous with softness, confusion, sentimentality, compassion and what not. From this point forward Marx and Engels used such concepts very sparingly—spaced where they would do the most good and the least harm.

The "Fragment from Fourier" also contained a note of unlimited hostility towards the bourgeoisie. Although exploitation of the proletariat might be the "main consideration" for sentencing the bourgeoisie, they deserved execution on other grounds, such as their "sweet commerce, their contemptible amusements that are not amusements, their organization of cuckoldry in married life, their general confusion" which Fourier had condemned in such a masterly fashion. Engels praised Fourier for also exposing the hypocrisy of respectable society, the boredom of its "clean morals." After such an indictment, it would seem almost superfluous to bring in the proletariat, except as executioners.

2. THE TRIP TO ENGLAND

AROUND the middle of July, 1845, Marx and Engels began a "study-tour" of England. For some time Engels had been planning a brief trip to Manchester. He wanted to retrieve the many books he had left behind when he returned to Barmen—a valid consideration that justified the cost of the excursion in the eyes of his parents. It is unlikely that he mentioned Mary Burns whom he also wanted to bring back to the continent with him.

Marx was interested in the trip for other reasons. With Engels as his guide, he would become acquainted with the most advanced country in the world and be introduced to its industrial society. This was important now that he had adopted the materialistic theory of history with its emphasis on economic forces. He also wanted to read some older English economic studies that had not been available in Brussels. Money for the trip was a problem. But, most opportunely, the publisher of his still unfinished *Economic and Philosophic Manuscripts of 1844* made an advance payment of 1500 *francs* in July, 1845.

Marx and Engels spent six weeks in England, most of it in Manchester, a major industrial center and the home of Mary Burns. Although the public library was far inferior to the one in London, Marx's notebooks nevertheless show that he consulted a variety of works on the general theme of economic history—treatises on political economy, big industry, prices, banking, machinery, trade, money and gold. The final week or ten days was spent in London, giving Engels the opportunity to renew old acquaintances and to introduce his partner to the more revolutionary trends, societies and individuals that the great city had to offer. They visited the London branch of the League of the Just where Marx met Schapper, Bauer, Moll and other members of that resolute group of Germans-in-exile. Engels renewed his contacts with the more radical and revolutionary wing of the English Chartists. George Julian Harney who was editor of the Chartist paper, *Northern Star,* thereafter welcomed Engels' journalistic contributions. Since the Owenite *New Moral World* had ceased publication, this new gateway to the English public helped to put an international stamp on their communist movement.

While in London, Marx and Engels helped to promote a radical and democratic alliance or fraternization of peoples, favored by many at that time as a counterpart to a supposed alliance of princes (Holy Alliance and others). Meeting with a group of English Chartists, certain members of the League of the Just, and some other individuals, Marx and Engels helped to plan a great "festival of nations." Engels proposed the following motion: "A *public meeting of democrats* of all nations residing in London is to be called to consider the founding of an association aimed at the promotion of the common cause, via joint periodic meetings and the exchange of information regarding the movements existing in each land."

Perhaps a shortage of money made it impossible for Marx and Engels to stay in London for the Festival of Nations that followed on September 22, the anniversary of the proclamation of the first French Republic, resulting in the organization of a society known as the Fraternal Democrats. Marx and Engels thereafter established contacts with that group, even if it proved to be too fraternal and mild to suit their tastes.

Marx and Engels returned to Brussels in a buoyant mood. From this point forward Marx could speak as one who had studied in England. Engels also had fulfilled his mission. He returned with his books and Mary Burns. This uneducated working girl remained a devoted lifelong companion with whom Engels could relax. She knew her own place, however, and accepted the fact that her unorthodox union acted as a social barrier. Engels soon found it unwise to bring her along when he called at the Marx home.

An incident at a banquet of the German Worker Society in Brussels late in 1847 has been described by Stephan Born, a communist recruit. Marx and Jenny were seated a safe distance from Engels and Mary. Marx, "through a look and a very expressive smile," gave Born to understand that his wife "rigidly rejected an acquaintanceship with that woman. In questions of marriage and purity or morals the noble woman was intransigent." Although Jenny Marx identified herself with the views of her husband in most matters, she believed in the sanctity and propriety of marriage. Perhaps Marx himself merely tolerated Engels' attachment to this virtually illiterate Irish girl. The one serious strain on the relationship between Marx and Engels occurred when Mary Burns died in 1863. Engels wrote to Marx that even his bourgeois friends had shown more sympathy and consideration for his bereavement. Marx made fulsome amends, and he was very careful thereafter to pay his respects to Lizzy Burns, Mary's sister and successor.

3. THE GERMAN IDEOLOGY

It is usually assumed that Marx went to England to gather additional material for his two-volume work on economics and politics. But the economic *Scheiss*, as he called it several years later, failed to hold his interest. Instead, he and Engels began a work on another polemic against Bruno Bauer and associates, a matter they had been considering for several months. *The Holy Family* had been designed to annihilate Bruno Bauer, but like the "damned spot" of Lady Macbeth, Bauer was not out; instead, he was alive and talking back. A new and unexpected competitor, Max Stirner (pseudonym of Johann Caspar Schmidt) also attracted attention with his *Der Einzige und sein Eigenthum* (*The Ego and His Own*, as it is entitled in an English translation), published in

1844. The book offended the eye with scattered and hostile references to communism.

Even while Engels was still in Barmen, he and Marx had exchanged views concerning the best way to handle Stirner. In the *New Moral World* of May 10, Engels spoke of a declaration of war on German philosophy. He specifically pointed to Stirner and Bauer, as the only important philosophical opponents of communism. It was also time to clarify their new position towards Feuerbach, though in a gentler manner. Marx and Engels began writing the new polemic in September, 1845. Several months later they expanded its scope to include a second declaration of war. The title and subtitle describe the dual purpose of the work: "The German Ideology. Critique of the latest German Philosophy in its Representatives, Feuerbach, B. Bauer and Stirner; and of German Socialism in its Various Prophets." (*"Die deutsche Ideologie. Kritik der neuesten deutschen Philosophie in ihren Repräsentanten Feuerbach, B. Bauer und Stirner, und des deutschen Sozialismus in seinen verschiedenen Propheten."*)

As Marx wrote later, the first volume of *The German Ideology* represented another settling of accounts with their own "past philosophical outlook." But "self-clarification" was not the major aim of the polemic. The purpose of the first volume, as stated in the preface, was to expose "these sheep who think they are wolves and whom others regard as such." They were the "biggest conservatives regardless of their pretended 'world-shattering phrases.'" They were to be stripped of all respectability so none would stop to admire their philosophic conclusions, instead of moving forward to the higher, more advanced and realistic findings of Marx and Engels.

None but the devotee or the dedicated scholar will read every line of *The German Ideology,* and even he soon finds that his devotion saddles him with a galling burden. There are the usual polemics, some wit, much straining for effect, a constant play with words, an unneeded verbosity and bushels of petty quibbling. Often a mountain is scraped up to bury a mouse. As an example of Marxian critique at full tilt, Stirner's book is introduced as " 'the book,' the book as such, absolutely the book, that is the perfected book, the holy book, the book as a sacred thing, the book as *the* holy thing—the book in heaven," all in one breath and sentence. Bruno Bauer is derided as "St. Bruno" and also as one of the "Church Fathers." Max Stirner is hobbled with holiness for nearly four hundred pages. That required some ingenuity. He appears as "St. Max," the "Holy Author," "Holy Max," "Holy Dialectician," the "Holy Juggler," the "Knight of the Sad Countenance," the "Holy Warrior," and finally as "St. Sancho."

Marx and Engels refused to add much to what they had already said about Bruno Bauer in *The Holy Family*. They announced that he was dead and filled just a few pages to certify that fact. The major assault was on Max Stirner. Their critique was longer than the book that they criticized.

The German Ideology handled Ludwig Feuerbach very gingerly. It reproached him for never having written a "critique of contemporary living conditions," for not applying materialism to history, and because his concept of man did not rise above an abstraction. Otherwise, the seventy or eighty pages addressed to Feuerbach concentrated mainly on a disjointed elaboration of Marx and Engels' own views and new concepts of history. Scattered paragraphs elsewhere in the two volumes, often in a ringing prose that ranks with their best, contain additional statements as to what communism stands for. This was a preview of much that was to appear later in a more compact and connected form in the *Communist Manifesto*.

As a critique of the idealistic philosophy of the Young Hegelians, *The German Ideology* stressed the economic basis and class character of all governments, ideals, religions, morals and culture in general. "The ideas of the ruling class are the ruling ideas in every age. . . . Liberal phrases are the idealistic expression of the real interests of the bourgeoisie." Lack of sugar and coffee was the "real basis of the glorious War of Liberation in 1813," causing the Germans to revolt against Napoleon. No other work of Marx and Engels was quite so crassly and even crudely materialistic.

By January, 1846, Marx and Engels decided that a declaration of war against True Socialism also was in order. This required a second volume for a full deployment of their polemical weapons. The main attack was directed against a successful school of socialist writers whom they derisively branded as "True Socialists," which included Karl Grün and Hermann Püttmann. Engels could truthfully write in 1888 that he and Marx fought harder against the socialists than against any others.

The True Socialists were accused of spoiling French and English socialism and communism via a two-fold distortion. First, they divorced such socialism and communism from the real world that gave them life. Second, the True Socialists tried to improve and clarify such theories by mixing them with the ideologies of Hegel and Feuerbach. The results were deplorable. The real "proletarian communism" was "transfigured" in the "heaven of the German intellect and German sentiment." This gave birth to an "esoteric literature" that appealed to sentiment and allowed a whole host of "young German writers and quacks" to exploit the social movement. Socialism and communism in the process "lost all revolutionary passion and in its place proclaimed a universal love of man."

The German Ideology confidently envisioned an early and inevitable decline of True Socialism. As soon as a "real communist party" appeared in Germany, the True Socialists "naturally would be restricted more and more to a public made up of the petty bourgeoisie and the impotent tatterdemalion writers who represented this public." At this time, however, the True Socialists had the greater following in Germany. They controlled certain newspapers, periodicals and a press, while Marx and Engels lacked even a single organ to propagate their views.

There was no quarrel with the True Socialists as to motives and general goals. The True Socialists had taken over the common stock of the socialists at large. They condemned the capitalist system, bourgeois society, competition and private property, which was to be replaced by the principle of "association," realized through social or cooperative ownership and control. The True Socialists also envisioned a richer society resulting from the "organization of industry," or labor—a planned economy consciously geared to the ideal of creating an abundance for all on an equitable basis. As heirs of Hegel, the True Socialists likewise spoke of overcoming man's "alienation" and "estrangement."

The True Socialists could not be denounced because they lacked humanity and good socialist goals. If anything, *The German Ideology* derided them for being too humanistic, in the wrong sentimental Feuerbachian manner. They were ignorant of, or ignored the laws of history and economics. Hence, they refused to recognize the necessity of class conflict, revolution, even terror and dictatorship as steps in the quest for the perfected society. They were as unrealistic as a coconut palm that demanded that the world provide it with the "appropriate soil, warmth, sun, air and rain at the North Pole."

The root of Marx and Engels' conflict with the True Socialists was over the ways and means of bringing about the mutually desired transformation of society. The dividing line was *"revolutionary* passion" and the will to act accordingly. Marx and Engels demanded that the drums be beaten unceasingly for an attack on the old society and especially the bourgeoisie. Class differences and hatred had to be accentuated, as another preliminary to revolution. Anything else was deception, hypocrisy, sentimentality and "humanity-dizziness." As for man himself, Marx and Engels believed that the real human being still had to be made. Only revolution could bring about the necessary change. Man had to be hammered on the anvil of revolution into a shape conforming to communist requirements.

The True Socialists, in contrast, had "lost all revolutionary passion and in place of it proclaimed a general love of humanity." They accepted the contemporary man, moved as he was by humanistic considerations, as an adequate foundation for an improved society. They had confidence in reason and therefore rejected the necessity of class conflict and revolution. The True Socialists wished to conciliate all human differences and to combine under the banner of humanity. The socialist *Rheinische Jahrbücher* optimistically insisted that "all quarrels over names are now being dissolved in humanism. Why Communists? Why Socialists? We are human beings." To which *The German Ideology* replied sardonically, "Why human beings, why beasts, why plants, why stones? We are all physical bodies." Marx and Engels scoffed at a reconciliation of all differences; revolution was impossible when all quarrels were "dissolved in humanism."

It was in *The German Ideology* that Marx and Engels established the practice of attaching a class label to opposing ideals and systems. True Socialism was branded as "petty bourgeois." The technique was consistent with their new philosophy of history. If all ideas, cultures, ideologies and institutions are an echo of the interests of a particular class, ultimately determined by its economic status, then every thought, ideal and system can be stabled in a particular stall, be it bourgeois, petty-bourgeois, feudal, proletarian or any other. But the method also can be used as a weapon. Once a phenomenon is classified and categorized, it is tied down and becomes manageable. Put a label on an ideology or a political principle, and people are influenced by the legend on the label. Once ideas are stamped with a class label, they immediately appear less universally human and reasonable. Such labeling also represents an assault on individual judgment, the chance that a particular set of ideas might rest on the findings of the intellect, logic and experience, free of any particular class or other bias.

By linking every idea or system with a particular class, Marx and Engels were able to display an appearance of personal detachment and objectivity now and then, in sharp contrast to their customary partisan vehemence. If an individual just replayed the ideas composed by the class to which he belonged, it was logical to absolve that person from all responsibility. Thus *The German Ideology* disavowed anything personal against the True Socialists. Their writings were merely the expression of an "inevitable tendency in a land so swampy as Germany"; they spoke for and to the "two most numerous classes in Germany, the petty-bourgeois world and its philanthropic illusions, and the ideologists of the same petty-bourgeois crowd—the philosophers and students of philosophy." While Marx and Engels professed to have nothing personal against such socialists, they did demand that they be silent, cease to mislead people and stop offering opposition. The penalty for nonconformity was illustrated in the *Ideology* where the popular Karl Grün was pushed through a gauntlet of forty or fifty pages and whipped for ignorance, stupidity, simple plagiarism, false pretenses and dishonesty.

Marx and Engels sandwiched the first fairly complete description of communism between attacks on the Young Hegelians and True Socialists. At a time when Europe was filled with a host of competing theories and ideologies, they insisted that their theories were not just another ideology. Their communism, instead, was the "*real* movement which will end the present condition." The word "Communist" meant the "adherent of a definite revolutionary party," their own. The Communists did not preach a "morality," nor did they confront human beings with the "moralistic demand: love each other; do not be egoists." Their aim was to "revolutionize the existing world, to attack the things of the present in a practical way and to change them." All this is vague enough. What stands out clearly is their emphasis on the *real* and revolution, with a parallel repudiation of the ideal and any moral preachments.

As always, Marx and Engels placed the greatest stress on history. When they unroll the tapestry of the past, pictured in a bold design, we witness the conflict of classes through the ages, as each dominant class in its turn imposes its ideals and institutions upon society. The viewer gets the impression that history gathers momentum as it progresses; change comes more rapidly as the historic process culminates in the rise of the proletariat.

In theory, communism would initially become a force in countries and localities with the biggest industries and most numerous proletariat. But this was no iron-clad rule, according to *The German Ideology*. No area was isolated from the rest of the world and even non-industrialized regions would be drawn into the maelstrom. In any given state, industry just did not develop at the same speed in all localities. This would not prevent the simultaneous growth of a proletarian movement everywhere. The competition of the machine would cause the non-industrial worker to experience hardships greater than those of the factory proletarian himself. This would enable the big industrial workers to take the lead, dragging all other workers along with them towards revolution and communism.

The same rule operated along international lines. The advanced industrial states would bring impoverishment and the communist consciousness to workers in the less industrialized countries. "The competition with more industrially-developed countries resulting from an expanded world trade is enough to create a similar conflict in countries with a less developed industry." (The Germans often complained that England was making another "India" out of Germany.) This explains why Marx and Engels soon placed their main hopes for an early communist triumph in Germany, even if that collection of German states referred to as Germany lagged far behind Britain, Belgium and France in an industrial sense.

125

Elsewhere in *The German Ideology* Marx and Engels asserted that the revolution had to occur fairly simultaneously in the leading countries —Britain, France and Germany. "Communism is empirically possible only as the act of the dominant peoples, simultaneously and at the same time, as conditioned by the universal development of the productive forces and the world trade associated with it." The proletariat could exist only in a "universal historical sense" (*Weltgeschichtlich*). Capitalism and private property everywhere produced the same relationship between classes, thus eliminating national differences.

An outline of the Marxian classless society of the future can be pieced together from scattered references in *The German Ideology*. Revolution stands as the beginning. The proletariat had to "conquer political power in order to present their own interest as the universal interest." Revolution was necessary not only because the dominant class could be overthrown in no other way, "but also because it is only through revolution that the *over-throwing* class can reach the point where it can shake off all of the old trash from its neck and become capable of founding a new society. . . . The creation of a large-scale communist consciousness and the introduction of communism itself demands a large-scale change in man, which can take place only in a practical movement, in a *revolution*." In harmony with this imperative, the True Socialists were condemned for "wanting to remain as they were, while demanding that society should produce a change which could result only from their *own* transformation." Marx and Engels insisted that the worker, mankind itself, first had to be transformed and remodelled, conditioned and cut to the pattern needed to make a classless, humanistic and most ideal communism work. Once this was accomplished, the communist revolution would "ultimately shelve the political institutions." Communism would subject all the forces of production and exchange to the "power of the united individuals."

The Communist Man whom Marx and Engels required was worthy of a humanist dream. He would dispense with the state "to give full play to his personality." Existence would become a "creative manifestation of life flowing from the free development of all abilities." But that man had to meet various requirements. "The abolition of private property depends on the all-sided development of the individuals, simply because the existing commerce and productive forces are all-sided and can only be mastered by individuals developed in an all-sided manner." Communism, as Marx and Engels envisioned it, was impossible without a great versatility in the individual and a willingness to work in the most diverse ways.

As one of the "first conditions of communism," the division between country and city had to disappear. There could be no separate "narrow city animal" and another "narrow country animal" leading to a conflict of interest, daily renewed. In fact, every division of labor where a person was, and had to remain, a "hunter, fisherman, herdsman or critical critic" would be ended. When society controlled production, it would be possible to do "this today, tomorrow that, go hunting in the morning, fish in the afternoon, be a cattle herder in the evening and a critic after dinner, just as one pleased, without ever becoming a hunter, fisherman, herdsman, or critic." Only in a communist society was the "original and free development of the individual no mere phrase." It was assumed that there would always be someone willing to do every needed job.

As for rewards and pay, one of the essential principles of communism states that "differences of the *head* and of the intellectual capacities in general in no way indicates a difference of the *stomach* and of *physical needs.*" The Communists rejected the "reactionary socialists'" rule, *"To each according to his capacity,"* at least "insofar as consumption in the narrow sense is involved." In its place they put the formula: *"To each according to his need; . . . A difference* in activity, in work, justifies no *inequality,* no *special right* of property or consumption."

Such were the few details which Marx and Engels sketched into the picture of a promised and destined world of the future. To reach it, man had to make his way through conflict, revolution and a rebirth or conditioning that would make him, or his children, fit to populate and shape a communist society.

Marx and Engels had worked on *The German Ideology* intermittently for nearly a year. It was the first major work containing their new philosophy of history, woven into their critique of philosophy and of True Socialism. Since the manuscript was never published during their lifetime, posterity can judge only from the surviving portions.* Some parts were lost and a few chapters probably were not in final form. More than half of the manuscript is in the handwriting of Engels, with occasional corrections and insertions by Marx. A part was copied by Joseph Weydemeyer, a former Prussian artillery officer and socialist writer from Westphalia who joined them temporarily in Brussels. It is impossible, however, to identify the author of any given part by the handwriting alone. Marx preferred to let others do the copying. His own handwriting was notoriously illegible, and the time had not yet come when Jenny Marx acted as his "usual secretary."

In a letter of December 28, 1846, to the Russian literary historian

---

* The manuscript of *The German Ideology* was first published in 1932 in the *Gesamtausgabe* (complete works of Marx and Engels). An abbreviated English edition appeared later. Here, as in all cases where English translations are available, the author has used the German edition exclusively.

P. W. Annenkow, Marx described the difficulties of publication. The "police" (censorship) stood on the one side. On the other was the barrier of the publishers themselves who were the "interested representatives of the views" that he attacked. As for their own "party," Marx explained, it not only was poor but also included a strong group that was angry at him for attacking their "utopias and declamation." Consequently there was no money to pay for publication.

In the beginning, however, Marx and Engels had not been concerned about the publication of their work. Joseph Weydemeyer had located two wealthy "communists" in Westphalia—Rudolf Rempel and Julius Meyer—who were ready to advance a small fortune to finance a publishing house that specialized in radical books. Marx and Engels seemed to have the inside track. Early in 1846 they were confident that the money was there to finance about everything they wished to publish—*The German Ideology,* the library of socialist writers, and even a new quarterly review that they hoped to edit with Moses Hess.

Rempel and Meyer, however, began to talk of business difficulties and losses when Weydemeyer showed them the manuscript of the *Ideology.* Even the first volume with its polemics against the Young Hegelians displeased them. The second volume against True Socialism settled the issue. Rempel and Meyer were both sympathetic to the socialist views that Marx and Engels attacked. In July, 1846, they informed Marx that they would not finance the publication of the two volumes.

The manuscript was then carried to Cologne where old friends in the past had repeatedly raised money for Marx. Moses Hess again used his flair for promotion, this time in behalf of a stock company that would publish for Marx and Engels. When this plan failed, it became necessary to find a commercial publisher. There were two handicaps. The length of the manuscript (about eight hundred pages) meant high printing costs. Moreover, Marx and Engels expected a good honorarium or advance payment. The contents and style of the two volumes pointed to a small sale.

Scattered information concerning efforts to find a publisher comes from Engels' letters after he moved to Paris in August, 1846. Enquiries were made all the way from Bremen to Switzerland, without result. Ultimately, in a letter of March 9, 1847, Engels proposed that Marx take *The German Ideology* and "hurl it into a corner, in the name of the devil," if it interfered with the publication of another work, the Proudhon critique, which Marx had just completed. The latter was more important. Engels then added his epitaph to the *Ideology:* "Neither of us bit off very much in our work on it." A generation later Marx added his own postscript: "We left the manuscript to the gnawing criticism of the mice, all the more willingly because we had achieved our main purpose—self-clarification." Fortunately, the mice found that the manuscript was largely indigestible.

The German Ideology was abandoned to the mice because no publisher would take it. In contrast, Marx did not publish his *Kritik der Politik und Nationalökonomie* (*Manuscripts of 1844*) even though he had a contract with a publisher, Leske from Darmstadt. In a letter to Leske dated August 1, 1846, Marx excused the repeated delay in completing the manuscript as follows: "It appeared to me to be very important that a polemical writing [referring to the *Ideology*] against German philosophy and the current German socialism should come out first, before the *positive* exposition. This is necessary to prepare the public, since my position on economics is diametrically opposed to past German knowledge." Writing to Annenkow on December 28, 1846, Marx gave an entirely different impression: "I would have gladly sent you my book on political economy (about which I told you in Brussels) with this letter, but up until now it has been impossible for us to get this work . . . published." Marx's statement to Annenkow is misleading since Leske did not cancel the contract until February 2, 1847, when he finally lost patience and demanded an early return of the advance payment, threatening to take "not very pleasant steps" in case of noncompliance. Marx never completed the work, nor did he refund the 1500 *francs*.

Why was this book which was to revolutionize the knowledge of economics never completed? Did Marx find that the proof for his theories rested on fragile foundations? He spend over twenty additional years, with many interruptions, before he was ready to publish the first of the big "learned volumes" on economics (*Das Kapital*) late in the 1860's.

Another question comes to mind. Did Marx decide that other portions of the manuscript were outmoded after the spring of 1845? In parts of the *Manuscripts of 1844* Marx had written copiously of humanity, alienation, estrangement, estranged labor, human essence, objectification of man, realization of humanity and much else. All this now seemed out of tune with the new tone and tactics in *The German Ideology* which derided the socialists for writing of humanity and for appealing to human sentiment. The *Ideology* hardly mentions estrangement (*Entfremdung*) and then only "so as to remain intelligible to the philosophers" or "to keep the philosophical expressions for the time being." Furthermore, it was almost apologetic about Marx's early articles in the *Deutsch-Französische Jahrbücher*. There the use of such "philosophical phraseology" as "human essence" gave rise to misunderstandings. In view of the above, it is evident that the *Manuscripts of 1844* needed to be revised and updated wherever they touched on humanity and alienation. Marx may not have felt equal to the task. There were so many other things to do, and the zest with which he had originally undertaken the work had evaporated.

4. MARX: EX-CITIZEN OF PRUSSIA

MARX severed his national ties with Prussia during the time he was working on *The German Ideology*. It was a step that he regretted later. In 1848, and again in the late 1850's when Prussia had a new King, he tried to reverse the process. According to the account that is generally accepted, the Prussian government tried to get Belgium to expel Marx because Brussels was too close to the Rhineland. In order to deprive Prussia of all legal rights over him, he boldly and contemptuously renounced his Prussian citizenship on December 1, 1845.

Hubert Schiel, the German scholar in Trier, published some curious documents in 1954 * that show that on October 17, 1845, Marx applied to the Prussian authorities in Trier for an emigration permit (*Auswanderungsschein*) to go to the "United North American States." In this application, Marx called attention to the fact that no military obligations stood in the way. The chief Prussian official, in sending on Marx's application to Berlin, declared that Marx had been released from all future military obligations in 1841, as "totally unfit," physically. The official, however, noted several technicalities that might be cited to deny Marx's request. He mentioned Marx's long absence from Trier and the probability that Marx had no intention of returning. Because of "criminal literary efforts," Marx also faced immediate arrest and a charge of lese majesty, if he appeared on Prussian soil. The Trier official nevertheless recommended that the above considerations be ignored since this was a good opportunity to bar forever the return of the "writer Marx, guilty of attempted high treason and lese majesty." The Interior Department in Berlin acted affirmatively on this advice and granted an *Auswanderungsschein* dated December 1, 1845. On December 3, this information was duly recorded in Trier; the "permission to emigrate," the "document of dismissal," had been delivered to Marx's mother-in-law and the stamp-duty of 15 silver *Groschen* had been forwarded to the Royal Government. Marx thus received a formal and legal dismissal from all ties to Prussia. There is no evidence of a bold, defiant or contemptuous renunciation of Prussian citizenship.

The question arises as to whether Marx actually considered emigrat-

* Hubert Schiel, "Die Umwelt des Jungen Karl Marx. Ein unbekanntes Auswanderungsgesuch von Karl Marx," *Trierisches Jahrbuch,* Trier, 1954, pp. 31–42.

ing to the United States. Hubert Schiel suggests the possibility that Edgar von Westphalen, Marx's brother-in-law who had visited America, may have prompted the idea. It seems most unlikely, however, that Marx even gave a passing thought to a move to the United States just then. He and Engels were so preoccupied with *The German Ideology,* so confident of the ultimate triumph of their cause and so personally engaged in the conflict that any move across the ocean makes no sense. Moreover, Marx only asked for an emigration permit for himself alone, in his initial application. When the official then enquired whether he wanted to include his wife and daughter, he replied affirmatively, "if it were necessary to get the permit for [himself]." Apparently Marx wanted the emigration permit for reasons other than its stated purpose. Having decided to abandon his Prussian citizenship, it might be useful to have a document that indicated the land of his origin and also showed that the Prussian state officially sanctioned his departure. A certificate of dismissal, as proof of a legal identity, would make entry into other countries easier. On January 15, 1847, when Engels tried to persuade Marx to visit him briefly in Paris, he advised Marx to get a passport from the French Embassy in Brussels "on the basis of your Prussian Emigration Certificate." (This was two years after Marx had been expelled from France.)

5. THE "YOUNG MARX," AND ENGELS TOO

A NUMBER of scholars and enthusiasts claim that the true Marx, or the clue to the true Marx, is to be found in the "Young Marx" and the "Early Writings." This interest in the "Early Writings" began to emerge when the previously unpublished manuscripts (as much of them as survived) were published in the 1930's. Translations into English and other languages followed, sometimes in an abbreviated form which omitted much that might be incomprehensible, boring or offensive. With the translation of the *Manuscripts of 1844,* in which Marx appears at his most "youthful," "humanist" and philosophical best, the idealization of a Young Marx reached an apex.

In a broader sense, Marx and Engels themselves became conscious of a change that distinguished their earlier works from the later writings. Marx commented on this when he reread Engels' *The Condition of the Working Class in England* in 1863. He did not repudiate their youth; instead, there was a touch of nostalgia and a tinge of regret over lost illusions. He found that "later developments since 1844" completely confirmed all of Engels' findings down to the minutest details, even the predictions of an imminent revolution in England. Marx flatly stated in regard to the latter that "only the petty German philistines, who measure world history by the yard and in the light of the latest interesting newspaper reports, could imagine that in such great developments twenty years amounted to no more than a day, although later days would appear into which twenty years would be telescoped." But he noted with regret that "an aging process" was also evident. In that first work, Engels had tackled every problem in a style that was "so fresh, passionate, boldly anticipatory and without learned and scientific misgivings. And the illusion itself, that the results would historically follow tomorrow or the day thereafter, gave the whole thing a warmth and a vital mood, which was in damned contrast to the later 'grey on grey.'" If an older Marx still felt the spell of their youthful work, it is possible to appreciate its impact a century later, for it possessed a chestiness, confidence, buoyancy and some idealism. The real age of enchantment for Marx and Engels ended soon after the Revolutions of 1848/49. A similar change affected many Europeans, young and old, after the experiences of 1848.

It is possible in a limited sense to separate a younger Marx from the more mature person, taking the spring of 1845 as the dividing line. A new tone appeared thereafter, as reflected in *The German Ideology*. If philosophical and humanistic terms were employed very cautiously later, spaced where they reaped the most dividends, it was mainly because their use tended to weaken revolutionary morale and the conflicts that breed revolution. It was a question of expediency and tactics that represented no fundamental shift in motives and goals.

Actually there is a monotonous consistency in the lives of Marx and Engels, whether young or old. They always advocated revolution and tried to promote it as the locomotive force in the dialectical process. They always used destructive criticism as the prime weapon to soften up an old society destined for destruction and to mobilize human passions for that work of destruction. They always demanded practical organization and action to carry through the anticipated revolution. Without ever revealing many of the details concerning the society that they envisioned as a replacement for the old, they always saw themselves as revolutionary leaders, and not as mere ideologues.

The question of motivation enters the picture. What caused Marx and Engels to devote their lives and talents to the aim of revolutionizing the existing world in favor of everything that they lumped together under the name of communism? Some assert that they were sheer humanists and theorists, first and always, undefiled by practical considerations, political machinations and *real* revolutionary aims.

A devil's advocate might pose a rhetorical question here. Could or would anyone justify a revolutionary program in the name of anything else than humanity and a better future for man? A religious zealot might do so in the name of virtue or the greater glory of God, all in accordance with some divine plan. But that description does not fit either Marx or Engels. Humanistic motives, the betterment of man, therefore remain as the ostensible answer. Marx and Engels had a highly idealistic concept, insofar as can be determined, as to the ultimate type of man and the society they envisioned—coming after the necessary revolutionary rounds and the conditioning needed to make man fit for communism. Their sights were set on a better world for man and a better man for the world.

What is surprising, however, is that some scholars point to this humanism as something almost unique in Marx and Engels, raising them above their century and all time to come. Yet for their contemporaries in the 19th century, a humanist was hardly a rarity.

Europeans were hedged in by humanity. In Germany, J. G. Herder earlier had formulated a theory of history woven about the concept of the evolution of humanity. National prophets like the Italian Mazzini propagated nationalism in the name of humanity. "Young Europe"—that society of liberal, republican, revolutionary internationalists—adopted the motto of "liberty, equality, humanity." No one would appear in public without wearing a ribbon of humanity.

Getting closer to Marx himself, his father was a humanist and so was the Baron von Westphalen. Many of the teachers in Prussian schools paid tribute to a concept of humanity. It was no mere accident that Marx, in the German essay exam preceding his graduation from the state *Gymnasium* in Trier, picked a topic that glorified the man who dedicated his life to benefiting mankind and whose grave, as a reward, would be wetted by the tears of a grateful humanity.

The same humanism was a factor in causing the 19th century to reject violent revolutions and extremes, for fear of another Terror, a replay of the bloody and tyrannical episode of the Great French Revolution. When Marx and Engels ridiculed various socialists, they were attacking persons who were inspired by an ideal of humanity and of human betterment. Humanism, veritably, had become even a bourgeois virtue! (Engels almost accused the English bourgeoisie of a boundless humanity, although a hypocritical one.) Marx later devoted a section of the *Communist Manifesto* to unmask the "conservative or bourgeois socialist" who favored social reform for humanitarian reasons. Marx and Engels utilized *"denunciation"* and *"pathos of indignation"* so widely in their critiques because of the widespread presence of humanist sentiment. The tactic would have been amiss in an age less humanistic and humane.

It is impossible to judge or accurately assess the inner motives of anyone. But something resembling egoism and ambition strikes one as being the moving factor in Marx and Engels. Some of their contemporaries accused Marx of vanity, egoism, ambition and the lust to command, making him capable of employing terror in the role of a proletarian dictator. Both Marx and Engels always rejected such charges, but they never indicated that they expected to be mere spectators. They believed that historical crises brought forward the leaders demanded by the times. They could point to examples from past revolutions when obscure persons such as Robespierre, Napoleon, and Cromwell had risen to power. Their personal correspondence points to the conclusion that they were confident that their time would come.

The existence of this ambition, or belief in their destiny, did not necessarily conflict with humanist motives and final goals. Marx and Engels apparently were convinced that their ambitions corresponded with what was bound to happen. They were sustained in the face of adversity by a conviction that they were destined for revolutionary leadership, because they had the true insight into the forces that were involved, coupled with the revolutionary energy that the circumstances would demand and the "courage to be ruthless." Similarly, they saw themselves in a role that coincided with what was good and inevitable for humanity. In promoting themselves and their views they were benefiting mankind.

What set Marx and Engels apart was not any particular fullness of humanism but the means they advocated and the path they selected as leading to a human millennium. Was class conflict and revolution the cheapest way (in suffering, lives and time) to gain their humanist ends? Even assuming that they wished such a revolution to be as humane as possible, we know that they were ready to take in stride the expected horrors, terror, executions, wars, repression and an extended "dictatorship of the proletariat." Various classes had to be eliminated until the total of all such subtractions left only a classless society. The bourgeoisie was destined to be destroyed or educated out of its past existence. Marx also saw no salvation for the *Lumpenproletariat*—that host of chronically unemployed, unemployable persons, beggars, shiftless characters, petty thieves and others. Marx spoke of a process extending over twenty, thirty, forty years during which the new man would be shaped, hammered into the form required for the realization and operation of that most humanistic and ideal communist future. Time was necessary not only to do away with the undesired classes and to develop the proper material conditions for a better society but also to create the indispensable Communist Man. Without the latter, communism was an illusion.

Were Marx and Engels realistic in staking everything on the conviction that the perfected man was a human possibility, or were they utopian? Was a "dictatorship of the proletariat," even when blessed with a planned abundance for all, the proper environment in which to breed that versatile, humanist and refined individual that communism required? The ultimate test of Marxism depends upon the answer to the above questions. Their humanism and the correctness of their critique of existing society alone are not enough to justify the upheavals they advocated. Revolution for them was not a parlor game or a mere palace revolution. It touched the lives of millions.

=IV=

The Genesis of
an Internationale

1. THE COMMUNIST CORRESPONDENCE
COMMITTEE

EARLY in 1846 Marx and Engels formed the Communist Correspondence Committee (*Kommunistische Korrespondenz-Komitee*) in Brussels, designed to serve as the center for the exchange, coordination and reconciliation of views among Communists and socialists everywhere, quite naturally in the direction of Marxian communism. Brussels thereafter became the intellectual and nerve center of communism.

Various German radicals, as they came to the Belgian capital, were drawn into the Marxian circle. At one time or another, the Brussels group included Moses Hess, Wilhelm Weitling, Joseph Weydemeyer, Wilhelm (*Lupus*) Wolff, Ferdinand Wolff, the poets Ferdinand Freiligrath and Georg Weerth, Edgar von Westphalen, Louis Heilberg, Sebastian Seiler, and Stephan Born. There were also a few German-speaking Belgian followers, notably Victor Tedesco and Philippe Gigot. The Committee apparently used Gigot's address as the safest destination for letters coming from the outside.

Under normal operations, the Brussels Committee depended on a regular correspondence with the branch committees to establish cooperation and a uniformity of view and policy. Beyond that, it hoped to distribute printed pamphlets. On special occasions a "circular" was printed or lithographed to be sent to all branches and persons who kept up a correspondence with Brussels, informing them of any special action taken by the Central Committee, or of anything significant.

A letter to G. A. Köttgen, the Elberfeld artist who planned to organize the Communists in the Wuppertal, reveals the minute details of the makeup and functions of a local correspondence committee. Dated June 15, 1846, and signed by Marx, Engels, Gigot and F. Wolff, the letter spoke of a regular correspondence with the Brussels Committee. Reading and discussion societies to guarantee regular meetings and to clarify communist questions were to be instituted "soon and energetically." Regular dues were to be assessed to cover the cost of printing cheap, communistic fly-sheets and pamphlets and also to help pay the expenses of the Brussels Committee. Each "communist society" was to inform the Central Committee of the names of its members.

Practical politics and preparation for the day of revolution were also on the agenda. The letter to Köttgen rejected the idea of a Communist Congress to be held in Germany. Only after communist societies existed everywhere, with the capacity to act, could such a congress meet with good chances for success. The Committee also advised Köttgen not to send a petition to the Prussian government, as a vehicle of communist protest. "A petition is of value only when it simultaneously offers a threat, backed by a compact and organized mass." Unless they could get over five hundred signatures, they would merely reveal the weakness of the Communist Party. It was better

> to act in a Jesuitical manner, to hang up on a nail your good German honesty, fidelity and frankness while signing and promoting the bourgeois petitions for freedom of press, constitutions, etc. If the latter are acquired, a new era begins for communist propaganda. The means at our disposal will be intensified. One must support anything in the party which is helpful without bothering oneself with any tiresome moral scruples.

Such were the instructions issued to Köttgen.

In line with its aim of producing clarity, uniformity and cohesion in the communist and socialist world, the Brussels Committee occasionally acted as a high tribunal that judged those who deviated, excluding them from the Correspondence Committee and exposing their errors for all Communists to see, ridicule and repudiate. Wilhelm Weitling was the first to face the new tribunal in Brussels. This was ironic because Marx had once held up the name of Weitling as proof of the intellectual capacity that lay slumbering in the proletariat. At this time Weitling had just come from London where the League of the Just had repudiated his program. Marx welcomed him most warmly and admitted him to the Committee in Brussels. But Marx lost patience when the "first German Communist" failed to accept the Marxian views and would not completely efface himself. A controversy also developed over the use of the money that Marx and Engels thought would soon be at their disposal, thanks to the wealthy Westphalian sympathizers.

A brutal confrontation occurred at a meeting of the Brussels Committee on March 30, 1846. Marx, Engels, Gigot, Heilberg, Seiler, Edgar von Westphalen and Weydemeyer were present. The Russian P. W. Annenkow who came to the meeting as Marx's guest, later wrote an account of the proceedings.

As Annenkow described the event, they all sat around a small table with Marx at the head, pencil in hand and his "lion's head" bent over a sheet of paper. The dependable "tall, erect and grave Engels with his British distinction" opened the meeting with a speech. The proceedings became heated and confused. It appeared as if Marx was using the power to grant or withhold the anticipated money from Westphalia as a bribe or threat. All along he harped on the need for proper tactics and comprehension, insisting that a "screening" of the ranks of the Communists was essential. He accused Weitling of leading German workers astray into actions that lost them their "jobs and bread." "Artisan" and "philosophical" communism had to be fought. Sentiment was a mere "dizziness." Tactically, the Communists had to drop their own propaganda, and even talk of propaganda, while helping the bourgeoisie seize power as the next logical step. At one point Marx spoke the classical dictum, "Ignorance never did anyone any good." Weitling was a pathetic figure when matched against Marxian anger and mental superiority, in the presence of a group already sold to Marx. The meeting ended when Marx stormed out in anger. Weitling was not expelled from the Committee, but from this point forward, he felt like an outsider. It was a pathetic ending for Weitling who was convinced that he had done much, suffered much and deserved more for his efforts in behalf of humanity and communism.

Weitling expressed his bitterness in a letter to Moses Hess. Marx was a man who had "authority over men of money" and was far "removed from the suffering world and the torments of the people. . . . I see in Marx's head nothing more than a good encyclopedia, but no genius . . . Rich people made him an editor, that is all."

Annenkow's description of Marx was more objective:

> Marx represented the type of human being who was an amalgam of energy, will power and an unyielding conviction, the type which was also distinctly notable in external appearances. He looked like a person who had the right and the power to demand respect, although his actions and appearance seemed peculiar enough—a thick black mane on his head, hands covered with hair, his coat buttoned irregularly. His movements were abrupt, but bold and self-assured; his manners were contrary to all forms of social intercourse. But they were proud, with a trace of contempt, and his sharp voice which had the ring of metal, harmonized remarkably with the radical judgments which he passed on men and things.

He spoke only in imperative terms which tolerated no opposition and which, moreover, were sharpened by a tone which affected me almost painfully. This man expressed the firm conviction of his mission to dominate minds and to dictate laws to them. Before me there stood the incarnation of a democratic dictator, as one sees him in moments of fantasy.

Several months later the Communist Correspondence Committee, again acting as a high tribunal, passed judgment on Hermann Kriege. Originally from Westphalia, Kriege had impressed Engels so favorably in 1844 that he sent him to Marx in Brussels, as a "superb agitator." Thereafter Kriege went to London and became a member of the League of the Just. Late in 1845 he landed in New York where he soon founded a socialist society and became the editor of a new paper, *Der Volks-Tribun* (*Popular Tribune*). The paper had a communist slant, but it mirrored all the sins of True Socialism—love, humanity and a peaceful solution of social ills.

On the basis of copies of the newspaper, Marx and Engels decided to criticize, expose and excommunicate Kriege. Since Kriege was in New York and lacked any substantial following in Germany, he was hardly important enough to be thrust into fame via such a formal action. Yet, formal action was taken at a meeting on May 11, 1846. Marx, Engels, Gigot, Heilberg, Seiler, Von Westphalen, Wolff and Weitling were present. The Committee drafted an indictment that was distributed in the form of a circular to all committees and persons in correspondence with Brussels. A copy was also sent to New York with the demand that it be printed in Kriege's own paper. The vote for the official indictment against Kriege was unanimous except for Weitling, "who voted against it." This courageous step was Weitling's last in Brussels; he left soon thereafter to find a better future in New York.

The indictment contained three major charges. First, the "tendency" that Kriege represented in his paper was not "communistic." Second, the "childish pompous" manner in which Kriege represented this tendency was "most highly compromising" for the Communist Party in Europe and America "insofar as he is regarded as the literary representative of German communism in New York." Third, the "fantastic sentimental fanaticism" that he preached in the name of communism was bound to act in a "most highly demoralizing" manner on workers who adopted it. Fourteen pages of proof and citations followed under the headings of "Transformation of Communism into Love-Giddiness"; "Economics of the *Popular Tribune* and its position toward Young America"; "Metaphysical Fanfaronades"; "Religious Flirtations"; and "Kriege's Personal Demeanor" (*Auftreten*). Such headings are enough to indicate that the measure of deviation had reached the point of overflowing. Numerous instances were cited to prove a "love-giddiness." In one issue of his paper, love ("by a rough count") appeared in thirty-five different connections. The effect was "enervating."

Kriege had suggested that the 1400 million acres in America be given to those who were in need, 160 acres for each. The Circular conceded that such an "agrarian" program might be adopted as a temporary tactical expedient that the Communists might have to adopt under certain circumstances, even if it was contrary to communist principles as such. Kriege, however, made the mistake of presenting it as a final aim of communism. (This was the first time, but not the last, that Marx and Engels stated that the Communists might pose as champions of "agrarian reform" if this were a necessary step in the direction of an ultimate triumph of communism.)

The bill of particulars against Kriege was overwhelming. "Kriege disappeared from the League stage," Engels wrote many years later. Whether the Circular speeded his way into obscurity is debatable; it did give him a certain publicity and immortality that could have come in no other way.

Weitling and Kriege were not the only ones who were unable or unwilling to follow the rigid line demanded by the Committee in Brussels. Even Moses Hess had trouble because he showed some of the inclinations of a True Socialist. As a man of sentiment and feeling, he failed to understand that it was necessary to "screen" the ranks of the Communists. He resented the manner in which the Brussels Committee had treated Weitling. Marx and Engels, however, were reluctant to precipitate an open break with him. He had influence and numerous contacts in the Rhineland. In the past he had been useful and might again be helpful in raising money to finance newspapers and other publications. Nevertheless, by May, 1846, the word got around that Hess had been "outlawed."

The break did not last long. Hess was wounded but still attracted to the man he admired. He wrote to Marx near the end of May stating that he would like to continue their personal association in the future, but he wanted nothing further to do with the "Party." He also wrote to Engels that he dreamt of again enjoying the "flesh-pots of Egypt, namely a carousel in Brussels with Engels and Company." So in the next months Hess made a laudable effort to make himself useful and to recast his thinking in the Marxian mold. It is evident that Marx demanded conformity in tactics as well as in theory. Hess accepted this fact when he wrote the following to Marx on July 28: "As it was necessary at first to link communist efforts to the German ideology, so it is now necessary to use historic and economic hypotheses as proof; otherwise one cannot dispose of either the 'socialists' or any other opponents. I am now concentrating completely on the reading of economic subjects." Hess, nevertheless, found that it was impossible to stay in step always. Some years later he wrote the following lament over Marx: "Too bad, deplorably bad, that the self-confidence of this undeniably most genial man of our party was not content with the deserved recognition bestowed upon him by all who knew and could appreciate his accomplishments. But he seemed to demand a personal submission" that Hess was unready to grant to any person.

The Communist Correspondence Committee in Brussels had only moderate success when it attempted to become the center for an international network of similar committees. Though it maintained connections with several followers in Cologne, results elsewhere in Germany apparently were too few to justify a regular correspondence. The most promising tie was in England with the London branch of the League of the Just which set up a corresponding committee under the active leadership of Schapper, Bauer and Moll. The Committee also maintained a contact with Julian Harney and the Fraternal Democrats. It was less successful in France.

A letter of May 5, 1846, signed by Marx, Engels and Gigot, had hopefully invited Proudhon to become a French correspondent for the Committee. Since Proudhon commanded considerable prestige and following, it would have been possible to reach many Frenchmen through him. Moreover, it appeared necessary just then to save him from certain ideological aberrations. It was reported that he had formed a compact with Karl Grün, the very Grün whom *The German Ideology* had denounced as ignorant and infected with True Socialism; Grün was teaching Proudhon more about Hegel and at the same time spreading Proudhon's ideas and writings among the Germans. No good could come from all that.

Marx added a confidential postscript to the Committee's letter, warning Proudhon to beware of the "parasite," Karl Grün. The latter was nothing but a "swindler, a sort of charlatan who would like to make a business out of modern ideas." Although Grün hid his "ignorance under pompous and arrogant phrases, he constantly made himself ridiculous." Grün was also "dangerous" as a person who shamelessly exploited the friendship that he made with noted authors for the purpose of building a "pedestal" for himself. Indeed Grün had even written of playing the schoolmaster to him (Proudhon) by revealing the most important axioms of German knowledge; otherwise Grün made fun of Proudhon's works.

As was to be expected, Proudhon was not taken in by the exaggerated subtlety of Marx's postscript. He defended Grün and preached a sermon to Marx in return.

"Perhaps you still have the opinion that no reform is really possible without an act of force, without that which one formerly called a revolution but which is nothing else than a smashup," Proudhon stated, adding that he himself had outgrown a belief in revolution, as being nothing more than a simple appeal to force and caprice. He then urged Marx not to issue anathemas or excommunications and to avoid being dogmatic. "Let us give the world the example of a wise and broad toleration; let us not pose as apostles of a new religion, even if it were the religion of logic and reason itself." He then warned Marx that the workers' thirst for knowledge called for more than a "drink of blood."

Having made his position clear, Proudhon nevertheless was ready to act as an occasional correspondent. A tolerant exchange of views could only be beneficial. Marx, however, regarded Proudhon's reply as a slap and not as an acceptance. Proudhon, without knowing it, was to become the target of Marxian attacks. For the next twenty years Marx fought to destroy Proudhon's influence.

The attempt to establish corresponding committees among the Germans in the three Paris branches of the League of the Just had not succeeded either. True Socialism ruled in Paris, but Marx and Engels were not ready to give up. No international movement could do without Paris and the Germans there. Engels therefore moved to Paris in August, 1846, to open up a whirlwind campaign to expunge the influence of Grün, Proudhon and Weitling from the German societies. Constituting himself as a Communist Correspondence Committee of one in Paris, he immediately began sending reports to Brussels.

Engels also hoped to enlist native French socialist and communist leaders as correspondents for the Brussels Committee. Soon after arriving in Paris he had an interview with Cabet, the very popular Utopian Communist. Engels reported that Cabet received him cordially; he in turn showed a great interest in all of Cabet's "trash" (*Dreck*). Nevertheless, Cabet refused to become a correspondent for the Brussels Committee; he was too busy and a little suspicious; this might be a trap to exploit his name in an improper manner. Engels also sensed that he and Marx did not yet represent a force sufficiently recognized to command respect; the French *Journal des économistes,* in an article on German Communists, had listed Marx as a "shoemaker" (*cordonnier*) by trade.

Engels' main task in Paris was to win the support of the radical Germans and through them to establish local Communist Correspondence Committees with ties to Brussels. The three branches of the League of the Just served as a starting point. August Ewerbeck, the leader of the League, was cooperative enough but lacked the force, resourcefulness and clarity that the Marxian outlook demanded. The members of the League were skilled craftsmen or journeymen—tailors, cabinet-makers and some tanners. They were *Straubinger* (scrubby persons), as Engels contemptuously called them. (The *Ideology* applied the term to the class of petty-bourgeois craftsmen.) Most of them associated in the name of communism or socialism, but Engels soon found that they were not true proletarians. Nevertheless he threw himself into the task of winning them for the new brand of communism as if the destiny of the world would be decided by a meeting of fifteen to twenty craftsmen from among the eighty to one hundred thousand Germans in Paris.

The first need, as Engels reported to Marx, was to expel Grün and his "empty phrases" from the League. This took time and required "some patience and a little terrorism." The majority was against him. After a number of stormy sessions, Engels demanded a vote to decide whether the society was "communist" according to his definition, or whether, as Grün's followers asserted, it stood "for the welfare of humanity," garnished with much talk of "mildness, compassions and fervent brotherhood." There were thirteen *ayes* against two who stuck by Grün. It was a triumph for Engels and Marxism.

The repudiation of Grün by a small group of cabinet-makers represented a turning point, so Engels optimistically reported. Now it was possible to start with a clean slate and to "make something out of the fellows, insofar as that was possible." They would soon have "a hundred followers from among the cabinetmakers alone, if they could hold public meetings." But Grün's ouster did not create a vacuum into which the Marxian concepts flowed either by gravity or any inexorable logic of history—even with Engels' help. By late October, 1846, he was again deploring the horrible harm that Grün had left behind. Everything "positive" in the "fellows" had been transformed into a "pure giddiness, humanity-striving, etc." By the end of the year he expressed relief when the police showed an extraordinary interest in the doings of the Germans in Paris. Here was an "honorable pretext" for refusing to attend any further meetings. He was tired of the "dirt"; nothing could be made out of the *Straubinger.*

Engels began to see the figures of policemen shadowing every move of his own. He amused himself by making it necessary for them to follow him into many byways and ballrooms. Thanks to them, he became acquainted with some "cute grisettes and much pleasure." Early in 1847 he began to urge Marx to come to Paris briefly, to join in some of the more innocent carousing—and probably to discuss the doldrums that had overtaken the Communist Correspondence Committee.

It was at this time that Engels became acquainted with Stephan Born, a typesetter by trade and a moderately capable writer. Born had come all the way from Berlin to learn from Engels. Under such tutoring he became a convert to the latest form of Marxian communism and in due course was expedited to Brussels where Marx also regarded him as a promising prospect. Many years later Born wrote that he had turned to communism as an anchor "for one who could not feel completely happy except through faith." Marx temporarily was able to dispel all doubts.

Marx and Engels could not show much profit from the operations of the Communist Correspondence Committee in 1846, as far as the French and the Germans were concerned. In England also, the Fraternal Democrats showed too much "peacefulness" and even failed to correspond with Brussels. The attitude of the Germans in the London League of the Just also brought Marx and Engels to the point of despair, as outlined in a long letter from Engels at the end of 1846. The situation was especially exasperating because it could affect their ties with Julian Harney. Moreover, the London group represented the only *Straubinger* with whom they could establish connections without any mental reservations. The League could not be accused of lacking energy for it had just circulated two "miserable" statements on current issues in Germany. But there was an "eternal jealousy" of Marx and Engels as "learned men." The members also posed as "proletarians," as the "people," while Marx and Engels could only refer to a communist proletariat that was supposed to develop behind them in Germany. If the Londoners "rebelled," it was best to allow the correspondence with them to fade away in sleep. Any discussion with them was impossible; they were all *Straubinger;* one could only get "dirty boots" out of a quarrel with them. Nevertheless Engels regretted the possible break, for the London League, when all was said, was "200 men strong and accredited among the English through Harney; in addition, it included the most acceptable of the *Straubinger.*" That was a lot to lose at the end of 1846.

In 1847 the Communist Correspondence Committee as such faded away. To the end, it remained largely as a soul in search of a body, a source of energy waiting for a machine through which it could operate. Later it was replaced by other organizations and agencies. At the start of the year, however, Marx was preoccupied with writing a critique against Proudhon whose latest book had appeared in the fall of 1846.

2. THE POVERTY OF PHILOSOPHY

MARX had experienced a distinct rebuff in May, 1846, when Proudhon blankly repudiated his revolutionary program and extolled the virtues of a wise tolerance. Proudhon, moreover, was considering the formation of an association among Germans, Swiss and French—perhaps another international—that would stand in the way of the Communist Correspondence Committee. To make matters worse, as Engels indignantly reported, some of the Germans were turning to Proudhon's latest "peaceful medicine for economic ills." Worse yet, Karl Grün had found a new life by adopting the "panaceas" offered in Proudhon's new book, *Système des contradictions économiques, ou philosophie de la misère* (*System of Economic Contradictions, or The Philosophy of Poverty*). Moreover, it was known that Grün was going to translate it into German and promote its sale. The competition from Proudhon could become serious.

Engels wrote Marx on October 23, 1846, that Proudhon's book was selling for 15 *francs*, too costly to buy. But he bought a copy anyway and by the end of December had taken copious notes on it. He still felt that the book was not worth 15 *francs*, but he offered the notes to Marx, just in case Marx wanted to write something on Proudhon in his "book," (presumably *The German Ideology*). Proudhon's newest plan for the peaceful transformation of society was a piece of "*completely limitless nonsense*," and the best way to trap Grün was not to hinder him from committing "himself body and soul to the Proudhon system of salvation." But Marx had already decided that the book was worth a critique, and the added effort of writing it in French.

Marx's letter of December 28, 1846, to P. W. Annenkow had a postscript that explained why the critique was being written in "poor French instead of good German." It was because he was "dealing with a French author." It seems self-evident, however, that it was written in French because it was aimed at the French reading public that would learn of Marx's own theories, economics and philosophy of history, juxtaposed against the ruins he would make out of Proudhon's work. There could be no better way for Marx to introduce himself to the French world than through a devastating critique of a writer and economist as important as Proudhon. The Germans would have an adequate introduction to the Marxian philosophy of history when *The German Ideology* appeared, as was still expected.

Cleverly inverting Proudhon's subtitle (*La philosophie de la misère*), Marx entitled his critique, *La Misère de la philosophie. Réponse à la philosophie de la misère de M. Proudhon* (*The Poverty of Philosophy. A Reply to the Philosophy of Poverty of Mr. Proudhon*). In this work Marx explicitly called himself an economist for the first time. He introduced Proudhon as a "misunderstood" person. In France, Proudhon had the right to be a poor economist because people regarded him as an expert in German philosophy; in Germany, however, he could be a poor philosopher because the Germans thought that he was the best French economist. As a "German and an economist," Marx declared that he would clear up the double error. Much of the book then ridicules Proudhon as being very naive and an inept economist. He is also accused of trying to scare the French by "throwing a few quasi-Hegelian phrases at their heads."

Marx demonstrated the sophomoric level of Proudhon's knowledge of German philosophy by initiating the French into the real complexities of the Hegelian dialectical process. The reader is confronted with the trio of:

> . . . position, opposition and composition. Putting it in Greek, we have thesis, antithesis and synthesis. For those who do not understand the Hegelian language we will add the initiation formula: affirmation, negation, negation of the negation. . . . Indeed, this is no Hebrew, with the permission of Mr. Proudhon; but it is the language of pure reason separated from the individual. . . .
>
> The yes becomes no, the no becomes yes, the yes simultaneously becomes yes and no, the no concurrently becomes no and yes; in this manner they contradict or counterbalance each other, neutralize each other, annul each other. The amalgamation of these two contradictory thoughts forms a new thought, the synthesis of the same.

But this was only the beginning of the world. Marx takes the reader through two additional levels of the dialectic before a higher and more complicated system of thought emerges. When this dialectical method was applied to political economy, so Marx declared, the well-known economic categories were "translated into a little known language in which they look as if they had just emerged sparkling-new from a pure head of reason."

At this point all mortal French readers could conclude that Proudhon had not met all of the dialectical requirements. Marx seconded their suspicions when he added that Proudhon had never climbed beyond the first two steps, and then only twice, "on which occasion, to top it off, he once fell flat on his back." Proudhon, out of a "hotch-potch of contradictions and antidotes for contradictions, produced two volumes of contradictions which he quite appropriately entitled System of Economic Contradictions." Marx also cited and quoted extensively from numerous English political economists, the acknowledged masters in this field, to demonstrate that Proudhon was an amateur as an economist as well.

As usual in critiques, Marx brought in his own views as a correct replacement for the ideas and systems that he attempted to destroy. In doing so, he presented a lucid sketch of the operation of material or economic forces in shaping history. The appearance of new forces of production that altered the manner in which people made a living also changed the class structure of society. The same changes produced a corresponding set of new principles and ideals. "Thus these ideas, these categories, are no more eternal than the conditions which they reflect.

They are *historical, mortal, evanescent products.*" For Marx there were no eternal verities.

Marx used the materialistic explanation to account for economic thought and social theories in general. "As the economists are the intellectual representatives of the bourgeois class, so the socialists and communists are the theorists of the class of the proletariat." Proudhon and all other non-revolutionary socialists are dismissed as living in the infancy of a movement that saw its maturity in Marx. Such socialists were bound to be merely of a "humanitarian," "philanthropic," utopian, non-revolutionary variety. They saw in "poverty only poverty, without seeing the revolutionary subversive side which would overthrow the old society." As a result, they hatched out theories purely in their own heads to cope with the problem. But all this would change once the proletariat appeared as a solid and self-conscious class. Socialists and Communists thereafter would not have to "look for the science in their own heads; they would only have to take note of that which takes place before their own eyes and make themselves the spokesmen of it." "Science" then would become the "conscious offspring of the historical movement"; it would stop being doctrinaire and become revolutionary.

Marx sketched the picture of the future in which there would be neither classes nor class rule with a few bold dialectical strokes. He used a quotation from the French romantic writer, George Sand, as the "last word of social science": "Conflict or death; bloody war or nothing. This is the inexorable choice."

The Poverty of Philosophy was printed simultaneously in Brussels and in Paris early in July, 1847. There was no question of royalties or the finding of a publisher; Marx paid for the printing costs. He also arranged for the Paris printer to send free review copies to various prominent writers in France, including Louis Blanc, A. M. L. Lamartine, the liberal romantic poet and politician, and François Vidal, the socialist economist.

When no reviews appeared, both Marx and Engels began to suspect that a "conspiracy of silence" was operating against them. Since they never believed in allowing chance, accident and the laxity or stupidity of publishers to determine the success of a book, Engels checked with the publisher, A. Frank, late in October. Engels was pleased to learn that ninety-six copies had been sold instead of only thirty-seven, as he had heard earlier. But he discovered that the free review copies had been accompanied by a bill of 15 *sous* to cover mailing costs when sent out. All of the copies had been returned—none of the hoped-for reviewers wanted to pay the 15 *sous*. Engels straightened out the mess and saw to it that the copies were sent again, this time without charge. He personally gave Louis Blanc a copy and the French socialist promised to write a review for *La Réforme,* the well-known social democratic paper. But when Engels again saw Blanc in January, he learned that Blanc had merely "paged through" the volume and noticed that it contained some lively attacks on Proudhon. As for a review, Blanc insisted that he did not have the time. When Engels persisted, Blanc finally suggested that Engels himself write the review which he would then have published in *La Réforme.* Engels agreed to write it immediately. In any event, he assured Marx, they would lose nothing in the process—he would portray Marx's views more correctly than Blanc could have done.

The book was no success, insofar as it aimed at discrediting Proudhon —Proudhon remained as the chief theorist and prophet of French labor. Yet it represented a landmark in the life of Marx. Since *The German Ideology* was never published, *The Poverty of Philosophy* was the first work in which the new materialistic concept of history—already more than a year old—was presented to the public. From this point forward, Marx's critique of Proudhon could be referred to as carrying "their program." A book was a book, even if it was not widely read.

3. TOWARDS A DEMOCRATIC FRONT

AT the start of 1848, Marx and Engels could count the names of their reasonably reliable and informed followers on the fingers of their four hands. Although they spoke of a Communist Party in a way which gave the impression that they commanded a multitude, that host was made up almost entirely of supposedly potential Communists, who would become professing and practicing Communists whenever the proletarian consciousness took hold of them. Marx and Engels might well have been discouraged, but they were braced by the conviction that they were moving with history and the play of gigantic forces. The few stones that they moved were hastening the release of an avalanche.

The events of 1847 in Prussia, as well as in Europe at large, quickened the hopes of those who looked to revolutionary solutions. Financial needs, which so often heralded the advent of revolution or constitutional concessions, caused the Prussian King to call for a meeting of the United Diet in Berlin early in 1847. Since it was made up of the eight Provincial Diets united in a single national diet, it was not a modern representative body. Yet the event evoked hopes that remained unfulfilled and forebodings that did not come to pass.

The eyes of the German world and of Europe were on Berlin. Metternich warned that the United Diet would go the way of the French Estates-General of 1789, which had met to solve a financial crisis and had ended by making a revolution. The Prussian liberals used the tried parliamentary tactic of keeping the purse strings tightly closed until royal concessions were made. Frederick William IV, however, refused to yield and dismissed the United Diet when the liberal majority stood equally firm. But the world was impressed by the show of strength, courage and moderation displayed by the liberal forces in Prussia. The belief persisted that another test of strength would follow soon, possibly in the shape of a revolution. Engels wrote a pamphlet, "The Status Quo in Germany" (submitted to Marx for approval and corrections) in which he joyfully declared, "The battle against the *status quo* in Germany reached a turning point with the convening of the Prussian United Diet." Now the liberal bourgeoisie had to seize power or perish. Prussia was about to experience a rerun of the Great Revolution, with certain more advanced features that reflected the fact that the world had moved ahead since 1789—Marx and Engels assumed that Germany at large, and notably Prussia, stood at about the same political, social and economic level as France had in 1789.

Mounting unrest in Switzerland, Denmark, Italy and France helped to magnify the impression that widespread revolution was possible. The French began to hold that series of banquets, which centered about toasts in favor of reform and speeches denouncing "corruption" and the "personal rule" of the King. While the masses seemed passive, there were those who sensed the danger and warned of revolution.

In 1847 Marx and Engels were in a better position to promote their views and to discredit their rivals. The old handicap, the lack of a party *Organ*, was partially removed when a German-language newspaper in Brussels, the *Deutsche-Brüsseler-Zeitung*, began to accept their writings regularly. Edited by Adalbert von Bornstedt, an ex-Prussian radical, its only drawback was a limited and uncertain circulation, except among the Germans in Brussels. Yet it helped fill an obvious need, and when Marx ultimately gained control over its editorial policy, it became almost the *Organ* of the Communists.

Marx and Engels used two major guidelines in setting forth their views in the *Brüsseler-Zeitung*. First, they advocated whatever policy appeared most likely to hasten the advent of revolution. Second, they took the stand that no reforms or changes in domestic policies could benefit the workers—only revolution would do that. Their object was to persuade their readers not to be misled by any panaceas of the day—anything short of a revolution was only an illusion.

One of the lively topics most widely discussed was the question of free trade versus protective tariffs. Liberal economists met in congresses to promote the adoption of free trade. Britain, generally, was turning towards a free trade policy. In Germany, on the other hand, there was an increased demand for protective tariffs as a guard against the influx of cheaper goods from industrially advanced England. The advocates of each bolstered their opposite cases by insisting that labor would benefit from the change.

Engels took up the issue of free trade versus protective tariffs in the *Brüsseler-Zeitung* of June 10, while Marx prepared a speech on the subject for an international congress of economists meeting in Brussels in September. The Congress did not find a place for Marx's talk, but Engels had it published in the *Northern Star* of October 9. On January 9, 1848, Marx gave a long lecture on free trade at a meeting of the Brussels Democratic Association, which the Association then published as a pamphlet.

Both Marx and Engels constantly cited the economists to show that wages were determined exclusively by the law of supply and demand. Therefore, it was immaterial whether a nation operated under free trade or protection; in either event the worker would get merely enough "to keep going as a working machine." Nevertheless, the proletariat and the Communists had a long-range interest in the matter. In a broader international sense, free trade fostered revolution; protection was conservative. "In this revolutionary sense alone," Marx voted for free trade. In Germany, however, a protective tariff would produce the more revolutionary results. Wherever the bourgeoisie was just getting on its feet, protective tariffs could be beneficial "as weapons against feudalism and the absolute power of the state," Marx declared. Since the Communists favored the rise of the bourgeoisie as the necessary prelude to their own subsequent conflict with that same bourgeoisie, they favored protective tariffs in Germany.

It is evident that Marx and Engels were trying to make the point that none should place their faith in anything short of a revolution, as the only reliable cure, or at least the first step in the direction of a final solution. The whole subject gave them an admirable opportunity to paint a gruesome picture of the presumed steadily deteriorating situation of labor under the capitalist system. The very progress of industry, by devising cheaper ways for keeping the worker alive, thus making possible lower and lower wages, was perpetually pulling him down to a still lower level. The more harmful gin or brandy (*Schnaps*, which Marx once called a poison, the opium of the poor) forced out the beer; cotton took the place of wool and linen; the potato supplanted bread. (It is not clear what industry had to do with the production of the potato.)

Another controversial issue was the question of an income tax instead of a sales tax. The Prussian government had proposed an income tax to replace the unpopular slaughter and milling tax (*Schlacht- und Mahlsteuer*) levied on flour and meat. The bourgeois Liberals in the

United Diet had opposed the income tax. The True Socialist paper, the *Rheinische Beobachter* (*Rhenish Observer*), asserted that the masses could expect more sympathy from the Prussian authorities than from the liberal bourgeoisie. Marx was incensed at the *Beobachter*. The Prussian government was merely trying to hoodwink the workers, he declared flatly. "An income tax eliminates a *boundless* penury only to put a limitless penury in its place." The worker gained nothing in the process. Ilis wages were set by the law of supply, with a tendency to remain at a level just adequate to keep him going and able to rear enough children to stock the labor market. Only the state profited. It cost less to collect the income tax, and it also freed the authorities from unpleasant daily contacts with the public while collecting an unpopular milling and slaughter tax, Marx asserted.

Before another year had passed, Marx and Engels were condemning the Prussian government because of that same sales tax. If the government proposed to eliminate the tax, economic laws could be cited to prove that this was a futile, hypocritical gesture. Later, the unpopular tax could be held against the same government. That was politics. Tactical considerations in 1847 made it appear vital to discredit the thought that the worker might fare better under a "social monarchy" than he would under a liberal bourgeois regime.

It is not difficult to grasp Marx's anger when the *Beobachter*, in the name of "communism," suggested that the workers might gain more through an alliance with the Prussian state against the liberal bourgeoisie than by a policy of opposition to the government. Socialism or popular well-being introduced from on high, via cooperation between people and their King, was shameful, Marx declared in the *Brüsseler-Zeitung* of September 12. The "real people" would make no such deal. The present King would be fortunate if the people allowed him to survive as a "public speechmonger" (Frederick William IV was a gifted speaker) in a Berlin artisan society on a pension of 250 *Taler* and a cool daily *Blonde* (glass of pale Berlin beer). Many years later Marx could cite this relatively obscure article as proof that the Communists had always opposed any compromise with an existing government, aiming at a "social monarchy."

Marx likewise scoffed at the *Beobachter* for its favorable comments on the "social principles of Christianity." Those principles through eighteen hundred years had "justified ancient slavery and glorified medieval serfdom; if need be, they were capable of defending the oppression of the proletariat, even if with a somewhat sorrowful face." Moreover, the "social principles of Christianity preached cowardice, self-denial, abasement, submission, humility—in short, all the characteristics of the rabble [*Kanaille*]; but the proletariat does not want to be treated like a rabble; it needs courage, self-confidence, pride and the feeling of independence—much more even than its bread." Marx wanted no part of Christian social principles or of Christians with social principles.

Since the Marxian theory regarded culture and thought as the product of the dominant class during a particular stage of history, literature fell within the scope of criticism when it did not reflect the proper proletarian outlook. In eight issues of the *Brüsseler-Zeitung*, beginning September 12, 1847, Engels critically reviewed literary works that did not meet the above criterion. He especially ridiculed the socialist poet, Karl Beck, whose poetry was permeated with a "womanly sentimentality" and vitiated by a cowardly petty-bourgeois glorification of the poor, the "proud pauper." There was no sign of the "proud, threatening and revolutionary proletarian." Instead of deploring the potato crop failure which brought misery to millions, Beck should have welcomed this catastrophe of the potato, "this bourgeois god and one of the pivots of the existing bourgeois society." Beck's poetry was an expression of a lower stage of civilization, soon to be superseded when the class struggle became sharper, more specific and revolutionary, Engels declared.

Engels' "Status Quo in Germany," which Marx checked and corrected, stated that the Communist Party, as the "youngest" of all parties, had to "clarify its position, its campaign plans and resources." Criticism might weaken and demoralize an old society, theory could tell what kind of a revolution was in the offing, but revolutions were won by the concentration of forces at a point where victory was possible. The general strategy of Marx and Engels called for a coalition of revolutionary elements behind the class that was historically destined to win. In Prussia and in Germany at large, that meant the liberal bourgeoisie which alone was capable of overthrowing feudalism and the "bureaucratic monarchy."

The proletariat, quite cold-bloodedly, would support the same liberal bourgeoisie that the Communists normally denounced as the exploiter; the proletariat would be on the winning side, even if another party were the big winner for the moment. The proletariat, Marx wrote in the *Brüsseler-Zeitung* of September 12, 1847, was not concerned over the fact that the bourgeoisie might use it as mere "cannon fodder." It acted with the knowledge that its own direct battle against the bourgeoisie had to be postponed until after the bourgeois Liberals controlled the government. Communists' chances also would improve thereafter because the bourgeoisie itself would hand the proletariat entirely new weapons: freedom of press, assembly and association. The proletariat then would be able to organize itself as a recognized Communist Party, in preparation for its own direct assault of bourgeois rule.

Influenced by the dialectic and the precedents of the French Revolution, Marx assumed that the bourgeois revolution could end in nothing less than a republic, liberal in form but dominated by the victorious bourgeoisie. There could be no compromise in the form of a constitutional monarchy such as the English enjoyed. "A rule of the people is pure nonsense when aristocracy and bourgeoisie still exist side-by-side," Marx declared on November 18. The arena had to be cleared of all other contestants so the people (*Volk*) and the bourgeoisie would directly face each other—in a war to the knife.

As for the fight that lay directly ahead, Marx and Engels naturally recognized that their few hundred followers, acting in the name of communism, would not attract much support, even if they backed the liberal bourgeoisie in their bid for power. To make a respectable showing, Marx and Engels needed more soldiers to man the barricades. Their search for allies in this cause was made easier because the various parties just then were ready to de-emphasize their differences in order to cooperate in a common assault on the status quo. Marx and Engels adopted the tactic of a democratic front, using democracy as the password.

Utter confusion existed as to what democracy would be like in practice. Guizot, the French historian and politician, was soon to complain that every party from the far right to the farthest left wrote democracy on its banners. Democracy, of course, had something to do with the will and power of the people, or perhaps only the interests of the masses, however determined and expressed. Could a government that ruled *for* the benefit of all the masses call itself a democracy, even if it were run *by* a dictator? This and many other questions were both affirmed and denied. But there was a fairly general agreement that democracy was an undefined force that none could ignore. No government could afford to flout it completely. No revolutionist could omit it from his platform. The very vagueness of the concept of democracy and its practical applications made it easy for Marx and Engels to appropriate the term, linking themselves with the broader masses.

Although Marx and Engels in private spoke contemptuously of Democrats and "vulgar" democracy, they had started to appropriate the word for their own movement as early as their joint excursion to England. Thus, Engels equated the democracy of 1845/46 with communism. When the Communists in Brussels congratulated the radical Chartist, Feargus O'Connor, on his parliamentary victory in England, the message was signed: "Engels, Ph. Gigot, Marx," in the name of the "German Democratic Communists in Brussels." In 1847, Marx and Engels used the words proletariat, democracy and people loosely and almost interchangeably, as if all three spelled out the same thing. It was a deliberate technique to make it appear that communism and the proletariat meant about the same thing as democracy and *Volk*. Engels tried to justify the substitution of the word proletariat for *Volk* with the explanation that he was replacing a "vast and uncertain expression with something definite." Elsewhere he spoke of the proletariat as the "crown of modern democracy" that provided the leadership for the peasants and the petty bourgeoisie—presumably under Marxian guidelines.

By 1847 Marx and Engels would "allow nothing democratic to happen" without having a hand in it. They actively sought contacts with democratic societies and worked through democratic associations. Their greatest success came in Brussels, thanks initially to the dexterity of Engels who had arrived early in August.

A dissident group of German Radicals, together with a select group of Belgians, secretly planned to create an international democratic association in Brussels, excluding Marx and his followers from any role in the organization. Marx knew nothing of their plans when he left for Holland late in September to visit his Dutch relatives in a successful effort to get some of the money he was to inherit when his mother died. Engels, however, heard of the plans and indignantly reported that something "democratic" was being plotted against them or without them. A Democratic Association (which was to have international connections on the order of the English Fraternal Democrats) was to be launched September 27 at a "cosmopolitan-democratic *souper*," as Engels derisively described it. Numerous Democrats—Belgians, Italians, Poles, Frenchmen and Germans—were invited to the affair, all but the followers of Marx. The Association was to be headed by a Belgian President (L. L. Jottrand) and two Vice Presidents. One of the Vice Presidents was to be French (the radical Jacques Imbert) and the other was to be a German —a worker, if possible.

The attempt to exclude the Communists boomeranged. Engels immediately began a countermining operation with the purpose of getting a Communist elected to fill the German vice-presidential post. Since no other qualified Communist was available, Engels himself became the candidate (though he regretted that he looked "so terribly young"). He was elected; the "whole intrigue fell apart and was thwarted." That was a day of triumph for the followers of Marx and Engels, more so because it was witnessed by Belgian Democrats and others. Before leaving for Paris again, Engels consolidated the victory by persuading the Belgian President to accept Marx as his replacement in the vice-presidency, as the person with the best right to represent "German democracy." All of this gave Engels an enormous lift. He and Marx were now recognized as the "representatives of German democracy in Brussels." With such credentials, and by working through the Brussels Democratic Association, it was easier to propose alliances with democrats in all lands.

Engels returned to Paris, eager to form such an alliance with the French Social Democrats. In preparation for this, he had written to Louis Blanc, whose influence was high just then; his recently published work, *The Organization of Labor*, was an enormous success, with three thousand copies in a cheap edition for the workers having been sold in two weeks. Engels assured Blanc that he came with a "formal mandate from the London, Brussels and Rhineland democracy, likewise as a Chartist agent." He even claimed that the Democrats in Switzerland and South Germany, together with the radical and well-known Johann Jacoby from distant East Prussia, were their "allies." Impressed by such formidable credentials, Blanc was "courtesy and friendship itself and appeared to want nothing more than the closest ties" with them. Engels improved the outlook by describing the status of their party as "extremely brilliant." He then stated that Blanc should consider Marx as the "*chef* of [their] party (namely, the most advanced faction of German democracy)." Blanc then showed the utmost interest in Marx and regretted that they had parted "somewhat coldly" when they had last met in Paris some years earlier.

Engels also visited Ferdinand Flocon, the editor of *La Réforme*. Posing as an Englishman at first, Engels asked "*père* Flocon" why *La Réforme* ignored the *Northern Star* and Chartist affairs in general. When Flocon explained that no one on the editorial staff read English, Engels thereupon offered to write a weekly article on English affairs. But this was just the opening wedge, he wrote Marx; he would take additional steps to get Flocon "entangled in their net." If things continued thus, they would soon control "the whole tendency" without having made any concessions on their part. An informal alliance with French Social Democracy seemed assured.

Articles by Engels covering the commercial crisis in England, the Chartist movement, the suffering of the Irish and similar matters began to appear in Flocon's paper after October 26, 1847. But Engels had less success when he tried to get Flocon to publish the speech that Marx had prepared for the International Congress of Economists held in Brussels in September. Engels first had sent the speech, "Protectionists, Free Traders and the Working Class," to Louis Blanc who promptly forgot about it until a reminder from Engels brought amends. Blanc thereupon passed it on to Flocon who agreed to publish it, though he protested that at that late date the subject seemed a little "old." But, Engels wrote in disgust, that "*Esel*" Flocon then gave another reason for not publishing it—he found it a "*peu confus!!!*" It needed changes to make it "clearer." At this point Engels gave up—*La Réforme* saw economic matters through the "eyes of a Parisian clerk of the third class working for a banker of the fourth rank."

Meanwhile, democratic contacts in England were not overlooked. On

October 9 Engels introduced Marx to the Fraternal Democratic and Chartist readers of the *Northern Star* as the most talented representative of German democracy by far. Engels reminded Marx that something "fraternally democratic" would probably take place in London on November 29, the anniversary of the Polish Revolution of 1830. (Marx and Engels were to be in London then, attending the second Communist Congress.) He suggested that Marx give a speech in French which he would then have printed in *La Réforme*. The Germans had to do something to impress the French. "A single speech will help more than ten articles and a hundred calls," he added. He also called Marx's attention to the *Northern Star* of October 2 in which Julian Harney and the Fraternal Democrats had called for an international democratic congress. He urged Marx to second the move in the name of the German and Brussels Democrats; he would do the same for the French.

The London events of late November, 1847, took the course that Engels anticipated, except that Marx gave his speech in German and not in French when the Fraternal Democrats hosted a Polish anniversary meeting on the 29th. Marx was greeted with "long sustained applause" when Karl Schapper announced that the Brussels Democratic Association had sent him a "German democrat and one of its vice presidents" to establish a regular correspondence with the London Society of Fraternal Democrats and to prepare for the calling of a "Democratic congress of the different nations of Europe." Engels, in turn, was presented as "Mr. Engels from Paris, a German Democrat," according to the short report of his own speech for *La Réforme*.

Later, during that same meeting, Julian Harney and Engels moved that the assembly recognize the "three big democratic newspapers of Europe" (*La Réforme, Northern Star, Deutsche-Brüsseler-Zeitung*) with a three-fold salvo of applause. It was done. This was followed by a motion to condemn three anti-democratic papers (*Le Journal des débats,* the London *Times* and the *Augsburger Allgemeine Zeitung*) with three successive grunts. This was also done. The meeting ended with the singing of the French *La Marseillaise,* while all bared their heads. Democracy was on the march.

Marx and Engels generally avoided any open criticism of the numerous democratic leaders during this period when they were placing the communist forces on the left wing of a revolutionary democratic front. The notable exceptions were Karl Heinzen, a Democrat who publicly attacked communism, and Louis Blanc who made a statement that provoked hostility between Democrats of different nationalities.

Karl Heinzen became the target of a double-barreled attack. It was another case of former collaborators becoming vehement opponents. Heinzen had once worked with Marx in editing the *Rheinische Zeitung.*

His democratic revolutionary credentials were beyond reproach. The federal republic of the United States was his model, except where it could be improved through the addition of the proper "social institutions." The conflict developed because Heinzen sensed that the liberty and "human realization" that he cherished were threatened by the principles of the socialists and Communists. A prolific writer, Heinzen first merely assailed the True Socialists. In the summer of 1847, however, his polemics against communism began to appear in the *Brüsseler-Zeitung*. This was a direct affront and challenge to Marx and Engels.

Engels' reply in two articles, on October 3 and 7, in the same newspaper made clear that democracy as such was not under attack. The Communists, Engels declared, avoided all useless controversy with democrats under the "present condition" and instead "posed as democrats in all practical party questions for the time being." Until the "battle of democracy was won" (an expression later repeated in the *Communist Manifesto*), the interests of the Communists coincided with those of the Democrats. Meanwhile, differences of a purely "theoretical character" need not interfere with a common program of action. "In short," Engels emphasized, "the Communists wanted to, and had to, work with the German radicals." (Democrats were then often classified as radicals.)

After making clear that democracy itself was not in question, Engels attacked the "person and personal idiosyncrasies" of Heinzen. The motives for Heinzen's conversion to "bloodthirsty radicalism" were impure and entirely selfish. Heinzen was inspired by "arbitrary, philistine world-improvement fantasies" that ignored existing realities and any objective examination of what was practical and possible. A party spokesman needed more than "sentiment, goodwill and a stentorian voice." Heinzen's incompetence as a writer would "confuse and betray any party for which he spoke. His every sentence carried a twofold nonsense; first, the nonsense which he wished to express, and, secondly, the nonsense which he did not want to say but nevertheless did say." But he did agree with one point of Heinzen's attack on the Communists. Yes, Engels affirmed, the Communists did laugh at "elevated ideas, virtue, justice, morality, etc.," as the supposed foundations upon which society rested. The Communists would continue to deride the *"eternal verities"*; they were not the bases upon which society developed but merely the product of such societies.

Engels' fusillade did not silence Heinzen. The battling democrat's reply in the same paper on October 12 struck Engels "like an avalanche of mud" plunging down from the "heights of the Alps," as he informed Marx on October 25–26. He could only answer such an attack with a "boxing of the ears." This may not have been meant entirely in a figurative sense; Engels did have a manly (even aristocratic) code that called for the use of force when wit and reason failed. Hence he was relieved when Marx felt the call to answer Heinzen, especially since Marx had spoken of being "entirely brief." A long reply would represent too much of a recognition of Heinzen.

Marxian brevity in answering the "Heinzen Manifesto" helped to fill the columns of five issues of the *Brüsseler-Zeitung* (October 28, 31; November 11, 18, 25) and doubled Engels' volume. The title of the articles, "The Moralizing Critique and the Critical Morality. A Contribution to German Cultural History," was a guarantee that Heinzen would be crowded aside most of the time in favor of an exposition of Marx's own theories, views and tactics. The polemic was seeded with some excellent Marxian gems on history, economics and revolutionary strategy. It was here that he called a government a "political husk . . . the natural cover for the old society" that later becomes an "unnatural fetter" of the newly evolving society and is "exploded." Since Heinzen admired the United States, Marx described it as the place where "social inequalities stand out most starkly." The articles contain some of Marx's best writing, even if they failed also to silence Heinzen.

The controversy might have continued in the *Brüsseler-Zeitung* for additional weeks, but Marx's influence over its editorial policy became so exclusive towards the close of 1847 that nothing more from Heinzen was printed. Heinzen, however, carried on the fight in writings elsewhere. He accused the Communists of "confusing the heads of the uneducated and of using the workers merely for their own purposes, while actually keeping them in ignorance as to their real aims."

Engels rose to the defense of an offended English democracy when Louis Blanc inadvertently displayed a national prejudice or superiority. With a national naivete that came naturally enough to a 19th century Frenchman, Blanc stated that anything French was inevitably cosmopolitan and that France always acted and thought for the good of all mankind. This might not have appeared offensive, but then Blanc added that England's role in history, in contrast, had been a perpetual "fight on the side of egoism and against fraternity." This was more than the *Northern Star* could take, even when a "union of democracy" was at stake. An angry retort followed. Engels stepped into the affray to soothe ruffled sensibilities.

"The union of democrats of the different nations does not exclude mutual criticism," Engels declared in the *Brüsseler-Zeitung* of December 30, 1847. But he warned Blanc of the consequences of such talk. If the Germans used Blanc's yardstick, they themselves could claim to be the true cosmopolitans. They, "as was generally recognized, had produced a larger number of magnanimous and cosmopolitan ideas than France and England combined." But the German Democrats were far removed from such "pretenses."

Engels himself was the great cosmopolite just then. He wrote in the French *La Réforme*, mainly on English affairs. He reported primarily on French developments in the English *Northern Star*. In the *Brüsseler-Zeitung* he wrote for German readers on subjects that embraced the wide world. All the while he held up a banner of democracy—at least in one hand. This flag was most evident when he faced the English and French public, less so when he addressed the Germans.

4. THE COMMUNIST LEAGUE AND ITS *STATUTES*

EVEN while Marx and Engels were recruiting future soldiers for a revolutionary army, via a democratic front, an officer corps was being established under their influence through the creation of the secret Communist League. This was accomplished by their joining the League of the Just and then using its external framework and membership as the foundation for a communist organization of their own.

The League of the Just originally was composed of the extreme radical and proletarian wing that seceded from the League of Exiles (a broader, democratic-republican organization of German expatriates and workers in Paris) and formed its own *Bund* in 1836. The new *Bund* was prosecuted and its members were dispersed in various lands after it had taken part in the abortive revolt of the French "Society of Seasons" in 1839. The *Bund* nevertheless survived as a secret organization with branches or communes (*Gemeinde*) in Paris, London, Switzerland and more uncertainly in Germany, with the Central Authority and leadership residing in Paris.

The three Paris branches of the League of the Just lost much of their revolutionary fervor in the next years, as Engels discovered in 1846. The London branch of the League, in contrast, was far more active. It had established the Workers' Educational Society which openly acted as a recruiting ground among Germans in London. Gradually the London group became slightly international in character when a few German-speaking Poles, Danes, Italians, English and others joined. The London League also entered into a lively correspondence with the Communist Correspondence Committee in Brussels. Through letters and lithographic circulars, the members became acquainted with the Marx-Engels concepts, as also with their objections to the various brands of socialism and communism. Nevertheless by the fall of 1846 Marx and Engels seem to have felt that they were not making any progress in converting the London branch to their views.

The League of the Just took on a new life and direction in November,

1846, when its Central Authority was shifted from Paris to the more active branch in London. Leadership in the League was now in the hands of a group led by Schapper, Moll and Bauer. They had been joined recently by two new men with a "greater capacity for theoretical comprehension," as Engels later described Karl Pfänder, a tailor from central Germany, and Georg Eccarius, the German miniature painter. This invigorated Central Authority, sensing that Germany was on the eve of a momentous revolution, recognized the need of an appropriate philosophy and program of action. Almost immediately it sent out an *Address* to all the League branches, calling for a clarification of views and policies. A "simple communist confession of faith to serve as a guide for all" was needed, as well as a policy in relationship to other radical movements. The various branches were instructed to discuss these matters and to prepare their recommendations. The *Address* then announced that a congress of the League would meet in London on May 1, 1847 (later postponed until June), to formulate a final statement of principles and a program of action.

In their search for a philosophy and program of action, the London group eliminated one possibility after another. They were disillusioned with Weitling, their earlier hero. Cabet was found unacceptable when he appeared in London in January, 1847. Then they turned to Marx, perhaps because the Marxian stress on economics and class warfare meant more to them, exposed as they were to the Chartist movement in the advanced industrial society in England.

In February the Central Authority therefore sent Joseph Moll to visit Marx in Brussels and Engels in Paris. Moll's mission was to persuade them to become members of the League of the Just. Both agreed to join. Evidently the latest League developments in London and Moll's arguments convinced Marx and Engels that the League could be persuaded to adopt their views as the official policy of the organization. This impression was certainly strengthened when the Central Authority circulated a second *Address* in February that spoke of the advent of a "terrible revolution" and the need for strong men ready to seize the sword. But it warned against premature riots and conspiracies, a view congenial to Marx who always opposed senseless and ill-timed actions. The *Address* also called on the communes to combat any "insipid love-giddiness" and to clarify the difference between communism and socialism as methods for achieving a socialist society. The outlook was favorable for Marx and Engels.

Marx immediately established a commune of the League of the Just in Brussels. This made it possible to send a delegate representing an organized group of reliable communist followers to the coming Congress in London. Marx himself was unable to go because of an acute shortage of money; perhaps he was also influenced by a lifetime reluctance to be personally present at a congress when results were not completely certain. Wilhelm Wolff (*Lupus*), a dependable Marxian though not a very articulate delegate, represented the Brussels branch. Much therefore depended on Engels' appearance as a delegate to present the Marxian point of view effectively.

Since the delegates were chosen in a democratic manner, it required some special efforts to get Engels elected as the Paris representative. He was hardly popular; he had not always concealed his contempt for the *Straubinger* and *Knoten* (boors), as he called the members. Fortunately, Engels' friend, Stephan Born, presided over the meeting. Voting was done by a show of hands. Born, however, executed a "presidential trick" by simply asking those who were opposed to Engels to raise their hands. When a majority failed to do so, Born declared that Engels was elected. After the meeting Engels, expressing his gratitude to Born, said: "You did that beautifully." Engels was then in a position to appear at the London Congress with formidable credentials, as the delegate of three Paris communes.

The Congress of the League of the Just met in June, 1847. It changed its name to *Communist League* and adopted the motto, "Proletarians of All Lands, Unite," in place of the former slogan, "All Men are Brothers." The "shrill and defiant proletarian rally cry" thus replaced a motto too reminiscent of the "love-giddiness, fraternization and humanity-talk of the True Socialists," Engels said. The author of the new slogan (which Marx later used at the end of the *Communist Manifesto*) is not known.

Statutes or rules of organization for the new Communist League were drafted by the Congress, subject to approval by the various local communes, with final ratification reserved for a second congress. It is commonly assumed that Engels played the decisive role in drafting the *Statutes*, which provided that the *Central Authority* (*Zentralbehörde*) of the new Communist League be located in the city where the next congress was to be held, namely London. Nominally at least, leadership of the League therefore remained in the hands of Karl Schapper and his group. As a guide for the League members, the *Central Authority* was expected to publish an official *Organ*. The first and only issue of such a Communist Journal (*Kommunistische Zeitschrift*), edited by Schapper, appeared in September, 1847. It carried the motto: "Proletarians of all lands, unite!" The Journal reflected Marx's views quite strongly, though apparently neither Marx nor Engels wrote any of the articles.

On the whole Engels and Wolff were moderately successful as delegates in getting their program adopted at this first Congress, but it was impossible to work out and adopt a full communist declaration of principles. The new *Central Authority* therefore had the responsibility for calling on the entire League for recommendations concerning questions of general interest, particularly a full "Confession of Faith" (*Glaubensbekenntniss*).

Accordingly, Schapper, Moll and perhaps several others drafted a tentative communist *Glaubensbekenntniss* to serve as a guideline for the communes. Copies were then sent (probably in August) to the various communes in London, Paris and Brussels for discussion and recommendations. As the final authority in such matters, a second congress was to meet in London later in 1847, to formulate and adopt a final draft of communist principles and program of action. Publication would follow.

The *Central Authority's* tentative *Glaubensbekenntniss* has not survived. Apparently it contained over twenty questions with the appropriate answers. This question-and-answer method was familiar to the Germans ever since Martin Luther had written his catechisms for instruction and guidance in Protestant faith and practice. In the early 19th century the catechistic device was also used for other purposes, when the education or indoctrination of the relatively uneducated masses was in the picture.

After the June Congress had converted the League of the Just into the Communist League, the local branches of the old League had to be reconstituted and reorientated. Marx and Engels had to make sure that the new Communist *Communes* would adopt their views when making recommendations concerning the *Glaubensbekenntniss*. The final adoption of the Marxian platform by the second Congress in London depended on it. Marx was enough in command of the situation in Brussels to prevent the development of any serious opposition there. The former League of the Just commune was converted into a *Commune* of the new Communist League and duly constituted on August 5, 1847. A brief note in Marx's own handwriting recorded the fact that he was elected President and Philippe Gigot, the Secretary-Treasurer. The district executive committee (*Kreisvorstand*) included Gigot, A. F. Junge (Junge had shown his mettle as an ally of Engels in Paris in the campaign against Grün's followers), Marx and Wilhelm Wolff—listed in that order. Engels' name does not appear because he was expected to play a vital role in the Paris *Communes*.

Since the Communist *Commune* operated secretly, another organization was needed as a recruiting agency. To serve this purpose a German *Arbeiterverein* (Worker-Society) under communist leadership was established in Brussels late in August. Karl Wallau, the compositor of the *Deutsche-Brüsseler-Zeitung*, was President; the ever staunch Wilhelm Wolff (*Lupus*) served as Secretary. Such worker-societies served a double purpose—social and educational. In Brussels, Saturday evenings were set aside for social purposes, to attract more people and perhaps to disguise the main aim of the society. Women were present. Music, dancing and singing (Germans were always a singing people, even in exile) could account for several hours. Literary declamations and the reading of poetry of a socialist and revolutionary tone soothed the thirst for culture. An occasional lecture gave food for thought. But human companionship was the major attraction.

For the serious business of the Brussels Worker-Society, another weekly meeting was devoted to discussion and talks on such subjects as the impact of the machine and factories, the position of the workers, free trade or protection, and the value of a liberal constitution. The worker thus received a piecemeal exposure to Marxian ideas.

While it appears that Marx had things pretty well under control in Brussels, Moses Hess' zeal was creating some problems that had repercussions in Paris. Late in October, 1847, Hess started publishing a whole series of articles in the *Brüsseler-Zeitung*. Engels, who was trying to get Marxism adopted by the Communist League in Paris, immediately asked Marx what kind of a "fly" had stung Moses—Hess' articles contradicted what he himself was saying. Later in November Engels' tone became angrier—it was incomprehensible why Marx had not called a halt to Hess' "chatter." The stuff was read in Paris and produced a "devilish confusion and wearisome objections" on the part of the workers. Marx, however, apparently felt that Hess could not be silenced or repudiated right on the eve of the London Congress. As Vice President of the Worker-Society, he still commanded too much of a following. It was necessary to indulge him a little longer.

Engels was having enough other troubles in Paris. He did succeed in getting himself included in the new *District Authority* of the Communist League in Paris, with control over its correspondence. But then he ran into a serious complication. While he was in Brussels in August, Moses Hess had been in Paris, sowing confusion in his wake. Hess could not resist the opportunity to improve upon the tentative confession of faith sent out by the *Central Authority* in London and had persuaded the Paris *Communes* to adopt his own "godly improved *Glaubensbekenntniss*" (as Engels derisively described it). Hess' "improved confession" was already in the hands of the *District Authority*, as the democratically adopted decision of all the Paris *Communes*, before Engels' return. Engels had to act fast. In an executive committee session on October 22, he played a "hellish trick" on Hess by taking up each point of Hess' *Glaubensbekenntniss* point by point, and tearing each of them apart. Before he had reached the halfway mark, the Committee declared that it was "satisfied"; Hess' work would not do. Describing the result to Marx, Engels wrote: "Without any opposition, I allowed myself to be instructed to draft a new one [confession of faith] which will then be discussed in the *District* [Authority] next Friday and sent to London *behind the backs of the Communes*. Naturally, no devil must know about this; otherwise we will all be ousted, and there will be a murderous scandal." This was democracy at work in Paris when Engels was under the pressure of time to get a statement of principles along Marxian lines.

Armed with this mandate from the *District Authority,* Engels proceeded to draft an improved confession of communist faith on short notice, keeping the catechism form (with twenty-five questions). He may have encountered some difficulties getting it adopted by the executive committee because he evidently had to prepare two drafts. As late as November 24 he had informed Marx that he hoped to get it adopted (by the *District Authority*) in a form which at least contained nothing contrary to their views. Although Engels' *Glaubensbekenntniss* was not printed until the 20th century when it appeared under the title "Principles of Communism" (*Grundsätze des Kommunismus*), it certainly played a significant role in 1847 as a preliminary draft of the *Communist Manifesto.*

On November 23 Engels wrote Marx that the London Congress had to be decisive, adding in English, "as this time we shall have it all our way." Urging Marx to give the *Glaubensbekenntniss* a little thought, he proposed that they drop the catechism form and "entitle the thing: Communist *Manifesto."* Since it was more or less a historical narrative, the catechistic pattern did not fit; some of his answers took up a full page, in violation of the brief form of a catechism. He was bringing his copy along; it was in a "simple narrative form, but miserably edited, in a terrible hurry." He then hastily sketched his main points, ending with a discussion of the "party policy of the Communists insofar as it belonged before the public." Engels evidently felt that not all could be told.

Engels did not have to "do any intriguing" to get himself elected as the delegate from the Paris district to the second Congress. After a "highly confusing" session, he was elected by a two-thirds majority—he had been careful not to do or say anything against Moses Hess and his "dull twaddle" (that was restricted to the session of the *District Authority*).

In contrast to Engels' activity in Paris, the Brussels branch of the Communist League seems not to have drafted anything like a black-on-white "confession of faith." With Moses Hess around, Marx may have decided that it was safer to appear as the spokesman of the group, unembarrassed and unbound by the ambiguities of a set of written definitions.

In any event there is no indication that Marx went to London with the draft of a statement of principles in his pocket.

Until the middle of November, Engels had worried that Marx and Victor Tedesco, the German-speaking Belgian delegate, might not have the money to go to London. It would be senseless for him to go "congressing" all by himself. He also was short of money just then and had to postpone seeing Marx and Tedesco until they met in Ostend on November 27, before embarking for London on the 28th. This gave them a day together, however, to plan for the second Communist Congress which met from November 29 until December 10, 1847.

No news of the Congress of the Communist League reached the public, though the Polish rally sponsored by the Fraternal Democrats at the same time was well publicized. The *Communist Manifesto* proudly states that the Communists had met in London and had drafted the *Manifesto*. But it was not until 1853, when the Prussian government seized and published the *Statutes* of the League during the course of a prosecution of the Communists in Cologne, that the general public read about the Congress and a part of its results. Much later, in 1885, Engels wrote the following brief sketch of the Congress:

> Here Marx was also present and defended the new theory in long debates—the Congress lasted at least ten days. All opposition and doubt were finally overcome; the new principles were unanimously adopted; and Marx and I were instructed to draft the *Manifesto*. This was done immediately afterwards.

The *Statutes* of the Communist League open with a brief statement of aims, calling for the "overthrow of the bourgeoisie, the rule of the proletariat, the destruction of the old bourgeois society based on class conflict and the founding of a new society without classes and without private property." The statement resembles the definition of aims that Engels formulated earlier during the fight against Karl Grün's followers in Paris. The *Statutes* became official when they were signed by Karl Schapper, the President of the second Congress, and by Engels, the Secretary, as of December 8, 1847.

In contrast to the almost dictatorial leadership that existed in some similar organizations, the League's *Statutes* sound most democratic. The circumstances would have permitted nothing else. It took considerable persuading and a little maneuvering just to get their principles adopted by the League. Any bid for dictatorial control by Marx and Engels would have been rejected; the League's leaders were suspicious of learned men. Moreover, neither Marx nor Engels possessed the peculiar qualities of the popular leader or prophet—the charismatic quality that enables some to command the dedicated following of many. However much they impressed others by their brilliant intellects, neither had the oratorical gift that could move masses to accept them as dictatorial leaders. With the retention of democratic processes, the members were left with the impressions that their votes remained decisive. Marx and Engels knew that "democratic techniques and parliamentary procedure allowed for a lot of maneuvering and machinations." As Marx observed later in connection with the International Workingmen's Association of 1864, it was not so difficult to put through one's views where only workers were involved.

Membership in the Communist League called for a complete submission and dedication to the principles and decisions of the party. This was to be reflected in the member's mode of living and activity. If he had any ties with other organizations, he was to inform the leaders of this fact. Members had to maintain secrecy regarding League affairs, make the needed confession of communism, and display "revolutionary energy and zeal in propaganda."

Starting from the bottom, the League was made up of various *Communes* of from three to twenty members in each. Discussion in the *Communes* was to be kept in line with the purposes of the League, as decided by a higher authority. Each *Commune* had a separate name and was to have no contacts with other *Communes*. Between the *Communes* and the *Congress*—the supreme authority in the League—lay three intervening *Authorities* (*Behörde*), or executive bodies, through which all communications were channeled. The League as a whole was organized along disciplined hierarchical lines.

Final legislative power rested in the *Congress* which met in August each year. It was made up of delegates from the various *Districts* (*Kreis*), but the *Statutes* are silent as to the method by which delegates were selected. After each annual session of the *Congress*, a *Circular Letter* and a *Manifesto* announcing its decisions were to be sent out to the *Communes*. Between meetings, executive power was exercised by the *Central Authority* which was to be located in the city selected by the *Congress* as the site of its next meeting. The *Central Authority* was composed of at least five members chosen by the *District Authority* (*Kreisbehörde*) in the same city. The *Central Authority* occupied a crucial position. All proposals regarding changes in the *Statutes* were to originate in the Leading District (*Leitende Kreis*) and then were submitted to the *Central Authority* which in turn presented them to the *Congress*. (There was no provision for any action from the floor or for proposals from any other source. Order and a disciplined procedure were the rule.)

Elaborate rules made certain that the individual Communist and the

ORGANIZATION OF THE COMMUNIST LEAGUE

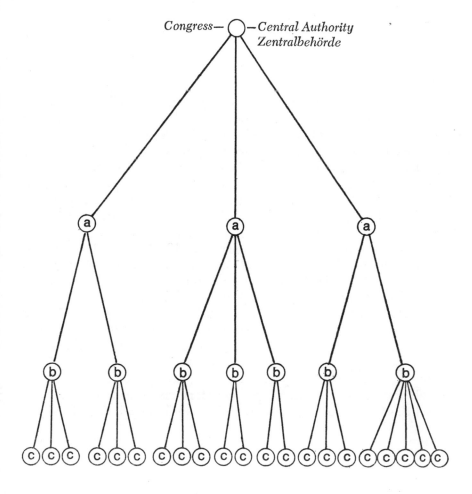

a. *Leading District—Leitende Kreis*—at the head of a country or province. *Leading District* designated by the Congress, upon recommendation of *Central Authority*.

b. *District Authority—Kreisbehörde*—at the head of a district (*Kreis*) including 2 to 10 *Communes*.

c. The local *Communes—Gemeinde*.

various *Authorities* did not go to sleep on the job. No more than two weeks were to pass without a meeting. Periodic reports were required all along the line. Even the individual members had to correspond at least once every three months with the *District Authority*. Regular dues, as established by the *Congress*, had to be paid by each member on pain of expulsion. Half of the money went to the *Central Authority* to pay for administrative expenses, printing and distributing "propaganda pamphlets," and the traveling expenses of "occasional emissaries" sent out from the center. The other half of the money remained with the various *Authorities* to be used for the same stated purpose on a local scale. Extraordinary costs and the annual *Congress* expenses called for special assessments. Thus, local contributions had helped to pay the expenses of Marx, Engels and Tedesco for the second Congress of 1847.

Membership in the League required the unanimous approval by the *Commune* and the prior recommendation of one member. Any violation of League rules could lead to expulsion. "Suspended and expelled individuals, as well as suspicious persons in general, are to be kept under surveillance by the League and made harmless." (There was no indication as to how far the last provision might go.)

The *Statutes* do not reveal the influence that Marx and Engels exercised in the League. The *Central Authority* was scheduled to remain in London for the following year. Yet when revolution occurred in 1848, that *Authority* was shifted overnight to Marx in Brussels, even though the *Statutes* contained no provision for such a sudden transfer of power. Again, though avowedly an international organization, the League was overwhelmingly German in leadership and personnel, with its interests focused primarily on Germany. As for the general purposes of the League, it was a "pure propaganda society," as Engels later stated, "at least during ordinary times of peace." Marx and Engels otherwise regarded the League as capable of preparing an informed, disciplined and energetic officer corps for revolutionary action.

=V=

The Communist Manifesto

Marx and Engels experienced their greatest triumph when the London Congress instructed them to draft a manifesto embodying their views, as the platform for the Communist Party. They were not even required to submit the finished *Manifesto* to the next Congress for final examination and endorsement. Evidently, all doubts had been stilled, as Engels wrote many years later.

After the Congress adjourned, Marx and Engels were together in London and Brussels for more than a week before Engels returned to Paris. Marx accepted Engels' suggestion that they drop the catechism form in favor of a "Communist *Manifesto*." Engels later stated that each of them separately drew up a copy; then the final draft was made. More customarily when the two worked together, they would first discuss the matter, after which Engels, who had the more facile and dexterous pen, would rough out a first copy. Then Marx usually made the final alterations and corrections. Responsibility for the final copy of the *Manifesto* was left to Marx after Engels returned to Paris. In later years, Marx once noted appreciatively that a German writer had used the *singular* verb when speaking of their activities. In the same sense he apparently wished to have it known that Marx-Engels *was* the author of the *Manifesto*. As for the contents, there is a marked similarity to the draft of the "Principles of Communism" which Engels brought along from Paris to the London Congress. But there are also conspicuous omissions, additions and changes in stress in the *Manifesto*. Only one page of a manuscript draft of the *Manifesto* has survived. It shows the effort that went into the work. Many words were crossed out as Marx filed away to give the text the desired pungency and edge.

Marx failed to complete the manuscript on schedule. An ultimatum from the *Central Authority* of the League, dated January 25, 1848, demanded delivery by February 1, threatening "further measures" in case of nonperformance. The manuscript then arrived in London before the deadline. It was printed immediately in a 23-page edition under the title, *Manifest der Kommunistischen Partei* (*Manifesto of the Communist Party*), and was ready for distribution to the *Communes* on the eve of the Revolutions of 1848. Later in the year it was reprinted with minor corrections in a 30-page form. In 1872 a new German edition changed the title to *Das Kommunistische Manifest* (*The Communist Manifesto*), as it has been called subsequently. The first edition, printed in the office of the Educational Society for Workers in London, February, 1848, did not carry the names of the authors, as was appropriate for a party platform. The names of Marx and Engels were first linked with the *Manifesto* in the *Foreword* to an English translation by Julian Harney in 1850.

It can be stated that almost everything in the *Manifesto* had already appeared, scattered through various works, especially in the unpublished *The German Ideology*. The *Manifesto*, however, brought it all together in a concentrated form. That was its major virtue. The particular militancy, confident tone, revolutionary élan, indignation, denunciation, survey of the historical past, condemnation of the present and optimistic peep into the bright future were standard items. But because of the comprehensive yet condensed scope of the *Manifesto*, it achieved a special orchestral effect not found elsewhere.

Since the function of the League was normally that of a "propaganda society," it may be assumed that Marx and Engels regarded the *Manifesto* mainly as a propaganda device to be distributed by members of the League. The *Manifesto* would tell its own story and extract the desired emotional response better than any person. Communism, moreover, could not be explained in a simple fashion. It was difficult to be elementary and brief when dealing with a theory that called for a certain understanding of the past, the right grasp of the present and a dialectical leap into the future. Communism was more than a stated set of facts, assumptions and conclusions—communism was equally a state of mind, a mood, a reaction to the world and a specific view of mankind. The force of the *Manifesto* is mainly of an emotional character. It employs the destructive "pathos of indignation" and "denunciation" formula, long recognized by Marx as an effective auxiliary for revolution.

It is commonly recognized that much of the *Manifesto*, in style and content, did not descend to the level of the rank-and-file members of the Communist League, much less to the proletariat in general. Yet by ending with a call to the proletariat to unite and shake off its chains, the impression is given that the *Manifesto* had been directed to the worker all along. Actually, Marx and Engels always assumed that a "Communist consciousness" would soon spring forth from the masses, without much theoretical pump-priming. Once that happened, it was enough that the worker sensed the mood and tone of the *Manifesto* which would stand out clearly in a few simpler paragraphs—above all in a few properly spaced catchwords, phrases and slogans (especially at the beginning and at the end). It did not matter if the proletariat were awed by nine-tenths of the text. A little awe was even helpful.

The contents of the *Manifesto* had little that was new or original. It was a synthesis of accepted or widely current ideas, impressions, prejudices, fears, hopes, historic and economic concepts. It harnessed much that was familiar in the service of revolution to overthrow the existent. Its impact was strongly emotional. Therein lies its strength and appeal. Humanity is asked to accept a supposedly inevitable conflict of classes, social warfare and the inhumanity of revolution, all in the name of humanity and with the promise of a higher humanity. It asked for a war to end all warfare.

Some critics have charged Marx with plagiarism. Indeed, all of the socialist ideas in the Marxian program did come from diverse French and other socialist sources. The Marxian theory of history was fore-shadowed in the works of the French bourgeois historians, Guizot and Thierry, as well as in others. It has even been said that the *Manifesto* was an outright copy of an earlier manifesto drafted by Victor Con-sidérant, a French socialist disciple of Fourier. Marx himself, in a moment of unusual frankness stated * that he was not the originator of many things usually attributed to him. He claimed merely to have discovered and "proved" that (1) the existence of classes was connected only with specific historic developments and conflicts of production; (2) class conflict of necessity led to a dictatorship of the proletariat; (3) this dictatorship in turn was only the transition that led to the abolition of all classes and to a classless society. In short, Marx's own chief claim to originality lay in a "proof" of what would happen in the future.

No attempt will be made here to give a complete analysis of the *Manifesto*. More stress will be placed on the work as a product of the year 1847 and the opening month of 1848 just before the Revolutions of 1848. The *Manifesto* is a reflection of the confidence so typical of Marx and Engels just then, with a program of action attuned to the realities of the age, as they saw them.

The *Manifesto* opens with a prelude that established the optimistic theme that communism was already a European force. A "spectre of communism" was abroad in Europe, with the Pope and Tsar, Metter-

* Letter to Joseph Weydemeyer, March 5, 1852.

nich and Guizot, French radicals and the German police in hot pursuit. Governments denounced the opposition as being Communist, while competing parties hurled the same charge against each other. The *Manifesto* then drew two conclusions from the preceding "data." First, all European states already recognized communism as a power. Second, it was high time that the Communists openly declared their views, aims and tendencies through a party manifesto. It then informed the public that "Communists from the most diverse nationalities" indeed had met already in London and had drafted the following *Manifesto*, to be published in English, French, German, Italian, Flemish and Danish.

Upon reading the above, the casual reader could get the impression that the Communist Party already represented a formidable international force. He could not know that the Congress of the "most diverse nationalities" had consisted almost exclusively of German expatriates, with only a handful of German-speaking persons of other national origins to make it an "international" event. Furthermore he might assume that the specific party that spoke through the *Manifesto* represented that force of "communism" which disturbed much of Europe. A show of confidence and strength is traditional in a party platform. Indeed, pretense and bluff were in the picture. In 1851 Engels stated (letter to Marx, February 13) that for "so and so many years" they had acted as if every Tom, Dick and Harry (*Krethi Plethi*) belonged to their party when they actually had none whatever. And they always regarded the few who were included in an "official" count of party members to be "incorrigible blockheads" who lacked even a most elemental knowledge of their "things" (*Sachen*). Marx and Engels were convinced, however, that the millions would soon be in their camp. So it might just be a case of affirming that which was soon to be.

Actually, as of January, 1848, Europe was completely undisturbed by any knowledge of the new Communist League. When the 1840's spoke of communism, Marx and Engels were not in mind. The age used the word as a collective label for a whole spectrum of labor unrest, fear of mass uprisings, social war and different schools of socialist and communist thought, including the True Socialists, Proudhon and others who were repudiated by the *Manifesto* itself. The *Manifesto* seemed to speak in the name of millions when hundreds were an exaggeration.

The *Manifesto* early asserts that the Communists would publicly reveal their views to all the world. The last paragraph proudly boasts that the "Communists disdain to hide their views." But the intervening pages do not carry out the promise completely. Absolute frankness can be a handicap in a party program. Not everything "belonged before the public," as Engels had put it in the letter of November 23–24. Therefore, the omissions in the *Manifesto* become as eloquent as the inclusions.

The first section, "Bourgeois and Proletarian," a good third of the *Manifesto*, is a survey of world history cut to a simple pattern, pointing to an eventual proletarian triumph and communism. It was necessary to present their principles as "flowing logically and historically out of existing views and past history, and as a necessary continuation thereof," as Engels said earlier. Nothing is more persuasive than the inevitable.

The meaning of all history was wrapped up in a simple sentence, "The history of all previous society is the history of class struggles." This was demonstrated for the Ancient and Medieval worlds by referring to the conflicts of "freeman and slave, patrician and plebian, baron and serf, master and journeyman"—all in two short paragraphs.

The gallop through the early ages slows down to a walk as the *Manifesto* reaches the modern age of capitalism. Much was to be seen and said on the road to the approaching conflict between bourgeoisie and proletariat. Oppression and exploitation became truly hideous with the advent of capitalism. The greater part of the first section of the *Manifesto* is devoted to Marxian proof of the misery of the proletariat, its exploitation by the bourgeoisie, and the certainty that the proletarian revolution would follow. Capitalism in producing the proletariat was rearing its own "gravedigger." So as to make capitalism appear all the more odious, Marx even joined the romanticists in making the Middle Ages seem almost golden. He denounced bourgeois rule for destroying the old "patriarchal, idyllic" conditions. An "unfeeling cash payment" mercilessly cut apart the "chequered feudal ties" that bound the individual to his "natural superior." The bourgeois man even robbed the family tie of its "moving-sentimental veil" and degraded it to a "pure money question." If such statements were taken out of context, it could be argued that Marx admired the good old ways. Nothing could be further from the truth. Normally, Marx and Engels referred to country life, agriculture and religious piety as being on par with barbarism, idiocy, and fanaticism. Cities, trade and industry meant progress and civilization.

The bourgeoisie receives a few words of praise. During less than a hundred years of its "class rule," it had produced "more colossal forces of production than all the preceding centuries." Illustrating this point, the *Manifesto* cites advances in chemistry, railroad construction, telegraphy and other advances that so justly excited the admiration and awe of all. Past centuries had not suspected that "such forces of production slumbered in the lap of social labor."

A few scholars have been awed by this Marxian praise of bourgeois capitalist accomplishments, as a wondrous illustration of Marxian objectivity and fair-mindedness towards the bourgeoisie. Yet it was only the least that he could do without denying his own philosophy of history and the political alliances he proposed elsewhere in the *Manifesto*. Marx and Engels constantly stressed the importance of the growth of bourgeoisie and capitalism. Cities, factories, trade and the bourgeoisie represented progress and civilization in contrast to rural life and agriculture. Capitalist production and the factory system had to appear; without them there could be no proletariat in the Marxian sense. Capitalism also had to produce the foundations for an industrial system that a communist revolution in turn could confiscate. Much as Marx and Engels denounced the bourgeoisie, for the time being they wished it every success.

Actually, the bourgeoisie was praised only for its material, technological and scientific progress. Even so, credit for such advances was attributed to "social labor." Often enough Marx and Engels made clear that under real "social" communist control much more would be accomplished. In Question 20 of the "Principles of Communism" Engels had stated, "Large industry, freed from the burden of private property, will grow to such a degree that its present development will appear just as petty as manufacturing by hand when compared to the large industries of our day."

The second section of the *Manifesto*, "Proletarians and Communists," staked out the ground that the Communist Party was to occupy, with reference to the proletarians at large (other labor parties). It disclaimed any special interests and principles that set it apart from the proletarian movement as a whole. But the Communists were unique because they spoke for all of the proletariat, regardless of national frontiers. They also represented the "interests of the total movement" throughout each of the successive stages of the bourgeois-proletarian conflict. Communism was an "expression of the actual conditions of an existing class conflict, of a historical movement going on before our own eyes." In practice, the Communists were the "most determined, ever-forward-driving party" of all the labor parties. In theory, they were in advance of the "remaining mass of the proletariat" because of their "understanding of the conditions, the course and the general results of the proletarian movement." The *Manifesto* wished to make clear that communism was not just another set of "ideas or principles invented or discovered by this or that world-improver"; communism was anchored in reality and historical facts.

The *Manifesto* then replied to the various charges that had been raised against the Communists, involving such sensitive issues as their stand on marriage, religion, the "eternal verities," patriotism and self-earned property. The *Manifesto* rarely answered in a frank, pertinent manner. Instead, it either raised a digressing question of its own or hurled back a counter charge against the bourgeoisie. In the process the reader often

1. Marx as a student at the
University in Bonn (1835).
A photograph taken from
a highly romantic
painting of a student
group in Bonn.

2. Friedrich Engels,
a youthful profile.

3. Friedrich Engels, as a Prussian artillerist in Berlin, 1841.

4. Jenny Marx, the daughter of a Prussian nobleman— the belle of the ballroom in her youth, circa 1843.

5. Jenny Marx with her oldest daughter, Jenny.

6. Pierre-Joseph Proudhon, the French socialist and reformer whose influence Marx attempted to destroy, unsuccessfully, over many years.

7. Title page of the *German-French Yearbooks*, one double issue which appeared in 1844.

8. Title page of *The Holy Family, or Critique of Critical Criticism*, the first joint work of Marx and Engels.

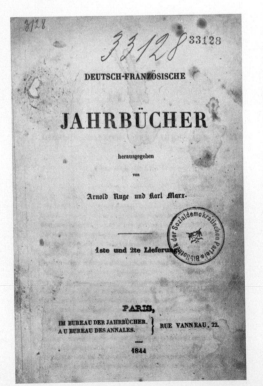

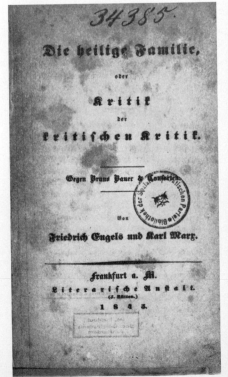

9. Moses Hess, the "first Communist," an early associate of Marx and Engels.

10. Title page of *The Poverty of Philosophy. Response to the Philosophy of Poverty of M. Proudhon*, written and published in French.

11. Title page of the *Communist Manifesto*, as it appeared in 1848 with the title, *Manifesto of the Communist Party*, without the names of Marx and Engels as the authors.

12. An allegorical presentation of Marx as Prometheus, chained to a printing press, following the suppression of the *Rheinische Zeitung* in 1843.

13. Karl Marx, the *Redakteur en chef,* in a formal, pensive pose, circa 1848/49.

14. Marx's passport, granted by the French Provisional Republican Government, to "Charles Marx," on March 30, 1848, and valid for one year.

15. The expulsion order of August 16, 1849, in which the French government ordered Marx to leave Paris, to reside in the Department of Morbihan.

loses track of the original question, or is apt to wonder how any persons as villainous and contemptible as the bourgeoisie ever had the right to raise questions in the first place, let alone throw stones. When the *Manifesto* does offer an answer in what appears to be a bold and forthright manner, the reply is usually limited to a harmless fraction of the original charge, or to a question so rephrased that a clear-cut yes or no gives nothing away. Denunciation was an easy substitute for an answer that was difficult to give or withhold. The success of the *Manifesto* in the century that followed proves that Marx had the right tactical touch. In contrast, Engels had provided answers in his "Principles of Communism" that were far clearer, more to the point and often more complete than those found in the *Manifesto*.

The section ends with a brief description of the Communists' policies after the overthrow of the bourgeoisie. The first step in the "worker revolution" was to be the elevation of the "proletariat to the position of ruling class, the winning of the battle of democracy (*die Erkämpfung der Demokratie*)." * Just as Marx and Engels made a point of being present when anything "democratic" was scheduled, so it was appropriate for the party platform to include some reference to the democracy with which they were trying to establish tactical alliances. What better way could there be than to declare that the first step of the Communists after seizing power was the same as winning the battle of democracy? Democracy was thus brought into the *Manifesto* in the briefest form, in a place where it would do the most good and the least harm.

Engels had been more explicit and detailed in Question 18 of his "Principles." He spoke of setting up a "*democratic constitution* and thereby the direct or indirect political domination of the proletariat." In such a democracy, the small farmers and the petty bourgeoisie would have to submit to the proletariat. He foresaw a probable second battle to conclude the process. Then he made it clear that "Democracy would be entirely useless for the proletariat if it were not used as a means whereby further steps would be taken immediately to attack private property directly and to secure the existence of the proletariat." Marx apparently thought that was saying too much; he recognized that the Communists were not yet capable of winning any revolutionary skirmishes in their own name.

For the time being it was necessary for them to gain the confidence of the potentially democratic masses—the workers, peasants and petty bourgeoisie—and to join them in order to speed up the process of revolution in general. It must not be known that the "proletariat" regarded democracy as a passing phase or as a mere expedient towards the

---

* This step was later called the establishment of a dictatorship of the proletariat, of course under communist leadership.

Communists' goal. Marx and Engels, moreover, always assumed that the peasants and petty bourgeoisie would follow the lead of the proletariat, as the ultimate revolutionary class to whom the future belonged. By running with the Democrats everywhere, joining them in a loose democratic front, the Communists could hope to impart the needed energy, decision and direction to each revolutionary movement. At the same time, this would place them in a good strategic position for the final round against the bourgeoisie.

The policies that the Communists would follow once they acquired power are outlined in two paragraphs: The state (the proletariat organized as the ruling class) would progressively seize all capital and instruments of production, which would be utilized to increase the productive forces as rapidly as possible.* Marx admitted that some of the measures would appear economically inadequate and untenable. Yet they were needed to keep things unsettled and moving in the direction of a complete revolution. The more specific measures to be adopted would vary with each country. Marx allowed for tactical adjustments to suit the circumstances.

There was nothing uniquely Marxian in the ten points of the socialist program in the *Manifesto,* which was to be "rather generally" initiated in the most advanced countries. (Marx always included Britain, France, Germany and the United States as leading states.) These steps correspond largely to the twelve demands that Engels listed in his "Principles." Marx, however, produced the shorter text, as when speaking of democracy. Other changes or omissions are interesting.

The most significant change in the *Manifesto* resulted from the fact that it was written with the coming revolution in Germany, notably in Prussia, in mind. In the historical process, Germany lagged one revolution behind France, Britain and Belgium. To speed history along, the Communists were to join the bourgeoisie in their destined role of toppling kings, aristocracy, church and bureaucracy in favor of liberal bourgeois institutions, parliamentary government, and a bill of rights.

The *Manifesto,* as a tactical guideline for the Communists, had to avoid advocating any drastic program that would frighten the bourgeoisie unduly. Therefore in that respect the *Manifesto* is even more cautious than Engels' "Principles of Communism." Thus, the "Principles" had called for the following: "gradual expropriation" of factory owners; the establishment of state factories that would force the "manufacturers, as long as they still survive," to pay the same "high wages" and "forced loans." The *Manifesto* merely asked for a "high progressive tax" and an "increase in national factories, instruments of production. . . ."

---

* This is the dictatorship-of-the-proletariat phase, comparable to the 20th century regime in Russia, lasting from 1917 to the present.

Whereas the "Principles" had asked for the "suppression of all private banks and bankers," the *Manifesto* softened the demand to a "centralization of credit in the hands of the state through a national bank with state capital and an exclusive monopoly."

On the other hand, the *Manifesto* actually placed a proportionally heavier stress on "agrarian reform," directed against the large estates and land holdings of the aristocracy and kings, as prevailed in Prussia, than did Engels' "Principles." The *Manifesto* demanded the following: "expropriation of property in land and the use of its income for state purposes"; "increased cultivation and improvement of land in accordance with a general plan," accompanied by the "creation of industrial armies, especially for agriculture"; the "union of the pursuit of agriculture and industry, aiming at the gradual elimination of the gap between country and city." Engels' "Principles" had merely advocated a "gradual expropriation" of land and does not mention state appropriation of its income.

It is interesting to speculate why the *Manifesto* failed to adopt certain other portions of Engels' "Principles," for example, Engels' demand for slum clearance, the "destruction of all unhealthy and badly constructed buildings in urban areas." Engels also had called for the confiscation of the property of "rebels against the majority of the people" (proletariat) whereas the *Manifesto* in the same connection spoke only of "rebels." Both the *Manifesto* and the "Principles" felt that children should work while getting an education so as to produce the well-rounded communist person. The *Manifesto*, however, merely wanted factory work for children abolished in its "contemporary form."

Just two paragraphs of the *Manifesto* are used to present a preview of the communist world of the future. The picture is hazy with only the miseries of the bourgeois capitalist world clearly visible far below and behind.

When in the "course of developments class differences disappear and all production is concentrated in the hands of the associated individuals, public power loses its political character." Presumably, as Marx and Engels put it, the government would just "wither away." The ensuing classless society, the final goal of the Communists, is described in exactly twenty-nine German words: "In place of the old civil society with its classes and class conflicts, an association appears in which the free development of each is the condition for the free development of all."

This look into a misty future is befogged still further by the use of the word "association." Marx and Engels usually avoided the word that (like "organization of labor") had become one of the passwords of every person with proper social sentiments. But "association" sounded well in a party platform. It carried the mystic appeal of a promised land where people would be "associated," in direct contrast to rough and rugged individualism, unlimited competition, and private initiative.

Concrete details in regard to the future were difficult to give. It was easy to promise that agricultural and industrial production would be vastly increased, with proper planning and organization by society. But that was merely socialism. The communism of Marx and Engels demanded much more—it required the creation of a new human being.

Engels' Question 20 of the "Principles" made clear that science and machines were not enough. Communist production, in order to succeed, "would require and would breed entirely new men." Training and education would rapidly acquaint young men with the "whole system of production," enabling them to turn from one branch of industry to the next, in "accordance with the needs of society and their own inclinations." The old division of labor under which "one was a farmer, the other a shoemaker, the third a factory worker, the fourth a speculator in stocks" would have to end. Mobility was needed. For this reason the gap between city and country also would have to disappear. Farming and manufacturing would go hand in hand, with farmers who manufactured, and manufacturers who farmed. The *Manifesto* merely hints at all of this.

The *Manifesto* could not project a clear picture of the future communist world, except in very general terms, and yet remain true to the Marxian theory of history. According to that theory, all ideas, principles, institutions, cultures, religion, laws, morals and social relations reflected the interests of the dominant class. There was no certainty, however, as to the shape of the institutions and ideals the new proletarian classless man would prefer. Engels illustrated the dilemma well in the 1870's when he wrote on the future form of marriage. After freeing the communist couple from every drawback and objection that he found in the existing institution of marriage, there still was no clear picture of wedlock in a communist society. He then asked rhetorically how could one expect to anticipate and to dictate the form that marriage would take in a classless society? The people then would have their own rules and laws.

What the *Manifesto* requires is the acceptance of the historical dialectic as interpreted by Marx and Engels. This in turn demands an act of faith, coupled with an emotional, intellectual and aesthetic repudiation of the existing society. But the dialectic was of little use in filling in the more concrete details of a future society. That would be left to the new Communist Man, created by forceful revolution, nurtured by a classless society, and conditioned by a proletarian dictatorship. Marx and Engels recognized that without the Communist Man, communism was impossible.

The whole case of the communist society hinges on the creation of this new man. Otherwise it remains only a dream or a deception. Many scholars, impressed by the apparent sameness of the basic instincts and motives that have governed the behavior of man throughout thousands of years of recorded history, will remain skeptical. Marx, an avid reader of history and literature (ranging from Homer through Shakespeare to Sir Walter Scott), seems to have had no such doubts.

The third part of the *Manifesto* carries a misleading title, "Socialist and Communist Literature." It was actually an attack on all other varieties of socialism and communism, which Marx and Engels attempted to dismiss as so much "literature." This part is frequently omitted in 20th century English reprints of the *Manifesto* on the grounds that it is outdated and contains so little on Marxian theory. But it contains much information on Marx and Engels—demonstrating the intensity of their attack on all competing schools of socialist and communist thought, and the application of their theory of history to explain away, discredit and overcome such views.

Marx and Engels, in effect, denied the validity of any solution and theory that differed from their own. Consistent with their theory that ideas reflected merely class and economic interests, they placed a bourgeois, petty-bourgeois or feudal label on most competing socialist systems. Such classification made it possible to denounce and deride them as being hypocritical, self-seeking and reactionary. Others were described as once having been progressive during an earlier stage of capitalist society. But they were now passé, purely utopian or reactionary, since they mirrored the realities of a period already dead and irrelevant.

Some socialist and communist writers were dismissed as literary opportunists who turned to social questions as the popular thing to do; they represented no real political force. Others, such as St. Simon, Fourier and Owen, listed under the classification of "critical-utopian socialism and communism," were shown some respect. As representatives of the "first, undeveloped period of conflict between proletariat and bourgeoisie," they had been the authors of good critiques of the old society and of "positive concepts regarding the future society." But their importance stood in an "inverse ratio" to historical progress. They had once been revolutionary, but now their followers were reactionary and wanted reform as a means of avoiding class conflict.

Under the heading, "Conservative or Bourgeois Socialism," are listed the bourgeois "economists, philanthropists, humanitarians, improvers-of-the-lot-of-the-workers, organizers of charity, repealers of cruelty to animals and petty reformers of the most chequered varieties." Their socialism consisted of the "claim that the bourgeois were bourgeois-in-the-interest of the working class." Proudhon was the only name mentioned.

As might be expected, the *Manifesto* directed its heaviest volley against the "German or the 'True' Socialism." Its "smutty, enervated literature" reflected a mixture of German philosophy and French socialism. Its garment was made out of a "speculative cobweb, embroidered with aesthetic metaphors, saturated with love-sticky sentimental dew." The True Socialists talked too much of "alienation" and the "realization of human essence." Marx was never more eloquent than when blasting his fellow Germans. He knew their language and had gone through the same schools.

The common denominator of all complaints against the socialists was their lack of revolutionary zeal. Engels likewise had classified the competing socialists and Communists in his "Principles." He, however, had employed a style that was briefer, more calmly analytical and less denunciatory. Furthermore, he had also listed another category, the *"Democratic Socialists,"* which certainly was justified by the facts. This omission from the *Manifesto* may have been due to the fact that Marx considered it impolitic to denounce anything democratic.

The final section of the *Manifesto,* less than two pages in length, outlines the "Position of the Communists toward the Oppositional Parties," namely, the parties in opposition to existing governments. The guideline was given in the sentence, "The Communists everywhere support every revolutionary movement against the existing social and political conditions." They joined with the Chartists in England, the "agrarian reformers" in the U.S.A. and with the Social-Democrats in France. Among the Poles, the Communists supported the party that carried the banner of "agrarian revolution" and had inspired the abortive uprising of 1846 in Cracow. Where no substantial bourgeoisie existed as a revolutionary force against aristocracy and feudalism, "agrarian reform" served as a revolutionary lever.

The *Manifesto* continues,

> In Germany, the Communist Party fights on the side of the bourgeoisie as soon as they act in a revolutionary way against the absolute monarchy, the feudal property in land and the petty bourgeoisie. But the Communists do not for a single moment neglect to bring to the workers a clear understanding of the hostile conflict between bourgeoisie and proletariat. This enables the worker to open the fight against the bourgeoisie immediately after the fall of the reactionary classes, using as so many weapons against the bourgeoisie the very social and political conditions [freedom of speech, press, assembly, association, etc.] which the bourgeoisie would have to introduce when it acquires power.

The Communists direct their main attention on Germany because it is on the eve of a bourgeois liberal revolution. This upheaval above all [will] take place under more advanced conditions of European civilization and with a more developed proletariat than in England in the 17th and France in the 18th century. The German bourgeois revolution therefore can only be the immediate prelude to a proletarian revolution.

Engels in his "Principles" had predicted that revolutions would take place concurrently in the "civilized lands," at least in England, America, France and Germany. The degree of industrialization and wealth would determine the pace of revolutionary developments in each case. An advanced England would move along with the greatest speed and ease, while a backward Germany would move "most slowly and with the greatest difficulty." Engels' predictions are more in harmony with the economic explanation of historical change. Perhaps Marx, in contrast, still hoped that the philosophic Germans could make no revolution without doing a thorough job. In any event, the *Manifesto*, which was directed mainly to the Germans, had to assure the German proletariat that their triumph lay close at hand, just one revolutionary hurdle away.

After making a final bow to democracy with the promise that the Communists everywhere promoted ties and agreements between democratic parties of all countries, the *Manifesto* closes in a revolutionary mood matched only by the confidence expressed in the preamble:

> The Communists disdain to hide their views and purposes. They declare openly that their aims can be reached only through the forceful subversion of all past social orders. May the ruling classes tremble before a communist revolution. The proletarians have nothing to lose by it except their chains. They have a world to win.
> Proletarians of all countries, unite!

Paradoxically, in respect to its success today, when the *Manifesto* first appeared in 1848, it suffered from the embarrassment that accompanies the birth of an untimely child. Marx and Engels showed none of the optimistic expectations so evident in connection with all their other publications. Nor did they make the usual attempt to publicize the work. Even in the following fifteen years, they seldom referred to it. A regular second edition did not appear until the 1870's, although there were various unauthorized printings. Ultimately however, Marx and Engels recognized the *Manifesto* as a child who had succeeded and brought honor to his parents.

PART THREE

The Revolution

=I=

Springtime of Revolution

1. THE LULL BEFORE THE STORM

Even while Marx was weighing every word and applying the last polish to the *Manifesto*, the revolution that was to introduce a series of revolutions in Europe was only weeks away. Though millions were expecting revolution, either with eagerness or fear, neither the place nor the time (Paris, February 22, 1848) was foreseen by anyone, not even by De Tocqueville, who had warned the French Parliament late in January that "France stood on top of a volcano."

Throughout 1847 the increasing liberal, national and social protests, followed by revolution and the granting of constitutions in small countries or peripheral areas, had pointed to the slow gathering of a general storm. Although a Polish national revolt in Cracow and Galicia (the Austrian share of partitioned Poland) had been suppressed in 1846, everybody was sure that the Poles were irrepressible. Switzerland had electrified Europe during the fall of 1847 when the progressive and nationally-minded cantons overpowered the reactionary cantons in a brief war to establish a closer union. The Germans celebrated the event with a song that opened with the words, "In the highlands the first shot was fired." Liberals and nationalists in Germany and Italy felt that they would be firing the next round. They also wanted their countries to be united and free.

In Germany all eyes had turned to Prussia when the United Diet met on April 11, 1847. Although the Liberals failed to gain their ends before the Diet was dismissed by the King on June 26, Germans everywhere were less impressed by the rebuff than inspired by the courageous stand of the liberal majority. In Bavaria public resentment, expressed by student demonstrations, ultimately forced the romantic King Ludwig to face a future without the charms of the Irish-born, Spanish-named Lola

Montez. It was a revolution of comic opera proportions, but the eviction of Lola nevertheless represented a victory over royal caprice. On September 12, 1847, a group of radical German Republicans, prompted by Gustav von Struve and Friedrich Hecker, met in Offenburg in South Germany where they drafted a program calling for a German Parliament in a free and united Germany. They also demanded protection for the worker and a guarantee of employment, in response to the social sentiments of the age. A group of moderate Liberals met in Heppenheim in October and adopted a platform requesting a constitutional monarchy for a united Germany as well as liberal institutions in the separate states. Similar petitions and parliamentary motions in other localities gave added proof of the increasing strength of national and liberal sentiments. Conversely, such actions demonstrated that governments were losing confidence in their capacity to stifle protests.

Austria, long regarded as the bastion of reaction and stable government, began to show signs of an internal collapse, apparent even in the censored theatre. The most popular hit of the day on the Vienna stage revolved about an old and faithful servant of the house who had outlived his usefulness. All Vienna knew that the servant represented Metternich, long identified with the House of Habsburg. Various noblemen published works outside of Austria, warning of disaster if Habsburg policy remained unchanged in a world that moved. Liberals in Vienna, Budapest and Prague, meanwhile, began to meet informally to reach agreement on a minimum program. But the gravest threat was barely recognized before 1848. Only a few sensed that national feeling—as nurtured by scholars, poets and historians—could develop into irreconcilable animosities that threatened to split the Habsburg monarchy apart. The conflicting aims of Germans, Czechs, Poles, Ukrainians, Hungarians, Slovaks, Rumanians, Serbs, Croats, Slovenes and Italians guaranteed a diversified, but unexpectedly brutal, show. Italian national fury against Austria was already inflamed by clashes between soldiers and civilians in areas under Habsburg rule.

Italy seemed to be on the brink of a liberal transformation at the start of 1848. Embarrassed and challenged by the reforms that Pius IX had introduced in the Papal States, Charles Albert, King of Sardinia, Ferdinand II, King of the Two Sicilies, and Grand Duke Leopold of Tuscany kept pace by granting liberal constitutions to their own people.

France concurrently seemed to be enjoying the most stable government in Europe. Guizot and Louis Philippe commanded a solid parliamentary majority in support of a program of immobility. But the French continued to protest by organizing banquets, climaxed by toasts and speeches that demanded reforms, denounced corruption and deplored the personal rule of Louis Philippe. Preparations were made for a spectacular banquet to be held right in Paris on the evening of February 22, 1848.

The climax of the Hungry Forties in Europe came when the depression of 1847 brought business failures, unemployment and frequent reduction in wages. Every third family in Cologne received public relief. The scope of this disaster attracted universal attention. We find it mentioned in the correspondence of an untold number of persons. The columns of the True Socialist *Trier'sche Zeitung*, edited by Karl Grün, were filled with the sombre details. Marx and Engels, however, stand out curiously as persons who wrote little, and then only casually, about the tragedy that struck millions, especially the laboring classes.

Engels, in deriding the poet Beck, almost seemed to welcome the potato crop failure as a blow against the bourgeois order. He and Marx even neglected to criticize the authorities (as others were doing) for not providing timely relief. Perhaps they felt that such criticism might be interpreted to mean that an existing government, if it did enough in the right way, could alleviate poverty. At this time Marx and Engels even seemed oblivious to the fact that food shortages and suffering might hasten the advent of the expected revolution. But they noted every other popular tremor and reported it as a revolutionary portent.

During this period Marx and Engels' major emphasis was on the creation of a democratic front. In connection with this, they were in a position to persuade members of the democratic and worker-societies that the existing bourgeois capitalist society was inherently incapable of producing a better world for which men yearned. They did not, however, openly propagate communism as such. They operated on the assumption that, once the faith in a capitalist economy and existing form of government vanished, people's minds would cast about for a new answer and find it in communism.

To educate the workers, Marx began a series of lectures on economic and social questions during the last half of December, 1847. He spoke before the German Worker-Society of Brussels, which the Communists had organized to serve as an open recruiting agency for the League and as a medium through which the Communists could reach other workers. (All of the officers of the Society were members of the Communist League.) Marx's lectures, on the subject of wages and capital, presented the well-thumbed proof that wages represented just another commodity, that they would be merely high enough to keep the workers alive and able to rear enough children to prevent any future labor shortage. Apparently he had the ability to expound his ideas patiently in a simple form that the workers could grasp. In any event he repeated the same lecture before other labor societies in the next years. Later, the lectures, obviously touched up for publication, were printed under the title, "Wages and Capital."

Bakunin, who attended sessions of the Worker-Society during a short stay in Brussels at the end of 1847, expressed his disgust in a letter shortly thereafter. He declared that Marx was still guilty of "the same theoretical insanity and unquenched self-satisfaction," and was spoiling the workers by making them argumentative. "Lies and stupidities, stupidities and lies," Bakunin stated. He refused to join such a society where it was impossible to breathe freely.

Marx's lectures in Brussels seem to have attracted considerable attention. In any event, Adolf Bartels, the well-known Belgian Liberal, writing in the *Journal de Bruxelles* attacked the outsiders who played the "schoolmaster" in Belgium by promoting "nasty and barbarian theories." Marx replied to Bartels' charges in the *Deutsche-Brüsseler-Zeitung* of December 19, 1847. He and Bornstedt followed this up with a personal call at the editorial offices of the *Journal de Bruxelles* to register a direct protest against this denunciation of "foreigners."

Marx remained undaunted by Belgian protests. Thereafter he proceeded to orientate the Belgian Democratic Association in a proletarian direction. He addressed the Association on January 9, 1848, on the subject of free trade, using the topic mainly as an introduction to the familiar speech on wages and the hopeless case of the worker in a capitalist society. Since he quoted extensively from the current catalog of economic concepts, the address was weighted with enough learning to command respect. Six sessions were devoted to discussing the subject. The address was then published as a pamphlet, at the expense of the Democratic Association.

The Belgian press again expressed an angry recognition of Marx's success among Belgian democrats. Without mentioning names, the Brussels *Le Débat social*, a radical democratic paper, referred to certain teachings at six meetings of the Democratic Association. It expressed confidence that those of its readers who were members of the Association wanted none of the "utopias pursued by certain democrats from countries whose social institutions ruled out any hope of practical reform" and where it was easy to "dream of castles in Spain" and "millions." Marx, replying in the *Brüsseler-Zeitung* of February 13, concluded that *Le Débat* was attacking Communists, not just Communists in general, but "*German Communists*." He in turn expressed confidence that Germany, a land of forty million, "would not look to the radicalism of small free lands for a pattern on which to base its own movement when it prepared for revolution."

As Vice President of the Democratic Association, Marx also was instrumental in the promotion of international connections. Responding to the initiative of the Fraternal Democrats, the Association opened a monthly correspondence with that English society. Arrangements were approved "unanimously and with great enthusiasm" for an international democratic congress to be held in Brussels the following September, according to the Democratic Association's report of February 13.

The same report also spoke of affiliated branches being organized in other Belgian communities. Marx himself was a member of a delegation that went to Ghent to establish a branch there. A second meeting in Ghent attracted over three thousand people; happily most of them were workers. This reflected a "revival of a pure democratic movement," and was decisive for the entire worker movement in Belgium. Belgian "democracy" was gravitating in a proletarian direction. Ultimately, it was hoped, there would be a "strong, united and democratic party."

The year 1848 began auspiciously for Marx in one other respect. For the first time he had enough money in hand to take care of the year ahead. Financial problems always plagued Karl and Jenny Marx and the year 1847 had been no exception.

Marx once admitted to Engels that his marriage, ironically, was "more productive than his work." Yet he was perhaps a little proud that he was a "family father who was strong in the loins." Two children were added during the Brussels period. A second daughter, Laura, was born in 1846, followed by the big event of 1847, a son named Edgar in honor of Jenny's brother, Edgar von Westphalen. This son was Marx's favorite and his early death was one of the great tragedies in Marx's life for which the three surviving girls offered no solace. Nonetheless, Marx's attachment to his daughters was very close.

When Stephan Born arrived in Brussels late in 1847, he found the Marx family living in a "highly modest, one can even say poorly furnished, small dwelling in a suburb of Brussels." But he saw nothing poor in the family relations. It was a most happy marriage. Jenny herself was a blonde, in striking contrast to the children who had the dark hair and eyes of the "Moor." She took a very direct interest in all of the affairs and aspirations of her husband. Externally and in her emotions and mind, Jenny Marx was "a most harmoniously constituted person." She was anything but the typical German *Hausfrau* whose skill was cooking and knitting. (They always had the services of the faithful servant, Lenchen Demuth, to take care of the drudgery.)

Expenses in the Marx household were always high. Jenny did not have the knack for good management, while Marx himself was constantly amazed and puzzled by the speed with which money passed through his hands. Moreover, he believed in putting up a pretense of well-being.

He just refused to live on a proletarian level. From a purely "mercantile" point of view, as he once wrote to Engels, it was necessary for him to put up a certain front.

The only surviving letter (dated May 15, 1847) from Marx to Engels written before 1848 shows Marx's financial desperation at that time. After informing Engels that he could not go to the first Communist Congress because of a lack of money, he stated that he was drafting several bills of exchange, payable on sight after thirty days and drawn against Moses Hess and Bernays. The step was so risky that he instructed Engels (in Paris) to take all necessary precautions to make sure that nothing backfired. To add to the general complications, he had just submitted to a blood-letting in his right arm. When he continued to work with that arm, an infection had set in and there was the danger that he might lose his writing arm.

To escape the chronic shortage of money, Marx visited his uncle in Holland late in September, 1848. He hoped to get an advance on the sum that he was to inherit from his father's estate, even though the will of Heinrich Marx stipulated that nothing was to be withdrawn until after the death of the mother. This business of getting "some coin" from a "marauding excursion into Holland, in the land of the fathers, of tobacco and of cheese," as Jenny Marx described a similar expedition many years later, required time and skill. (Jenny's letters reflected the mood, tone and cynicism of Marx himself to a remarkable degree.) "It was necessary to find the right tack, to express diplomacy and to maneuvre enormously." But Marx, who could play the part of a first rate diplomat and solicitor, was equal to the occasion.

Before relief came from Holland, however, Marx had to resort to other expedients. On November 9, he had asked his brother-in-law in Maastricht, W. R. Schmalhausen (Sophie's husband), to loan him a "bigger sum." Schmalhausen did send 150 *francs* on November 15. While in London for the second Communist Congress, Marx anticipated another shortage. At that time he wrote to the Russian Annenkow, then in Paris, asking him to send a loan of 100 to 200 *francs* to Brussels.

The Dutch "raid" of 1847 ultimately brought relief in 1848. In January, Marx received 6000 *francs* from his future inheritance; he was also freed from the obligations of 1200 *Taler* advanced to him by his mother in 1843. Thus Marx was free from pecuniary worries during the Revolutions of 1848/49 that lay just ahead.

Engels was equally on the move during the two months preceding the Revolutions of 1848. Following the London Congress, he spent a week or so with Marx in Brussels and then hurried off to Paris around December 21. Engels was in a confident mood. Both the Fraternal Democrats in London and the Democratic Association in Brussels had asked him to represent them in Paris. With the weight of these two new credentials in his pocket, he hoped to establish an alliance with French democracy—as initiated earlier and as outlined again in the forthcoming *Manifesto.*

Engels' first task was to persuade Louis Blanc to work with them, but he had a difficult time trying to see Blanc. No one had taken the trouble to tell him that the "little literary would-be-great" received people only on Thursday and then only in the afternoon. When he finally broke through that barrier, he found that Blanc was too impressed with his own success to risk anything in an alliance of doubtful value.

Engels had better results with Flocon, the editor of *La Réforme,* though Flocon was initially disturbed when Engels informed him that he and Marx had decided to "appear publicly as Communists." Flocon ruefully remarked: "You show a tendency toward despotism; you will kill revolution in France. We have eleven million small peasants who are the most fanatic owners of property." Nevertheless, after much bluster and protest, Flocon stated that the views of the Social Democrats and the Communists were close enough for them to move forward together; they would support the Communists as much as possible.

Engels had less success getting the rank-and-file members of the three Communist *Communes* in Paris to behave like Marxian Communists. In a gloomy report to Marx on January 14 he wrote that the affairs of the League in Paris were going "miserably." Petty jealousy and sleepiness were the order of the day. He did his utmost to facilitate the distribution of the *Brüsseler-Zeitung,* now almost the official Marxian *Organ,* among the German workers, but the ideas of Weitling and Proudhon best expressed the "mode of living of these donkeys." He would make one more attempt to promote their views, but if that failed, he was withdrawing from that type of propaganda. He hoped that the "London papers" would arrive soon and liven things up a bit.

As for the anticipated "London papers," this probably meant the circular letter that the *Central Authority* was supposed to send out covering the decisions of the Congress. Some scholars assume that Engels meant the *Manifesto.* Perhaps he did think of the *Manifesto* as included in a pack of "London papers"—such a casual reference to it would not have been out of line with the thinking of Marx and Engels just then.

Engels was responsible for most of the journalistic writings on the eve of revolution. In presenting news of an oncoming tide of unrest, Engels helped to encourage incipient revolutionary movements and simultaneously to orient the Communists in regard to their proper role in each particular revolution. When he wrote for the English in the *Northern Star* and for the French in *La Réforme,* he emphasized democracy and the growth of democratic protest. When he wrote for the German reader of the *Brüsseler-Zeitung*, he turned to the growth of bourgeois confidence and the promise of early bourgeois liberal triumphs.

On January 27, Engels optimistically predicted "The Beginning of the End in Austria." A bourgeois victory was near in that land of "concentrated barbarism" (rural life was not civilized in Engels' view) and "organized jumble of ten languages and nationalities." He hoped that the bourgeoisie who seized power in Vienna would be a "real low, real dirty, real Jewish bourgeoisie." Austria deserved no better; she gave the Germans the reputation of being despicable mercenaries of a despotism that had oppressed Poles, Czechs and Italians—and had pilloried the Germans also. Even the disruptive force of national feeling did not temper Engels' optimism. Trade, better communications and the growth of the bourgeoisie and a proletariat produced "certain common tendencies and interests" that would close the gap between ten different nations in the Austrian Empire. In a second article, mainly dealing with the events of 1847, Engels reviewed bourgeois triumphs in Italy, Switzerland, Belgium, Britain and the United States (referring to the American conquest of Mexican territory).

There was one curious omission in Engels' survey of events in 1847—he completely ignored the bold and provocative meeting of South German Liberals at Heppenheim and the radical platform drafted by equally outspoken Republicans at Offenburg. Engels did not approve of the South Germans—they were too doctrinaire in politics. Moreover, the South Germans tended to favor a federal union of all German states. Salvation could not come from them. Anyway, Marx and Engels never believed that small states could make history. Prussia, however, cast a bigger shadow.

In Prussia, Engels anticipated another crisis soon, perhaps in 1849. So confident was he of bourgeois successes that he already congratulated them on their victory and day of triumph. But he concluded with the quotation from Heine, "The hangman waits outside the door."

Engels' final article before the actual outbreak of revolution continued the tale of bourgeois triumphs outside Germany. Everything was moving along splendidly—only the forty million Germans remained inactive. They were hesitating because they recognized that their revolution would be a most serious affair. It would occur in the context of a war between East and West (reminiscent of the French Revolutionary wars). Moreover, the German bourgeoisie was acting in a cowardly, indecisive manner, because they already feared the threat of a growing proletariat as much as they disliked the existing governments. Engels apparently sensed that the liberal bourgeoisie might refuse to act as the witless instruments of history, automatically destined to destroy monarchy and aristocracy.

Engels did not remain long in Paris. On January 29, the French government ordered him to leave France; he rejoined Marx in Brussels on the 31st. The circumstances surrounding his expulsion remained unclear. A Paris journal stated that the expulsion was not for political reasons. The *Brüsseler-Zeitung* of February 24, 1848, reported that Engels "in a few words explained the circumstances surrounding his eviction" at a meeting of the Brussels Democratic Association. But the paper did not print the account, except to say that the Association was satisfied with the explanation. Engels himself never claimed the laurels that went to those who were the victims of governmental action on political grounds. Yet some scholars insist that he was expelled because of revolutionary activity among the workers. The workers, however, were Germans—Engels' success among members of the Communist League in Paris was no cause for alarm.

Stephan Born may well have given the correct explanation. He was close to Marx and Engels at this time, and Engels confided in him. According to Born, Engels was outraged when he heard of the affair of a certain French aristocrat, Count X, who had rejected his established mistress without making any appropriate financial arrangement for her future. Engels then threatened the Count with an exposé of the whole affair. The account is consistent with Engels' personality. (Engels himself always considered his own arrangement with Mary Burns as having the same sanctity as a legal tie, entailing certain obligations in the event of a rupture.) It also explains Engels' own silence in the matter. He had found that others did not grasp the essence of his code of morals, in the question of women and marriage.

2. THE FEBRUARY BARRICADES

EUROPE was still in the late winter doldrums when the Revolutions of 1848 began with a flourish that only France, the *grand* nation, could provide. When the French government belatedly forbade the holding of a gigantic reform banquet in Paris on February 22, a restless crowd gathered anyway, robbed of the opportunity to protest, or to watch others do so. On the 23rd, the masses shouted "Reform" and "Down with Guizot." The issue was decided by the 24th, once the celebrated barricades appeared in the streets as a defense and rallying point of revolution and as a barrier to the movement of troops. France had called for reform and stumbled into revolution. The King, Louis Philippe, lost courage, gave up his Crown and with unroyal haste left for the safety of England. Paris made the revolution. The rest of France heard of it via telegraphic dispatch, as one French official proudly stated—a tribute to the 19th century revolution in communications.

Marx, in retrospect, derided the February Revolution as the "beautiful revolution." There was none of the class warfare that people had feared and predicted for a decade. Instead, a spirit of fraternization ruled, reassuring to the millions who abhorred the fratricidal strife, vengeance and terror that had marred the Great French Revolution. The old opposition parties and the editorial offices of the republican newspapers (*La Réforme* and *National*) each prepared a list of persons to serve in a new provisional government. The original group, moderately republican in sentiment, was broadened to include Louis Blanc and Ferdinand Flocon, in response to popular clamor in Paris, mass demonstrations and the social inclinations of the age. Ultimately, an almost nameless worker (usually referred to merely as Albert, his first name) was added to the list and he served his country well by not trying to make a name for himself.

The Provisional Government proclaimed a republic, although most observers noted that there were few Republicans in France. Yielding to the force of socialist sentiment and the presence of thousands of unemployed workers, the Provisional Government then rather reluctantly adopted certain socialist principles. The "right to work," a guarantee of a job for all, was added to the list of human rights. An awkward experiment began in the name of "national workshops" and the "organization of labor." Work was made for the jobless, to be paid through an extraordinary boost in taxes for the millions who were in a position to be taxed. Paris staked out much new ground before the rest of France, 29/30 of the population, had the opportunity to speak.

For the time being, however, France yielded to the concept of popular sovereignty and democracy—as well as revolutionary tradition. Universal manhood suffrage was decreed. The Provisional Government arranged for the popular election of a constitutional assembly that would decide on the future of France—to accept, reject, alter or enlarge upon the action taken in Paris.

The February Revolution influenced the revolutions that followed in other lands. When France proclaimed the Second Republic, it gave an initial boost to republicanism everywhere. Other countries also took up the call for universal manhood suffrage, the election of constitutional assemblies and even the "right to work." Contrary to general expectations and the wishes of the more radical elements in France, Lamartine, as Foreign Minister in the Provisional Government, immediately assured the world that the Republic stood for peace. There would be no wars or "liberation" of other peoples—no march to the Rhine. The Germans, in particular, needed such assurances from the French before dropping everything in favor of revolution.

3. THE BRUSSELS FIASCO

WHEN revolution began on February 22 in Paris, Marx and Engels were together at a banquet sponsored by the Brussels Democratic Association in honor of the second anniversary of the Polish uprising in Cracow. It was becoming traditional for them to give a speech on all such Polish occasions. Marx, speaking somewhat didactically, singled out an agrarian movement and the emancipation of the peasants as the particular contribution of the Cracow revolution to the cause of the Polish nation. The fate of Poland therewith became inseparable from that of democracy and the liberation of suppressed classes.

Engels spoke more eloquently as he praised Joachim Lewelel, the Polish historian and revolutionist who was present as a member of the Executive Committee of the Democratic Association. His speech was in harmony with that of Marx when he cited the agrarian and peasant emancipation as proof of the victory of a young democratic Poland in Cracow over the traditionally aristocratic Poland. This showed that the peasant could take the lead in the struggle of class against class, the "driving force back of social progress," where other revolutionary classes were weak or missing. Engels then predicted an alliance between German and Polish "democracy." The Germans, like the Poles, could only be freed through a revolution that destroyed Prussia and Austria, accompanied by a rollback of Russian frontiers to the Duna and Dniester (he probably meant the Dnieper) rivers. Germany stood on the eve of a "democratic" revolution in which the Germans would fight the "barbaric hordes of Austria and Russia."

Brussels was in suspense after the first rumors of revolution in Paris. The Burgomaster tried to rally the civic guard in defense of public order and Belgian institutions adopted in 1830. The "more exalted democrats" were equally active in an opposite direction. The news from Paris, arriving with each train from France, could be decisive in giving them a moral advantage.

The train was late on the night of February 24 as a group of people waited in the Brussels station to hear the results of the Paris barricades. When it arrived at 12:30 A.M., the engineer jumped from the cab even before the locomotive came to a full stop. In a ringing voice he called out the dramatic news, "The red flag flies over the towers of Valenciennes. The Republic is declared!" As if this were the news they were hoping to hear, the crowd replied with the cry of *"Vive la République."* A whole mass of people from all classes were present, according to Engels' contemporary account. Stephan Born, who actually was at the station, later wrote that the group was small, and mainly German. Only the French Ambassador and his wife who also had waited for the news were distressed.

The Paris events were psychologically impressive and seemed to confirm the view that kings and aristocracies everywhere would be washed away by a republican tidal wave. Engels' dramatic account of the February Revolution, published in the *Deutsche-Brüsseler-Zeitung* on the 27th, was filled with revolutionary exuberance. The revolution was a triumph for democracy in all of Europe. "The people, the workers alone," Engels declared, had manned the barricades. "The flames of the Tuileries and of the Palais Royal are the rosy dawn of the proletariat. If the Germans show a little courage and pride, in four weeks it will be possible to cry out, 'Long live the German Republic!'" The paper was suppressed by the Belgian authorities on the same day, though the article did not specifically mention Belgium.

Marx, Engels and the communist followers, however, did not allow such visions of greater revolutions to distract them from the immediate task, that of promoting a Belgian revolution. But they had to work from behind the scenes. If the Germans became too conspicuous, it might provoke a Belgian national reaction against them. It was safer to work through their Belgian followers and to utilize the Brussels Democratic Association for revolutionary purposes. Victor Tedesco, who had accompanied Marx and Engels to the Communist Congress in London, was especially active in attempting to excite the people in favor of a republic, as he went from café to café, using the tops of tables as a revolutionary rostrum. The Democrats in Brussels enjoyed a brief moral ascendancy, while the *philistines* were abashed. Less eyecatching preparations for an armed republican uprising were underway. Marx himself gave money to pay for the arming of workers, according to a traditional account.

February 27 was a memorable day for Marx and Engels. First, the *Central Authority* of the Communist League in London notified Marx that it was transferring its powers and functions to the Brussels *District Authority* over which Marx presided. (This was a realistic response to a revolutionary situation for which the *Statutes* had made no provision. The transfer was also a recognition of the fact that Marx and Engels represented the leading brains and revolutionary energy in the League.) Second, the Brussels Democratic Association, after deciding to meet every day, drafted a letter (dated the 28th) congratulating the Provisional Government in Paris and expressing the confidence that the countries located next to France would be the first to follow the Parisian example. Marx's signature stood right below that of L. L. Jottrand, the Belgian President of the Association. The Association also sent a message to the Fraternal Democrats in London, likewise signed by Marx, suggesting "peaceful but energetic agitation" to acquire, via legal means, the advantages that France had just won. Third, Marx signed an *Address* from the Democratic Association to the City Council of Brussels, demanding that the Council create a general Civic Guard, in accordance with the laws of the land. Such a Guard, made up of those "citizens" who were armed in normal times, should be expanded to include the workers who could be armed in extraordinary times. The available arms were to be divided equally between the middle classes and the workers. Thus the workers would be armed, via legal means. (The City Council rejected this demand several days later.) Through such highly important decisions, the Association assumed leadership of the "movement," as Engels succinctly summed up the results of that day.

In Belgium, however, the opposition to revolution developed a movement of its own. With an instinct for sound statesmanship, Leopold I indicated that he was ready to abdicate if the people so wished. No blood should be shed because of him. The gesture inspired confidence, but revolutions are seldom averted by a mere gesture. Brussels simultaneously prepared the necessary safeguards. Most of the citizens rallied around the throne as Belgian Liberals grew suspicious of any revolution inspired by the Democratic Association with the German Communists behind the scenes.

The crisis came on the evening of February 27, a Sunday. Vast crowds gathered in the streets, surrounded the City Hall and raised the cry of "*Vive la république.*" When the masses refused to disperse, infantry and cavalry appeared on the scene. The revolution was over except for the arrest of the apparent ringleaders and a more arbitrary, or calculated, seizure of some bystanders.

There is no record of Marx being anywhere within sight that evening. He could later assert that the German Communists had refrained from open provocations and any obvious participation in public demonstrations. Engels, Born, Wilhelm Wolff (*Lupus*) and several other German Communists, however, had watched events from the detached angle of a sidewalk position in front of a café. It was there that *Lupus*, always one of the most popular of the German Communists and an effective agitator, was grabbed by the collar by a mounted policeman and dragged away. The gesture was typical of the reaction that followed.

Brussels had experienced a revolutionary scare. The Belgian authorities traced the whole democratic agitation to the "exalted Germans." A week later in Paris, Marx proudly admitted that the Germans had played a part, but "without exaltation." In any event, there was a tendency in 1848 to blame foreign elements for the unrest and subversion. The anti-foreign trend was also helpful to governments, employers and workers who had a common interest in eliminating the competition of foreigners in the face of wholesale unemployment. In Brussels, the first arrests affected mainly those who were politically suspect. Then a more general order of expulsion struck those whose passports were not "in order," people without jobs and almost any suspicious persons. The normal legal formalities were often disregarded in the process.

Because all Germans were suspect and any meeting of Germans appeared doubly suspicious, the new *Central Authority* of the Communist League was unable to operate in Brussels. A transfer to France became possible when the Provisional Government rescinded the expulsion order of 1845 against Marx, and Ferdinand Flocon personally invited him to come to Paris. On March 3, Marx risked calling a meeting of the *Central Authority* to provide for its own dissolution in favor of a move to Paris. "League member, Karl Marx" received absolute control of the new *Central Authority*, with the right to select its members. The way to Paris was open and Marx was in command.

Thus far Marx himself had not been molested perhaps because he was not on the scene when the riots occurred in Brussels on February 27. The Belgian authorities thereafter avoided the sensationalism of an arrest during broad daylight. Since the Communists were aware of this fact, Marx, Engels and Stephan Born took the precaution of spending several successive nights in the home of a Belgian friend outside the city. But the police finally caught up with Marx at 5 P.M. on March 3. Though they did not arrest him at that time, he was handed a Royal Order directing him to get out of Belgium within twenty-four hours.

Marx then made the mistake of staying with his family for the night while preparing for the trip to Paris. Although Belgian law guaranteed the sanctity of the home between sunset and sunrise, ten armed policemen led by a commissioner entered Marx's home at one o'clock in the morning, and arrested him on the pretext that his passport was not in proper order. Marx submitted without protest. He was released from the prison before noon the following day. This gave him six hours to prepare for his departure and to board the train for Paris.

Jenny Marx became a pathetic victim of the events that swept up her husband. Although a woman of great fortitude, she was not prepared for the raw realities of revolutionary times. When her husband was arrested, she was frightened and lost her composure. Perhaps she had heard too much talk of Belgian "police brutality" since February 27. She first rushed out to solicit help from Jottrand who was a lawyer. Then she was joined by Gigot, the Belgian Communist who had been active with

Marx for three years. Returning home, she accosted the two policemen who were stationed at the door and demanded information as to the whereabouts of her husband. One of the officers (with "exquisite courtesy," according to Marx's account in *La Réforme* of March 8) told her to follow him. Accompanied by Gigot, the policeman led her to the City Hall where, instead of seeing her husband, she was charged with vagrancy and put in a "dark cell" occupied by prostitutes. (The latter were of the lowest sort, according to Engels, the "street sweepings of humanity," in the words of Stephan Born.) The protests of Gigot were ineffective. The three Marx children, however, slept at home in the always competent safekeeping of Lenchen Demuth during that harrowing night.

In the morning an "escort of gendarmes" brought Jenny out of her cell for a hearing. But then they kept her waiting for another three hours, exposed to the chill of the late winter and the "shameless talk of the gendarmes." Finally she was released. (Marx later informed the readers of *La Réforme* in newly-republican France that Jenny Marx's only crime was that she shared the democratic views of her husband, "in spite of her membership in the Prussian aristocracy.")

It is not clear where Engels was during the dramatic hours of March 4. Since he also expected arrest and expulsion, he probably felt that he could not help Jenny when so many officers were on the scene. In any event, it was Gigot and Stephan Born who helped her prepare for the trip to Paris. Born accompanied her to the train.

The "unheard-of brutalities" committed by the police against the "German democrats" were fully publicized by both Marx and Engels. On March 5, Engels wrote a "fulminating article" for the *Northern Star*. Two articles by Marx appeared in *La Réforme* on March 8 and 12. In these articles, Marx accused the Belgian authorities of having previously drawn up a list of persons who were to be arrested as disturbers of the peace. Marx claimed that the Germans were arrested so as to divert attention from the seizure of Belgian republicans and also to excite nationally sensitive souls. This plan was executed in a manner all the more "perfidious and brutal" because the arrested persons had avoided every provocation. The police then mistreated and abused the prisoners, all in the presence of the "philanthropist" Hody (A. G. Hody, a Police Commissioner). The prisoners were kicked and beaten with fists and sabres; the police spit in the faces of these "Republicans." Ultimately, after six days in prison, the prisoners were placed in railroad cell coaches and hauled to the frontier. Marx's own expulsion from Brussels had been less physically direct and brusque.

Although Marx wrote of the "arrest and brutalities" that he himself had experienced, he gave no specific details. According to Engels' "fulminating article," Marx was locked in a cell with a raging madman against whom he had to defend himself constantly. On top of this, he was subjected to a most brutal treatment on the part of the jailor. Engels then stated that he himself daily expected an order of expulsion. There was no telling how far the "Belgian-Russian" government would go. But Engels was not molested and left of his own free will several weeks later. Since he had been in Paris most of the preceding year, he was less a marked man. The Belgian authorities had acted arbitrarily but not completely without discrimination.

In the next weeks, the Liberals in Belgium raised questions concerning the irregular proceedings, arrests and expulsion of foreigners. Engels played a part (although in an unostentatious way) by promoting a campaign of protest over the treatment of Karl and Jenny Marx. The matter was brought to the attention of the Chamber of Deputies. Jules Bartels interpellated the City Council concerning police excesses against the Marxes. An official investigation followed, which led to the dismissal of an over-zealous Police Commissioner, G. Daxbeck. It was a vindication of a sort for Marx, and many Belgians became aware of his existence for the first time. Engels also encouraged Marx to write letters of appreciation to such Belgians as rose to his defense. The publicity surrounding this second expulsion was not without some benefit.

4. INTERLUDE IN PARIS

Paris still retained some of the signs and spirit of the revolution when Marx arrived March 5. A few barricades survived as physical reminders. There was much singing in the streets. New newspapers of every political view appeared by the dozens. Societies, clubs and associations of all sorts met and propagated a wide choice of systems for the political and social regeneration of France. The revolution was not ended; it was merely marking time. France was to have an election for a constitutional assembly on the basis of universal and equal manhood suffrage. Only Paris had fought behind the barricades. All of France would speak through the new Constitutional Assembly.

As if to make amends for his expulsion three years earlier, Paris welcomed Marx most profusely, all the more so because he now came as the victim of reaction in Belgium. He (also the other Communists from Brussels) was warmly received by Jacques Imbert who had been French Vice President of the Brussels Democratic Association and now reigned briefly as "Governor of the Tuileries." Ferdinand Flocon was especially cordial.

There is no evidence that Marx and his communist followers became involved in French affairs. An American scholar did indeed discover that the minutes of *The Society of the Rights of Man* mentioned a "Marx" as taking the floor during March and April. It was easy to conclude that a Marx in Paris just then had to be Karl Marx. Later research then revealed that the Paris Marx spoke before Karl Marx's probable arrival and continued to hold forth after the verified appearance of the latter in Germany. The Paris Marx was merely one of the dozen persons with the name of Marx listed as living in Paris in 1848.

Marx's arrival in Paris happened none too soon. The thousands of Germans who had joined the French behind the barricades as well as other Germans were considering the formation of a German Democratic Legion that would transport republicanism into South Germany through an armed invasion. Bornstedt, the late editor of the *Deutsche-Brüsseler-Zeitung*, and Herwegh, the German revolutionary poet, promoted the idea. The ubiquitous Bakunin also favored the plan. The French Provisional Government encouraged the undertaking by providing marching quarters and a 50 *centime* daily allowance for each legionnaire enroute to the Rhine. France also experienced that revolutionary urge of 1848 to get rid of the competition of foreign workers.

Marx bitterly opposed the creation of a German Legion. Such a well-advertised force, with a marching route and night quarters marked out by the French Government, would be met and crushed by a superior and organized German army. (Marx's prediction proved to be accurate.) Marx's own plan demanded that the Germans return separately or in small groups, without any fanfare or display of colors. They could then go to all parts of Germany, to work from within in harmony with a common revolutionary goal.

Marx attended a meeting in Paris, open to all Germans, on the evening after his arrival. The majority voted in favor of the creation of a German Legion in the face of Marx's vehement opposition. Some of the artisans may have turned against him out of hostility to Engels. Marx reported to Engels that the "*Straubinger* dedicated more or less fury" to him. Marx, in turn, denounced Bornstedt and Herwegh as scoundrels, for forming a "Black-Red-Gold Society" (the colors of an envisioned free and united Germany) in opposition to the Communists. Thereafter, on a motion by Marx, Bornstedt was expelled from the Communist League because of this breach of discipline.

Acting with the full energy he expected of every Communist, Marx set out to reorganize and enlarge the Communist League for the work that lay ahead in Germany. On March 8 he called for a joint meeting of all the Paris Communist *Communes*. Karl Schapper, Heinrich Bauer and Joseph Moll of the late London *Central Authority*, together with two English Chartists, George Julian Harney and Ernest C. Jones had arrived in Paris and were present at the meeting. The three *Communes* were consolidated into one Paris *District,* which would meet as a unit under one set of officers—with Schapper as President and Marx as Secretary. A number of new members were accepted including three former followers of Weitling. Since the hour called for an increase in League strength, revolutionary zeal and the readiness to follow the Marxian plan of operations for Germany were the prime considerations.

The League also created the customary, not avowedly communist, open worker-society as a recruiting agency for the secret League and as a device to reach the German workers at large. Marx was instructed to draft the *Statutes* for the projected "Club of German Workers," as it was called. Eight officers, including Bauer, Moll, Born and Schapper, were selected for the club. Marx, as in Brussels, avoided a position in an open worker-society. The new *Statutes* with five articles were adopted as drafted by Marx at a Communist League meeting on March 9.

This second meeting of the League proceeded with that seriousness which allows nothing to be left to chance. The sparse, factual minutes jotted down by Marx give just a few clues with respect to the revolutionary passion that directed the decisions. Formal reports were followed by the selection of additional officers. Members who spoke at the meeting were instructed to rise and to remove their hats. Stephan Born was sent out to spy on the rival Democratic Legion group. Marx made a motion that all League members wear a *red* ribbon. Since a uniform shade was desired, one person was delegated to purchase a "blood-red" ribbon for general use. The next meeting was set for March 11, 8 P.M.

Marx immediately used the discretionary power granted to him in Brussels to organize a new *Central Authority* of the League. No Frenchman or German residing in Paris was on the list that included Karl Wallau, W. Wolff (*Lupus*), Moll, Bauer and Engels, with Marx himself as President and Schapper as Secretary. Wallau, the compositor of the late *Brüsseler-Zeitung,* had followed Marx to Paris. Wolff had been thrust across the French frontier at Valenciennes. Engels alone remained behind in Brussels.

Marx's will was decisive in the hand-picked *Central Authority.* He instructed Engels to oust Gigot from the League in Brussels, if he failed to be "more energetic at this moment." Marx was kept informed of developments in Cologne (where the "first Communist uprising" had occurred on March 3) by Roland Daniels and Georg Weerth. From London he had heard that the former Duke of Brunswick (ousted during the Revolutions of 1830) appeared ready to furnish money for revolutionary purposes. It was a quixotic situation, but money was money if there were no strings attached. Marx encouraged the London Communists to pursue the affair and then sent Schapper to clinch negotiations. Before the end of March, Schapper had to report that no money was to be had from the Duke's private fortune.

A temporary shortage of money forced Engels to mark time in Brussels until around March 21, before rejoining Marx in preparation for the expected return to Germany. During this time, Engels confirmed the admission of Ernst Dronke to the Communist League, after examining him closely and giving him additional instruction in Marxian views. Dronke had already been admitted to the League by the *Commune* in Cologne, but Engels was suspicious of the True Socialist trends and the influence of Moses Hess in that Rhenish city. As a writer, moreover, Dronke was expected to measure up to more rigid standards. Engels ultimately informed Marx that he still had a few reservations, but "with some supervision and study," Dronke might become good. (Two months later Dronke was included on Marx's editorial staff.)

The *Commune* in Cologne had been established in the summer of 1847 by Andreas Gottschalk, a popular leader and a physician among the poor. Two former Prussian officers (Friedrich Anneke and August Willich) gave the group the benefit of their military training and ties with other Prussian officers. Several of Marx's friends (two physicians— Roland Daniels and Karl L. J. d'Ester—and a writer, Heinrich Bürgers) were also members. The group was active enough, met twice a week, read, debated and sang—and engaged in the "retail business of propaganda." While Marx and Engels had mental reservations regarding the Cologne *Commune*, it was this group that prompted and organized the March 3 demonstrations, commonly referred to as the first communist uprising in Germany.

The local Communists had been exploiting the popular unrest and friction with the Prussian authorities that had existed in Cologne for over a year. After the news from Paris provided the final spark, a mass of five thousand people, led by Gottschalk, gathered before the City Hall with a petition, requesting the traditional freedoms, together with a few distinctly socialist demands. The demonstrators dispersed when a battalion of infantry appeared to the roll of drums. Gottschalk, Willich and Anneke were arrested in the aftermath, but soon released. Cologne thereafter turned its thoughts to the coming carnival.

Engels, on the basis of a first-hand report from one of the Cologne Communists, disgustedly wrote to Marx on March 8–9 that everything had been botched and planned in a "terribly stupid" manner. Most of the troops, so Engels believed, had been in sympathy with the movement. But the demonstrators failed to arm themselves, although weapons were easily obtainable. They allowed themselves to be dispersed by the soldiers when they might have been on top in two hours. What

Engels did not know was that the Prussian authorities were fully informed as to what was in the air. The police forces and army were on the alert.

Since the Cologne demonstration occurred even before Marx left Brussels, the question can be raised whether he and Engels had a hand in instigating the affair. This seems unlikely even though the Prussian Ambassador in Brussels notified an official in Aachen on February 29 that the Brussels Democratic Association was directing its efforts towards the Rhine Province, with Cologne and Aachen as places where revolts would be started. The information, allegedly, came from Wilhelm Wolff, after his arrest. Wolff, however, was not the type of person to give officials any true information on revolutionary plans. It seems improbable, moreover, that a mainly Belgian Association after a shattering reverse in Brussels would immediately set its sights on the promotion of revolution in Prussia.

Posterity has also linked Engels' name with an anonymous appeal of March 10, 1848, that was circulated in the Prussian Rhineland, calling for a secession from Prussia and the creation of a Republic of the Lower Rhine. Most of the army favored a republic, so the appeal declared. The South German states were ready for a Republic of the Upper Rhine. Hesse-Darmstadt, Nassau and other adjacent states would merge into a Republic of the Middle Rhine. The new republics would form a federal union like that of North America. Belgium and Holland were looking forward to the hour when they could join such a union. The appeal called on the people to raise the republican flag, to seize the armories and to have done with the matter.

The above appeal normally would be catalogued with other oddities that sprout from revolutionary soil. But an eminent German historian * of the Prussian Rhineland, on the basis of some circumstantial evidence, has asserted that the appeal must have been drafted by Engels. Other considerations, however, contradict this possibility. There is no reference to any such work in the Marx-Engels correspondence. Moreover, both Marx and Engels always insisted on a unitary German state, not a patchwork of republics tied up with the Low Countries. As for a federal union like the U.S.A., that sounded too much like the idea of Karl Heinzen whom they derided. They might have resorted to such a plan as a tactical expedient in a desperate situation. But Engels was not desperate or even discouraged just then. Except for the recorded fiasco in Cologne, his letter to Marx on March 8–9 was optimistic about everything.

"The reports from Germany are otherwise splendid," he wrote. He merely hoped that the Prussian King would remain stubborn in clinging

* Joseph Hansen, *Rheinische Briefe und Akten zur Geschichte der politische Bewegung, 1830–1852*, Bonn, 1942, Vol. II, First Half.

to his feudal ways. "Then everything is won, and we have a German revolution in a couple of months." Ten days later things were going even better, "truly very beautiful; everywhere riots; and the Prussians are not yielding." Engels then expressed the hope that their stay in Paris would be brief (he moved there in the next days). This was not the tone of a person ready to resort to a tactical expedient, in contradiction to their basic aims, just to get something started.

5. THE MARCH REVOLUTIONS

THE March Revolution among the Germans occurred at a time when there was no Germany as such, except a German Confederation (*Bund*) that was barely more than a loose league of thirty-nine sovereign states, ranging in size from Austria and Prussia with big-power status down to the pocket-sized free republican city-states, Bremen, Hamburg and Frankfurt am Main. Neither did the Confederation embrace all areas whose inhabitants considered themselves German. On the other hand, it included some non-German territories.

Within the Austrian Empire, Austria proper, Bohemia and Moravia, which had been associated with the German world for centuries, belonged to the Confederation. Austria proper was overwhelmingly German in nationality. Bohemia and Moravia, the homeland of the Czechs, had a longstanding German minority. The areas of the Austrian Empire outside of the Confederation included such extensive kingdoms and territories as Hungary, Galicia, Dalmatia, and Lombardy-Venetia in northern Italy. Prussia, largely a German state, also was located partly within and partly outside of the Confederation. East Prussia, though distinctly German in population, was not in the *Bund*. Prussia was also enmeshed in the Polish problem, especially in connection with her rule over the Grand Duchy of Posen, with its Polish majority. The above considerations, plus the fact that certain foreign kings ruled German states, made it impossible for the Germans to reorganize their own political arrangements without in some way affecting the destinies of outside princes and peoples.

The desire for a unified and strong Germany which would command respect in the world and uphold German interests was more widely shared in 1848 than any other sentiment. This national feeling was fortified by the confidence that German culture, intellectual and scientific advances placed Germany on par with the great nations. Germans from all classes, from the workers to the industrialists, felt the humiliations and frustrations that resulted from the lack of a strong Germany to protect their interests. Much disagreement and uncertainty existed, however, as to the exact form that a unified Germany would take. Most Germans apparently favored a federal government, under which the separate states would survive with reduced powers and functions. Only a minority (mainly republicans and radicals) demanded a unitary state wherein all the old historic divisions and landmarks would be erased completely, as in France.

In questions of politics and government, the trend in Germany was in the direction of the traditional liberal program, which called for representative institutions, parliamentary control over legislation and taxation, and the usual written constitution guaranteeing the rights of the individual. After decades of repression, most Germans yearned for freedom of speech, press, assembly, association and religion. The majority apparently preferred a constitutional monarchy, similar to that of Great Britain or Belgium (the latter especially was favored by many German Catholics). The republican minority, however, was unwilling to compromise on anything less than a complete elimination of princes and aristocracy, as untrustworthy, unnecessary and expensive. A democratic trend was pronounced enough so that a demand for universal manhood suffrage proved to be irresistible in 1848.

Similarly, the "social question" was in the thoughts of most Germans. Some felt that nothing short of a reorganization of society would suffice. The *Trier'sche Zeitung*, a socialist paper, declared flatly that political reforms and personal liberty were secondary; the times called for a decision on the prosaic issue of wages and the poverty of the masses. Most Germans did not go that far. Sympathy for the worker, side by side with the dread of class warfare, nevertheless was prevalent in Germany.

Since Germany was still mainly an agricultural land, the city worker represented a minority. Factory labor, or the proletariat in the Marxian sense, existed only as a minority within the urban minority. Most of the workers, ranging from apprentices to skilled craftsmen, belonged to one of the dozens of guilds whose position was becoming desperate because of factory and machine competition. They were in a disgruntled and revolutionary mood, in an inverted sense. Their revolution demanded a return to the good old times with a guarantee of old privileges and monopolies. The nail smiths wished to outlaw the machine that produced nails in a faster and cheaper way. The tailors protested against large establishments that turned out ready-made clothes. The men who had made a living towing boats up the Rhine denounced the advent of the steam tugboat. The mood of the workers was indeed revolutionary, but many of them were more interested in reclaiming the advantages of the past rather than striking out on entirely new paths.

Germany also had a peasant and agrarian problem. Marx himself had once pointed to peasant poverty in the Rhine Province, an area that had harvested all the benefits of the Great French Revolution and Napoleonic change. Serfdom as such had generally disappeared from the German world, yet in East Prussia, and other localities as well, the peasant still was obliged to make various payments and to perform some labor services, usually for the benefit of a former manorial lord. The aristocratic landowner in some places also functioned as the local sheriff, justice of peace, jailor and chief administrator. The odds were against the hapless peasant and the simple farm worker.

The grievances, the problems, the hopes and demands that make revolution likely were all present, in adequate proportions. But it required the news of something big and inspiring to bring on a relatively simultaneous uprising in all of the German states. The Paris events provided the spark. The immediate response of many Germans was that now something would have to be done by the Germans also. The reaction of others was one of resignation to the inevitable, an attitude that accounts for the slight resistance offered by governments.

A revolution in Germany, however, could not display the same dramatic qualities as a Parisian affair wherein all was decided in one city in barely three days. Germany had no one capital and center of power that could set the same pace. A revolution in Germany meant action on thirty-nine fronts against thirty-nine separate governments with thirty-nine sets of local grievances and demands to distract attention from a full concentration on general German issues. Since size and power are factors even in revolutions, the events in Vienna and Berlin were bound to be crucial. The lesser states, however, gained revolutionary merit by being among the first to recognize the advent of a new world.

Most of the March revolutions in Germany never reached the barricade stage, with bloodshed and a display of the corpses. Warned by the fate of Louis Philippe, most German princes and their advisors offered almost no resistance. By accepting the revolution, they survived. A siege of popular petitions, demonstrations and a riot or two were generally enough to cause the princes and governments to promise everything. Liberal Ministers rose to power in the various states already having constitutions and parliamentary institutions of a limited sort (Baden, Bavaria, Württemberg, Saxony, Hesse-Darmstadt, etc.). A promise of reform, the abolition of censorship (always a cardinal demand), and an assurance of real popular government accompanied the change in ministries. Everywhere the Black-Red-Gold colors of the envisioned free and united Germany were also raised, while princes and governments promised to cooperate with the people in the creation of a new Germany.

The March Revolution was an especially exhilarating experience for the German, as he saw the people in state after state raising the same demands and receiving similar concessions. A sense of national birth and fulfillment captured the people as the revolutionary movements everywhere called for a united and free Germany.

Private individuals, acting without official sanction, took the initiative in calling for a national constituent parliament, elected by the whole German people. A group of fifty-one Liberals and Republicans, self-appointed or invited, met in Heidelberg on March 5 and called for an immediate election for a German parliament. It appointed a Committee of Seven to make the necessary preparations. The Committee in its turn scheduled another larger meeting of a pre-parliament (*Vorparlament*) to assemble in Frankfurt on March 30, to settle the last details for the popular election of an all-German parliament, which would also meet in Frankfurt.

March 13, which began with demonstrations and minor street clashes in Vienna, became a cardinal day on the Austrian revolutionary calendar. The most popular demand, comprehensible to all, was "Down with Metternich." Emperor Ferdinand, acting on Habsburg family advice, dismissed Metternich. This was done in the hope that sacrifice of the person might save the system popularly identified with the name of Metternich. Courteous and correctly dressed as usual, Metternich bowed his way out of Austrian politics and prepared for a trip to England, host of so many refugees in 1848. His dismissal was a European event. It seemed to symbolize the fall of the old order in Central Europe.

But the people of Vienna and the Austrian Empire were not content with mere shadows. The thirst for reform and change was not slaked. In the end the Habsburgs also gave way to the demands for popular government, individual freedom and the election of a constitutional assembly. Meanwhile, the Empire seemed to be falling apart along national and historical lines. Louis Kossuth had demanded a separate constitution and status for the Kingdom of Hungary. Now the Hungarians were going their own way with the helpless approval of Vienna. The Italians in Lombardy-Venetia prepared for an uprising. The Czechs aimed at a dominant and autonomous position for themselves in Bohemia and Moravia. The Austrian Germans, in turn, were ready to play a part in the construction of a united Germany.

Prussia was free from serious convulsions during the first two weeks of March. Aside from local disturbances, protest took the form of a growing flood of petitions, demanding various liberal concessions. The liberal bourgeoisie, especially from the Rhineland cities, advised the government in Berlin of the urgent need of broad reform. Ludolf Camphausen, David Hansemann and others impressed the King with the moderation of their demands and evident loyalty. Conscious of his own personal integrity and bound by deep convictions, Frederick William IV, however, moved slowly and reluctantly at first.

On March 6, the King promised that in the future, the United Diet would meet periodically—a demand of the Liberals that he had resolutely refused less than a year earlier. Two days later the Prussian government indicated that censorship might soon be abandoned. All the while, tension in Berlin increased as the masses became bolder and more disgruntled. Unemployment spread with the closing of some factories and business stagnation in general.

When the news of the revolution in Vienna reached Berlin on March 16, when even the Habsburgs had yielded to revolutionary pressure, it became easier for Frederick William IV to overcome his conscientious objections. At the same time the Berlin populace was emboldened. Surely Prussia alone would not hold back when all the rest of Germany had accepted the liberal and national demands!

Through a series of patents and announcements on March 18, Frederick William IV showed how far he had moved towards meeting the liberal and national wishes of the month. Censorship was now abolished. The Prussian United Diet was summoned for a meeting on April 5. (Though hardly the desired representative body, it had earned popular acclaim for its courageous and liberal stand in 1847.) The King also indicated that he was ready to take part in the formation of a unified Germany. Such concessions brought joy to Berlin. Crowds gathered before the royal palace to cheer the King and the event. Two accidental shots were fired later, apparently by soldiers who ultimately moved to clear the people out of the square. Although no one was hurt, the shots angered the masses and excited their distrust. Radical agitators exploited the situation to provoke a violent revolution.

The fighting that followed in Berlin made March 18–19 memorable as "The March Days" of 1848. Barricades sprang up in many quarters. Serious and sustained fighting occurred between the revolutionary forces and the Prussian regiments. The French Ambassador in Berlin noted the fact that the Berliners behind the barricades were doing even better than the Parisians had done. The outcome, however, was hardly in doubt. The Prussian army was at the point of winning the street warfare when the fight was abandoned. The Prussian King was responsible for the troop withdrawal order that left the losing revolutionary forces in possession of the battlefield. He could not bear the thought of his soldiers and civilians fighting each other. He would not believe that his "dear Berliners" were responsible. Foreign elements and outsiders were the instigators. Or, there was a misunderstanding in the picture. An armistice, a halt in the fighting would clear up the misunderstanding. With this in mind, the troops had been ordered to withdraw even before there was a real assurance that the barricades would also be cleared away. When the soldiers then withdrew from Berlin, the barricades could claim the victory. They were still there.

A Civic Guard was established to maintain a semblance of order. The revolution then had its triumphs and spectacles to show that the King had identified himself with the wishes of the people. The casualties of March 18 and 19 (except for the soldiers who were buried without fanfare) were carried aloft on biers past the royal palace, where the King had to appear on a balcony to pay his respects to the dead. Upon a cry from the crowd, Frederick William IV was forced to take off his cap. The King's brother and heir to the throne, Prince William of Prussia, left for England because it was widely believed that he had been responsible for the shooting and for wanting to continue the fight.

Liberal Ministers began to supplant the less liberal group in the Prussian government. By the end of the month, two Rhineland Liberals occupied key positions—Camphausen as Minister President and Hansemann as Finance Minister. It was also clear that the United Diet would meet mainly to arrange for the early election of a constitutional assembly, after which it would meet no more.

With the triumph of the March Revolution in Berlin, the way was open for the return of any political refugees. It was now possible to write freely without the interference of censorship. Political societies, clubs and parties could meet and organize from one end of Germany to the other. The opportunity was there for any political talent and revolutionary leader to gain recognition and power—or to turn the revolutions into a new direction.

== II ==

Return of the Natives

1. THE IMMEDIATE STRATEGY

ABOUT two days after the fighting ended in Berlin, Engels left Brussels to join Marx in Paris and take up the seat that had been reserved for him on the *Central Authority* of the Communist League. With the door to Germany now open, there was nothing to prevent either of them from returning immediately. Nevertheless they remained in Paris for another fifteen days to prepare for the work ahead in Germany.

A thousand copies of the original printing of the *Communist Manifesto* had arrived in Paris late in March, but Marx and Engels felt that the practical requirements of the hour demanded another set of revolutionary guidelines. To meet this need, they prepared a brief, seventeen-point platform—the "Demands of the Communist Party in Germany"—which was printed in handbill form for easy distribution. The "Demands," simple to read and remember, are significant because they illustrate Marx's tactical elasticity, his readiness to advocate measures that apparently contradict his principles but that would help to promote revolution and to enable the Communists to play the guiding role in such a revolution.

The first five points covered politics, the national question and the political rights of the individual. All Germany was to be united into a single, indivisible republic, including the German areas of Austria. Every German male, over twenty-one and not a criminal, was to have the right to vote and to be elected. Representatives of the people were to be paid so that a worker could take a seat in future parliaments. There was to be universal arming of the people. Future armies would also be armies of workers; the military would not merely consume but would produce more than the cost of its upkeep. The creation of worker armies, moreover, would offer the opportunity to promote the "organization of labor" (whatever that meant).

The next four points were distinctly "agrarian" and anti-feudal. All feudal burdens, payments, tithes and labor obligations that oppressed the rural population were to be abolished without compensation. All princely and other feudal estates, mines, "etc." were to become state property. On the confiscated estates, farming would be done on a large scale with the help of the most modern scientific aids, all for the benefit of society as a whole. All mortgages on individual peasant farms would become state property, with the peasant paying interest to the state. In areas where the tenant system prevailed, the rental would also go to the state in the guise of a tax. Marx inserted an explanatory paragraph here to point out that the above measures were designed to "reduce the public and other burdens of the peasant and small tenant, without thereby endangering production and lowering the sums needed for state expenditures."

Point 10 demanded the creation of a state bank to replace all private banks; its paper money would serve as legal tender. In an explanatory digression Marx stated that this step would regulate credit in favor of the "whole people," thereby undermining the "rule of the big money men." Paper money would gradually replace gold and silver, cheapening the indispensable medium of exchange. Finally, these steps were necessary in order to make the interests of the conservative bourgeoisie dependent on the revolution.

Point 11 placed all means of transportation—railroads, canals, steamboats, highways, postal system, "etc." in the hands of the state. (The various German states controlled most of them already, except the boats.) As state property, these would be available without cost for the use of the "poor class."

Point 12 made the unpopular bureaucrat the pacesetter on the road to egalitarian communism. All state officials would be paid the same salaries, except that the persons "*with* a family, therefore with greater needs, would also get higher salaries than the rest."

Point 13 called for the complete separation of Church and State. Clergymen would be paid entirely from voluntary contributions of the parishes.

Point 14 merely reads as follows: "Limitation of the right of inheritance." It dealt more gently with people who had property to bequeath and was less alarming than the *Manifesto* which had called for the "abolition of the right of inheritance."

Point 15, like the *Manifesto,* demanded a "strong progressive tax." But it also added the "abolition of consumption taxes." Although Marx less than a year earlier had cited all the economists to bolster his contention that the removal of such taxes would be of no permanent benefit to the worker, he now joined in the popular outcry—grassroots opposition to the consumer tax on bread and meat in Prussia and some other German states was convincing.

Point 16, the only one specifically dedicated to the worker, promised the "erection of national workshops. The state guarantees all workers their existence and takes care of those incapable of work." Marx and Engels here took up the Parisian calls for "national workshops," a cry that was also being heard in Germany.

Point 17, the last, merely called for "Universal and free popular education." Like Point 14, it used just three German words.

A concluding unnumbered paragraph, addressed to the German proletariat, the petty bourgeoisie and the peasantry, stated that it was to the interest of these three classes "to work with all energy to put through the above measures. Only through the realization of the same, could the millions previously exploited by a small number gain their rights and that power which properly belonged to them as the creators of all wealth."

There was little that was distinctly proletarian in the seventeen points, although the "Demands" were headed with the slogan, "Proletarians of all lands, Unite!" Also, the proletariat, though smallest in number, was listed before the petty bourgeoisie and the peasantry, as the classes to be mobilized for revolutionary action. In other respects, however, the appeal was directed mainly at the agrarian masses. The revolutionary potential of the 80 percent of the population in Germany that lived on the land could not be ignored. Even in the Rhine Province, probably the most industrialized area of Germany, no more than 27 percent of the people resided in cities.

Only the princes, feudal aristocracy, large land owners, the holders of peasant mortgages, "big money men" and bankers were explicitly accused in the "Demands," as comprising the small number who exploited the millions. Large landowners and agriculture in general were threatened with the most drastic and immediate change. The bourgeoisie at large, the factory owner, merchant, and capitalist as such were not mentioned. Nor was there any specific reference to a clash of classes between bourgeoisie and proletariat. The bourgeoisie, the indispensable actor and ostensible victor in the current revolutionary drama, was not to be alarmed prematurely.

There is one conspicuous omission in the "Demands of the Communist Party"—there is no mention of a guarantee of individual rights as found in most other declarations of 1848, liberal or radical. Freedom of speech, press, assembly, association, education and religion are not there; nor trial by jury and writ of *habeas corpus*. The administration of justice, however, would be free, as promised in Point 5. The *Manifesto* is equally silent on the question of individual freedom. When history is merely a story of class conflict with culture a reflection of class interest, there is little room left for individual expression. Marx and Engels were logical in omitting the "freedoms" from their party program, except for a vague reference in connection with the ultimate communist society.

By the first of April, Marx and Engels had been able to recruit between three and four hundred Germans in Paris to return to the Fatherland. Perhaps a fourth of them were actually members of the League, but the rest seemed willing to follow Marxian guidance. Marx's bargaining position in relation to the Democratic Legion had improved greatly after the March Revolution removed all barriers to the return of any German. Now there was less need for an armed Democratic Legion to crash its way into the Fatherland. Furthermore, Marx also could offer his followers the same financial subsidy from the French government that it had promised to the Democratic Legion, to cover the cost of their exit from France. The French government paid for this communist exodus. The London Communists (nine of the ten London *Communes* were German) were less fortunate—they also were instructed to play their part in Germany, but they received no monetary aid from the British government.

Those who returned to Germany under Marx's sponsorship were instructed on how to proceed. They were to leave Paris separately or in small groups, carrying copies of the "Demands of the Communist Party in Germany" in their baggage for distribution as propaganda material. Once in Germany, they were to go to all parts of the Fatherland, preferably to their native locality. There they could agitate on familiar ground, with all of the advantages of a native son. They were instructed to establish the usual secret Communist *Communes,* if possible. Of greater immediate importance, they were to organize open worker-societies. Germany was to be covered with a network of such societies, as the media through which the Communists could reach the wider masses.

Marx himself acquired a passport from the French government on March 30, valid for one year. He, Engels, W. Wolff, Dronke and several others then left Paris around April 6 with Cologne as their destination. Marx and Wolff had to take the longer route through Lorraine, since they could not travel through Belgium due to their recent expulsion. Marx's passport was stamped "Habkirchen, April 7," as the place and date of entry into Germany. The *Central Authority* of the League moved along with him—the third change in a month and a half.

Gottschalk had suggested that Marx return to Trier and Engels to Barmen, to get themselves elected to one of the expected constitutional assemblies. Gottschalk himself had early decided to cash in on his "bit of martyrdom" (his imprisonment after the March 3 demonstration in Cologne) by being a candidate from Cologne. Parliamentary opportunities promised to become abundant just then. Prussia was certain to have an election for a constitutional assembly; Germany at large would choose delegates for an all-German parliament to meet in Frankfurt. The challenge to help in the creation of a great national state with an appropriate liberal constitution was already attracting some of the best German talent. Marx and Engels, however, spurned the suggestion of serving as popular delegates in any constituent assembly. They both lacked the gift of oratory, so useful in influencing a revolutionary assembly or in appealing to the gallery. Nor did they ever respect the deliberate proceedings of any parliamentary body—English, French or German. (They were soon to deride the Frankfurt Parliament as the "Frankfurter Frogpond.") The French Revolution, moreover, had shown that he who controlled the populace and could whip up a demonstration might influence the decisions of a parliament by methods that were faster than formal motions.

While still in Paris, Marx and Engels had decided that they could accomplish most by living in Cologne and operating out of the Prussian Rhine Province. In some respects Cologne was not the logical location for revolutionary action and propaganda. It was only the third largest city in Prussia, with somewhat fewer than ninety thousand people. The city was not a governmental center. No constitutional assembly would meet there. It was not even the provincial capital of the Rhine Province. As a fortified city, moreover, it usually had a large garrison of Prussian troops, generally drawn from the eastern provinces. This was true especially in 1848/49 when a third of the Prussian army was concentrated in the western province, ostensibly as a defensive measure against France, but also available for action in case of domestic disturbances. Cologne had its drawbacks.

Marx and Engels selected Cologne as their base of operation nevertheless. Above all, it was the logical place for them to publish a great revolutionary newspaper, the always indispensable *Organ*, and to find the money to finance the undertaking. Only in Cologne, moreover, could they capitalize on the name and prestige of the earlier *Rheinische Zeitung*. It was possible that many of the former stockholders and subscribers would support a revival of that suppressed paper as a competitor for the liberal *Kölnische Zeitung* which had become the largest newspaper in all of Germany, with seventeen thousand subscribers.

Of crucial importance to Marx and Engels, however, was the fact that the Rhine Province in 1848/49 continued to enjoy the status of a privileged sanctuary in Prussia. There they could count on a greater immunity from governmental action than was possible elsewhere in Prussia, or in any other German state. Press offenses were subject to trial by jury, and a Rhineland jury was likely to operate on the assumption that any native prosecuted by the Prussian state deserved all the benefits of the doubts harbored by many Rhinelanders in connection with anything distinctly Prussian. Engels later stated that this consideration was decisive in causing him and Marx to go to Cologne and not to Berlin.

Marx and Engels also recognized that they could operate in the Rhineland with all the advantages of native sons. They knew the moods, prejudices, traditions and ways of the Rhinelander, even if they did not share in them. Furthermore, the Rhine Province was the most advanced industrial area in Germany, with an active liberal bourgeoisie and the nucleus of a small proletariat. The class structure and economy were closest to the pattern that they considered best for a mid-century revolution in Germany.

2. WORKER-SOCIETIES

BEFORE going on to Cologne, Marx and Engels spent April 8–9 in the city of Mainz on the middle Rhine, to consult with two trusted emissaries sent there in March to organize a worker movement. The two Communists (Karl Wallau, a member of the new *Central Authority* who had proved his competence as President of the late German Worker-Society in Brussels, and Adolph Cluss, an engineer by profession) had acted energetically to found an Educational Society (*Bildungsverein*) for workers. With Wallau as President and Cluss as Secretary, the Society then launched a broader program aimed at the creation of a network of worker-societies all over Germany, with Mainz as the center. It is usually assumed that they acted on instruction given to them before they left Paris.

Marx and Engels recognized the importance of covering Germany with a network of worker-societies as the vital link in their strategy of a Democratic Front. Though the peasants and the petty bourgeoisie constituted the largest elements in such a front, Marx and Engels looked to the proletariat, the class historically destined for leadership, for real revolutionary energy, passion and leadership. By mobilizing and disciplining the workers, the Communists, although a minority, could expect to play a significant and ultimately the dominant role in the revolution.

Wallau and Cluss had already made considerable progress before

Marx and Engels arrived in Mainz. Several days earlier, they had composed a handbill directed "To All Workers of Germany! Brothers and Workers!" which was also reprinted in various newspapers. It called on the workers in cities and villages to unite and organize into an "irresistible force" based on worker-societies through which they could explore all of their problems, agree on candidates who would speak for them in the coming German parliament, and take all necessary steps to protect their interests. The handbill envisioned a congress of representatives from all societies to decide on the permanent location of a central committee. This appeal to the workers represented the first ambitious attempt to create a network of worker-societies under the sponsorship of a member of the *Central Authority* of the Communist League. Marx and Engels could only applaud and confirm the work that had been done. The outlook was hopeful early in April.

Marx and Engels sent out other trusted emissaries to various cities to create worker-societies and, wherever possible, Communist *Communes*. Stephan Born had gone to Berlin near the end of March, where he had considerable success in promoting a general association of German workers. Wilhelm Wolff returned to his native Silesia where he worked efficiently for several months. Schapper went on numerous missions to cities along the Main and central Rhine rivers; later he made a trip to London to keep alive the ties with the *Communes* there. Ernst Dronke formed a *Commune* of four members in Koblenz. On April 23, the Society in Mainz, probably prompted by the Communist *Central Authority*, even took the bold step of calling itself the provisional Central Committee of the worker-societies in Germany. The move was premature.

By the end of April, it was clear that the attempt to dot the German landscape with open worker-societies and secret Communist *Communes* was utopian. The reports of Marx's emissaries depicted the obstacles. The workers still lacked a proper "proletarian" orientation. They did indeed combine, organize, protest and even hold congresses. But they tended to coalesce along guild lines. Many workers were more interested in regaining old guild privileges and in recapturing an imagined golden age that had passed away than in revolutionizing the world in response to a strange vision of a better future.

Marx and Engels arrived in Cologne on April 11. As an expatriate, Marx requested and was granted permission by the City Council to reside there. He also inaugurated the formalities needed to regain the Prussian citizenship that he had given up late in 1845. During the first two months in the Rhineland, Marx and Engels escaped all official notice as troublesome or dangerous persons. Indeed, Albrecht von

Roon—a salty conservative and later War Minister and organizer of Prussian victories in the 1860's—reported, when he appeared for duty in Koblenz early in June, that the popular mood was generally good, except in Cologne and Aachen where a revolutionary party was still active. The army had information that a new *Putsch* would be tried in a few days in the big cities. There was no reference to Marx and Engels. Only Gottschalk and Anneke were mentioned. Aside from the leading role that they had played in the Cologne demonstrations of March 3, they appeared dangerous because they had organized a large worker-society in Cologne.

Before the arrival of Marx and Engels, Gottschalk had inserted a notice in the *Kölnische Zeitung* (on April 6) announcing that he and several friends intended to organize a "Democratic-Socialistic Club." More than three hundred people, mostly workers, appeared at a meeting on April 13 to form the Cologne Worker-Society. Gottschalk became the President and the uncontested leader of the Society which soon had a membership exceeding five thousand, organized along guild lines with a large Executive Committee composed of separate representatives for the various types of workers.

Gottschalk's success among the workers was phenomenal, a "veritable terror for the bourgeoisie," as he himself had written to Moses Hess as early as March 26. After years of contact with the workers as a physician among the poor, Gottschalk had developed the qualities needed by a popular leader and organizer. Engels once described him as a true demagogue.

The success of Gottschalk was embarrassing to Marx, painfully so because Gottschalk was not following a fundamental Marxian principle in the organization of the Cologne Worker-Society. Instead of treating the proletariat as one great undifferentiated mass, he had divided them along guild lines. Marx, however, did have the satisfaction of seeing a purer proletarian instinct asserting itself in the selection of a name for the Society. The first issue of the Worker-Society paper on April 23 laconically reported the proceedings as follows: "Democratic-Socialist Club [proposed by Gottschalk] was not favored; the designation, Peoples-Society, was likewise rejected; the name, Worker-Society, universally accepted."

Gottschalk, although a founding member of the Cologne *Commune* of the Communist League, continually displayed a lack of party discipline by refusing to bow to all of the directives of the *Central Authority*, now operating in Cologne and dominated by Marx. Thus, Gottschalk for a time was willing to compromise in favor of a constitutional monarchy for Germany, contrary to the "Demands of the Communist Party." He felt that agitation in favor of a republic was impractical because of popular opposition. The very name republic frightened the bourgeoisie who placed it on par with "robbery, murder and an invasion by Russia," so Gottschalk had written to Hess earlier, on March 26.

The question of tactics in connection with the upcoming elections led to new divisions between Gottschalk and Marx. Elections were to be held on two separate days early in May—for delegates to the Prussian Constitutional Assembly and for the All-German Frankfurt Parliament. Although Prussia granted universal manhood suffrage (except for persons receiving public relief), the elections were to be indirect. Every five hundred qualified citizens were to vote directly for an "elector." The electors then were to meet as a group eight days later to select the constitutional delegates. Since indirect elections appeared undemocratic, many Democrats and workers were ready to boycott the elections, to register their direct protest. Gottschalk persuaded the Worker-Society to adopt such a boycott.

Marx and Engels vigorously took the position that more could be gained by voting, even if there were no hope that a representative of labor, or a Communist might be elected. Instead of abstaining in the name of a principle, the Communists should join with the Democrats, mainly petty bourgeois voters in Cologne, so as to get as many Democrats as possible elected. Also, participation with the Democrats in the election would help to establish a link with democracy. The Democrats' platform, as printed in the *Kölnische Zeitung* of April 21 and 23, came close enough to the political points in the seventeen "Demands" of the Communists so that Marx and Engels actually could feel more at home with the Democrats than with the workers, as led by Gottschalk. As the election turned out, the Cologne delegation of six was equally divided among the three main political parties or groupings—Democrats, Constitutional Liberals, and Catholics.

A second clash between Marx and Gottschalk occurred early in May. Prussia's new liberal Ministry, headed by Ludolf Camphausen of Cologne, had asked William, Prince of Prussia, to return from his "diplomatic" mission in England. Since it was commonly assumed that Prince William left Prussia to escape the "popular fury" (he was blamed for the bloodshed in Berlin on March 18 and 19), the news of his impending return provoked fear and anger. It was felt that the Prince, as the oldest brother of the King and heir to the throne, might provide the forces of reaction with a courageous leadership that Frederick William IV himself was unable to offer. Those who wished to see monarchy destroyed also recognized that an attack on the heir to the throne was an indirect blow against monarchy as such.

The Democratic Society of Cologne, with which Marx was in close association, called a big popular meeting that produced the expected protest against the return of Prince William. It was now up to the Worker-Society to second that move. Marx himself did not attend any meetings of the Worker-Society. But Joseph Moll, a member of the *Central Authority* of the League and a finished diplomat in handling workers, was present when the question was taken up in a Committee meeting on May 15. Moll, with the support of Anneke, urged the Worker-Society to support the democratic protest. Gottschalk, in contrast, argued against the justice and wisdom of such a move. He asserted that it would be unjust to banish the Prince without a proper hearing, since the accusations against him rested on newspaper reports and popular rumor. Furthermore, the denunciation of Prince William's recall represented an oblique attack on monarchy as such. If the people wanted a republic, Gottschalk continued, they should have the courage to say so directly. Gottschalk again remained the victor in a contest in which a trusted Marxian supporter vigorously backed an opposite stand.

Gottschalk's continuing opposition had produced a crisis in his relationship with the Communist League even before the Worker-Society Committee meeting of May 15. The *Statutes* demanded a discipline that permitted no such independence of thought and action. The final break occurred in a meeting of the Cologne *Commune* on May 11, presided over by Heinrich Bürgers. Marx raised all of the questions, asking Gottschalk what his decision was with respect to the League and what position he now wanted to take. (It is evident from the context of the brief minutes of the meeting that the matter had come up earlier.) Gottschalk then repeated his decision to withdraw, unless the *Statutes* were revised. His "personal freedom was endangered" under the existing rules. In all other respects, Gottschalk added, he would be willing to cooperate fully whenever the League wanted his services.

The experiences with Gottschalk and the breakdown of discipline in the Cologne *Commune* may have been the decisive factor in causing Marx to dissolve the Communist League early in June. As early as April 18 Wilhelm Wolff had written: "In Cologne the League continues to vegetate in a great state of incoherence." Even the presence of Marx and the *Central Authority* failed to improve matters. The organization had become more of an embarrassment than an asset. When some of the Communists opposed the disbanding, Marx used the dictatorial powers voted to him in Brussels to declare that the League was dissolved. To justify the act, he stated that the League was no longer needed as a secret propaganda society since freedom of press now prevailed. Although the League thereafter ceased to operate as a formal organization, Stephan Born perhaps best described the situation in a letter to Marx: "The League is dissolved—everywhere and nowhere." The Communist *Communes* in London certainly continued an uncertain existence.

The conflict with Gottschalk illustrates the problem the Communists faced when they attempted to form a network of worker-societies throughout revolutionary Germany. The workers usually favored the local leaders who spoke their own language and were familiar with their immediate grievances. When Wallau (probably prompted by the Communist *Central Authority*) on April 23 took the bold step of proclaiming the Mainz society as the provisional Central Committee of all worker-societies in Germany, the move was ignored by most worker groups, including the one in Cologne. Gottschalk's independent position, furthermore, created difficulties for Marx and Engels in sustaining that democratic front in which the proletariat would provide an energetic leadership for the petty bourgeoisie and peasantry.

The failure to control the Cologne Worker-Society was an irritating setback for Marx and Engels. This disappointment was all the more acute because the Cologne Worker-Society immediately became a recognized force backed by over five thousand members. The Cologne city authorities allowed the Worker-Society to hold its general meetings in the celebrated *Gürzenich* (the city's largest meeting place and a status symbol). Worker-societies in other Rhineland cities, like Düsseldorf and Trier, copied the Cologne model by adopting the same motto and similar rules of order. The Cologne group soon corresponded with societies in many German cities, extending as far east as Leipzig.

In view of Gottschalk's personal influence, there was nothing the Communists could do except to promote a grassroots movement within the Cologne Worker-Society, aimed at converting the rank-and-file members. An opening was made in the Committee meeting on May 11 when Moll and Anneke successfully proposed that the Society be split into smaller local units. This would give the members a greater opportunity for mutual clarification and education. Moll noted that it was time to prepare the workers for the position they would have to assume in the near future. Six local societies were accordingly established, where the overwhelming presence of Gottschalk would be felt only indirectly.

Karl Schapper began to assist Moll in the task of educating the workers in a Marxian sense. Very soon they began to circulate the seventeen "Demands," as recommended by Marx, to counteract Gottschalk's "hazy talks." A few of the local societies began to spend an evening discussing the separate Communist "Demands." But progress was slow, although Gottschalk apparently made no attempt to interfere with such efforts.

On June 1, Marx and Engels began publishing the *Neue* (New) *Rheinische Zeitung,* which was to become the vehicle through which they not only directed their followers, but also reached a wider public. They later placed this paper (a daily record of their reaction to an actual revolution) on par with their best theoretical and historical works.

3. *"ORGAN DER DEMOKRATIE"*

It was almost inevitable that persons who had been connected with the founding of the *Rheinische Zeitung* in 1842 would be the first to plan its revival in 1848. The popular fame which that paper had gained as a result of its suppression in 1843 was an asset in a year that saw the birth of hundreds of journals and the failure of more than half of them.

Gottschalk was the first to broach the subject of reviving the *Rheinische Zeitung.* In a letter of March 26 to Moses Hess, Gottschalk envisioned a democratic paper financed through the sale of stocks. Hess immediately moved to Cologne from Belgium to have a hand in the affair. Others came forward with the same idea. When it became known that Marx was returning, several individuals referred to him (and also Engels) as other interested persons. Hess and Anneke published a notice in the *Kölnische Zeitung* of April 7, calling for the revival of the *Rheinische Zeitung.* Since speed was essential, they hoped to raise enough money through a flood of subscriptions to get started in a few weeks. The tendency of the paper would be "purely democratic," but it would also take up the no longer to be avoided "social question." Any plan to support the "position of certain theories, ideas, principles and systems" was disavowed—the paper would explore social questions only from a practical point of view.

Heinrich Bürgers, who was also busy promoting the paper, testified later that he had written to Marx in Paris, inviting him to return to take over the post of editor-in-chief. If such an invitation were sent, it was by no means clear that Marx was to be in command. When he and Engels appeared, there was a tense test of strength. But it took only twenty-four hours for Marx to "capture the terrain," as Engels wrote much later. Of all the original promoters, Heinrich Bürgers alone was included on the editorial staff of the *Neue Rheinische Zeitung.* Gottschalk and Hess who had done the original spadework were completely pushed aside.

Marx and Engels insisted that subscriptions alone would not be sufficient, that stocks had to be sold to finance the undertaking. Engels went to his native Wuppertal to raise money (and also to start a Communist *Commune*). Marx himself promoted the sale of stocks in Cologne and attended to such business details as arranging for a contract with a printer. As editor-in-chief he immediately began to line up correspondents in all parts of Germany and in several foreign lands. Writing to Engels in Barmen on April 24, he stated that they surely would be able to get started soon. It was now necessary for Engels to "raise demands" from his "old man" and to report definitely on what was to be had out of Barmen and Elberfeld.

Engels' reply of April 25, however, spoke only of difficulties. Although he had used the "most beautiful rhetoric and all possible diplomacy," they could "count damn little on any stocks" from the Wuppertal. People admitted privately that social questions now belonged on the agenda, but they were unwilling to rush such matters. Even Emil Blank (the brother-in-law Engels had once called a Communist) was now a bourgeois in practice. People avoided airing the social problem like the pest, Engels lamented. That was "incitement to rebellion." The radical bourgeoisie basically regarded them as future enemies and did not want to furnish weapons that would soon be used against them. As for his father, he would rather aim 1000 bullets at them, instead of 1000 *Taler*. Engels then warned Marx that if just one copy of their seventeen "Demands" appeared in the Wuppertal, all would be lost for them.

At a meeting of the stockholders in the *Gürzenich* on May 9, the outlook was not encouraging. By the end of May, only 13,000 *Taler* in shares (at 50 *Taler* each) of an anticipated 30,000 had been sold, with only 10 percent paid at the time of purchase. July 1, the start of the third quarter for newspaper subscriptions, appeared to be the earliest practical date to begin publication. But Marx, claiming a growing reaction in Germany as the reason, refused to wait. The first issue of the *Neue Rheinische Zeitung* (dated June 1) appeared on the evening of May 31.

June then became a crucial month for the new paper. Paid advertisements and subscriptions had to make up for the lack of capital. Communist followers all over Germany were directed to act as agents to promote circulation. In Cologne, large placards advertising the paper were placed on the city's walls; subscribers could sign up on lists posted in all beer and wine dispensaries. Towards the end of June a large advertisement was prominently placed in the competing *Kölnische Zeitung* where it would attract maximum attention.

The new paper won a certain official recognition in democratic circles when the first general German Democratic Congress, attended by over two hundred delegates including half a dozen of Marx's trusted followers, met in Frankfurt on June 14–16. Marx's paper was chosen as one of three newspapers to be used as party *Organs* by the newly elected Democratic Central Committee which was to have its headquarters in

Berlin. But that gain was largely offset when many stockholders, shocked by the editorial tone of the paper, withdrew support.

The *Neue Rheinische Zeitung* had a labor problem prior to publication, ending in the triumph of management over labor. The details appeared in the June 11 edition of the Cologne Worker-Society paper, the *Zeitung des Arbeiter-Vereines zu Köln. Freiheit, Brüderlichkeit, Arbeit* (Newspaper of the Worker-Society in Cologne. Freedom, Brotherhood, Work). In an extra-supplement, the paper denounced the "pompous" subtitle of the *Neue Rheinische Zeitung, "Organ der Demokratie,"* as a malicious lie. The appearance of the paper indeed represented a "formal act of suppression of the proletariat, a betrayal of the people." The newspaper of the Worker-Society further accused the *Neue Rheinische Zeitung* of exploiting the existing unemployment to get a "submissive" labor force at a low cost. "A law [was] needed to protect the workers from falling into the hands of such Democrats." Additional details and supporting evidence appeared on June 18 and 25.

The Worker-Society paper did not directly accuse Marx. It appears, however, that his concern in the matter did not extend beyond the conclusion of a favorable printing contract for his paper—a plain business transaction. The immediate dispute had been between ten journeymen typesetters and W. Clouth, the printer and business manager of the *Neue Rheinische Zeitung*. The journeymen, prompted by the spirit of 1848 and the new right of association, had tried to improve their lot by asking Mr. Clouth to consider certain work rules (*Reglement*) which had been approved by the journeymen typesetters in Cologne. Clouth, in turn, took his stand on the fact that he was "bound by contract to get the paper out at a definite price and hour." When a meeting between Mr. Clouth and the journeymen was set for May 27, Clouth kept the workers waiting for half an hour and then refused to discuss even the terms suggested by them. He would have nothing to do with such "coalitions." Instead, he confronted the journeymen with his own rules of employment which all had to sign. The typesetters especially objected to two of the stipulations under which they had to accept a collective responsibility for any loss incurred by the employer because of a strike or the failure of any of the workers to appear for work. They also had to agree that no more than one of them would quit the job in any given week. All ten typesetters refused. Marx's paper came out on schedule, however, because there were enough unemployed typesetters who were willing to accept the terms. The Worker-Society paper considered such labor practices to be all the more unfair because the wages paid by this *Organ der Demokratie* were lower than those of the *Kölnische Zeitung*, a paper Marx always denounced as a bourgeois organ.

The format of the *Neue Rheinische Zeitung* was impressive, comparable to that of the leading *Kölnische Zeitung*. None of the other new journals (labor, democratic or Catholic) which appeared in Cologne in 1848 equalled its appearance. It was a four-page daily, with all the features of a big paper. Often there was a supplement (*Beilage*), occasionally a second supplement and even an extra edition. The subscription price per quarter in Cologne was one *Taler* and 15 silver *Groschen* (slightly over a dollar). Even the first issue contained two-thirds of a page of paid advertisements, ranging from lifelike daguerreotypes, fresh cherry tarts, English steel pens, to a church fair (*Kirmes*).

The first five issues conspicuously listed the names of the editors in alphabetical order, headed by Karl Marx as "*Redakteur en chef*": Heinrich Bürgers, Ernst Dronke, Friedrich Engels, Georg Weerth, Ferdinand Wolff, Wilhelm Wolff. All of them were Communists. Five had returned to Germany in the wake of Marx, while the sixth, Heinrich Bürgers, was from the local Cologne *Commune*. Bürgers never measured up to Marx's requirements and was dropped in August.

Marx exercised an editorial dictatorship over the tendency and policy of the paper, as confirmed by Engels in 1884 in an article on Marx and the *Neue Rheinische Zeitung*. Engels willingly accepted a subordinate role, convinced that Marx had the surer touch and sounder judgment in a revolutionary situation, even if in ordinary times the opposite was often true. In any event, the views of Marx and Engels always rested on the same fundamental assumptions, and Marx recognized Engels' mastery in certain areas, thus allowing for a division of labor. In general, Marx concentrated on constitutional and German domestic issues; Engels, on foreign policy, nationality conflicts and military affairs. All leading articles appeared unsigned at the top of the first page under the dateline "Cologne," followed by a single or a double asterisk. Engels made the somewhat mysterious statement in 1885 that it was virtually impossible to separate his "things" from those of Marx during this time, "because of a deliberate division of labor." * In the first month, Engels did most of the writing. Marx was busy cultivating foreign contacts and looking for money.

Engels, whose facility as a writer Marx admired, envied and occasionally overtaxed, could become irritated when his partner shoved too much into his lap. Stephan Born once caught Engels in such a mood, when he called at the office of the *Neue Rheinische Zeitung* in 1849. Engels, feeling as if the whole world rested on his editorial shoulders,

---

* Scholars have assigned the authorship of most of the major articles to either Marx or Engels, according to the style, clues in their correspondence, as well as the subject matter. Often, however, Marx and Engels worked together in drafting an article. As chief editor, Marx always felt free to alter Engels' work.

complained that Marx was no journalist and would never be one. Marx "altered and filed away, and again changed what he had altered, and never got anything out in time because of pure thoroughness." It took him a full day to write a leading article which another could finish in two hours.

Among the lesser editors, the ever dependable *Lupus* was valuable for his articles on the peasant question, especially drawn from his native Silesia. Georg Weerth was responsible for the *Feuilletons*—the light satirical prose and verse spread below the leading articles on the front page. His serial, "Humorous Sketches from German Business Life" and a chain of poems on "The Comical Emperors" began with the first issue.

The avowed editorial trend of the *Neue Rheinische Zeitung* was spelled out in the subtitle, "*Organ der Demokratie*." The word "communism" was never mentioned in a way that would identify the journal with that cause. There were no references to the *Communist Manifesto*, nor did it reprint the "Demands of the Communist Party in Germany" as a few other papers had done. This editorial policy was a continuation of the democratic front idea adopted earlier, that of gaining the support of peasants, petty bourgeoisie and workers by joining with, and acting as, Democrats.

Engels stated very frankly in 1884 that they had no choice except to operate under the flag of democracy in 1848—a democracy which stressed a proletarian character that could not yet be openly displayed. He acknowledged that if they had not adopted such a tactic in 1848, they would have been confined to the small role of promoting communism in a minute local paper, supported by only a minor sect instead of a large mass party. They, however, did not relish the role of a preacher in the wilderness, Engels added.

The aim of the *Neue Rheinische Zeitung* was to promote and ignite a second revolution, and to provide guidelines for it. The March gains represented just the start of a revolutionary process and not the conclusion. Hence, the *Zeitung* opposed any stabilization of the revolution along moderately liberal lines, at a time when German hopes for a free, liberal and united Germany on a federal basis were brightest. Any persons or parties who stopped short of the Marxian goal were subjected to the weapons of ridicule, innuendo, denunciation and contempt. Stating that the paper was not at all "solemn, serious or inspired," Engels later recommended that his heirs study it as a model for a party newspaper.

The first issue carried a note in bold-faced type at the top of the first page, signed by the Editorial Committee:

. . . But since the revived and bold appearance of reaction points to the enactment of German September Laws [a reference to the repressive

French September Laws of 1835, which curbed freedom of press and other liberties] in the near future, we wanted to use every free day that was left and so we are appearing on June 1. Our readers will have to forgive us if we are unable in the first days to give the manifold reports and correspondences which our extensive contacts make possible. In a few days we will be in a position to meet all demands along this line.

The pronouncement set a certain tone that became characteristic of the paper. Without being explicit, it implies the necessity of revolution, as needed against the threatening reaction which Marx saw advancing from all sides. (Even the early appearance of the *Neue Rheinische Zeitung* was presented as an extraordinary effort designed to utilize "every free day" that remained.) The apology for the shortcomings of the first issue conveys the impression that it would be an extraordinary journal indeed. Actually it already carried reports from such cities as Vienna, Brussels, Trieste, London, Verona, Dublin, Paris and Naples.

=III=

Between "Reaction and Anarchy"

1. UNFINISHED REVOLUTION

WITH the appearance of the *Neue Rheinische Zeitung,* Marx and Engels at last were in a position to praise, denounce, ridicule, exhort, direct, inspire and influence the men and events of 1848. There was much to be said and done. It was clear that the revolutions had not produced the results that they considered to be historically destined. It appeared that people were ready to compromise on something short of communist expectations. It was possible that some of the gains of February and March might even be surrendered in the process.

In France, a National Assembly had been elected on the basis of universal manhood suffrage to draft the Constitution by which the nation would be governed. But the results represented a reaction against the pace set by Paris because France was far less radical than the capital that had made the revolution. (Engels on June 11 denounced the French Assembly as an "Assembly of capitalists.") Universal manhood suffrage, long dreaded because of its supposedly radical tendency, gained respectability by showing that it could produce moderate and even conservative results in France and elsewhere. That was one of the lasting gains of 1848.

In Germany, likewise, order had been generally restored after the March days. The princes had conceded much and were on the defensive, but they continued to reign as the nominal masters of the machinery of government—bureaucracy, police, army and courts. From the point of view of most Liberals, all that remained was for the popularly elected constitutional assemblies to give permanent form to the gains of the revolution.

228

The Frankfurt Parliament opened its sessions on May 18. It was a festive occasion, with church bells ringing and cannons booming as the delegates filed to St. Paul's Church, a tall, circular structure—the only building in Frankfurt architecturally suited for a parliamentary body. Heinrich von Gagern, a courageous moderate Liberal from Hesse-Darmstadt, was elected to preside over the sessions. The delegates ranged from the Prussian Prince Lichnowski of the conservative Right to a radical democratic minority with Robert Blum of Leipzig as its most popular spokesman. The Parliament included many talented men but it often appeared to lack revolutionary energy. The vast majority were moderate Liberals, favoring a constitutional monarchy for a large Germany united on a *federal* basis, with ample guarantees for the latest version of individual freedoms. Most members took for granted that the level of civilization in the 19th century made it possible for reasonable men to arrive at a constitution through calm deliberation, debates and orderly procedures.

The usual verdict against the Frankfurt Parliament is headlined by the charge that that body deliberated too long when speed was essential. Newspapers, many petitions, even the delegates themselves spoke of the need for action. Others, for diverse reasons, welcomed and worked for delay. The Parliament faced no easy task. Division of opinion among the delegates and among Germans at large led to the postponement of vital constitutional decisions, to allow a clearer consensus of view to ripen. The delegates also had to defend the national interests of the Germany they were creating, as well as the frequently ignored rights of Germans in foreign lands. They were faced with the agonizing question of the Poles and Germans in Posen, which led to additional days spent in emotional debate. When Danish naval forces seized German ships and swept German commerce from the seas (in connection with the war with Denmark that had been going on since April), the Parliament set out to correct this costly and humiliating situation by creating an Imperial navy.

The Frankfurt Parliament is customarily criticized for spending too much time drafting an elaborate bill of rights. It might have expedited the matter by simply copying the French Declaration of the Rights of Man. But experience had shown that such brief and doctrinaire statements were not adequate for protecting the liberty of the individual in all of the complex situations of life. After experiencing years of repression the Germans took their liberty very seriously; they wanted to be certain that their new-found freedom would be fully documented so as to cover every contingency. This required endless committee meetings and debate before satisfactory definitions were hammered out.

The Parliament took the first step towards the creation of a central government when it responded to the "bold stroke" proposed by its President, Heinrich von Gagern, on June 24 by passing a law that established a provisional Imperial Government. The Archduke John of Austria was selected as the Imperial Administrator on June 29, to act in behalf of an emperor to be selected later. The choice was a popular one because the Archduke, although a Habsburg, was regarded as a warmly romantic advocate of national unity and as a Liberal (confirmed by his marriage to a commoner).

The Archduke John was soon joined by several subordinate Ministers as heads of the most vital departments—finance, justice and war. But it remained a government without hands and feet, in the absence of an Imperial governmental machine, treasury, courts and an army to enforce the decisions of the Imperial Administrator and the Parliament for which he spoke. A first serious test came on July 16 when the new Minister of War called for a review before the Imperial Administrator of army units from all German states, as an expression of the allegiance to the new Germany. Austria and Prussia evaded the order. Of the nations of the world, only Belgium, Holland, Switzerland and Naples— plus the distant U.S.A.—granted recognition to the new Black-Red-Gold flag, the symbol of the German will to form a great liberal, united Germany. All the great powers of Europe held back in disbelief, disapproval and diplomatic uncertainty. Facts and power, not the mere national aspirations of the Germans, commanded recognition.

With respect to the drafting of constitutions for the separate states of the envisioned federal union, Prussia provided a classic example of the 1848 shift from absolute monarchy to constitutional government, accomplished with a pretense of legal continuity. The role played by the revolution had been tactfully ignored when arrangements were made for the election of a Prussian Constitutional Assembly in May, with the power to draft a constitution, but in "agreement" (*Vereinbarung*) with the King. The new liberal government headed by Ludolf Camphausen (a Catholic and former stockholder of the *Rheinische Zeitung*) with David Hansemann as finance Minister, aimed at a peaceful transition to a liberal constitution, representation of the people, and the traditional guarantees of individual liberty. Monarchy was to be preserved to provide the continuity that a hereditary ruler can give. But the Ministers and the Parliament were to have enough power to prevent the King from acting contrary to the popular will.

The Prussian Assembly suffered, or benefited, from the fact that most Germans regarded service in the Frankfurt Parliament as the higher honor and responsibility. The Assembly's membership was less illustrious but younger, more inclined to action and ultimately radical decisions. As is typical of such bodies, most of the delegates were professional people

—mainly lawyers, officials, some professors and teachers. Only a few came from the lower classes. Neither was there a sizeable Right, or conservative wing. The vast majority were to the Right or Left of Center—moderate liberal monarchists who accepted the idea of *Vereinbarung* and wanted the existing agencies of power to operate as a guarantee against the "anarchy" that might result from an immediate and full adoption of the revolution and the principle of unlimited popular sovereignty. But the men of the Center were also men of principle, capable of reacting in a more radical sense when they feared that individual rights and true representative government were endangered by reactionary moves. This gave the minority on the Left, usually confined to a role of criticizing and obstruction, an occasional opportunity to win majority support for their motions. It was this minority that the *Neue Rheinische Zeitung* encouraged, incited and applauded—or reproached and denounced when it showed a lack of energy and boldness in opposition.

The Left included a variety of Democrats, Republicans and Radicals. This democratic wing was led by a group of active publicists and eloquent popular leaders. One of them, B. F. L. Waldeck, was Vice President of the Assembly and prepared the draft of a new constitution, usually referred to as the Waldeck Charter. Johann Jacoby, a physician from East Prussia, was a well-known, courageous, incisive but somewhat doctrinaire writer. Julius Berends was President of the Berlin Artisan Society. Julius Stein, a writer and teacher from Breslau was President of the Democratic Club in Berlin. Georg Jung from Cologne was an old associate of Marx. Karl d'Ester had been a charter member of the Communist *Commune* in Cologne. Their program generally called for an acknowledgment of popular sovereignty, democratic government, perhaps a republic. Their success was greatest in the next months, as reaction outside the Assembly evinced a new boldness. Through their criticism, interpellations and radical motions they were able to impede the work of the Government.

Contrary to the expectations of Marx and Engels, the liberal bourgeoisie in Prussia failed to destroy monarchy and aristocracy. Instead of proclaiming a republic, they favored a *Vereinbarung* with the old powers. A similar pattern prevailed in the other German states. Even in the Frankfurt Parliament an overwhelming majority repudiated a republic in favor of an emperor of a united Germany. Marx and Engels later stated that special circumstances accounted for this error in German ways. First, the liberal bourgeoisie did not have to fight for their revolution because, after the July Monarchy fell in Paris, the German rulers gave in without much resistance. Second, the German bourgeoisie became frightened from the first, when the Paris masses raised proletarian and socialist demands. Hence, they were ready to compromise with the old authorities to preserve the existing bureaucracy, police forces and army for the purpose of keeping the masses in order.

The two explanations are persuasively deceptive in their simplicity. They underrate the fact that most German bourgeois liberals recognized the virtues of the British model and favored a constitutional monarchy before, during and after the revolution. This does not rule out the possibility that the bourgeoisie, in the course of a sustained and bitter revolutionary struggle with King and aristocracy, might have become republican in spite of themselves.

As for a fear of the proletariat, mass upheavals and socialism, it was present even before February. For the time being, the news from Paris had been reassuring: the Parisians had demonstrated how civilized and restrained a mid-nineteenth century revolution could be. Well before the revolution had made much progress in Germany, the liberal *Kölnische Zeitung* (March 7, 1848) reminded its readers that France, in the short and nearly bloodless revolution of 1830, had escaped the "horrors of 1793" because of the "better spirit of the times," a "higher morality, progress and the universalization of humane ideas." Europe surely would fare no worse eighteen years later. This was a reassurance as well as an admonishment.

After the revolutionary concessions of March, most bourgeois liberals were interested in the preservation of order, allowing the various constitutional assemblies to complete their work free from undue popular pressure and the fear of mob violence. Stability was also needed to revive business and industry, to create new jobs. Governments and municipalities undertook public works to provide employment. Telegraphic lines connecting Cologne with Frankfurt and with Aachen were built. Harbor improvements provided work in Cologne. The installation of gas lighting in Cologne Cathedral was rushed towards completion before Christmas, 1848. There was a general recognition that constitutions and individual liberties were not enough.

If the bourgeois liberals had been left undisturbed to draft their constitutions, the future status of the German states might have been decided in a few months. In revolutionary times, however, there is little respect for even a popularly-elected majority. The Great French Revolution had shown that revolutions could take a more radical course when the faith of the people in the promises of princes and governments wavered. Disillusionment usually follows the first intoxication that revolutions bring. Discontent could be promoted by discrediting the motives, policies and accomplishments of the liberals in Germany. The people might become alarmed that the gains of the revolution were being endangered by a new reaction and counterrevolutionary plots.

In Prussia and Germany at large, the temporarily depressed forces on the Right (reactionary or conservative) and the disappointed groups to the Left (Republicans, Democrats, Radicals and the few Communists) had one thing in common: both were in the minority in the constitutional assemblies and had everything to gain by delay. By slowing the process of drafting a constitution through endless debate, petitions, protests and interrogations, both the Left and the Right could prevent any rapid consolidation of a liberal government. Yet each expressed alarm over the growing boldness and reputed machinations of the other.

As early as June 26, 1848, the *Kölnische Zeitung* complained that the "new still-to-be-built ship of state had to find its way between two equally dangerous cliffs, the Charybdis and Scylla of reaction and anarchy." It accused both sides of trying to prolong the drafting of a constitution so as to keep "freedom away from a firm legal basis as long as was possible. . . . Murder and fiery red republicans stood on one side; clever reactionaries stood on the other side in a conspiracy against the creation of a German constitution."

The Liberals increasingly sensed that the "republican ultras" were as intolerant and tyrannical as the old-style reactionary. The *Kölnische Zeitung* cogently expressed this view on July 1:

> The old system, which we fought for years, was characterized by two qualities. First, it thought it had a monopoly on wisdom; it regarded everyone who did not accept this wisdom as guilty of high treason. Second, it never believed in the purity of motives of its opponents, but assumed that selfishness, malice, etc. were involved.
>
> And our current republican ultras? Our criers of reaction, those people who everywhere suspect treason against the people, selfishness, etc., who never regard their opponents as erring persons, but solely as conscious enemies of the good, of the people, of their freedom. Now, take a look at them. If they do not resemble the old system, as one basilisk egg the other, there is no longer any similarity in the world.

The Democrats, Republicans and Radicals, meanwhile, apparently were haunted by a spectre of reaction, as the Conservatives again raised their voices after having been silenced in March. They derided the reactionary as a "howler" (*Heuler*) at one moment; in the next they used the words "reaction" and "reactionary" as synonyms for "poisoning" and "poisoner." They accused the reaction of instigating police and army provocations, designed to stir up popular revolts which could then be forcefully suppressed, to preserve order and to avert "anarchy"; but all the while the real aim of the reaction was to rob the people of the gains of March. Revolutionists, by harping on the danger and the machination of the reaction, could hope to rouse the people in defense of their newly-gained liberties. A second revolutionary round was possible. Even Gottschalk, after earlier resigning himself to a constitutional monarchy, began to favor a republic and even predicted its inevitable victory.

Beginning with the first issue of the *Neue Rheinische Zeitung* on June 1 and continuing to the end, the dominant motif was an exposé of the machinations of reaction with the assurance of the ultimate triumph of revolution. This program appears in the leading articles written by Marx and Engels as well as in the reports from distant correspondents who either adopted the tone and theme as their own or had their reports retouched after they reached Cologne. The full impact of the *Neue Rheinische Zeitung* can be appreciated only by a study of the whole paper.

Reaction, according to the first issue, had just celebrated its major victory in the Kingdom of the Two Sicilies where the Bourbon King, aided by the *lazzaroni* (the Italian equivalent of the *Lumpenproletariat*, always denounced as ready mercenaries of reaction and as incapable of being socially reconstructed), had just crushed the revolution in Sicily. But the "revolutionary flood" that had swamped Europe could not be dammed by any absolutist conspiracy.

Turning to Germany, the paper pointed to a "big plan" hatched by the reaction in Berlin. The Prussian army had imposed martial law in Mainz, in conformity with a specific "method." Two or more drunken soldiers had been sent out, and they quite naturally started a fight with civilians. When the police stepped in to arrest the soldiers, martial law was proclaimed so all weapons in Mainz could be confiscated. The citizens then were exposed to the mercies of a "brutal licentious soldiery" (*Soldeska*, soldiers lacking discipline, morals and respect, the term that Marx and Engels usually used). The paper then suggested that all of the Rhineland faced the same danger. All Civic Guards would be disarmed, making the people helpless in the face of a largely strange army which could be easily provoked or was already hostile to civilians.

Incidents involving soldiers and civilians were a frequent source of friction in 1848/49. Many Democrats, Radicals and even Liberals were anti-militaristic and suspicious of armies as the alleged instruments of tyranny. This mood was pronounced in the Rhineland where a certain coolness towards everything Prussian was aggravated by the fact that most of the regiments were made up of conscripts from the distant, eastern provinces. The provocation sometimes came from civilians who made life unpleasant for the soldier when he appeared in the streets or in public places. Civilian scorn and hostility was all the greater because many soldiers appeared rough and uncouth, mere peasant lads, fresh from the country. The soldiers in turn, as conscripts drafted for service for two years, resented being treated like pariahs. Incidents were likely to happen, unless the soldiers exercised extreme self-discipline. The soldiers were also exposed to revolutionary attempts to undermine discipline and to convert them to the cause of revolution. Marx and Engels, with a respect for big battalions, recognized the value of the demoralization of armies. Conversely, they valued the services of experienced officers in the cause of revolution. A number of Prussian ex-officers served on the side of revolution in 1848.

Continuing with the reactionary theme on June 6, the *Neue Rheinische Zeitung* declared in a short leading article under the dramatic title, "*Comité de sûreté générale*" (the name of a major revolutionary agency of the French Terror of 1793) that Berlin now had such a committee, but it operated in a reactionary sense against the revolutionary people. But the loudest alarm sounded on the evening of June 10 when Engels, writing under the headline COLOGNE IN DANGER warned that a reactionary "coup" was being prepared for the two Pentecostal days (June 11 and 12) "when the holy spirit of the reaction would be poured out over all states on the same day." With a penchant for military detail, Engels described the deployment of Prussian troops in the Rhineland to prove that a "big blow" was being prepared. He emphasized the steps aimed "*directly against*" Cologne, as "*entirely unprovoked*" because the city had never been more quiet than in recent times.

According to the plans as described by Engels, a general rumor was being "diligently spread" that things would happen on the second day of Pentecost. Attempts would be made to provoke a "little scandal" as the signal for military action. Cologne would be threatened with a bombardment, the Civic Guard would be disarmed and the chief agitators would be imprisoned. Engels warned the workers not to step into the trap set by the reaction, by providing an excuse for action.

June 12 passed by quietly, with the troops on the alert and ready. This caused the *Bonner Wochenblatt* (*Bonn Weekly,* a moderately conservative paper with a perceptive and balanced correspondent in Cologne) to comment wryly on June 15 that the "prophet of the *Neue Rheinische Zeitung* certainly erred on the date." The *Cologne Peoples' Comic Calendar* needed only to say: "On this day nothing at all is happening." But the *Neue Rheinische Zeitung* could always boast that the calm behavior of the people thwarted the reactionary plot. The Worker-Society paper, which seldom referred to Marx's paper otherwise, stated that the *Organ der Demokratie* had served the people well in this case.

The Prussian army certainly was prepared for any eventuality on the Pentecostal days, not in the service of a reactionary plot but in defense against an anticipated revolutionary uprising. Gottschalk had just come out openly in favor of a republic, to be gained by "legal means." The

Worker-Society called for the resignation of the Camphausen Ministry and posters in Cologne raised similar demands. Various newspapers expressed concern over a possible eruption in Cologne. Impressed by such signs, Albrecht von Roon, Chief of Staff of the 8th Army Corps on the Rhine, believed that Anneke and Gottschalk, the Cologne Worker-Society, and their accomplices in other cities planned a simultaneous revolt in many places—a *"Putsch* in an anarchist sense." The elaborate military precautions that followed may, in turn, have suggested the suspicion that reaction was plotting a general offensive, culminating in Engels' vivid exposé.

The *Neue Rheinische Zeitung* accompanied its exposure of reaction with an incessant attack on the popularly elected constitutional assemblies, where reaction certainly was less visible. In its very first issue, Engels criticized the Frankfurt Parliament by deriding its lack of achievement. The Parliament, first of all, should have issued a loud and open declaration of the sovereignty of the German people. Second, it should have constructed a constitution on this basis, annihilating everything that denied the concept of popular sovereignty. (Presumably the Parliament should have been able to accomplish all of this within the first fourteen days of its existence.) But it had done nothing of the sort.

Engels then proceeded to ridicule everything that the Parliament had done. First, it adopted a rule of parliamentary procedure because it knew that "when two or three Germans meet there had to be rules [*Reglement*]; otherwise the fools would get the best of them." It discussed the "brutalities of the Prussian military" in Mainz but did nothing about it except to set up a committee to make an inquiry. It heard various petitions; it listened to the "national will" as expressed in the endless speeches of the delegates. But then every session adjourned because it was time to eat. The need to eat took precedence over all other considerations; it never lacked a majority and tolerated no delays, judging from Engels' review of the proceedings.

The flippant tone of Engels' article offended many readers and caused half of the stockholders to withdraw their financial support, according to the traditional account. Marx and Engels thereafter generally avoided the same blanket condemnation and sustained ridicule. The Frankfurt Parliament was too close to the hearts of most Germans—including Democrats and Radicals. Marx could not afford to offend too many subscribers.

On June 7, another leading article (probably by Marx) compared the Frankfurt Parliament unfavorably with the ideal revolutionary body. Instead of carrying the people along, and being swept forward by them, the Frankfurt Parliament merely bored them. It showed that it was afflicted with a "peculiarly German disease," by holding its meetings in

Frankfurt which was merely an "ideal" center of Germany. This was the first time in world history when such a body met in a small city, lacking a "large revolutionary population standing behind the assembly, partly in defense, and partly as a forward-driving force." In London and Paris, revolutionary assemblies had met on "fire-spewing soil." But the Germans considered themselves lucky to be functioning on neutral ground, "where they could cogitate on the best constitution and order of the day in a relaxed and quiet mood," Marx lamented.

The *Neue Rheinische Zeitung's* most sustained polemics against popular assemblies were reserved for the Prussian Constituent Assembly. Fundamentally, Marx and Engels were opposed to the drafting of constitutions by the separate German states as such. They wanted a unitary republic embracing all of Germany, in which there was no place for such separate states, governments and constitutions—regardless of how liberal, democratic and even socialistic they might be. Revolution and progress moved faster in a unitary state, where all power was concentrated in one central national government. If the Assembly succeeded in providing Prussia with a liberal constitution, Prussia might even gain an added lease on life because of popular support under her new institutions. Marx and Engels did not want this to happen; instead, they insisted that the large monarchies, especially Prussia, should be fragmented, presumably into departmental units, as in France. The "Demands of the Communist Party in Germany" explicitly called for a unitary republic. The *Neue Rheinische Zeitung* was less explicit. Marx and Engels' views on this matter are brought out best in only two articles, neither of which deals directly with the Prussian Constituent Assembly. In one of them—a discussion on June 25 of the wider problems of revolution and German unification—the paper states: "We want the unification of Germany, but the elements of unification can be made only through the fragmentation of the big monarchies. Only in the tempest of war and revolution will they be welded together." In another article (on August 27), one attempting to exploit Rhineland provincial opposition to Prussia, Engels asserted that German unity was impossible as long as the Rhine Province remained a part of a specific Prussian state, regardless of whether that state were an "absolutist, constitutional or a democratic Prussia."

From a practical political point of view, however, the *Neue Rheinische Zeitung* could not baldly demand that the Prussian Assembly preside over the liquidation of a separate Prussian state, as its only justifiable course. That would have repelled most liberal and even democratic Prussians, including an influential minority in the Rhine Province, who wanted to preserve Prussia within the confines of a liberal and federal union. Therefore, a more devious method, ridicule and denunciation, was employed against the Constitutional Assembly and the liberal Ministers in Berlin for failing to act in an energetic and avowedly revolutionary manner.

Marx opened the *Neue Rheinische Zeitung*'s attack on Camphausen on June 3 and 4, referring to him as a person who spoke in a "solemn exalted manner, with that so-called earnest solidity which concealed the lack of a soul," and accusing him of compromising with the reaction. Marx warned that such machinations would not succeed in converting a "revolution into a peaceful reform"; the French had failed to do this under more favorable circumstances in 1789. (French parallels were always a source of inspiration and confidence for Marx.)

The popularly-elected Assembly was incessantly derided as the *Vereinbarung* Assembly, going through *Vereinbarung* debates during *Vereinbarung* sessions. Using the stenographic reports of the debates (as published in a supplement to the *Preussischer Staats-Anzeiger*), Engels reported ironically on the "most gratifying progress" the Assembly was making. Motion after motion was offered, most of them four or five times so they would not get lost on the long road through the committees. Every measure then had to run through a parliamentary gauntlet of "preliminary questions, incidental questions, questions in between, inquiries and main questions." Then there was the "great debate" interspersed with quieter explanations by the Ministers. The drama always ended with the victory of the "virtuous right and almost always when the conservative army called for a vote."

Beginning June 13, the *Neue Rheinische Zeitung* took up the Prussian Assembly's rejection of a motion by Julius Berends, a democratic Deputy from Berlin, proposing that the Berlin dead of March 18 be recognized as having served their Fatherland well. The first leading article, impressive in its brevity—about ninety words in all, with all but twenty italicized—declared that the Assembly in rejecting Berends' motion had solemnly recorded its own "incompetence." The Assembly thereby denied the revolution and admitted that it was there merely to "reach an agreement on the constitution."

Analyzing the situation the next four days in a series of articles, "The Berlin Debates on the Revolution," Engels reviewed the events of March 18. He asserted that the victorious people had won liberties of a decided democratic character. But the upper bourgeoisie had seized power and had formed a "defensive and offensive alliance with the reaction" out of fear of the people. It was "a half revolution, merely the start of a long revolutionary movement." Engels then stated that even the spirit and tone of the debates on the Revolution had been ridiculous. "Instead of the great passion of party conflict, a calm mood had prevailed, which constantly was on the verge of degenerating into a conversational tone."

Nor had the Left distinguished itself. Although Berends phrased his motion in the "old Roman, laconic" wording of the French Revolution model, he had justified it in a conciliatory style. Instead of voicing the "rage of the insulted barricade fighters," he had lectured calmly and dryly, as if he were teaching the Berlin Artisan Society. If the fighters of March 18 had shown no more "energy and passion in battle," Germany would be in a sad way. Passion was needed, and not reason.

Some of that passion already had been displayed on June 14. Alarmed by repeated rumors of reactionary plots and incited by popular leaders over the rejection of the Berends' motion honoring the fighters of March 18, the Berlin masses demanded weapons and stormed the Berlin *Zeughaus* (Armory) to get them. The soldiers fled from the scene in panic. People compared the event to the storming of the Bastille in 1789. The *Neue Rheinische Zeitung* of June 18 called it the "first distant lightning of the second revolution." The Assembly was frightened and placed itself under the protection of the people of Berlin. Such a "vote of confidence" in the people, however, was not enough for the *Zeitung* because—"*The Bastille has not yet been stormed.*" Engels accused the Deputies of the Left of cowardice, because none of them had stepped forward as leaders on June 14 to make the victory complete. Berlin had experienced an alarm but not a second revolution.

The Prussian Constituent Assembly at this time began a slow shift to the Left, as the majority, including some Deputies from the Right, rejected the constitution that had been prepared by the Camphausen Ministry. Bowing to a concept of popular sovereignty, the Assembly decided to write its own constitution, opening the way to months of delay and later crises. Ironically, it finally came up with a copy that differed little from the original Camphausen draft. With this rebuff from the Assembly, Camphausen resigned as Minister President on June 20. He was succeeded by Rudolf von Auerswald, a spokesman of the liberal aristocracy. But this new Government which survived until September, 1848, is usually called the Hansemann Ministry because that Rhineland Liberal, publicist, banker and promoter was the real leader.

After constantly calling for the fall of Camphausen, the *Neue Rheinische Zeitung* now interpreted his resignation as new proof of the growing reaction. In serving the high bourgeoisie, Camphausen had been forced into an alliance with the aristocratic party against democracy, making him the tool of reaction. The *Zeitung* declared that he had tried to cover the counterrevolution with a liberal-bourgeois mantle, only to discover that the counterrevolution now felt strong enough to shed this burdensome disguise.

The next day the paper predicted an even shorter life for the Hansemann Ministry. Hansemann could find glory in his "gigantic financial plans, his boundless projects for the elimination of all poverty and misery." But he would fall from the "dizzy heights before the rooster had crowed three times. The hangman stands before the door," this time in the form of "reaction and the Russians."

2. MARX AND THE DEMOCRATS

WHEN revolution began, a Democratic Party as such did not exist in Germany. Democracy represented no more than a political tendency groping its way towards a clearly defined platform calling for a larger measure of popular rule than the first fruits of March had brought. In an article for the New York *Daily Tribune* (November 28, 1851), written for and published under Marx's name,* Engels described the "Democratic Party" of 1848 as being headed by the "petty trading and shopkeeping class and uniting under its banner, in the beginning of the Revolution, a large majority of the working class." The Party demands included direct and universal suffrage, a single legislative body and the recognition of March 18 as the revolutionary foundation on which the new order would rest. Engels stated that the Democrats regarded the Frankfurt Parliament as the supreme body representing the German nation (i.e. superior to the constituent and legislative bodies of the separate states). The moderate wing was satisfied with a "democratized Monarchy," while the more advanced faction wanted a republic. In joining with the Democrats Engels admitted that the Communists kept their real aims hidden—"the immediate wants and circumstances of the moment were such as not to allow any of the specific demands of the Proletarian Party to be put in the foreground," Engels stated. He clearly pointed out how the Communists differed from the Democrats. First, the "Proletarian Party" insisted on a "German Republic, one and indivisible, while the very extremist ultras among the Democrats only dared to sigh for a Federative Republic." Second, the "Proletarian Party showed upon every occasion that revolutionary boldness and readiness for action, in which any party headed by and composed principally of petty tradesmen will always be deficient." Third, the Communists and Democrats disagreed diametrically in their respective reactions to the Paris Insurrection in June.

It was only by posing as Democrats and identifying themselves with

---

* This article was one in a series of nineteen articles published in the *Tribune* between October 25, 1851, and October 23, 1852, which later came out in book form under the title, *Germany: Revolution and Counter-Revolution*. All the evidence from the Marx-Engels correspondence indicates that Marx fully endorsed everything Engels wrote.

democracy that Marx and Engels could hope to excite the majority of the people and guide them into more advanced revolutionary channels. Soon after their arrival in Cologne, both of them joined the Democratic Society formed there early in April. Two Communists (Bürgers and d'Ester) were on the committee that drafted its political platform published on April 16. Marx soon played a prominent role in the Society although it published its own newspaper, *Der Wächter am Rhein* (*The Watch on the Rhine*). (The conservative *Bonner Wochenblatt* later characterized it as "comical, witty.")

The first efforts to launch an All-German Democratic Party culminated in a Democratic Congress that met in Frankfurt on June 14–17. In order to give the new party a wider popular base, the various democratic societies which arranged for the Congress also invited the worker-societies throughout Germany to send delegates. As a result, several of Marx's trusted followers (Schapper, Moll and Dronke in particular, as well as Cluss, Weydemeyer and Freiligrath) were able to attend. Only Gottschalk, however, appeared as a delegate from Cologne proper, as the spokesman of the Worker-Society.

The first Democratic Congress accomplished little enough, beyond agreeing on a limited program and recommending a democratic organization embracing all of Germany. A Central Committee with headquarters in Berlin was selected, with a provision for district headquarters in Cologne and other leading provincial cities. The new Central Committee was headed by Hermann Kriege, the very person whom the Communist Correspondence Committee in Brussels had ousted from its ranks. This may account for the fact that Marx and Engels, regardless of ties with the Democratic Society in Cologne, generally ignored the Central Committee and failed to attend a second National Congress which later met in Berlin.

Gottschalk returned to Cologne after having played a prominent role at the Frankfurt Democratic Congress, eager to establish a union of all democratically inclined organizations in Cologne. His plan was to combine three organizations—his own Worker-Society, the Democratic Society led by the lawyer, Karl Schneider (but referred to as Schneider II) and the weaker Society for Workers and Employers—to form one "Republican Society." Two delegates from each of the three societies were entrusted with the negotiations to achieve this union.

Marx and Schneider II were chosen as the representatives for the Democratic Society. Both were opposed to the union in which Gottschalk's influence might predominate. In any event, Marx always believed in keeping democratic and worker-societies separate, even though he hoped to operate through both of them. A compromise was arranged on June 24, whereby the three societies would cooperate but not combine. For this purpose, a Committee of Six was established, two from each society, to act as the local coordinating body and as a District Committee for the Rhineland at large. Marx and Schneider II were on this Committee. This put Marx in a key position where he could influence democratic councils affecting the whole Rhine Province.

Through the *Neue Rheinische Zeitung,* as well as by personal participation, Marx constantly offered guidelines to the Democrats, exhorting, criticizing and occasionally praising them. As one Democrat to another, he announced in a leading article, "The Democratic Party" (June 2), that he would not "gild with deceptive illusions" the defeats the Democratic Party had experienced. Carried away by the "staggers of the first intoxication of victory" and drunk with joy because it could finally express its principles openly and aloud, it lived under the impression that it merely had to proclaim its principles in order to guarantee their realization. As a result, the "Peoples Party" had been outwitted by the "Party of the prudent, moderate bourgeoisie." But the Democrats were sobering up, now that they were being denounced as "agitators" (*Wühler*). The situation would not become disastrous unless the Democratic Party allowed itself to fall back into that German idealistic habit of "recommending to the distant future that which could not be brought to life at once." Marx especially warned against "hypocritical friends" who said that they agreed with the Democrats in principle but doubted that their program was practical because "the world was not ripe for it." Later that week (June 7) he appraised the "Program of the Radical-Democrats and the Left in Frankfurt."

The Left in the Frankfurt Parliament had two highly popular leaders —Carl Vogt, a noted science professor and ultimately a bitter foe of communism, and Robert Blum from Saxony. The views of the Radical-Democrats were somewhat to the left of the Left and were closest to those of the *Neue Rheinische Zeitung.* Marx had little confidence in two of its leaders: Julius Fröbel, the well-known publisher of radical literature who was chosen by the Frankfurt Democratic Congress to be a member of the Central Committee in Berlin, and Arnold Ruge. To make cooperation with the Democrats possible in 1848/49, Marx, however, muffled his dislike and scorn for Ruge and other democratic leaders.

Writing in the *Zeitung,* Marx stated that he did not demand the impossible of this democratic minority. (The two factions together had only about 100 followers in a body of 831, with an average attendance of 400–500 during the daily sessions.) It would be utopian to insist that an "indivisible German republic" be proclaimed at once. No constitution could be decreed, Marx continued; "German unity, as also the German constitution, can only be the product of a movement in which internal conflict and a war with the East [Russia] will equally force a decision." Marx's strongest criticism was directed at the "notion" of the editor of the "Democratic Manifesto," Arnold Ruge, which pointed to the "North American federal state" as a model to be kept in mind. A federal system, Marx insisted, was out of place in Germany where the conflict between centralization and the federal setup was identical with the battle between "modern culture and feudalism."

During the last half of June, Democrats, Republicans and Radicals were confident that they were winning new followers, in spite of or because of the reaction. Obviously impressed by his experiences at the Democratic Congress, Gottschalk, as reported in the Worker-Society paper, repeatedly expressed the certainty that a republican victory lay ahead. The *Freie Volksblätter* (*Free Peoples Paper*), another of the five 1848 democratic papers in Cologne, on June 28 predicted confidently that the "Republican Party" would soon be on top in Germany, if all Democrats became active. The *Neue Rheinische Zeitung* of June 18 had cited the statistics of a by-election in Cologne two days earlier to illustrate the same trend. On the next day, very appropriately, the *Zeitung* began publishing a translation of the Proceedings of the French Revolutionary Convention dealing with the condemnation to death of the King, Louis XVI.

3. JUNE DAYS

On June 23, 1848, Paris again held Europe in suspense when new barricades appeared in the streets with guns pointing at the National Assembly recently elected by the French nation on the basis of universal manhood suffrage. From the beginning of its sessions on May 4, the new Assembly faced a situation that called for much tact and a little luck. Though nominally republican in sentiment (there seemed to be no other choice just then), its republicanism was distinctly suspicious of the Provisional Government installed after the February barricades. In the election, France, in effect, had repudiated Paris. A clash with the Paris masses was expected, and dreaded.

The Assembly represented a nation that was suspicious of and even hostile to the situation resulting from the introduction of the "right to work" and "national workshops," really gigantic relief projects in the form of public works. In Paris, every man who needed work was given a job with a good wage of 2 *francs* a day. Workers, and some idlers, from all parts of France moved to Paris to share in the new deal. Ultimately up to 120,000 workers had to be accommodated while some private employers found it impossible to hire needed workers.

The first confrontation occurred on May 15 when a restless mob, without any clear leadership, invaded the hall where the National Assembly was meeting, and demanded war against Russia and Prussia to prepare the way for the resurrection of Poland. It was easy for all sorts of people to join in a collective emotional release over the question of distant Poland when experience showed that nothing practical would ever come of it. The demonstrators temporarily terrorized the Assembly and even proclaimed a new provisional government. Units of the National Guard then restored order, without bloodshed. Armand Barbès, Louis-Auguste Blanqui and other less known advocates of revolution were arrested in the next days.

The events of May 15 shocked and frightened the National Assembly. In Paris, to cite De Tocqueville, "society was cut in two. Those who owned nothing were united in a common greed. Those who had property were united in a common terror." From this point forward the pressure to end the National Workshops mounted. Experienced hands by the thousands were concentrated there for a third resort to the barricades if the occasion arose. An English observer (Florence Bone) noted on June 8, "No one believes that the present republic can last a fortnight, and yet one almost dreads its downfall, as it is more likely we shall be upset in the direction of a Red Republic than that of a restoration."

Early in June the National Assembly adopted repressive measures against political clubs, forbidding meetings at which armed men were present. The Assembly also prepared to disperse the workers in the National Workshops. The unmarried men were to enlist in the army. Workers who had flocked to Paris were to return to their native localities, at governmental expense. Individuals who refused jobs in private industry were to be dropped from the public payroll. Other groups were to be employed on public works outside of Paris. The pay of those who remained in Paris was to be based on performance.

The reaction of the workers was one of hostility and distrust. Since the first group to leave Paris was to go to the swampy, reputedly unhealthy region of Sologne, it looked as if the workers were being sent away to their death, as one way of solving an unemployment problem (such suspicions were commonplace in that age). The provision regarding the dismissal of workers who refused an offer of private employment was interpreted as designed to give the employer a free hand to hire workers at low wages.

Revolutionary elements in Paris, counting on a force of 200,000 men, meanwhile were planning a revolt on July 14, the anniversary of the fall of the Bastille. But the action, real or expected, of the government then precipitated an earlier crisis. On June 22 the *Moniteur* (the official gazette) called on workers aged twenty to twenty-five to appear for enlistment in the army. It was known that the Assembly planned to act on a proposal to close the workshops the following day. The Assembly actually rejected the proposal but by then barricades had been rising since early morning (June 23), at first without police or military interference.

The republican Assembly then acted with an energy that contrasted sharply with that which Paris had witnessed under a monarchy both in 1830 and in February, 1848. General Cavaignac, a lifelong republican, was given dictatorial power to crush the revolt. A methodical fighter who had won his military laurels in Algiers, Cavaignac refused to rush into battle without careful preparation. This gave rise to the charge that he waited until the insurrection had gained full dimensions so as to bring all rebellious elements together where they could be seen and crushed. The National Guard also hesitated to attack until they were sure of their ground. Nothing could be more demoralizing than an early defeat for the part-time citizen-soldier in the Guard. The workers had time to erect the highest and most elaborate barricades ever seen.

Perhaps fifty to sixty thousand insurrectionists fought behind the well-constructed barricades. Much of France was drawn into the battle, as National Guard units appeared upon request from distant cities and departments. Those units fought with a special intensity and occasional ferocity, as if they were there to defend France against a new conquest of Paris by the insurrectionists who were fighting with an equally desperate tenacity. It took four days to overcome the last resistance. All attempts made to reach a peaceful settlement with the workers had failed. In one of them, the Archbishop of Paris, a recognized friend of the worker, was mortally wounded. Shooting had started again even while he stood between the two lines. It will never be known from which side the bullet came.

France and Europe stood agape and horrified by the shape and dimensions of the fight in Paris. No one was completely sure as to the immediate causes and the concrete aims of the insurrection. Slogans like "bread or death" were heard and posted. Misery and despair unquestionably did exist. It has been called the "revolution of despair." But hope and defiance were there also. It was a protest against the alleged attitude of the National Assembly and its policies towards the workshops. The barricades again might decide the political and social destiny of the nation, as had happened before.

Marx and Engels have sometimes been credited with a special insight and interpretation because they immediately proclaimed that the June uprising was the first big clash between proletariat and bourgeoisie. But they actually were saying what nearly everybody else was saying, with some variation in vocabulary. No other conclusion was possible in

Europe which had dreaded and talked about a spectre of communism for ten years. De Tocqueville stated that the June uprising differed from other struggles because this was not an attempt to overthrow the government, but to alter the form of society. It was sort of a "Servile War" with class arrayed against class. People had an "erroneous notion of right. . . . They believed that society was built upon injustice and they wished to give it another foundation." Had the revolt been "less radical and ferocious," it would have succeeded—most of the bourgeoisie would have stayed home; all of France would not have come to Paris to combat the insurrection, De Tocqueville asserted. The Count of Cavour, the liberal Italian statesman, saw the battle as between the "salvation of order from absolute destruction, of keeping intact and sacrosanct the principle of the family and of property menaced by socialism and anarchy, of preserving modern civilization from a new invasion of barbarism." A Deputy from Lyon called the struggle one between "order and disorder, liberty versus anarchy." "Distress and famine were the primary causes of this great struggle," according to Greville, the famous English diarist.

Most Europeans, including the Rhinelanders, were shocked and appalled by the June Days. On June 30 the *Bonner Wochenblatt* stated that for the past five days only a few republicans in Cologne were recognizable by the red ribbons they wore. Two days later the same correspondent commented on how the horrors and dreadful events in Paris were affecting everybody. Many emigrants to the U.S.A. from South Germany were passing through Cologne and thousands would follow. Some stated that the "upheavals in Germany were a factor in causing every man with property to decide to go to America." *

Most democratic papers in Cologne, including that of the Worker-Society, originally were sympathetic to the insurgents. Only the *Neue Rheinische Zeitung,* however, glorified the June Days in Paris in a sustained manner. Its first account on June 25 merely noted that a "battle between the people and the National Guard" had broken out, as told by a courier who passed through Cologne. Direct reports from Paris were still lacking on the 26th, but Engels enlarged the "confused and contradictory accounts" from Belgian newspapers with his own first-hand knowledge of the streets, byways and quarters of Paris.

"The rebellion is a pure worker uprising," Engels declared in the opening sentence. On the other side were the bourgeoisie, "these heroes,

* There is a common myth to the effect that the great flood of emigrants in the late 1840's represented a flight from tyranny and the failure of the Revolutions of 1848/49. But the flood was already in full flow in 1847, mainly because of economic reasons. It continued unabated during 1848 when revolutionary hopes were most high. This is confirmed by statistics and all sources of information. In fact, one of the minor demands of 1848 was government protection and facilitation of emigration.

who were threatened first and foremost by the Red Republic." Then using his flair for describing military operations, he took the reader through the various streets and quarters where the barricades were located. A cloudburst interrupted the fighting for a time. The battle had not yet reached a decisive stage, but the government had two counts against it at the end of the first day: It had used grapeshot without defeating the insurrection and night brought only an armistice. Therewith, "*the insurrection comes to an end and the Revolution starts,*" Engels optimistically concluded the first installment of the Paris events of June 23.

The *Neue Rheinische Zeitung's* "Reports from Paris" on the following day (June 27) were made up almost entirely of dramatic headlines, plus a few sentences:

> *Cavaignac military dictatorship from Algiers transplanted to Paris* . . . *Paris swimming in blood,* the **insurrection** develops into *the greatest Revolution which ever took place,* into *a revolution of the proletariat against the bourgeoisie.* The gigantic scope of this *June Revolution* requires more than the three days each needed for the *July Revolution* and the *February Revolution,* but the *victory of the people is more certain than ever.*

In the second installment on June 28 concerning the events of the 23rd, Engels declared that the "June Revolution" was unique in the "absence of all illusions and enthusiasm." It was the first wherein the "entire society is split into two big hostile camps, represented by East-Paris and West-Paris. The unanimity of the February Revolution has vanished, that poetic harmony filled with dazzling deception, full of beautiful lies, so well represented by the beautiful-speaking traitor Lamartine." The February fighters were now fighting each other. Engels immortalized as glamorous heroines the two prostitutes (*Grisettes*) who were shot down as they defied the enemy with immodest posture and phrase. He stressed the "unexampled brutality" of the governmental forces and described the Paris bourgeoisie as even worse than the Austrian generals Radetzky and Windischgrätz (hitherto pilloried as paragons of brutality). The following day he excoriated the *Mobil Guard,* mainly recruited from the *Lumpenproletariat* at 30 *sous* a day and ready to serve any master, as having excelled as ferocious fighters against the *real* workers.

Moving forward to the events of June 24, Engels spoke increasingly of the use of cannon fire—cannon balls, grapeshot, grenades, Congreve rockets and ultimately incendiary rockets. By noon of that day the insurgents had gained a decisive advantage, only to lose it when National Guard reinforcements from all over France began to arrive in Paris. The most striking thing about the battle was the "fury with which the 'defenders of order' fought," as the bourgeoisie, "with a clear awareness of what they were doing," conducted a war of annihilation against the workers. "Terrorism" alone was possible after such a struggle—on both sides. The account closed with an eye-witness report of the shooting of some prisoners.

After so much savage fighting and slaughter in which the barricades were held to the last man (Engels compared the fight with the Battle of Nations or Leipzig in 1813, in the number of combatants involved), the battle toll was less than fifteen hundred dead on both sides, including prisoners who were shot or bayoneted. While this official count probably fell below the actual losses, the figure does suggest that the ferocity and desperate character of the contest were more episodic than general. Many thousands, however, were rounded up and arrested after the battle; some were kept imprisoned; others were exiled to Algeria.

Marx's celebrated epilogue, "The June Revolution," appeared in the *Neue Rheinische Zeitung* on the 29th. He interpreted the defeat as a victory, as a gigantic proof of class conflict and as a foreplay of bigger battles to come. The workers were *defeated,* "but their opponents were *beaten,*" Marx declared.

> The momentary triumph of brutal force was purchased with the destruction of all illusions and fancies of the February Revolution . . . with the splitting of the French nation into two parts, the nation of the property owners and the nation of the worker. . . . The tricolor republic now would fly only *one color,* the color of the defeated, the color *of blood.* It has become the Red Republic.

Marx saw victory in this defeat of the workers because he believed that the bloody battle would create a permanent cleavage, hatred and conflict between the two classes.

The February Revolution was the "beautiful Revolution," Marx mocked. In contrast the June Revolution was the "odious Revolution," because it tampered with the desire for "order," thereby replacing phrases with hard facts. Marx then parodied the 1848 stress on order:

> "*Order!*" that had been the battlecry of Guizot. "*Order!*" cried another French politician when Warsaw became Russian (in 1831). "*Order!*" cried Cavaignac, the "brutal echo" of the French Assembly and the republican bourgeoisie. "*Order!*" thundered Cavaignac's grapeshot as it tore apart the body of the proletarian. The June Revolution had laid its hands on "*Order.* Woe to June!"

But Marx had some second thoughts. It was a republic in France, with a National Assembly elected by universal manhood suffrage, that had crushed the workers. This might cause the workers to conclude that they could do no worse under a king. Various socialists, and especially

Karl Grün's *Trier'sche Zeitung*, had insisted all along that political forms were irrelevant. They could now point to Paris as proof.

Addressing the Democrats, Marx warned that they had to keep the republic as their only goal and that social conflict was unavoidable. "Only weak, cowardly characters" would be led astray by the thought that the "struggles over political forms were meaningless, illusory, nil. . . . The best form of government is the one in which social conflicts are not blotted out, are not forcibly, but only ostensibly and artificially, chained. The best political system is the one in which [social conflicts] develop into an uninhibited struggle, thereby reaching a solution."

Marx affirmed that it was the "privilege and the right" of the democratic press to place a crown of laurels on the "dark threatening brow of the plebians," who had been torn by hunger, despised by the press, abandoned by the surgeon and denounced as thieves, incendiaries and galley slaves. As for those who fell before the "wrath of the people, the government would take care of the fallen, and their widows and children," he concluded sardonically.

On July 1 and 2, Engels gave a "purely military presentation" of the June Days for the benefit of the workers and as a demonstration of the "heroic bravery, the unanimity, the discipline and military skill" with which the Paris workers had fought, with odds of four to one against them. Yet they had missed by "only a hair." The heroism of the workers and the odds against them did not diminish in the retelling. The Paris battle, so Engels stated, had proven that "the worker would win before very long, even if considered only from a purely military point of view. If only 40,000 workers in Paris had accomplished so much, what could the combined force of workers not accomplish if they acted together!" With this farewell to the June Days and their significance, the *Neue Rheinische Zeitung* returned to the more prosaic debates of the Prussian Assembly which had been neglected between June 25 and July 3. In the meantime the paper had acquired a unique character and personality through its positive glorification of the June Revolution.

Most German newspapers and most Germans continued to deplore the extremes of the Paris insurrection. (According to the traditional account the last half of the stockholders of the *Neue Rheinische Zeitung* now withdrew their support.) Some German newspapers openly attacked Marx's paper, a type of recognition more welcome than silence. But the *Kölnische Zeitung* * in its own self-assured way which Marx and Engels were seldom capable of ruffling, merely reprinted on July 1 an

---

* The *Kölnische Zeitung* refused to be drawn into any polemical exchanges with the *Neue Rheinische Zeitung*. Only rarely did it refer to Marx's paper—or to Marx and Engels themselves—except within the context of an occasional news item.

article that had appeared in a Bonn newspaper (the *Bonner Zeitung,* a distinctly republican as well as democratic paper) as being worthy of a wider distribution:

> The *Neue Rheinische Zeitung* calls itself an *Organ of Democracy.* We call it an *Organ* of the Red Republic. No one who preaches riot and anarchy is a supporter of democracy. Is the *Neue Rheinische Zeitung* perhaps interested in the social question and takes the part of the insurgents because of an exaggerated friendship for the human race?

The *Bonner Zeitung* thereupon reaffirmed its own commitment to the social question and concluded:

> We want freedom, but we also want order, without which no freedom can exist. Was the *Neue Rheinische Zeitung* truly defending democracy when it praised a wild insurrection which endangered the republic, the first fundamental basis for a democracy?

The June Days represented a turning point in the Revolutions of 1848/49, with France again leading the way, this time in a retrograde manner. France was determined that the National Assembly would never again be terrorized by mob demonstrations. The National Assembly consented to a virtual dictatorship under General Cavaignac and various repressive measures, which deprived the press of much of its freedom, outlawed many political clubs and restricted the right of assembly. In December, 1848, after the task of drafting a republican constitution was concluded, the French people overwhelmingly elected Louis Napoleon as the President of the Second French Republic. The choice was determined by the fact that the name Napoleon stood for strong government and order, in addition to glory.

In Germany, the June Insurrection evoked a horror and fear that placed a damper on republican and democratic hopes regarding an early victory. The very defeat of the "people" in Paris discouraged similar uprisings by dispelling the mystique of invincibility that had hovered over the popularly-manned barricade. Above all, German Democrats and Republicans were divided temporarily. Moderate Republicans and the Social Democrats who wanted reform via orderly democratic procedures were appalled by the Paris Insurrection. Even the *Organ* of the Democratic Society in Cologne, *Der Wächter am Rhein,* welcomed the French government's victory over the "anarchy" that would have proclaimed a "Red Republic." Time was required before a popular anger over new grievances and the fear of reaction would draw the Democrats together again.

The June events above all played into the hands of the reactionary and counterrevolutionary forces in Germany. Democratic- republican- and worker-societies, clubs and parties became more suspect. The bourgeois Liberals and many Democrats developed a common interest with the existing governments so that order might be preserved and peaceful change not endangered.

Marx and Engels, however, were undaunted. Indeed, they developed a new confidence in the correctness of their own interpretation of events. The June Insurrection was a mere forerunner of an immense and decisive struggle between proletariat and bourgeoisie. If the Paris worker —or the small fraction of the proletariat that had taken its position back of the barricades—had missed by "just a hair," as Engels had written, it was possible to envision more than a near-miss in the months to come.

The paper of the Worker-Society (under Gottschalk's editorial control) expressed a similar confidence when it asserted on July 2 that the June battle was only a start of a fight to death. It condemned the *Kölnische Zeitung* for rejoicing over the defeat of the workers, who had been overcome only because they refused to murder and burn as Cavaignac had done. In the next round, the workers would be less magnanimous. "Between you and us there no longer is peace," the little paper of the Worker-Society informed the great *Kölnische Zeitung*.

4. THE FRUIT OF REACTION

"AFTER the tragedy the idyll, after the thunder of the Paris June Days, the drumming of the Berlin *Vereinbarer* [members of the Prussian Constituent Assembly attempting to reach *Vereinbarung* with the King on a constitution]." With those words the *Neue Rheinische Zeitung* on July 4 renewed its attack on the Prussian Constituent Assembly and the Hansemann Ministry. In the months to follow, Marx and Engels scanned the stenographic reports of the Prussian Assembly for information on proposed laws and ministerial interpellations—to be denounced or derided, but rarely applauded. The list of subjects is instructive only because it reveals the wide range of problems that the Assembly had to consider, making the task of reaching an agreement on a constitution appear almost incidental.

To mention just a few of the subjects, Engels castigated the handling of the Polish question, a proposal to raise a "forced loan" to meet extraordinary expenses, the lack of a service manual for the army, and a law regulating the new Civic Guard. Marx contributed an article on a new press law being considered by the Assembly. Turning to the question of the abolition of feudal burdens still resting on the Prussian peasants, Marx reminded the bourgeoisie of their historic role as liberators and accused them of shamelessly betraying their "natural allies," the peasants. He declared that the revolution in Germany was *"only a parody of the French Revolution of 1789"* which had destroyed all feudal vestiges during the course of one long night session of the Assembly.

In contrast to 1789, the various constitutional assemblies of 1848 had indeed avoided such feverish night sessions, when the power to discriminate may falter or be frightened away by goblins. Though the Hansemann Ministry did emphasize the need for speed in consolidating a constitutional monarchy, it was to be a deliberate speed accompanied by the preservation of law and order. Like most of his contemporaries, Hansemann recognized too that the "social question" would not be solved by a mere bill of rights. An economic revival was needed to provide jobs and better pay for the worker, with public works to take up the slack. But there had to be stability to inspire business confidence and also to enable the Prussian state to borrow the money to finance public works. Hansemann therefore stressed law and order as the first requirement.

Engels on July 4 confidently predicted that the Hansemann "Ministry of Action" would fall before much action occurred along this line. The stress on law and order, as a prerequisite for improved economic conditions to alleviate the hardships of the working class, was cited as proof that Hansemann was entrusting the well-being of the worker to the Minister of War—"repressive laws in the first instance, followed by grapeshot and bayonets." All exaggerations aside, Marx and Engels regarded every attempt to stabilize the revolution along liberal constitutional lines as nothing less than a reactionary plot, inspired by reactionaries.

Therefore, during the first days of July, the *Neue Rheinische Zeitung* resumed its hunt for reactionaries on the loose. By now the visible proof was more abundant. Since late June the reactionary and conservative elements in Prussia had been expressing themselves aggressively through newspapers and new societies, to match those of the Liberals and Democrats. A new journal, the *Neue Preussische Zeitung* (*New Prussian Gazette*) began to appear in Berlin under the motto: "Forward with God, for King and Fatherland!" Since the paper carried the Prussian cross as a symbol, it was often called the *Kreuzzeitung*. It offered the masses the positive alternative of uniting under a conservative banner, as it boldly attacked the Liberals and Democrats. The catchy rhyme: *"Gegen Demokraten helfen nur Soldaten"* (against Democrats only soldiers can help) was occasionally heard in reactionary and military quarters. Alarmed by the June Insurrection in Paris, and emboldened by its defeat, the governments of various German states arrested some Republicans, Democrats and leaders of worker-societies. (Repressive measures, however, were less extensive than in republican France.) On July 3, Dr. Gottschalk and Lieutenant Anneke were arrested.

The *Neue Rheinische Zeitung* reported the events in two articles, on July 4 and 5. Under the bold headline, "Arrests," the paper charged that Gottschalk and Anneke were arrested in order to provoke a popular uprising that would give the army an opportunity to crush the workers. The workers, however, would be "smart enough" not to allow any provocation to bring on a clash. The second article called attention to the extensive military alert that had accompanied the arrests. Moreover there were plans for new arrests. J. J. Jansen (an officer of the Worker-Society) had placed posters on city walls, exhorting the workers to remain quiet, but these placards had been torn down by the police during the night. "Was this done in the interest of order?" the *Zeitung* enquired. "Or was one looking for a pretext to carry out long cherished plans in the good city of Cologne?"

Aside from mentioning the fact that both Gottschalk and Anneke had been arrested between six and seven in the morning, the *Zeitung* confined its account of the arrests proper to a detailed description of Anneke's seizure. (The explanation for the omission was that the paper lacked concrete information concerning Gottschalk.) Six or seven *Gendarmes* appeared at Anneke's house, "mistreated" the servant girl at the door and quietly sneaked upstairs to the bedroom of Anneke and his wife (who was in an advanced state of pregnancy). Anneke was obliged to dress, then was pushed down the stairs and driven away to prison. The homes of Gottschalk and Anneke were searched but nothing was found except the membership list of the Worker-Society. Mrs. Anneke (a progressive, militant feminist and an accomplished person in her own right) lodged a protest with State Procurator Hecker against the "brutal arrest" of her husband. Hecker replied that he had given "no orders for brutalities." Mrs. Anneke thereupon charged that the *Gendarmes* had been sent alone so no official could be held accountable for the "brutalities" that occurred.

To buttress the charge of an organized Prussian plot against Cologne, Marx brought the First Procurator, Zweiffel, into the account. He accused Zweiffel (who was away in Berlin serving as one of Cologne's delegates to the Prussian Assembly) of having specifically stated that he "would put an end to the 19th of March, the clubs, freedom of press and other manifestations of the evils of 1848 in Cologne" within eight days. Such were the "acts of the Ministry of Action" in Prussia. Marx concluded by warning the Left in the Berlin Assembly that any "small parliamentary victories and big constitutional drafts" were useless if the revolution "outside" of the Assembly was disarmed.

State Procurator Hecker replied at once to the *Neue Rheinische Zeitung*, denying emphatically that he had spoken to Mrs. Anneke as alleged in the article. Explicitly Hecker stated, "I did not say 'I have given *no order for brutalities*.' I merely said I must deplore it, if the

Gendarmes really did behave themselves improperly!" After replying briefly to other incorrect charges, Hecker announced that judicial action was being instituted against the paper because of the "slanders and insults against the High *Prokurator* Zweiffel and the *Gendarmes* who carried out the arrests."

Marx published Hecker's statement as an introduction to his own lengthy rebuttal on July 7, gleefully commenting that the worthy reader would see that the paper had acquired a "new and highly promising collaborator." Admitting that his paper had erred in a minor manner, Marx insisted that the "brutalities" which "Mr. Hecker had *deplored*" remained illegal. As for any slandering of the *Gendarmes,* that could only have occurred when the *Neue Rheinische Zeitung* stated that one of them had " 'staggered' as a result of more or less spiritual or spiritous causes." Holding his ground, Marx stated that the "slanders" against Zweiffel were based on "rumors" coming from good sources and seemed entirely probable in view of his record in the Prussian Assembly. Recent events in Berlin, moreover, offered proof of a big "offensive plan undertaken by the Ministry of Action." As a final thrust, Marx reported that the imprisoned Gottschalk and Anneke were denied the privilege of reading the *Zeitung.* Were accused persons being sentenced to read only the *Kölnische Zeitung?*

The Prussian authorities, trying to obtain proof of the authorship of the offending article (unsigned though written by Marx), pursued a policy of harassment against the *Neue Rheinische Zeitung* and Marx in particular. Hermann Korff, a former Prussian officer and the responsible publisher refused to give the desired information. The editorial offices of the paper were searched. Mr. Clouth and his eleven compositors were questioned. Engels and Dronke (suspected of having obtained the information for the article from Mrs. Anneke) were interrogated. The case against "Marx and Associate" remained weak. Libel and slander were difficult to establish under existing laws, and Marx was careful not to print anything upon which certain legal action could be based. The trial was ultimately postponed until December. Meanwhile, Marx every now and then printed a reminder of the several actions that were pending against him and his newspaper, enhancing his position in the eyes of Democrats and workers, and irritating the Prussian officials who shrank from anything blatantly repressive, especially in the Rhine Province.

The articles in the *Neue Rheinische Zeitung* glorifying the Paris June Insurrection, the attacks on Prussian officials, and the general tone of the paper unquestionably were factors in causing the Prussian state to refuse the request of the *Redakteur en chef* for a renewal of his Prussian citizenship. Marx's prospects for regaining citizenship had appeared good in April when the doors to all German states were opened even to political refugees and expatriates. The City Council in Cologne had granted him permission to reside there. Marx claimed, moreover, that the Police Director had assured him at that time that no obstacles would stand in the way of his renaturalization. (Marx had solicited this statement with the plea that he wanted some positive assurance before moving his family from Trier where they had been staying after leaving Paris.) The final endorsement, however, had to come from the Prussian government in Berlin.

Early in August, Marx received a notice (dated August 3) from Wilhelm Geiger (the Police Director who had protested against the *Neue Rheinische Zeitung*'s account of the arrest of Anneke) stating that the Royal Government had decided not to exercise its "power to grant the attributes of a Prussian subject to a foreigner" in Marx's behalf. The state thus reserved the right to expel Marx as an unwanted foreigner without any legal formalities or trial. Though this forced him to be more careful thereafter, it also provided the opportunity for a democratic denunciation of Prussia.

The Democratic Society met on August 11, with Marx as temporary President. Prussia's refusal to grant him citizenship was on the agenda. The moment was well chosen since the Democrats in Cologne were in a militant mood just then, as is evident from the account in the Society's paper, *Der Wächter am Rhein* (August 25). They were incensed against both Berlin and the Frankfurt Parliament in connection with the ever popular Polish cause and enthusiastically adopted a protest to send to Berlin and Frankfurt in favor of the Poles. Immediately thereafter, Moritz Rittinghausen (a radical Democrat, perhaps even a Communist, who occasionally contributed to the *Neue Rheinische Zeitung*) rose to defend Marx's right to Prussian citizenship. Marx himself then took the floor to expound Prussia's real motives for denying him citizenship. It was because "one had earlier attempted in vain to enlist his services in favor of the Government." (Marx asserted that he had been asked to work with Camphausen in Berlin.) The entire assembly recognized the "cogency" of these remarks by its applause. Rittinghausen then proposed sending a deputation (himself, Schneider II and Bürgers) to the Prussian officials in Cologne to request a "reversal of this illegal and entirely ridiculous step." A direct protest to the Minister of Interior in Berlin was also drafted and signed by the Democrats in attendance. Engels then spoke of a "new, fatal police measure" against Karl Schapper who was a proofreader for the *Neue Rheinische Zeitung* and a leading figure in the Worker-Society since the arrest of Gottschalk and Anneke. Schapper was threatened with expulsion from Prussia as a foreigner, although he was a citizen of the German state of Nassau. The Democratic Society then agreed to a double protest to the Cologne authorities—in behalf of Schapper as well as Marx.

Police Director Geiger had ordered Schapper to leave Cologne within twenty-four hours, but then allowed him eight days of grace. The *Neue Rheinische Zeitung* took up Schapper's case on August 12, claiming that Schapper's only crime was membership in the Democratic Society and the Worker-Society, plus his position with the *Neue Rheinische Zeitung* —"indeed, three simultaneous crimes." Furthermore, the expulsion order was a violation of Schapper's rights as a German, the *Zeitung* stated, citing as proof a decision of the Frankfurt Parliament popularly regarded as the will of the German nation. Geiger had distorted the first article of the German Bill of Rights which reads, "Every German possesses a general German citizenship" to mean "Every German has the right to be expelled from 37 German states." The *Zeitung* then charged that Prussia was determined to purge Cologne of all "foreigners" and to allow only "Prussian subjects" to be there. If this were carried to its logical conclusion, none but the police, army bureaucracy and people from old Prussia, including Geiger himself would survive as the "last of the Mohicans." (Most native Rhinelanders were somewhat reluctant to think of themselves as Prussians.)

Marx's account of his own citizenship problem was published in the *Neue Rheinische Zeitung* on September 5 when he was away on a trip to Vienna. It was mainly the text of a letter he had sent to the Prussian Minister of Interior, dated August 22. The contents and tone of the letter indicate that it was written to be read by the public rather than as an appeal to the Prussian government from which Marx expected no favorable reply. Briefly reviewing his relations with Prussia since 1843, Marx explained that he had asked for a release from Prussian citizenship only in order to escape further persecution. To prove that this occurred only in "self-defense," Marx called attention to the fact that he had not accepted citizenship in any other country, even though the French Provisional Government had made him an offer.

Marx then argued that it was illegal to deny him citizenship. The (extinct and often denounced) Diet of the German Confederation had decreed on March 30 that any political refugee who returned and declared his intention of resuming his German citizenship (as he had done in Cologne) was eligible to vote and be elected to the Frankfurt Parliament. As a voter and as a person eligible to be elected, Marx stated that he at least had "German Imperial citizenship." If he had this highest right granted to any German, surely the "lesser claim to *Prussian* citizenship" could not be denied him. Marx also pointed out in protest that Geiger had used the word *Untertan* (subject) after the Camphausen and Hansemann ministries had banished the word from all official documents and spoke only of "citizens." Marx affirmed that he was a "German Imperial citizen," and he challenged the propriety of classifying him as a "foreigner." He concluded the presentation of his case with the accusation that he was denied citizenship only because of his "activity as *Redakteur en Chef* of the '*Neue Rheinische Zeitung*,'" the "nature of his 'democratic convictions'" and his "oppositionist attitude toward the existing government." As a final thrust he stated that the refusal to grant citizenship belonged in the "old police state, but not in a revolutionary Prussia with a responsible government."

Neither the letter to the Minister of Interior nor the article of September 5 were designed to promote a favorable reconsideration of Marx's case. Marx unquestionably wanted the benefits of such citizenship, but he was already persuaded that his chances were nil. The Minister of Interior duly reaffirmed the decision of the officials in the Rhine Province on September 12, denying the renewal of citizenship. Marx, however, pocketed whatever gains resulted from the publicity that depicted him as a special victim of Prussian discrimination and of a denial of his rights as a "German Imperial citizen." As a foreigner, however, Marx had to be more careful in his public actions and utterances than would have been necessary otherwise. An expulsion from Prussia was the last thing he wanted.

The reaction under the Hansemann Ministry was of a limited variety that actually helped Marx and Engels more than it hindered. It allowed them to recover and strengthen their position in the Democratic Society, after relations had become strained because of the *Neue Rheinische Zeitung's* glorification of the June Insurrection which many Democrats had deplored. Above all, the arrests of Gottschalk and Anneke, plus the attempted arrest of four other leading figures in the Society who escaped through flight, gave Marx the opportunity to gain the dominant influence over the huge Worker-Society, which by then could boast of seven thousand members.

There is some evidence that a number of the members of the Worker-Society were abashed and lost heart after the arrest of their revered leader, Gottschalk. Some of the succeeding meetings were more lightly attended. The Society, nevertheless, continued to hold its general meetings in the celebrated *Gürzenich,* and its paper, *Die Zeitung des Arbeiter-Vereines zu Köln,* showed no panic, dejection or resignation. Instead, the paper began to appear as a semi-weekly after the first week in July. It is the main source of information covering the frequent sessions of the select Committee and the occasional general meetings of the Society.

Joseph Moll and Karl Schapper, two of Marx's most trusted followers with years of experience in dealing with the German workers in London, were ready to step into the leadership gap in the Cologne Worker-Society. Since their return to Germany, both had been active in the Society where they had gained the confidence of many of the workers. Joseph Moll was elected President of the Worker-Society at a Committee meeting on July 13. Karl Schapper became Vice President.

In his maiden speech as President, Moll immediately attempted to dispel the impression that the Worker-Society would falter because of the loss of Gottschalk. He assured the workers that the police might arrest one president after another, but they would show that they were "not dependent on any particular person." Any of the seven or eight thousand members could step into the gap, if the need arose. Such statements certainly suggested that the loss of Gottschalk was not irreparable. Continuing his address, Moll stated that reports indicated that the bourgeoisie, frightened by Paris events, welcomed the arrest of the former leaders. He urged the workers not to be provoked into any suicidal action, such as the bourgeoisie, the police and the military expected. Reaction must be allowed to make the first provocative move, Moll reiterated. In its blind fury and fright, the reaction would take steps to curb the right of assembly and freedom of press. When that happened, the petty bourgeoisie, "the whole world of shopkeepers," would feel that their rights and liberties were being attacked. They would then join the workers in a new revolution. The future would belong to the workers sooner or later, Moll promised. It was a statement of policy that reflected the views expressed in the *Neue Rheinische Zeitung*, adjusted to a worker audience.

The meetings and activities of the Society continued without interference or pause. Since the police continued their surveillance, the workers were told to note closely who sat in front, behind and beside them, on the assumption that police spies were likely to be present. When a rumor was spread that the Society was to be dissolved, Moll assured the members that this was done to test popular reaction to such a move. The police had appeared at his house, presumably with the aim of frightening him into flight from Cologne. Then there was the attempt to expel Schapper, because he was not a citizen of Prussia, Moll reminded the workers.

Moll and Schapper exercised an almost unchallenged leadership over the Worker-Society until late in September. They also represented that Society on the Cologne, six-member District Democratic Committee of the Rhine Province (Marx and Schneider II were the two delegates from the Democratic Society). Under the influence of Moll and Schapper, the correct Marxian views and tactics gradually supplanted the less orthodox influence of Gottschalk. The task was made easier by

Gottschalk's alleged behavior in prison during the months prior to his trial for treason and conspiracy to overthrow the existing government.

Rumors were heard immediately that Gottschalk was "weary of the business" and would go to America, once he was free again. Although the Worker-Society paper at first stated that none would believe such "false rumors" and "stupid miserable lies," on July 20 it reported, without comment, that Gottschalk had proposed to the police authorities that he be allowed to go to England, or to America if need be, to escape the "tediousness" of imprisonment, which might also impair his health, while awaiting trial. Although other information indicated that the imprisoned Gottschalk was hardly humble, repentant or frightened, the mere fact that he had sought a release from a long arrest detracted from his status as a "martyr," as the Worker-Society paper originally called him and Anneke. Gottschalk, moreover, seems to have made some ambiguous statements which suggested that he was not firmly committed to the republican ideal. Additional rumors probably did their part. In the Düsseldorf Worker-Society (which looked to Cologne for leadership) it was stated that Gottschalk had been arrested because he kept for his "own private use!!!" money which had been sent from Paris for the German workers. Such rumors reduced resistance to new leadership.

In order to introduce specific Marxian proletarian ideas to the Worker-Society, Schapper proposed on July 13 that the Committee meetings thereafter concentrate on a "discussion of issues," so that the coming revolution would represent "an intellectual victory as well as a physical one." Moll seconded the move. From this point forward Committee meetings centered around the discussion of familiar and often popular concepts, leading to their elimination or correction in line with the proper Marxian view. Taking up such a characteristic issue as whether the machine was beneficial to the human race, Schapper brought out in summation that the machine would no longer be harmful "when all machines become the property of the state, namely of everybody [Gesamtheit]." The machine had to be accepted as an instrument of progress which made goods more abundant and brought the workers closer together through improved communications. Capitalist control and ownership alone prevented the people from reaping the blessings of the machine. Another topic, "organization of labor," ultimately exposed the Committee to Point 16 (the state guarantees all workers a living and takes care of those who are incapacitated) of the "Demands of the Communist Party." Schapper here declared emphatically that this applied only to people who wanted to work. "The lazybones would have to live on air, if he could." This was a position that the honest worker could applaud.

Only a select few, however, were benefiting from this discussion of issues as conducted in Committee meetings. To remedy the situation so that more members of the Worker-Society would become acquainted with the proper point of view, Schapper urged the Committee members to participate actively in the meetings of the local branches. Moll then proposed on July 31 that all officers of the branch societies be included in the Committee, to benefit from the discussion of "issues" and to enable them to transmit the same enlightenment to the rank and file members.

Concurrently with the discussion of the labor question, Schapper also introduced the "agrarian question," as part of the general theme of "organization of labor." The peasants were as much involved as the worker in the city, since there was also a "proletariat" on the land. Fallow land should be turned over to this agricultural "proletariat" and state domains should be administered for the benefit of society. This would introduce improved agricultural methods through large-scale farming. Schapper's discussion of an agrarian program was in harmony with the Marxian "Demands," which aimed at enlisting the revolutionary potential of the peasants and farm workers. The time was opportune because peasant distress was great and the Prussian Assembly seemed to favor only half measures concerning peasant emancipation.

To put an agrarian program in action (as also recommended by the first Rhineland Democratic Congress which met in Cologne, August 13–14), several members of the Worker-Society went to Worringen, a short distance north of Cologne, on Sunday, August 26, to meet with the peasants. A discussion of "political and social conditions" revealed that the peasant knew "where the shoe pinched." That same day a Society was formed in Worringen, with over forty members. The Worker-Society paper, the *Zeitung des Arbeiter-Vereines,* of September 7 optimistically reported the results. Since the peasants and workers were the main pillars of the state, the real revolutionary power was to be found in the peasant and working classes. "The end of the rule of money" would come, if the two joined hands. The paper exhorted the members of the Worker-Society to open and maintain ties with their brothers on the land.

The educational program inaugurated by Moll and Schapper for the Worker-Society progressed satisfactorily. Engels appeared to give the final talk on September 11—a "long lecture" on the subject of organization of labor—as reported by the *Zeitung des Arbeiter-Vereines.* Moll and Schapper did not have the same success in controlling the editorial policy of that bi-weekly paper.

Theoretically, the President of the Worker-Society had been responsible for the contents of the paper, but in practice the real work of preparing the copy was done by others. When Gottschalk was imprisoned, it appeared neither politic nor practical to replace the persons in immediate charge. Since Moll had to earn his living in the watch-maker trade, he could not exercise the presidential prerogative of checking every item and issue. As a result, articles appeared that contradicted the policies advocated by Marx and Engels—an intolerable situation since the paper which had a circulation of fourteen to eighteen hundred copies was a "substantial power among the workers."

The Communist leadership ignored the July 25 issue of the *Zeitung des Arbeiter-Vereines* which, most fittingly, denounced the *Kölnische Zeitung* as "below all criticism," but then continued as follows: "And the *Neue Rheinische Zeitung?* Your Servant my Lords! But the music is pitched so high we, unfortunately, can't whistle the tune. Your *Rheinische Zeitung* needs an interpreter." The item suggested the need for another democratic paper.

The climax came on July 30 when the *Zeitung des Arbeiter-Vereines* published an article entitled "Politics." Because people in Berlin were citing the late events in Paris to prove that republicans were enemies of the Fatherland and of property, the article attempted to show that the French example was irrelevant. French power was fully centralized in Paris, whereas Germany wanted a "federal republic, unity with and in spite of diversity." This call for a federal republic was a blatant contradiction to the first "Demand" of the Communists for a "united indivisible republic," a program constantly advanced in the *Neue Rheinische Zeitung.* Moll protested vigorously at a Committee session of the Worker-Society on July 31, roundly condemning the offending article for advocating a federal state when the "most able men of our times" insisted on a "free, unitary republic." Moll asked to be relieved of all responsibility for the paper since he could not check every issue before it went to press. Ultimately, as proposed by Schapper, a committee was selected to pass on all questionable items in the paper.

The *Zeitung des Arbeiter-Vereines* made some amends on August 10. In a short item from Vienna complimenting the *Neue Rheinische Zeitung,* it stated that the *Kölnische Zeitung* was read very little there. "All the greater, therefore, is the recognition accorded to the *Neue Rheinische Zeitung,* which arouses general interest because of its superior interpretation of conditions." Three days later, however, the Worker-Society paper again erred when it gave way to some "Festival Thoughts."

The particular Festival was to mark the 600th anniversary of the start of construction on the famous Cologne Cathedral. For centuries that Gothic structure had stood as a gigantic torso, with a crane on one of its unfinished towers dominating the skyline. At a similar Festival in 1842, the German nation had dedicated itself to the completion of the great Cathedral. Frederick William IV, a romantic admirer of the Gothic and an enthusiastic supporter of the undertaking, had been the main speaker. The Archduke John, now the Imperial Administrator, also had been a distinguished guest. Both princes again were to be present at the coming Festival on August 13–16, together with a delegation from the Frankfurt Parliament. German princes, diplomats, politicians, churchmen and commoners together would join in the Festival, because the completion of the Cathedral had become a national undertaking that united Catholics and Protestants. Many Germans regarded the Cathedral as a symbol of Germany's capacity for unity and greatness. It was a mood that was difficult to resist in 1848.

Some Liberals and Democrats, and quite a number of radicals, scoffed at this Gothic enthusiasm, dangerous because Frederick William IV of Prussia was so closely identified with it. Those who opposed the Church also resented any link between a religious building and the rising 19th century force of national sentiment. Yet it was difficult to be openly critical of the Festival in 1848 when German hopes for unity were so high. Marx and Engels themselves studiously avoided any comments in the *Neue Rheinische Zeitung*. In fact, the paper ignored the coming event completely; only the extraordinary volume of paid advertisements bearing on the coming Festival informed the reader that something big lay ahead in Cologne. Marx and Engels recognized in 1848 that silence was better than valor when religious sensibilities were involved. Nor did they dare to offend the popular yearning for a strong united Germany, which the Cathedral also represented.

The *Zeitung des Arbeiter-Vereines*, however, felt that something had to be said about the biggest event in Cologne in years. In its "Festival Thoughts" the paper stated that it "gladly greeted" a Prussian King who listened to the wishes of the people, and it then saluted the Archduke John with "unfeigned joy," as a pledge of a "united powerful happy Germany." This was too much for the Communists and other strongly republican members of the Worker-Society. Princes and kings were not to be "greeted gladly," anywhere or on any occasion. The Committee met on August 14 and unanimously rejected the article, demanding also that their protest be printed in the next issue of the paper.

In the end, the Communists themselves had to take over full editorial responsibilities for the paper to guard against future lapses. Since Schapper's services with the *Neue Rheinische Zeitung* were indispensable, he proposed on September 14 that the Committee select one editor who would be "completely responsible for the paper." Since the editing, proofreading and distribution of the paper would require four or five days per week, a salary was to be paid. Vice President Schapper nominated President Moll for the position. An opponent of the Com-

munists then offered to do the job without pay. This proposal was rejected with the remark that every worker deserved to be paid; Moll
became the new editor with a salary of 3 *Taler* per week (about $2.40).
The paper was now in sure hands. It followed the line of the *Neue
Rheinische Zeitung.*

Moll and Schapper also substantially altered the organization of the
Worker-Society. As set up under Gottschalk, a Central Committee made
up of fifty members was the real policy-making body, representing the
many crafts, guilds or types of workers. It met twice a week, decided
on policy, held "discussions" and later listened to reports on current
political developments. At the infrequent general meetings of the
Society, there was a report from the President, an occasional speech,
and general endorsement of the policies recommended by the Committee. The local branches of the Society were more important. Because
of their smaller size and weekly meetings, indoctrination and educational work were more possible on the local level.

At the Committee meeting of September 4, Moll called for the reorganization of the Worker-Society. The Committee was reduced to
twenty-five members and the principle of representation by the various
crafts, so offensive to Marx and Engels, was dropped. The new Committee included only those who in the previous months—in short, since
Gottschalk's arrest—had shown the greatest interest and capacity. Moll
also succeeded in winning approval for fixed dues on one silver *Groschen*
(less than three cents) per month. This provided a better financial basis
for the Society and a closer count of the members, since contribution
previously had been on a voluntary basis. The vital Worker-Society Committee was now safely in Communist hands, with provisions for a steady
income from dues. But it would require time to gain the unquestioning
allegiance of thousands of workers.

Marx's role and influence in the Cologne Democratic Society, consistent with his pose as a Democrat, was direct and open and in contrast to his relations with the Worker-Society during the summer of
1848. As an officer in the Democratic Society, he attended most of its
meetings. He and Schneider II represented the Society on that Central
Committee which served as a coordinating agency for the three democratic and worker-societies in Cologne and ultimately in the Rhine
Province at large. Marx's greatest success with the Democratic Society
came when their general views, hopes and fears aroused them to action consistent with his revolutionary tactics.

The arrests in Cologne early in July particularly roused the fears of
the Democrats. In two South German states, Württemberg and Baden,
democratic societies were suppressed. This was followed by a rumor

that the Cologne Society was going to be outlawed. The loud alarm expressed by the *Neue Rheinische Zeitung* helped to confirm and to magnify such fears. In response to the circumstances, the Democratic Society sponsored a popular meeting on July 9 in the *Gürzenich*, producing a signed protest against the alleged counterrevolutionary actions of the Hansemann Ministry. The petition, which was sent to the Prussian Assembly, asked that body to declare that said Ministry "did not possess the confidence of the country." The protest brought no change in Berlin, but the Democratic Society and similar organizations in Prussia continued to exist, to protest and to propagate themselves throughout the summer.

The stalking of reaction, however, helped to bring a certain unity into the ranks of Democrats and radicals and aided the Communists' strivings towards a common front. Marx gained an additional advantage when Wilhelm Wolff, who served on the editorial board of the *Neue Rheinische Zeitung*, began to give regular surveys of current events at meetings of the Democratic Society. This was important because his selection and interpretation of the news were dependably cast in a Marxian mold. Marx himself, however, was distinctly rebuffed when he tried to exclude certain democratic views from even being heard in the Democratic Society.

The disputed views were those of the once renowned "first Communist," Wilhelm Weitling, formerly admired by Marx but later condemned. Like Banquo's ghost, Weitling appeared in Cologne to propagate his own communistic views as outlined in a pamphlet that he distributed among workers and Democrats. Marx responded without fanfare by having copies of the *Communist Manifesto* handed out in the same quarters. The matter became serious, however, when Dr. H. Becker, a leader in the Democratic Society as well as one of the two delegates of the Society of Workers and Employers in the Democratic Central Committee in Cologne, granted Weitling the opportunity to expound his "system" at a meeting of the Democratic Society. Marx called on Becker privately and protested vigorously, asking, "Don't we have enough of the Gottschalk form of nonsense around without having you bring Weitling on the platform!" But Becker stuck to his decision, granting to Marx the right to reply in return.

Weitling, accordingly, spoke at the Society's meeting on July 22, when he was given the recognition due a veteran of the fight against the status quo. But the views which he expressed did not have a democratic ring. Because the masses were not yet ready to rule, Weitling declared that those who had the "best insight" should exercise power after the revolution. He also argued that it was necessary to handle political and social questions separately. Clearly he had not hit the right note and did not gain much of a following.

Marx did not reply until the next meeting on August 4. In contrast to the forthright Weitling, Marx asserted that the democratic republican government, established after the next revolutionary round, would have to represent the different classes. While it was necessary to emphasize class conflict, Marx insisted that no one class could exercise authority during a transitional period. The new government would have to represent the "heterogeneous elements" that made the revolution, like the February Provisional Government in Paris—sort of a democratic front. Karl Schapper similarly spoke to the Worker-Society to counteract Weitling's more elemental appeal to the workers.

Early in August the Democratic District Committee suddenly called a congress to organize a Democratic Party in the Rhine Province. Hitherto this Committee had been rather remiss in its efforts towards furthering the cause of a Democratic Party in Germany. Possibly this was due to a certain coolness and suspicion on the part of the three Communists on the Committee towards the German Democratic Central Committee in Berlin, which included Hermann Kriege and Julius Fröbel.

A mere notice in the *Neue Rheinische Zeitung* served as a general invitation to all societies with a "democratic tendency" (to include worker-societies) to send delegates to a Democratic Congress in Cologne on August 13 and 14. The notice was signed by Marx and Schneider II for the Democratic Society, by Moll and Schapper for the Worker-Society, and H. Becker and H. Schützendorf for the Society of Workers and Employers. The fact that individual invitations had not been sent to various democratic societies led to protests and demands for an explanation during the Congress. The *Zeitung des Arbeiter-Vereines*, not yet under control by the Communists, also called for an explanation. No satisfactory answer was given. Perhaps the District Committee members in charge of arrangements had assumed that an invitation in the *Neue Rheinische Zeitung* would be noticed by all societies with a democratic tendency.

The date selected for the Congress coincided with that of the Cologne Cathedral Festival when Cologne would play host to numerous kings, princes, parliamentary delegates, archbishops, priests and thousands of people from all ranks. The Festival was to be the most spectacular event in many years, bigger than several carnivals. Special trains and extra steamboats would carry thousands to Cologne. After several hungry years, all this would give the city an enormous boost. There would be something for everybody and for every hour—special operas, balls, Cathedral albums, medallions and good food. Most spectacular of all, a certain A. Coxwell of London would be there to take his 104th flight in a "Big War Balloon" over Cologne. A large advertisement on successive days in the *Neue Rheinische Zeitung* stated that Coxwell would bombard the city from the air. The balloon was described as a "terrible and useful machine," capable of destroying a city or a whole army. No congress had a chance in the face of such a performance.

If the Democratic District Committee deliberately scheduled the Congress as a democratic demonstration with republican overtones and as an alternative attraction to the princes who would be in Cologne, the move was a blunder that backfired. The Democrats were widely condemned for holding their Congress at the same time as the Festival. The *Kölnische Zeitung* reprinted, without comment, the observations of an Elberfeld paper that could not understand why such a congress of democratic-republican societies was tolerated at that time. It charged that the purpose of the meeting was to incite the masses with talk of a "republic and communism" at a time when so many princes and high clergy were present. A riot during the festivities would be scandalous. Anyone who read the *Neue Rheinische Zeitung* and the *Zeitung des Arbeiter-Vereines* could see that "freshness and not freedom ruled there." The article ended with the suggestion that the meeting place of the Democratic Society be closed and all republican societies be suspended.

Faced with so much hostility, the Democratic Congress conducted its sessions quietly. There were no public pronouncements. Even the *Neue Rheinische Zeitung* said nothing about the Congress until exactly a month later when it published a brief, factual summary of the meetings. The delegates themselves recognized that their meeting during the Cathedral celebration was being used against them in a "perfidious way." They therefore decided to ignore the issue. But this did not prevent Wilhelm Wolff from stating, "The current Cathedral Festival has nothing to do with Germany's unity; it is a Cologne moneybag affair." H. Becker proclaimed, "We here are also building a cathedral, the Cathedral of Freedom. We also are workers. May our cathedral not become a ruin" like the torso of the Cologne Cathedral.

The accomplishments of the Congress can be pieced together from Joseph Moll's report to the Worker-Society and the account in the *Neue Rheinische Zeitung*. Moll spoke of forty-one delegates representing sixteen democratic or worker-societies. The *Zeitung's* report counted seventeen societies by including a Rhineland Westphalian Society in Berlin. Other Democrats were present without credentials as delegates.

Three main questions were listed on the agenda: (1) How to expand the number of democratic societies and create a closer coordination between them; (2) What action and propaganda the societies should follow towards the outside world; (3) How to raise money and how much. Some progress was made towards establishing a Rhineland provincial democratic organization with Cologne as the center. The Cologne Central Committee in turn was approved as the Central (District) Democratic Committee for the Rhine Province. Contrary to the intentions of the Central Committee in Berlin, the Congress also favored bringing the neighboring Prussian province of Westphalia under Cologne's jurisdiction. Arrangements were made for constant correspondence between each Society and the District Committee in Cologne. A second Congress was scheduled to meet on September 24.

Missionary work for the cause of democracy was strongly urged. It was pointed out that the countryside was ripe for a democratic harvest, because of agrarian discontent. The peasants, harassed by the bureaucrats and burdened by taxes and feudal obligations, were ready to join with democracy, if the Democrats showed an interest in their cause. Members were urged to go out into the country among the peasants and factory workers, to create new societies in the villages and to maintain ties with them.

This matter of going to the land, of using agrarian discontent, of organizing societies and holding meetings in the country was pressed by Marx, Engels and their faithful supporters. The stress on an "agrarian" appeal, already pronounced in the "Demands of the Communist Party in Germany," grew even stronger as it became evident that the needed revolutionary forces in the cities were too small and even lacked the right spirit. It was the Worker-Society, however, directed and inspired by Moll and Schapper, that did the most to carry out this agrarian approach. The regular Democratic Society was less active.

Miscellaneous items on the program of the Congress included the idea of looking to France for revolutionary help; that idea was explored and rejected as impractical. A certain Giolina from Cincinnati, Ohio spoke hopefully of proletarian prospects in the U.S.A. Engels gave a talk, but the report merely summarized the contents as follows: "The chief character trait of the Rhineland was hatred of the officials and of stock Prussianism; this state of mind, it was hoped, would persist."

The Congress adjourned on August 14 without any public pronouncements. If Marx had hoped to gain a solid personal following from the Democrats there, he must have been disappointed. Only two delegates became devoted to him—Peter Imandt, a teacher from Krefeld, and Victor Schily, a lawyer from Trier. Both men became faithful followers during 1848/49 and in the years ahead.

Marx had no success with the important delegation from Bonn— Gottfried Kinkel and Karl Schurz. Kinkel was a well-known professor, poet and Social Democrat who had just become the editor of the *Bonner*

Zeitung. Karl Schurz was then a university student at Bonn and a follower of Kinkel.

Later, when in America, Schurz recalled how he had looked forward to seeing Marx, only to find that his reactions were unpleasantly mixed. He saw Marx as a man who spoke clearly, logically and solidly—a daring man fired by an inner passion. Yet Schurz also found that he had never seen any person who showed such an "insulting unbearable arrogance in demeanor. No opinion which differed from his own was given the honor of a somewhat respectful consideration." Marx treated everyone who contradicted him with contempt that was barely concealed. When an argument displeased him, he showed his scorn over peoples' ignorance or openly doubted their motives. He always used the word *bourgeois* with contempt, as if he were spitting it out. Thus Marx won no supporters and had very little success, as Schurz recalled.

Marx himself recognized the limits of his influence on a mixed body such as the Democratic Congress; he could accomplish most in a group of that kind by working behind the scenes, allowing others to push the policies he favored. The Cologne Central Committee (with Marx, Schapper, and Moll as three of its six members) emerged from the Congress as the District Committee of the rudimentary Democratic Party in the Rhineland. From an organizational standpoint, Marx was in a good position to influence the future policies of all who flew the democratic flag in a large and important area of Prussia. Marx registered another gain when the Congress specifically recommended the *Neue Rheinische Zeitung* by name as an *Organ of Democracy.* The major proposal of the Congress calling for the exploitation of agrarian and peasant unrest certainly was Marxian-inspired.

The *Neue Rheinische Zeitung* continued to be of utmost importance to Marx and Engels, as a medium through which their revolutionary guidelines, exhortations to action, and denunciations of existing governments reached a far wider public. But it required a tremendous exertion on the part of Marx to keep the paper alive, after having launched it with insufficient capital. The traditional account (based on an assertion of Engels years later) that half of the stockholders withdrew their support early in June while the second half allegedly followed suit at the end of the month, unquestionably is exaggerated. There are references to stockholders in the paper throughout 1848 and into 1849. A contract and statute regulating the affairs of the company was agreed on late in July. Still later, around November 10, Marx himself wrote to Engels (temporarily a refugee in Switzerland) that he had thwarted some "imbecile reactionary stockholders" who had demanded that he drop Engels from the Editorial Committee of the paper. But exaggerated or not, the fact remained that there was not enough money from subscriptions and paid advertisements to maintain publication. Marx had to spend a great deal of time soliciting funds.

Reputedly, Marx sacrificed some of his personal fortune to keep the paper solvent at critical moments. But his "fortune," the 6000 *francs* he had received early in 1848, also had to cover the cost of moving from Brussels to Paris and thence to Cologne, plus the living expenses of his family until May, 1849, when he was expelled from Prussia. At the very best, Marx may have placed back into the *Zeitung's* till some of the compensation he counted as his due for services to the paper.

The finances and the financing of the *Neue Rheinische Zeitung* will remain something of a mystery. It will never be known just how many persons Marx approached for financial support, either by letter or in person. But unquestionably Marx was successful in convincing a number of people that his unprofitable paper might turn into a financial success, or that it deserved support in any event. People were always impressed by his undoubted mental powers, especially when he allowed himself to be as charming and diplomatic as he was capable of being. Some of the money he received was nothing less than a subsidy or gift, occasionally dressed up in the guise of a loan.

Soliciting money and subscribers for the *Neue Rheinische Zeitung* was one of the main purposes of an excursion to Berlin, Vienna and back to Berlin again. The *Zeitung* of August 24, however, merely reported that *"Der Redakteur en chef,* Karl Marx, left yesterday to go to Vienna for some days." Perhaps to mislead the authorities, the fact that he was also going to Berlin was not mentioned. Such business excursions apparently were very enjoyable for Marx. As a diplomat for the cause, and as *Redakteur en chef* of a great newspaper, he believed in preserving appearances by staying in first-rate hotels and living as became a man of his stature. He liked to go out in the company of others for an evening, warmed by an indulgence in good wine. The trip which was to be brief lasted nearly three weeks.

Marx had not been in Berlin since his student days. He arrived from Cologne on the 24th and remained until the 27th. A nostalgic reunion took place with Friedrich Köppen, an old associate and fellow member of the Doctors' Club. Several years later Marx took pains to point out that he also "renewed his friendship" with Bakunin who was in Berlin at the time—a friendship that had just been severely taxed. Before going on to Vienna Marx also met various members of the Left in the Prussian Assembly, including Jung and d'Ester of Cologne.

Marx arrived in turbulent Vienna on August 28 for a longer stay than in Berlin. The Austrian capital deserved special attention because of its unparalleled revolutionary ferment and happy chaos which made it unique in 1848. Marx's first public appearance was at a meeting of the Democratic Society where he gave a talk on the latest disturbances which had shaken that city. But he had to share the stage with Julius Fröbel who was then a leading Democrat in the Frankfurt Parliament and who very probably overshadowed Marx in popular esteem. The Vienna paper, *Der Radikale* of August 31 reported that this meeting of the Democratic Society was interesting and most important, because several guests were present—"the well-known political writer, *Julius Fröbel;* and the editor of the *Neue Rheinische Zeitung,* Mr. *Karl Marx;* both men have become important because of their peculiar destiny." According to several accounts, Marx and Fröbel advocated contrasting policies for the Vienna Democrats. Marx argued that it mattered little who was in the Austrian Ministry (there were frequent shifts in 1848) because the battle was now between the proletariat and the bourgeoisie, as in Paris. This was a little too advanced for the Democrats in Vienna, although Marx's speech was described as "intelligent, sharp and instructive."

Marx's next public appearance in Vienna was on September 2 at a meeting of the Worker-Society. A number of newspapers referred briefly to the speech of "*Herr* Dr. Marx." He told the members of the Worker-Society that he felt honored to speak before them, as he had already spoken to similar societies in Paris, London and Brussels. After this reference to his international contacts and credentials, he recited his litany against the capitalist system, the already familiar discourse on "Wages and Capital," as the best introduction for the uninitiated workers. It taught them that under the capitalist system they could only fare worse and worse, regardless of remedial measures of any sort.

Marx remained in Vienna about eleven days. On the whole he was very gratified with his reception. He had met diverse democratic, radical and nationality leaders and had been able to explore the nationality conflicts, especially with reference to their effects on Czech and German workers. Marx also became personally acquainted with Eduard von Müller-Tellering, the Vienna correspondent for the *Neue Rheinische Zeitung.* They were mutually impressed with each other, and Müller-Tellering thereafter became the leading Communist contact in Vienna. He followed Marx into exile in 1849 and remained a loyal supporter until 1850 when a breach occurred.

Around September 8 Marx returned to Berlin again, just as a ministerial crisis was developing. He had the opportunity to consult with various Democrats and radicals and to watch them in action, by attending a session of the Prussian Constituent Assembly. The stay in Berlin ended rather abruptly because of the growing crisis. He wanted to be back at the helm in Cologne, in the safer surroundings of the Rhineland, which he reached around September 11.

The tour to the capital cities had been financially rewarding. In Berlin, he negotiated with Wladyslaw (Leon) Koscielski, a representative of the Polish National Democrats in exile. Thereafter, on September 18, Marx received 2000 *Taler* from the Poles as a subsidy for the *Neue Rheinische Zeitung*, in view of numerous past and expected services of the paper in favor of Poland. Writing to Engels around November 10, Marx spoke of only 1950 *Taler* from that source. Perhaps he had a poor memory for round numbers or he deducted the difference to cover his expenses. The same letter mentioned an additional 1850 *Taler* derived from other sources, apparently from Vienna.

=IV=

The September Crisis

1. THE POLISH DEBATES

THE Cologne Cathedral celebration demonstrated clearly that the popular force of national sentiment in 1848/49 was not one that Marx and Engels could afford to offend. National hopes or grievances were capable of commanding a wider popular following than any particular political platform or ideology. They were the grounds on which diverse radical, democratic and even liberal elements could unite for revolutionary action. Hence, Marx and Engels exploited national feeling as an ally against the status quo and especially against the old bulwarks of reaction—Prussia, Austria and Russia.

The enlistment of national feeling as a revolutionary force appears to be a contradiction to Marx and Engels' theory of history which rejects nationalism. (The future was to show that they seriously underestimated the nature and durability of national differences.) According to their theory, national hostility and divisions were bound to vanish when it became clear that the decisive conflict in human affairs was along class lines, as determined by economic factors. As workers everywhere realized that they had the same common interests and enemies, national differences resting on diverging languages, cultures, historical traditions and past conflicts would become irrelevant and fade away. The proletarians of the world would indeed unite.

In 1848, however, Marx and Engels seldom allowed theoretical and long-range considerations to control their decisions. The practical revolutionist draws on the forces that are immediately available. Marx and Engels, accordingly, glorified and defended every national movement as being "revolutionary," if such a movement acted as an ally against the status quo which they wanted to destroy. Contrariwise, they denounced as reactionary every national manifestation that barred revolutionary progress.

Marx and Engels also recognized that existing states still had a brief role to play. Until the dawn of the communist classless and stateless millennium, the separate states served as the stage on which revolution occurred, leading to the rule of the proletariat. Since Marx and Engels looked to the German world especially, as destined to play a big revolutionary role, they supported the national drive for a united Germany. Such a Germany, fused together in an unconditional, militantly revolutionary sense, with German Vienna and Austria proper included, was entitled to greatness in the name of historical progress.

Revolutionary considerations caused Marx and Engels to place the cause of Poland on par with that of Germany. They believed that the restoration of a large Poland was necessary to help usher in, and to guarantee the survival of, a revolutionary Germany. Such a Poland would be constructed largely out of land that Russia had seized earlier, thus shoving back the frontiers of Russian "barbarism" and facilitating the triumph of revolution among the Germans by relieving them from the pressure of a reactionary Russia. This latter view was shared by radicals, democrats and certainly many liberals in Germany.

The progress of revolution, however, could be seriously endangered when the national aims of neighboring peoples clashed, creating division, even deadly enmity among the democrats and liberals of competing nations. National considerations caused certain parties and even a whole people to side with reaction, or, in the name of their own national hopes, to fight against the aspirations of another people. This spirit was most graphically expressed by a Czech patriot who voiced an emphatic preference for the Russian *knout* rather than freedom in the liberal German empire that the Frankfurt Parliament was to construct. Tyranny under the rule of the racially-related Slavic Russia was better than freedom in a German context. When the chips were down, nationality came before freedom in the case of most Poles, Germans, Czechs, Hungarians, Italians, Croats and others. That was one of the major surprises of 1848 and a cause of much disillusionment. Marx and Engels bitterly denounced this trend which gave priority to national claims at the cost of revolutionary gains. In particular, the Pan-Slavic program of Bakunin was anathema to them, even though his credentials as an anarchist and democrat were unassailable.

Bakunin's program of democratic Pan-Slavism, with its appeal to the small Slavic nationalities within the Austrian Empire, could be realized only at the expense of the Germans and Hungarians whom the Slavic nationalists viewed as their competitors, oppressors or enemies, past or potential. In the opinion of Marx and Engels, this Pan-Slavism was directed at the very Germans and Hungarians who were destined to play the major revolutionary role. Hence, it was easy for them to assume that Bakunin was trying to split the ranks of international "democracy" by advocating the cause of a Pan-Slavic empire at the cost of revolution in general. Indeed, Bakunin was even trying to win a following among the Poles whom Marx and Engels regarded as the revolutionary allies of Germany against Russia. Since Marx and Engels always suspected Pan-Slavism of being a Russian device, or one that could be exploited by the Tsar to extend Russian power, it was easy for them to sense the presence of a sinister plot in which ·Bakunin, consciously or unconsciously, acted as a Russian agent. In any event, Bakunin's volcanic energy and capacity to win a popular following made him a dangerous competitor. His efforts had to be checked.

It appeared most opportune, therefore, for the *Neue Rheinische Zeitung* of July 6 to publish a curious report under the dateline, "**Paris, July 3." After commenting on the fact that the people of Paris, in spite of their own domestic ferment, were following the struggles of the Slavic race in Bohemia, Hungary and Poland with a vigilant eye, the *Zeitung* stated:

> With reference to Slavic propaganda, we were assured yesterday that George Sand [the social novelist, feminist and long time companion of Chopin] had gained possession of papers which strongly compromised the banned Russian, M. Bakunin, by portraying him as a tool, or as a recently acquired *agent of Russia,* who was guilty of bringing about the recent arrest of Polish patriots. George Sand showed the papers to several trusted friends. We have nothing against a Slavic empire, but it will never, never come into being through the betrayal of Polish patriots.

The *Neue Rheinische Zeitung*'s report of the alleged evidence obtained by George Sand, linking Bakunin with the arrest of Polish patriots, carried a devastating impact that could destroy his influence among radicals and democrats. Bakunin keenly sensed the danger.

Bakunin's reply was published in a Breslau newspaper, together with a copy of a letter that he sent to George Sand, asking her either to make public the alleged papers or to certify their non-existence. In regard to the editor of the *Neue Rheinische Zeitung,* Bakunin wrote:

> I am dealing with a powerful and irreconcilable enemy who has pursued me systematically and tirelessly ever since I openly attacked him in a speech in Paris. He even uses and exploits my natural allies, Democracy and its *Organs,* as a means for his purposes. In the eyes of governments, he depicts me as a demagogue capable of any crime; at the same time he tries to discredit me in the public mind by spreading the rumor that I am an agent. Evidently he hopes thereby to discourage me and to make me harmless. But he will have made his efforts in vain.

Marx published Bakunin's communication to the Breslau paper in the *Zeitung* of July 16. He had everything to gain by doing so. If George Sand indeed possessed the incriminating documents, the case against Bakunin would only be strengthened. If the accusation proved false, the *Neue Rheinische Zeitung* could claim that it had been fair when it printed Bakunin's communication from the columns of another paper.

George Sand's denial soon came. Marx printed it in the *Zeitung* on August 3, preceded by a statement that the original report which he printed had come to him from two correspondents in Paris who were strangers to each other. "We thereby fulfilled the duty of the press to keep a close eye on public characters; simultaneously, we gave Bakunin the chance to deny the suspicion which already was circulating in Paris." Marx then quoted the relevant part of George Sand's letter: "The facts that were given me are totally false and do not even have the least appearance of the truth," George Sand wrote, further stating that she had never entertained the least doubt as to the loyalty of Bakunin's character and the liberality of his views. She ended her communication with a postscript, which Marx also published, in which she appealed to Marx's honor and conscientiousness to publish her letter immediately.

Marx was able to turn the episode into another gain for himself. Wladyslaw Koscielski, the Polish democrat and supporter of Bakunin, had carried George Sand's letter to Marx from Paris. It seems that at that meeting, Marx succeeded in turning Koscielski against Bakunin, for the Pole immediately wrote to Bakunin that he would no longer serve him as a "second." It was this same Koscielski who was instrumental in providing Marx with a substantial subsidy from the democratic Poles in September.

The Bakunin case was closed, but never quite ended. When the charge against Bakunin was revived in London in 1853, it was noted that the "same calumny" had been printed in a German paper in 1848. Since this obviously was in reference to the *Neue Rheinische Zeitung*, Marx, who was living in London, then explained that the Paris reports accusing Bakunin had come from the Havas-Bureau, a news agency, and from a "Polish refugee" (a misleading designation, as Marx confided to Engels, for August Ewerbeck—an East Prussian, a Communist and formerly head of the League of the Just in Paris); he had published Ewerbeck's report and not that of the Havas-Bureau.

The Polish issue was one on which Marx and Engels could meet with most German democrats, radicals and even some liberal and Catholic elements. Opinions were divided over the June Insurrection, various social questions and such specifically German matters as the choice between a federal or a unitary state. But differences of this nature sank out of sight when a question like Poland temporarily stirred up a tidal wave of emotions. The case for Poland even had some of the qualities of the seven virtues—many might sin against it, but few would openly repudiate its claim to a fundamental validity.

But there was a more important reason for Marx and Engels to champion energetically the Polish cause in 1848. Poland, for them, was a key to success in the revolution. It offered the surest guarantee of a big war—the needed war against Russia. War, a life and death struggle against a formidable enemy, was necessary to produce the domestic strains, tensions and passions required to usher in and to accompany the complete revolution in Prussia and Germany at large. The example of the French Revolution always stood before their eyes. France, when faced with the threat of a national disaster, had experienced an upsurge of patriotism and anger which led to the downfall of the King, a radical turn in French politics, a national concentration and centralization of power, dictatorship and a regime of executions and terror.

"Only in the tempest of war and revolution" would Germany be welded together, the *Neue Rheinische Zeitung* stated on June 25. Marx and Engels were even urging the necessity of war as a tonic for Germany. Germany should support the cause of freedom of other peoples, the *Neue Rheinische Zeitung* demanded on July 3, to atone for a long "register of sins." The theme of past sins, repentance and a new life was repeated on July 12, ending with the following exhortation: "Only *war with Russia* is a proper war for *revolutionary Germany*, a war in which she will wash away the sins of the past, in which she can build up her own courage, in which she can defeat her own autocrats. . . ."

Most German democrats hesitated to follow the Marxian demand for a deliberate plunge into a war with Russia, aimed at the restoration of Poland as she had existed before the first partitioning in 1772. But most of them were all the more vehement in wanting to do the right thing by such Poles as were included in a German state—even at the expense of some of their own fellow Germans. The immediate issue in 1848 involved the Grand Duchy of Posen, with a Polish majority together with German and Jewish minorities. Posen was a part of the Prussian state, but the Polish majority was highly nationalistic and repudiated the thought of remaining united with a free Prussia or Germany.

The prospects for the Poles in Posen proper looked good in March, 1848, when the Germans were almost more pro-Polish than pro-German. The Polish revolutionary leaders were applauded more vigorously in Berlin than any German heroes of the barricades. The liberalized Prussian government almost immediately granted national autonomy to the Grand Duchy of Posen, with the Poles in command. It was a risky move, but in line with the optimistic mood which prevailed early in 1848, the

Prussian authorities evidently felt that there was no need for asking the Poles to guarantee the rights of the German minority residing in Poland. There was also the danger that Russia might intervene to crush the newly-established autonomy of the Poles in Posen. (Russia was certain to regard a Polish national government at her frontiers as a nest of sedition and conspiracy which would try to promote a national revolution and to raise claims to the far more numerous Polish elements in the Russian Empire.) Unknown to the public, the Prussian government even proposed a war, in alliance with France, against Russia for the very purpose of liberating all of Poland. But Lamartine, the French Foreign Minister, was not ready for such an adventure. In any event, the mood in Berlin soon changed.

The news that came from Posen prompted the change. Once the Poles were in control, they apparently acted in a highly nationalistic fashion. The German minority in Posen complained of discrimination, persecution and a Polish terror. Influenced by such reports, the Prussian military forces returned to Posen to protect the alarmed and endangered Germans. This in turn led to a brief but ferocious conflict in which the outmatched Polish national forces (many were armed with terrifying scythes) were crushed early in May. Engels denounced this Prussian military action as a "war of the Huns" (*Hunnenkrieg*). The democrats out of sympathy with the Poles were generally angry at Prussia.

The Prussian state then tried to solve the conflict of the two nationalities by drawing a new frontier between them. In four successive steps certain regions that supposedly were mainly German in population were separated from Posen and annexed to Prussia proper, with strategic considerations leading to the inclusion of certain areas that were distinctly Polish. The *Neue Rheinische Zeitung* called this the first of a long train of reactionary steps taken by the Camphausen Ministry—it was tantamount to a fourth, fifth, sixth and seventh partitioning of Poland, added to the three historic ones.

The question of Posen embarrassed the new liberal ministries in Prussia. Democrats, radicals and some Catholics in the Prussian Assembly repeatedly brought up the matter. The Germans in general were in a painful dilemma, accustomed as they were to a position sympathetic to the Polish national cause. Yet they could not deny protection to their fellow nationals in Posen. The matter was brought directly home when contributions were solicited to relieve the distress of the Germans there.

The Frankfurt Parliament was faced with this unhappy problem in July when it had to decide whether those areas that Prussia had detached from the Grand Duchy of Posen were to be included in the German Empire they were creating. The matter could not be evaded or postponed because the Parliament had to vote on granting or denying the admission of representatives of the people living in those regions. The debates on the Polish-Posen question took place on July 24–27. The majority of the Frankfurt Parliament upheld the Prussian decision by voting to admit those areas in Posen that appeared to be mainly German. The Parliament thereby accepted the nationality principle as decisive in frontier questions. Some of its members took into account the strategic need for a good defensive frontier against Russia.

The sentiments of many Germans were perhaps best expressed by the *Kölnische Zeitung* on June 27 and 28. Granting that the past partitionings of Poland had been unjust, it maintained that such injustices in the past would only be compounded if a new act of force were applied against the national wishes of some of the present day inhabitants of Posen. The soil itself was neutral, neither specifically Polish nor German, the paper reasoned. Those who inhabited and cultivated the land should be the masters, as "free, self-determined human beings," an argument that sounds almost Wilsonian. (The Constitution drafted later by the Frankfurt Parliament also contained a full guarantee of equality and the cultural rights of such minorities as would be included in the new Germany.)

The Democrats and the Left in the Frankfurt Parliament, with a few exceptions, passionately opposed the decision of the majority. They were joined by a few Catholic delegates, prompted by a sympathy for Polish Catholicism and a pinch of anti-Prussian feeling. The issue provided another angle from which Prussia could be attacked and rebuffed, because the Parliament in effect was being asked to endorse annexations initiated by Prussia. A few Democrats, however—notably Wilhelm Jordan, a well-known democratic writer—adopted the German national view. Jordan defended his decision by stating that it was time for the Germans to act realistically by looking out for themselves, rather than playing the cosmopolitan who wished all others well while neglecting vital German interests.

Initially the Polish Debates were reported in the *Neue Rheinische Zeitung* merely within the context of news from Frankfurt. It is surprising that neither Marx nor Engels wrote any leading articles on the debates for nearly two weeks. Perhaps they personally hesitated to assail the decision of the all-German Parliament in a matter where German national interests clashed with Polish national claims. But between August 9 and September 7, Engels wrote nine leading articles on the subject. This emphasis was justified because the way to war with Russia lay through Poland.

The Germans, "with weapons in their hands," Engels declared, should have demanded from Russia the surrender of her Polish territories so Poland could be restored to the dimensions of 1772. War with Russia, moreover, would have brought about a complete, open and real break with Germany's "shameful past." War would have meant the "downfall of the German and French bourgeoisie," followed by the victory of democracy erected on the ruins of feudalism and the "short dream of power on the part of the bourgeoisie." The creation of a democratic Poland remained a necessity for the establishment of a democratic Germany.

The Polish question likewise gave Engels the opportunity to denounce Prussia's military campaign against the national revolutionary elements in Posen as having been ferociously conducted. In any event, Prussia had merely pretended that she was protecting the Germans in the areas detached from Posen, when the real reasons for the annexations were of a fiscal and economic nature. The Prussian treasury just did not want to lose the large income from the extensive estates that the King owned in Posen. As for the annexation of the Posen areas by the Frankfurt Parliament, Engels compared it to the *Reunion* policies of Louis XIV. This argument was designed to hit the Germans directly; many still grieved over the French annexation of Strassburg and much of Alsace back in the 1680's.

In demanding the restoration of Poland, Engels was determined that the Poles should not be shortchanged. After having spoken of a Poland as great as that of 1772, by August 20 he was ready to grant Poland even more, including the mouths of her important rivers and a big coastal frontage on the Baltic Sea. He was confident that frontier questions would raise no problems between the Poles and Germans. Naturally, many Germans would have to become Poles in the process, and many Poles would turn into Germans. It is not clear where the "many Poles" would come from to match the "many Germans" in this peaceful shift in nationality. But his proposal had a true ring, in harmony with the belief that national feeling represented no barrier between two revolutionary peoples.

Engels' pro-Polish ardor declined in the next few years when he developed a greater appreciation for the defense needs of Germany, because of her destined revolutionary role. Writing for Marx in the New York *Daily Tribune* in 1852, he no longer could see why whole tracts of land, largely peopled by Germans, should be turned over to a nation that had shown no proof of its "capability" to progress beyond a feudal order. Never again did either Marx or Engels explicitly state, as in 1848, a willingness to disregard Germany's strategic and other interests in favor of Poland. War with Russia still remained as the one solution that could solve the boundary question. The Poles would just help themselves to more Russian soil, making them more "tractable and reasonable in their demands on Germany."

In 1848, however, Engels attributed a special revolutionary task and historic mission to the Poles. They were the first to recognize and propagate the idea that the Slavic peoples, as also every other nation between the Black and Baltic seas, could liberate themselves only via an "agrarian democracy," and advance only through an "agrarian revolution." But all this demanded that Poland simultaneously regain national independence on a grand scale—a prerequisite for a nation with a revolutionary mission. Engels, therefore, gave free rein to his genius for satire and denunciation when he applied it to those who spoke against the Polish national case in the Frankfurt Parliament, above all to the Prussian delegates from Silesia.

Gustav Stenzel, the liberal professor and historian who presented a history and population figures for Posen favorable to the Germans, was derided throughout the length of two articles in the *Neue Rheinische Zeitung*. But Engels' main target was Prince Felix Maria von Lichnowski.

There was an aura of mystery, irresponsibility, romance and even danger about the wealthy Prince and landowner from Silesia. Although essentially a conservative, he was likely to take a position in the opposition where the stones flew thickest. He had defended the Silesian weavers in the Prussian Diet. He had stood by the Prussian King on that dark March day when Frederick William IV was forced to appear on a balcony to pay homage to the barricade dead. In the Frankfurt Parliament he sat among the conservatives, without however conforming to the formulas of any fixed party. An able parliamentarian, skilled in interpellation, witty and cogent in debate, Prince Lichnowski used his brilliant gifts to bait and deflate the Democrats and the Left. He would call upon Robert Blum—perhaps the best-known and most loquacious figure in Parliament—to identify himself whenever he rose to speak. The Prince's actions, manner, figure, position and misdirected abilities were an offense to the egalitarian eye. The Prince was a Mephistopheles who dogged the steps of the earnest, upward-striving Faust like a shadow.

Directing his flair for verbal inventiveness squarely against the suave, able and striking personality of the Prince, Engels called him a "Prussianized Pole," the "German Bayard without fear and reproach," and much more. The attack was pursued by Georg Weerth in a series of *Feuilletons* under the title, "The Life and Deeds of the Celebrated Knight Schnapphahnski" (*Schnapphahn*, a highwayman, plus the Slavic *ski* ending of Lichnowski's name).

When Weerth temporarily ran out of ideas or tired of the subject, the *Schnapphahnski* series was interrupted late in August. A Breslau (Silesia) newspaper thereupon published a report, ostensibly coming from Berlin, that Lichnowski had bought a large block of stocks in the *Neue Rheinische Zeitung*, causing the paper to drop the subject "because a newspaper could not possibly carry on a polemic against its own stockholders." A democratic paper reprinted the same information in nearby Düsseldorf—uncomfortably close to Cologne. The *Neue Rheinische Zeitung* then published a denial on September 3, asserting that as a party newspaper it had given adequate proof that it "could not be bought." Perhaps to prove the point, the *Schnapphahnski* series was thereafter resumed with a new verve and vigor. The Prince was even pursued beyond the grave, months after the September day when he was killed by a mob in Frankfurt. Perhaps this was a fitting though unconscious tribute to the life and ways of Prince Felix von Lichnowski.

If the conservatives and liberals in the Frankfurt Parliament were flayed unmercifully by the *Neue Rheinische Zeitung,* the pro-Polish Left did not escape blame. Robert Blum never got beyond "mere declamation," Engels declared. Arnold Ruge, Marx's old foe, was recognized as important enough to be pummeled throughout two successive issues. Since the "Democratic Party" included such multiple and diverging elements, Engels insisted on watching them more closely than any other. A vote alone in favor of the Polish cause was not enough. Posen, after all, was important only because of its revolutionary potentialities, which had to be defended with the proper stance and passion. Engels demanded that the "decided Left" dismiss all "indulgent mildness" and abandon all hope of getting anything accepted by the majority. Only one delegate was praised for his elemental passion—a lone Pole from Posen, elected from an area whose annexation the Frankfurt Parliament was about to sanction. Engels quoted this Pole at the end of his final article on the subject: "You have swallowed Poland, but, by God, you won't digest her."

2. MINISTERIAL CRISIS IN PRUSSIA

EVEN before Engels had published the last of his articles on the Polish Debates early in September, serious crises were approaching in both Frankfurt and Berlin. The situation was doubly grave for Prussia since there was an anti-Prussian edge to the all-German crisis in Frankfurt. The Prussian crisis simultaneously came to a head in connection with a matter concerning the army, always the source of much opposition and suspicion.

The Prussian army, while recruited on the basis of universal military service, had a tradition of loyalty to the King, all the more so because most officers came from the ranks of the aristocracy (*Junkers*). Since that army had fired on the people of Berlin at the time of the barricades in March, it could be used again as the right arm of the reaction to destroy the newly won liberties of the people. The democrats and radicals were generally anti-militaristic and talked of the need of a "peoples' army," or a people-in-arms. But many moderate liberals also were critical of the old military setup, with its professional officers drawn mainly from the *Junker* class. Hence it was possible for democrats, radicals and many liberals to join hands in the Prussian Constituent Assembly meeting in Berlin when army issues were involved. This happened in August and September, 1848.

The conflict began with an incident in Silesia which gave the army some luridly unfavorable publicity. The members of the Civic Guard in the city of Schweidnitz demonstrated against their Commandant in a manner that was typical of 1848, by investing his house and smashing the windows. The Commandant, fearing for his own safety, asked for the protection of the regular Prussian military garrison. On August 3 an exchange of shots took place between the soldiers and members of the Civic Guard. Fourteen civilians were killed and others were injured. The incident was universally condemned and deplored. The democratic and radical press exploited the situation by asserting that the Prussian Commander had ordered his soldiers to fire.

Since the event created a furor in the Prussian Constituent Assembly, the Democrats and the Left were able to rally a solid majority in favor of a motion proposed by Julius Stein, the Democrat from Breslau. The motion (of August 9) demanded that the Minister of War should instruct the officers to avoid all reactionary agitation. Officers were not only to avoid every clash with civilians but they also were to associate with the burghers in a manner that would demonstrate their desire to cooperate in the achievement of a legal constitutional system. An amendment added to the above motion furthermore requested all officers who found this motion inconsistent with their political views to resign, as a matter of duty and honor. Stein's motion, passed by a substantial majority, placed the Hansemann Ministry in an impossible position.

The demand that the officers fraternize with the burghers might undermine discipline and make the army unreliable in the event of another revolutionary clash. But more important, the Stein Motion offended the King who insisted that the army owed loyalty to him alone. He denied the Assembly this right to interfere with the powers of the Crown. The program of *Vereinbarung*, of a peaceful agreement between Assembly and King, faced a breakdown. The Hansemann Ministry postponed the crisis by keeping the Assembly ignorant of the King's hostile reaction while it placated Frederick William IV by neglecting to issue the necessary instructions to the army, as demanded by the majority in the Assembly. But a variety of developments made a later explosion all the more certain.

Tensions, mutual rancors and provocations increased during the month of August. On the one side, "reaction" showed a new boldness and began to mobilize its forces. The new tendency was dramatically illustrated by the meeting of a *Junker* Parliament on August 18–19 in Berlin, which was nothing more than a congress of large landowners, with the *Junkers* playing a conspicuous role. A congress was no rarity in 1848. The Democrats had had one in June and were to meet again in October. A labor congress would meet in Berlin at the end of August. Various interests and even specific trades, such as the artisans in general and the tailors in particular, had had their own national get-togethers. But the congress known as the *Junker* Parliament appeared especially sinister because it took an open stand in favor of Prussia, the King and property. Only reaction could rest on such a foundation.

The day after the adjournment of the *Junker* Parliament, the Prussian capital witnessed the curious spectacle of a mob attacking the Democratic Society's headquarters in Charlottenburg, a suburb of Berlin. It is not clear what prompted the action, but it was easy to assume that the reaction, in some form, was behind it. To emphasize the importance of the Charlottenburg affair, the *Neue Rheinische Zeitung* published an extra-supplement to an already published supplement to the daily edition for August 23. It stated that the assault on the Democratic Society's headquarters was the work of a mob and citizens, including some members of the Civic Guard. The account stressed the usual "brutalities," giving specific details concerning the treatment meted out to two of the Bauer brothers, Bruno and Egbert (Marx's former friends). The Bauers had been seized by the hair, dragged down the stairs and hustled out into the street, with the military all the while standing by and making no move in defense of the Democrats. The "officials" were back of it all, the *Extra* charged; they had stirred up a mob by bribing the *Lumpenproletariat* with 10 silver *Groschen* per person (a scandalously large day's wage).

The Democrats of Berlin struck back the following day. Popular gatherings, demonstrations and violence occurred, aimed at forcing the resignation of the Hansemann Ministry and punishment for those involved in the attack on the Democratic Society. The democratic masses invested the building in which the leading Prussian Ministers were assembled, with the usual shattering results for the glass windows. The government replied with a decree prohibiting armed assemblies and demonstrations. Berlin remained in an inflammatory mood that was bound to affect the deliberations of the Prussian Assembly. It was during this period of growing unrest that Marx returned to Berlin from Vienna, to consult with democratic and leftist leaders.

The *Neue Rheinische Zeitung* (and other papers also) contained daily accounts of revolutionary ferment and clashes in cities. Simultaneously the papers reported that the peasants were in a sullen mood and appeared ready to strike. In September a new newspaper began to appear in Cologne, in line with the Marx-Engels attempt to cultivate the revolutionary potential of the peasants. This paper, with popularized versions of many of the views of the *Neue Rheinische Zeitung*, was edited by Anneke (still in prison) and Friedrich von Beust, a former Prussian officer and currently a Committee member of the Worker-Society in Cologne. Both were Communists, or at least close to Marx in their views. This *Neue Kölnische Zeitung für Bürger, Bauern und Soldaten* (*New Cologne Newspaper for Townsmen, Peasants and Soldiers*) was to follow a "social-democratic" slant, and would represent the interests of the "working people, whether in the city or on the land, whether in civilian clothes or in a soldier's uniform."

The ministerial crisis in Berlin came to a head during the first week of September. In reply to interpellations from the Left on September 4, the Hansemann Ministry took the position that it could not, and would not, issue the instructions to the army demanded by the Stein Motion of August 9. This appeared as a direct challenge to the Assembly, which showed no patience towards Hansemann's attempt to avert a crisis. The Prussian Assembly thereupon forced the issue with the following motion: "It is the urgent duty of the State Ministry to execute without delay the motion passed on August 9, in order to calm the country and to avoid a break with the Assembly." Heated sessions followed, accompanied by growing unrest in Berlin. On September 8 a strong majority of the Assembly repeated the demand that the government enforce the Stein Motion. (It is possible that this was the session of the Assembly that Marx attended.) The Hansemann Ministry resigned. The resignation was accepted by the King two days later.

The deliberations of the Assembly during that crucial session of September 8 occurred in an atmosphere that was far from calm. Descriptions in the *Neue Rheinische Zeitung* and the *Kölnische Zeitung* are in essential agreement, though from opposite points of view. According to the *Neue Rheinische Zeitung* of September 10, "Thousands of men surrounded the meeting place of the Assembly." The Deputies of the Left were acclaimed by the people and carried aloft, shoulder-high, in a "triumphal march."

The report in the *Kölnische Zeitung* (September 12) which had supported the liberal Hansemann Ministry, spoke of a terrorizing mob-pressure on the Assembly. Various leaders of "decided progress" and of "the sovereign voters" led the crowd which blocked the doors, halls, and steps of the Singing Academy (the meeting place of the Assembly).

The mob even made itself at home in a refreshment room reserved for the Deputies. As described by the Berlin wit of the hour, the demonstrators there smoked "ministerial cigars lit with a barricade fire."

The *Kölnische Zeitung* then repeated an earlier warning, or suggestion, that the Assembly would have to meet elsewhere, if it lacked the opportunity to deliberate freely due to the threatening posture of the Berlin masses. Otherwise, the laws and the constitution that the Assembly drafted would not reflect the views of the elected Deputies. Instead, the results would be dictated by the leaders of those political clubs who wore "red feathers" in their hats. Nothing was "more dangerous to freedom than a *Convention,* the absolutism of a big and therefore, by nature, irresponsible assembly of popular representatives." Other liberal newspapers and organizations joined in the protest against the mob pressure mobilized by the Left, as reminiscent of the French Revolutionary Reign of Terror. The move to transfer the Constitutional Assembly from Berlin, taken by the government two months later, was already anticipated by many liberals.

Berlin, meanwhile, seemed face-to-face with a revolutionary crisis. On the one hand, a Democratic and Left-Center Ministry, headed by Waldeck and the economist, Johann Karl Rodbertus, seemed assured of the support of a solid majority of the Assembly. On the other extreme, Frederick William IV might install a Ministry of reaction, backed by the presence of the military. The *Neue Rheinische Zeitung* predicted this second alternative, and appeared to welcome it. Such a reactionary step would relight the fires of revolution and bring a repetition of the March Days, followed this time by the fall of the monarchy.

Frederick William IV, however, confounded everybody by his inability to move rapidly and decisively. He also refused to follow either of the two simple alternatives. He did make General F. H. E. von Wrangel, who had just returned with his troops from war with Denmark, commander of all military forces in the vicinity of Berlin on September 13. But the selection of a new Ministry was delayed for nearly two weeks. During the interval, the people were uncertain what kind of a policy, or crisis, the yet unnamed Ministry would represent. Almost symbolically, the Prussian Assembly at this time shifted its meeting place from the halls of the Singing Academy to the Berlin Theater. The Berlin wit interpreted the move as follows: "The operetta has ended; the drama starts." But no one was sure how the plot would develop.

The crisis in Berlin was not exclusively domestic and ministerial. It coincided with the all-German crisis on the Schleswig-Holstein issue with its potentialities for revolution and war—revolution against Prussia and a war with Russia, Denmark, and perhaps Britain and Sweden.

3. SCHLESWIG-HOLSTEIN, SEA-SURROUNDED

THE Schleswig-Holstein question, in the words of a contemporary, was the "thermometer" that registered most sensitively the degree to which national feeling had developed among the Germans. Nothing could arouse them more strongly and unanimously, except perhaps a French threat to the Rhine. It appeared as if all past German frustrations and all promises of a happier future were associated with the destiny of those two disputed territories.

Schleswig and Holstein were two sovereign dukedoms which for centuries had been under the personal rule of the Kings of Denmark, without however being a part of Denmark proper. Holstein was one of the thirty-nine states in the German Confederation, while Schleswig was not. The arrangement created no special difficulties as long as the supremacy of princes, hereditary rule and the principles of legitimacy governed the destinies of a particular land. But with the advent of national feeling and the growth of constitutional government after 1815, Schleswig-Holstein became a source of bitter conflict between German and Danish national claims and aspirations.

Denmark, after the loss of Norway to Sweden in 1814, attempted a comeback through an extension of Danish influence in Schleswig-Holstein. The Danes acted with the confidence of a small nation that can count on the support of some of the major powers. They also had a backing from the Pan-Scandinavian movement which stressed the common culture and destiny of the Scandinavian states. As constitutional government progressed, the Danish liberals wanted to apply every extension of parliamentary power and legislation to all lands ruled by the King, even if those lands lay outside the Kingdom of Denmark proper, as was the case with Schleswig-Holstein. Most of the German inhabitants resisted this trend which pointed towards full annexation. Holstein was wholly German and only the northern third of Schleswig had a Danish majority. Every new constitutional gain in the 1840's brought another crisis; the principle of national self-determination favored a closer union with Germany.

A simultaneous growth of national feeling among the Germans at large assured the people of Schleswig-Holstein of German support. This was best expressed in the sentimentally romantic and heroic song, *Schleswig-Holstein, Meer-Umschlungen* (Sea-Surrounded), which became almost a national anthem after 1844. Schleswig-Holstein became the test case of the Germans' readiness for national unity and future greatness, conscious as they were of all the German-speaking areas they had lost during the preceding centuries, because they lacked national strength and unity—Alsace, parts of Lorraine, much of Switzerland, Holland and half of Belgium. If the Germans could not now prevent a small state like Denmark from taking over some more German land, then all hope and talk of future German greatness was worth no more than an indulgent smile. The fact that this area was bound to be of economic and strategic importance (the Kiel Canal was not put through the peninsula until 1895) played no important role in German emotions at that time. The readiness of the Germans to react strongly over Schleswig-Holstein made a war with Denmark likely sooner or later. Furthermore, the issue provoked such a widespread emotional response that it could also become a mainspring of revolutionary action, if the Germans felt that their own governments had failed to defend their national rights in Schleswig-Holstein.

Marx and Engels, with Engels setting the tone as the expert on nationality and international affairs, at first derided this national enthusiasm and readiness to sacrifice all in behalf of Schleswig-Holstein. In 1846 Engels sent Marx a mocking parody he had written to the song, *Schleswig-Holstein, Meer Umschlungen.* Later that year, he was upset when the League of the Just in London circulated an *Address* that was sympathetic to the German cause. His interest in the subject, however, led him to a broader study of Denmark and other Scandinavian countries, "as an innocent distraction" along with the "girls" in Paris. The net result of his study was the consoling thought that the "smallest German was preferable to the greatest Dane." Though he did not accept the German national claim to Schleswig-Holstein, this new knowledge gave him the self-confidence, and doubts, that reward the person who examines both sides of a question.

The next Schleswig-Holstein crisis came at the start of 1848 when the new Danish King, Frederick VII, was forced to accept a new, liberal constitution which, in effect, absorbed the duchies of Schleswig and Holstein. It granted the people of Schleswig-Holstein representation in the Danish Parliament and placed them under the government and laws of that Parliament, with extensive concessions to the Germans in the duchies. The offer was so liberal that it caused the *Kölnische Zeitung* of February 25 to observe that the inhabitants of Schleswig-Holstein were being offered more in the way of personal freedom and self-government than could be found in most European states just then. But the Germans in the duchies (like the Poles in Posen and the Czechs in Bohemia) placed nationality above immediate personal freedom; they preferred a union with their fellow Germans to any larger measure of individual freedom within the framework of a predominantly non-German state.

In March, 1848, the people of Schleswig and Holstein had their own March revolutions, directed against their Danish Duke (the King of Denmark) and all ties with Denmark. They established their own provisional governments, drafted constitutions, asked for admission to the projected German Empire, and later elected delegates to the Frankfurt Parliament. When the Parliament met, it accepted the Schleswig-Holstein representatives and the responsibility for defending the right of the two duchies to be included in the new German union. Denmark, however, was not overwhelmed or even greatly impressed by such developments. Confident of Russian and British support, perhaps of Swedish aid also, Denmark took military action against Schleswig and Holstein as two rebellious provinces, certain that it would not be a conflict between a dwarf and an awakening giant.

The typical German response to the Danish military operations was expressed by the *Kölnische Zeitung* of April 8. Speaking of the "coarse fury" with which the Danes proceeded against the Germans in the two duchies, the paper exhorted the Germans to show that they would not allow another nation to lay hands on territories inhabited by Germans. They must not permit a repetition of the loss of Alsace. "Do not allow the shame of having Denmark defeat a country of forty million," the paper pleaded.

The German popular response was certainly sufficient. But the Frankfurt Parliament and the new Imperial Ministry were powerless without an army. It was necessary for the Imperial Ministry to request Prussian help to defend German honor, interests and national rights in this struggle with Denmark. The war began in the spring and extended into the summer of 1848.

The military operations actually appeared to be so staged that each side might win a few brilliant skirmishes but no one could win the war in a strategic sense. The heart of Frederick William IV was not entirely in a war in which Prussian troops assisted the Schleswig-Holstein rebels against their divinely-ordained Duke, who was also the Danish King. Moreover, every vigorous Prussian advance was checked by diplomatic intervention and the knowledge that no conclusive victory over the Danes would be permitted by Britain and Russia. The Danes, in turn, lacked the strength to drive out the Prussians, but they were buoyed up by a confidence that Prussia would not be permitted to win.

Engels derisively pointed to the indecisive Prussian military operations as additional proof of the perfidy of the Hansemann Ministry. On June 5, he called it a "comedy of war," and a "belligerent ballet" presented by Prussia for the glory of the German nation.

Small Danish naval forces, meanwhile, had chased German shipping from the seas and captured various Prussian vessels, bringing German commerce to a standstill and making the Germans bitterly conscious of their impotence. As a result, the Germans became angrily and over-whelmingly conscious of the virtues of naval strength. Voluntary contributions poured into Frankfurt to finance a navy. Even the German woman of 1848, otherwise active in such innocent diversions as the emancipation of women and the organization of mothers to breed and educate a new democratic generation, sacrificed her pin money, trinkets and silver to help buy another ton of naval power.

From the first, naval power was regarded as an Imperial question, in contrast to the land forces already existing in each of the separate states. But ships were not built, manned and commissioned overnight. The Danish command of the seas was not challenged by Germans during the Schleswig-Holstein War.

Diplomatic pressure finally stopped the fighting. Faced with the threat of war with Russia, Britain and perhaps Sweden, Prussia signed an armistice at Malmö on August 26, 1848, after many agonizing weeks. It meant the surrender of Schleswig-Holstein and of the right of the people there to join a united Germany.

The Prussian government had acted upon a realistic appraisal of the forces involved. The German public, however, showed less appreciation for the realities of international politics. Nothing in 1848 affected the Germans more unanimously and strongly than the national frustration, pain and anger which they now experienced over the surrender of Schleswig-Holstein. Prussia was accused of selling out or betraying the German cause. There was a general demand that Prussia be forced to renounce the Armistice and to renew the war, regardless of consequences. It was a good psychological setting for a revolution directed against Prussia, and a war with Russia, and perhaps against all the world.

At this point Marx and Engels became rabidly and belligerently nationalistic. When it appeared that the broadest road to war and revolution (better even than the one via Posen) passed through Schleswig-Holstein, the cause of the "Sea-Surrounded" duchies suddenly became revolutionary and sacred.

The Malmö armistice shook the Frankfurt Parliament like the faulting process of an earthquake, as it separated one salient of the German world from the new Empire. There was an outburst of anger against Prussia for having concluded such an armistice without the prior approval of the Parliament and the new Imperial Ministry of the nation as such. On September 5, the Frankfurt Parliament reasserted its authority by refusing to ratify the Armistice.

It was now up to the Imperial Ministry to carry out the decision of the Parliament, but the responsibility looked more appalling than challenging. The Ministry recognized that Prussia would not willingly renew the war with Denmark, with all the attendant risks. It also saw that Frankfurt lacked the power to force Prussia to conform, except through an appeal to the people in Prussia and Germany at large to exert pressure on Berlin, even to the point of revolution. It might be difficult, however, to keep such a revolution within safe bounds. The renewal of war with Denmark also would almost certainly bring about the armed intervention of Russia and Britain. The prospects were not without a touch of grandeur which called for the courageous conviction that a revolutionary, sovereign and free people—or one that was fanatically united in a national sense—could triumph in the face of all odds. Since the Imperial Ministry lacked that confidence, it resigned as a body.

The Imperial Administrator, Archduke John, accepted the resignation of the Ministers and called upon Friedrich Dahlmann to assemble a new Ministry that would represent the majority and carry out its decisions. Dahlmann, the well-known historian and admirer of British constitutional practices, was a moderate liberal and normally a supporter of Prussia. Now, however, he was one of the most vehement advocates of continuing the war in defense of German claims to Schleswig-Holstein.

An aroused Germany, meanwhile, expected Frankfurt to defend the honor of Germany, so shamefully betrayed by Prussia! Concurrently, Prussia and especially the Hansemann Ministry were widely denounced. (The emotionalism of the hour certainly did not help Hansemann in Berlin, as he faced the crisis growing out of the Stein Motion.) All eyes were on Frankfurt to see whether the Parliament would stand by its rejection of the Malmö armistice. It was the first decisive test that would reveal whether Germany had reached the point where she could uphold her interests and command respect in Europe.

There were some, however, who recognized that the test was too much for the still disjointed strength of the infant German giant. But it took much courage to tell this to an aroused public—the *Kölnische Zeitung* was almost apologetic on September 8 when it suggested that there was also a "moderate" point of view concerning the Malmö armistice. To illustrate the "bitter truth" of the matter, the paper merely cited the explanation offered by the Prussian King when bowing to the harsh, humiliating and nearly Carthaginian terms imposed by Napoleon in the Treaty of Tilsit of 1807: "The peace had to be concluded as the circumstances demanded." The comment was almost proverbial in its unrhetorical realism. But few were ready just then to apply the same standards to the Malmö armistice.

Numerous popular petitions urged the Frankfurt Parliament to stand firm in defense of German honor. Assurances were given that the people would support the national Parliament in any action against Prussia.

The long-standing and justified grievances against the separate German states and princes for standing in the way of national unity, freedom and greatness helped to feed this anti-Prussian mood. The situation was favorable for a second round of revolution and war.

As late as July 22, when the general terms of the impending Armistice were already known, Engels had reaffirmed the *Neue Rheinische Zeitung's* refusal (a certain "cold-bloodedness") to be identified with the "raging bluster of the nationalists or the eternal litany of the Schleswig-Holstein-Sea-Surrounded straw-enthusiasm." At the same time, however, Marx and Engels had been employing in the *Neue Rheinische Zeitung* such emotion-packed, nationalistic items as the Prussian army abandoning Schleswig to "devastation and plundering by the Danes," on a stage "lit with burning Schleswig villages" to the chorus of the "vengeful cry of Danish pillagers and armed insurgents." But they had used the items as a means to denounce and deride the Hansemann Ministry. It was this cold, detached state of mind that facilitated their policy of manipulating German national anger, hopes and frustrations in accordance with their aims. But would the Parliament "protect the honor of Germany in Schleswig-Holstein after disregarding it in the Polish question?" Engels challenged on September 8. Analyzing the alternatives the Frankfurt Parliament faced, Engels forecast that if Parliament ratified the Armistice after all, "the Central [Imperial] Government would come under the yoke of Prussia, the Central Government and Parliament would earn the universal contempt of all Europe." The other alternative, the rejection of the Armistice—the one which Engels favored—would mean a "European war, a rupture between Prussia and Germany, new revolutions, the collapse of Prussia and the *real unity of Germany.*" This would be brought about because the demands and strains of such a civil conflict occurring simultaneously with a major war would call for a national concentration of power which would not tolerate the distractions and divisions associated with the continued presence of thirty-nine separate state governments and armies. Monarchy, aristocracy and feudalism in general would be swept aside with the unmasking of the treachery, inadequacy and obsoleteness of kings, princes and feudal aristocracy. A republican government would rule over a unitary Germany, with the annihilation of a separate Prussia, Austria and all other states. At this moment, however, Engels stressed the anti-Prussian factor most strongly. He exhorted the Parliament not to shrink back or to be intimidated: "At least two-thirds of Prussia sides with Germany, against the Prussian government."

Marx and Engels were fully in character when they hailed the Schleswig-Holstein movement and the accompanying German national sentiment as revolutionary, with all the higher rights of revolution. Schleswig-Holstein, Engels explained on September 10, developed a splendidly revolutionary character in 1848, after having been a "purely bourgeois-peaceful, legal philistine agitation." It had been popular with the people from the beginning because it was the first *"revolutionary war"* waged by the Germans (a fact which Marx and Engels had not noted earlier). Under the stress of this revolutionary war, the people of Schleswig-Holstein had become most democratic, with the best democratic constitution in the German language and the "most civilized institutions" (a very questionable assertion). As a proof of the revolutionary character of the German cause in Schleswig-Holstein, Engels cited the fact that the three "counterrevolutionary" powers, *Russia, England* and the *"Prussian Government"* had sided with Denmark from the first. (Prussia's presence in this lineup was justified because she merely "pretended" to fight.) Those countries had the most to fear from a German revolution and its results—the unification of Germany. It would mean the end of Prussia's existence, England would lose her past liberty to exploit German markets, while Russia would see democracy advanced not only to the Vistula but to the Duna and Dnieper rivers. Hence, the three powers conspired against Schleswig-Holstein and against revolution.

Engels justified Germany's claim to Schleswig-Holstein above all in the name of a higher civilization, progress and the rights of revolution. Denmark was a "half-civilized nation," as none would deny. Germany therefore had the same right to take Schleswig as France had exercised when she took Flanders, Alsace, Lorraine, and would take Belgium sooner or later. It was the "right of civilization against barbarism, of progress against stability." This right was "superior to all treaties because it is the right of historical evolution." The right to greatness and conquest belonged to the revolutionary powers.

War was a revolutionary necessity just then because the German "movement" was going to sleep. War, Engels stated, would "endanger the Fatherland and thereby save it," because the Germans would see that victory depended on the internal triumph of "democracy." German nationalism was revolutionary and progressive for the time being, because its demands would bring war and an accentuation of revolution in Germany.

The popular excitement brought on by the Malmö armistice was at its height when the Hansemann Ministry resigned on September 8. Marx, who was then in Berlin, had hurried back to the Rhineland where he wrote a series of articles entitled, "The Crisis and the Counterrevolution," which appeared in the *Neue Rheinische Zeitung* on September 12, 13, 14 and 16.

The signs Marx had seen in Berlin caused him to predict that they were moving towards a "decisive battle." He discounted all rumors that a democratic Ministry would be formed in Prussia, and forecast instead that the reaction would not be satisfied with anything less than a Ministry of the Prince of Prussia. As a sop for the liberals, a few liberal bourgeois conservatives such as Hermann von Beckerath (from the Rhineland) would be included.

Triumphantly confident, Marx predicted that the reaction would provoke a showdown. The reaction or counterrevolution, faced with the simultaneous crises in Berlin and Frankfurt, now would be forced to fight its last battle. If it dared to trample on the constitutional principle of the rule of the majority in Berlin, if it confronted the 219 votes of the majority with 219 cannon, if the new Ministry in Frankfurt also disregarded the majority, "*if they provoke a civil war between Prussia and the Germans in this way, the Democrats would know what to do.*" The italicized parts appeared in large and bold print.

In the second article of the series Marx declared that the ministerial crisis in Berlin was really a conflict between the Constituent Assembly and the King, the *Crown*. One or the other would triumph. If the King won, the Assembly would be dissolved, the right of association ended, freedom of press destroyed, suffrage limited—all under the protection of a "military dictatorship, cannon and bayonets." The attitude of the people, namely, of the Democratic Party, would determine who would win. "There is certainly no lack of good will, but of courage, courage!" Marx concluded with words which were both an exhortation and a question.

Continuing his analysis of the revolutionary situation in Prussia and the specific requirements of any revolution, Marx stated that every provisional revolutionary government required dictatorial power, and "indeed an energetic dictatorship." The principle of "public welfare" alone counted under revolutionary circumstances. To make sure that his readers did not misunderstand him, Marx added the French words, "*mesures de salut public.*" (In the name of public welfare, the French Revolution had resorted to a general terror.) In contrast to the above revolutionary requirements, Prussia had been operating merely under the principle of *Vereinbarung*. But now an unavoidable collision between Assembly and Crown was at hand. "The side which acted with the greatest courage and consequence would win!" Marx asserted. Marx invariably was very outspoken on the eve of, or during a crisis, as well as immediately after a revolutionary defeat, in contrast to his more normal "democratic" stance of 1848/49.

Several incidents occurred in Potsdam and Nauen involving the refusal of two regiments to obey orders. Marx interpreted such "military revolts" as proof of a general defection in the army. It might not even be necessary to do much fighting to make a new revolution, when the conflict between "democracy and the aristocracy" had erupted even in the guard regiments. "Thereby the sword is wrenched from the hands of the counterrevolution," Marx declared optimistically, ending his reports on the crisis.

The following day Marx replied to the charges of the "counterrevolutionary press" that the Constituent Assembly in Berlin lacked freedom of deliberation because of the pressure from the masses. He did not deny the charge—instead, he boldly affirmed that the "Center" (moderate liberals) indeed had been intimidated by the masses at the time of the fall of the Hansemann Ministry. "Whether its [the Center's] fears were justified or not, we will not say." Marx gloried in the right of the masses to exert such pressure. "The right of the democratic masses to exercise their presence is an old revolutionary right of the people . . . which cannot be spared in any stormy time. History owes its thanks to this right for all energetic steps taken by such bodies."

Freedom of deliberation has always been a "hollow phrase," Marx continued. It is a "completely senseless phrase," in a time of revolution. When two powers, two parties, face each other in arms, when the battle can erupt at any moment, the Deputies have only one choice. They either place themselves *under the protection of the people* and submit to a little lecture from time to time," or they place themselves *under the protection of the Crown*" and move to a small town, away from the masses, under the protection of bayonets and cannon. It is a choice of "intimidation by the unarmed people or intimidation by the armed *Soldeska*." The alternatives were simple!

4. BLOOD-RED AND THE BLACK-RED-GOLD

ALL the hopes of the German nation seemed to depend on Dahlmann's ability to form a new Imperial Ministry which was willing to accept the challenge implicit in the repudiation of the Malmö armistice. Whatever the outcome, new domestic convulsions, perhaps a second round of revolution and war seemed most probable in view of continuing high tension in Germany. Marx and Engels identified themselves with the anger and national frustration resulting from the Schleswig-Holstein disaster through the medium of their *Organ of Democracy*. They spoke as German patriots and as the most energetic defenders of German honor and national hopes against Prussian perfidy and foreign opposition. Journalistic interpretations of events, exhortations to courage, and appeals to the passions of the day, however, were no longer enough. A public and energetic display of the Party's colors was the demand of the hour, now that the time for action on the part of the masses was fast approaching. To inspire and direct them, Marx had the help of that small but dedicated group of followers—Schapper, Wilhelm Wolff (*Lupus*), Dronke, Weerth, Moll, and occasionally Bürgers, all except the last two currently connected with the *Neue Rheinische Zeitung*.

In the ensuing revolutionary agitation in Cologne, the Communists were evident everywhere. They appeared to be in command, almost like a party, or at least an overwhelming presence. Newspapers commented on the fact that the editorial staff of the *Neue Rheinische Zeitung* occupied the public platform, gave many speeches, and initiated motions. Marx alone kept away from the stage. Having been informed on September 12 that his petition for reinstatement of Prussian citizenship had been denied, he undoubtedly felt it best as an "alien" to avoid public meetings and applause.

On September 7, before Marx's return from Berlin, the Democratic Society had sponsored a large popular meeting in the arena of a riding academy in Cologne. The crowd which perhaps exceeded twenty-five hundred (the *Neue Rheinische Zeitung* reported that five thousand had been turned away for lack of room) approved an *Address* to the Frankfurt Parliament demanding the rejection of the Malmö armistice. Carried away by the spirit of that meeting, several hundred persons joined the Democratic Society the next evening when it met with more than three thousand people in attendance, according to the Worker-Society paper.

A "stormy unanimity" reigned at that meeting of the Democratic Society. An *Address* to the Frankfurt Parliament, which ultimately carried four thousand signatures, condemned Prussia for having ignored the Imperial Ministry in concluding the Armistice and demanded that the Parliament stand by its repudiation of said Armistice in the face of a European war. But the declaration did concede that the Danish-speaking areas of northern Schleswig should not be forced to join Germany against the will of its inhabitants. The meeting reached a climax with a storm of loud "hurrahs and bravos" when Ernst Dronke appeared to announce the news that the Hansemann Ministry had fallen.

The Communists concurrently were counting heavily on agrarian unrest. Both the *Neue Rheinische Zeitung* and the Worker-Society paper carried numerous reports of peasant disturbances, large protest meetings and scattered acts of violence throughout Germany. Such accounts encouraged the workers and Democrats in the cities to look to the peasants for help, and conversely, local agrarian ferment was more likely to crystallize if the peasants saw that their grievances were part of a nationwide pattern. Early in September the Communists ordered a large new printing of the "Demands of the Communist Party," with its four distinctly agrarian clauses, for wide distribution in the countryside.

At the Committee meeting of the Worker-Society on September 11 (Engels' first appearance), Ernst Dronke presented a stirring analysis of the ministerial crisis in Berlin. He predicted a Ministry of Reaction behind which absolutism would stand out in all of its "greatness, boldness and presumption." The Berlin Assembly undoubtedly would be dispersed with the help of "Pomeranian bayonets." (No one expected anything good out of Pomerania, generally regarded as a most backward province in Prussia.) A fight between the King and the people was unavoidable. Perhaps at that very moment the people were taking to the barricades in Berlin, Dronke declared. It was a presentation that certainly produced an atmosphere of suspense. But the first serious clash was not in Berlin.

Even as Dronke was speaking that evening of September 11, a clash was taking place between Prussian soldiers and civilians right there in Cologne, where memories and resentments were still alive concerning a similar incident that had occurred in August two years earlier. This "small Rhineland intermezzo" (as General von Roon described it from headquarters in Koblenz the following day) was nothing less than a senseless brawl started by soldiers of the 27th Regiment from Saxony. The outbreak occurred in a city square when a girl fled from the attentions of several soldiers to the protection of civilians who were out walking. Verbal exchanges and insults followed. The enraged soldiers called for help from their comrades in nearby establishments. The soldiers went on a rampage, almost berserk, as an over-indulgence in drink caused an explosion of their resentment over the coolness and hostility of the civilian population. Feeling had been so high that soldiers from regiments passing through Cologne sometimes refused to eat in public places unless the proprietor joined them; they had heard that they might be poisoned.

In the melee which followed, the soldiers struck about with drawn weapons at both men and women and refused to obey the commands of their officers when they appeared. It required the intervention of the Civic Guard to restore order. Where so much fury was in the picture, it was surprising that there were no casualties. But a number of civilians were wounded, some with several sabre wounds. Witnesses also noted that the soldiers had made insulting remarks about the German national colors, the Black-Red-Gold.

The first reaction in Cologne was one of anger and outrage. The City Council met immediately the next morning to deliberate on the events and to decide what action to recommend to the Prussian authorities. The democratic and radical forces, in turn, surrounded the City Hall and besieged the Council with their demands. Although the offending 27th Regiment had been confined to the forts as a precautionary and disciplinary measure, the crowd insisted that the unit be entirely removed from the environs of the city. It also demanded that the Civic Guard (armed and five thousand strong) be completely mobilized to defend the populace against the Prussian "Soldeska," as reported in the *Neue Rheinische Zeitung*.

The City Council called out the Civic Guard to patrol the streets while the army transferred the 27th Regiment to another locality. Such steps had a reassuring effect. After the first angry reaction, it likewise seemed clear that the soldiers had acted in such a rage that it ruled out the possibility of the incident being a deliberate plot aimed at provoking a clash. Nevertheless a minority in Cologne remained doubtful, on the assumption that there was a "method in such a display of madness." The Democrats and radicals were not appeased—or they recognized that the circumstances were favorable for a revolutionary move.

A first attempt to organize a revolutionary apparatus was made within the ranks of the Civic Guard, after it had been armed on September 12. One unit, the 9th Company—commonly called the "Red Company"— was commanded by Karl Wachter, a radical Democrat. Karl Schapper was in this Company as well as other Communists, many Democrats and members of the Worker-Society. Demands were raised that the defense of the city gates be turned over to the Guard, thereby sealing off the city from the military. It was also proposed that a Committee of Public Safety be created, reminiscent of the body that had exercised dictatorial powers during the French Reign of Terror. The *Neue Rheinische Zeitung* of September 13 related that the Committee was to be elected by a direct, popular vote, thus representing all of the people in Cologne, in contrast to the City Council which was elected by restricted suffrage resting on property qualifications (*Zensus*), as related in the *Neue Rheinische Zeitung* of September 13. The Committee would have the power to call popular meetings when "serious situations" called for it. The Commanders and guardsmen of other companies, however, refused to back such a revolutionary step. Although it is difficult to connect Marx and Engels with this event, the *Zeitung* indicates that they at least were well-informed about what was going on behind the scenes.

After the Civic Guard had refused to approve such a Committee of Public Safety, an "appeal to the people" was considered necessary, as the *Neue Rheinische Zeitung* described developments. Late that same evening (September 12), the leaders of both the Democratic and Worker-Society decided to call a meeting for the following day at noon. They also prepared a list of names to serve on the Committee of Public Safety, to be endorsed by popular acclamation. Placards and announcements summoning people to the meeting were printed and posted everywhere that night. The following morning, according to an official Prussian report, the editors of the *Neue Rheinische Zeitung* "did not disdain . . . to go through the streets with a bell inviting the public to attend the meeting." * "Something novel to satisfy the precious search for novelty," as the *Kölnische Zeitung* contemptuously described it.

The Prussian authorities, uncertain of the attitude of the Civic Guard, made no attempt to prohibit the meeting. Reports on the size of the crowd that met in the *Frankenplatz* vary greatly. The *Kölnische Zeitung* reported only a small number around the speaker's platform while several hundred others, largely drawn out of curiosity, stood discreetly apart. Cologne's correspondent for the *Bonner Wochenblatt,* who was always reasonably objective in his appraisals, stated that the square was about one-fifth filled, probably several thousand people. The *Neue Rheinische Zeitung* raised the figure to five to six thousand.

All reports agree that the editors of the *Neue Rheinische Zeitung* were the chief participants in this "grotesque spectacle of the election of a committee of Public Safety," as the *Bonner Wochenblatt* described the event. Engels, Dronke, Wilhelm Wolff and Heinrich Bürgers followed one another to the improvised speakers' platform set up on a cart that was draped with the Black-Red-Gold flag. It was the type of popular meeting where no serious dissent is expected and none is heard. Heinrich Bürgers presided, as moved by Wilhelm Wolff and seconded by a few "hurrahs." The speakers talked of the excesses of the soldiers and of worse threats to freedom that were being launched by the reaction, the camarilla and the *Soldeska.* Wolff, always the trusted and efficient executor of the Marxian will, then proposed that a Committee of Public Safety be created, since the municipal authorities were too weak to guarantee the necessary security for citizens. The motion was adopted with "stormy applause." The assembly then approved the thirty members of the new Committee, as their names were read one by one from the prepared list. (The *Bonner Wochenblatt* commented on the "astounding sureness of vision" shown by Bürgers, as he counted by 10's the votes endorsing each candidate.) There were no rejections, but when the showing of hats appeared too thin, the chair gave the candidate an extra boost by describing him as a member of the Worker-Society and a good Democrat. Marx, Engels, Wilhelm Wolff, Karl Schapper, Joseph Moll, Ernst Dronke and Heinrich Bürgers were on this Committee of Public Safety. (Actually, thirty-two persons were elected, since Gottschalk and Anneke were on the list but could not serve until released from prison.) In the next days, Schapper informed the Communist-led Committee of the Worker-Society that the new Committee "belongs to our party bag and baggage."

After the Committee was duly elected, Engels addressed the meeting.

* Cited by the East German historian, Gerhard Becker, in *Karl Marx und Friedrich Engels in Köln 1848–1849. Zur Geschichte des Kölner Arbeitervereines* (Berlin, 1963), p. 122.

He spoke mainly of the late events in Berlin, to direct attention to the work ahead. Reviewing the ministerial crisis in Berlin, Engels stressed that the reactionary Ministry which he anticipated would dissolve the National Constituent Assembly—nothing less than a *"coup d'état."* He asked the people assembled in the *Frankenplatz* to approve a declaration calling on the Assembly in Berlin "to do its duty in defiance of any attempt to dissolve the Assembly and to defend their places even in the face of the power of bayonettes." The resolution was unanimously adopted. The meeting was adjourned.

The Committee of Public Safety, however, had been launched without a revolutionary tide sufficient to keep it afloat. Most of the citizens of Cologne saw no need for it. Instead, many regarded such a Committee as an actual threat to public safety and took steps to counteract it, even before it had been acclaimed in the *Frankenplatz*. As described by the *Neue Rheinische Zeitung* two days later, many emissaries of the *Bürgerverein* (Citizens-Society, composed of moderate constitutional liberals) had appeared as observers, occupying the higher areas of the *Frankenplatz*. It was also alleged that several "well-known howlers" tried, unsuccessfully, to bribe people to provoke a disturbance.

The Commanders of the Civic Guard met at the City Hall that same day (September 13) to prepare for action against the anticipated unrest. Leaders of the *Bürgerverein* were present to warn them that Cologne was in danger; the Committee of Public Safety was the first step towards revolution, and the "Red Republic" would soon be declared. Therewith the *Bürgerverein* offered its services to the Guard to preserve order. As a first step it printed a protest against the Committee of Public Safety and posted copies on the walls of Cologne.

The *Bürgerverein* also prepared a handbill in "bold lettering, printed in the shop of the *Kölnische Zeitung* and distributed to its subscribers" (according to the *Neue Rheinische Zeitung*) which accused the "Social Democrats" of trying to regain lost ground by exploiting the discontent resulting from the latest actions of Berlin and Frankfurt. The handbill further stated that, to provoke a conflict at any cost, the Social Democrats "deliberately exaggerated" the late disturbances in Cologne. It flatly declared that no one could recognize a committee selected by a "casually-assembled popular meeting" as having any legal authority. The "pretended danger" from the military no longer existed. The "real danger" resulted from the creation of the Committee of Public Safety. True freedom and order demanded the support of the existing authorities in preserving law and order.

The Committee of Public Safety recognized almost at once that they had misjudged the popular temper in Cologne. A statement was issued clarifying its position so as to mollify the public and avoid legal complications. As a first step the Committee formally notified the authorities of its existence and purpose, denying that it was a revolutionary body with power to operate parallel or in opposition to the constituted legal and political agencies. The Committee explicitly declared that it "aimed to preserve the peace, whenever possible in cooperation with the authorities, but to guard simultaneously the continuation of popular rights." In the face of this avowal, the Prussian authorities found no ground for legal action against the Committee of Public Safety.

The *Neue Rheinische Zeitung* published the above clarification on September 15, followed by its own comments, designed to counteract the unfavorable reaction. Making light of popular apprehensions, the *Zeitung* stated that people were already losing their fears of yesterday which saw in the "Committee a provisional government, a *comité de salut public,* a conspiracy to create the Red Republic"—in short, everything except what the Committee actually was, "a *Committee* publicly and directly elected by the people, which is here to represent the interests of that part of the population not represented by legal authorities." The Committee would only operate legally; it would usurp no power whatever, except for the "moral influence which the right of free association, the laws and the confidence of the voters bestow on it." By spelling out what the Committee was and what it was not, this public disclaimer simultaneously called attention to what the Committee might do under more favorable revolutionary circumstances.

This denial of revolutionary intent and purposes, however, did not prevent even radical members of the Democratic Society from disavowing the Committee of Public Safety, after some reflection. Seven of its members, including Schneider II, the President of the Democratic Society, and Karl Wachter, the Commander of the "Red Company," informed the public of their resignations through notices in the *Kölnische Zeitung.* The Committee of Public Safety thus represented a premature hope rather than a significant milestone in the mobilization of revolutionary forces in a more radical direction.

In view of the setback with the Democratic Society, Marx and Engels had to rely mainly on the Worker-Society as a propaganda and organizational agency during the remainder of the September crisis. Schapper confidently asked its Committee to approve and recognize the Committee of Public Safety. Wilhelm Wolff, perhaps less sure of the outcome of such a vote, suggested that it was superfluous to vote since the five thousand people who had approved it on September 13 represented a "true expression of the will of the people." The ensuing vote allayed all doubts when the Worker-Society Committee unanimously added its endorsement.

A gigantic popular meeting sponsored by the Worker-Society was scheduled for Sunday, September 17 at Worringen, ten miles north of Cologne. It was to be the culmination of the missionary work of the Cologne Society "in the direction of social reform," and was designed to give an enormous boost to the movement. Members of the worker-societies recently organized in the small towns, peasants from the surrounding countryside, and delegations from Cologne and Düsseldorf would cement the new revolutionary alliance between worker and peasant, city and small town. Elaborate preparations were made to insure a big turnout, with large advertisements in many newspapers. Transportation from Cologne to Worringen, by land or river, was to be furnished for one silver *Groschen*—a reasonable price for a Sunday outing.

Optimistic reports from Worringen indicated that almost all the people, townsmen and peasants, in that area had adopted the "new view." The mayor, on the other side, sent alarming reports to the Prussian authorities in Cologne, speaking of dangerous "rebels" from Cologne spreading atheistic, communistic and treasonable ideas among the peasants. The "Demands of the Communist Party" were being distributed. He even reported that Marx and Schapper had been there spreading Communist ideas. (Marx certainly was not there, but evidently his name was being used in connection with some of the principles that were being propagated.)

When the 17th arrived, the police in Cologne tried to hamper the flow of celebrants to Worringen. Boats were studiously inspected to see if they were seaworthy; the credentials of the pilots were examined to check upon their qualifications; delays and confusion were multiplied because embarkation was denied at certain appointed places along the river. But the *Neue Rheinische Zeitung* was able to announce triumphantly that five or six big boats (canal barges), each carrying about two hundred people behind the "red flag" at the bow, left Cologne for Worringen. The Worker-Society paper reported that 10,000 people from all points assembled in a meadow. The *Neue Rheinische Zeitung*, seldom guilty of understatement in such matters, saw "at least 6000–8000." This number included the usual contingent of real or suspected informers and police spies. Several of them were treated roughly and thrown into the Rhine. One nearly drowned before being mercifully rescued. There was no lack of revolutionary energy.

Sunday, September 17, 1848, stands out as a red letter day for the Communists. The organizational *éclat* and the unanimity of sentiment made it a testimonial to the success of the Communist-led Worker-Society in recruiting a following among the peasants and villages. It brought the new Committee of Public Safety a recognition that the

Cologne Democratic Society had withheld. The "blood-red flag" dominated the center of the speakers' platform, flanked by the Black-Red-Gold national colors.

Joseph Moll, the Communist President of the Cologne Worker-Society, opened the proceedings with the motion that Karl Schapper (the Communist Vice President) be elected as President of the meeting, with Friedrich Engels as Secretary. There were no other nominations. Schapper took the chair and then proposed a unanimous declaration in favor of a "republic, and specifically the democratic-social, the *Red Republic.*" The response was unanimously affirmative, except for one vote, as reported in the *Neue Rheinische Zeitung* two days later.

Unanimity continued to rule at Worringen as the crowd approved Ernst Dronke's motion calling upon the Berlin Assembly to stand firm in the face of bayonets (the same resolution endorsed by the Cologne popular meeting on September 7). This was followed by the adoption of Moll's proposal recognizing the Committee of Public Safety as elected in Cologne. That Committee was then honored by a "thundering, triple *Hoch.*"

The same enthusiasm prevailed when Engels asked the assembly to support the Frankfurt Parliament with their "fortunes and blood" in behalf of Schleswig-Holstein. They, the "assembled imperial citizens," were to pledge their allegiance to Germany, if a conflict developed between Germany and Prussia because of a Prussian refusal to accept the decisions of the Central (Imperial) Government and Parliament in Frankfurt. A vote on the matter was superfluous, except as a formality and as a demonstration. This was a rejection of legal and concrete obligations to Prussia in favor of citizenship in an empire yet to be created.

In line with the prevailing unanimity, the *Neue Rheinische Zeitung* was designated as the paper which Democrats were to recommend everywhere, whereas they were to outlaw the *Kölnische Zeitung*, this "reactionary, slanderous paper wherever they met." If a proprietor of a public place subscribed to "this vulgar paper," the Democrats should patronize a more acceptable establishment.

Only a small part of the Sunday at Worringen was spent on declarations and resolutions. A long line of speakers took up most of the time. Wilhelm Wolff took the floor for the Cologne Communists. Because of his Silesian peasant background, he was the most suitable speaker for a crowd such as this. Ferdinand Lassalle also spoke. Though only twenty-three years old, he was the leader of a large delegation from Düsseldorf. Thereafter, a leader from every locality, including tiny Worringen, had to be recognized. The meeting ended with a short speech by "Henri [Albert] Brisbane of New York, the well-known editor of the democratic-socialist New York *Tribune.*"

The success of the Worringen meeting immediately led to the scheduling of a similar one for "Wesslingen" (probably Wesseling) on October 1. A meeting at "Wesslingen" (a small community like Worringen, with a newly-organized Worker-Society) would have an extra punch because that was the place where the *Bürgermeister* had earlier arrested two emissaries of the Cologne Society in a futile attempt to stop their agitation.

There is no record that Marx appeared at that Sunday meeting at Worringen, although there no longer was a Monday edition of the paper to be prepared on that day. (Reluctantly, and only after all other newspapers had agreed to grant Sunday as a day of rest for the typesetters, had Marx notified his subscribers of this change late in August.) Marx's insecure status in Prussia, however, called for caution, a policy that paid off a week later.

Actually the Worringen meeting represented only a mobilization of revolutionary forces for an anticipated crisis rather than a rally for immediate action. It was necessary to wait until the crisis came to a head, as would occur when the Frankfurt Parliament took its final stand on the Schleswig-Holstein question or when the ministerial crisis in Berlin brought a reactionary usurpation of power. For the time being, the forces of order held the advantage. With thirty to forty thousand troops available in the Rhine Province as a whole, General von Roon was confident of the power to maintain order.

Joseph Moll expounded the Marxian policy of caution before the Committee of the Worker-Society. Opposing immediate action, as Hermann Kriege was then advocating, Moll stated that it was still necessary to "restrict the battle to the mouth and the pen." The Party was growing constantly. Many people, especially those on the land, were waiting for someone to bring them the "humanist doctrines of democracy and socialism." It was necessary to gain the support of the peasants (80 percent of the population) and to overcome the resistance of the army. Even the soldiers had a human heart and a sound mind. They were not "robber gangs without a will of their own. . . . A bullet-proof shirt of mail could not resist the truth," Moll asserted.

In Frankfurt, meanwhile, Dahlmann was attempting vainly to form a Ministry that would accept responsibility for the rejection of the Malmö armistice and its consequences. But most of the persons who were acceptable to him refused to serve in this particular crisis. He undoubtedly could have found others from the ranks of the Democrats and the Left who were eager to chastise Prussia and to resume the war. But such persons, because of their radical views in other matters, did not command the confidence of the moderately liberal majority. Moreover, coldly realistic considerations began to enter the picture more strongly. Helmuth von Moltke (who was not a member of the Parliament) expressed the situation well when he asked quite bluntly how any sensible man in Frankfurt could expect Prussia to break the Armistice, resume military operations against Denmark, expose her ships to seizure, provoke a war with Sweden and Russia, to mention only the major complications. Many also recognized that some of the most vocal supporters of a repudiation of the Armistice hoped to exploit the ensuing confusion for their revolutionary purposes. Because of this fact, August Reichensperger, a Catholic delegate from the Rhineland, extracted a little comfort when he finally voted to accept the Armistice. Thereby, he wrote, "the hopes of our subversives for chaos at home and in foreign affairs are destroyed or their realization delayed in any event."

After ten agonizing days Friedrich Dahlmann finally notified the Parliament that he was unable to form a new Ministry. That body then bowed before the unhappy reality when a slender majority voted on September 16 to accept the Malmö armistice, thus reversing its former stand. The Imperial Ministers who had resigned returned to their posts. The impotence of the Parliament was unsparingly exposed by this humiliating reversal. The response in Germany was an angry popular outcry on the one hand, a fatalistic resignation on the other.

Popular excitement and anger were especially pronounced right in Frankfurt. The masses, inspired by the Radical-Democrats and the Left, undertook action to force that body to act courageously by purging or persuading the timid majority which had accepted the Armistice. A group of radical Deputies, emboldened by the revolutionary potentialities of the situation and bolstered by popular acclaim, met separately the following day. The more audacious members proposed that they secede from the Parliament and set themselves up as a separate body meeting in permanence and backed by an aroused populace.

A gigantic rally under the open skies of a large meadow took place that same day (September 17). The crowd wanted action and demanded the courage that an angry or enthusiastic mass itself experiences. It denounced the 257 Deputies who had voted to accept the Armistice as traitors to the Fatherland and called on the minority to form a separate government. In response to fiery exhortations, the people then rushed back to the city to construct and man the customary barricades. This popular uprising was sullied that afternoon by the senseless killing of Prince Lichnowski and General Hans von Auerswald who were foolhardy enough to go out riding.

Insurrection and revolution reigned in the streets of Frankfurt that day. The angry mob even attacked St. Paul's Church. With no troops of its own, the Imperial Ministry was helpless. It finally had to submit to the ultimate ignominy of asking for Prussian, Austrian, Hessian and other nearby military units to restore order. The workers of Frankfurt and neighboring localities, supported by an influx of peasants (as reported by

Engels on September 20) fought a heroic though hopeless battle against the disciplined, regular soldiers. The revolt was crushed in less than forty-eight hours.

The first news of the insurrection brought new hope to Marx and Engels, after the frustrations they had experienced when the Frankfurt Parliament refused to stand by its initial repudiation of the Malmö armistice. If the revolt succeeded and a democratic-radical minority took control of the Parliament, the armistice again might be rejected. German national feeling, angered and aggrieved over Schleswig-Holstein, might be ready to take such a radical turn in its stride if it promised to fulfill their national aims. Engels, as the expert on Schleswig-Holstein, bayonets and barricades, wrote three articles on the events that were transpiring in Frankfurt.

Although Engels had little confidence that the workers themselves could win the battle of the barricades, he expected the peasants to intervene in a decisive manner. He spoke of an influx of peasants from "countless localities." If the insurrection held its own for a day, the "whole population" of designated areas in South, Central and West Germany would be under arms. There would not be enough troops to suppress the revolt. Even after the Frankfurt revolt had been extinguished, the "raging peasants" would not just put aside their arms. Engels hopefully predicted that they would continue the war against six or eight capital cities and hundreds of knightly manors until feudalism was destroyed.

Philosophizing in the familiar Marxian style, Engels then analyzed the reasons why "Order" always triumphed. The red flag, as the "standard of the fraternized European proletariat," had flown from every barricade in the past five months; nevertheless the people would not win until the army was tied up in war, until there were inner divisions, or until "some development" drove the people into a desperate struggle and demoralized their opponents. If everything else failed, help would come from beyond the horizon when another "crowing of the Gallic cock" would signal the hour of liberation and revenge. Paris would act, "striking the hour of liberation for Europe."

The next hope and challenge, however, came from Berlin with the installation of a new Prussian Ministry headed by a conservative general, E. H. A. von Pfuel. The Neue Rheinische Zeitung of September 23 (probably in Marx's words) flatly labeled the new government as a Ministry of the Prince of Prussia, the instrument with which the "counterrevolution wants to risk the last decisive blow." The army would disperse the Prussian Assembly, giving the "Don Quixotes of Further Pomerania . . . the chance to wash their rusty swords clean in the blood of agitators." The article ended with a challenge to reaction, "Go to it! Forward with God for King and Fatherland!"

The *Kölnische Zeitung* of the same day came closer to the mark by classifying the new Ministry as a purely "administrative, a neutral one," which represented a transition, or a bridge across "the abyss of counter-revolution or a second revolution." Anyone could see what a second revolution would look like, in view of the "prevailing social tensions." The alternative was a moderate *coup d'état*, accompanied by the Royal concession of "an otherwise entirely satisfactory constitution." The latter was an accurate forecast of things to come. Or was it a suggestion?

The Pfuel Ministry actually avoided hasty, reactionary steps. It preserved a neutral position by not identifying itself clearly with any party or person. It indicated a readiness to work with the Prussian Assembly to complete a constitution. If the course was somewhat to the right, there was no broad, overtly reactionary shift to provoke popular anger, demonstrations and a renewal of the March Days, as Marx and Engels hoped.

Cologne, however, was moving towards a September Crisis of its own. Popular fever had arisen when the Frankfurt Parliament made the humiliating reversal on the question of the Malmö armistice. The news of the insurrection and barricades in Frankfurt thereafter led to demonstrations in Cologne in support of the people who were defending Germany's honor. The Committee of Public Safety came to life again and jointly sponsored with the Democratic Society and Worker-Society a popular meeting on September 20. At this meeting Engels reported on the barricade battle in Frankfurt and denounced the Frankfurt Parliament. The crowd then adopted two resolutions, the first of which denounced the "honorless Armistice" as a betrayal of Germany and the "honor of German arms," and branded as traitors to the people those members of the "Frankfurter so-called National Assembly" who had ratified the Armistice. The second resolution simply stated that the barricade fighters in Frankfurt served their Fatherland well. The resolutions were printed as a *Proclamation* in the *Neue Rheinische Zeitung* of September 23, which urged that it be reprinted on placards and in other papers. The *Zeitung* also solicited contributions for the families of the insurgents.

In view of the persisting popular excitement, the Prussian authorities decided to forestall any popular disturbances growing out of the events scheduled for the immediate future. The gigantic worker-peasant meeting at "Wesslingen" lay ahead, patterned after the Sunday at Worringen with its "blood-red" flag and endorsement of a Red Republic. The second Rhineland Democratic Congress was to open in Cologne on September 25. Concurrently, the revivified Committee of Public Safety had helped to organize the protest meeting on the 20th. All of this led many solid citizens of Cologne to share the fears of the authorities. This caused the Worker-Society paper of September 24 to complain that the bourgeoisie were "howling" in a heartrending manner about a threat from the "bloodthirsty Democrats and Proletarians." In turn, the paper accused the bourgeoisie of "despising, maltreating and murdering the workers," and of threatening "to hang the Democrats by their legs."

During the weekend of September 23–24, preparations were made to arrest those who had been especially active at the recent popular meetings—Schapper, Moll, Wilhelm Wolff, Bürgers, Becker, Wachter and finally Engels—on the charge of "conspiracy aimed at revolution." Specific reference was made to the speeches given at the Worringen meeting. Police action began at 6:00 A.M., Monday, September 25, the day set for the opening of the second Rhineland Democratic Congress. Schapper and Becker were arrested. The elusive Wilhelm Wolff could not be found. Moll and Wachter were seized, but then released when the six- or seven-man police squad felt inadequate in the face of the hostile crowd that had gathered. When the police finally went to Engels' residence, he was no longer at home. Marx charged later that the choice of Monday for the arrests was part of a deliberate plot to create a "little June battle" in Cologne, which could be crushed easily. He had made the same charge when Gottschalk and Anneke were arrested. (Monday was a day when most of the workers were idle and would, consequently, be on hand to protest forcibly against such arrests.)

Popular unrest indeed did reign throughout the day. Minor brushes with the police occurred and some looting took place. In some parts of the city all the gas lights in the streets were demolished and the gas lines cut. The windows of the police administration building were smashed. It was rumored that the Police Commissioner had been hanged from a pump at the north end of Cologne, while the masses danced around. A popular protest meeting took place at one o'clock in the Old Market Place, even though the police had prohibited such a meeting and had called on the Civic Guard to handle the explosive situation. Peter Imandt, who had just arrived from Krefeld to attend the Democratic Congress, opened the meeting. The Civic Guard stood in the background, more irresolute and sympathetic than active. When Imandt asked the Guard whether they were there to act as a police force or as the defender of the people, many guardsmen replied that they were there to protect the people.

Wilhelm Wolff, who had eluded the police earlier, then presided over the meeting. Joseph Moll, having been released from arrest through popular intervention, was the hero of the hour. This Communist leadership successfully persuaded the crowd to restrict its protest to a disciplined assemblage, in defiance of police orders. The Communist tactics of the moment, as outlined the preceding day in the Worker-Society paper now edited by Joseph Moll, rested on the following assumption: "The destiny of Prussia and of all Germany will be decided in Berlin. Both sides are preparing for the decisive battle which can be expected at any moment." The success of any local action depended on the situation in the country as a whole, notably in Berlin. In line with this assumption, the Communists were now marking time until they heard what was happening in Berlin and elsewhere; they were uncertain whether the arrests in Cologne represented an isolated incident or a small part of a far broader reactionary push, which would provoke a general revolutionary kickback.

Marx himself was very active on that day of uncertain revolution. With one ear turned to Berlin, he was everywhere advocating caution, pending favorable news from the East. There could not be a false move; too many troops were in the forts around Cologne. Even the Civic Guard might hesitate to support an insurrection triggered by the arrest of Schapper and Becker and the planned arrest of Moll, Wolff, Wachter and Engels. There was no sense fighting alone when it meant going down in a heroic defeat, even if it might set an inspirational precedent for future generations. (Marx and Engels always paid full tribute to such failures. But in 1848 they themselves hoped to continue operating from a base in Cologne, until the expected revolutionary conflagration, on a grander scale, improved the odds.)

Early in the morning (September 25), Marx appeared at the meeting place of the second Rhineland Democratic Congress. It would appear as an heroic gesture if the Congress were to go ahead with its plans and meet, in defiance of Prussian authorities. But with half of the Provincial Democratic Committee (Schapper, Moll and Becker) arrested or threatened with arrest, the role of the Communists in such a congress certainly would be weakened. The Congress was cancelled.

With the Democratic Congress disposed of, Marx next appeared at the headquarters of the Worker-Society, to advise the workers not to allow themselves to be baited by the police into any hopeless action. When the Democratic Society hurriedly met early in the afternoon, Marx and Moll repeated the same warning. This was not the time for a *Putsch*. No "big issue" was driving the whole country into battle. The people were to save their strength because "momentous events" might occur within a few days. It was senseless to act sooner and to be defeated and disarmed before the decisive hour arrived.

The Cologne crowd, however, found it hard to preserve a disciplined ferment without some action. Late in the afternoon there was another popular meeting in the Old Market Place, attended mostly by workers. Simultaneously, the Prussian troops began to move into the city to occupy the strategic positions and to assist in a second, though futile, attempt to arrest Joseph Moll. When the workers in the Old Market Place heard that the "Prussians" were coming, they hurriedly dispersed, calling for "barricades."

According to the official report to the Prussian Constituent Assembly, between thirty and forty barricades were erected during the evening, using furniture from adjacent houses, all sorts of upturned vehicles (including the Protestant hearse), scaffolding from Cologne Cathedral, trees felled across the streets, cobblestones and other typical ingredients. The tocsin sounded from the tower of St. Columba Church. Hardware and gun stores were plundered in the quest for weapons. The Red Flag was raised over some of the barricades, with the "Red Company" guarding one of them. A barricade defender was wounded by the accidental discharge of a gun. A bloody battle seemed in sight.

There would have been a sharp though perhaps brief encounter, if the soldiers had attacked. But the Commander decided to wait until daylight. Meanwhile, the defenders of the barricades were having second thoughts during the long hours of a quiet night as they waited for an attack that did not come. When the morning of September 26 arrived, there was nothing for the army to do except to supervise the removal of the barricades; all the defenders had gone home.

After the nightmare of barricades in Cologne was ended, several newspapers described the affair as a "poor Carnival joke" (Cologne's annual Carnival was famous throughout Europe). The barricades—the symbol and substance of revolutionary defiance and valor—appeared comical when they were neither attacked nor defended. It was even suggested that those who had built them lacked the courage to defend them. The accusation of cowardice was embarrassing to the workers, the more radical Democrats, the Communists, the Neue Rheinische Zeitung and, Marx and Engels themselves.

Often enough Marx and Engels had berated and belittled democratic and leftist leaders and delegates in the Berlin and Frankfurt assemblies for failing to take the initiative—boldly, energetically and actively— during revolutionary demonstrations and even barricade fighting. Only five days earlier Engels had criticized the same Left (with a few honored exceptions) for inciting the people in Frankfurt, but then betraying and deserting them at the decisive moment when the barricades sprang up. "Eternal shame on this double betrayal," the paper had declared.

After the "Cologne Revolution" of September 25, Marx became the victim of similar jibes. But he had to wait until October 13 before he could reply, in behalf of the workers and the Democrats. The joke, Marx then declared, was on the "Cavaignac of the Cologne Revolution" because he could not be a single inch taller than the revolution he opposed. As for the workers, they had acted with the knowledge that a "decisive counterrevolutionary blow" could come from Berlin at any moment. They abandoned the barricades only after vainly waiting through most of the night for the enemy to attack. Meanwhile, they had also heard that no "momentous reports had come from Berlin." It was ridiculous to call the workers cowardly. If some looting occurred in Cologne, it was only because every city has its contingents of thieves who take advantage of the popular turmoil to exercise their craft. Marx then accused the editors of the *Kölnische Zeitung* and similar newspapers of wanting blood and then being disappointed when the soft-hearted Democrats, "because of *cowardice*" allowed no blood to flow. But the charge that the men of the *Neue Rheinische Zeitung* disliked the smell of gunpowder persisted during the ensuing months.

Although the barricades appeared comical in retrospect, fear and alarm had accompanied the "Revolution." The *Kölnische Zeitung* initially described the event as "most highly damnatory," as the result of "widely-ramified plans of the Democrats" inspired by the republicans and Communists. Unquestionably most of the people of Cologne were equally disturbed. In view of this public reaction, the Commander of the Cologne fortresses (a certain Colonel Engels, not related to the Wuppertal Engelses) found that the imposition of martial law was almost welcomed when he proposed it at a meeting of civic officials the morning after the barricades. The decision was announced to the public at twelve noon (September 26) to the roll of drums and in the presence of troops. The regulations governing the city under martial law were posted everywhere.

Martial law meant the suspension of all societies organized for political and social purposes, as well as the listed democratic and workers' newspapers: the *Neue Rheinische Zeitung, Neue Kölnische Zeitung, Der Wächter am Rhein* and the *Zeitung des Arbeiter-Vereines*. The Civic Guard was disbanded and obliged to surrender its weapons, pending a later reorganization. Street meetings of more than twenty persons by day and ten at night were prohibited. Taverns were closed at 10 P.M. The existing civil authorities continued to function, but the military courts would handle all cases of resistance. Martial law would end as soon as quiet and order prevailed in Cologne. The order for the arrest of certain persons, including Engels, Dronke, Wilhelm Wolff and Moll, remained in effect.

Marx apparently had received a tip that martial law would be imposed —including information on the time and the terms. Hence he hastily prepared a September 27 edition of the *Neue Rheinische Zeitung* before noon of the 26th, writing: "We are hurrying to get the paper to the press. We hear from reliable sources that martial law will be declared in the city within 1–2 hours, the Civic Guard will be dissolved and disarmed." After correctly listing the papers that were to be suspended, he continued with less accurate details: "Military courts will be introduced and all rights won in March are to be suppressed. It is said that the Civic Guard is not in the mood to allow itself to be disarmed." (The Guard offered no resistance.) On the above note, the *Neue Rheinische Zeitung* disappeared until October 12, nine days after the end of martial law in Cologne.

Most of the people accepted martial law with a sense of relief. There were no popular protests or hostile demonstrations. One of the suspended papers, the *Neue Kölnische Zeitung*, attempted to reappear under a new name, the "Newspaper for Women," edited by Anneke's militant wife, but the authorities allowed no such evasions. The *Bonner Wochenblatt* spoke whimsically of the "harmless, leisurely martial law, certainly the most wonderful that ever existed anywhere in the world," which even the "honest Democrats" enjoyed. The liberal *Kölnische Zeitung* wrote that there was nothing very terrible about martial law, as a change from the "terrorism" of the preceding days. But then the paper began to voice reservations; the suspension of newspapers began to appear unduly severe and doubly harmful because it occurred at a time when subscriptions were to be renewed for the final quarter of the year.

An "Extra-Ordinary Supplement" to the *Kölnische Zeitung* of October 1 carried the news that martial law would end on the 4th. In that same paper there was also a notice that the *Neue Rheinische Zeitung* would reappear on the 5th. In the meantime, Berlin interceded to speed up the process. D'Ester (who was in correspondence with Marx) and several others had denounced the "sabre rule" before the Prussian Assembly, already uneasy over the prolonged suspension of many rights in Cologne. The Pfuel Ministry also did not want to bear the onus for the continuation of repressive measures. On orders from Berlin, therefore, martial law in Cologne came to an end a day earlier (on October 3). All suspended newspapers were again free to appear. The right of assembly was restored. The Civic Guard was not reconstructed, however, nor did its members recover the weapons they had turned in. The persons who had been arrested on September 25 were not released.

The orders for the arrests in Cologne forced most of the leading Communists into flight, or into prison cells. Aside from some harassment by threat of an investigation, Marx was left untouched. He had avoided all overt actions which were legally compromising. And the Prussian authorities, although sorely provoked and suspicious, did not take the risk of expelling him as an undesirable and dangerous "alien." He was looked upon as a native in the Rhineland, regardless of his legal status. Prussia, as so often, avoided wounding Rhineland sensibilities. Marx was free to make a comeback.

=V=

Marx Holds the *"Fort"*

1. AFTER THE "RULE OF
THE SABRE"

With Engels in exile, the last three months of 1848 stand out as the heroic period for Marx. After the end of the "Rule of the Sabre" (as many radicals called martial law) in Cologne, Marx at first stood almost alone, laboring mightily to "hold the *fort* and to preserve the political position at all cost," as he wrote to Engels around November 10. The *Neue Rheinische Zeitung* was the "fort" and the "political position" included the influence that the Communists exercised in both the Worker-Society and the Democratic Society.

To hold the "political position" Marx had to exert himself more openly, directly and boldly. He was ready to take more chances, perhaps reassured by the immunity he had experienced during the September Crisis. He was practically alone, a chief without a group of trustworthy subalterns to aid in the execution of policy. The broken lines with the Democratic Society, growing out of the division in regard to the Committee of Public Safety, had to be repaired. Marx also had to keep the Worker-Society from drifting and foundering during the enforced absence of Schapper and Moll. Karl Schapper was not released from prison until November 15. Joseph Moll, after eluding arrest, left the Rhineland and found a refuge in his old surroundings in London. He reappeared during the winter but kept mainly under cover while attempting to revive the Communist League in Germany.

Marx maintained his position in the Cologne Democratic Society, at least in a formal sense. He continued to act as one of its two representatives in the Rhineland Provincial Democratic Committee of Six. During the September Crisis, however, Marx again found that many Democrats refused to follow him along a more radical course of action. Consequently his influence in the Society was small at the moment. But the situation could change overnight.

The Editorial Committee of the *Neue Rheinische Zeitung* was decimated. Marx's sole assistant was Georg Weerth, editor of the *Feuilletons*. Wilhelm Wolff, the extremely able, popular agitator, had fled to the Bavarian Palatinate. Being a resourceful person and a dedicated Communist, Wolff was the first to return to Cologne, but he remained in hiding for awhile. Ernst Dronke, and above all the nearly indispensable Engels, also had fled. Engels did not return until January.

Initially Engels found a shelter in the parental home in Barmen, probably the last place the police expected him to go. He arrived at a time when the family was not at home. It is usually assumed that this was when he burned his papers, as a precautionary measure, to keep them out of the hands of the police. Most of the earlier letters from Marx went up in flames.

When the Engels family returned after several days, an unhappy reunion took place. The family was shocked because the Engels' name had been mentioned openly in connection with the Worringen meeting and other revolutionary activities. Now the gifted oldest son was being dogged with an order for his arrest. The family tried to persuade him to abandon a career that could lead to a final rupture. His mother, as always, played a moderating role. Once more it became evident that Engels had not miscalculated when he turned to his home for a refuge. Family devotion existed side-by-side with, or perhaps at the heart of, the bourgeois values which the son otherwise derided. After a few days, Engels proceeded to Brussels, with the assurance that money would be sent to him there.

Ernst Dronke was with Engels during the flight to Brussels, where they arrived around October 4. Meanwhile, the Prussian authorities in Cologne had posted and published a "Wanted" notice, calling for the apprehension of Heinrich Bürgers and Friedrich Engels.

The description of Engels read as follows:

Profession: merchant
Birthplace and residence: Barmen
Religion: Evangelical
Age: 27 years
Height: 5 feet, 8 inches
Forehead: ordinary
Eyes: grey
Nose and mouth: proportionate
Teeth: good
Beard: brown
Chin and face: oval

Complexion: healthy
Figure: slim

Engels and Dronke appeared in the Belgian capital under their own names, without any attempt to conceal their identity. During the anti-foreign campaign in March, neither of them had been molested or expelled from Brussels. Now, however, the authorities were less considerate. Undoubtedly they knew that Engels and Dronke were on the Editorial Committee of the *Neue Rheinische Zeitung,* which had repeatedly insulted Belgium, ridiculing it as the "model constitutional state" and denouncing it unsparingly for imposing draconian sentences on various Belgian revolutionists (including Tedesco). Both Engels and Dronke were arrested almost immediately, kept in prison overnight, and then hauled to the frontier where they were ejected as vagrants—across the French border, and not the Prussian.

Engels and Dronke immediately went to Paris. Engels remained there only five days, Dronke for a longer period. Engels may have kept a diary during the next weeks. Later, after arriving in Geneva, he began an account of his migrations and observations, probably for publication in the *Neue Rheinische Zeitung.* Ultimately entitled, "From Paris to Bern," the journal ends while he is still a long distance from Switzerland, on the plateau that separates the Seine, Rhône and Loire valleys.

Engels' descriptions of his travels on foot through France stand out strangely as a lyrical and bucolic intermezzo in an otherwise drab revolutionary year. He apparently was tired of revolution and discouraged by the turn of events since September 25. Once before, towards the end of 1846, when Communist agitation had proved fruitless and dangerous, Engels had turned to the *grisettes* and other diversions of Paris for relief. This time, however, even Paris was impossible. The grenades of Cavaignac had destroyed the old irresistible gaiety. He had to get away from it all. After composing a verbal rhapsody to the Paris of yesteryear, he started off, to the south and east towards Switzerland. He had to walk since he had very little money (the stay in Brussels had been too short to allow the promised parental subsidy to reach him), leaving Paris on October 10 and arriving in Geneva around the 24th. During this interval he was cut off from all news and was little interested in what was happening.

Engels' travelogue reveals a superb narrative gift, almost a poetic quality. Descriptions of customs, people and scenery were interspersed with the reflections of an epicure. It was the time of the grape harvest. Engels ate that fruit with the peasant girls in Burgundy, chatted and lay in the grass with them. He expressed his preference for the slender figure of the French girl, compared to the thick-waisted, heavy-boned German girl. He discovered that every type of wine produced its own style of intoxication, conforming to every human mood. At Dampierre he observed directly one of the public works projects that had replaced the Paris "workshops" suppressed in June. He noted the general well-being of the workers and commented that they were entirely spoiled in a revolutionary sense. He was struck by the conservative character of the peasant and his fanatical hatred of radical Paris. The peasant was the "barbarian in the midst of civilization." In between such distractions and reflections, Engels walked from Paris to Geneva in fourteen days.

During the month-long interval when Marx and Engels were out of contact with each other, attempts were made from opposite directions to create dissension between the two. On the one hand, Engels' brother-in-law tried to persuade Engels that his partner had deserted him. Information on the subject is only fragmentary since Engels' letter to Marx on this matter has not survived. But it appears that Engels had some doubts about Marx when he failed to receive the money he had expected from his partner. (Marx's letter and the money may have gone astray when Engels moved from Geneva to Lausanne.) In any event, Marx must have felt that some explanation and reassurances were necessary when he replied to Engels on November 10. He was "truly surprised" that his partner had not yet received the money; the Editorial Committee of the *Neue Rheinische Zeitung* remained the same—he had thwarted the efforts of "stupid reactionary stockholders" to oust Engels. Marx then added the following assurance: "That I would leave you in the lurch even for a moment is pure fantasy. You ever remain my intimate friend as I remain yours, let us hope." Engels evidently was reassured.

From the other direction, August Ewerbeck, Moses Hess and Karl d'Ester tried to get Marx to abandon Engels. It is evident that often enough Engels had wounded the sensibilities of other Communists because he was likely to act as the hatchet-man for Marx. As a result he was sometimes impetuous, brusque and even brutal. The offended group was unsuccessful, however, in persuading Marx that Engels was a party liability. Ewerbeck, writing to Hess on November 14, had to concede that Marx was "extremely enthusiastic over Engels, whom he describes as being extraordinary in an intellectual and moral sense, as well as in character." The Marx-Engels partnership survived the test. Eventually Engels received some money from Marx's "till" (*Kasse*); Marx also informed Engels that his father was trying to locate him so he could send money to his needy son.

The assurance of a family remittance probably reached Engels by mid-November when he applied for permission to reside in Bern as a "political refugee." With the promise of money from home, Engels was able to guarantee that he had the means to support himself. Even so, at the end of November when Marx's own till was empty, Marx came forward with a "surefire plan" to "extort" money from Engels' "old man." Engels was to write Marx a "money letter," as "crass as possible," describing his past misfortunes and composing it in such a way that it could be forwarded to his mother. Engels, apparently, did not go through with Marx's "plan."

The acute financial distress of the *Neue Rheinische Zeitung* was Marx's major problem. The temporary suspension of the paper proved to be nearly fatal. Stockholders withheld payment of the fifth 10 percent installment, which had been due towards the end of September. Renewal of subscriptions for the fall quarter (starting October 1) likewise came during the time of suspension. In view of the uncertainty resulting from martial law, very few subscribers responded, even though Marx sent out notices on September 28, and again on October 3, stating that the paper would appear just as soon as martial law ended. He also promised a bigger and better paper with "an enlarged format, backed by large new resources" and a speedier publication due to a fast new printing press that had been ordered.

As late as October 10 there was still some doubt that the *Neue Rheinische Zeitung* would ever appear again. But Marx managed somehow. "Finally," as the *Bonner Wochenblatt* described the proceedings, "after much faltering and the most wonderful financial operations, which even included loan certificates [*Darlehnscheine*]," the paper went to press on the evening of October 11. No one was "under any illusion that he would ever recover a penny" from the *Darlehnscheine* he had purchased.

Marx's resort to *Darlehnscheine* represented a boldly-conceived plan to finance the paper through the financial sacrifices of the little man, the petty-bourgeoisie. Many of them were strongly democratic. But the plan was not too successful because many Democrats had their doubts regarding Marx. Persons like Ferdinand Lassalle in Düsseldorf who were active in promoting the "loan certificates" discovered that "men of decidedly radical views accused the said newspaper of perfidy and would like to see some other democratic organ founded in its place."

It is usually asserted that Marx sacrificed a part of his personal fortune to revive the paper. Marx's letter of November 10 to Engels throws some light on the transactions. He does write that he took money out of his *Kasse*. In a rough accounting which follows, he lists the contents of that till as including "the 1850 *Taler*" he had brought back from his trip to Berlin and Vienna, together with the "1950 *Taler*" which the Polish Democrats had sent him, minus 100 *Taler* expended on the trip. Whether such sums were intended as an outright gift to Marx personally, or as a subsidy to the *Neue Rheinische Zeitung*, is not clear. Marx apparently considered the money as sort of a personal war chest, to be used as he saw fit. Out of this *Kasse*, the letter continued, he "loaned" 1000 *Taler* to the *Zeitung*. He used another 500 *Taler* to pay for the new, fast press. The money he sent to Engels, Dronke and others came from the same source. At the same time, Marx mentioned that he had not received a single "Cent" from the paper. "Rationally-wise," he probably should not have "loaned" the money to the paper, in view of his own needs. He might be thrown into prison any day and then he would have to "cry out for money like the deer for fresh water." But it was a question of holding the "fort" under all circumstances, he concluded.

When the *Neue Rheinische Zeitung* reappeared on October 12, Marx announced that the Editorial Committee remained the same. (Only Georg Weerth was still around.) The poet, Ferdinand Freiligrath was added to the staff. He had just been acquitted of the charge that one of his revolutionary poems incited people to revolution. As the lion of the hour, his name on the editorial staff was worth several hundred subscriptions. A fiery poem meant more than three columns of prose. The literary quality, though not the spirit, of the *Neue Rheinische Zeitung* suffered from the absence of Engels. Marx complained that he was busy "to up over his ear" and never found the time for any "polished works." The results were evident in the brevity, rough style and poor development of the comparatively few leading articles. The first numbers were also rather thin in other respects.

Besides the responsibilities of the *Neue Rheinische Zeitung*, Marx found that he had to play a directly personal role in the affairs of the Cologne Worker-Society, to assure a continuing Communist control over that dependable agency. The removal of Moll and Schapper, irreplaceable as popular leaders, had led to a short period of uncertainty and confusion. The *Bonner Wochenblatt* reported from Cologne on October 12 that the Society, deprived of its leaders, seemed dead. But this lack of public manifestation of life was only temporary.

Actually, the Worker-Society had reappeared almost immediately after the "Rule of the Sabre," reduced in numbers but with an added spirit of defiance. Its Committee, with thinned ranks and no fanfare, had a meeting on October 5. A nucleus of steady Communist followers (Peter Röser, cigarmaker; Peter Nothjung, tailor; Christian Esser, cooper; and Christian Moll, Joseph's brother) remained in control. Röser was accepted as the provisional President of the Society. The group, however, lacked the capacity to control the Committee with the same sure hand as Moll and Schapper. Around October 10 Peter Nothjung and several others asked Marx to serve as President of the Worker-Society. A week later Röser was able to report to the Committee that Marx had agreed to be President. As a matter of fact, Marx was already present and stepped forward to take the chair.

Speaking as the new President of the Cologne Worker-Society, Marx enumerated the difficulties he faced. His position was precarious; Prussia's rejection of his renaturalization application was like a "concealed expulsion order." He also faced court action in connection with several press offenses. Moreover, he was overburdened with work because of the dispersal of the Editorial Committee of the *Neue Rheinische Zeitung*. But he was ready "to accede to the wishes of the workers, provisionally, until Dr. Gottschalk were freed." (Marx always paid tribute to Gottschalk, but when Gottschalk was freed on December 23, Marx made no move to vacate the chair in favor of the former President.) The "government and the bourgeoisie" had to be shown that there would always be people ready to make themselves available to the workers, in spite of persecution. The Committee was favorably impressed.

Marx then took complete charge of the meeting. After introductory remarks concerning the revolutionary activity of the German workers in other states, Marx singled out the workers in Vienna for having played the decisive role in the uprising that had just occurred in the Austrian capital. He proposed that the Cologne Society express its appreciation to its counterpart in Vienna. The proposal was adopted via acclamation. Marx thereafter announced the order of business for the Committee in the future. Meetings would start at 8:30 P.M. The first hour would be taken up with internal affairs and external operations of the Society. During the second hour, they would discuss "social and political questions." The Committee accepted the Marxian agenda.

A general meeting of the Worker-Society followed on October 22, with Marx presiding. The assembly confirmed his selection as President, and accepted Röser as Vice President. Röser and a certain B. Ross, both dependable supporters of Marx, were elected to represent the Worker-Society on the Rhineland District Democratic Committee, to fill the seats involuntarily vacated by Schapper and Moll. Marx had every reason to be pleased.

In conformity with a previous Committee decision (certainly influenced by Marx), the Society rejected the suggestion of sending a delegate jointly with the Cologne Democratic Society to the second German Democratic Congress in Berlin from October 26–30. Instead, Friedrich von Beust was elected as the delegate who would act upon the instructions of the Worker-Society alone. Drafted later, those instructions included the proposal that Von Beust should attempt to persuade the Berlin Congress to adopt some of the "Demands of the Communist Party in Germany." Marx evidently felt that no such communistically-oriented mandate would have been possible in cooperation with the Cologne Democratic Society.

Marx, after an impressive beginning, did not attend many of the biweekly Committee meetings of the Worker-Society. He continued to serve as President but appeared only on climactic and dramatic occasions, or when the weight of his presence was needed to tilt the scales properly. Vice President Röser presided in his place until November 15 when the former Vice President, Karl Schapper, was freed from prison. Röser then yielded the chair to Schapper who was formally named "First Vice President" (a new position), while Röser continued as plain Vice President.

Under the safe guidance of Schapper, the Committee carried on a program of self-education, methodically examining the seventeen "Demands of the Communist Party in Germany" point by point. The study advanced through Point 4 by the end of the year. Thoroughness and full comprehension were the goals—and the removal of all doubt.

Externally, the Worker-Society continued its missionary work in small towns and among the peasants. It sponsored another big rally, appropriately enough at Worringen on October 15, a Sunday when many peasants were there in connection with a church fair. Although the Prussian officials forbade the meeting and assembled troops to stop it, the leaders from the Cologne Worker-Society insisted on their right of assembly. The authorities yielded in the face of this recognized right, withdrew the soldiers and permitted the crowd to meet in a big tent. After listening to speeches comparing the relative values of a monarchy and a republic, the assembly declared unanimously that it favored a "social republican system." Marx did not appear at the affair.

Throughout the fall new societies were formed in the small towns and among the peasants. The distribution of the "Demands of the Communist Party" continued. When revolutionary tension again was high in November, the Committee urged the members of the Cologne Worker-Society to organize and participate in regular Sunday rallies in the country. The Society's paper reported that their emissaries were everywhere received with "joy and enthusiasm." One group literally took along a drum to attract a crowd which followed the speeches thereafter with sustained attention.

Marxian Communist control over the policy of the Worker-Society was disturbed only by a later revival of Gottschalk's influence among some of the members. Controversy developed first over the editorial control of the Society's paper. A certain W. Prinz just stepped in to assume the editorial responsibility vacated by Joseph Moll. When the paper reappeared on October 5, it carried a new masthead: "Responsible Editor: W. Prinz." (Formerly it had been: "Edited under the responsibility of the President.") This caused no immediate alarm, and Marx was too busy otherwise to insist on his presidential prerogatives. Only later did Prinz's anti-Marxian and pro-Gottschalk views become evident.

The Prussian state, after the abortive move to stop the Worringen meeting, did not seriously interfere with the activities of the Worker-

Society. There was only one exception. The *Gerant* of its paper was brought to trial on October 24 and 25 for having slandered "the honor and delicate feelings" of the Prussian First Procurator, Zweiffel, and the *Gendarmes* who had played a part in the arrests of Gottschalk and Anneke early in July. The jury, by a simple majority, found the paper guilty. The judge then sentenced the publisher to a month in prison and stipulated that the Worker-Society had to post a bond (*Kaution*) of 4000 *Taler* before it could appear in print again.

The month in prison was not fatal for the printer nor did it put him out of business. The Worker-Society, however, could not post the 4000 *Taler* bond. Technically therefore, the paper ceased to exist. The Worker-Society, however, enjoyed a minor triumph by continuing to publish its newspaper under a new title, or rather, an abbreviation of the old title. Not a single issue was missed in the process. The *Zeitung des Arbeiter-Vereines zu Köln. Freiheit, Brüderlichkeit, Arbeit* dropped its main title and appeared thereafter as simply *Freiheit, Brüderlichkeit, Arbeit*. Under its new name the paper even printed an ironic obituary of its old self, informing the public that it had died as a result of a "press trial" and because it lacked the 4000 *Taler* prescribed by the physician as the medicine to keep it alive. Nobody was fooled by the change in the name of the Worker-Society paper. Newspapers accurately reported the nature of this new incarnation. Another newspaper, the small, democratic *Freie Volksblätter* (Free People's News-Sheets) reappeared as the *Freie Blätter* (Free News-Sheets) after it likewise had been found guilty of the same offense.

Marx's *Neue Rheinische Zeitung*, faced with similar charges for publishing calumnies against Zweiffel and the *Gendarmes*, was spared meanwhile. When Marx and Korff, the responsible publisher, were finally summoned for trial on December 20, 1848, the action was postponed until 1849, on the technicality that the defendants had not received a proper ten-day notice.

2. REVOLUTION IN VIENNA

MARX had greeted the world with unfeigned confidence when the *Neue Rheinische Zeitung* reappeared on October 12. Revolution was on the march again. He had always predicted that the counterrevolutionary plots of the reaction would provoke explosions which would blow up the old order. Nothing of the sort had happened in September. But on the 6th and 7th of October a splendidly successful revolution had occurred in Vienna. Buoyantly he wrote that the revolution in the Austrian capital would produce repercussions in Hungary, Italy and Germany, strong enough to nullify the "entire plan of the counterrevolutionary campaign."

Throughout the spring and summer of 1848, Marx and Engels had maintained an interest in the fortunes of the old Austrian Empire, and in August Marx had visited its capital. This Empire, a collection of historic kingdoms, duchies and counties brought under the rule of the Habsburg family over many centuries, was one of the citadels of reaction. No Great-German revolutionary state could come into being without its fall.

After the March Revolution, very few people in Europe would have bet on the survival of the Habsburg Empire. The usual problems associated with every revolution were compounded in Austria by the unusual presence of eight or ten separate nationalities, each seeking recognition, self-realization and power. These nationalities, for all of their ideal aspirations, could be ferociously, fanatically and murderously hostile to each other. The Italian national prophet, Giuseppe Mazzini, had expressed the ideal when he stated that the individual through nationality arrived at humanity. The Austrian dramatist, Franz Grillparzer, after noting the 1848 realities, came back with the conclusion that the individual through nationality arrived at bestiality.

In the beginning of the revolutionary process in 1848, the force of nationalism was on the side of revolution and liberalism. The voice of the nationalists in general joined the liberal and democratic chorus in calling for a reduction of Habsburg power and a disruption of the Austrian Empire. Later, however, the clash of separate nationalities helped to defeat the revolution and restore Habsburg rule. It became clear that national feeling would become the ally of that force—liberal or reactionary—which best served the interests of the particular nationality.

During the first months of the revolution, it appeared that the multinational Habsburg Empire was disintegrating along national lines. The Hungarians, fired by the democratic and vehemently nationalistic ardor and oratory of Louis Kossuth, had gained a position of virtual independence for their historic kingdom, with a separate constitution and full control of its own domestic policies. Aside from that, the Hungarians were ready to keep a Habsburg as their constitutionally-limited monarch. In addition, certain still undefined financial, military and diplomatic ties would be retained with the government in Vienna.

The chances for the survival of Austrian rule seemed even more desperate in Italy. The Italian patriot hated the Austrian as a national oppressor whose grip had to be broken before Italy could be free and united. The Austrian Commander, Marshal Radetzky—able, courageous and energetic for all of his eighty years—grudgingly abandoned most of

Lombardy and Venetia. Charles Albert, ruler of the north-Italian Kingdom of Sardinia (he regarded himself as a man with a special mission —to free, unite and rule all of Italy), declared war against Austria, confident that Radetzky and the last of the Austrian White-Coats would soon be expelled.

To the north of Vienna, the traditional Kingdom of Bohemia with Prague as its capital was granted special concessions which virtually eliminated Habsburg power in another key possession. In German Vienna itself, revolutionary turmoil reigned for months, as in no other major capital city in 1848. When the ground became too shaky for the Habsburg throne in that city on the banks of the Danube, the Imperial court took refuge in the Tyrol (at Innsbruck) where the mountains and the relatively free German peasants were steadfast. But Vienna remained the governmental center and had its own elected Constitutional Assembly during the summer of 1848.

The question of constitutional government with guarantees for individual liberties, however, was only one and often the lesser of two major issues which confronted each of the peoples in the Habsburg lands. The emerging, aspiring and self-asserting nationalities in the Austrian Empire (Germans, Poles, Czechs, Ukrainians, Hungarians, Slovaks, Rumanians, Croats, Slovenes, Serbs and Italians) faced two choices. On the one hand, each nationality could aim at the total breakup of the Habsburg monarchy by constituting itself as a separate national state, or by uniting with an outside state of the same nationality. Such a disruption of the Austrian Empire, however, would mean the loss of the political, economic, strategic, diplomatic and emotional advantages associated with greatness. Influenced by such considerations, the various nationalities might decide, on the other hand, to preserve the external framework of the Austrian Empire, as a matter of convenience or necessity. The numerically-small nationalities needed the protection and well-being that a large state could offer.

The Germans in the Austrian Empire were in a dilemma in 1848. Austria proper was German, with Italian and Slovene minorities to the south. Vienna was a German city. The German-Austrians through centuries had played a significant role in all of the German world. The Habsburg dynasty also had drawn extensively on the strength of Germany at large in extending its rule to the north, east and south over areas mainly non-German in population. The people of Bohemia and Moravia (that Kingdom of Bohemia which the Czechs claimed for themselves) were about one-third German. Those Germans (called Sudeten Germans after World War I) were concentrated heavily in the cities and very solidly along the northern and western frontiers, adjacent to German areas across the border. On the basis of history, culture and tradition, the German in the

Austrian Empire felt that his destiny was inseparable from the German world at large.

The German in Austria nevertheless felt a twofold pull in 1848. Inspired by national feeling, he wanted a closer union with the German nation as a whole. But there was also a certain Black-Yellow (the Austrian colors) patriotism which caused many German-Austrians to want to preserve a tie with the non-German Habsburg possessions. They had a certain pride in the "civilizing" role of the German throughout the Empire. They did not want Vienna to sink to the level of a mere capital city of just another German state. Without the Empire, it might not have remained the Vienna of the Strauss waltzes to come. The Black-Yellow patriots wanted to keep the best of two possible worlds.

It was the democratic and radical elements, notably in Vienna, who flew the Black-Red-Gold flag and wanted German-Austria to sever connections with Hungary, Galicia, Italy and the Dalmatian coast in order to facilitate a union with the other German states in a Great-German state. In harmony with this position, they strongly supported the work of the National Parliament in Frankfurt. For the same reason they sympathized with the attempts of the Hungarians, Italians and others in throwing off Habsburg rule, as simplifying the complications involved in a merger of Austria with Germany at large.

The conflict of loyalties and aspirations which the German-Austrians faced is illustrated by the fact that they elected delegates to two constitutional assemblies with conflicting aims. They sent representatives to the Frankfurt Parliament to help draft a constitution for an *all*-German union. At the same time, another set of German-Austrian delegates joined representatives of the other nationalities in the Constitutional Assembly (*Reichstag*) meeting in Vienna to agree on a constitution for *all* Habsburg lands, except the Kingdom of Hungary, pointing to a continuation of the existing ties with the Czechs, Poles, Ukrainians, Serbs, Rumanians, Slovenes and Italians.

The Austrian Empire owed its survival in 1848/49 mainly to two factors. It had the services of several loyal generals and armies which first stamped out the revolutionary fire at the edges and then joined forces to subdue Vienna. Secondly, the conflict between adjoining and intermingling nationalities helped to divide the original opposition, as some of the weaker nationalities began to look to the Habsburgs for aid and protection. From that point forward, such nationalities ceased to be very revolutionary and favored the preservation of the Austrian Empire.

The Austrian government traditionally has been accused of exploiting such nationality conflicts to wear down and divide the opposition. This was the reprehensible divide-and-rule technique. But it took two to play the game. The nationalities and their leaders were not simple dupes or puppets in 1848 and thereafter. They played the game in return for protection and the hope of equality, or even a preferred position and a dominant role.

The first nationality clash occurred most dramatically (unexpectedly for the Germans) in Bohemia. The large German minority in Bohemia naturally expected to cast their lot with their fellow Germans. Since Bohemia's three million Czechs taken together looked like a mere Slavic thumb thrust into an otherwise solidly German body, the Germans expected the Czechs to associate themselves with the liberal German empire to be created by the Frankfurt Parliament.

The Czech national leaders in turn refused, with a ringing *nay*, the German offer to join them in creating a liberal German empire. The Czech historian, Palacky, came back with the demand that the Austrian Empire be kept intact. His doctrine of "Austro-Slavism" preached the necessity of the Habsburg state where the small Slavic nations could survive and collectively be dominant, since the Slavs outnumbered the Germans in the Austrian Empire. The Czechs, as the most advanced Slavic nation, naturally would play a leading role in such an Austro-Slav empire. (If Austria had not existed, Palacky declared, it would have to be created, as a convenience for the small Slavic nations, too weak to stand alone.)

As a challenge to the All-German Parliament meeting in Frankfurt, the Czechs convoked a Pan-Slav Congress which met in Prague early in June. The meeting was dominated by spokesmen of the Slavic nations in Austria, but it also included some leading Bohemian aristocrats (with such German names as Schwarzenberg and Thun) and Bakunin. The majority favored the Austro-Slav program advocated by Palacky, but the deliberations of the Congress were interrupted by street demonstrations inspired by the more radical Czechs who opposed continued Habsburg rule, as both nationally and politically repugnant. The wife of the Austrian Commander in Prague, Prince Alfred von Windischgrätz, was killed in the course of the disturbances by a stray, though possibly deliberate, bullet. When the army of Windischgrätz thereafter threatened Prague with action, the insurrection collapsed with virtually no resistance. Habsburg power was restored in Bohemia, and the Czech supporters of an Austro-Slav empire seemed ready to support the ruling dynasty in recovering control over the rest of the Empire. Though strongly anti-German, these Czechs wanted German-Austria and Vienna to be included in their Austro-Slav realm, but in a subordinate position.

Just as Marx and Engels favored the Polish cause as being revolutionary, so they initially acclaimed the national aspirations of all the peoples under Habsburg control. They were for a free Italy, Hungary and Bohemia—a prerequisite for the fall of Habsburg rule. Their views coincided with those of many liberals and democrats who had grown up in an age haunted by the spectre of a "Holy Alliance"—the supposed alliance of reactionary Russia, Austria and Prussia. It was easy to believe that the national movements threatening to tear the Austrian Empire apart were serving the cause of revolution by destroying one of the pillars of reaction.

It is not surprising, therefore, that the *Neue Rheinische Zeitung* should boast on July 12 that it had championed the Poles in Posen, the Italians in Italy and the "Czech Party" in Bohemia. After Windischgrätz had crushed the radical Czech uprising in Prague, Engels wrote, in denouncing the action, that the Germans should have proclaimed the "freedom of all nations." Instead, the "Austrian Soldeska" had choked in "Czech blood" the possibility of a peaceful union between Bohemia and Germany. This made a war of annihilation against the Czechs inevitable, he concluded. The Czechs were to be pitied. Because of the German (Austrian) action, they would throw themselves into the arms of the Russians and perish while fighting on the side of despotism. Engels did not anticipate that the same Habsburg government which had suppressed the Prague revolt in "Czech blood" would have the Czechs as willing allies in suppressing revolution in German Vienna. When that happened, Engels denounced Czech nationalism as being reactionary.

With Windischgrätz in control in Prague, a second Habsburg army was restoring the Austrian position in Northern Italy. Marshal Radetzky defeated the Italian forces of Charles Albert of Sardinia in a series of battles. Radetzky reentered Milan in triumph. Austrian prestige in Northern Italy was revived, even if the pre-1848 position was not fully regained. It was at this time that the Austrian dramatist, Grillparzer, summarized the new situation by saying that Austria was to be found in Radetzky's camp.

Engels placed the blame for the Italian defeat by Radetzky on the treachery, ambitions and ineptitude of Charles Albert. If the Italians had "retired" all their princes at once in favor of a democratic union, the soil of Italy would "probably be free of all Austrian troops." Instead, the Italians had to endure Radetzky. Attila with his Huns appeared as an "angel of mercy" in comparison to Radetzky with his White-Coats. But Engels was confident that new revolutionary tremors would follow. He and Marx never wavered in their support of a free and united Italy. Marx took pride in the fact that the *Neue Rheinische Zeitung* exchanged news items with an Italian democratic paper.

Meanwhile, Vienna went its own free way during the summer, unhampered by the presence of a large army. The *Reichstag* took up the task of drafting a constitution. German, Ukrainian, Polish, Czech, Slovene and Italian delegates jostled each other amidst a great confusion of tongues. The *Reichstag* did vote to free the peasant from labor obligations (*Robot*), but the conflict of nationalities and languages otherwise stood in the way of progress. It was the Czech delegation that generally defended the Habsburgs and the Empire, in opposition to the more radical Germans representing Vienna. By September the *Neue Rheinische Zeitung* was beginning to comment on the reactionary position of the Czechs and on their venomous hatred of the Germans.

Vienna, meanwhile, was in a perpetual turmoil. Revolution had a special flair and flambuoyancy on the banks of the Danube. The university students, taking the lead, formed a revolutionary "Academic Legion" and joined the workers to give Vienna a special radical stamp. An ecstatic report in the *Neue Rheinische Zeitung* declared that the students "do everything, experience everything and are everything." In the face of so much turmoil, it is little wonder that Vienna had to form a Committee of Safety with over two hundred members, to preserve some order. The general tone of the student-democratic-worker combine was patriotically Great-German. They favored the work of the Frankfurt Parliament and proudly flew the Black-Red-Gold colors from the spires of St. Stephen's Cathedral. They stood for an independent Hungary, as easing the way for the union of German-Austria with the other German states, and as barring the revival of Habsburg power and reaction.

A public works program was begun in Vienna, to give employment to those without work and for some who were looking for something better. The situation got out of hand when too many of the unemployed and others from all over Austria flocked to Vienna. As in Paris earlier, taxpayers, employers and the government became alarmed at the cost and the unproductive character of the work.

In August the Ministry of Public Works acted to eliminate some of the laxity in the program and announced a reduction in wages. A clash occurred on the 23rd between workers and the National Guard (an armed citizen-guard drawn largely from the middle classes). Vienna seemed to be approaching a replay of the Paris June Insurrection, attended by the customary 1848 fear of "anarchy." It was during this time that Marx had visited Vienna.

The crisis came late in September and early October when the Austrian government made the next counterrevolutionary move. An invasion of Hungary was begun to crush the revolution there. Conditions in Hungary and the pro-Imperial attitude of her numerous minorities pointed to an easy victory.

The Kingdom of Hungary since March, 1848, had been operating under its own Parliament and constitution, liberalized and democratized considerably through the influence of the energetic revolutionist and fiery orator, Louis Kossuth. But his democracy went hand-in-hand with a highly demanding Hungarian national intolerance. As a result, the Croat, Serb, Rumanian and Slovak minorities in Hungary looked to the Imperial government in Vienna for help, professing a preference for the old ties with Austria and soliciting Habsburg protection.

The most compact resistance to the Hungarians was found in Croatia, an old historic kingdom, long embodied and overshadowed in the broader Kingdom of Hungary. Croat national feeling was well-developed and articulate, with a distinct anti-Hungarian accent. But more important in 1848, the Croats had an army of reputedly ferocious soldiers, enhanced by colorful uniforms and unorthodox fighting tactics. Baron Joseph Jellačić, an Imperial general who professed an undying loyalty to the Habsburgs, associated with a strong commitment to the Croat nation and to the Slavic cause at large, was the Commander of this army. Jellačić's opportunity came in September when the Austrian government commissioned him to restore Imperial authority in Hungary. His first invasion of Hungary, however, was repulsed before Budapest.

Jellačić's actions in Hungary alarmed and angered the students, democrats and workers in Vienna. If the Habsburgs—aided by the Croats, Serbs, Rumanians and Slovaks—regained power in Hungary, Vienna's turn would come next. Furthermore, if Habsburg power were restored over Hungary, it would be most unlikely that the Austrian government would consent to the union of German areas of the Empire (including Vienna) with the rest of the German states. The Black-Yellow colors would supplant the Black-Red-Gold in Vienna. Hence, the more revolutionary and Great-German nationalist elements in Vienna were ready to fight in behalf of a free Hungary.

The disturbances began when it became known that certain regiments stationed in Vienna had received orders to join the forces of Jellačić against the Hungarians. A popular deputation called on Latour, the Minister of War, on October 5, asking him to rescind the order. When Latour refused, popular tumults, demonstrations and fighting followed. Barricades appeared. Latour was mobbed, struck with hammers and iron pipes, stabbed innumerable times, almost torn apart, and then left hanging from a lamp post—a victim of the "popular wrath." There were other casualties. The insurrectionists, armed with modern weapons and museum pieces taken from the arsenal in Vienna, gained control of the city. The *Neue Rheinische Zeitung* of October 13, praising the "determined courage" of the people, stated that, aside from the French, there were no people as ready to "meet death with a good-humored sportiveness" as the Viennese. They acted as if they were on their way to a coffee shop.

Meanwhile, the Emperor and his court again slipped out of the city, this time to the north, to Olmütz in Moravia. Most of the Austrian Constituent Assembly—the representatives of the people—remained in Vienna, meeting "in permanence" with conscious regularity during the tumultuous weeks that followed. But the President of the Constituent Assembly, a Czech, together with most of the Czech delegates, slipped away to Prague. Such behavior strengthened the impression that a Slavic-Habsburg reactionary conspiracy was at work, against Hungary and the Germans. Marx repeatedly denounced the Czechs as favoring reaction, but he waited for Engels, the expert in nationality questions and international affairs, to draft the final verdict against the Slavic peoples.

Revolution reigned in Vienna for several weeks. A new municipal government was established to mobilize manpower and materials for the decisive fight that lay ahead. Vienna's attempt to enlist the support of the peasants and other cities in Austria yielded only minor returns. To the end Vienna looked hopefully to Louis Kossuth and the aid of the Hungarian army in defense of a common cause.

Many of the citizens of Vienna, meanwhile, were becoming alarmed or weary of the radical character and actions of the revolutionary leaders (most of them new men with a nondescript past). Towards the end, Vienna seemed to be drifting towards anarchy, or a confused reign of terror, as the army of Windischgrätz from the north and the army of Jellačić from the southeast methodically closed in on the Austrian capital. There was nothing for Vienna to do except to wait for the final siege—and the hoped-for help of the Hungarians.

Sympathy for Vienna was widespread in Germany. When the armies of Windischgrätz and Jellačić began moving towards Vienna, most Germans viewed this as a reactionary Habsburg assault, with the Slavic peoples (notably Czechs and Croats) as allies against the revolutionary and German capital of Austria. For many Germans it was not merely a question of saving the revolution but of defending German Vienna from the "Slavic hordes." This theme was most pronounced in democratic and radical circles. But even the *Kölnische Zeitung* of October 22 saw Vienna threatened by Ukrainians, Czechs, Croats, Rumanians and some Austrians who felt that the time had come to submerge the German people and their "hated power" through the weight of their masses.

The *Rheinische Volks-Halle* (*Rhineland Forum*), a new Catholic paper, stated that Vienna had taken up arms against the Austrian government which, in order to regain its old power, was at the point of becoming a Slavic empire. Vienna was fighting to preserve its German rights, its nationality. Citing Jellačić to the effect that he fought to make Austria a Slavic empire, the paper declared that that would be tantamount to making German-Austria the Alsace-Lorraine of a Slavic state.

The Frankfurt Parliament and the Imperial Ministry intervened to the extent of sending two Imperial emissaries to mediate between revolutionary Vienna and the Austrian government. Frankfurt could do no more, unless it issued a general revolutionary manifesto in support of Vienna. Not content with the Parliament's action, the Democrats and the Left in Frankfurt sent their own delegation of five members—including Robert Blum and Julius Fröbel—directly to Vienna. The delegation carried an address of appreciation, signed by 130 members, applauding the "magnificent insurrection."

For Marx, the Vienna Revolution was as refreshing as a thunderstorm after a long drought. Here at last was the revolutionary *yea* in response to the counterrevolutionary *nay*. The dialectics of history were being asserted. Marx, however, qualified his optimistic forecast with a cautionary question: Would the bourgeois mistrust of the proletariat hobble the revolution in Vienna? (His most confident predictions usually had a dangling reservation to which he could point later as proof that the unexpected was no surprise.) Yet at this time Marx was certain that the bourgeoisie had no choice except to fight against the Imperial government which appeared like an irreconcilable foreign force, operating from the outside and demanding unconditional surrender. Simultaneously, the hostile acts of the Czechs looked like a Slavic declaration of war on German Vienna.

Marx was equally convinced that the Hungarians under Louis Kossuth had a national and revolutionary stake in defending Vienna. The Hungarians knew that a Habsburg victory over Vienna would be followed by another counterrevolutionary assault against them. The Hungarians, like Vienna, also had an interest in blocking the Slavic aim of preserving the Austrian Empire as a national haven for numerous small Slavic peoples. Vienna could count on Hungarian aid, Marx reasoned.

Throughout Germany there was much talk of supporting revolutionary Vienna in its fight against the Habsburg counterrevolution, aided, so it appeared, by the Slavic hordes of Windischgrätz and Jellačić. In Berlin there were riotous demonstrations at the end of October. A paid notice calling for volunteers from Cologne appeared in the *Neue Rheinische Zeitung*. Those who could not go should contribute money so others could go. The paper, however, did not support the undertaking.

Marx all along insisted that the Germans could help Vienna only by conquering reaction and really revolutionizing their own home governments. He argued that a ground swell of revolution in Germany at large would aid Vienna more than a rash of sympathy, money and volunteers. Marx, in fact, bitterly ridiculed a proclamation drafted by the second German National Democratic Congress which was meeting in Berlin at that time. The proclamation, written by Arnold Ruge, called on the German people to save German freedom in Vienna from the "barbaric hordes." The people should send help, but above all should demand that their own governments act to assist Vienna.

Without mentioning Ruge's name, Marx scoffed at the proclamation for revealing a "preacher-like howler-pathos" in place of "revolutionary energy." Emphasizing that the only way to help revolutionary Vienna was to conquer the counterrevolution at home, Marx warned that speed and action were necessary. Instead, the proclamation had indulged in a "humanistic phraseology" directed at a "cosmopolitan land of fog" populated by "noble hearts in general." That was no comfort to revolutionary Vienna. When Marx wrote the above, Vienna had already fallen.

During the weeks of waiting in October, Vienna had prepared somewhat haphazardly for the coming siege, cheered only by the arrival of a few volunteers and the recollection of past heroic deeds. On October 14, Vienna celebrated the anniversary of the 1683 repulse of the Turks from the walls of Vienna, following a long and desperate siege. On that same day, General Joseph Bem, a Polish officer in exile, offered his services in defense of Vienna—no revolutionary force in 1848 was complete without the presence of a Polish officer. On October 23, Robert Blum, the highly-respected Democrat from the Frankfurt Parliament volunteered in a similar capacity. One hundred and fifty Tyrol mountaineers appeared with green feather brushes in their hats, according to the *Neue Rheinische Zeitung*. A little color went a long way in a revolutionary army.

Vienna otherwise watched rather helplessly while the armies of Windischgrätz and Jellačić moved in to invest the city. The bombardment of Vienna started on October 28 and lasted for nearly four days. For the defenders, the sight of a Hungarian army, visible in the distance from the spires of St. Stephen's Cathedral, brought only temporary hope. The Hungarians moved a little, hesitated and waited again, insisting all the while that they would march as soon as requested by Vienna. The Hungarians insisted on a formal invitation because their advance might later be denounced as a hostile invasion. Protocol and caution were as strong as revolutionary audacity. On the other side, Vienna, while hoping the Hungarians would come, was reluctant to request formally the intervention of a "foreign" army. When the Hungarians finally moved, it was too late. In any event, they lacked the strength and also the strategic audacity that might have offset their weakness.

The German revolutionary ardor in Vienna was matched by the zeal of the attacking forces. Heroic defensive improvisation could not withstand the methodical siege and final assault of the Imperial armies. During the last days, moreover, many of the more solid citizens lost faith in revolution when a reign of terror, mitigated only by a certain chaos and lack of organization, ruled in Vienna. The city fell on October 31.

Martial law went into effect, characterized by a number of executions. Robert Blum was shot on November 9 for aiding the rebels. He had served with distinction in the defense of Vienna; his position in the Frankfurt Parliament gained him no immunity.

To the end and beyond, Marx held out hope of a Viennese victory. His accounts of the siege of Vienna were stirring. He saluted Joseph Bem's role with a threefold "hail." Here as elsewhere the Poles were the "noble-minded *generals of the revolution*." Five days after the fall of the city, he was still reporting that the situation was unclear. The army of Windisch-grätz lay between Vienna and eighty thousand Hungarians. Salvation might still come from the east. As always during a desperate revolutionary crisis, Marx grasped at straws. The trembling of a leaf was interpreted as the forerunner of a hurricane. The grousing of a peasant in the market place appeared like the rumble of an unleashed agrarian avalanche. Real revolutions often start with no more audible portents. Reports of revolutionary unrest, moreover, serve a purpose by helping to ignite unrest in other places. It was necessary, above all, to show courage.

The gloom which settled over Vienna after its fall was dispelled in the *Neue Rheinische Zeitung* by reports of lightning on all horizons. Windischgrätz's actions were giving the "signal for revolt in all provinces or at least to very threatening movements." Even the "Czech fanatics" in Prague were having second thoughts. There were hints of unrest in Berlin. With a seismographic sense, Marx heard the "first subterranean rumbling announcing the approach of an earthquake" in distant Paris.

By the 7th of November, Marx had to concede that "Croatian freedom and order" were the victors in Vienna and were celebrating their success with "incendiarism, rape, plundering, atrocities without name." Denouncing the Slavic peoples who had aided the Habsburg cause, he stated that the "national fanaticism of the Czechs" had been the most powerful weapon in the armory of the "Vienna Camarilla." Marx was always at his fervidly eloquent best in such denunciations.

Analyzing the Vienna uprising in the broader context of revolution, Marx asserted that the events in the Austrian capital represented the second act of a drama which had opened in Paris under the name of the "June Days." The third act would follow soon in Berlin. The chief malefactors were the same in all cases. In Acts I and II, "an armed and hired *Lumpenproletariat*" had fought against the "working and thinking proletariat." (Just where the ragged ones entered the action in Vienna is not clear, but the caste of class characters would be incomplete without them.) Six times, as in a Greek tragedy, Marx then asked who was guilty of "betrayal." The reply to each of the six separate charges was a paragraph of two words, as coming from a tragic chorus: "The *Bourgeoisie*."

Though a dozen Viennas might fall, Marx never doubted that the day of revolutionary reckoning was near. The Gallic cock again would shatter the night with his crowing. In Paris, a "destructive counter-blow" would wipe out the defeat of the June Insurrection and set up a "Red Republic." France would then "spit out" revolutionary armies across her frontiers. "Then we will remember June and October, and we also will call: Woe to the vanquished!"

After the massacres of June and October, Marx continued, "the cannibalism of the counterrevolution would convince even the people" that there was only one way of *"shortening,* simplifying and concentrating the death agony of the old society—only *one way, revolutionary terrorism."* Marx was, in effect, using the argument that the terror was the quickest and therefore the more humane way to accomplish the inevitable, the collapse of the old society.

Marx capitalized on the fall of Vienna and its aftermath to instil a greater revolutionary ardor in both the Worker and Democratic societies. Reporting to the Worker-Society, he stressed the point that the city had fallen only because of betrayal by the bourgeoisie. Several days later he dramatically interrupted a meeting of the Cologne Democratic Society. Waving a telegram he then read the following dispatch that had just come to him from Breslau: "The Murder-Hound Windischgrätz has had Robert Blum, the German Reichstag Deputy, shot under martial law at 7:30 A.M. on November 9." After a moment of stunned silence, the hall resounded with a cry of wrath and an emotional call for revenge. Blum was a popular and revered democratic leader. Moreover, he was a native of Cologne.

Marx had never thought very highly of Blum. Blum lacked the desired revolutionary energy, but he had served the revolution well through the manner of his death. He deserved full tribute, which could be best expressed in verse by Freiligrath who had already honored revolutionary Vienna.

The Robert Blum poem, not one of Freiligrath's best, declared that Blum would be revenged. They that sang dirges now would seize the sword in a "sublime wrath." A great blow would be struck. "The dread avenger, dressed in red and besmirched and stained with blood and tears," would carry the "red banner." It was hardly a fitting requiem for a man of Blum's character and views. But the *Neue Rheinische Zeitung* was not interested in honoring the memory of Robert Blum as he was; it was using his tragic death for revolutionary purposes.

Marx himself dropped the subject of Austria, except for occasional denunciations of the "Slavic Party" which, allied to the "Camarilla," looked to the counterrevolution for emancipation. At the end of November he asked Engels, as a "good geographer," to write fully on the "Hungarian

Scheiss" and the "beehive of nationalities." Engels' articles, written later, certainly were in accord with Marx's views.

Vienna, meanwhile, experienced the fate that follows revolutionary failure. The reaction tolerated no academic legions, no worker-societies, nor any club with an unorthodox purpose. The Habsburg return was followed by ministerial changes that produced a remarkable revival of Imperial power, with Prince Felix von Schwarzenberg as the leading Minister and the real force behind the government. Schwarzenberg, like General Windischgrätz, was a member of the wealthy and highest aristocracy in Bohemia. It was his sister, the wife of Windischgrätz, who had been killed during the June riots in Prague. Schwarzenberg, as he himself deplored, had wasted his talents and best years on play, women, minor diplomatic posts and some military service. But in 1848 the world discovered that he was a man of iron will, courage and intellect, and an embodiment of energy in the service of the counterrevolution and the Habsburg dynasty. Under him, Austria experienced a comeback, almost a miraculous rejuvenation that astounded the contemporary world. The transformation of the Habsburg ménage was completed when the simple-minded, easy-going, congenial and popular figurehead, the Emperor Ferdinand I somewhat reluctantly abdicated on December 2. He was succeeded by youth itself in the form of Franz Joseph, then eighteen years old and destined for a long reign, until 1916 when the Empire was groaning under the strains of World War I.

The revival of Habsburg power complicated the work of establishing a liberal, united Germany. The students, democrats, and radicals of Vienna had been among the warmest advocates of a Great Germany, which would include Vienna and the German areas of the Austrian Empire. Power now lay in the hands of those who favored the preservation of Austrian preeminence and the Habsburg Empire. Vienna became a city that Marx did not care to visit again.

The struggle for the full restoration of Habsburg power was not yet concluded, however. Charles Albert, the King of Sardinia, made a second attempt to improve his fortunes in 1849. But more important, the Kingdom of Hungary, aided somewhat by the coming of winter, was still unsubdued. Hungary under Louis Kossuth put up an unexpectedly tough fight. Months were to pass before the issue was decided.

If the Austrians failed to overcome revolutionary Hungary, then German-Austria, even under Habsburg rule, might yet cast her lot with the rest of the German states—in a Great-German empire-to-be. Those who fervently wished for such an empire, preferably of a revolutionary character, therefore cheered the Hungarians in their fight against the invading armies of Windischgrätz and Jellačić. A Hungarian victory, also, might still produce new revolutionary repercussions in Vienna itself. The situation was fluid enough to permit hope. Marx and Engels in the months to follow regarded Kossuth and the Hungarians as revolutionary and progressive, fit to play a history-making role beside the Poles, Germans, Italians and French. (Engels called Kossuth the greatest man of 1848.)

Among liberals and moderates in Germany, however, a shift in opinion was taking place. Originally there had been a great emphasis on the nationality question—of Slavic and other non-German hordes moving in to gain mastery over German Vienna. After the fall of the city, however, many liberals were appalled by the information they received, describing the radical character of the revolutionary regime that had prevailed in Vienna towards the end. The shift in opinion was exemplified in the *Kölnische Zeitung*.

When the news of the fall of Vienna was first received, the *Kölnische Zeitung* expressed deep sympathy for the cause of the defeated city. On November 8, the paper reversed itself, stating that the battle for Vienna had not been a "conflict of nationalities as the press believed, or pretended to believe." It was, instead, a struggle of "order against anarchy, of legal power against a reign of terror." Hungarian gold had prompted the revolt which was primarily the work of the mob and the students. Vienna had become a "seat of anarchy," the paper concluded. Political and ideological considerations occasionally transcended the national viewpoint, even in 1848.

The Catholic *Rheinische Volks-Halle* registered an equally pronounced change of views on November 10, evidently in response to similar information. It even made the "defeat of the men of terror" in Vienna appear as a victory of the German cause against two enemies at one time. First, it was a victory over the proponents of the subversion of all existing conditions. Secondly, it was a defeat of the "*Junkers* of the Hungarian Magyar race."

As had happened earlier in the course of the Schleswig-Holstein crisis, many moderates and liberals became suspicious of, or denied, the national motif when democrats, radicals and Communists appeared to exploit national sentiment for extreme revolutionary purposes. Nevertheless, the democrats and radicals on the whole made popular gains because of their unreserved support of the Vienna Revolution. It certainly helped the Democrats in Cologne to overcome the divisions and depression that had resulted from the September Crisis. Marx, for his part, regained standing among the Democrats, because of the common support of revolutionary Vienna.

The Cologne correspondent of the *Bonner Wochenblatt* accurately assessed the situation when it reported on November 4 that the "Democratic Party in the Rhineland was displaying a militant disposition and activity which the most demoralizing results had not dampened." For the moment the Democratic Party controlled "the easily-fired part of the masses, the people who had nothing to lose and everything to gain." The *Wochenblatt* warned the liberal constitutional party to stop resting on its laurels, or it might have cause to regret it later.

3. "NO MORE TAXES!!!"

THE September Crisis left most Germans bitter, disillusioned, alarmed, or just weary. There was widespread disappointment with the Frankfurt Parliament which had failed its first big test when it capitulated in the Schleswig-Holstein question. The democrats, viewing this as a betrayal of the people's trust, lost some of their faith in the national Parliament and developed a more reckless, revolutionary response. The moderate liberals (the constitutional monarchists who commanded the widest support in Germany) likewise were disappointed. But they had been equally alarmed over the way the radicals and some democrats had tried to exploit the national anger over Schleswig-Holstein to foment a new and more radical round of revolutions.

With everything still in a state of flux and uncertainty, the liberals called for more speed in the drafting and adoption of a constitution, as the prerequisite for the return of stability and order. This caused them to concentrate on their own separate states which alone commanded the machinery and power needed to preserve law and order. The Frankfurt Parliament, to a degree, receded into the background. Thus a Congress of Constitutional Societies, representing the moderate liberals in the Rhine Province and Westphalia, urged the Constituent Assembly in Berlin to expedite its work. Dozens of separate societies sent similar pleas to Berlin.

The desire for order became a compelling passion that prepared the liberal for a compromise on something less than his original hopes. This was a European phenomenon, not confined to Prussia and Germany at large. The same development was apparent in France. Marx, however, failed to recognize the full force of this essentially anti-revolutionary sentiment that, in effect, reflected a shrinking from the results a revolution might entail. In the case of France, Marx continued to expect a new eruption in Paris into 1849 and beyond. Lorenz von Stein, the Young Hegelian professor and author, came to a far more accurate conclusion in 1848. Noting the hostility of the bourgeoisie towards the principle of revolution after the June Insurrection, Stein predicted that there was no alternative except a "dictatorship of *Order*." People would surrender a portion of their liberty in return for stability. The French soon confirmed this view when they elected Louis Napoleon as President of the Second French Republic, followed by a colossal popular endorsement several years later when he became Emperor with dictatorial powers. The Germans were to go less far.

Two other forces, operating from different directions, helped to diminish revolutionary ardor during 1848. Although the year remained generally depressing in a material sense, there was a noticeable economic recovery, with a reduction in unemployment. Better crops helped to reduce the scarcity and high cost of food (even the potato began its comeback, with the Rhineland reporting a 50 percent yield). Tens of thousands of Germans, however, emigrated to the United States, Brazil or elsewhere in search for a better existence, unwilling to wait for the millennium in Germany.

The 1848/49 revolutionary years, as in 1830/31, again brought the ravages of Asiatic cholera which moved relentlessly out of Russia like a dreaded reaction and ultimately engulfed much of Europe. By September, 1848, the deadly cholera had invaded the Prussian provinces east of the Elbe River. Even Vienna reported its arrival. The terror of the cholera, with its extremely high mortality, may have turned the thoughts of many away from revolution and the prospects of a better future on this earth. The advance of the plague appeared more insidious than any approaching reaction.

While the spectre of the cholera and a gradual economic recovery slowly eroded the earlier revolutionary ardor, continued crises in Germany produced a temporary revival of the old spirit. Popular excitement over the revolution in Vienna was just subsiding when a developing clash between Frederick William IV and the Prussian Constituent Assembly produced new alarms, or hopes. The Pfuel Ministry which had assumed power on September 22 was not a Ministry of armed reaction in practice, as Marx and many others asserted. On instructions from the King, Pfuel continued to cooperate with the Assembly towards completing a constitution. It is impossible to know whether this was a mere ruse to gain time or a last sincere attempt to continue the program of *Vereinbarung*. Pfuel himself honestly attempted to work with the Assembly, even if he was distrusted generally and condemned from the first by the Democrats and the Left. Georg Jung, a leader of the Left in the Assembly, openly admitted after the fall of the Pfuel Ministry that, although his group continually denounced the Ministry as one of armed reaction, Pfuel himself had always acted in a "fully honorable manner." Even Marx conceded, again after Pfuel's fall, that Pfuel still had shown "some grains of sense."

Pfuel actually instructed the army to conform to the demands of the Stein Motion which had angered the King and had brought about the resignation of the Hansemann Ministry. The enforcement of the Stein Motion, however, angered many officers and helped to turn the army against the Assembly. This, in turn, may have been a factor in hardening Frederick William IV against the Assembly in the month that followed. Though a most unmilitaristic King in nine out of ten respects, Frederick William always felt that the army owed its first loyalty to him.

During the latter half of October, the program of cooperation between the Assembly and King faced a severe test as the changing fortunes of the revolution in distant Vienna unquestionably influenced both sides. The debate on each separate clause of the new constitution, previously drafted by a special committee, began on October 12, when revolution was ascendant in Vienna. The Assembly struck out the phrase that referred to the King as "King by the Grace of God." (The age took such questions seriously, although English monarchs bear that title to this day without alarming anyone.) This was a direct affront to Frederick William IV who did indeed believe that kings owed their power to God. Later the Assembly also abolished all titles of nobility, thereby offending the aristocracy which was influential and strongly represented in the army and the government. A showdown between Assembly and King seemed inevitable.

The position of the Prussian King and government had been strengthened during the September Crisis by the return of the army of General von Wrangel, which had fought against the Danes in Schleswig-Holstein. On September 13, Von Wrangel had been named Commander of all military forces concentrated in the vicinity of Berlin. Though relatively undistinguished as a field general, he was energetic, dramatic, cool and untrammeled by constitutional scruples when confronted with a revolutionary situation. Yet his bluntness and businesslike demeanor were not those of a humorless martinet. He could place himself on the level of the crowd in a manner that commanded a grudging admiration instead of provoking an angry reaction. He used the language of the Berliners while in Berlin, successfully adopting their local dialect.

The revolution in Vienna and reactionary moves in Berlin, each in their own way, helped to nurture popular unrest and to bring on a governmental crisis, or were used as an excuse for counterrevolutionary measures. A clash between the populace and the Civic Guard occurred on October 16, followed four days later by a demonstrative funeral for the victims. The meeting of the second German National Democratic Congress in Berlin on October 26–30 came at this crucial time. Some of the 230 delegates representing 260 societies in 140 cities played a special role in organizing and mobilizing the revolutionary masses.

A brief account of the Democratic Congress appeared in the *Neue Rheinische Zeitung* of November 5. The Congress got off to a slow start.

With Kriege in charge, the first day was wasted on a lot of formalities and useless speeches, all terribly boring, the *Zeitung* deplored. Things went better on the second day. A party of action emerged from within the broader ranks of the Democrats. This "Decided Party" called for a "Red Republic" and demanded action. Thereafter the sessions became highly turbulent. Delegates "stamped their feet and drummed with their hands" to drown out the opposition. Most of the moderate delegates became discouraged and left. Towards the end, only the left wing remained, the fifty to sixty who belonged to the "Decided Party." This group then elected a new Central Committee. D'Ester, the Cologne Communist who was also a Deputy in the Berlin Assembly, replaced Kriege as the key figure. Von Beust's report on the social question (drafted by the Cologne Worker-Society), which included some of the Communist demands, was adopted. Marx was not displeased with their work.

It was this radical faction of the Democratic Congress that helped to organize popular unrest in Berlin. On the 30th there was a large popular meeting, followed the next day by a scene reminiscent of the Great French Revolution. The Decided Party rallied a gigantic crowd to present a petition to the Prussian Assembly and, at the same time, impress the Assembly with its physical presence. The petition was in support of a motion by Waldeck calling on the "Prussian Government to act with all forces for the purpose of assisting threatened Vienna," the emotional issue of the hour. An eerie evening followed. The crowd, carrying numerous torches, surrounded the *Schauspielhaus* (Theatre) where the Assembly was meeting, nailed shut or blocked all doors, to force the Deputies to adopt the motion. Some of the demonstrators carried long ropes. Ultimately the Civic Guard arrived to relieve the pressure. The Deputies left the *Schauspielhaus* under the protection of the Civic Guard, but a few were roughed up in the process. Before adjourning, however, the Assembly bravely voted down the Waldeck Motion.

The events of October 31 produced a crisis, or served as a pretext for reactionary steps already contemplated. The Prussian King decided to end the "constitutional comedy." He dismissed the Pfuel Ministry on November 2 and replaced it with a real Ministry of reaction. Simultaneously, Berlin was notified that the army would move in, if the Civic Guard proved unable to prevent a renewal of popular demonstrations.

The new Ministry was headed by Count Brandenburg, the illegitimate son of a former Prussian King, Frederick William II and his beautiful mistress, the Countess Dönhoff. Brandenburg, a general with years of military experience, had shown a steadiness, tact and capacity in dealing with revolutionary unrest in Breslau. He and General Wrangel now acted with an energy that allowed no doubt regarding their capacity to maintain order. Marx scornfully described the two as "men without heads, without hearts, without political views—nothing but moustaches." But even moustaches sometimes play a vital, though brief, role in history. The brains of the new Ministry were supplied by Baron Otto von Manteuffel who served as Minister of Interior.

The Prussian Constituent Assembly refused to accept the Brandenburg Ministry because it lacked the confidence of the majority. A deputation was sent to the King, to ask him to reconsider the matter and select a person more acceptable to the Assembly. The reception by the King was cool and the gap between the King and Assembly widened into a gulf when Johann Jacoby, the radical from East Prussia, bluntly told Frederick William IV, "It is the misfortune of kings that they never want to hear the truth." The remark was bold, but impolitic. It conjured up the memory of an English King, Charles I, deposed and executed in the 1640's. Historical precedents can cut two ways.

Now that an open conflict between the Prussian Assembly and the King seemed at hand, Marx no longer used the disdainful designation "Vereinbarungsversammlung" (Assembly to reach an agreement) when speaking of the Prussian Assembly. From this point forward, he honored that body with the title, "National Assembly" (perhaps in memory of the French Estates-General which changed itself into the revolutionary National Assembly in 1789).

Once again Marx envisioned a crisis that certainly would lead to the revolution September had failed to bring. Once again Marx hoped that monarchy and feudalism would fall, leading to a republic temporarily under the rule of the liberal bourgeoisie. Then the field would be finally cleared for the last revolutionary round, the decisive battle between proletariat and bourgeoisie, ending in the Communist victory. This final step, however, was never explicitly mentioned in the Organ der Demokratie. If Marx's repeated attacks on the bourgeoisie were somewhat disturbing, they might be but negative straws pointing to no more than a strong "social democratic" slant.

Even though Berlin was quiet during the first days of November, Marx's paper forecast revolution. The people were merely keeping their powder dry for the day of decision. To set the issues straight, Marx explained the situation in dramatic contrasts. Once the attempt to reach an agreement between the Assembly and the King failed, the two parties would be transformed into hostile forces with the right to challenge each other to combat. All "talk of right" (Rechtsphrase) was a sign of impotence. The advantages were on the side of the King. But "the greater right was on the side of the greater power," Marx declared.

Momentarily the populace seemed united in opposition to the Brandenburg Ministry. Already aroused by events in Vienna, excitement in the Rhineland reached an acute pitch. Cologne had a torchlight parade, accompanied by two choruses. Though it was a dark and rainy night, fifteen hundred torch and lantern bearers honored Ulrich Kyll, a Deputy of the Left in the Prussian Assembly. To make their meaning clear, they serenaded Heinrich von Wittgenstein, the chief Prussian official in Cologne, with a "most highly solemn *Katzenmusik*" (literally, "cat music," a derisively hostile serenade). The same noisy, derisive ceremony was repeated at the book store of Joseph Dumont, the owner of the *Kölnische Zeitung* and a member of the Cologne City Council, whom Marx always denounced in both capacities.

The *Neue Rheinische Zeitung* made the most of this popular unrest. Marx spared no expense to bring out the latest and greatest coverage of the news. Second editions were frequent, alternating with or augmented by supplementary editions, extra-supplements and extraordinary supplements, depending on the gravity of the hour. Marx made every effort to increase the circulation of the paper. For more than a week he ran a large notice at the top of the front page stating that people everywhere could enjoy the advantages of following the "current important happenings" for only one *Taler* for the remainder of the quarter. Postal officials everywhere would handle subscriptions. Though often enough Marx had accused Prussian officials of hindering the distribution of his paper, in this case they certainly were obliging by even facilitating wider subscriptions. By November 29, Marx could inform Engels that the *Neue Rheinische Zeitung* was very much "*en vogue.*"

The counterrevolution in Berlin, however, was even more in fashion. The Brandenburg Ministry, faced with the continuing hostility of the Constituent Assembly, decided to insulate that Assembly against the atmosphere in Berlin. On November 9, Count Brandenburg adjourned the Assembly until the 27th, when it was to reconvene in the small city of Brandenburg about thirty-five miles due west of Berlin. This was done, allegedly, to restore to the Assembly that freedom of deliberation which had disappeared in Berlin because of mob pressure.

The Brandenburg Ministry's choice of Brandenburg as the new meeting place for the Assembly gave rise to the couplet: "Brandenburg in the Assembly, and the Assembly in Brandenburg." Marx himself repeated the pungent line five times in one short article, creating the lingering effect of a martial leitmotif.

In Berlin, only the conservative Deputies and some moderate liberals obeyed the order to adjourn. The majority of the Assembly defiantly continued to hold sessions "in permanence." Even most of the moderate constitutional liberals protested against the adjournment and transfer of the Assembly to Brandenburg. It was feared that a dissolution of the Assembly would follow, ending with the restoration of absolute power. It appeared as if most of the Assembly, backed by the people, were on the eve of a new and perhaps mortal conflict with the King and the Brandenburg Ministry.

Count Brandenburg, however, did not allow the opposition much time to organize in Berlin. General von Wrangel entered the city on November 10 with over ten thousand troops. Momentarily, it appeared as if part of the Civic Guard might offer some resistance. The Democratic Central Committee, headed by D'Ester, attempted to stir up the masses. But many people were happy to see the soldiers again, as a guarantee of order; the occupation of Berlin proceeded without serious opposition.

The Constituent Assembly protested bravely and firmly when Von Wrangel ordered the Deputies to adjourn and to clear out of their meeting place in the Berlin Theater. The General thereupon commanded them to leave within fifteen minutes or be physically evicted. He then coolly took out his watch and waited for the minutes to tick by. The Deputies left before the appointed moment, in time to make an upright exit. It was impossible to argue with the "Moustache."

Martial law followed in Berlin on the 14th and the Prussian capital experienced the restriction that Cologne had in September. The members of the Constituent Assembly alone enjoyed a certain immunity. They met in a Shooting Gallery when they found that the Theater was locked and under guard. They moved again and again as each meeting place was successfully closed, constantly passing more and more revolutionary resolutions and appealing to the country at large.

Marx was again convinced that the decisive moment was indeed at hand. He demonstrated historically in three installments of the "Counter-revolution in Berlin" that people always found it easier to dispose of kings than parliamentary bodies. His epitaph for the tombstone of the Hohenzollerns was the oft repeated phrase: "Brandenburg in the Assembly and the Assembly in Brandenburg." The ideal revolutionary lineup which he and Engels had always envisioned was about to take shape. Now that the King had dropped the pretense of *Vereinbarung* by thrusting the reactionary Brandenburg Ministry into the lap of an unwilling Assembly, the bourgeoisie could no longer compromise in favor of a "half-revolution." They now had no other choice than to join the people in a direct battle against the King. In Berlin "the *dilemma* was posed, *King* or *People*," and the people would win. It might be necessary to go through a hard school, he warned, but it was the preparatory school of the *"total revolution."*

Marx was indignant that the Deputies had allowed General von Wrangel to order them out of their meeting place. "Why did not the Assembly outlaw the General?" Marx inquired. "Why did not some Deputy walk right into the midst of Wrangel's bayonets to proclaim the outlawry of the General and to harangue the soldiers?" He advised the Assembly to look for inspiration in the pages of the *Moniteur* of 1789/95, the official gazette of revolutionary France. Engels, writing for Marx in the New York *Daily Tribune* in 1852, granted that several hundred lives might have been lost if Berlin had revolted at this time. "But they would have fallen gloriously and would have left behind themselves, in the minds of the survivors, a wish for revenge, which in revolutionary times is one of the highest incentives for energetic and passionate action." A "well-contested defeat" was as good as an "easily-won victory." In any event, risks had to be taken. Curiously, however, Marx always cautioned against suicidal action in Cologne, when the odds were against him and his followers.

Evidently the Deputies of the Assembly reviewed their French revolutionary history, read the *Moniteur,* and may even have acted on cue from Cologne. (Marx was in contact with some of them, notably D'Ester.) Marx lauded them when they continued to meet in defiance of orders, comparing their move to the Shooting Gallery to that of the French National Assembly in 1789 when it had moved to an indoor Tennis Court upon finding the entrance to their usual meeting place likewise barred. He again praised the Berlin Assembly when it unanimously (the 242 who continued to meet in the Shooting Gallery) decreed on November 11 that Count Brandenburg was guilty of high treason for ordering the dissolution of the Civic Guard.

Concurrently in Cologne, Marx was using every means to arouse and mobilize popular resistance to the government. On November 12, after Brandenburg had adjourned the Assembly, Marx asked, "And what do *we* do in these moments?" The answer, "We refuse to pay taxes." Since the Prussian monarchy defied not only the people but also the bourgeoisie, it was best to defeat monarchy in a "bourgeois way"—by "starving it," by refusing to pay taxes. All the princes of Prussia, the Brandenburgs and the Von Wrangels produced no "army rations." The people did that. Two days later, after hearing that the Assembly had proclaimed the Brandenburg Ministry guilty of high treason, Marx declared that the obligation to pay taxes automatically ceased. "One does not owe taxes to a treasonable government." With an inevitable clash ahead, it was the "duty of the Rhine Province to rush to the aid of the Berlin National Assembly with men and weapons," Marx advised.

The revolutionary tone of the *Neue Rheinische Zeitung* was merely a more extensive manifestation of the popular ferment in Cologne, the Rhineland and Prussia at large. When the Brandenburg Ministry was decreed on November 4, all parties from the bourgeois Constitutional Liberals to the unavowed Communists supported the Assembly's opposition to the new Ministry. In Cologne, green placards bearing the caption, "Cologne is in Danger," announced a popular meeting in the *Eiser'sche Saal* (Eiser Hall) on the 11th. The *Neue Rheinische Zeitung,* stressing the unity of all parties, reported that workers, merchants and officials crowded the hall. Speakers from all classes were heard. Events in Berlin had ended all divisions among the people in Cologne, Marx reported exuberantly.

The *Eiser'sche Saal* meeting adopted a resolution that declared: "The Crown does not have the right to suspend the Assembly, or to transfer its sessions to another place, or to dissolve it." Deposited in nine localities (including the offices of the *Neue Rheinische Zeitung*), it was endorsed by more than seven thousand signatures in two days. The popular meeting decided that it would not adjourn, continuing instead as a body operating "in permanence." On the second day it sent a deputation to the City Council to persuade the latter to adopt the above resolution, which was done by a narrow margin. The following day the Cologne Citizens-Society (representing the bourgeois Constitutional Liberals) voluntarily endorsed the same resolution. All political parties in Cologne then sent a joint committee to Berlin to inform the government of the sentiments of the city. The *Zeitung* again confidently boasted that all were united now and "determined to go hand-in-hand with the National Assembly in the most decided fashion."

Organization for action began on November 13 when the popular meeting-in-permanence elected an executive committee of twenty-five, soon called the Peoples-Committee (*Volkskomitee*). The name, "Committee of Public Safety" was avoided this time. Five Communist members of the Worker-Society Committee—Marx, Von Beust, Röser, Nothjung and Christian Moll—were elected to this Peoples-Committee. Schneider II, the President of the Democratic Society, who was to associate actively with Marx during the next weeks, was also chosen. The members of the Committee were deliberately selected to represent all political parties and societies in Cologne.

The meeting-in-permanence instructed this Peoples-Committee to ask all civil and military authorities to declare publicly whether they sided with the King or the Berlin Assembly. That was the decisive question that would put all such officials on the spot. But when it became evident in the next days that the Committee (which included many moderate Democrats and Constitutional Liberals) refused to support such a radical line of action, Marx utilized other agencies and means to bring about revolutionary action.

As in all similar crises, the *Neue Rheinische Zeitung* was filled with reports from all corners of Prussia, pointing towards a gathering storm of popular indignation burgeoning into revolutionary action. Many accounts rested on a mere rumor, or the anticipation of a rumor. But even rumors serve a purpose—revolutionary action is often inspired by reports of actions allegedly taken already. Among other untold items, it was said that the people in Berlin mocked at martial law and refused to give up their weapons. The soldiers were fraternizing more and more with the people. Armed people from outside Berlin had arrived to help the beleaguered city. A popular revolt in Breslau had led to the expulsion of the army from that leading city in Silesia. The provinces of Silesia and Thuringia were in full revolt. Fifty thousand men were being marshalled in Halle, ready to march in a few days. Even in Pomerania a popular militia (*Landsturm*) of thirty thousand was organized in the vicinity of Greifswald to rush to the aid of Berlin. If that had happened in Pomerania (always depicted by Marx as the most benighted, bigoted and brutal area in Prussia), much more must be brewing in all other areas not covered in the reports.

Marx maintained close contacts with D'Ester, the newly-elected head of the Democratic Central Committee in Berlin, who called on people everywhere in Prussia to hold protest meetings. Peasants were to write to their sons in the army to inform them that they were traitors if they supported the government against the Assembly. When D'Ester appealed to the people through the *Neue Rheinische Zeitung* for money to ease the desperate financial status of the Committee, Marx urged that the money withheld from taxes be sent to the Democratic Central Committee instead. The *Zeitung* accepted such contributions and printed the initials of donors.

Marx and Schneider II issued a Proclamation (*Aufruf*) in the name of the Democratic District Committee, calling on all democratic societies throughout the Rhineland to encourage the non-payment of taxes, as the most effective weapon against the government. There should not, however, be any forceful resistance at this time. Passive resistance was to be the watchword, but additional action was anticipated. All societies were invited to send delegates to a second Rhineland Democratic Congress in Cologne on November 23, to deliberate on such matters. The Proclamation, published in the *Neue Rheinische Zeitung* of November 15 appeared in Cologne on the evening of the 14th.

As the crisis was developing, Marx made special appeals to all parties and minority groups, to turn them against the Prussian government. He wasted little effort on the Conservatives, except to advise them that they would be rewarded with a "tip and a kick" for their support of the government. More might be accomplished with the Catholics.

Throughout 1848 Marx had avoided attacks on religion and had advised others likewise. He had, on the other hand, exploited the fears, sensibilities and suspicions of the Catholic minority in Prussia. At this time he attempted to show that the essential spirit of Prussia found its expression in a Protestant "Evangelical government." . . . "It is known," Marx stated, "that even under the *Camphausen* Ministry the *Poles* were plundered,

burned and clubbed equally as much because they were *Catholics* as because they were *Poles*." (Camphausen, incidentally, was both Catholic
and liberal.) The "Pomeranians" had taken a special delight in "*spearing
the image of the Blessed Virgin and in hanging* Catholic priests." Marx
warned the Catholics in the Rhine Province, Westphalia and Silesia of
the horrors they faced if the Brandenburg-Manteuffel Ministry stayed in
power. Instead of being beaten with canes, they would then be "scourged
with scorpions." Marx could use Biblical imagery when addressing those
to whom the Church meant much.

Marx also turned to the Jews who had been emancipated by the
March Revolution. "Nevertheless," he charged, "leading representatives
of the Jews everywhere are at the head of the counterrevolution." But
what fate awaited them if the reaction won? He cited isolated incidents
to show that Prussia was already restricting their freedom of movement
and was hurling them back into the ghetto.

Three days after Marx had openly advocated non-payment of taxes,
the Prussian Assembly adopted the policy. The motion had been pushed
by D'Ester and the Radical-Democrats. Many Deputies were at first opposed to it, but after having been evicted from several successive meeting places by the army, the Assembly (by the unanimous vote of 226–0)
decreed on November 15 that the Brandenburg Ministry did not have
the right to spend state funds and to collect taxes as long as the Assembly could not meet freely in Berlin. The denial of taxes was to go into
effect on the 17th. "No-More-Taxes" ultimately became the battle cry
in the conflict between the Brandenburg Ministry and the majority of
the Prussian Constituent Assembly that refused to adjourn.

The non-payment of taxes program raised the possibility of daily incidents. It meant the refusal to pay the tolls collected at bridges. The
peasant would be confronted with the milling and slaughtering taxes
assessed on grain and cattle entering the gates of cities on their way to
the market places. At first it appeared as if the refusal to pay taxes would
be widely followed in Prussia. The radicals and democrats immediately
attempted to make it effective and to mobilize the necessary forces to
intimidate all officials. Some newspapers reported that the whole country was in a state of riot. As always, however, action made the news,
whereas the refusal of the majority to go along was less noticeable at
first.

On November 17, the day that the Assembly's decree was to go into
effect, an extraordinary edition of the *Neue Rheinische Zeitung* carried
the exhortation and battle cry, "*Keine Steuern mehr!!!*" (No-more-Taxes!!!)
that Marx made famous. It appeared as the headline of an article that he
wrote on the developments in Berlin. The article closed with the commandments, "Beginning today all taxes are therefore abolished!!! The pay-

ment of taxes is high treason; the refusal to pay taxes is the first duty of citizens!" Thereafter the *Keine Steuern mehr!!!* appeared in large, broad print across the top of the paper. Since headlines were uncommon in the 1840's, it certainly caught the eye. It became a new fighting trademark for the paper until December 17, weeks after it had lost all practical meaning.

The highest Prussian official in the Rhineland, F. A. Eickmann, issued an order on November 17, warning the people to disregard the agitation for non-payment of taxes. Marx answered Eickmann on the 19th by declaring that said official was an "open enemy of the National Assembly," and as such, was deprived of his office. Marx then warned all lesser officials that those who followed Eickmann's orders did so at their own risk. The revolutionary threat was implicit. Thereafter Marx drafted a program for *"active resistance,"* without which *"passive resistance"* was meaningless. Force had to be met with force. He demanded that all refractory officials be *"deposed,* declared guilty of *high treason* and replaced by provisional committees of public safety, whose orders alone would be accepted as legal." Wherever the "counterrevolutionary officials" tried to prevent the creation and functioning of such committees, force was to be met with force. This was a program for revolutionary action and seizure of power on all levels.

A second *Aufruf* issued in the name of the Rhineland Democratic District Committee (a diluted and less explicit version of the above program) appeared in the *Neue Rheinische Zeitung* later in the day. This *Aufruf,* as the earlier one, was signed by Marx and Schneider II, and also by Karl Schapper who had just been released from prison. It called upon all democratic societies in the Rhine Province to adopt and carry out the following measures:

(1) Since the National Assembly itself had decreed non-payment of taxes, all attempts at forceful collection were to be met with resistance of every type.

(2) A popular militia (*Landsturm*—the equivalent of a nation at arms) was to be organized everywhere for defense against the enemy. If arms were lacking, they were to be furnished by the local governments or through voluntary contributions.

(3) Officials everywhere were to be asked to declare publicly whether they were willing to recognize and enforce the decisions of the National Assembly. In case they refused, Committees of Public Safety were to be selected, if possible in cooperation with the municipal councils. City councils which opposed the National Assembly were to be replaced through universal elections.

The immediate revolutionary response in the Rhineland looked promising. The first days were turbulent. Reports from all sides, though often

346

exaggerated, told of refusals to pay taxes and of organized attempts to prevent the collection of taxes. In Bonn, the Democratic Society, students, and other groups persuaded or coerced the City Council to join them in a solid front. The Civic Guards generally went along. Prussian officials and guards were dislodged and intimidated. Casualties and physical injuries were negligible, however. Most of the damage was confined to toll stations and booths which were smashed and burned. As a result, flour and cattle entered the city gates tax-free. The same thing happened in Düsseldorf, Koblenz and some other cities. The small towns and the peasants were also on the move. Barricades allegedly were constructed in one community. In Bernkastel on the Moselle River, people were "sharpening old lances and manufacturing scythes." The scythes had the right ring, ever since the Polish peasants armed with them had done everything but gain the victory against the cannon, bullets and bayonets of Prussian armies with a fourfold numerical superiority earlier in 1848.

While Marx had looked to Berlin to initiate revolutionary action during the September Crisis, this time the situation was reversed. Now it was a case of going to the assistance of Berlin. Berlin could be saved only through the "revolutionary energy" of the provinces, their main cities and the open country, so Marx declared on November 19. Force had to be met with force. Even earlier, during the popular meeting in the *Eiser'sche Saal*, Friedrich von Beust had attempted to create a fighting force. Von Beust was a former Prussian officer who enjoyed the confidence of Marx. On the 15th, he had drafted a plan to utilize the *Landwehr* (National Guard) as a popular revolutionary army. An appeal went out to *Landwehr* units elsewhere in Prussia to do the same.

The *Landwehr*, subject to recall in case of war or a national emergency, included most men between the ages of twenty-five and forty who had completed two years of active service and two years in the reserve forces. Here was a vast body of civilians with past military training which might be utilized, it was hoped, against the government. But only about thirteen hundred of the eleven thousand *Landwehr* men in Cologne signed a pledge to defend the Berlin Assembly.

The Cologne Worker-Society created its own shock force, a "Flying Corps," which also accepted Democrats because the emphasis was on the unity of all parties. The *Turnverein* (Turner or gymnastic society) established its "Free Corps." A third group solicited the enlistment of masons, carpenters, locksmiths, cabinetmakers, etc. A notice in the *Neue Rheinische Zeitung* of November 23 asked for an additional "Free Corps" of persons who were not members of the Prussian *Landwehr*, but were ready to give their "blood and fortunes in defense of German freedom." Attempts were also made to revive the Civic Guard. But there was a shortage of weapons and the money to buy them. Von Beust was elected

Commander of all forces in Cologne on November 21. The situation became critical when these forces attempted to prevent the movement of regular army units. The climax came on November 23 when a meeting of all the Corps and *Landwehr* men was scheduled in an open square, as announced on placards signed by Von Beust. The Prussian army intervened and prevented the meeting from taking place. Immediately thereafter, when an investigation of his revolutionary activities was started, Von Beust hurriedly left Cologne for Paris. There were no further attempts to organize and consolidate a revolutionary armed force.

The Democratic Society and the Worker-Society (once again under the guidance of Karl Schapper) tried to get the Cologne City Council to cooperate, as advocated in the *Aufruf* issued by Marx, Schapper and Schneider II. But the Council from the very first refused to join the tax-refusal campaign. It did, however, send a petition to the Prussian King asking him to dismiss the Brandenburg Ministry in order to restore confidence, as a step needed to save the Crown.

Marx furiously denounced the Cologne City Council for sending such a petition to the King. Centering his main attack on Joseph Dumont of the *Kölnische Zeitung,* Marx accused the Council of trying to save the King when the Rhine Province was turning against him. The Council instead should have seized control of the city gates to stop the collection of taxes. Because it had failed to do this, Marx demanded categorically that it be deposed without delay. All judicial and financial officials who refused to oppose the payment of taxes "with all energy" were also to be treated as persons guilty of high treason. If Cologne did not depose the City Council, Marx declared, it deserved the *"knout."* After listing the major cities that had halted the collection of taxes, Marx then asked Cologne, the metropolis of the Rhineland, not to allow itself to come to shame by doing less.

Minor demonstrations took place on November 22. Perhaps they were designed to test the popular temper, with the hope that a display of action would touch off a general conflagration. The home of the *Bürgermeister* and an adjacent building were attacked, with the usual stoning of windows. As a vengeful gesture against Councilman Dumont, the windows of the editorial offices of the *Kölnische Zeitung* also were smashed. That paper further reported that one of its carriers was stopped on the street and offered money to destroy the copies he was delivering. He was beaten up when he refused. In view of such incidents, the *Kölnische Zeitung* could only conclude that the "Democrats, really anarchists," had celebrated a "triumph and enriched the annals of the city with a shameful page."

Cologne never got beyond protest meetings, demonstrations, remonstrances, organization of revolutionary corps, minor street brawls, breaking of some windows, and hit-and-run skirmishes. The needed revolutionary energy, will, decision and planning were perhaps abundant enough, but too many soldiers manned the gates and forts around Cologne to allow for any interference with the collection of taxes. Since the September Crisis, Cologne also lacked the armed Civic Guard which had proved useful against regular soldiers in some other cities. Although Marx expected and demanded that Cologne act more decisively, all the evidence indicates that he also advised against a hopeless test of strength. He did not want Cologne to be added to the small list of cities which went down heroically in defeat, as an inspiration for later times.

The *Kölnische Zeitung* reported on November 23 that an "obvious reversal of public opinion" had taken place during the preceding week. Most people initially backed the Assembly in its protest against adjournment and the move to Brandenburg. But when the Assembly voted to halt the collection of taxes, it opened the "floodgates of anarchy." People then began to recognize that the plans and proclamations of a "certain party" (the Republicans) were aimed at converting a constitutional struggle into a life and death battle which threatened monarchy and the whole existing order. The Catholic *Rheinische Volks-Halle,* while insisting that the King had no right to move or dissolve the Assembly, likewise called attention to the manner in which the "party of terror" was exploiting the situation. That party, with "unashamed ruthlessness" called for the overthrow of the throne in favor of a republic, and a "socialistic republic" in particular. The All-German Parliament and Imperial Ministry in Frankfurt, claiming that its decisions were the supreme law for all Germans, issued an *Aufruf* to the German people on November 22. The *Aufruf* declared that the motion to end tax collections was illegal, therefore null and void, and exhorted the Prussians to avoid violence and illegal acts. At the same time, it promised that the Parliament would protect the liberties of all Prussians and called on Frederick William IV to select Ministers who commanded the confidence of the people. The intervention of Frankfurt did not help the Berlin Assembly in its fight with the King; the Prussian government simply rejected it as meddling in a "domestic issue." But the vote of the Frankfurt Parliament, freely arrived at, strengthened the position of those who questioned the validity of the No-More-Taxes decision.

Encouraged by such a shift of public opinion, the Prussian officials had little difficulty in curbing further revolutionary moves. Martial law squelched lingering resistance in Düsseldorf. In Bonn, order was established by the "Croats" as the *Zeitung* termed the Prussian soldiers. Elsewhere the story was the same. The "Flying Corps" in Cologne never had the opportunity to swing into action. The "golden sun of freedom, order and peace" was returning, the *Bonner Wochenblatt* wrote on November

23. The brief union of all parties, the combination that Marx always considered essential in 1848, came to an end. The crisis in Prussia was over a week after the Assembly called on the people to refuse to pay taxes. Marx miscalculated when he concluded that this "bourgeois" way of fighting the government would command the continued support of the bourgeois liberals. Instead, it was this very step that may have defeated the prospects for a united stand against the Brandenburg Ministry. The liberals had second thoughts and scented anarchy. It was all very well to think of English revolutionary precedents, of the role played by the refusal to vote money in contests between parliaments and kings. In Prussia, however, parliamentary control over the purse strings was just in the process of being established. Moreover, the 19th century state already had such extensive functions that a paralysis of governmental services could have many unfavorable side effects. Marx himself never went to the point of refusing to pay postal charges (the Prussian postal system operated in the black and maintained a large body of officials) for the distribution of the *Neue Rheinische Zeitung*.

Marx was able to capitalize on a minor judicial harassment during the aftermath. On November 20, Marx, Schneider II and Schapper were charged with "public incitement to rebellion" and ordered to appear for a hearing the following day. The charge, which ignored the more inflammatory material in the *Neue Rheinische Zeitung* as involving freedom of press, was based on the second *Aufruf* that the three had issued in the name of the Democratic District Committee. That *Aufruf*, however, had been carefully drafted. It was full of incitement, without a doubt, but it steered clear of advocating specific, concrete action. Marx was well-acquainted with the niceties of the Napoleonic Code and Schneider II was a skilled lawyer. Marx confidently informed Engels on November 29 that their paper "constantly operated on the level of insurrection." But all legal summons to the contrary, it "sailed clear" of the "*Code* penal. . . . Revolution was on the march," Marx exulted.

Marx boldly answered the judicial summons with another *Aufruf* addressed to the "Democrats of the Rhine Province!" This *Aufruf*, appearing in the *Neue Rheinische Zeitung* the evening of the 20th, charged that the officials, acting on orders from the highly treasonable Prussian Ministry, were counting on the populace to create a "*Skandal*" in favor of their accused leaders. Such a "row" then would be exploited to impose martial law on Cologne. No matter what happened to the accused, the *Aufruf* continued, the people were to remain quiet so as to "frustrate this hope. . . . The Rhine Province would rather shed its last drop of blood than submit to the regime of the sabre." The Democratic Congress was to convene under any circumstances. (It later met as scheduled on the 23rd.) The *Aufruf* was signed by the accused, Marx, Schapper and Schneider II.

The *Aufruf* was a skilled stroke. It alerted the people to the fact that the three faced a hearing and possible imprisonment. By accusing the authorities of employing this odious device to provoke an uprising which would justify martial law, it simultaneously implied that the people were ready to fight to protect Marx, Schapper and Schneider II. It also suggested that the three were ready to face any fate rather than to have the people engage in a suicidal struggle in their behalf. Their admonition to the Democrats to remain calm could likewise be cited as evidence to contradict charges of "public incitement to rebellion."

At the hearing on November 21, Marx, Schapper and Schneider II were merely asked to confirm that they were the authors of the *Aufruf*. Their replies were recorded and that was the end of the affair, for the time being. But the threat of future action remained.

During the following weeks, Marx repeatedly called attention to various charges that were pending against the *Neue Rheinische Zeitung*, like so many feathers in his hat. On November 26 he listed three such cases. Beyond that, he had reliable information that at least a dozen "inquisitions" were being considered against the "scandal paper," as the officials called his paper. Furthermore, the Imperial Ministry in Frankfurt allegedly recognized it as the "worst newspaper of the wretched press." Marx obviously enjoyed acknowledging such notoriety. By making it appear that the authorities were out to get him, he also improved his chances for a sympathetic hearing, if it ever came to a jury trial. He felt reasonably confident that a Rhineland jury would never return a guilty verdict. The recent acquittal of Freiligrath was a reassuring precedent. Marx, moreover, remained careful not to overstep the limits of the law, and enough could be done within its borders.

Though the crisis in Prussia was over, Marx continued his No-More-Taxes campaign, scorchingly denouncing those who questioned its validity. On November 23 he had denounced the Frankfurt Parliament as an "assembly of professors," and declared it guilty of treason. A week later, eighty real professors from the University of Berlin (including the famous Grimm brothers) and nineteen from Halle came in for a lacing. The professors had justified the transfer of the Prussian Assembly to Brandenburg, asserting that the mob had deprived the Assembly of freedom of deliberation by confronting it with a "rule of terror" that threatened the "lives of the Deputies," the dignity of the Constituent Assembly, and the honor of the nation.

The "money-greedy professorial clique," feeling that the source of their salaries was being threatened by the tax-refusal program, were guilty of "brash lies," Marx asserted. They would line up just as speedily in defense of the "sovereignty of the people which they now damn so much," if the people were to win the final victory. But the people would meet them with the cry, "Too late" and make short shrift of the "whole poverty of privileged learning." (It is not clear whether the people then would have no need for professors and learning, or whether they would require an entirely new brand.)

Developments in Prussia followed the expected course, but with an unanticipated corollary. When the Constituent Assembly reconvened in Brandenburg on November 27, a quorum was lacking. Most of the Deputies had remained away in Berlin, in continued protest against the change. An increasing number, however, began drifting in, but they did not take their seats in the Assembly, waiting instead for the Brandenburg Ministry to make concessions. The Brandenburg Ministry, however, ultimately used the lack of a quorum as a pretext for dissolving the Assembly, stating that it was impossible to work out an "agreement" on the constitution when the Assembly was incapable of operating. The dismissal of the Assembly appeared as a decided counterrevolutionary stroke. But most of the sting was taken out of the move when the King simultaneously granted a surprisingly liberal constitution to Prussia on December 5.

The Constitution, as a matter of fact, was strikingly similar to the draft that the Assembly itself had nearly completed. The main differences represented concessions to the King, who recovered the title of "King by the Grace of God," and was granted a full veto power and authority over the choice of Ministers. But a solid residue remained to satisfy the minimum expectations of most liberals. The way was left open for further revisions resulting from agreement (*Vereinbarung* again) between the King and the two legislative bodies which were to be elected in late January and early February, as provided by the Constitution. Much therefore depended on the decisions and events of the next months and years. Unfortunately, the trend in Europe was in a reactionary direction.

The liberals were surprised at the liberal character of the Constitution, though displeased over the manner in which it was acquired. A constitution coming as a gift from the King (*octroyirt*) was distrusted. What had been granted presumably could be taken back later, or altered at the will of the King. Marx mockingly cited Scripture to express the situation, "*The Lord giveth, the Lord taketh away. Blessed is the name of the Lord.*"

Many Rhineland communities expressed their appreciation to the government in signed statements. The *Kölnische Zeitung*, though initially displeased, stated that the spirit of the Constitution was one of "true freedom," which allowed for a constant, free and legal development of a democratic humanity, hostile to every despotic and revolutionary caprice. The Catholics were especially pleased because the Constitution gave them a freedom almost unparalleled anywhere except in Belgium. Religious liberty was a first consideration, the *Rheinische*

Volks-Halle declared on December 13. Without it all the other freedoms were like a "silver apple given to a starving person." The *Neue Rheinische Zeitung* stood almost alone in its derision and defiance of the new Constitution.

Perhaps Marx kept the headline "NO-MORE-TAXES!!!" until December 17, 1848 as a challenge to the counterrevolution in Prussia, to see how reactionary and repressive it was. Since nothing happened, there was little that he could do except to analyze what had occurred in four installments, "The Bourgeoisie and the Counterrevolution," which appeared between December 10 and 31 in the *Neue Rheinische Zeitung*.

Marx, as Engels always insisted, was at his best in these "historic" essays and chapters. In such writings his characteristic and astounding capacity for manipulating history allowed him to trim the facts so that they fit beautifully, and were comfortable, in the procrustean bed of his theories. It was done with a verve and confidence that have since commanded the admiration, and faith, of many. But the human being, always the chief actor in history, was submerged in the process.

The long-deferred political trial of the imprisoned Gottschalk, the first President of the Worker-Society, and his two associates, Friedrich Anneke and Joseph Esser, took place in Cologne from December 21–23. Marx wrote two articles on the subject while the trial was in progress. Jury trials, as then constituted, were institutions to preserve the privileges of a few and not the rights of all, Marx asserted. The idea that the "conscience" of the juror acted as a guarantee of justice was ridiculous, since a conscience was determined by the "knowledge and way of life of a man." It would take a miracle for an accused person who had opposed the privileged class and the existing government to be acquitted. Marx nevertheless accurately predicted that Gottschalk and the others would be acquitted.

The news that Gottschalk and Anneke had been freed caused Engels' hopes to soar. On December 28 he wrote to Marx from Bern, asking whether the time had come for him to return. Surely the "Prussian dogs" would not want to deal with juries thereafter. He was ready to come at once if there were some assurances that he would not be thrown in prison while awaiting trial. He could not endure that; in prison one "could not smoke." But he was ready to face ten thousand juries.

During the stay in Switzerland, Engels had lost some of his usual enthusiasm for work. Marx had urged him to write articles on Proudhon, the "Hungarian *Scheiss*" or the "beehive of nationalities," and something against the federal system, using Switzerland as proof. But he completed none of them before the end of the year, except several articles on Switzerland which portrayed that country as producing nothing but mediocrity, boredom and little men, all the smaller because of the federal character of the state. But the articles failed to convert the German democrats and republicans who generally favored a federal system, much to Marx's disgust.

Marx had surmounted the financial hurdles of the resurrected *Neue Rheinische Zeitung* and was still holding the "fort" at the end of the year. Journalistic ingenuity, including his handling of the Prussian crisis, had attracted many new subscribers. For the rest, a certain business acumen paid off. He began the quarterly subscription drive on December 19 with a large, front-page advertisement which claimed that the "*N. Rh. Ztg.*" was not only the *Organ* of German but of European democracy. On December 25 he bought space in the *Kölnische Zeitung* for a particularly large advertisement, prominently blocked off across two columns, which asserted that the *Neue Rheinische Zeitung* during its short life had acquired a wider distribution than any other German newspaper. On all occasions the leading foreign newspapers spoke of it as being distinguished. "Mr. Dr. Carl Marx," as "*Redacteur en chef,*" controlled the paper. Because of extensive contacts with "leading men of the movement in England, France, Italy, etc. and because of numerous correspondents in all parts of Germany" the *Zeitung* was in a position to keep the public informed in the "speediest and most detailed manner." Marx never undersold his paper, or himself.

Marx continued to publish his paper without official interference, even though he never ceased attacking the government in Berlin. In other respects also, he was still free to organize, associate, assemble and agitate. As President of the Worker-Society and as a force in Rhineland democratic circles, he was in a position to make the most of the opportunities. Though he had miscalculated twice in reading the revolutionary weather-map for Germany in regard to the second and decisive round of revolutions, there was nothing catastrophic in the situation, except in distant Vienna. Marx remained confident. The people would be more receptive to real revolutionary agitation in the coming year.

The chief loss for the people of 1848, so Marx declared, was the loss of their illusions (the belief that revolutions came easily, without extraordinary upheavals, sustained action and the complete destruction of the old order). Freed of such illusions, they would be more responsive to the revolutionary verities, corresponding to his interpretation of history regarding the requirements of the times.

=VI=

1849

1. NEW PREDICTIONS
AND OLD SCORES

THE customary New Year's greetings, "renewed each year by every pastor and choir leader, barber and night-watchman, gravedigger, etc." left Marx cold. He did, however, note the advent of 1849 by celebrating New Year's Eve with a correspondent of the English *Daily News* and two revolutionary poets, Freiligrath and Alfred Meissner. Just a year ago Marx had greeted the New Year at a celebration sponsored by the German Worker-Society in Brussels. Engels had been in Paris.

The year 1848 had been one of alternating hope and disappointment for Marx and Engels. Convinced that they had a role and mission in life, they expected a replay of the Great French Revolution when unknown men had risen from the ranks to play a decisive part in history. Their relative youth was no disqualification—Marx was thirty, Engels, twenty-eight. Yet time and again events had seemed at the point of taking their destined course, only to stop short. The "complete revolution" had not come. Marx assessed the reasons for these failures on New Year's Day in an article entitled, "The Revolutionary Movement."

No revolution, Marx declared, had started with a more "inspiring overture" than that of 1848. "Nothing was more philanthropic, more humane and weaker than the February and March revolutions; nothing was more brutal than the consequences of this *humanity of weakness*," as was illustrated in the fate of Italy, Poland, Germany and, above all, in the June defeat of the workers in Paris. Why had all this happened? Marx now picked out Britain as the missing piece in the revolutionary puzzle.

Britain was the rock on which the waves of revolution broke. The massive protest that the Chartists had planned in April (1848) had been choked off prematurely by the presence of thousands of constables. As a master of world trade, English control of the world markets was fatal to all other countries. "Every partial social reform" in France and all of Europe therefore remained a hollow hope as long as Britain was not "overthrown through a world war." A victory of the French proletariat was needed to start a chain reaction of revolution and war. Therefore, the watchword of European liberation in 1849, Marx announced confidently, was the fall of the bourgeoisie in France. Britain again, as during the Napoleonic era, would lead and finance the counterrevolutionary armies. Such a war would give the Chartists, "the organized English worker party," the opportunity to carry through a successful revolution in England. Britain, by virtue of her highly developed industries and proletariat, then would reverse her role to take the lead in the revolutionary movement, Marx predicted.

Marx did not expect an immediate crisis in Prussia. A new confrontation would occur when the elected Parliament, as provided for in the Constitution of December 5, rejected that Constitution. Marx declared that no compromise in the form of a *"constitutional* monarchy" was possible in Prussia or in Germany at large. The choice lay between two extremes, either a "feudal absolutist counterrevolution or the social-republican revolution." When that "part of the bourgeoisie which was fit to survive" recognized this fact, they would awaken from their "apathy." Marx still counted on the bourgeoisie in Germany to play its destined role.

Engels started the New Year in Bern, depressed and impatient because he could only kill time and accomplish nothing. His celebration of New Year's Eve, nevertheless, took him to places where he could observe that every second *philistine* in Switzerland was "simultaneously a spy and an assassin." Writing to Marx on January 7–8, Engels asked if there was any chance that he might be treated as favorably as others who had been arrested in September, and then released. Even a brief arrest in Cologne might be preferable to life in free Switzerland—a person was freer in Prussia, even under the latest Constitution, than in "free Switzerland."

Marx's reply must have been reassuring. In any event, Engels returned to Cologne around the middle of January, without incident. The *Neue Rheinische Zeitung* reported on January 28 that another of the "September refugees," Friedrich Engels, had appeared before a judicial magistrate two days earlier. After a short hearing, he was dismissed with the statement that there "were no charges against him."

Engels' article, "The Magyar Struggle," which Marx had requested in November, appeared in the *Zeitung* on January 13, having been mailed from Bern. It represented a settlement of old scores against the Slavic peoples in the Austrian Empire for their betrayal of the revolution in Vienna and Hungary. As a backdrop, Engels eulogized the Hungarians, or Magyars, who were at that time engaged in a heroically desperate fight against the same armies that had conquered revolutionary Vienna. For the first time in the revolutionary movements of 1848, Engels exulted, a nation surrounded by superior forces had the courage to mobilize a "revolutionary passion and the red terror against the cowardly counterrevolutionary fury." The odds were terrible. "All Austria, headed by 16 million fanaticized Slavs, against four million Magyars!"

The article then broadened into a historical glorification of the civilizing and revolutionary role of the Germans and Hungarians, often in the face of opposition from the "barbarian Slavs" (the Poles always excepted). Engels found that the whole history of Austria demonstrated that only three nationalities were "bearers of progress who played an active role in history, who [were] still fit to live—Germans, Poles, Magyars." For this reason they were revolutionary in 1848/49, Engels declared.

In condemning the Slavs, Engels used the same criterion as he had used against the Danes during the Schleswig-Holstein crisis. There was nothing specifically anti-Slavic about it. Since the right of revolution overrode all other considerations, the leading revolutionary states were entitled to greatness and had the right to crush any interference. The small nations would be annihilated, if their claims to a separate, independent national existence impeded the course of the revolutionary nations.

The various peoples of the Austrian Empire represented so many "national scraps and ruins," destined to be fanatically reactionary until their "complete destruction or denationalization." Engels especially condemned the Pan-Slavism of the Czechs and the South Slavs, which originated in Prague and Agram. He declared that its aim was to create a Slavic empire under Russian tutelage. Palacky, the Czech, was the spokesman and Jellačić, the Croat, was the military leader for this Pan-Slavism. They represented the counterrrevolution. The Germans and Hungarians represented the revolution. It was as simple as that.

Taking his cue from Marx's predictions for 1849, Engels likewise predicted that there would be a victorious uprising of the French proletariat which would bring immediate freedom to the Austrian Germans and the Hungarians. Then they would exact a "bloody revenge on the Slavic barbarians." The general war that would follow would destroy the Slavic league and would annihilate all these "small, ox-headed nations down to their very names." The next world war would not only destroy "reactionary classes and dynasties, it would also wipe out whole reactionary nations from the face of the earth. And that also is progress," Engels concluded.

The Slavic peoples in the Austrian Empire, however, refused to bow to the verdict of history and the threat of future annihilation, as expounded in Marx's newspaper. Pan-Slavism was bound to appeal to them. Taken separately, none of the small Slavic nations could be in a position to assert their nationality fully in competition with the otherwise more numerous Germans and Hungarians.

Marx and Engels became especially angry when Bakunin published a mesmeric "Appeal to the Slavs," which ardently advocated a democratic federation of free Slavic nations in a broader European confederation of democratic states. The matter was all the more serious because some German Democrats, notably Arnold Ruge, appeared to be receptive to Bakunin's call. Marx therefore was overjoyed when the Polish Democratic Society in Paris published its own appeal to all "Slavic Brothers," urging them to oppose Bakunin's program and the Austro-Slav ideal. He printed this Polish "Manifesto" in the *Neue Rheinische Zeitung* on January 22 and added a hearty endorsement. Engels, the expert on nationality questions in the Marx-Engels partnership, answered Bakunin's "Appeal" on February 15–16 in an article entitled, "The Democratic Pan-Slavism."

The fact that "Bakunin is our friend" would not prevent them from criticizing the pamphlet, Engels asserted. He began by ridiculing and denouncing all "enthusiasm over the universal fraternization of nations, a European federal republic and eternal world peace." With an almost Bismarckian accent Engels stated that the fraternization of European nations could not be accomplished through "mere phrases and pious wishes, but only through a thorough revolution and bloody battles."

Engels then repeated all the old arguments and added some new ones to prove that the Slavic peoples in the Austrian Empire lacked the historic, literary, political, commercial and industrial potential to emerge as independent nations. The Slavs, moreover, sinned against revolution everywhere by placing the interests of their respective nationalities ahead of the "*revolution.*" They were destined to experience the vengeance of the revolution and the revolutionary nations.

Hatred of the Russian had been the "*first revolutionary passion*" among the Germans, Engels asserted. Since then, hatred of the Czechs and Croats had been added. The Germans now recognized that they, in alliance with the Poles and Hungarians, could not make the revolution secure without a "decided terrorism against the Slavic peoples." He forecast a merciless life and death battle against the revolution-betraying Slavic race—"a battle of annihilation and ruthless terrorism, not in the interest of Germany, but in the interest of revolution!" Such was the verdict against the Slavs, for failing to answer the revolutionary roll call.

2. THE PRUSSIAN ELECTIONS

ELECTIONS for the new Parliament provided by the Constitution of December 5 were held as scheduled in late January and early February, 1849. The chief issue in the campaign was the Constitution itself. Disregarding the views of the extreme right, public opinion ranged all the way from acceptance without change to outright refusal of any constitution granted by a king.

All male citizens who met a six-month residence requirement (except persons with a criminal record or those on public relief) were eligible to vote for the lower of the two-house legislature. (Since about one-third of the inhabitants of Cologne were on public relief, this restriction hurt the Democrats. On the other hand, it also excluded the *Lumpenproletariat*, always denounced by Marx and Engels as useless and reactionary.) The elections to the Lower House were indirect. In the first stage —the "primary election" (*Urwahlen*) on January 22—all the voters in a district chose a specified number of "electors" (*Wahlmänner*). For the second one about two weeks later, the electors of each district were to meet and elect the actual representatives for their respective districts.

Eligibility as a voter for the Upper House depended on a high income, property, or tax qualification. Consequently there was little interest there, for that house was bound to be moderately liberal, perhaps even conservative in makeup. (Marx hoped that it would be most reactionary so as to guarantee a conflict with the Lower House.)

The major contest involved a test of strength between the moderate or Constitutional Liberals and that somewhat inchoate mass which flocked together under the banner of a Democratic Party. In the Rhine Province, the Catholic interest could be the decisive factor. The Constitutional Liberals, favoring a constitutional monarchy, were ready and even happy to accept the Constitution as the foundation for the political future of Prussia. Some wanted to take it just as it was, postponing any changes to later and more settled times. Their first consideration was order on a constitutional basis. A majority of the liberals, however, wanted a few immediate alterations, while accepting the document as a whole.

The Democrats insisted on drastic changes or even outright repudiation of the Constitution. Some refused, as a matter of principle, to accept any constitution handed down from on high. Others saw the rejection of the Constitution as opening the way for a new clash between King and People—the prelude to a more radical revolution, ending in the downfall of monarchy and feudalism.

The Communists again joined with the Democrats, even though Marx was becoming increasingly disillusioned with them. Writing in the *Neue Rheinische Zeitung* after the election (February 18), Marx stated unequivocally: "The party which we represent, the Party of the People (*Volk*), until now exists only in an elementary form in Germany." (Marx avoided the term "Communist" in 1848/49.) As an explanation for their union with the Democrats during the election, he flatly stated: "Where it is a question of a battle against the existing government, we ally ourselves even with our enemies."

The *Neue Rheinische Zeitung* took an active part in the election campaign. In a positive sense, it defended the Democratic position in regard to the Constitution, and it extended advice on the requirements of a successful campaign. But the main emphasis was on attack, an unceasing denunciation of the Prussian government and the Constitutional Liberals. They were accused of endless intrigues, bribery, dishonesty and a vast expenditure of funds. The indirect elections gave the "government and its sworn allies against the people—the aristocratic-bureaucratic-moneybag caste"—a thousand opportunities for deceptive maneuvers. The government was flooding the country with placards and fly sheets designed to fool the peasants, while the *Kölnische Zeitung* printed and distributed 182,000 pamphlets and 162,000 reprints. The Prussian army was made to appear more odious and brutal than ever, with the soldiers habitually labeled as "Croats," thus linking them with the alleged brutalities and ferocity of the Croats during the siege of Vienna. The *Zeitung*, however, was on the defensive when the *Kölnische Zeitung* and some other papers accused those who opposed the Constitution as wanting a republic—and not just a "simple republic, but the Red Republic."

Marx, neither then nor later, found cause to reproach the Democrats for lack of zeal during the campaign. He himself was somewhat remiss in the matter. He did not bring up the subject of the elections with the Worker-Society until a mere week before the primary. The delay may have been deliberate to avoid a conflict with the Gottschalk-inclined minority which opposed cooperation with the Democrats. Finally, on January 15, the matter came up at a Committee meeting. Marx did most of the talking, arguing emphatically that it was now too late to organize a successful campaign for any worker candidates. Since it was hopeless to base a campaign on their "own principles," it was best to unite with other parties to assure the victory of a large opposition to governmental absolutism and feudal rule. Just "ordinary Democrats, so-called liberals," Marx assured the Committee, would suffice for this purpose. Karl Schapper, as always, supported Marx's view. The Committee, accordingly, decided to support the "democratic principles" and selected Schapper and Röser to meet with the leaders of the Democratic Society to promote the desired unity.

Opposition to the Marxian tactics, nevertheless, made itself heard at the next Committee meeting three days later. Friedrich Anneke, who disliked "pale Democrats who merely chattered and protested," proposed that the workers field their own candidates and that they join the Democrats only where their own men had no chance. Schapper, in defending Marx's position, declared that he disliked Democrats equally as much as Anneke but it was necessary for the workers to get their help against a common foe. Schapper then proposed a criterion by which the worker should judge every candidate: If a candidate replied affirmatively to the question, "Are you satisfied with this or any granted constitution?" he was to be opposed as a "howler, a peace-at-any-price man." The Committee, as a concession to Anneke, thereupon agreed that the workers could set up their own candidates unless it appeared impossible to get such "socialists" elected. Since the chances for success at that late date were non-existent, the Marxian tactics prevailed in practice.

A few days before the election Marx appealed to the liberal bourgeoisie themselves to reject the Constitution. The *Kölnische Zeitung* had urged all people who did not want communism, another revolution and renewed conflict to vote only for outright acceptance of the Constitution. Deriding the position of the *Kölnische Zeitung*, Marx argued that the actual choice lay between "absolutism or a bourgeois representative system." He claimed that the Constituent Assembly had been dissolved because it represented the interests of the bourgeoisie against feudalism. The bourgeoisie, therefore, had to get an "appropriate form of government or perish." Industry had to break the fetters of absolutism and feudalism. Prussia needed a government that represented the "modern society" and not the past centuries, with a constitution that would uphold "bourgeois property relationships" against "feudal property, King, army, bureaucracy and *Krautjunkern* [Cabbage-Junkers]." Marx's article of January 22 certainly made it appear that the *Neue Rheinische Zeitung* advocated all that was best for the bourgeoisie.

Lest the above appeal to the bourgeoisie appear like a betrayal, Marx remarked that the *Neue Rheinische Zeitung* surely was the last to want bourgeois rule. But he asked the workers and the petty bourgeoisie "to suffer preferably in a modern bourgeois society" rather than to fall back into "medieval barbarism." Through industry the bourgeois society developed the material foundations for the appearance of a new society that would satisfy all workers and the petty bourgeoisie.

Marx's paper scored first in publishing the election results from many localities. Even the *Kölnische Zeitung* cited its competitor as the source for some of its reports. The election proved to be a "splendid [the adjective invariably used] victory" for the Democrats in the Rhine Province. Two-thirds of the 360 electors chosen in Cologne were Democrats, including "very many" from the working class. Worringen, that "powerful seat of democracy," had gone solidly Democratic. (The Worker-Society there had picked its own candidates, after a visit by Schapper and Esser.) Though the liberal conservatives won in Barmen, the election of only "one Engels" by a bare majority of one vote was a cause for joy. If the other Prussian provinces had voted only half as "decidedly" as the Rhineland, the *Neue Rheinische Zeitung* rejoiced, nothing would be left to uphold the granted Constitution except the "Grace of God."

The *Kölnische Zeitung* blamed the "shocking indifference among the middle bourgeois elements" for the defeat of the liberals. Many moderates were tired of the struggle and failed to vote. By February 1, however, the *Kölnische Zeitung* was consoled by the fact that not all the democratic electors were "full thoroughbreds" with a social-democratic republic as their aim. Many were mere "half-breeds," and some did not even favor a plain republic.

Looking forward to the meeting of the electors on February 5, the *Neue Rheinische Zeitung* warned that further efforts were needed to make the "end worthy of the beginning." The people had to be on guard against the "tricks of the officials, Junkers, the howler party, plus the evil influence of the Christian-Germanic Jesuits and the agents of the money-bags." The people wanted Deputies of the "most decided color and character" who were ready to show their "courage even in the face of bayonets." Various meetings of the Democratic and Worker-Societies accordingly produced a full agreement on candidates—Ulrich Kyll and Schneider II. A competing Democratic candidate, H. Schützendorf, who represented the Society of Workers and Employers on the Democratic District Committee was hounded out of the race. Any "pale Democrat," Marx declared, was better than a master shoemaker like Schützendorf, who served the reaction and favored the return to the "barbarism" of former ages by advocating the revival of old guild privileges as a solution to the worker problem. When Schützendorf tried to present his views, he was howled down and nearly mobbed.

Kyll and Schneider II won by more than a two-thirds majority. The *Neue Rheinische Zeitung* of February 7 reminded its readers that Schneider II was the President of the Democratic District Committee, and that he was about to face a trial for incitement to rebellion, together with Marx and Schapper.

Election results elsewhere in the Rhine Province were less "splendid." In Prussia at large the results failed to produce a majority committed to a rejection of the Constitution. An immediate crisis was therefore unlikely. But enough unsettled questions remained.

3. RHINELAND JUSTICE

IMMEDIATELY after the elections, Marx, Engels and Korff were brought to trial for calumny and slander against the First Procurator, Zweiffel, and the *Gendarmes* who had arrested Gottschalk and Anneke the previous July, the "oldest of many charges against the *Neue Rheinische Zeitung*." Marx's second trial, in which he, Schapper and Schneider II were charged with incitement to rebellion, followed on the next day. Since both were jury trials, Marx's fate depended on the verdict of the "bourgeois conscience" which he considered incapable of rendering justice.

At the first trial on February 7, Marx and Engels themselves addressed the jury, though they had the services of two qualified lawyers. Most of Marx's appeal dealt with proof that the charges against them were questionable under the *Code Napoléon* which ruled in the Rhineland. Establishing a certain emotional tone unspoiled by self-defeating histrionics, Marx made it appear that the arrests in July (which his paper denounced) had been part of an alarming and general counterrevolutionary campaign already in progress.

Marx complimented the jury for being responsive to a lofty calling. He maintained that they, as jurors, were there to correct the law, rather than to reach a verdict under the law. The jury was to help out where the "antiquated commands of the law and the living demands of society" conflicted, where "existing laws were in open contradiction to the newly-won level of social developments." That function was the "noblest attribute of the jury court," Marx asserted. All the jury had to do was to interpret the "letter of the law" in the light of the "understanding of our times, our political rights and the needs of society." No Rhineland jury was ever honored with a more august responsibility.

Marx made it appear that freedom of press, the right "to denounce villainy," was at stake. He did not deny that the *Neue Rheinische Zeitung* had aimed to "offend and slander"—the paper merely fulfilled its duty when it denounced. The press was the "public guardian, the tireless denunciator of those in power, the omnipresent eye and mouth of the spirit of the people, jealously guarding its freedom." Marx then made a statement that has impressed posterity, as it probably did the jury, when he assured the jurors that he personally would rather follow "the big world developments" and "analyze the course of history" than watch "local idols, *Gendarmes* and the judicial system." The latter stood for "absolutely *nothing* in the colossal conflicts of the present." He regarded it as a "true sacrifice" on his part to have to fight such opponents. But it was the duty of the press to defend the oppressed. Moreover, "the edifice of slavery had its real props" in such subordinate officials. The March Revolution had failed because it left them untouched. Marx closed his appeal with the ringing call, "The first duty of the press, therefore, is to undermine all foundations of the existing political order [applause in the auditorium]." This statement, as published in the *Neue Rheinische Zeitung*, with the acknowledged applause appears surprisingly frank. Yet, due to its context, it certainly seemed far less revolutionary to the bourgeois jurors.

Engels spoke almost as long as Marx. He also paid the proper respect to the jury and likewise charged them: "It is the particular privilege of the jurymen to interpret the law in accordance with their healthy understanding and conscience, independently of all traditional practice." The jury was there to "adjust the old laws to the new conditions through their interpretations."

"What if the *Neue Rheinische Zeitung* had stated that the *Gendarme* had drunk one more *Schnaps* than was necessary to quench his thirst?" Engels asked. He then called upon "public opinion in the whole Rhine Province" to judge whether this were a slanderous remark. In a concluding statement, he informed the jurors that they "in that moment had to decide on the fate of the press in the Rhine Province." He did not mention Prussia as a whole.

The jury deliberated for a respectful half hour and returned with an acquittal. The verdict, according to the *Neue Rheinische Zeitung* of February 9, was "a new guarantee of freedom of press in the Rhineland."

At the second trial of Marx, Schapper and Schneider II the following day, Marx again addressed the jury. Seeming proof of "incitement to rebellion" lay in the *Aufruf* of the Democratic District Committee of the Rhine Province, published on November 19 and signed by the three defendants. Marx did not deny that the *Aufruf* had appealed to the use of force, but he justified it by declaring that the King himself had resorted to revolution, violence and a disregard for the law, culminating in the dissolution of the Prussian Assembly and the grant of a constitution. "If the *Crown* made a counterrevolution, the people were right in replying with a revolution." Marx even cited a conservative Prussian newspaper to support his contention that in such situations, force was the judge, and power, the law. As in his appeal to the jury of the previous day, Marx was respectful and flattering. He made it appear that his revolutionary aims coincided with the interests, liberties and ideals of the bourgeois liberal. He could do this with a straight face by stopping short, at the point where the proletariat and communism entered the picture. He did, however, present a thumbnail sketch of his theory of law.

Human society did not rest on law. That was a "juristic illusion." Instead, law was based on the makeup of a given society. Law had to reflect a society's "common interests and needs, which also expressed the existing material modes of production." (The way human beings produced food and goods, together with the corresponding division of labor and the class structure.) Applying the above theory to the late conflict in Prussia, Marx stated that it had not been an ordinary political struggle between two factions. Instead, it was a *"conflict of two societies . . . of the old feudal-bureaucratic society with the modern bourgeois society,"* of the guild system against free competition, of a society based on landed property against a new one founded on industry, of faith versus knowledge. In Prussia, the Crown had represented the feudal-aristocratic society while the Constituent Assembly stood for the "modern bourgeois society." Thereafter, when Marx reaffirmed the right of revolution, the jury could feel that there was no conflict between the interests and aspirations of Marx and the bourgeois liberal.

The prosecuting attorney did not even bother to reply to the defense. The judge then summarized the proceedings with "as much impartiality as clarity," as the *Kölnische Zeitung* reported ironically. The jury retired and returned half an hour later with a unanimous verdict: "Not Guilty." The foreman of the jury thanked Marx for his informative analysis.

A resume of the trial and its significance appeared in the *Neue Rheinische Zeitung* of February 10, with Marx using the opportunity to reprint the very *Aufruf* that had led to the charge against him. He stated that the main issue had been a "political question": Had the defendants been justified in calling for the use of force against the power of the state, in organizing an armed force against the state and in deposing and installing officials? "The jury," Marx declared, "had answered in the affirmative after a very short deliberation." The complete text of Marx and Engels' appeals to the juries were printed in the *Zeitung* on February 14, 25, and 27, and then sold in pamphlet form under the title, *Two Political Trials.*

After these jury verdicts, Marx predicted that Ferdinand Lassalle and others who had been imprisoned and were awaiting trial would soon be freed. "The government just has no luck in political trials before a jury." But the machinery of justice did not speed up in the case of Lassalle. Marx's immediate followers were more fortunate. Charges against Wilhelm Wolff were dismissed at a hearing on March 1. Ernst Dronke returned from Paris on March 9. The editorial staff of the paper was again virtually intact.

On several occasions during the first part of March, however, Marx himself was personally threatened by Prussian soldiers. In his mission of chopping away at the "real props" of the old order, Marx sought to discredit the army by repeatedly denouncing individual army officers and the general conduct of the soldiers. The alleged infractions apparently were minor, judging from the lack of reaction in Cologne, always quick to protest any military irregularities. The officers and soldiers, however, were angered by what they considered exaggerations and unwarranted slanders. Matters never went beyond threats, however, because Prussia maintained a tight rein on the soldiers in the sensitive Rhine Province.

In 1884, a year after Marx's death, Engels reminisced proudly that people outside of Prussia expressed wonder over the way in which they continued to operate so coolly right in the middle of a first-rate Prussian fortress (Cologne was a fortified city), confronted by eight thousand troops. Engels boasted that it was because the army officers considered the editorial offices of the *Neue Rheinische Zeitung* as a fortress, not easily taken because it contained eight guns with bayonets (perhaps one for each member of the editorial staff), 250 live cartridges, and the red Jacobin caps of the typesetters. This probably was the sort of bravado in which old warriors sometimes indulge. Marx and Engels were secure because the Prussian government, though anxious to be rid of the pair, was sensitive to the particularism of the Rhine Province.

The Prussian authorities, however, began to be a little less accommodating than they had been three months earlier. When the *Neue Rheinische Zeitung*, faced with the "greatest financial difficulties," again tried to solicit new subscribers in February during the middle of the subscription quarter, the Prussian postal officials no longer were willing to handle them. But Marx remained free to bring this refusal to the attention of his readers. For six days he ran a prominent, front-page advertisement which read: "In response to many inquiries from the outside, we regret that we have to reply that our requests along this line have met with obstacles from the postal authorities."

4. TOWARDS A PROLETARIAN PARTY

A MORE pronounced proletarian orientation became evident in Marxian tactics in 1849. This was reflected in the contents of the *Organ der Demokratie*, though that paper never openly avowed its Communist purposes. In a negative sense, this proletarian emphasis reflected Marx's disillusionment with the Democrats, or with his capacity to mobilize them for revolutionary purposes. The weakness of the Democrats as allies had been demonstrated in the various crises since September when they displayed a lack of revolutionary decision and energy, the two qualities demanded by Marx. Too many Democrats were satisfied with something less than a "complete revolution." Furthermore, most of them preferred a German union along federal lines. Worst of all, many of them were convinced that democracy was possible even in the shadow of a throne, under a king. These shortcomings had again become evident through the popularity and proliferation of the March-Society (*Märzverein*), founded in November, 1848, by the Left in the Frankfurt Parliament (ultimately, there were more than nine hundred branches throughout Germany).

Although the *Märzverein* was denounced as dangerous by many moderate liberals, its avowed aim did not go beyond the use of "all lawful resistance in the defense of the imperiled gains of the March Revolution [hence its name] which are threatened from all sides." As early as December 29, Marx stated in the *Neue Rheinische Zeitung* that it was the duty of all Democrats to oppose the *Märzverein*, whose lofty purposes were vitiated by the decision to use only "legal resistance." This was another victory for reaction, "a disguise for half measures, a lack of decision and honesty," Marx declared. Revolution, which "elevates a people and transfuses them with its moral strength," alone sufficed.

Marx again denounced the *Märzverein* on March 11, angrily declaring that it was "pure slander" for that Society to have given the *Neue Rheinische Zeitung* an "honoring star" for being a paper that opened its columns to the *Märzverein*. (This is another illustration of the fact that Marx's paper was indeed viewed as an *Organ of Democracy*, and that outside of a rather limited circle, the public generally considered Marx himself as a bona fide Democrat, even if somewhat "social" or "red.") A week later, Marx repeated his denunciation of the *Märzverein* by calling it the "unconscious tool of the counterrevolution," a most derogatory epithet. In all such attacks, however, he was careful not to wound the sensibilities of local Rhineland Democrats.

Marx's break with the Rhineland Democrats was gradual and did not close the door to tactical cooperation later, whenever that might appear useful for revolutionary purposes. Marx and Engels joined with the local Democrats in giving a series of banquets commemorating the various revolutions of 1848, even though they repeatedly castigated the newly-elected Democratic Deputies in the Prussian Parliament for being cowardly. The banquets were remindful of the numerous French banquets held in 1847 and early 1848, so effective in voicing opposition to the regime of Louis Philippe, which reached a climax in the February Revolution. The German version, however, included a mixture of music and song in addition to the toasts and speeches that had characterized the French model.

The first such banquet took place at Mülheim-am-Rhein and actually occurred before the anniversary season arrived, on February 11. It was sponsored by the local Worker-Society, although the idea probably came from Cologne, across the Rhine a few miles away. Members of both the Democratic and Worker-Societies in Cologne were invited.

Instrumental music and song alternated with toasts at the Mülheim banquet. All toasts in turn were followed by "long speeches explaining the reasons for the toast." A special toast was offered to the guests from Cologne, notably the "*Redakteur en chef*, Karl Marx," who had "championed the working class through word and deed long before the February Revolution," according to the *Neue Rheinische Zeitung* report on the affair. Marx replied with one of his favorite talks—the role of the workers in the "battles in France, England, Belgium and Switzerland." Engels was also there to toast Louis Kossuth and the fighting Hungarians whose battle against the Habsburgs he continually described in glowing terms. It was left to Schapper to say the word for the "democratic-republic." Hopefully the *Zeitung* predicted that "this first Democratic banquet in the Rhine Province was so appealing it will surely be imitated."

Several days later Engels duly proposed that the Cologne Worker-Society sponsor a banquet on February 24 to honor the Paris Revolution of 1848. Marx was selected by acclamation to preside over the affair, but he declined because of other commitments. Schapper took his place in the presidential chair, as so often on such occasions. The banquet hall was filled to capacity with two to three thousand persons. The toasts and speeches, punctuated by music and song, went on endlessly to include all current revolutions and revolutionary leaders, potential revolutionary groups, as well as the ashes of past revolutions, a vision of the future "social revolution," and the women who were present at the banquet. Engels toasted revolutionary Italy, notably the Roman Republic which had been declared after Pope Pius IX fled to Gaeta. The French Revolution of 1848 was almost slighted in favor of Robespierre, Saint-Just, other heroes of 1793, and the music and songs of the Great Revolution (*La Marseillaise*, etc.). The banquet moved along in an atmosphere of "order and calm," as the *Neue Rheinische Zeitung* invariably reported such events, and it ended with a "*Hoch*" to the "general democratic social republic." Troops patrolled the streets during the banquet, but they found no cause to interfere.

The German March Revolutions, notably the Berlin barricades of March 18 and 19, were next on the anniversary calendar. But Marx himself had had enough of such banqueting, with its music, toasts and song, which offered an emotional release without being an inspiration for another round of revolution. Anyway, the very name *March* had become odious to him because of the futile talk of the gains of March, March hopes and the proliferation of March-Societies. The March Revolution in Berlin, Marx wrote on March 18, left him cold. After reminding the Berliners that they had sung "Jesus My Salvation" following the victory of March 19, 1848, he sardonically advised them to sing "Wrangel my Salvation" to commemorate the event in 1849. He thereupon announced pontifically that the *Neue Rheinische Zeitung* for its part would celebrate its first anniversary on June 25, honoring the Paris Insurrection of 1848.

The Communists, however, were unable to ignore the March celebrations. The moderate Constitutional Liberals in Cologne had spoiled things by planning and extensively advertising (even in the *Neue Rheinische Zeitung*) a large banquet and concert to be held in the *Gürzenich* on March 18, with the proceeds going to help unemployed workers. To counteract the effect of this "Howler-Concert" (as the *Zeitung* derisively called the affair), the Worker-Society had to join with the Democratic Society in sponsoring a "Big Democratic Banquet" for the 19th, also in the *Gürzenich*. Schapper again presided at the banquet after Marx had excused himself because of the press of "accumulated" business. Engels, Wolff and Dronke (recently returned from Paris), plus numerous Worker-Society leaders and Democrats were on hand to run through the full scale of revolutionary toasts. Freiligrath even wrote a special song for the occasion (also published in the *Zeitung*) to be sung to the tune of *La Marseillaise*, with the following refrain:

The New Rebellion!
The Complete Rebellion!
March! March!
March! March!
March!—ev'n to death! (*Tod!*)
And our flag is red! (*rot!*)

The tune was good, the spirit appropriate, the words were martial—pointing to revolution to come, rather than commemorating the Berlin days as a closed chapter.

Perhaps as a by-product of the enthusiasm generated by the first revolutionary banquets late in February, the Primary Voters (*Urwähler*) in Cologne began to organize to exercise a certain vigilance over their elected Deputies in the Prussian Assembly and to inform them of the will of the people. At the first meeting of the Primary Voters on March 4, attended mainly by Democrats, a Committee of nine (including Friedrich Anneke and H. Becker) were elected to maintain constant communication with Berlin. When this Committee called for a bigger "Primary Voter Meeting" to be held in the *Gürzenich* on March 11, Marx and his followers began to take note of the movement. After the *Neue Rheinische Zeitung* had repeatedly condemned the Democratic Deputies for a lack of energy and boldness, the Primary Voter movement appeared like an effective agency for exerting pressure on the elected representatives, with the purpose of provoking another crisis.

The meeting on March 11 attracted from two to three thousand, according to the most optimistic reports. (The *Kölnische Zeitung*, however, stated that it was "thinly attended.") The people, with appropriate energy, despatched an order to Berlin demanding the cessation of martial law in the Prussian capital; until then, the Deputies of the Left were to boycott all sessions of the Assembly. Furthermore, the order reproached the Left for having allowed two weeks to pass, during which the Assembly met under the "Rule of the Sabre"—that martial law which a wit of the day defined as the *"Katzenjammer* [hangover] of a freedom-intoxicated city."

Four of the original nine members of the Primary Voter Committee now resigned to make room for Marx himself, Wilhelm Wolff, Nothjung and Bartholomäus Weyll, all dependable Marxians. Marx's presence was noteworthy because he was not even a voter, being no longer a Prussian citizen. For a week thereafter the Primary Voters endorsed the moves and views advocated by the *Neue Rheinische Zeitung*. They adopted the substance of Marx's devastating denunciation of three laws, drafted by the Prussian government for consideration by the Parliament, which defined and regulated the unrestricted 1848 freedom of assembly, of press, and of the posting of placards. The *Neue Rheinische Zeitung* (Marx writing) claimed that the purpose of the proposed laws was to force the Rhinelanders "to become Prussians at any price" and called on the Rhineland Deputies to secede from the Prussian Parliament if anything remotely resembling such laws was adopted.

After such a hopeful beginning, the Primary Voter Committee began to disappear from the news, probably because too many democratic voters refused to endorse the extreme views and tactics advocated by Marx. This development merely helped to hasten that formal but amicable break between Marx and the democratic societies in the Rhine Province early in April.

As Marx's disillusionment with the Democrats grew, the importance of the Worker-Society increased as a vehicle for revolutionary purposes and as the nucleus of a proletarian party to come. Marx continued to act as President of the Society, with Karl Schapper as the First Vice President. The policy-making Committee, likewise, was controlled by the Communists. Although thousands of the seven thousand members that the Worker-Society had claimed in the summer of 1848 had lost interest and drifted away, most of the remaining active members seemed to have confidence in their Communist leaders. A minority, however, remained loyal to the founder and first President of the Society—Andreas Gottschalk, the physician of the poor, a man who knew their misery from his work among them.

Marx was hardly sincere when he stated in the fall of 1848 that he was only provisionally accepting the Presidency of the Worker-Society, until Gottschalk was free; he had made no move to surrender the position when Gottschalk was acquitted in December. A clash of personalities, policies and principles was in the picture. Marx could justify his refusal to return the Presidency of the Society by pointing to the contents and spirit of Gottschalk's address to the jury in his own defense (later published and widely advertised). Gottschalk had failed to take an unequivocal stand against monarchy. Furthermore, he had appealed to the example of Jesus Christ to justify his own actions in the past. Marx was not ready to surrender leadership in the Worker-Society to such a person.

Gottschalk recognized the futility of a direct attempt to contest Marx's leadership when the Society's Committee was stacked against him. Even two of Gottschalk's former associates, Anneke and Esser, generally were supporting the Marxian program. Gottschalk therefore left Cologne at the end of 1848, shortly after his release from prison, to go into a self-imposed exile. In Bonn, Paris and then Brussels, he cultivated contacts with the poet Herwegh, Moses Hess and others whom Marx had offended. On January 9, while in Brussels, Gottschalk issued a declaration which was inserted in various Rhineland papers, including the *Neue Rheinische Zeitung*, stating that he would not return to Prussia until he received a call from the people or the "still highest judge." Since the latter reference could mean the King, Marx's followers were in a position to denounce this seeming abeyance to royalty. They also derided Gottschalk's exile as a bid for martyrdom.

All the while, Gottschalk was conducting guerrilla operations against Marx, mainly through Prinz who edited and partly financed the Worker-Society *Organ, Freiheit, Brüderlichkeit, Arbeit*. The first blow fell when Prinz stopped publishing that paper, after filling the last issue on January 1 with Gottschalk's address to the jury. This left the Worker-Society without an *Organ* to start out the New Year, all without a previous notice. After two weeks of expostulation, Prinz resumed publication of the paper with an abbreviated name, *Freiheit, Arbeit* (Freedom, Work). The intermediate *Brüderlichkeit* (Brotherhood) thus disappeared from the old title, perhaps symbolically so. Prinz's new paper continued to pose as the official *Organ* of the Worker-Society, by printing the protocols of the Committee meetings and other official matters. In all other respects, however, it continually condemned the official views, tactics and leadership of the Society—those of Marx and his followers.

The very first issue of *Freiheit, Arbeit* on January 14 roundly condemned the two Democratic candidates whom Marx was supporting for the Prussian election—Schneider II and especially Franz Raveaux (a Cologne tobacco dealer and a radical, Marx's pet candidate). An angry Marx appeared at the Committee meeting of the Worker-Society on the following day, determined to demand an explanation from Prinz and to impose discipline. Although Prinz had left the meeting early, probably sensing what was in the air, Marx and Schapper nevertheless brought up the matter and moved that the "editor of the official *Organ* of the Society" be subjected to the supervision of an Editorial Committee, to guarantee that the *Organ* really represented the interests of the "party" and be edited in the spirit of that party. The motion was "widely supported" and three Marxian supporters—Schapper, Röser and Wilhelm Reiff—were named to the Editorial Committee.

Gottschalk's declaration of January 9 from Brussels was also brought up and generally disapproved at the same Committee meeting. Marx, however, wished to avoid a public controversy just then—on the eve of the Prussian elections. An open break with Gottschalk also appeared impolitic, in view of the wide sympathy that the latter enjoyed among some Democrats and the workers in general. Hence, the question was referred to a special committee for further study, in accordance with a motion by Marx and Schapper that was "generally applauded." Since Marx and Schapper were on this committee (together with Anneke, Röser and Esser), they were in a position to decide when, and if, the conclusions on Gottschalk were to be published and acted upon.

The attempt to keep Prinz's paper within acceptable bounds by subjecting everything to the scrutiny of an Editorial Committee proved ineffectual. Prinz merely by-passed the Committee when he again attacked Franz Raveaux on the 26th. This produced a scandalous situation. At a time when the Worker-Society was backing Democratic candidates in the elections, the avowed *Organ* of that Society was attacking a favorite Democrat. The Editorial Committee, in behalf of the Worker-Society, found it necessary to offer a public explanation in the *Neue Rheinische Zeitung*.

The Committee of the Worker-Society now took energetic action. It could not dismiss Prinz because the paper was partly financed by him. There was no other choice except to defrock *Freiheit, Arbeit* as the *Organ* of the Society and to create a new one in its place. On February 4, the *Neue Rheinische Zeitung* notified the public that *Freiheit, Arbeit* was no longer the official *Organ* of the Worker-Society and that a new one was being prepared under the earlier name, *Freiheit, Brüderlichkeit, Arbeit*. After that the situation became a little confusing, with two papers bearing similar names and vignettes at the top of the front page. Prinz's paper depicted a blue-shirted worker (*Blousenmann*) with a hammer in his belt, holding a red flag in his left hand and a shovel and ax in the other, standing back of a woman seated with a child. The vignette of the new paper showed a worker equipped for action. The red flag was also there, but the worker brandished a sword and was unencumbered by tools, woman and child.

Prinz's repudiated paper thereafter conducted a sustained attack on Marx, Marxian policies and the *Neue Rheinische Zeitung*. On February 11 Prinz derided the members of the late Editorial Committee as "red republicans, defenders of unrestricted freedom" who nonetheless had acted as "censors" of his paper. He asked why a similar censorship was not applied to the papers of "Mr. Marx and Mrs. Anneke." Prinz then assured his readers that he would "sooner be quiet than accept the slovenly polemics of the *Neue Rheinische Zeitung* as a model." Later he listed the "party of the *Neue Rheinische Zeitung*" as belonging to the "reactionary parties." That was a foul blow.

Gottschalk himself directly attacked Marx in an open letter addressed "To Mr. Karl Marx, Editor of the *Neue Rheinische Zeitung*" and published in *Freiheit, Arbeit* on February 25. Though the letter was unsigned, it was easy to guess the author, as one who had enjoyed the confidence of Marx and knew the workings of the Marxian mind. Gottschalk began with the whimsical and ironic comment that a small "local workers' paper" would not be attacking the "mighty of the earth" if it hoped to gain anything from the "movement of the present." People would smile indulgently over the "dwarf" who threw down the gauntlet to the "giant Marx, the big *Neue Rheinische Zeitung*, and Friedrich Engels who had the manner and speech of a boxer."

Marx was an "angry Jehovah" and a "modern Jeremiah" who prophesied the fall of the bourgeoisie, Gottschalk continued. Yet Marx was asking the people to endure the rule of capital and a bourgeois triumph rather than return to the "barbarism" of the earlier craft guilds and privileges. The workers, to avoid the "hell of the Middle Ages" were to enter voluntarily into the "purgatory of a decrepit rule of capital," in order ultimately to enter the "nebulous heaven" promised in the Marxian confession of faith. Gottschalk then charged that Marx was not in earnest regarding the liberation of the oppressed. He accused Marx of being a person unmoved by that which stirred the hearts of men. The misery of the workers and the hunger of the poor had only a scientific, a doctrinaire interest for him.

Revolution had become a mere secret cult for "Mr. Carl Marx and his followers," Gottschalk continued. Marx would bemoan the divisions in the party which this letter would produce. But the worker at least would know that Marx was not, and could not be, their friend, Gottschalk concluded.

Gottschalk's attack angered Marx very much. But since an acrimonious reply just then would have led to an open brawl and recriminations which might produce a sharp cleavage in the ranks of the Worker-Society, Marx kept silent. Furthermore, he may have learned the effectiveness of the technique of silence from his own experience with the *Kölnische Zeitung* which refused to respond to the many "kicks" he had given it. Others could take care of Gottschalk.

Marx was away from Cologne when an open letter appeared in both the *Neue Rheinische Zeitung* and the official Worker-Society paper on April 22. It was signed by two workers, "in the name of many comrades." Among a host of charges, it stated that Gottschalk despised the proletariat and was more dangerous than all the reactionaries. Marx, in turn, was depicted as one who stood in the breach for the cause of the proletariat, as a person who had "defied imprisonment and persecution" all his life. That same day the leading branch of the Worker-Society in Cologne also published a long bill of grievances against Gottschalk which then was adopted by the Committee of the Worker-Society. On May 2, the business was concluded (but not quite ended) at a general meeting of the Worker-Society when those present and voting adopted the verdict as their own.

The followers of Gottschalk struck back in kind. On May 6 Prinz's paper carried a letter signed by four workers "in the name of many workers," stating that most of the workers rejected the attacks on Gottschalk as "ordinary vileness." Simultaneously, the paper announced the creation of a "Society for the Attainment of Freedom and Well-being for All," as a home for those who opposed the present Worker-Society. Whether the new Gottschalk society would have prospered remains an open question. The reaction that followed the revolutionary crisis then in process stymied the operation of all worker-societies.

Marx's triumph over the Gottschalk faction in the Cologne Worker-Society had become certain when a reorganization was carried through in February, 1849. It was Karl Schapper, always acting on instructions from Marx, who had proposed on January 25 that new *Statutes* be drafted for the Worker-Society. After the proposal had been accepted by the full Society on February 4, the new regulations were prepared by a committee composed of Schapper, Esser, Hubert Salget and a Friedrich Wilhelm Carstens (the pseudonym for Friedrich Wilhelm Lessner, a German journeyman tailor who had come from London in August, 1848, and was to be a dedicated follower of Marx for many years). The completed *Statutes* then were adopted at another general meeting on February 22.

As defined in the new *Statutes:*

> The Worker-Society in Cologne aims at the education of its members in political, social and scientific respects, through the acquisition of books, newspapers, pamphlets and through *wissenschaftliche* [learned, scholarly

or scientific] lectures and discussions. The Society furthermore, will protect its members from all oppression, and help them in case of need, insofar as it is possible.

Such purposes could be grasped by any worker and yet not give any government ground for repressive action. The *Statutes* did not mention any communistic or even mere revolutionary goals. Marx was not one to set up his own standard and hope that others would rally around him. Instead, he created an organization in which all sorts could gather. "Education," time and management would do the rest.

The Society was organized on geographical lines with all workers in a given locale brought together on a straight "proletarian" basis, and not along guild or craft lines, as favored by Gottschalk and others. The number of local branches (*Filiale*) in Cologne was increased from three to nine, to allow for better education, clarification and discussion in weekly meetings. General meetings were also scheduled regularly each week.

The Committee of the Society, reconstituted to include the Presidents of the nine local branches, remained the major policy-making body. It exercised a centralized control over "education" by setting up the program for every branch meeting and also for the general one. The old Committee, upon which Marx could depend, initially selected two-thirds of the members of the reconstituted Committee. Marx did not remain as President of the reorganized Society because he often was unable to appear for meetings and the organization was in dependable hands. The new Committee selected Schapper as President, Röser as Vice President, Reiff as Secretary and Bedorf as Treasurer.

The reorganization also represented a sifting process that eliminated from membership most of the followers of Gottschalk, as well as other dissident or indifferent elements. Each member had to enroll anew in one of the nine branch societies, after receiving a copy of the new *Statutes* so he would be acquainted with the principles and organization of the revised Worker-Society. The anticipated membership was small compared to the seven thousand usually cited in September, 1848; the Committee of February 28, 1849, merely ordered two thousand copies of the *Statutes* and the same number of membership cards (printed on red paper with the vignette of the worker holding a sword and a red flag).

With "education" as the avowed major aim of the reorganized Worker-Society, Marx and Engels were there to provide the guidelines and texts. They had two objectives in mind. First, the worker was to be prepared for the more immediate revolution leading to the downfall of existing governments, notably in Prussia. The subjects discussed coincided rather regularly with the contents and viewpoint of leading articles in the *Neue Rheinische Zeitung*, which set the tone for the politics of the Worker-

Society. Secondly, the worker was also to be conditioned so he would develop the proper proletarian reflexes. As the text for this education of the worker, Marx wrote a popularized critique of the capitalist society, "Wage-Labor and Capital" (*Lohnarbeit und Kapital*), published in the *Zeitung* in five installments between April 5 and 11, when the series was interrupted. The articles were later published as a classical Marxian treatise brought down to a near-proletarian level.

"Wage-Labor and Capital," as Marx acknowledged in 1864, was a warmed-over elaboration of lectures first given to the German Worker-Society in Brussels in 1847. The subject, handled "as simply as was possible, in a popular manner," was designed to turn the worker against the existing or any capitalist system. Marx again adroitly marshalled the laws and conclusions of the political economists to prove that "the forest of uplifted arms asking for work" would become ever thicker and the "arms themselves ever more emaciated."

The Committee of the Worker-Society asked all other worker-societies throughout Germany to take up the "social question" with "Wage-Labor and Capital" as a guide. It likewise sent along copies of the *Neue Rheinische Zeitung* for this purpose. This represented an attempt to get German labor in general to think and organize along Marxian lines.

Concurrently, Marx published a series of articles, usually under the title, "The Silesian Billion," to educate the peasants concerning their wrongs. Wilhelm Wolff, the son of a peasant and a native of Silesia, wrote most of them, though they unquestionably were prompted by Marx who always kept the revolutionary potential of the peasants in mind.

The inspiration for the "billion" came from France. In 1825 the French government had agreed to compensate the nobles and others whose property had been confiscated more than thirty years earlier during the Great Revolution. Since a large figure was involved, it grew into a "billion" (*i. e., francs*) in the popular mind, an appalling and striking figure in the early 19th century. The actual sum was considerably less. This "billion" returned to haunt France in 1848/49. The workers were the first to raise a cry for the "return of the billion." Then the peasants took up the same demand for themselves early in 1849. Marx, always alert to anything that would produce a peasant revolt, wrote a leading article on "The Billion" (*Die Milliarde*) on March 16, asserting: "The billion is the first revolutionary measure which hurls the peasant into the revolution."

If a "billion" produced such results in France, the same formula should work in Germany, Marx evidently concluded. Some sort of "billion" certainly could be found and certified, especially in Prussia. Marx made a lame beginning with "The Prussian Billion" on March 17. This was followed by "Also a Billion" on the 22nd, when Wilhelm Wolff began to concentrate on figures for Silesia. The next seven or eight articles were simply called, "The Silesian Billion," with ample indications that other "billions" were there to be reclaimed elsewhere in Prussia and Germany at large. The official Prussian *Taler* (equal to nearly 4 *francs*) was always converted into *francs* in order to keep the sensational but still believable "billion" in the picture.

Wolff's "Silesian Billion" articles present a moving and detailed account of how the "little men"—the peasants—had been fleeced by the "robber barons," "bloodsuckers," and the government during the preceding thirty years. Various feudal dues, supplemented by labor services and a disproportionate burden of taxation were listed successively until the "billion" was reached and surpassed. Wolff repeatedly stated that the peasant would not be content with anything less than "full compensation." The next revolution would give the peasant his "lost billion," but only after the fall of the existing government and the "robber barons." Silesian conditions, moreover, were merely representative of the status in most of Germany.

The prospect of a "billion" failed to arouse the peasants, however. No serious unrest developed in Silesia, even though the Democratic Society in Breslau printed ten thousand copies of the articles for distribution among the peasants. The same was true for the rest of Germany. A "billion" was not enough to "hurl" the peasant into the revolutionary movement—not even in France.

The initiative for a general union of worker-societies throughout Germany originally came from the *Arbeiterverbrüderung* (Worker-Brotherhood)—a worker organization originally founded in Berlin by Stephan Born, a member of the Communist League and an associate of Engels and Marx in Paris and Brussels. The *Arbeiterverbrüderung* had held a Worker-Congress in the Prussian capital between August 23 and September 3, 1848, for the purpose of creating a wider union of German workers. The Congress set up a Central Committee to pursue that end, operating out of the perhaps safer environment of Leipzig (in Saxony) under Born's leadership.

Marx and Engels, however, had discreetly ignored Born's achievements in Berlin and Leipzig. In fact, they silently disapproved of much that Born was doing throughout 1848. Born, as he confessed later, had indeed forgotten a part of his communism after his arrival in Berlin, in order to adjust himself to the conditions that he found in 1848. Thus, the *Arbeiterverbrüderung* was organized along the popularly-preferred craft lines rather than on a straight proletarian basis. It was more interested in immediate action to improve the material well-being of the workers than in politics and revolution. Even the Berlin Worker-Congress had spent

most of its time drafting a Workers' Charter, defining all the requirements needed to better the material lot of the worker.

The Leipzig Central Committee had considerable success in establishing links with various worker-societies. Even the Worker-Society in distant Lausanne advocated a union of all Swiss societies with the Committee, as appears in its instructions to Friedrich Engels on December 8,
1848, when it asked him, "as an old fighter for the proletariat," to act
as its delegate at a Swiss Worker-Congress in Bern.

Marx and Engels became increasingly interested in this trend towards
a union of worker-societies when the German workers began to display
a greater interest in political action. An increase in unemployment during
the winter may have helped to produce the changed mood. Many workers, who had hoped for a revival of guild privileges and protection
against the competition of the machine, also discovered that they could
expect little help from the liberal, *laissez-faire* views which prevailed in
the parliaments in Frankfurt, Berlin and elsewhere. Although this caused
some workers to become almost reactionary, as they turned their backs
on politics and the work of the parliaments, others went to the opposite
extreme, developing a greater interest in politics, the possibility of
further revolutions, and a union of the workers for action.

A Congress of Southwest German Worker-Societies, meeting in Heidelberg on January 28 and 29, became a pacesetter in this drive towards a
union. Stephan Born and another member of the Leipzig Committee were
present, upon invitation, with the object of working towards a general
union of German workers. Joseph Weydemeyer, an old associate of Marx
then living in Frankfurt, was there to expound the Marxian point of view.

The Heidelberg Congress decided that the Southwest worker-societies
were to abolish their own regional Committee (in Frankfurt) in favor of
a union with the Leipzig Central Committee, as a big step towards a
"general German Worker-Confederation" (*Arbeiter-Bund*). It called for
a general congress of German workers in the near future to establish said
confederation. All questions regarding aims, organization, principles and
a confession of faith were to be postponed until that congress met.

Marx and Engels were patently pleased with the course of events at
Heidelberg. Such a union of worker-societies could become the organizational basis for a worker-party, or the "Party of the People" (*Partei des
Volks*), as Marx called it on February 18. The *Neue Rheinische Zeitung*
of February 4 commented favorably on the decisions of the Congress
that had rejected the old guild point of view. The paper referred to
Stephan Born for the first time as a speaker for the "revolutionary workers" who wanted to exploit the machine for their own purposes, rather
than destroy them, as advocated by the champions of the guild privileges.
In view of the spirit that had prevailed at Heidelberg, Marx and Engels

could hope to get their own minimum program adopted when the General German Congress of Workers met. The decisions of a North German congress of workers meeting in Hamburg in the next weeks seemed to confirm the trend.

Stephan Born, under the circumstances, was cordially received as a guest of the Marxes when he arrived in Cologne (most likely upon invitation) after the Congress in Heidelberg. An occasional favorable comment about Born in the *Neue Rheinische Zeitung* in the next weeks indicated that Marx and Engels felt that they could work with the Leipzig Central Committee under Born's leadership.

From this point forward it became evident that the views of the Cologne Worker-Society (safely Marxian since the reorganization) would carry more weight in the coming general Congress if it established and spoke for an organization embracing all Rhineland-Westphalian Worker-Societies. As a first step in that direction, the Worker-Society in Cologne had to gather a complete list of such societies, including the so-called democratic societies with a marked "social democratic" bias. A sifting process was necessary because hitherto all democratic and worker-societies had been combined indiscriminately under the leadership of the Rhineland District Democratic Committee in Cologne. Accordingly, an urgent call to all "Democratic Societies" to send their addresses to the *Neue Rheinische Zeitung* appeared daily at the top of the first page of that paper from March 11 to 25. No explanation was given. Anneke's *Neue Kölnische Zeitung* printed the same appeal.

The Committee of the Cologne Worker-Society then called on all worker-societies in the Rhine Province to create a separate organization of their own, apart from the democratic societies. Marx and his followers were now ready to sever all formal ties with the Democrats. This occurred when Marx called a meeting of the District Democratic Committee in Cologne on April 14. As reported in the *Neue Rheinische Zeitung*, the following declaration was read:

> The Citizens Marx, Schapper, Anneke and Wolff declare unanimously:
> We believe that the present organization of Democratic Societies includes too many heterogeneous elements to allow any beneficial action in behalf of the cause.
> We, moreover, believe that a closer union of the worker-societies is to be preferred, because the latter are made up of identical elements. We, therefore, from this day forward withdraw from the Rhineland District Committee of the Democratic Societies."

The declaration was signed by all of the "Citizens" listed above.

The break between the Worker-Society and the Democratic Society occurred without recriminations. Although this represented an abandonment of a policy of a democratic front, Marx certainly did not want to foreclose all possibilities of future tactical cooperation with the Democrats.

A general meeting of the Cologne Worker-Society on April 16 endorsed the steps already taken by the Committee and its leaders. Furthermore, it acclaimed a proposed tie with the emerging union of German worker-societies, headed by the Leipzig Central Committee. The meeting then empowered the Worker-Society Committee to call a regional congress of worker-societies of the Rhine Province and Westphalia, to meet soon (before the General German Congress scheduled for June) so as to establish a "closer union of the purely social party."

The Cologne Worker-Society Committee acted rapidly thereafter. A committee, composed of Marx, Wilhelm Wolff, Schapper, Anneke, Esser and K. W. Ott (a Communist member of the Committee, a chemist by profession) was set up to make all the arrangements. It selected the first Sunday in May (the 6th) as the date for the Congress and extended invitations to all worker-societies, plus any others with a different name which "nevertheless decisively support the principles of a social democracy." All communications were to be addressed to Karl Schapper (Marx himself was away from Cologne in the next weeks). The address given was that of the editorial offices of the *Neue Rheinische Zeitung*.

Simultaneously, the Cologne Worker-Society, as indicated earlier, attempted to acquaint all worker-societies elsewhere in Germany with the Marxian line of thought by sending them "Wage-Labor and Capital," as printed in the *Neue Rheinische Zeitung*. It also sent copies of its own *Statutes* and newspaper to provide information on the Cologne model. It is impossible to know how successful these efforts of the Communist-led Cologne Worker-Society might have been. In the end, the General German Congress of Workers never met. Even the local Rhineland-Westphalian Congress which met on May 6 was distracted from its original purposes by new revolutionary complications and the need for immediate action, in concert with the Democrats.

5. THE RED EXIT

DURING the spring of 1849, Marx and Engels displayed a boldness that exceeded anything of the previous year. The Prussian government, from the Hohenzollern family down to the most subordinate local *Gendarme*, never had been attacked so vehemently or insulted so unsparingly as it was then. Perhaps as if to emphasize personal responsibility for the contents of the *Neue Rheinische Zeitung*, the name of Karl Marx, *Redacteur en chef*, began to appear daily in place of Hermann Korff, the

Gerant. The confidence of Marx and Engels rested on the conviction that they were secure in the Rhineland. Had not a Rhenish jury acquitted first Gottschalk, then Marx himself, Schapper, Schneider II, Gottfried Kinkel and finally Ferdinand Lassalle of political charges? Moreover, Marx and Engels remained persuaded that their day, the complete revolution, was approaching. They did not, however, count on the Germans to start it, since the Prussian elections had produced a moderately liberal majority ready to accept the Constitution of December 5. They believed instead that the impulse would come from outside, most likely from Paris. With each change of the moon they predicted a new eruption of that "revolutionary volcano," ending in a Red Republic, which would bring on a European and then a world war. Other combinations, however, looked equally promising at times.

As the specialist on war and foreign affairs, Engels wrote on events in Italy and Hungary. He expected Austria to collapse. Though Radetzky had decisively defeated the army of the Kingdom of Sardinia, Engels insisted that nothing was lost, if the people of that Kingdom would declare a republic and wage war with revolutionary means. A people that fought for its independence could not rely solely on "ordinary methods of warfare." Engels was a proponent of guerrilla warfare, such as the Spaniards had used against Napoleon when ordinary methods failed. "Mass revolts, revolutionary war, guerrillas everywhere—and terrorism" were needed.

As for the war in Hungary, the early successes of the Habsburg forces during the winter of 1848/49 had been followed by a slow and then dramatic shift in fortune. When the Hungarians began to advance on all fronts, the *Neue Rheinische Zeitung* celebrated Kossuth's forty-third birthday with an extraordinary supplement. Kossuth spoke of being in Vienna by May 10 and he knew how to keep his word, Engels asserted. Once the Leitha River were crossed, separating Hungary from German-Austria, there would be a *"fifth* revolution" in Vienna. The impact on Germany at large would be shattering, Engels predicted. The Austrian revolution would inaugurate a European revolution. Salvation could come from the east, as well as from Paris.

Back in Germany, the Schleswig-Holstein war had been resumed after the Danes refused to extend the six-month Malmö armistice. The 1849 war, however, merely provided an illustration of the Marxian contention that, when history repeats itself, the second round is always a travesty of the original one. Again the Danes and Germans fought each other indecisively for months. Again the Danes blockaded the German ports and sailed unchallenged on the North and Baltic seas. On April 18, the *Neue Rheinische Zeitung* declared, "A German navy will first be possible when the red flag flies from the masts." But it never came to that. Again the Germans relived the old agony of humiliation and of national helplessness, as in 1848. But the fate of Schleswig-Holstein no longer provoked the same intense emotions and willingness to risk everything in a fight.

The next and final revolutionary crisis in Germany developed out of a purely German question. It began when the German national Frankfurt Parliament completed the work for which it had been called.

For ten long months the Frankfurt Parliament met and deliberated before defining the makeup of a unified German empire and completing its Constitution. Most of the members of the Parliament recognized the danger of delay. Gustav Mevissen, a prominent Rhineland liberal, expressed the despair of many when he wrote on December 2, 1848: "If we fail to achieve unity here, it will be because it is being literally talked to death by the many unnecessary speeches." But the Parliament believed in framing a free constitution, freely adopted, with no foreclosures on debate. The resultant Constitution stands out as a monument of mid-19th century liberalism, but it never went into effect.

As the revolutionary scare of March, 1848, wore off, the princes and governments who would be sacrificing a portion of their power to the new Empire regained self-confidence and the strength to resist. On the other side, popular confidence and interest in the Frankfurt Parliament declined when that body proved ineffective in the Schleswig-Holstein conflict, the revolution in Vienna, and the clash between the Prussian King and the Constituent Assembly—current issues that touched the vital interests of millions.

The Austrian question, an issue that defied a quick and easy solution, caused the Frankfurt Parliament the most perplexities. Initially, most Germans wanted to include in their unified empire all areas of the Austrian Empire that belonged to the German Confederation and earlier Holy Roman Empire. This meant Austria proper (west of the Leitha River and mainly German in population) and Bohemia-Moravia (with a Czech majority and a substantial German minority). It was impossible, however, to get a concrete answer from the Habsburgs whether or not they were willing to abandon their non-German areas, perhaps in exchange for the honor of being named hereditary emperors of the new Germany. Even the German-Austrians themselves were divided on the question. In the fall of 1848, the Frankfurt Parliament tried to hasten a decision on the part of the Habsburgs by adopting a constitutional clause which forbade any governmental tie between a state in the German union and an outside country. As applied to Austria, this clause meant that only the areas defined as German could join the new German Empire, and that, unless the Habsburgs relinquished control over the rest of their Empire, all of Austria would be excluded. Even then, however, the Austrian government refused (and probably was unable) to state its position. Until the revolution and power struggle in Vienna were decided, it could not be known what the official position of the Austrian government would be. As a result, the Austrian delegates remained in Frankfurt to vote on all questions affecting the Constitution and organization of a united Germany that ultimately might not include them.

In view of the uncertainty of Austria's position, a Small-German (*Kleindeutsch*) Party began to gain in numbers (there had always been a few). It advocated a small German union that would exclude all Austrian German lands, as a matter of practical necessity. Gustav Mevissen described such a union as a "practicably possible Germany of 36 million— a big European power, strong enough to stand on its own feet, but not strong enough to disturb the balance of power in Europe." Almost inescapably the *Kleindeutsch* Party looked to the Prussian King for leadership.

It was hard, nevertheless, for the Germans to think of excluding millions of Austrian Germans, when they were unifying Germany. The Catholics wanted Catholic Austria included as a balance against predominantly Protestant Prussia. The South German states also preferred Austrian laxity to the sterner Prussian mettle. Under the circumstances, the Great-German (*Grossdeutsch*) Party continued to hold a majority in the Frankfurt Parliament.

Only after March 4, 1849, when the Schwarzenberg government of Austria published a Constitution (it never went into effect) which stated explicitly that the Austrian Empire was an "indivisible monarchy" with one government and army, did it become clear that the German areas alone could not be admitted. Several days later Schwarzenberg specifically informed the Frankfurt Parliament that all of the Austrian Empire with its multi-nationalities would have to be admitted, thus creating that "empire of 70 million" favored by a few enthusiasts. The Germans, however, did not want to be united with areas populated mainly by non-Germans with whom historic ties were lacking. The only practical choice left was a *Kleindeutsch* empire.

Even so the Frankfurt Parliament remained passionately divided. The crucial motion in favor of a *Kleindeutsch* empire (with Austrian delegates voting) was passed on March 27 by a bare majority of four votes. A few concessions to the Democrats and the Left were required to get even that small majority. The vote on March 28 for Frederick William IV of Prussia as the new hereditary Emperor of the Germans was unanimous, however, but only because nearly half of the members of the Parliament remained silent.

Frederick William's election was announced to the people of Frankfurt by the ringing of bells and the booming of cannon. But the unity which the Parliament had decreed was far from being established. Catholic Germany, above all in Bavaria, opposed a union around Prussia. Some people, believing that a large Prussian state would overshadow all the rest, felt that Prussia somehow should have been "merged" in Germany, or reduced in size, perhaps into eight parts. The middle-sized German states—the kingdoms of Bavaria, Hanover, Saxony and Württemberg—generally were reluctant to surrender the needed power to any new central government. Kinkel's *Neue Bonner Zeitung,* pointing to a growing gap between North and South Germany, stated on March 31 that a "Black-White empire" (the Prussian colors) made a national union impossible. Civil War was anticipated by many, even if Frederick William willingly grasped the Imperial sceptre. But it was questionable from the first whether he would voluntarily accept.

The idea of forcing the hand of the Prussian King, by making it impossible for him to refuse, certainly was in the minds of many who welcomed the *Kleindeutsch* Empire as the best that could then be expected. The thought had been expressed earlier by the poet, Max von Schenkendorf, when he exhorted the Parliament to "pick yourself an emperor and force him to accept." Mevissen wrote in the same vein on March 21 when he recommended celebrations and demonstrations: "Public opinion in Germany must make it completely impossible for the Prussian King to refuse."

The large deputation, headed by Eduard Simson (President of the Parliament since December), left Frankfurt almost at once to offer the Crown to the Prussian King but met a mixed reception on its way to Berlin. In Cologne, as the *Neue Rheinische Zeitung* jubilantly reported, the deputation was joyously welcomed by the bourgeois liberals, only to be greeted later by a *Katzenmusik* (once facetiously described as a "musical vote of no confidence") furnished by an inspired crowd. The catcalls, whistles and jeers, accompanied by noise-making instruments, ceased only when the police and military cleared the streets.

In Berlin, Frederick William took the one position that was fully consistent with his general principles. The answer was neither yes nor no. As Count Brandenburg explained to the Lower House of the Prussian Parliament on April 2, the King was willing to accept the Crown, but he could not ignore the wishes of the thirty or more sovereign princes and governments that existed in Germany. The decision of the Frankfurt Parliament could be valid only after the numerous princes consented freely, and only for those who did consent.

Frederick William IV, as a believer in the Divine Right of Kings, could not admit that the Frankfurt Parliament, speaking for the people, had the right to hand out a crown, to give and to withdraw political power. The Prussian King, in a private letter to the King of Saxony, had earlier compared the situation to the Devil's temptation of Christ, with the

Frankfurt Parliament approaching him with the offer, "Fall down and worship me, and I will give you all the glory." The King's position represented a denial of popular sovereignty; it angered people who might otherwise have welcomed a refusal. This was true especially when the public began to hear that Frederick William referred to the proferred Imperial Crown as a gift from "the butcher and baker," a "swine's crown," a thing of "mud and straw."

Frederick William's reply was an appalling though not surprising blow for those who favored the Small-German union. The *Kölnische Zeitung* of April 6 declared that the King had given an "impossible answer" that would provoke a cry of anger from the Baltic to the Rhine. It was an impossible ending to the "great, German movement of 1848." The paper warned that Prussia was encouraging *"anarchy"* if it questioned the validity of the new Imperial Constitution. It would double the ranks of revolution if a congress of Princes (a reference to Frederick William's insistence that all the princes had to be consulted) met to pass on the work of the Frankfurt Parliament.

Tension in Germany mounted during April as the people recognized that the last chance for a united and free Germany seemed to be slipping away. The feeling grew that Frederick William must be forced to accept the Imperial Crown. Most people, however, hoped that the threat and fear of revolution would be enough.

By the middle of April, a collective note of the governments of twenty-eight small German states, the ones least capable of resisting popular pressure, indicated that said governments accepted the new Imperial Constitution and Frederick William IV as Emperor. The number (about 80 percent of the sovereign states) would have been impressive if it had included Prussia and the other four kingdoms—Bavaria, Hanover, Saxony and Württemberg (80 percent of the area and population). Moreover, Austria declared that the Frankfurt Parliament was a pack of rebels whose work was null and void. Many suspected that the Habsburgs spoke so boldly only because of a promise of Russian aid against the Hungarians, and if need be, the Germans—in return for Austrian opposition to the creation of a strong, liberal German empire adjoining Russia.

Some Germans proposed that the Frankfurt Parliament itself proclaim a general insurrection against the unwilling princes and governments, supported by the soldiers of the states that had accepted the Imperial Constitution. But the Parliament refused to unleash a full revolution and civil war to unite Germany. Certain republican and radical groups might use such an insurrection to demolish kings, instead of merely persuading them to accept the work of the Frankfurt Parliament.

A feeling of weariness and disillusionment was also asserting itself, as represented by Ludolf Camphausen, now active in Frankfurt. It caused his wife to comment on the "horrible truth"—the past year had stripped her husband of all zest for action and the striving to create an ideal future for the Fatherland. "The ideal is buried, the energies are used up," she deplored.

Marx did not consider the adoption of a most liberal Constitution and the establishment of a federal German empire under Frederick William to be worthy of a leading article. The *Neue Rheinische Zeitung* merely reported the news from Frankfurt, with derogatory comments. Several *Feuilletons* derisively disposed of the new Empire and the coronation of the "Christian, Germanic, Holy Imperial Majesty." But the paper did give a detailed account of the hostile reception of the deputation from Frankfurt when it stopped in Cologne on its way to Berlin.

The final revolutionary movement in Germany took place under the national Black-Red-Gold banner, even if many revolutionists tried to give it another twist. Marx was not in Cologne when the crisis was coming to a head. Having dismissed the new Imperial Constitution, both Marx and Engels failed to gauge the most serious revolutionary rumblings since March, 1848. Surely the great issues that precipitate revolutions did not include the banal combination of a Small Germany, a federal union and a hereditary monarchy with Frederick William IV as the Monarch. At the moment the financial problems of the *Neue Rheinische Zeitung* were far more important than the whole "Imperial comedy."

The subscription drive for the second quarter (April to July) had brought cheerless results, even though Engels later boasted that the paper "more than guaranteed its survival through an unheard-of rapidly expanding circulation." From April 14 to May 9, 1849, Marx therefore was in Bremen and Hamburg trying to raise funds. The one surviving letter from his trip, written in Hamburg, illustrated the seriousness of the financial situation, when Marx advised Engels not to let his "head sink." Though obliged to report, "In Bremen, nothing," Marx nevertheless expressed confidence that he surely would "get out of the ice" in Hamburg. He merely regretted that the *Neue Rheinische Zeitung* looked "very lean" that week, a fact that did not help his "present mission."

The "mission" in Hamburg was also fruitless, as far as the *Neue Rheinische Zeitung* was concerned. Furthermore, Marx found himself in an awkward situation. Confident that the expected contributions would take care of all personal expenses for the trip, he had registered at a "first rate hotel," fittingly. When no contributions came in, he found himself unable to pay for a fourteen-day stay in the expensive hotel. He did not even have the money to return to Cologne. In this emergency he turned to a Baron Frisch who gave him 60 *Taler* (almost $50) to take care of the matter. Marx protested that he would not take the money as a "gift," and Frisch, in his turn, declared that he did not want it back. The dilemma was solved through an understanding that Marx would pay the sum to Karl von Bruhn, a needy leftist writer. (Marx thereupon forgot about the whole "*Scheiss*" until Bruhn brought up the matter sixteen years later.)

As a last resort to raise money for the *Neue Rheinische Zeitung*, Marx stopped in Bielefeld to see Rudolf Rempel. Rempel was the True Socialist who had reneged on an offer to finance the publishing of *The German Ideology;* he was again unable or unwilling to help. But he did refer Marx to an A. Henze (an ex-lieutenant and a Communist living in Hamm) who "loaned" Marx 300 *Taler*. Marx at least did not have to return to Cologne with empty hands. Also he had made contacts with known Communists in North Germany and had dispatched emissaries with instructions to East and Central Germany. But in the meantime, revolution was in full progress throughout much of Germany.

The final German crisis was precipitated by developments in Berlin. Prompted by a widespread popular demand, the Lower House of the Prussian Parliament declared that the Imperial Constitution drafted in Frankfurt was legal and binding in Prussia. Almost simultaneously it demanded that martial law be ended in Berlin. The King and the Brandenburg Ministry responded immediately by dissolving the Lower House on April 27. On the following day, Frederick William IV informed the Frankfurt Parliament that he would not accept the Imperial Crown and Constitution. Minor clashes followed in Berlin. The *Neue Rheinische Zeitung* and other sources from Berlin reported that the Democrats and the Left were happy in anticipation of the showdown that lay ahead. Their joy was shared by reactionaries and many conservatives for different reasons. The Constitutional Liberals, in contrast, felt beaten and depressed.

A similar chain of events took place in other parts of Germany. Parliaments were dissolved in the kingdoms of Saxony and Hanover when the representatives of the people declared their allegiance to the new Imperial Constitution, in opposition to their respective kings. The King of Bavaria took the less drastic step of merely adjourning parliamentary sessions. Popular excitement grew as people everywhere expressed their determination to support the decisions of the Frankfurt Parliament, in defiance of their own governments.

In one sense, the ensuing crisis early in May was a conscious rerun of March, 1848, in that again it appeared necessary to force the princes to yield to the wishes of the people. The Black-Red-Gold demand that the decisions of the Frankfurt Parliament be accepted stands out most clearly. But other issues were involved. The dissolution of parliaments in various states made it appear that the liberal gains of 1848 within the separate states also were endangered. Beyond that, it was possible for radical elements to hope that the popular wrath during the battle for the Black-Red-Gold Empire might be inflamed to a point where the recalcitrant kings and even the governments of the separate states would be destroyed. The conflict, moreover, had an anti-Prussian tinge because of Frederick William's refusal of the proferred Imperial Crown. This raised the likelihood that the Prussian government, in turn, might act to quell revolution not only in Prussia but in other states where revolutionary forces demanded the adoption of the Imperial Constitution.

Tension in the Rhineland increased rapidly during late April and early May. This time the liberal bourgeois members of the numerous *Bürger-Vereine* were most active in petitioning the Prussian government to reconsider its decisions. The people of Elberfeld, noted for their loyalty to Prussia, gained a certain distinction even earlier (April 15) when a large, popular meeting unanimously agreed to send a declaration to the Frankfurt Parliament, pledging their loyalty to the new Imperial Constitution as the highest and only fundamental law of the land. Two weeks later the *Bürger-Verein* in Cologne proceeded more cautiously by merely informing the Prussian King that the rejection of the Imperial Crown ran contrary to the will of the people. But then, after news of the dissolution of the Lower House reached Cologne, the *Bürger-Verein* decided that it was necessary to oppose what appeared like a naked counterrevolution in Berlin. Such action seemed to endanger the Constitution of December 5 itself. Thus, a constitutional crisis gave an added impulse to the disappointment and anger over Frederick William's rejection of the Black-Red-Gold Empire. The *Bürger-Verein* thereupon asked the City Council of Cologne to join in a protest to Berlin and to invite all city councils in the Rhine Province to do the same. The Cologne City Council responded immediately by calling for a congress of city councils on May 5 (later postponed to the 8th), to consider the "critical political situation of the Fatherland."

Even the cautious *Kölnische Zeitung* declared on May 1 that the time for patience had ended. The Prussian people had to protest energetically their lack of confidence in the Brandenburg Ministry. Since Berlin was paralyzed by martial law, the provinces had to act, with Cologne taking the lead in the Rhineland.

Simultaneously, the Democrats in Cologne and elsewhere were aroused and welcomed the prospects of battle. The Cologne Democratic Society discussed the practical question of building barricades for the greater part of an evening. Only the Communist-oriented Worker-Society remained unmoved.

For the time being, the Communists disdainfully refused to join the hue and cry. Marx was not there to speak the decisive word. Engels merely exploited the dissolution of the Prussian Lower House and the King's refusal to accept the "gilded paper crown of an imaginary empire" to excite popular ire against the Hohenzollern monarchy. He originally dismissed the revolutions which broke out in South Germany in behalf of the Black-Red-Gold as little more than a "storm in a glass of water."

Before long, however, Engels conceded that the Frankfurt Parliament might become a new "momentary center" for a revolutionary movement backed by the advancing Hungarians and the anticipated fall of Vienna, if it had the courage. But it would have to *proclaim civil war* and even *"the one and indivisible German Republic."* Anyone who believed that the Frankfurters were capable of that erred greatly, Engels mocked.

Engels' natural buoyancy in any atmosphere that promised stormy weather thereafter began to assert itself. But he continued to see the initiative as coming from the Hungarian advance, or as resulting from an angry German reaction to a Russian armed intervention against the Hungarians. An extraordinary supplement to the *Neue Rheinische Zeitung* of May 2 envisioned the appearance of fifteen thousand Russians destined to garrison and hold down any revolutionary movement in German-Vienna. On May 4, Engels published an alleged Prussian despatch, instructing the railroads in Silesia to transport thirty thousand Russians into Bohemia, in support of the Habsburgs. Prussia herself, he stated, had agreed to send forty thousand troops into Bohemia. Appealing to the indignation of the Rhinelanders, he deplored the fact that "Rhinelanders like us" might be sent, perhaps even to fight against Hungary. "Now we feel what a shame it is to bear the name of Prussians!"

Three congresses met in Cologne and Deutz, directly across the Rhine, on May 6. The worker-societies of the Rhine Province and Westphalia assembled in accordance with earlier plans. The other two, a Democratic Congress and a Congress of the *Bürger-Vereine* of the Rhineland and Westphalia, met specifically to consider the critical situation in Prussia and Germany. The three congresses showed a remarkable unity of views. Since the Communist leaders of the worker-societies felt that a united front was now most important, they joined the Democrats in the afternoon to agree on a common strategy. The *Bürger-Vereine,* for their part, declared that the Brandenburg Ministry had lost the confidence of the people and had to be replaced. It simultaneously recognized the Imperial Constitution of March 28 as the supreme law of the land.

On the eve of May 6, as so often in the past, Engels had accused the Prussian government of planning to exploit the situation to provoke a clash *"at any price"* between the people and the military, to justify a renewal of martial law in Cologne. He urged the "Democrats and namely the *workers*" to show an unperturbable indifference to all provocations.

Cologne would do its part in the decisive events that lay ahead, but it could not start anything important.

Engels, in advising caution, stressed the point that the latest counter-revolutionary blows in Berlin struck the bourgeoisie most directly. They would hold their own "city congress" on May 8 (in defiance of Prussian authorities). "One must leave the *bourgeoisie the honor of speaking the first word,*" Engels advised. They had to commit themselves first; otherwise the workers would merely be *"pulling the chestnuts out of the fire* for the *bourgeoisie* and the *government.*" Any rash action was to be avoided; Germany was on the eve of a "civil war" in which the workers soon might have the opportunity *"to step forward with their own demands."*

Meanwhile, unrest increased in Germany, with insurrections everywhere. Dresden, the capital of the Kingdom of Saxony, had its barricades from May 3–8, with the Russian Bakunin and young Richard Wagner participating in the battle. The King fled for safety. Since his army had proven inadequate and unreliable, he requested help from Prussia. In the meantime a provisional government was established.

All of South Germany was on the verge of insurrection. In Baden, both the people and the army came out in favor of the Black-Red-Gold Empire. When the Grand Duke fled, a provisional government took over. The army and resources of Baden seemed available for the use of the Frankfurt Parliament. Catholic Bavaria did not succumb to the Black-Red-Gold cause, but the Bavarian Palatinate, lying west of the Rhine and south of the Prussian Rhine Province, rebelled successfully and set up its own provisional government. Even the Frankfurt Parliament faced a "terrorism of the masses" comparable to that of the previous September, when it refused to invoke civil war by calling on the people to help enforce its decisions.

In the Rhineland, open resistance and rebellion erupted on May 7 and 8 when the Prussian *Landwehr* was mobilized. Since the *Landwehr* was not to be mobilized except during time of war, the order to appear for duty was resented very much. It tore men away from their families and civilian pursuits. Moreover, the *Landwehr* resented being used to defend Prussia's reaction at home and opposition to the decisions of the Frankfurt Parliament everywhere. Resistance in the Rhineland, as elsewhere, carried the Black-Red-Gold banner.

Elberfeld once again distinguished itself by becoming the center of revolutionary resistance under the Black-Red-Gold. The Civic Guard and many armed "proletarians" built barricades when a small military force arrived to restore order. When the troops withdrew, revolution was in command, looking to Frankfurt for orders. The nearby cities of Solingen, Iserlohn and Hagen followed suit. Exaggerated accounts made it appear that the entire Wupper and Ruhr river valleys were up in arms. Barmen, however, refused to join the insurrection, although its citizens urged the King to dismiss the Brandenburg Ministry. Other quiet pockets escaped attention in the general turmoil.

During this time, Engels missed Marx's "surer" and more sanguine judgment in revolutionary situations. As it was, Engels had pursued a policy of caution and had braced himself against making any precipitate move. But at this stage, he could no longer hold out—the Communists would join the so-called "German Imperial Constitution Campaign" (*Reichsverfassungskampagne*) to fight under the Black-Red-Gold banner in support of the decisions of the Frankfurt Parliament. It was a little awkward of course to be in the ranks of those who fought to force Frederick William IV to wear the Imperial Crown—and perhaps a black-red-gold rosette. But any revolution quickened the pace of history, regardless of the banner under which it was fought initially.

Engels envisioned all sorts of revolutionary prospects. Help would come from the Hungarians who were moving westward. Nearer by, revolutionary forces from Baden and the Palatinate might cross the Moselle and Rhine rivers, sweeping into the Rhine Province like a prairie fire. He recognized that the left (west) bank of the Rhine had too many Prussian troops (around thirty thousand) for any action to be initiated there. Cologne, above all, was a fortified city with a large garrison. But action could start elsewhere, along the Moselle, in the Eifels and in the Krefeld district where the *Landwehr* had violently resisted mobilization. The east bank of the Rhine, with its wooded hills and valleys, was ideally suited for guerrilla warfare, Engels concluded.

Drafting the appropriate strategy for the above situation, Engels advised Cologne and other cities to avoid all incidents for the time being. The peasants and the small towns on the left bank should create revolutionary diversions, to keep the troops tied down and running in circles, thus demoralizing the military. The area of insurrection centering in Elberfeld on the right bank should receive help from all "disposable forces" in Cologne and other quiet cities, thus expanding the area of insurrection. Simultaneously, the angry *Landwehr* should be organized to create the "nucleus of a revolutionary army."

The *Landwehr*, however, had to be armed. This led to numerous raids on widely scattered armories. One night a group led by ex-Lieutenant Anneke and some Democrats from Bonn, including Carl Schurz and Gottfried Kinkel, attempted to seize the armory at Siegburg across the river from Bonn. The *Neue Rheinische Zeitung* of May 13 reported that the raid had succeeded and dramatically described how the "*Landwehr* men" had used the newly acquired "guns, sabres and pistols" to repel a body of dragoons who suddenly appeared on the scene. The account must have been written in advance, in anticipation of success. Actually the raid was a total failure.

When Marx returned to Cologne, Engels could not resist the urge to play a revolutionary role in his native Wuppertal. He arrived in Elberfeld on May 11 in a confident mood, with two chests filled with cartridges that he had picked up in Solingen. In a leading article written just before he left Cologne, he spoke of "big events" that would soon give the German movement a new unity and a powerful anchor from the outside: Hungary had declared her independence from Austria and had proclaimed a republic; revolution was still the standing order of the day in Paris.

By the time Engels arrived in Elberfeld, a Committee of Public Safety had already replaced the Mayor and City Council. Also, more than forty barricades, with much costly furniture and a large number of plush equipages serving as building blocks, graced the streets like monuments of revolutionary resolve. "Exemplary order and quiet prevailed," the *Neue Rheinische Zeitung* reported. The people were "truly great and noble," as Elberfeld raised the banner of rebellion higher than any other city. All classes had armed themselves to join the barricade heroes "who have committed themselves to a battle to death against monarchy." (The Black-Red-Gold Empire was not the aim of the insurrection, judging from this report in the *Zeitung*.) Volunteers appeared from surrounding localities, including a troop of armed girls from Solingen. All the country between Elberfeld, Hagen, and Iserlohn was in full revolt. The area was ideal for guerrilla warfare, the *Zeitung* declared. The Prussian army would learn what it meant when a whole province rose as one man.

According to Engels' account of his own participation, he had presented himself to the Committee of Public Safety immediately after his arrival, where he reported on conditions in Cologne and offered his services. He evidently impressed a special Military Committee because he was appointed inspector of the barricades with the duty of strengthening defenses in general. This was broadened on the next day to include control over the artillery and the posting of cannon, plus the authority to requisition workers. His recommendation also led to the appointment of Otto von Mirbach, a former Prussian officer, as the Supreme Commander in Elberfeld. (Von Mirbach's credentials included action in the Polish and Greek revolutions, followed by service in Egypt.)

Engels' personal appearance in Elberfeld soon caused some raised eyebrows. On the very first day, Karl Riotte, a Democrat and a member of the Committee of Public Safety, asked Engels to explain his intentions and presence. Engels listed three reasons: First, he had been "deputized from Cologne for this purpose" (it is not clear who deputized him); secondly, he was there because he might be of some help "in a military sense"; thirdly, as a native of the area, he considered it a "question of honor" to be present during the first armed insurrection of its people. Assuring Riotte that he intended to stick to military matters, Engels promised that he would not try to influence the "political character of the movement, since it was evident that only a Black-Red-Gold program was possible up to that point." He recognized that it was necessary to avoid any stand against the Imperial Constitution. Riotte appeared satisfied with this explanation.

On the following day, nevertheless, the chief of the Committee of Public Safety asked Engels to leave the precincts of the city that very day. While his behavior had been above reproach, the Elberfeld bourgeoisie were alarmed to the highest degree that he might declare the "Red Republic" at any moment. But Engels refused to be shoved out so unceremoniously; the Committee had to put the request in black and white. Even then he refused to leave, unless Von Mirbach, the Commander, approved. When Von Mirbach signed the necessary order on May 15, Engels as a good soldier then had no choice but to obey. Elberfeld meanwhile had been informed through placards that Engels had been asked to leave "since his presence could lead to misunderstanding regarding the character of the movement." Another placard carried the order that only the Black-Red-Gold colors were to be displayed in the city.

According to Engels, the armed workers and the free corps were most indignant over his ouster and vowed that they would defend him with their lives. But he asked them to desist. After that, he made a final reconnaissance of the area, formally surrendered his command, and leisurely left for Cologne.

An episode occurred on Sunday, May 13, that might have had disastrous consequences for Marx and Engels' future financially. As Engels was inspecting the barricade that barred the bridge over the Wupper to Barmen, looking very jaunty with a red sash, his father unexpectedly appeared on the opposite bank. The older man was appalled at the sight of his son standing cockily on a barricade. A painful scene ensued. The father nevertheless overlooked even this when he offered his son employment in the Manchester branch of the family firm in November, 1850.

With the exception of the above incident which he did not mention, Engels recorded his role in the *Neue Rheinische Zeitung* of May 17, immediately after his return to Cologne. He began the account with the proud statement: "The *Neue Rheinische Zeitung* was represented on the Elberfeld barricades. . . ." He ended with an assurance to the workers who had followed him with "such surprising affection and devotion" that the current movement was just a prelude to another one, a thousand times more serious, which would affect the interests of the workers themselves. When it came, they could count on him as well as all the other editors of the *Neue Rheinische Zeitung* to be in their places. No power on earth would cause him to withdraw from his position then.

Engels painted a less idyllic picture of the Elberfeld experience later in 1849 when he wrote "The German Constitutional Campaign." In it he described the workers, who had emerged too recently from the "swamp of *Schnaps* and of pietism," as being less united and revolutionary. The *Rotfärber* (red-dyers)—a "robust, well-paid working class, crude and therefore reactionary like all worker groups whose labor depended more on physical strength than on skill"—had refused to leave their jobs for the barricades. Other workers were fully employed again, after a depression of five months. "As is well known, you cannot make a revolution with fully employed workers," Engels explained.

The despised *Lumpenproletariat* in Elberfeld, Engels avowed, "could be bought after the second day of the movement, as everywhere." In the morning, they asked the Committee of Public Safety for money and wages; in the afternoon they were ready to sell themselves to the bourgeoisie. It had been a mistake to give weapons to the "*Schnaps*-happy" *Lumpenproletariat* who sold them to the bourgeoisie the same evening, perhaps to buy more *Schnaps*.

This account also indicates that Engels had proposed more "terroristic measures" than he had reported earlier in the *Neue Rheinische Zeitung*. From the first he had advocated that the largely bourgeois Civic Guard in Elberfeld be disarmed and that the confiscated weapons be distributed to the workers. He had also proposed a forced tax to support the armed workers and had acted to expand the area of insurgency.

Meanwhile in Cologne, Marx had resumed command with a fighting article, "The Deeds of the Hohenzollern Dynasty," which appeared on May 10. It was Marx's summary of two centuries of Hohenzollern rule, marked by unalloyed perfidy, pusillanimity, brutality, tyranny, aristocratic rule, police despotism, arbitrary bureaucracy, censorship and— the lack of a constitution! Although Marx certainly gave the impression of being on the side of those who were trying to force the King to accept the Imperial Crown, he at the same time obviously was trying to discredit and destroy the Hohenzollerns who were to wear that Crown, according to the current script.

On May 16, Marx expressed obvious delight because the conservative *Kreuzzeitung* in Berlin, the "Prussian Gallows-Paper," had denounced the *Neue Rheinische Zeitung* for its "Chimborazo-insolence" during the past weeks. (Mt. Chimborazo, rising to more than twenty thousand feet in isolated white splendor in Ecuador, was familiar to the Germans because Alexander von Humboldt had climbed to three-fourths of its height shortly after 1800.) Marx invited the "Gallows-Paper" to reprint his own article on the Hohenzollern family, stating that it rose to even greater heights than Chimborazo. It would make good reading for the Queen, Marx added defiantly.

That same day Marx published another brutal attack on the Prussian government, "The New Martial-Law Charter," in which he denounced a new set of more stringent rules for the application of martial law. He uttered a frenetic vow that the vengeance of the people soon would be fulfilled against the "lying, cowardly, plague-on-the-country family," the Hohenzollerns.

For a person who was no longer a citizen, expulsion might have been the anticipated corollary to such an intemperate attack on the ruler and government. Yet Marx was surprised when a formal order to leave Prussia was handed to him on May 16, soon after the appearance of the above articles. He was convinced that he was riding on the waves of a revolutionary destiny that was certain to destroy the very Prussian dynasty he had insulted. He fully expected to remain in Cologne and continue publishing his paper. The *Neue Rheinische Zeitung* of May 17 carried the first of the usual mid-quarter advertisements for subscribers for the remainder of the quarter, to July 1.

The Prussian authorities, however, had judged the situation more accurately. Much had changed since May 8 when all classes were united against the Prussian government. At that time (May 9) Prince William of Prussia could merely express the hope that his state would have enough power to reconquer the Rhine Province, if it seceded. But within less than a week, the danger of any serious revolution had evaporated. The "betrayal by the bourgeoisie," as Marx and Engels called it, was at work. Actually, it was a refusal by the liberal bourgeoisie and many Democrats to continue the fight to force Frederick William IV to accept the Black-Red-Gold Empire, after it became evident that many revolutionists were exploiting the situation for other purposes. Here and there the red flag had supplanted the Black-Red-Gold. In Düsseldorf, Heinrich Bürgers openly denounced the Frankfurt Parliament and declared that the approaching revolution would drive out all princes and usher in an indivisible republic. In Berlin, with typical Berlin wit and abandon, the Democrats were saying, "Go to it! If the kings become *absolute*, the people will become *resolute* and the armies *dissolute*."

Already on May 11, the *Kölnische Zeitung* reported that the presence of many "impure elements in the German movement" which threatened the "lives of the citizens and the free expression of their views" was producing a revulsion of feeling in favor of the governments. A private letter of Hermann von Beckerath, a Rhineland liberal, spoke of a "Red Republic which raised the Imperial Constitution as its transitory banner." All people with property "will prefer the absolute monarchy to a red republic," after the experiences of Elberfeld. In the next days, the *Kölnische Zeitung* stated that the party of order and legal progress could not overlook the policies of its "temporary allies," the democratic-republican party, and the more deadly elements—socialism and communism—which merely raised the Black-Red-Gold banner as a ruse to conceal their real colors. By May 13, the paper conceded unhappily that the diversion of the revolutionary movement into republican and socialist channels had produced divisions, opening the way for a victory of reaction. "The intelligent propertied class of citizens, the kernel and center of the nation" was beginning to waver, even to retreat to a counterrevolutionary position.

Under the circumstances, the revolution did not spread like a prairie fire, as Engels had anticipated. A revolt in Düsseldorf, with barricades and the red flag, was crushed with only minor casualties. Martial law followed. The *Landwehr* in most places failed to play its intended revolutionary role, initially because of a lack of arms. In Elberfeld, the revolution was disowned by most people who had helped to produce it, without any military intervention.

The Prussian authorities in Cologne therefore concluded that the moment had come when they could expel Marx without fear of more than a minor murmur in the Rhineland. They already had been authorized to proceed against him whenever the local situation seemed favorable. On May 11, immediately after Marx's attack on the Hohenzollern dynasty, Cologne authorities prepared the following order for the chief police official, the familiar Wilhelm Geiger, to be used at a suitable moment:

> In the most recent numbers, the *Neue Rheinische Zeitung* is constantly becoming more decisively outspoken in its incitement to contempt for the existing government, to violent revolution and to the introduction of a social republic. For this reason, its *Redakteur en chef*, Dr. Karl Marx is deprived of the right of hospitality which he violates so disgracefully, and, since the said person has not gained permission for a further stay, he is to leave within 24 hours. If he fails to follow voluntarily the order given to him, he is to be forcefully taken across the frontiers.

When the expulsion order was handed to Marx on May 16, he and Engels were still confident that a revolutionary resurgence on an even grander scale lay immediately ahead. Hence, Marx faced the order with the courage and defiance of one who knows he is on the winning side. He and Engels immediately tried to persuade the Prussian authorities that his expulsion would be a futile gesture, that it would not accomplish its intended purpose—killing the *Neue Rheinische Zeitung*. But the authorities convincingly demonstrated that they had enough evidence against all the other editors to either arrest or expel them. That settled the case.

"Nothing could be done about it, as long as the government was backed by an entire army corps," Engels concluded.

While the above parleys were going on, the police did not enforce the 24-hour ultimatum. Although no paper appeared on the 18th, Marx had the opportunity to concentrate on a large farewell issue with a supplement (No. 301), dated May 19. The entire paper was printed in red ink. The red print attracted attention and the issue soon became a collector's item. (When the official Worker-Society paper expired on June 24, it also was printed in red ink. Isolated, radical papers elsewhere in Germany made a similar red exit.) Engels could claim later, "We had to surrender our Fort, but we withdrew with arms and baggage, with ringing music and the flag of the last red number." The police did not interfere with its distribution—there was no official suppression of the paper as such. No serious repercussions in the Rhineland followed the ouster of Marx and the death of the *Neue Rheinische Zeitung*.

This last red number was defiant, belligerent and contemptuous. It came closer to declaring Communist aims than all the preceding three hundred issues, without spelling out the details. In tune with an age that honored the poet and expressed itself best in poetry, Ferdinand Freiligrath's "Word of Farewell from the *Neue Rheinische Zeitung*," spread across the three columns at the top of page one, set the tone for No. 301. "No open blow in an open conflict," but an attack from behind killed the *Zeitung*, the poem declared. But the "corpse of the proud rebel" would rise again. When the last crown broke like glass, when the people rendered their last "guilty!", the rebel would be there again, on the Rhine and on the Danube, "with the word, with the sword." "Rebel" runs through the entire poem like a refrain.

Immediately below the poem and set off in the same striking manner was an address from the editorial staff "To the Workers of Cologne." It warned the workers not to attempt a *Putsch*. That would be fatal and merely lead to martial law again. Elberfeld had demonstrated how the bourgeoisie betrayed the workers in the vilest manner. Thanking them for their "proven sympathy," the editors affirmed that their last word everywhere and always would be *Emancipation for the working class!*

Weerth's customary *Feuilleton* at the bottom of the front page took the form of a "Proclamation to the Women," opening with an astral image that compared the *Neue Rheinische Zeitung* to the rise of an "amazing star, menacing and splendid over land and seas," with the *Feuilleton* flickering behind like the "humorous tail of a comet." In this red issue the "humorous tail" paid its respects to the "beautiful women." From the first, Weerth avowed, he had found that the women were wiser than the educated men and the *philistines*, and also more passionate. What more could be said!

The Prussian expulsion order, prefaced by Marx's analysis, was also displayed prominently on the front page. Marx charged that "some time ago" an order from Berlin had called for a second round of martial law in Cologne, to provide a "martial-law ending" for the *Neue Rheinische Zeitung*. When that plan met unexpected difficulties, the Prussian authorities thought of gaining the same end through "arbitrary arrests." But this was rejected as impractical because the "healthy common sense of the Rhineland jurymen" was of no help to the government. Only one method remained—a "police trick"—the expulsion of Marx. As for the charge that the *Neue Rheinische Zeitung* had become more provocative lately, more open in its advocacy of violent revolution and a "social republic," Marx denounced this as a lie.

Marx wanted to show now that his paper had ever been the same. He cited passages from certain numbers, such as the glorification of the Paris Insurrection and the call for "revolutionary terrorism" in the fall of 1848, to demonstrate the point. He said that he did this explicitly for the benefit of the "feeble-minded" who had failed to see the *"red* thread" which ran through every account and interpretation of the "European movement." In conclusion, Marx defiantly informed the Prussians that it was unnecessary to resort to hypocritical phrases to justify his expulsion. *"We are ruthless,"* he continued, *"we ask for no consideration from you. When our turn comes, we will not embellish the terrorism. The royalist terrorists,* the terrorists by the Grace of God and the law, however, are brutal, contemptible and vulgar in practice; in theory they are cowardly, sly and double tongued; in both respects they are *without honor."* Terrorism in the service of the "movement," presumably, could have a contrasting grandeur, courage, refinement, frankness and honor.

Marx obviously did not want the red issue to look lean. An extensive survey of the great world followed, with spectres of threatening revolutions leaping like dry lightning on all horizons. Engels gave proper recognition to Elberfeld. He also offered a history and analysis of Hungary's revolution and its role in the broader European movement—an oft repeated tale, impressive through its length alone. The last report from Paris, not surprisingly, started with the words, *"Rouge! Rouge! Rouge!* Red wins! The red republic is on the eve of victory." Decisive events lay ahead—in "a few weeks, perhaps only a few days," there would be a festival of fraternization on the field of battle under the walls of Berlin by the French, Hungarian, Polish, and German revolutionary armies. As for Britain, "The fall of old Britain is the fall of the modern bourgeois society; the fall of the rule of the bourgeoisie is the victory of the working class." It all seemed so near to anyone who took the red No. 301 *Neue Rheinische Zeitung* at face value.

Marx and Engels left Cologne after this red farewell, perhaps during the morning of May 19. Before leaving, Marx paid all the business debts of the paper and the wages of all employees. It is often claimed that he dipped into his private fortune to do so. Marx himself stated that he used the 300 *Taler* he had brought back from his last trip, 1500 *Taler* that remained from the subscription money and from the sale of the fast press purchased the previous fall. The *Neue Kölnische Zeitung*, edited by Anneke, was named as the successor to the *Neue Rheinische Zeitung*.

Most of the editorial staff also left Cologne and Prussia, either because they faced a likely expulsion as non-Prussians (Dronke and Weerth) or because they feared arrest. A warrant for Engels' arrest in connection with the Elberfeld troubles was actually issued, and wanted signs were posted. But the Prussian authorities did not move until all had ample time to leave.

Marx and Engels had been forced to abandon their "Fort," the strategic center from which they commanded and exhorted, condemned and excited, denounced and derided. Self-confidence and the dialectical process of history, however, blinded them to what lay ahead. Hence, they set out from Cologne with the faith of a Don Quixote, not to tilt with windmills, but to help raise a wind that would turn the mills of history. They went directly to the focal areas of revolution from whence power might be derived for the necessary push to give momentum to the inevitable. It was imperative to give the German Imperial Constitution Campaign a boost and they hoped to give it. During the next weeks their lives were crowded with the pathetic and the heroic, near-tragedy and semi-comedy.

Frankfurt was their first stop, where they hoped to make their voices heard above the clamor of the "frog pond." By working through the democratic and radical Left there, they hoped to put decision and sense into the national Parliament afflicted with the "cretinism" they attributed to all such bodies. They wanted the Parliament to order the revolutionary armies in Baden and the Palatinate to rush to Frankfurt and come under its command. They hoped that the Parliament, inspired by the presence of such a revolutionary army, would promote revolutions against the separate princes and governments who refused to accept the Imperial Constitution and the Black-Red-Gold flag. Once the Central and South German states were brought into line, the movement would engulf the Rhineland and northern Germany.

The majority of the Frankfurt Parliament, however, was not at all persuaded that such a revolutionary gamble would produce the desired result. It appeared inconsistent to achieve unity through civil war. It was evident, moreover, that the radical parties were exploiting the situation for purposes that went far beyond a mere Black-Red-Gold empire. When uncompromising republicans were willing to fight to death to compel a Prussian king to become the hereditary emperor of a unified Germany, there was cause to suspect that something was askew.

The Frankfurt Parliament, in any event, was fading away. The mandate of the delegates from Prussia had lapsed, on orders from Berlin. The Bavarian delegates were withdrawing. Many others began to pack up and go, until only a radical rump remained. Marx and Engels saw immediately that they could accomplish nothing in Frankfurt. Leaving Wilhelm Wolff behind to occupy the seat in the Parliament to which he had been elected from his native Silesia (but which he previously had scorned to occupy), they themselves rushed on to Baden on a whirlwind course to get revolution rolling.

Marx and Engels now tried to induce the provisional government in Baden to gain the support of the peasant masses by abolishing all feudal burdens. Above all, they wanted Baden to send ten thousand troops to the defense of the Frankfurt Parliament, where the presence of such an army would place the "trembling so-called German national assembly under the terrorizing influence of an insurgent people and an insurgent army," as Engels wrote shortly thereafter. But the Baden revolutionary government of 1848 likewise failed to recognize that its historic hour had come.

After several fruitless days in Baden, Marx and Engels next moved on to the Palatinate where they caught up with its mobile provisional insurrectionary government at Kaiserslautern on May 25. There they were well received by D'Ester of the Democratic Central Committee of Berlin, which had moved to the Palatinate, together with the "flower of German democracy." But even the presence of D'Ester who stood behind the provisional government like a "sort of secret secretary-general," a "red camarilla," was not enough to convince that government that it possessed the capacity to play a decisive revolutionary role.

On their way to Bingen on the Rhine, perhaps a day later, Marx and Engels were captured by soldiers of Hesse-Darmstadt, but released after several days when it was established that they had not been involved in an uprising in the Hessian state. After this unplanned detour, they finally reached Bingen at the end of May, where they resurveyed the terrain and planned a future course of action. Their decisions took them on separate ways.

Marx, as Engels described the move, "went to Paris, where a decisive event was in the offing, with a mandate from the Democratic Central Committee [headed by D'Ester] to represent the German revolutionary party in connection with the French Social-Democrats." Since the revolutionary governments in Baden and the Palatinate already had sent representatives to Paris to solicit French aid, Marx wanted to establish himself as the spokesman of the real German revolution. Once the "Red Republic" triumphed in Paris, French revolutionary intervention in Germany would follow.

In Paris, Marx at first resided under the pseudonym of M. Ramboz. Writing to Engels on June 7, he declared that a shameless royalist reaction reigned side-by-side with an equally rampant epidemic of cholera. Nevertheless, a "colossal eruption of the revolutionary crater" was never nearer. He had met with the "entire revolutionary party" in Paris, while avoiding the "exiled Germans." He asked Engels to publicize the fact that he was in Paris as the representative of the German Democratic Central Committee—so as to counteract a report in the *Kölnische Zeitung* which cited Marx as having said that "his time had not yet come" and that he was withdrawing temporarily.

Marx's hopes for a "Red Republic" in France again proved most illusory. Paris attempted an insurrection on June 13, but it was a pitiful failure, a mere "ridiculous, worthless caricature of June, 1848," as Marx called it in disgust. Moreover, the fiasco left Marx without either a mission or the opportunity to remain in the French capital. Sooner or later the police were bound to take note of his contacts with French worker-societies, members of the *Mountain* and a certain "Secret Committee." To add to his problems, there was the money question, a most distressing distraction, especially after his family arrived in Paris on July 7.

Marx's family originally had accompanied him to Frankfurt where they stayed at the home of Joseph Weydemeyer for a few days. Although the Marxes had sold their furniture in Cologne, Jenny Marx was obliged to pawn the family silver, except for certain treasured heirlooms, to meet current needs. After that, the family seems to have gone to Trier, while Marx himself was trying to get the needed revolution going somewhere. Jenny was approaching an *"état par trop intéressant"* (Marx always put the matter in French). The one thing stable in the Marxian ménage was Lenchen Demuth who stayed with the family regardless of shifts and hardships, then as well as later.*

In the current financial emergency, Marx turned to his mother who again helped him by disposing of another parcel of property. Marx also wrote to Freiligrath, Lassalle and others in Cologne concerning his "most

---

* Only once did Lenchen's simple devotion lead her to a situation that was nearly disastrous. Early in the 1860's she became pregnant, with Marx as the father. To spare Marx a break with Jenny, whose marital code tolerated no such excursions, Engels (so often Marx's buffer) gallantly posed as the father. The child, Frederick (Freddy) Demuth, was shelved somewhere out of sight. To preserve a certain image of Marx, the matter was hushed up even after Jenny's death. (See Werner Blumenberg, *Karl Marx. In Selbstzeugnissen und Bilddokumenten* [*Karl Marx. In Self-Testimonials and Pictorial Documents*], Rowohlt Taschenbuch Verlag, Reinbeck bei Hamburg, 1962, pp. 115–117.) After Marx's death in 1883, Engels took care of Lenchen until she died.

serious lack of money." Lassalle immediately collected around 200 *Taler* for Marx, but apparently he had been somewhat indiscriminate in soliciting help. "I prefer the greatest hardship to public beggary," Marx protested angrily (he never hesitated to ask for help, but he did not want many people to know about it). Nevertheless the money proved useful when the Marxes again had to move.

On July 19 the French government ordered Marx to leave Paris, to reside in the Department of Morbihan in Brittany, far from any center of population—an impossible place for him. He immediately took steps to persuade the Ministry of Interior that the order was unwarranted. To help dispel the "misunderstanding," Marx wrote an open letter to the newspaper, *La Presse,* on July 30, ostensibly to correct various misstatements which that paper had published. Marx ended the letter with the gratuitous statement that he had come to Paris, not as a refugee, but of his own free will with the general aim of completing his research for the history of political economy that he had started five years earlier. The so-called *Manuscripts of 1844* were continuing to make history.

A month passed by while the French government reviewed the case. Meanwhile Marx heard from friends in Cologne that Morbihan was most unhealthful. He immediately concluded, or broadcast the impression, that this banishment to the "Pontine Marshes" represented a concealed attempt to murder him. ". . . I will not agree to this disguised attempt to murder me," he wrote Engels on August 23. He went to London instead where he remained for most of his life. His family arrived on September 25.

Engels had remained behind in Germany when Marx went to Paris late in May. He decided to "play the only role which the '*Neue Rheinische Zeitung*' could play in this movement, that of a soldier," if a suitable opportunity presented itself. But he first wrote an article for the June 3 issue of *Der Bote für Stadt und Land (Courier for City and Land),* the official organ of the Baden revolutionary government. Engels admitted that persons were being sent to Paris "to get information on the new direction which the French Republic will take." But he argued that this was no betrayal of the Fatherland to France because the Germans stood on the "threshold of a European, the Peoples' war," in which the military masses of the Republican West and the enslaved East would meet head-on for the big war on German soil. In this war, Engels declared, Baden and the Palatinate would stand on the "side of freedom against servitude." He wrote a second article but it was not printed, because it was too "seditious."

Engels' adventures during the following weeks are recorded in a letter to Jenny Marx, written on July 25, after he had reached Vevey, Switzerland. (He had heard that Marx himself had been arrested.) Engels wrote that he could not resist the urge to fight in the Palatinate when the Prussians appeared. He became the adjutant to August Willich, the Prussian ex-lieutenant who had played a role in the Cologne demonstrations of March 3, 1848. Engels fought in four battles and found that the so "highly-honored courage to attack" was a most ordinary thing and that the whistling of bullets was an "entirely trifling consideration." It was good that one person from the *Neue Rheinische Zeitung* was present because all of the "democratic rabble" were now boasting of heroic acts that were never performed. Otherwise, it would be said again, "The fellows from the *Neue Rheinische Zeitung* are too cowardly to fight." None of the "Democrats except [he himself] and Gottfried Kinkel really fought." (Kinkel was wounded, captured, tried and sentenced to a prison term by the Prussians.) Engels later paid effusive tribute to Joseph Moll, after hearing that Moll had died of battle wounds.

Actually the fight in the Palatinate and Baden was hopeless from the first. The Bavarian government had welcomed Prussia's invasion of the Palatinate, a part of Bavaria. A superior Prussian army outnumbered and almost leisurely outmaneuvred the revolutionary forces there and in Baden. Engels, however, could boast that his unit was the last to seek safety across the Swiss frontier on July 12, twenty-four hours after all the rest.

Marx was overjoyed when he finally heard that Engels was safe in Switzerland. It pleased him enormously that his partner had participated in the campaign. This would give Engels the "most beautiful opportunity to write a history or a pamphlet on the Baden-Palatinate revolution." Otherwise, it would have been impossible for them to "express their views on this lark." As it was, Engels could "brilliantly expound the position of the *Neue Rheinische Zeitung* toward the Democratic Party." The work would be a success and "bring in money."

With that encouragement and cue, Engels wrote an account of the "German Imperial Constitution Campaign." (It appeared in Marx's new revue early in 1850.) True to Marx's expectations, he treated the experiences as a "lark" in which the Democrats stand out as beer-drinking, easy-going, half-hearted, indecisive, cowardly, braggardly and traitorous heroes. He dismissed the whole Black-Red-Gold movement of 1849 as a typical expression of the boundless incapacity of the democratic petty bourgeoisie. In contrast to the Democrats, the "most decided Communists were the most courageous soldiers." The workers deserved this recognition as soldiers who fought and died bravely for a cause that was not their own. But nobody mentioned them because the "official Democrats" were so accustomed to the exploitation of labor that they regarded the workers as mere "raw material, as pure cannon fodder." Engels was doing his part in the preliminary campaign to discredit and denounce the Democrats—the petty-bourgeois class—as the major enemy of the future.

Epilogue

MARX AND ENGELS did not know that their one and only opportunity to play a part in an actual revolution was over when they left Germany, that for them personally it was the end of a dream, a calling, a destiny to help make and to be made by a revolution. When Marx wrote to Engels on August 17, 1849, he was still anticipating an "early revolutionary resurrection" in France; political developments in England were also taking a course that pointed to "incalculable consequences." Hungary was "stupendous." (The Russians had invaded Hungary late in June, but Marx evidently had not heard that Kossuth had fled across the frontier on August 11 and that all Hungarian resistance had collapsed on the 13th.) Marx, never one merely to watch the world go by, then asked rhetorically: "*Maintenant, mon cher, que faire de notre part? Il faut nous lancer dans une entreprise littéraire et mercantile. J'attends tes propositions.*"

Marx had the publication of a German revue in mind before he left Paris. He claimed that part of the money to finance it was already assured (from what source is not clear). It was to be a continuation of the *Neue Rheinische Zeitung,* in revue form, to allow a more detailed and learned investigation of economic conditions, the foundation of the entire political movement. It also was necessary to "clarify" the recent past during the "apparent pause" in the revolution. Marx had grandiose plans for this new *Neue Rheinische Zeitung,* which was to appear at first as a monthly, then a bi-weekly, or if possible, as a "big weekly similar to American and English journals." After their anticipated return to Germany, it would again become a daily. The old sub-title, *Organ der Demokratie,* was dropped in favor of *Politisch-ökonomische Revue.* It was published in Hamburg and remained a monthly through its irregular career which ran from March (the January issue) to the end of November, 1850, when the last number appeared. Marx had expected to finance the venture through the sale of stocks but, in spite of extravagant advertisements, few were sold. Likewise there were few subscribers.

The failure of the *Revue* was a keen disappointment for Marx and

405

Engels; Marx had counted on it as a means of a livelihood. They were bitter because their German friends were unable to enlist subscribers. For posterity, the *Revue* has one main virtue—it forced Marx and Engels to write certain things which they might not otherwise have written. But that consideration carried no weight in 1850. The *Revue* did not succeed because it analyzed a revolution that people wanted to forget and predicted eruptions that the Germans did not care to see. It also offended many subscribers because of its "ruthless criticism of pretended friends," namely, the Democrats.

"Revolution is the locomotive in history," Marx wrote in the *Revue*. Theory and historical analysis might be the instruments to determine the course and speed, but it required direct action to release the throttle. Almost immediately after he arrived in London, Marx acted to establish control over the local Communist League, which had survived in London despite the dissolution he had announced in 1848. He reconstituted the *Central Authority* to include himself and such reliable followers as Heinrich Bauer, Karl Pfänder, Georg Eccarius, Konrad Schramm, plus Engels and Schapper after their arrival in London late in 1849. Marx's aim was to revive and extend the secret Communist League in Germany, as a medium through which the Communists could organize and exercise control over open worker-societies throughout the land. In London, Marx himself joined the German Education Society for Workers where he began giving the now familiar lectures on the capitalist system and the hopeless lot of the workers in the existing society, to make the workers receptive to a higher level of instruction in communism. He likewise established contacts with many German political refugees by serving prominently on a committee that solicited and distributed funds to help needy expatriates.

The reconstituted *Central Authority* of the League prepared an *Address* (March, 1850) which was to serve as a guide for the Communists in preparation for the next revolutionary round momentarily expected. Heinrich Bauer was sent to Germany as a special emissary, carrying this *Address* with him. It was a secret document that outlined the strategy and tactics the Communists were to pursue during and after the revolution which would establish a democratic government.

It was clear from this *Address* that Marx and Engels no longer counted on the bourgeoisie as a revolutionary force; the bourgeoisie had reached a compromise with monarchy and feudalism in 1848/49 that satisfied their interests and desire for power within the framework of the existing order. In 1850, therefore, the Democrats were destined to be the major and indispensable force in overthrowing the existing governments, the *Address* declared. Hence, the "revolutionary worker-party" would have to join with them, accepting the fact that the Democrats would have the "greatest influence for the moment." At the same time, it warned the workers that the Democratic Party would be far more dangerous than the bourgeois liberals had been in 1848. Nevertheless, once the Democrats had overthrown the old regime and seized power for themselves, the war of the workers against democracy would start. (Marx and Engels later referred to this *Address* as a "Declaration of War on Democracy.")

The *Address* stated that democracy was not acceptable because it aimed merely at popular government, reforms and some improvement in the lot of the workers. It gave detailed instructions on how the workers (the Communists) were to operate after a democratic government seized power. The first requirement was that the Democrats must not be allowed to consolidate their position through the restoration of law and order. Revolutionary excitement was to be kept alive. Far from opposing "so-called excesses" the workers were to take the lead in exciting the "popular wrath against hated persons and public buildings." Popular distrust was to be inflamed from the first—not against the conquered reactionary party, but against the workers' own allies in the revolution, the Democrats themselves.

The *Address* further instructed the workers to set up their own revolutionary government immediately after they had helped the Democrats to win the revolution. For this purpose, the workers were to create communal boards or councils, or they could operate through worker clubs and committees (tactics similar to Lenin's utilization of the Soviets, or councils, in 1917). Through such bodies, they were to exercise vigilance over every move of the government, confronting it with threats backed by the workers *en masse.* The *Central Authority* of the League would come to Germany as soon as was possible, to assume control and to hold a congress. The workers were to be armed and organized, so as to confront the democratic government effectively and energetically. The creation of proletarian guards, with their own general staff under orders from the communal councils, was one of the possibilities suggested.

The *Address* stressed the imperative need for opposing every type of a federal republic, in favor of the most decisive centralization in a "one and indivisible German republic." In national elections, the workers were to put up their own candidates (League members if possible). They were to oppose or outbid the Democrats on every issue—so as to force the latter to go to greater and more compromising extremes. With regard to the question of confiscated feudal estates, the workers should demand that such property be controlled by the state, to be cultivated by worker colonies. This would prepare the ground for an "associated land proletariat." Naturally, the workers were to join forces with the land proletariat in general.

The *Address* assumed that the Democrats would have to introduce some "more or less socialistic measures." Although the workers at first could not advocate any of their own "direct communist measures" (this is the only time the adjective "communist" appears in the *Address*), they were to take advantage of this fact to force the Democrats to compromise themselves by proposing measures that would undermine the system of private ownership. Democratic motions aimed merely at reform and not revolution were to be driven to extremes. Thus, if the Democrats advocated a progressive income tax, the workers were to insist on a tax so steeply graduated that it would destroy big capital. The battle cry of the "Party of the Proletariat" was ever to be "Revolution in Permanence."

As noted above, the word "communist" appears only once in this long *Address*. There is only one reference to the *Communist Manifesto* itself, and then merely as one of three sources that embodied the "conception of the movement." The designation *Communist,* as such, is entirely lacking. Instead, the following words are used endlessly: worker, worker party, party of the proletariat, revolutionary proletarians. This seemingly studious avoidance of most everything specifically "communist" suggests that Marx and Engels considered it advisable to use the word very sparingly, in the immediate future at least.

The *Address,* above all, brought out clearly that Marx and Engels considered democracy their major obstacle—no matter how progressive, reformist and even socialistic a democratic government might be. Outlined in detail in the *Address* are diversified tactics that would undermine, compromise and destroy democracy, before giving it a fair opportunity to prove itself. The League was to be expanded, disciplined and instructed for the task.

In London, however, Marx and Engels soon were to encounter difficulties within the Communist League itself. The proposal of the European Democrats-in-Exile (led by Arnold Ruge, Mazzini and other less familiar figures) which called for the union of all revolutionary forces, produced a division extending into the membership of the League and the *Central Authority* itself. Ex-Lieutenant Willich and even the hitherto entirely reliable and devoted Karl Schapper supported the plan of the exiled Democrats.

Under normal circumstances, Marx and Engels undoubtedly would have settled the issue through a decision of a majority of the League membership in London. But in this matter, they did not have the majority on their side. Democratic procedures and the will of a majority could not be tolerated when erroneous views were upheld thereby. Hence the matter was settled in the *Central Authority* where Marx and Engels still commanded a slight majority.

The decisive meeting of the *Central Authority* occurred on September

15, 1850. Marx proposed that the *Authority* be shifted to Cologne (he had enough reliable supporters there). A vote of 6 to 4 decided the issue, with Marx, Engels, Bauer, Schramm, Pfänder and Eccarius comprising the majority. To counteract the argument of those who favored union with the Democrats for immediate revolutionary purposes, Marx spoke of probably "15, 20, 50 years of civil war and popular conflicts" before they could change circumstances and themselves enough to be ready for political power. (By then Marx had concluded that there would be no immediate renewal of active revolution.)

By shifting the *Central Authority* to Cologne, Marx saved the League from tactics and principles that he considered false. To save an orthodox minority among the Communists in London itself from being overwhelmed by a dissident majority, the League in London was split into two societies, completely separate from each other.

The new *Central Authority* in Cologne (guided by Marx from London) started out actively enough. A new *Statute* of the League was prepared, differing mainly from the old one in its first requirement for every Communist: "Freedom from all religious belief and the rejection in practice of every tie with the church and all ceremonies, unless they are required by civil law."

The activities of the League in Germany, however, were soon curbed. In May, 1851, the Prussian police arrested a Communist emissary, Nothjung of Cologne, who had in his possession various compromising documents. Most of the members of the new *Central Authority* and other followers of Marx in Cologne were arrested. Seven were sentenced to prison terms in a giant Communist trial in Cologne. The Communist League ceased to operate as an effective agency in Germany after 1852.

In the last issue of his *Revue* (November, 1850) Marx forecast no revolution in the immediate future with the same assurance with which he had prophesied an imminent renewal six months earlier. He based his latest conclusions on the "real foundations" on which party strife, political crises and revolutionary tensions played their superficial roles. As the commercial crisis and depression of 1847 had been the real factor in causing the Revolutions of 1848, Marx now asserted, a return of prosperity in 1849 just as inevitably had led to a waning of revolutionary fervor. However, with pontifical certainty he advanced to the conclusion: "A *new revolution* is only possible following a new crisis. But it is as certain as the latter." The revolution was just as inevitable as a new economic depression that Marx expected in 1852. Marx recognized that meanwhile he and Engels were in "public and authentic isolation," as he expressed it to Engels on February 11, 1851. But such isolation was in harmony with their "position" and "principles."

Except for their faith in the recurrence of revolution and in their destiny as entrepreneurs of revolution, Marx and Engels might well have lost hope. They were entering the darkest period of their careers.

Even before the failure of the *Revue,* the question of physical survival until the revolution became paramount for Marx. In April, 1850, the Marxes had been evicted from their living quarters and their furniture was seized as a pledge for the unpaid rent. After a brief stay in a run-down hotel, the family then settled in a two-room apartment at 64 Dean Street, Soho Square. Engels' family connections and his talents for making his way in the capitalist world now came in handy. His father offered him employment in the office of the Ermen and Engels textile plant in Manchester in November, 1850. Within the first year he was earning more than 200 £ yearly. This enabled him to send constant remittances to Marx, usually in the form of 5£ notes enclosed in letters. Marx concurrently could only remark that his marriage was more fruitful than his work. His journalistic and other writings, occasional windfalls, gifts, inheritances and loans never kept him from being a frequent patron of the pawnshops over the next fifteen years.

During these years of waiting for revolution, Marx had the time for research and writing. He had not yet completed that learned volume or two, *Das Buch,* proving that the capitalist system was inherently inhuman and destined for a certain fall. Marx always believed that the work would carry a devastating impact by persuading man to commit himself and his fortunes to the inevitable—revolution and ultimately communism.

Marx returned to the study of economics late in 1850, to that "History of Political Economy and Politics" which he had started in 1844 (remnants of which were published in the 20th century). Much of the old manuscript, however, could not be used. The extravaganza on alienation and humanity had become stylistically, conceptually and tactically unfit even in 1845. His unpublished *"Die grossen Männer des Exils"* ("The Great Men of the Exile," 1852), wherein he refers to humanism as "that phrase with which all muddle-headed persons in Germany, from Reuchlin to Herder, hid their confusion," clearly indicates that the 1844 terminology was definitely passé. There was no place for sentimental confusion in revolution, or in any work that prepared man for revolution. *Das Kapital* reflects this more mature judgment and added study.

Revolution itself continued to be the major preoccupation of Marx to the end. His private correspondence with Engels over the years shows them scanning the news, market reports and the diplomacy of nations, looking for signs of the next economic crisis or a war that would bring on a new revolution. Dozens of times they believed their hour was near. But they never lived to see it.

BIBLIOGRAPHICAL NOTES

The author found his way to the present work on Marx and Engels by an indirect route that began several decades ago with a doctoral dissertation on the separatist tendencies in the Prussian Rhine Province, 1815/1850, the homeland of both Marx and Engels and the period treated here. Thereafter he pursued an extensive and intensive investigation of the revolutionary generation in Europe from 1830/1850, which went far beyond the perusal of general works and specific monographs. It included far-reaching (though certainly not exhaustive) studies of the economic thought, the ideological trends, the culture and the politics of the age. His special interest and emphasis, however, was always on research in German history, 1830/1850. As the figures of Marx and Engels repeatedly entered the picture over the years, it became evident that they were not mere abstractions, born in an abstract world and breeding new abstractions. This writer then concentrated on the present work.

No attempt will be made to list all the sources that were, or might have been utilized. The indispensable source, Marx and Engels' own writings and correspondence, are readily available in the *Gesamtausgabe* (Complete Edition) and the newer *Werke* (Works). The *Gesamtausgabe*, the first planned publication of their complete works (*Werke, Schriften, Briefe. Historisch-kritische Gesamtausgabe* [*Works, Writings, Letters. Historical-Critical Complete Edition*], Frankfurt a. M., 1927–1935) was interrupted after the appearance of the twelfth volume and never completed—except in the Russian edition. To fill the gap for the German world, the East German Institute of Marxism-Leninism is currently publishing the complete works in thirty-six volumes, as estimated (Karl Marx. Friedrich Engels. *Werke*, Berlin: Dietz Verlag, 1957–). The *Karl Marx. Chronik seines Lebens in Einzeldaten* (*Karl Marx. Chronicle of His Life in Individual Dates*), compiled by the Marx-Engels-Lenin Institute (Moscow, 1934) provides a valuable, though not entirely infallible chronicle of the bare dates and events in the life of Marx.

This writer consulted innumerable contemporary governmental reports, writings, diaries, correspondences and memoirs in his attempt to place Marx and Engels in the proper historical context. Towards this same end,

411

he found he could draw upon his own broad background in the literature of the 19th century writers (especially English and German) whom Marx and Engels praised, damned or just ignored. But most useful of all in this connection have been the newspapers of the age, of every view in the political spectrum, notably from Cologne and the Rhineland in 1848/49, when the press was relatively uninhibited. The *Zeitung des Arbeiter-Vereines zu Köln* and the *Kölnische Zeitung* were especially important in this category. Marx and Engels' own *Neue Rheinische Zeitung. Organ der Demokratie* remains, of course, the major source of information on Marxian thought and tactics during the time of revolution. Although the newspaper articles usually ascribed to Marx and Engels are published in the *Werke*, the full impact of the *Neue Rheinische Zeitung*, as it appeared under Marx's "editorial dictatorship" cannot be appreciated without an actual examination of the original paper.

Gustav Mayer's *Friedrich Engels. Eine Biographie*, 2 vols., 2nd. ed., The Hague, 1934, stands out as a scholarly biography of Engels. Among the numerous biographies of Marx, none occupies the same eminent position. The short biography by Werner Blumenberg, *Karl Marx. In Selbstzeugnissen und Bilddokumenten*, Reinbek bei Hamburg: Rowohlt Taschenbuch Verlag, 1962, nonetheless deserves special recognition. This brief, sympathetic portrayal of Marx is designed to bring out the real Marx behind the several Marxian masks which the world customarily sees.

Recent East German scholarship, although operating in a specific ideological milieu, demands consideration because of its emphasis on the direct and practical revolutionary activities of Marx and Engels. Special attention is called to Herwig Förder, *Marx und Engels am Vorabend der Revolution, die Ausarbeitung der politischen Richtlinien für die deutschen Kommunisten* (*1846–1848*), Berlin: Akademie-Verlag, 1960, Gerhard Becker, *Karl Marx und Friedrich Engels in Köln 1848–1849. Zur Geschichte des Kölner Arbeitervereins*, Berlin: Rütten & Loening, 1963. The latter volume in some respects anticipates this present work.

This writer has generally avoided formal footnotes. Frequent references in the text, however, provide the reader, particularly the Marxian scholar, with a guide to the sources.

Index

INDEX

Index

Labor
  concept of, in Hegelianism, 101
  division of, 115
    Communist Manifesto and, 178
    end to, 126-27
Lassalle, Ferdinand, 302, 316, 365, 381, 401-2
Law, theory of, 365
League of the Just, 40, 84, 119, 159-60
  attempt to enlist, 142-43
  German, 93
  See also Communist League
Leipziger Allgemeine Zeitung, 45, 54, 64
Liberalism
  development of, 91
  fears of, 233
  government by, 44-45
  positions of, 231-32
  in Prussia, 72
  See also Democratic societies
Lichnowski, Prince Felix Maria, 229, 280-81, 304

Marx, Heinrich (father)
  conversion to Christianity of, 6-8
  relationship with son, 8, 10-15, 19
Marx, Henriette (mother), Marx as favorite of, 8-10
Marx, Jenny von Westphalen (wife), 8, 402
  children of, 189
  first child, 80
  pregnancy (1849), 401
  engagement with, 11-12, 27, 42
  marriage of, 64-66
    belief in institution of marriage, 120
  Marx's arrest and (1845), 198-200
  money and, 190
  poems for, 13, 14
  as secretary to Marx, 127
Marx, Karl
  adherence to communism of, 66-67, 69
  age of (1848), 355
  anti-religiousness of, 73-74
  Bakunin and, 84-85
    Bakunin attacked, 274-75
    on Marx, 188
  Bauer and
    collaboration, 26-27
    on Marx, 28

Marx's Ph.D. and, 24-25
Marx's professorship and, 25-27
  on censorship (1842), 48-49
  characteristics of
    Annenkow on, 138-39
    Bakunin on, 188
    Bauer on, 28
    compulsion to break with past, 79
    Engels on, 28, 37
    Flocon on, 191
    Hess on, 27, 29, 141
    motivation, 132-35
    Schurz on, 268
  citizenship of
    Marx's renunciation, 130-31
    refusal to reinstate, 254-55, 256-57
  in Committee of Public Safety, 298
  control, 408-9
  leadership, 196-97, 202
  on criticism, 74-75
  "Demands of the Communist Party in Germany" and, 211-14; *see also* "Demands of the Communist Party in Germany"
  democrats and
    advice given by Marx, 242-43
    control over Communist League, 408-9
    cooperation, 267-68
    disillusionment of Marx, 366-67
    distance maintained between, 241-42
    influence on Cologne democrats, 312-13
    on June uprising, 249
    new alliance (1850), 406-8
    role and influence of Marx, 263-64
    severing of ties, 379
    Vienna democrats and, 269-70
  Deutsch-Französische Jahrbücher and, 70-80
  1842 writings of, 42-44
    for *Rheinische Zeitung*, 47-51, 53-57
  Engels and
    Address (Mar. 1850) and, 406-8
    confidence, 380-82
    critique of Bauer, 94-98; *see also* Bauer, Bruno
    defense of Cologne barricades and, 309-10
    dissension between, 315
    first meeting, 39

422

Index